JONES & BARTLETT LEARNING INFORMATION SYSTEMS SE... ES

Network Security, Firewalls, and VPNs

J. MICHAEL STEWART

JONES & BARTLETT LEARNING

World Headquarters
Jones & Bartlett Learning
40 Tall Pine Drive
Sudbury, MA 01776
978-443-5000
info@jblearning.com
www.jblearning.com

Jones & Bartlett Learning Canada
6339 Ormindale Way
Mississauga, Ontario L5V 1J2
Canada

Jones & Bartlett Learning
International
Barb House, Barb Mews
London W6 7PA
United Kingdom

Jones & Bartlett Learning books and products are available through most bookstores and online booksellers. To contact Jones & Bartlett Learning directly, call 800-832-0034, fax 978-443-8000, or visit our website, www.jblearning.com.

Substantial discounts on bulk quantities of Jones & Bartlett Learning publications are available to corporations, professional associations, and other qualified organizations. For details and specific discount information, contact the special sales department at Jones & Bartlett Learning via the above contact information or send an email to specialsales@jblearning.com.

Production Credits
Chief Executive Officer: Ty Field
President: James Homer
SVP, Chief Operating Officer: Don Jones, Jr.
SVP, Chief Technology Officer: Dean Fossella
SVP, Chief Marketing Officer: Alison M. Pendergast
SVP, Chief Financial Officer: Ruth Siporin
SVP, Business Development: Christopher Will
VP, Design and Production: Anne Spencer
VP, Manufacturing and Inventory Control: Therese Connell
Editorial Management: High Stakes Writing, LLC, Editor and Publisher: Lawrence J. Goodrich
Reprints and Special Projects Manager: Susan Schultz
Associate Production Editor: Tina Chen
Director of Marketing: Alisha Weisman
Associate Marketing Manager: Meagan Norlund
Cover Design: Anne Spencer
Composition: Mia Saunders Design
Cover Image: © ErickN/ShutterStock, Inc.
Chapter Opener Image: © Rodolfo Clix/Dreamstime.com
Printing and Binding: Malloy, Inc.
Cover Printing: Malloy, Inc.

ISBN: 978-0-7637-9130-8

Library of Congress Cataloging-in-Publication Data
Unavailable at time of printing

6048
Printed in the United States of America
14 13 12 11 10   10 9 8 7 6 5 4 3 2 1

Contents

Preface

Purpose of This Book

This book is part of the Information Systems Security & Assurance Series from Jones & Bartlett Learning (*www.jblearning.com*). Designed for courses and curriculums in IT Security, Cyber Security, Information Assurance, and Information Systems Security, this series features a comprehensive, consistent treatment of the most current thinking and trends in this critical subject area. These titles deliver fundamental information-security principles packed with real-world applications and examples. Authored by Certified Information Systems Security Professionals (CISSPs), they deliver comprehensive information on all aspects of information security. Reviewed word for word by leading technical experts in the field, these books are not just current, but forward-thinking—putting you in the position to solve the cyber security challenges not just of today, but of tomorrow, as well.

The first part of this book on network security focuses on the business challenges and threats that you face as soon as you physically connect your organization's network to the public Internet. It will present you with key concepts and terms, and reveal what hackers do when trying to access your network, thus providing you with the necessary foundation in network security for the discussions that follow. It will define firewalls and virtual private networks (VPNs), providing you with an understanding of how to use them as security countermeasures to solve business challenges.

Part 2 discusses how to implement network security and reviews best practices. It discusses to how select and deploy firewalls and the tools for managing and monitoring them. It also reviews implementing a VPN, the technologies involved, and VPN-management best practices.

Part 3 focuses on the practical, giving concrete, step-by-step examples of how to implement a firewall and a VPN. It also discusses what challenges the future holds for information security professionals involved in network security. It covers the tools and resources available to the professional and scans the horizon of emerging technologies.

Learning Features

The writing style of this book is practical and conversational. Step-by-step examples of information security concepts and procedures are presented throughout the text. Each chapter begins with a statement of learning objectives. Illustrations are used both to clarify the material and to vary the presentation. The text is sprinkled with Notes, Tips,

FYIs, Warnings, and sidebars to alert the reader to additional and helpful information related to the subject under discussion. Chapter Assessments appear at the end of each chapter, with solutions provided in the back of the book.

Chapter summaries are included in the text to provide a rapid review or preview of the material and to help students understand the relative importance of the concepts presented.

Audience

The material is suitable for undergraduate or graduate computer science majors or information science majors, students at a two-year technical college or community college who have a basic technical background, or readers who have a basic understanding of IT security and want to expand their knowledge.

About the Author

James Michael Stewart has been working with computers and technology for more than 25 years. His work focuses on security, certification, and various operating systems. Recently, Michael has been teaching job-skill and certification courses such as CISSP, CEH, and Security+. He is the primary author on the *CISSP Study Guide, 4th Edition* and the *Security+ 2008 Review Guide*. In addition, Michael has written numerous books on other security and Microsoft certification and administration topics. He has developed certification courseware and training materials as well as presented these materials in the classroom. Michael holds the following certifications: CISSP, ISSAP, SSCP, MCT, CEI, CEH, TICSA, CIW SA, Security+, MCSE+Security: Windows 2000, MCSA Windows Server 2003, MCDST, MCSE NT & W2K, MCP+I, Network+, iNet+. He graduated in 1992 from the University of Texas at Austin with a bachelor's degree in philosophy.

PART ONE

Foundations of Network Security

CHAPTER 1

Fundamentals of Network Security

COMPUTER NETWORK SECURITY is very complex. New threats from inside and outside networks appear constantly. Just as constantly, the security community is always developing new products and procedures to defend against threats of the past and unknowns of the future.

As companies merge, people lose their jobs, new equipment comes on line, and business tasks change, people do not always do what we expect. Network security configurations that worked well yesterday, might not work quite as well tomorrow. In an ever-changing business climate, whom should you trust? Has your trust been violated? How would you even know? Who is attempting to harm your network this time?

Because of these complex issues, you need to understand the essentials of network security. This chapter will introduce you to the basic elements of network security. Once you have a firm grasp of these fundamentals, you will be well equipped to put effective security measures into practice on your organization's network.

While this textbook focuses on general network security, including firewalls and virtual private networks (VPNs), many of the important basics of network security are introduced in this chapter. In Chapters 1–4, network security fundamentals, concepts business challenges, and common threats are introduced. Chapters 2, 7–10, and 13 cover the issues and implementations of firewalls. Chapters 3, 11–12, and 14 discuss the use of VPNs and their implementation. Finally, Chapters 13–15 present real-world firewall and VPN implementation, best practices, and additional resources available regarding network security solutions.

This book is a foundation, and many of the topics covered here in a few paragraphs could easily fill multiple volumes. Other resources listed at the end of the book will help you learn more about the topics of greatest interest to you.

Chapter 1 Topics

In this chapter the following topics and concepts will be covered:

- What network security is
- What you are trying to protect within the seven domains of a typical IT infrastructure
- What the goals of network security are
- How you can assess the success of your network security implementation
- Why written network security policies are important
- Who is responsible for network security
- What some examples of network infrastructures and related security concerns are
- Which controls can enhance the security of wired vs. wireless local access network (LAN) infrastructures
- What some examples of internal and external network issues are
- Which common network security components are used to mitigate threats throughout the IT infrastructure

Chapter 1 Goals

Upon completion of this chapter, you will be able to:

- Describe the key concepts and terms associated with network security
- Describe the importance of a written security policy and explain how policies help mitigate risk exposure and threats to a network infrastructure
- Define network security roles and responsibilities and who within an IT organization is accountable for these security implementations
- Identify examples of network security concerns or threats that require enhanced security countermeasures to properly mitigate risk exposure and threats
- Describe the security requirements needed for wired versus wireless LAN infrastructures in order to provide an enhanced level of security
- Compare and contrast common network security components and devices and their use throughout the IT infrastructure

What Is Network Security?

Network security is the control of unwanted intrusion into, use of, or damage to communications on your organization's computer network. This includes **monitoring** for abuses, looking for protocol errors, blocking non-approved transmissions, and responding to problems promptly. Network security is also about supporting essential communication necessary to the organization's mission and goals.

Network security includes elements that prevent unwanted activities while supporting desirable activities. This is hard to do efficiently, cost effectively, and transparently. Efficient network security provides quick and easy access to **resources** for users. Cost effective network security controls user access to resources and services without excessive expense. Transparent network security supports the mission and goals of the organization through enforcement of the organization's network security policies, without getting in the way of valid users performing valid tasks.

Computer networking technology is changing and improving faster today than ever before. Wireless connectivity is now a realistic option for most companies and individuals. Malicious hackers are becoming more adept at stealing identities and money using every means available.

Today, many companies spend more time, money, and effort protecting their assets than they do on the initial installation of the network. And little wonder. **Threats**, both internal and external, can cause a catastrophic system failure or compromise. Such security breaches can even result in a company going out of business. Without network security, many businesses and even individuals would not be able to work productively.

Network security must focus on the needs of workers, producing products and services, protecting against compromise, maintaining high performance, and keeping costs to a minimum. This can be an incredibly challenging job, but it is one that many organizations have successfully tackled.

Network security has to start somewhere. It has to start with trust.

What Is Trust?

Trust is confidence in your expectation that others will act in your best interest. With computers and networks, trust is the confidence that other users will act in accordance with your organization's security rules. You trust that they will not attempt to violate stability, privacy, or integrity of the network and its resources. Trust is the belief that others are trustworthy.

Unfortunately, people sometimes violate our trust. Sometimes they do this by accident, oversight, or ignorance that the expectation even existed. In other situations, they violate our trust deliberately. Because these people can be either internal personnel or external hackers, it's difficult to know whom to trust.

So how can you answer the question, "Who is trustworthy?" You begin by realizing that trust is based on past experiences and behaviors. Trust is usually possible between people who already know each other. It's neither easy nor desirable to trust strangers.

However, once you've defined a set of rules and everyone agrees to abide by those rules, you have established a conditional trust. Over time, as people demonstrate that they are willing to abide by the rules and meet expectations of conduct, then you can consider them "trustworthy."

Trust can also come from using a third-party method. If a trustworthy third party knows you and me, and that third party states that you and I are both trustworthy people, then you and I can assume that we can conditionally trust each other. Over time, someone's behavior shows whether the initial conditional trust was merited or not.

A common example of a third-party trust system is the use of digital certificates that a public certificate authority issues over the Internet. As shown in Figure 1-1, a user communicates with a Web e-commerce **server**. The user does not initially know whether a Web server is what it claims to be or if someone is "spoofing" its identity. Once the user examines the digital certificate issued to the Web server from the same certificate authority that issued the user's digital certificate, the user can then trust that the identity of the Web site is valid. This occurs because both the user and the Web site have a common, trustworthy third party that they both know.

Ultimately, network security is based on trust. Companies assume that their employees are trustworthy and that all of the computers and network devices are trustworthy. But not all trust is necessarily the same. You can (and probably should) operate with different levels or layers of trust. Those with a higher level of trust can be assigned greater **permissions** and **privileges**. If someone or something violates your trust, then you remove

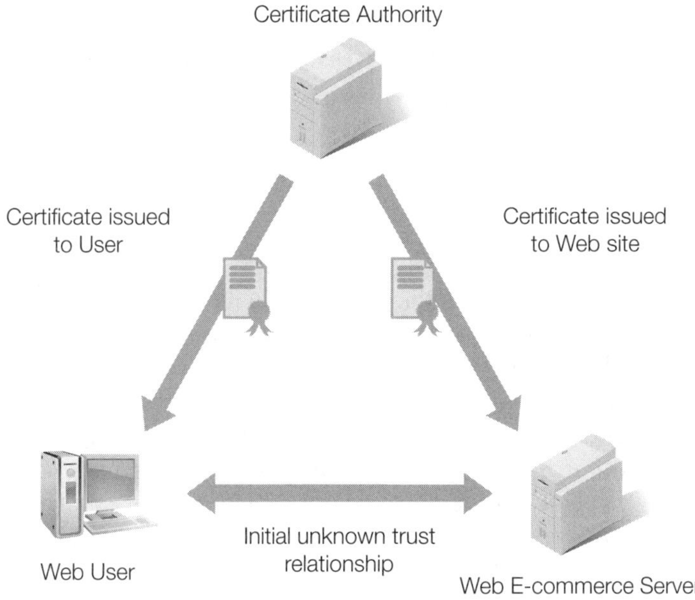

FIGURE 1-1 An example of a third-party trust system.

the violator's access to the secure environment. For example, companies terminate an untrustworthy employee or replace a defective operating system.

Who—or What—Is Trustworthy?

Determining who or what is trustworthy is an ongoing activity of every organization, both global corporations and a family's home network. In both cases, you offer trust to others on a conditional basis. This conditional trust grows over time based on adherence to or violation of desired and prescribed behaviors.

If a program causes problems, it loses your trust and you remove it from the system. If a user violates security, that person loses your trust and might have access privileges revoked. If a worker abides by the rules, your trust grows and privileges increase. If an Internet site does not cause harm, you deem it trustworthy and allow access to that site.

To review, trust is subjective, tentative, and changes over time. You can offer trust based on the reputation of a third party. You withhold trust when others violate the rules. Trust stems from actions in the past and can grow based on future behaviors.

In network security, trust is complex. Extending trust to others without proper background investigation can be devastating. A network is only as secure as its weakest link. You need to vet every aspect of a network, including software, hardware, configuration, communication patterns, content, and users to maintain network security. Otherwise, you will not be able to accomplish the security objectives of your organization's network.

What Are Security Objectives?

Security objectives are goals an organization strives to achieve through its security efforts. Typically, organizations recognize three primary security objectives:

- Confidentiality
- Integrity
- Availability

Confidentiality is the protection against unauthorized access, while providing authorized users access to resources without obstruction. Confidentiality ensures that data is not intentionally or unintentionally disclosed to anyone without a valid need to know. A **job description** defines the person's "need to know." If a task does not require access to a specific resource, then you do not have a "need to know" that resource.

Integrity is the protection against unauthorized changes, while allowing for authorized changes performed by authorized users. Integrity ensures that data remain consistent, both internally and externally. Consistent data do not change over time and remain in sync with the real world. Integrity also protects against accidents and hacker modification by malicious code.

Availability is the protection against **downtime**, loss of data, and blocked access, while providing consistent uptime, protecting data, and supporting authorized access to resources. Availability ensures that users can get their work done in a timely manner with access to the proper resources.

Several other objectives support network security in addition to the three primary goals:

- Authentication
- Authorization
- Non-repudiation
- Privacy

Authentication is the proof or verification of a user's identity before granting access to a secured area. This can occur both on a network as well as in the physical, real world. While the most common form of authentication is a password, password access is also the least secure method of authentication. Multi-factor authentication, therefore, is the method most network administrators prefer for secure logon.

Authorization is controlling what users are allowed and not allowed to do. Authorization is dictated by the organization's security structure, which may focus on discretionary access control (DAC), mandatory access control (MAC), or role-based access control (RBAC). Authorization restricts access based on need to know and users' job descriptions. Authorization is also known as access control.

Non-repudiation is the security service that prevents a user from being able to deny having performed an action. For example, non-repudiation prevents a sender from denying having sent a message. **Auditing** and public-key cryptography commonly provide non-repudiation services.

Privacy protects the confidentiality, integrity, and availability of personally identifiable or sensitive data. Private data often includes financial records and medical information. Privacy prevents unauthorized watching and monitoring of users and employees.

Maintaining and protecting these security objectives can be a challenge. As with most difficult tasks, breaking security down into simpler or smaller components will help you to understand and ultimately accomplish this objective. To support security objectives, you need to know clearly what you are trying to protect.

What Are You Trying to Protect?

In terms of security, the things you want to protect are known as assets. An **asset** is anything used to conduct business over a computer network. Any object, computer, program, piece of data, or other logical or physical component employees need to accomplish a task is an asset.

Assets do not have to be expensive, complicated, or large. In fact, many assets are relatively inexpensive, common-place, and variable in size. But no matter the characteristics, an asset needs protection. When assets are unavailable for whatever reason, people can't get their work done.

For most organizations, including **SOHO (small office, home office)** environments, the assets of most concern include business and personal data. If this information is lost, damaged, or stolen, serious complications result. Businesses can fail. Individuals can lose money. Identities can be stolen. Even lives can be ruined.

What causes these problems? What violates network security? The answer includes accidents, ignorance, oversight, and hackers. Accidents happen, including hardware failures and natural disasters. Poor training equals ignorance. Workers with the best of intentions damage systems if they don't know proper procedures and have necessary skills. Overworked and rushed personnel overlook issues that can result in asset compromise or loss. Malicious **hackers** can launch attacks and exploits against the network, seeking to gain access or just to cause damage.

"**Hacking**" originally meant tinkering or modifying systems to learn and explore. However, the term has come to refer to malicious and possibly criminal intrusion into and manipulation of computers. In either case, a malicious hacker or criminal hacker is a serious threat. Every network administrator should be concerned about hacking.

Some important aspects of security stem from understanding the techniques, methods, and motivations of hackers. Once you learn to think like a hacker, you may be able to anticipate future attacks. This enables you to devise new defenses before a hacker can successfully **breach** your organization's network.

So how do hackers think? Hackers think along the lines of manipulation or change. They look into the rules to create new ways of bending, breaking, or changing them. Many successful security breaches have been little more than slight variations or violations of network communication rules.

Hackers look for easy targets or overlooked vulnerabilities. Hackers seek out targets that provide them the most gain, often financial rewards. Hackers turn things over, inside out, and in the wrong direction. Hackers attempt to perform tasks in different orders,

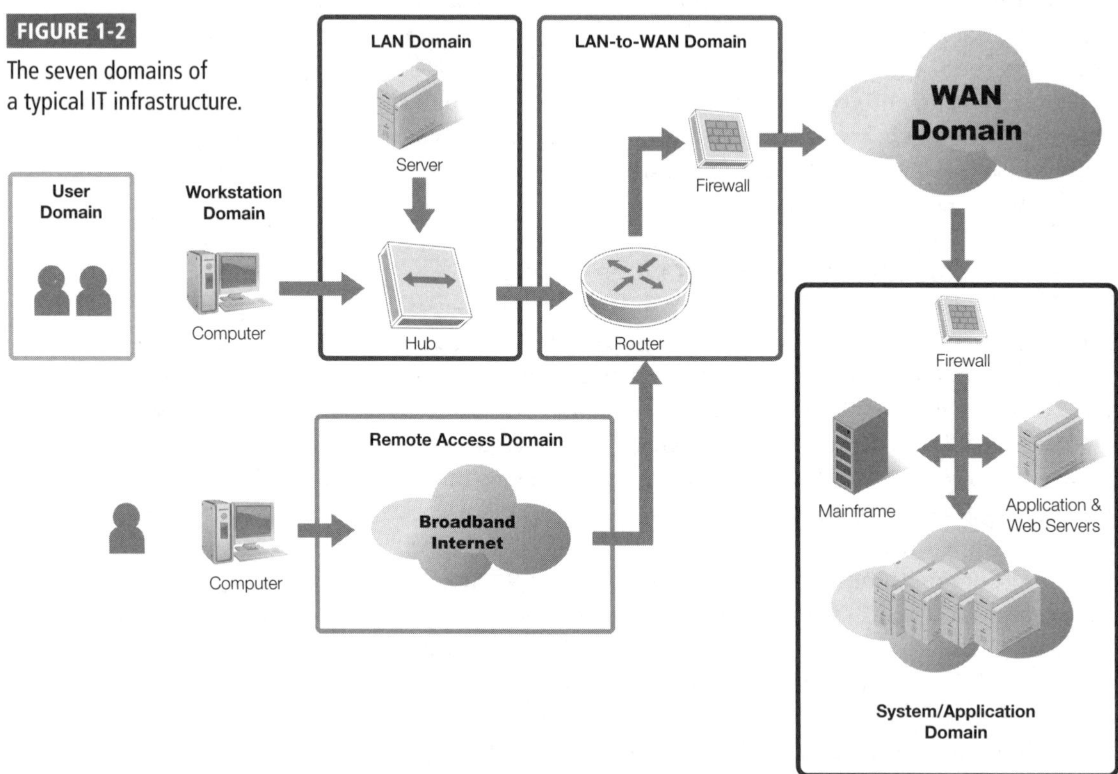

FIGURE 1-2

The seven domains of a typical IT infrastructure.

with incorrect values, outside the boundaries, and with a purpose to cause a reaction. Hackers learn from and exploit mistakes, especially mistakes of the network security professionals who fail to properly protect an organization's assets.

Why is thinking like a "hacker" critically important? A sixth century Chinese general and author, Sun Tzu, in his famous military text *The Art of War*, stated: "If you know the enemy and know yourself you need not fear the results of a hundred battles." Once you understand how hackers think, the tools they use, their exploits, and attack techniques they employ, you can then create effective defenses to protect against them.

You've often heard that "the best defense is a good offense." While this statement may have merit elsewhere, most network security administrators do not have the luxury—or legal right—to attack hackers. Instead, you need to turn this strategic phrase around: The best offense is a good defense. While network security administrators cannot legally or ethically attack hackers, they are fully empowered to defend networks and assets against hacker onslaughts.

Chapter 4 further discusses hacking and other threats in greater detail.

Seven Domains of a Typical IT Infrastructure

Hackers look for any and every opportunity to exploit a target. No aspect of an IT infrastructure is without **risk** nor is immune to the scrutiny of a hacker. When thinking like a hacker, analyze every one of the seven **domains** of a typical IT infrastructure (Figure 1-2) for potential vulnerabilities and weaknesses. Be thorough. A hacker only needs one crack in the protections to begin chipping away at the defenses. You need to find every possible breach point to secure it and **harden** the network.

The seven domains of a typical IT infrastructure are:

- **User Domain**—this domain refers to actual users whether they are employees, consultants, contractors, or other third-party users. Any user who accesses and uses the organization's IT infrastructure must review and sign an acceptable use policy (AUP) prior to being granted access to the organization's IT resources and infrastructure.
- **Workstation Domain**—this domain refers to the end user's desktop devices such as a desktop computer, laptop, VoIP telephone, or other end-point device. Workstation devices typically require security countermeasures such as antivirus, anti-spyware, and **vulnerability** software patch management to maintain the integrity of the device.
- **LAN Domain**—this domain refers to the physical and logical **local area network (LAN)** technologies (i.e., 100Mbps/1000Mbps switched Ethernet, 802.11-family of wireless LAN technologies) used to support workstation connectivity to the organization's network infrastructure.
- **LAN-to-WAN Domain**—this domain refers to the organization's internetworking and interconnectivity point between the LAN and the WAN network infrastructures. Routers, firewalls, **demilitarized zones (DMZs)**, and **intrusion detection systems (IDS)** and **intrusion prevention systems (IPS)** are commonly used as security monitoring devices in this domain.

- **Remote Access Domain**—his domain refers to the authorized and authenticated remote access procedures for users to remotely access the organization's IT infrastructure, systems, and data. Remote access solutions typically involve SSL-128 bit encrypted remote browser access or encrypted VPN tunnels for secure remote communications.
- **WAN Domain**—organizations with remote locations require a **wide area network (WAN)** to interconnect them. Organizations typically outsource WAN connectivity from service providers for end-to-end connectivity and bandwidth. This domain typically includes routers, circuits, switches, firewalls, and equivalent gear at remote locations sometimes under a managed service offering by the service provider.
- **Systems/Applications Domain**—this domain refers to the hardware, operating system software, database software, client/server applications, and data that is typically housed in the organization's data center and/or computer rooms.

Recognizing the potential for compromise exists throughout an organization. The next step is to comprehend the goals of network security.

Goals of Network Security

Network **security goals** vary from organization to organization. Often they include a few common mandates:

- Ensure the confidentiality of resources
- Protect the integrity of data
- Maintain availability of the IT infrastructure
- Ensure the privacy of personally identifiable data
- Enforce access control
- Monitor the IT environment for violations of policy
- Support **business tasks** and the overall mission of the organization

Whatever your organization's security goals, to accomplish them you need to write down those goals and develop a thorough plan to execute them. Without a written plan, security will be haphazard at best and will likely fail to protect your assets. With a written plan, network security is on the path to success. Once you define your security goals, these goals will become your organization's roadmap for securing the entire IT infrastructure.

How Can You Measure the Success of Network Security?

Organizations measure the success of network security by how well the stated, written security goals are accomplished or maintained. In essence, this becomes the organization's baseline definition for information systems security. For example, if private information on the network does not leak to outsiders, then your efforts to maintain confidentiality were successful. Or, if employees are able to complete their work on time and on budget, then your efforts to provide system integrity protection were successful.

If violations take place that compromise your assets or prevent maintaining a security goal, however, then network security was less than successful. But let's face it, security is never perfect. In fact, even with well-designed and executed security, accidents, mistakes, and even intentional harmful exploits will dog your best efforts. The perfect security components do not exist. All of them have weaknesses, limitations, **backdoors**, work-arounds, programming bugs, finite areas of affect, or some other exploitable element.

Fortunately, though, successful security doesn't rely on the installation of just a single defensive component. Instead, good network security relies on an interweaving of multiple, effective security components. You don't have just one lock on your house. By combining multiple protections, defenses, and detection systems you can rebuff many common, easy hacker exploits.

Network security success is not about preventing all possible attacks or compromises. Instead, you work to continually improve the state of security, so that in the future the network is better protected than it was in the past. As hackers create new exploits, security professionals learn about them, adapt their methods and systems, and establish new defenses. Successful network security is all about constant vigilance, not creating an end product. Security is an ongoing effort that constantly changes to meet the challenge of new threats.

Why Are Written Network Security Policies Important?

A clearly written **security policy** establishes tangible goals. Without solid and defined goals, your security efforts would be chaotic and hard to manage. Written plans and procedures focus security efforts and resources on the most important tasks to support your organization's overall security objectives.

A written security policy is a road map. With this map, you can determine whether your efforts are on track or going in the wrong direction. The plan provides a common reference against which security tasks are compared. It serves as a measuring tool to judge that security efforts are helping rather than hurting maintenance of your organization's security objectives.

With a written security policy, all security professionals strive to accomplish the same end: a successful, secure work environment. By following the written plan, you can track progress so that you install and configure all the necessary components. A written plan validates what you do, defines what you still need to do, and guides you on how to repair the infrastructure when necessary.

Without a written security policy, you cannot trust that your network is secure. Without a written security policy, workers won't have a reliable guide on what to do and judging security success will be impossible. Without a written policy, you have no security.

Planning for the Worst

Things invariably go wrong. Users make mistakes. Malicious code finds its way into your network. Hackers discover vulnerabilities and exploit them. In anticipating problems that threaten security, you must plan for the worst.

This type of planning has many names, including contingency planning, worst-case scenario planning, business continuity planning, disaster recovery planning, and continuation of operations planning. The name is not important. What's crucial is that you do the planning itself.

When problems occur, shift into response gear: respond, contain, and repair. Respond to all failures or security breaches to minimize damage, cost, and downtime. Contain threats to prevent them from spreading or affecting other areas of the infrastructure. Repair damage promptly to return systems to normal status quickly and efficiently. Remember the goals of security are confidentiality, integrity, and availability. Keep these foremost in mind as you plan for the worst.

The key purpose of planning for problems is to be properly prepared to protect your infrastructure. With a little luck, a major catastrophe won't occur. But better to prepare and not need the response plan, than to allow problems to cause your business to fail.

Who Is Responsible for Network Security?

Network security is the responsibility of everyone who uses the network. Within an organization, no one has the luxury of ignoring security rules. This applies to global corporations as well as home networks. Every person is responsible for understanding his or her role in supporting and maintaining network security. The weakest link rule applies here: If only one person fails to fulfill this responsibility, security for all will suffer.

Senior management has the ultimate and final responsibility for security. For good reason—senior management is the most concerned about the protection of the organization's assets. Without the approval and support of senior management, no security effort can succeed. Senior management must ensure the creation of a written security policy that all personnel understand and follow.

Senior management also assigns the responsibility for designing, writing, and executing the security plan to the IT staff. Ideally, the result of these efforts is a secure network infrastructure. The security staff, in turn, must thoroughly manage all assets, system vulnerabilities, imminent threats, and all pertinent defenses. Their task is to design, execute, and maintain security throughout the organization.

In their role as overseers of groups of personnel, managers and supervisors must ensure that employees have all the tools and resources to accomplish their work. Managers must also ensure that workers are properly trained in skills, procedures, policies, boundaries, and restrictions. Employees can mount a legitimate legal case against an organization that requires them to perform work for which they are not properly trained.

Network administrators manage all the organization's computer resources. Resources include file servers, network access, databases, printer pools, and applications. The network administrator's job is to ensure that resources are functional and available for users while enforcing confidentiality and network integrity.

An organization's workers are the network users and operators. They ultimately do the work the business needs to accomplish. Users create products, provide services, perform tasks, input data, respond to queries, and much more. Job descriptions may apply to a single user or a group of users. Each job description defines a user's tasks. Users must perform these tasks within the limitations of network security.

Auditors watch for problems and violations. Auditors investigate the network, looking for anything not in compliance with the written security policy. Auditors watch the activity of systems and users to look for violations, trends toward **bottlenecks**, and attempts to perform violations. The information uncovered by auditors can help improve the security policy, adjust security configurations, or guide investigators toward apprehending security violators.

All of these **roles** exist within every organization. Sometimes different individuals perform these roles. In other situations, a single person performs all of these roles. In either case, these roles are essential to the creation, maintenance, and improvement of security.

Examples of Network Infrastructures and Related Security Concerns

As you design a network, you need to evaluate every aspect in light of its security consequences. With limited budgets, personnel, and time, you must also minimize risk and maximize protection. Consider how each of the following network security aspects affects security for large corporations, small companies, and even home-based businesses.

Workgroups

A **workgroup** is a form of networking in which each computer is a peer or equal. Peers are equal in how much power or controlling authority any one system has over the other members of the same workgroup. All workgroup members are able to manage their own local resources and assets, but not those of any other workgroup member.

Workgroups are an excellent network design for very small environments, such as home family networks or very small companies. In most cases, a workgroup comprises fewer than 10 computers and rarely contains more than 20 computers. No single rule dictates the size of a workgroup. Instead, the administrative overhead of larger workgroups encourages network managers to move to a client/server configuration.

Figure 1-3 shows a typical workgroup configuration. In this example, a switch interconnects the four desktop workgroup members as well as an Internet connection device and a wireless access point. Additional clients can connect wirelessly via the access point or wired via a cable connecting to the switch.

Workgroups do not have a central authority that controls or restricts network activity or resource access. Instead, each individual workgroup member makes the rules and restrictions over resources and assets. The security defined for one member does not apply to nor affect any other computer in the workgroup.

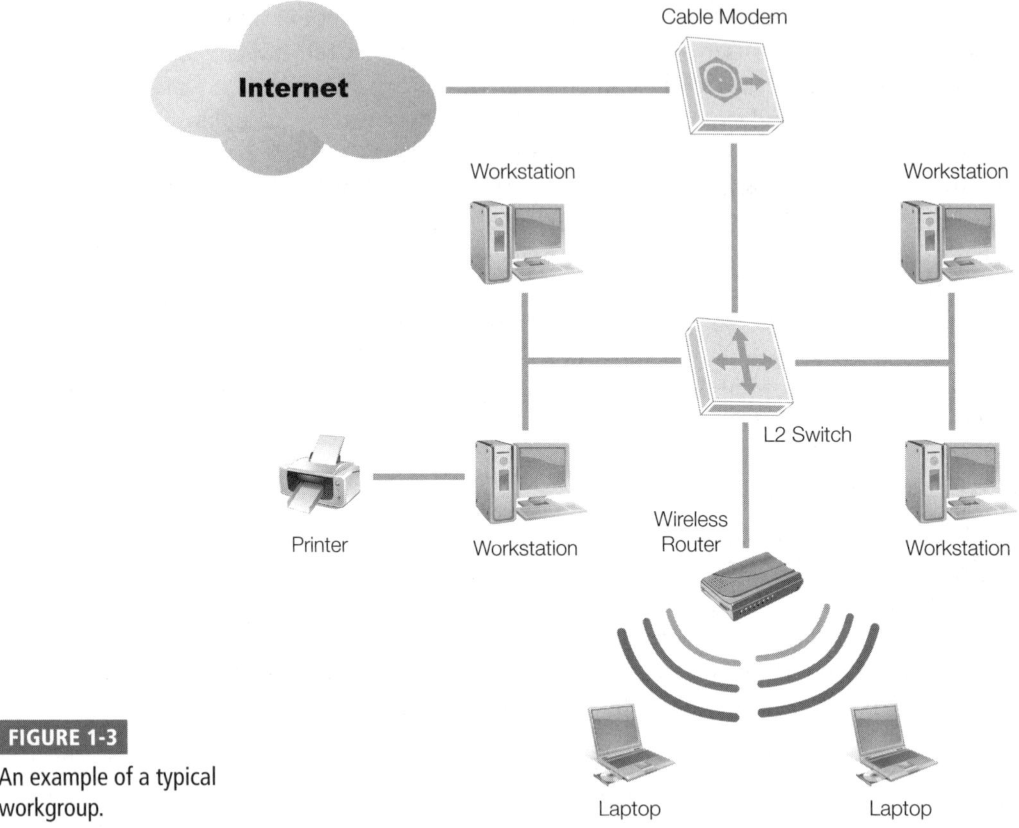

FIGURE 1-3
An example of a typical workgroup.

Due to system-by-system–based security, a worker or a workgroup member needs to have a user account defined on each of the other workgroup members to access resources on those systems. Each of these accounts is technically a unique user account, even if created by using the same characters for the username and password.

This results in either several unique user accounts with different names and different passwords or several unique user accounts with the same name and same password. In either case, security is poor. In the former case, the user must remember several sets of credentials. This often results in the user writing down the credentials. In the later case, an intruder need compromise only one set of credentials.

This lack of central authority is both a strength and weakness of workgroups. This characteristic is a strength in that each user of each computer can make his or her own choices about sharing resources with others. However, this is at the same time a weakness because of the inconsistent levels of access.

Workgroups are easy to create. Often the default network configuration of operating systems is to be a member of a workgroup. A new workgroup is created by just defining a unique name on a computer. Once one computer names the workgroup, it now exists. Other computers become members of the new workgroup just by using the same name.

Since workgroups lack a central authority, anyone can join or leave a workgroup at any time. This includes unauthorized systems owned by rogue employees or external parties.

Most workgroups use only basic resource-share protections, fail to use encrypted protocols, and are lax on monitoring intrusions. While imposing some security on workgroups is possible, usually each workgroup member is configured individually. Fortunately, since workgroups are small, this does not represent a significant amount of effort.

SOHO Networks

SOHO stands for small office, home office. SOHO is a popular term that describes smaller networks commonly found in small businesses, often deployed in someone's home, garage, portable building, or leased office space. A SOHO environment can be a workgroup or a client/server network. Usually a SOHO network implies purposeful design with business and security in mind.

SOHO networks generally are more secure than a typical workgroup, usually because a manager or owner enforces network security. Security settings defined on each workgroup member are more likely to be consistent when the workgroup has a security administrator. Additionally, SOHO networks are more likely to employ security tools such as antivirus software, firewalls, and auditing.

Client/Server Networks

A **client/server network** is a form of network where you designate some computers as servers and others as **clients**. Servers host resources shared with the network. Clients access resources and perform tasks. Users work from a client computer to interact with resources hosted by servers. In a client/server network, access is managed centrally from the servers. Thus, consistent security is easily imposed across all network members.

Figure 1-4 shows a possible basic layout of a client/server network. In this example, three servers host the resources, such as printers, Internet connectivity, and file storage shared with the network. Both wired and wireless clients are possible. Switches interconnect all nodes. Client/server networks are more likely to use hardware or **appliance** firewalls.

> **NOTE**
> This book will explore more complex network layouts, designs, and components in later sections.

Client/server networks also employ **single sign-on (SSO)**. SSO allows for a single but stronger set of credentials per user. With SSO, each user must perform authentication to gain access to the client and the network. Once the user has logged in, **access control** manages resource use. In other words, client/server authentication with SSO is often more complex than workgroup authentication—but it's more secure. Users only need to log in once, not every time they contact a resource host server.

Because of their complexity, client/server networks are invariably more secure than SOHO and workgroup networks. But complexity alone is not security. Instead, because they are more complex, client/server networks require more thorough design and planning. Security is an important aspect of infrastructure planning and thus becomes integrated into the network's design.

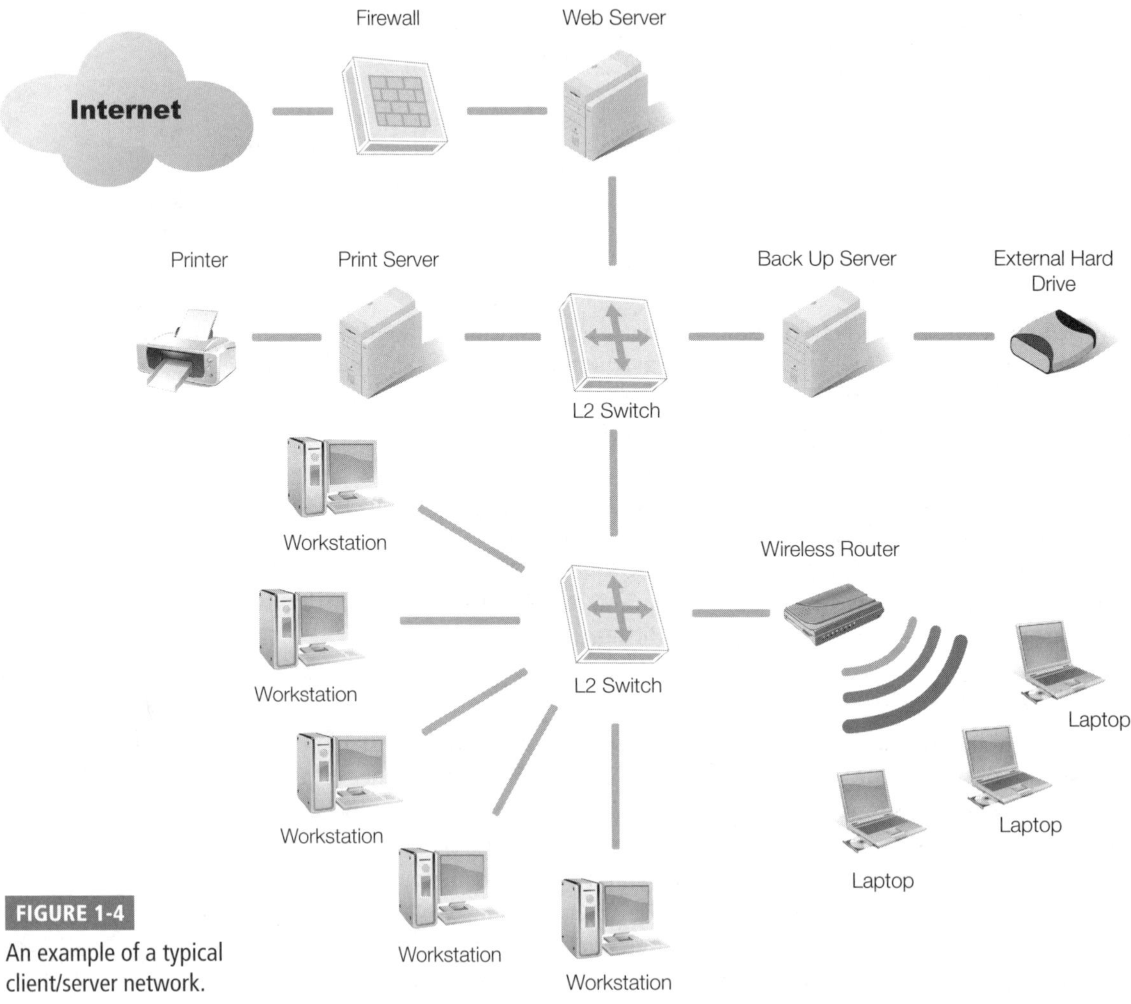

FIGURE 1-4

An example of a typical client/server network.

Client/server networks are not necessarily secure because you can deploy a client/server network without any thought toward security. But most organizations understand that if they overlook network security, they are insuring their ultimate technological downfall. Security is rarely excluded from the deployment process. And some networks are by nature more secure than others.

LAN Versus WAN

LAN stands for local area network. A LAN is a network within a limited geographic area. This means that a LAN network is located in a single physical location rather than spreading across multiple locations. Some LANs are quite large, while others are very small. A more distinguishing characteristic of a LAN is that all of the segments or links of a LAN are owned and controlled by the organization. A LAN does not contain or use any leased or externally owned connections.

WAN stands for wide area network. A WAN is a network not limited by any geographic boundaries. This means that a WAN network can span a few city blocks, reach across the globe, and even extend into outer space. A distinguishing characteristic of a WAN is that it uses leased or external connections and links. Most organizations rely on telecommunication service providers (often referred to as **telcos**) for WAN circuits and links to physical buildings and facilities, including the last-mile connection to the physical demarcation point. Both LAN and WAN networks can be secure or insecure. They are secure if a written security policy guides their use. With a LAN, the owner of the network has the sole responsibility of ensuring that security is enforced. With a WAN, the leasing entity must select a telco that has a secure WAN infrastructure and incorporate service level agreements (SLAs) that define the level of service and performance that is to be provided on a monthly basis for the customer. In most cases, WAN data is secure only if the data sent across leased lines is encrypted before transmission. This service is the responsibility of the data owner, not the telecommunications service provider, unless this option is offered as a value-added service.

Thin Clients and Terminal Services

"**Thin client** computing," also known as **terminal services**, is an old computing idea that has made a comeback in the modern era. In the early days of computers, the main computing core, commonly called a mainframe, was controlled through an interface called a terminal. The terminal was nothing more than a video screen (usually monochrome) and a keyboard. The terminal had no local processing or storage capabilities. All activities took place on the mainframe and the results appeared on the screen of the terminal.

With the advent of personal computers (PCs), a computer at a worker's desk offered local processing and storage capabilities. These PCs became the clients of client/server computers. Modern networking environments can offer a wide range of options for end users. Fully capable PCs used as workstations or client systems are the most common. PCs can run thin-client software, which emulates the terminal system of the past. That means they perform all tasks on the server or mainframe system and use the PC only as a display screen with a keyboard and mouse. Even modern thin client terminals can connect into a server or mainframe without using a full PC.

Remote Control, Remote Access, and VPN

Remote control is the ability to use a local computer system to remotely take over control of another computer over a network connection. In a way, this is the application of the thin client concept on a modern fully capable workstation to simulate working against a mainframe or to virtualize your physical presence.

With remote control connection, the local monitor, keyboard, and mouse control a remote system. This looks and feels like you are physically present at the keyboard of the remote system, which could be located in another city or even on the other side of the world. Every action you perform locally takes place at that remote computer via the remote control connection. The only limitations are speed of the intermediary network link and inability to physically insert or remove media such as a flash drive and use peripherals such as a printer.

You might consider remote control as a form of software-based thin client or terminal client. In fact, many thin client and terminal client products sell as remote control solutions.

Many modern operating systems include remote control features, such as Remote Desktop found in most versions of Windows. Once enabled, a Remote Desktop Connection remotely controls another Windows system from across the network. Chapter 14 discusses Remote Desktop in more detail.

Remote access is different from remote control. A remote access link enables access to network resources using a WAN link to connect to the geographically distant network. In effect, remote access creates a local network link for a system not physically local to the network. Over a remote access connection, a client system can technically perform all the same tasks as a locally connected client, with the only difference being the speed of the connection. Network administrators can impose restrictions on what resources and services a remote access client can use.

Remote access originally took place over dial-up telephone links using modems. Today, remote access encompasses a variety of connection types including ISDN, DSL, cable modem, satellite, mobile broadband, and more.

In most cases, a remote access connection links from a remote client back to a primary network. A **remote access server (RAS)** accepts the inbound connection from the remote client. Once the connection goes through, the remote client now interacts with the network as if it were locally connected.

Another variant of remote connections is the **virtual private network (VPN)**. A VPN is a form of network connection created over other network connections. In most cases, a VPN link connects a remote system and a LAN, but only after a normal network connection links to an intermediary network.

In Figure 1-5, a LAN has a normal network connection to the Internet and a remote client has established a normal network connection to the Internet as well. These two connections work independently of each other. The LAN's connection is usually a permanent or dedicated connection supporting both inbound and outbound activities with the Internet. The remote client's connection to the Internet can be dedicated or non-dedicated. In the latter case, the connection precedes the VPN creation. Once both endpoints of the future VPN link have a connection to the intermediary network (in this example, the Internet), then the VPN exists.

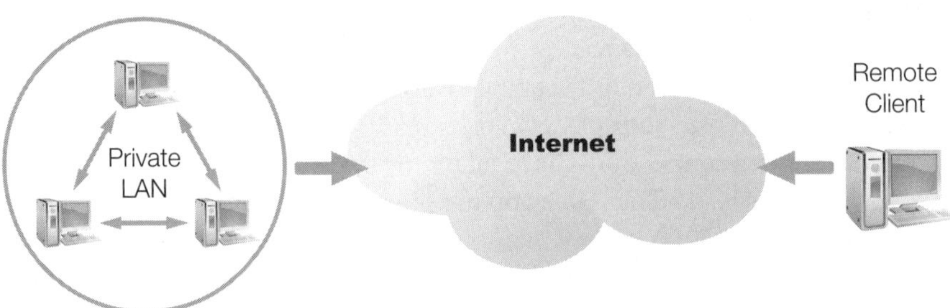

FIGURE 1-5
Common resource access connections.

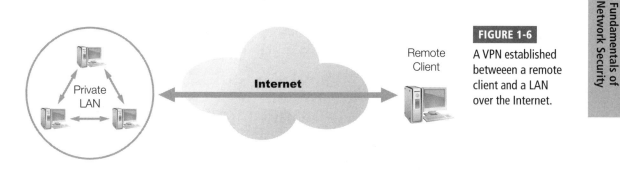

FIGURE 1-6
A VPN established betweeen a remote client and a LAN over the Internet.

In Figure 1-6, a new network connection connects the remote client to the LAN across the intermediary network. This new network connection is the VPN.

A VPN is a mechanism to establish a remote access connection across an intermediary network, often the Internet. VPNs allow for cheap long-distance connections over the Internet, as both endpoints only need a local Internet link. The Internet itself serves as a "free" long-distance carrier.

A VPN uses "**tunneling**" or **encapsulation** protocols. Tunneling protocols encase the original network protocol so that it can traverse the intermediary network. In many cases, the tunneling protocol employs **encryption** so that the original data securely traverses the intermediary network.

Boundary Networks

A boundary network is a subnetwork or "subnet" positioned on the edge of a LAN. A boundary network isolates certain activities from the production environment, such as programming or research and development. External users can also access resources hosted in a boundary network. Such a subnet is known as a demilitarized zone (DMZ) or "**extranet**."

A DMZ is a boundary network that hosts resource servers for the public Internet. An extranet is a boundary network that hosts resource servers for a limited and controlled group of external users, such as business partners, suppliers, distributors, contractors, and so forth.

A DMZ subnet is a common network design component used to host public information services, such as Web sites. The DMZ concept allows for anyone on the public Internet to access resources without needing to authenticate. But at the same time, the DMZ provides some **filtering** of obvious malicious traffic and prevents Internet users from accessing the private LAN.

An extranet subnet allows companies that need to exchange data with external partners a safe place for that activity. An extranet is secured so only the intended external users can access it. Often, accessing an extranet requires VPN connections. An extranet configuration keeps public users from the Internet out and keeps the external partners out of the private LAN.

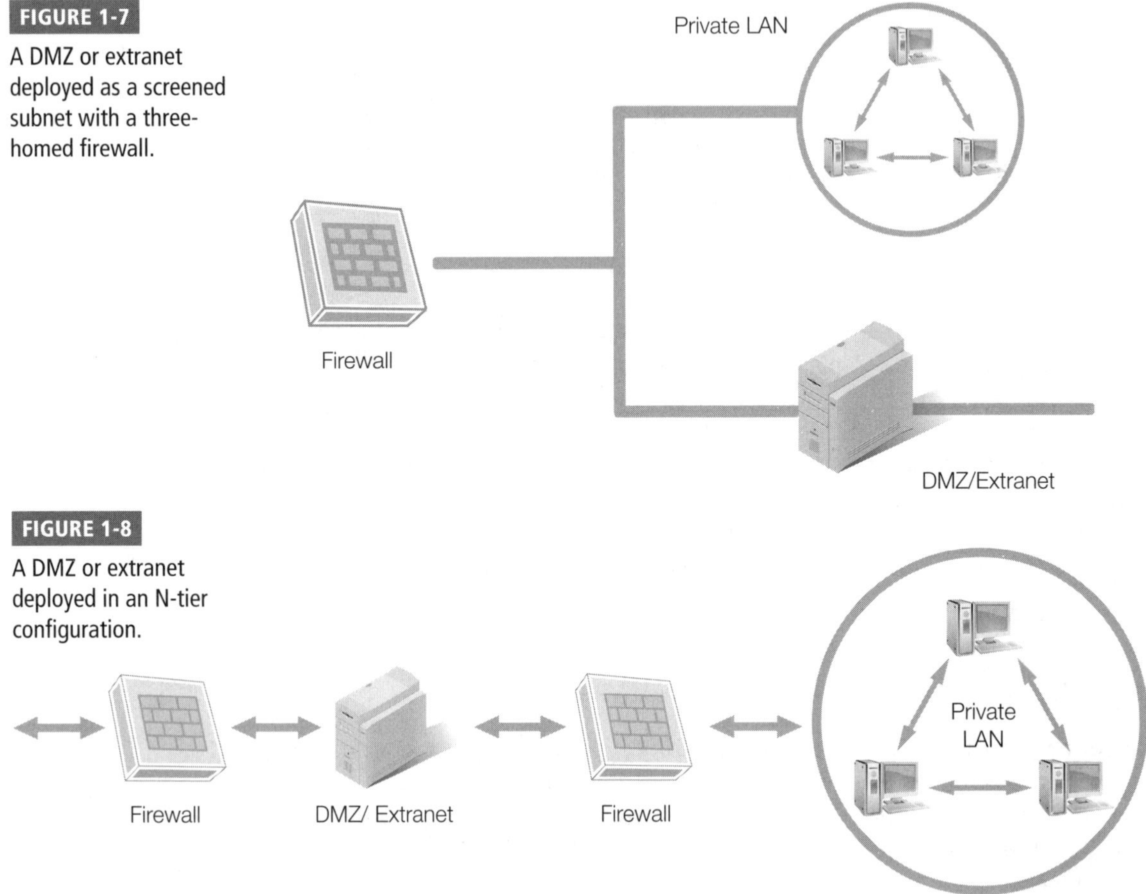

FIGURE 1-7 A DMZ or extranet deployed as a screened subnet with a three-homed firewall.

FIGURE 1-8 A DMZ or extranet deployed in an N-tier configuration.

You can deploy both DMZ and extranet subnets in different ways. Two of the most common designs are a screened subnet using a three-homed firewall (Figure 1-7) and N-tier deployment (Figure 1-8). A screened subnet using a three-homed firewall creates a network segment for the private LAN and a network segment for the DMZ or extranet. The three-homed firewall serves as a filtering device as well as a router to control traffic entering these two segments.

The N-tier deployment creates a series of subnets separated by firewalls. The DMZ or extranet subnet serves as a buffer network between the Internet and the private LAN.

Strengths and Weaknesses of Network Design

You need to evaluate every network design or layout for its security strengths and weaknesses. While there are no perfect deployments, some provide better security for a given set of parameters than others. For example, a network with only a single connection to the Internet is easier to secure than a network with multiple connections to the Internet.

When you are designing a network, consider the paths that malicious traffic could use to reach the interior of your private LAN. The more potential pathways, the more challenging securing the network will be. However, consider **redundancy**, as well. If your primary connection to the Internet fails, do you have an alternate connection? Remember, security is not just about preventing malicious events but also about ensuring that users can perform essential business tasks.

Try to avoid network designs that have a **single point of failure**. Always try to have redundant options to ensure that your mission-critical functions can take place. Keep in mind that bottlenecks are still likely to happen even with redundant pathways. Over time, monitor traffic and use levels on every segment across the network to look for trends towards reduced throughput or productivity. A bottleneck may at first be a slight hindrance to high performance and productivity, but it can later become a form of **denial of service (DoS)**.

Another consideration is traffic control and filtering. Blocking or allowing traffic is an important element in network security. You control what traffic enters or leaves the network. Traffic filtering often takes place at network choke points. A **choke point** is a form of bottleneck and is a single controlled pathway between two different levels of network trust where a firewall or other filtering devices blocks or allows traffic based on a set of rules. Thus, rather than being only a benefit for filtering, a choke point can slow throughput or become a target for DoS attacks.

Another network design issue is the location of authorized users. Often we assume valid users are internal users. With the proliferation of telecommuting and out-sourcing, however, valid users can often be external users as well. Realizing this, you must design networks to support inbound connections from valid external users. This can involve traditional remote access connections, but more likely will use VPN links. VPNs provide connections for remote users that function like local connections and encryptions to keep the content of those connections confidential.

Enhancing the Security of Wired Versus Wireless LAN Infrastructures

Wired networks offer a form of security that wireless networks lack. That security is the direct physical connection to a wired or cabled network. A hacker requires physical access to your facility or building. Usually, access control of the building can sufficiently prevent most external parties from accessing your private LAN.

Realize, however, that if you allow remote connection via telephone modem, high-speed broadband, or even basic Internet service, then you lose the advantage of a physical access limitation. Once remote access is allowed, the benefits of physical isolation disappear.

The same is true if you allow wireless connections into the network. Wireless networking grants valid and unknown users the ability to interact with the network. This completely eliminates the need to be physically present in the building to connect to the network. With the right type of antenna, an attacker could be over a mile away from your office building and still be able to affect your wireless network.

To regain some of the security offered by physical isolation, try to incorporate physical isolation into your network design. Isolate all remote access and wireless access points from the main wired network. You can achieve this by using separate subnets and filtering communications using firewalls. While design does not offer the same level of security as physical isolation, the arrangement provides a significant improvement over having no control over remote or wireless connections.

All remote connections should go through a rigorous gauntlet of verification before you grant access to the internal LAN. Think of a castle design in the Middle Ages that used multiple layers of defense: a moat, a drawbridge, thick riveted walls, an inner battlement, and finally, a strong keep or inner fortress. Your multi-layer defensive design should include multi-factor authentication and communication encryption, such as a VPN. Additional checks can include verification of operating system and patch level, confirmation of physical or logical location origin (such as caller ID, MAC address, or IP address), limitations to time of day, and limitation on protocols above the transport layer. Any intruder would need to circumvent layer after layer, making intrusion more and more difficult.

NOTE

An attack known as "Van Eck phreaking" allows an attacker to eavesdrop on electronic devices from a distance. This technique is not perfect or simple to perform, but has been demonstrated on LCD and CRT monitors as well as keyboard cables. With minor shielding, you can eliminate most of the risk from such an attack.

Internal and External Network Issues

When deploying a new network or modifying an existing infrastructure, carefully evaluate impacts on security and security's impact on the infrastructure. When you or your team overlook or sidestep standard security practices, good business stops. Business interruptions can result not only in lost profits, but also in lost opportunities and even in lost jobs. If the compromise is serious enough, the business might not recover.

The threats facing business are numerous and constantly changing. Often these issues arise daily. Malicious code, information leakage, zero day exploits, unauthorized software, unethical employees, and complex network infrastructures are just a few of the concerns that every organization and network manager faces.

Malicious code can make its way into a computer through any communication channel. This includes file transfers, e-mail, portable device syncing, removable media, and Web sites. Precautions against malicious code include network traffic filtering with a firewall, anti-malware scanning, and user behavior modification.

Information leakage stems from malicious employees who purposefully release internal documentation to the public. It can also result from accidents, when a storage device is lost, recycled, donated, stolen, or thrown away. Or, it occurs when users accidentally publish documents to P2P file sharing services or Web sites. Precautions against information leakage include doing thorough background checks on employees, using the principle of least privilege, detail auditing and monitoring of all user activity, classifying all information and controlling communication pathways, using more stringent controls on use of portable devices, and enforcing **zeroization** procedures for storage devices.

Zero day exploits are new and previously unknown attacks for which no current specific defenses exist. Think of them as surprise attacks on your defenses. "Zero day" refers to the newness of an exploit, which may be known in the hacker community for days or weeks, but about which vendors and security professionals are just learning.

The zero day label comes from the idea that work to develop a patch begins the moment a vendor learns of a problem. The moment of discovery of the new exploit is called "day zero." No specific defenses against zero day attacks exist, but general security management, use of intrusion detection and intrusion prevention, along with detailed **logging** and monitoring can assist in discovering and preventing new attacks quickly. Once you know of an attack or exploit, you can begin taking steps to contain damage or minimize the extent of the compromise.

Unauthorized software is any piece of code that a user chooses to run on a client system that was not approved nor provided by the company. Not all unauthorized software is directly problematic, but you should prevent its use for many reasons. Such software might be a waste of time and productivity that costs the company money, time, and effort. The software could be a license violation. Software could include hidden malicious components, known or unknown to the user, which could compromise the security of the network. Steps you can take to prevent the use of unauthorized software should include limiting installation privileges of normal users and using **white lists** to block the execution of any program not on the approved list.

Unethical employees purposefully violate the stated rules and goals of the organization. These employees often believe the rules are not important, do not really apply to them, or are not really enforced. Most believe they will never get caught. When users violate the mission and goals of the organization, consequences could be catastrophic.

Users are the final link in security and are often the weakest link in network security. If a user chooses to violate a security policy and release information to the public or execute malicious code, the results could devastate the organization or land the perpetrator in court. Methods of preventing unethical employees from doing damage include better background screening, detail auditing and monitoring of all user activity, and regular management oversight and job performance reviews. When you discover a problematic person, you might be able to grant the employee a second chance after re-training, but in many cases, the safest choice for the organization is to terminate employment.

Complex network infrastructures lend themselves to complex vulnerabilities. The larger a network becomes, the more servers, clients, network devices, and segments it includes. The sheer number of "moving parts" almost guarantees that something is bound to be mis-configured, be improperly installed, lack current firmware or patches, have a bottleneck, or be used incorrectly. Any of these conditions could result in vulnerability that internal or external attackers can exploit. The larger and more complex a network, the more thoroughly the security team needs to watch over the infrastructure and investigate every symptom, trend, or alert. Preventing complexity from becoming a liability involves detailed planning, careful implementation, regular security management, and constant review of the effectiveness of the infrastructure.

Studies have shown that most threats come from internal sources, but too many organizations focus on external sources and discount the internal threats. A better stance is to count all threats—regardless of their source—as worthy of investigation. Once a potential threat is understood, its risk, potential loss, and likelihood can be better understood and evaluated.

One of the most obvious external threats is the Internet. The Internet is a global network linking people and resources with high-speed real-time communications. Unfortunately, this wonderful infrastructure also makes great abuse more possible. Once your company installs an Internet connection, the world is at your door—or rather, at the fingertips of every employee. That world includes both potential customers and potential attackers.

Without a global communication infrastructure, hackers had to be physically present—wired in—in or near your building to launch attacks. With the advent of the Internet and wireless technology, any hacker anywhere can initiate attempts to breach your network security. It's helpful, therefore, to think of the Internet as a threat. It's not one that you should lightly dismiss nor should you discard the Internet as a powerful tool. The benefits of Internet access are well worth the effort and expense you should expend to defend against its negative features.

Some of the best defenses against Internet threats include a well-researched, written security policy; thoroughly trained personnel; use of firewalls to filter traffic intrusion, detection, and prevention systems; use of encrypted communications (such as VPNs); and thorough auditing and monitoring of all user and node activity.

Again, perfect security solutions don't exist. Some form of attack, compromise, or exploit can get past any single defense. The point of network security is to interweave and interconnect multiple security components to construct a multi-faceted scheme of protection. This is often called multiple layers of defense or "**defense in depth.**"

The goal is to balance the strengths and weaknesses of multiple security components. The ultimate functions of network security are to lock things down in the best way possible, then monitor for all attempts to violate the established defense. Since the perfect lock doesn't exist, improve on the best locks available with auditing and monitoring. Knowing this, your next step is to understand the common network security components and their uses.

Common Network Security Components Used to Mitigate Threats

When considering the deployment of a network or the modification of an existing network, evaluate each network component to determine its security strengths and weaknesses. This section discusses many common network security components.

Hosts and Nodes

A **node** is any device on the network. This includes client computers, servers, switches, routers, firewalls, and anything with a network interface that has a MAC address.

A **Media Access Control (MAC) address** is the 48-bit physical hardware address of a network interface card (NIC) assigned by the manufacturer. A node is a component that can be communicated with, rather than only through or across. For example, network cables and patch panels are not nodes, but a printer is.

A **host** is a form of node that has a logical address assigned to it, usually an Internet Protocol (IP) address. This addressing typically implies that the node operates at or above the network layer. The network layer includes clients, servers, firewalls, proxies, and even routers. But it excludes switches, bridges, and other physical devices such as repeaters and hubs. In most cases, a host either shares or accesses resources and services from other hosts.

In terms of network security, node and host security does vary. Nodes and hosts can both be harmed by physical attacks and DoS attacks. However, a host can also be harmed by **malicious code**, authentication attacks, and might even be remotely controlled by hackers. Node protection is mostly physical access control along with basic network filtering against flooding.

Host security can be much more involved because the host itself should be hardened and you will need to perform general network security. **Hardening** is the process of securing or locking down a host against threats and attacks. This can include removing unnecessary software, installing updates, and imposing secure configuration settings.

IPv4 Versus IPv6

Internet Protocol version 4 (IPv4) has been in use as the predominate protocol on the Internet for nearly three decades. It was originally defined in **Request for Comment (RFC)** 791 in 1981. IPv4 is a connectionless protocol that operates at the network layer of the **open system interconnection reference model (OSI model)**. IPv4 is the foundation of the TCP/IP protocol suite as we know and use it today.

IPv4 was designed with several assumptions in mind, many of which have been proven inaccurate, grossly overestimated, or simply non-applicable. While IPv4 has served well as the predominate protocol on the Internet, a replacement has been long overdue. Some of the key issues of concern are a dwindling, if not exhausted, address space of only 32 bits, subnetting complexity, and lack of integrated security. Some of these issues have been minimized with the advent of **network address translation (NAT)**, classless inter-domain routing (CIDR), and **Internet Protocol Security (IPSec)**. But in spite of these advancements, IPv4 is being replaced with IPv6.

IPv6 was defined in 1998 in RFC 2460. The new version was designed specifically as the successor to IPv4 mainly due to the dwindling availability of public addresses. IPv6 uses a 128-bit address, which is significantly larger than IPv4. Additionally, changes to subnetting, address assignment, packet header, and simpler routing processing make IPv6 much preferred over its predecessor. Another significant improvement is native network layer security. Figure 1-9 below compares an IPv4 address to an IPv6 address.

> **NOTE**
>
> If an IPv6 address has one or more consecutive 4-digit sections of all zeros, the sections of zeros can be dropped and replaced by just a double colon. For example: 2001:0f58:0000:0000:0000:0000:1986:62af can be shortened to 2001:0f58::1986:62af. However, if there are two sections of zero sets, only a single section can be replaced by double colons.

technical TIP

A **man-in-the-middle** attack occurs when a hacker is positioned between a client and a server and the client is fooled into connecting with the hacker computer instead of the real server. The hacker performs a spoofing attack in order to trick the client. The result is the connection between the client and server is proxied by the hacker. This allows the hacker to eavesdrop and manipulate the communications.

A **hijacking** attack occurs when a hacker uses a network sniffer to watch a communications session to learn its parameters. The hacker then disconnects one of the session's hosts, impersonates the offline system, and begins injecting crafted packets into the communication stream. If successful, the hacker takes over the session of the offline host, while the other host is unaware of the switch.

A **replay attack** occurs when a hacker uses a network sniffer to capture network traffic, and then retransmits that traffic back on to the network at a later time. Replay attacks often focus on authentication traffic in the hope that retransmitting the same packets that allowed the real user to log into a system will grant the hacker the same access.

Chapter 4 discusses a wide range of various attacks and **exploits**.

The security features native to IPv6 were crafted into an add-on packet for IPv4 known as IPSec. While in IPv4, IPSec is an optional add-on; it is a built-in feature of and used by default with IPv6. This use is a significant change in the inherent security issues surrounding networking and the use of the Internet. With native network layer encryption, most forms of eavesdropping, man-in-the-middle attacks, hijacking, and replay attacks are no longer possible. This does not mean that IPv6 will be security problem-free, but at least most of the common security flaws experienced with IPv4 will be fixed.

IPv4

In dotted decimal notation: 192.168.12.153

In binary: 110000001010100000000110010011001

IPv6

In hexadecimal notation: 2001:0db8:8fa3:dc94:1a2e:a370:7334:7337

In binary:
0010000000000000100001101101110001000111100010011110111001001010000011010001011101010001101110000

FIGURE 1-9

Comparing a typical IPv4 address to an IPv6 address.

As you use and manage computers and manage networks, use IPSec with IPv4 or switch over to IPv6. Most protocols that operate over IPv4 will operate without issue over IPv6. You will need to replace some applications that embed network-layer addresses into their application-level protocol, such as FTP and NTP. But valid IPv6 replacements already exist.

The complete industry transition from IPv4 to IPv6 will likely take upwards of a decade, mainly because of the need to upgrade, replace, or re-configure the millions of hosts and nodes spread across the world to support IPv6. During the transition, many techniques are available to allow a host to interact with both IPv4 and IPv6 network connections. These include:

- **Dual IP stacks**—a computer system that runs both IPv4 and IPv6 at the same time. Windows Vista and Windows Server 7 both have dual IP stacks by default.
- **IPv4 addresses embedded into an IPv6 notation**—a method of representing an IPv4 address using the common notation of IPv6. For example, ::ffff:192.168.3.125 is the IPv4-mapped IPv6 address for the IPv4 address: 192.168.3.125.

  Note: The IPv6 address is 80 zero bits, followed by 16 one bits, then the 32-bit IPv4 address (in dotted decimal notation), which adds up to 128 bits total.
- **Tunneling**—encapsulating IPv6 packets inside IPv4 packets, effectively creating a VPN-like tunnel out of IPv4 for IPv6.
- **IPv4/IPv6 NAT**—using a network address translation service to translate between two networks, one running IPv4 and the other IPv6.

Whatever the hurdles of transition, the benefits of native network layer encryption are immeasurable. Long story short: when you have the option to use IPv6, take it because you will be helping the world IT community upgrade sooner rather than later.

Firewall

Not all traffic on your network is from an authorized source, so you shouldn't allow it to enter or leave the network. Not all traffic is for an authorized purpose, so you should block it from reaching its destination. Not all traffic is within the boundaries of normal or acceptable network activity, so you should drop it before it causes compromises.

All of these protections are the job of a firewall. As its name implies, a **firewall** is a tool designed to stop damage, just as the firewall in an engine compartment protects the passengers in a vehicle from harm in an accident. A firewall is either a hardware device or a software product you deploy to enforce the access control policy on network communications. In other words, a firewall filters network traffic for harmful exploits, incursions, data, messages, or other events.

Firewalls are often positioned on the edge of a network or subnet. Firewalls protect networks against numerous threats from the Internet. Firewalls also protect the Internet from rogue users or applications on private networks. Firewalls protect the throughput or bandwidth of a private network so authorized users can get work done. Without firewalls, most of your network's capabilities would be consumed by worthless or malicious traffic from the Internet. Think of how a dam on a river works; without the dam, the river is prone to flooding and overflow. The dam prevents the flooding and damage.

Without firewalls, the security and stability of a network would depend mostly on the security of the nodes and hosts within the network. Based on the sordid security history of most host operating systems, having no firewall would not be a secure solution. Hardened hosts and nodes are important for network security, but they should not be the only component of reliable network security.

You also install firewalls on client and server computers. These host software firewalls protect a single host from threats from the Internet, and threats from the network itself, as well as threats from other internal network components.

In any case, a firewall is usually configured to control traffic based on a "deny-by-default / allow-by-exception" stance. This means that nothing passes the firewall just because it exists on the network (or is attempting to reach the network). Instead, all traffic that reaches the firewall must meet a set of requirements to continue on its path.

As a network administrator or IT security officer, you get to choose what traffic is allowed to pass through the firewalls, and what traffic is not. Additionally, you can also determine whether the filtering takes place on inbound traffic (known as "**ingress filtering**"), on outbound traffic (called "**egress filtering**")—or both.

Firewalls are an essential component of both host and network security. Additional firewall specifics and details are covered throughout this book in subsequent chapters.

VPN

A virtual private network (VPN) is a mechanism to establish a remote access connection across an intermediary network, often over the Internet. VPNs allow for cheap long-distance connections when established over the Internet, since both endpoints only need a local Internet link. The Internet itself serves as a "free" long-distance carrier.

A VPN uses tunneling or encapsulation protocols. Tunneling protocols encase the original network protocol so that it can traverse the intermediary network. In many cases, the tunneling protocol employs encryption so that the original data traverses the intermediary network securely.

You can use VPNs for remote access, remote control, or highly secured communications within a private network. Additional VPN specifics and details are covered throughout this book in subsequent chapters.

Proxy

A **proxy** server is a variation of a firewall. A proxy server filters traffic, but also acts upon that traffic in a few specific ways. First, a proxy server acts as a "middle-man" between the internal client and the external server. Or, in the case of reverse proxy, this relationship can be inverted with an internal server and an external host. Second, a proxy server will hide the identity of the original requester from the server through a process known as network address translation (NAT) (see the following section).

Another feature of a proxy server can be content filtering. This type of filtering focuses either on the address of the server (typically by domain name or IP address) or on keywords appearing in the transmitted context. You can employ this form of filtering to block employee access to Internet resources that are not relevant or beneficial to business tasks or that might have direct impact on the business network. This could include malicious code, hacker tools, and excessive bandwidth consumption (such as video streaming or P2P file exchange).

Proxy servers can also provide caching services. Proxy server **caching** is a data storage mechanism that keeps a local copy of content that is fairly static in nature and which numerous internal clients have a pattern of requesting. Front pages of popular Web sites are commonly cached by a proxy server. When a user then requests a page from the Internet in cache, the proxy server provides that page to the user from cache rather than pulling it again from the Internet site. This provides the user with faster performance and reduces the load on the Internet link.

Caching of this type often results in all users experiencing faster Internet performance, even when the pages served to them are pulled from the Internet. Obviously, such caching must be tuned to prevent stale pages in the cache. Tuning is setting the time-out value on cached pages so they expire at a reasonable rate. All expired cache pages are replaced by fresh content from the original source server on the Internet.

NAT

Network address translation (NAT) converts between internal addresses and external public addresses. The network performs this conversion on packets as they enter or leave the network to mask and modify the internal client's configuration. The primary purpose of NAT is to prevent internal IP and network configuration details from being discovered by external entities, such as hackers.

Figure 1-10 shows an example pathway from an internal client to an external server across a proxy or firewall using NAT. In this example, the external server is a Web server operating on the default HTTP port 80. The Web server is using IP address 208.40.235.38 (used by *www.itttech.edu*). The requesting internal client is using IP address 192.168.12.153. The client randomly selects a source port between 1024 and 65,535 (such as 13571). With these source details, the client generates the initial request packet. This is step 1. This packet is sent over the network towards the external server, where it encounters the NAT service.

FIGURE 1-10

An example of how NAT functions.

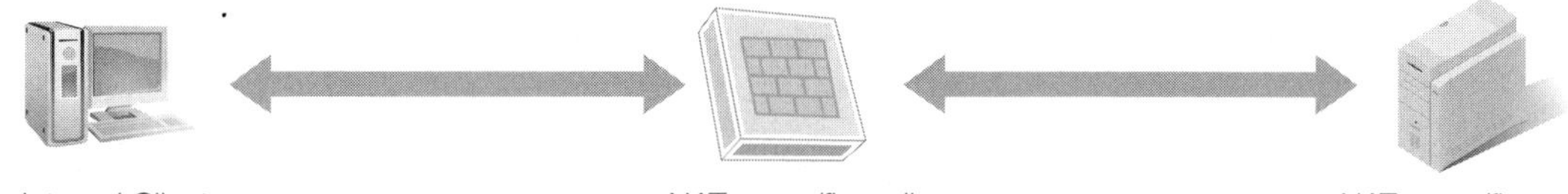

STEP 1 Initial request:

```
S: 192.168.12.153: 13571
D: 208.40.235.38: 80
```

STEP 2 NAT creates entry in translation mapping table:

```
Internal:                      External:
192.168.12.153: 13571 <- -> 72.254.149.76: 27409
```

The NAT service creates an entry in its translation or mapping table for the request. The table contains the source IP address and port and the translated IP address and port. The NAT server uses its own public IP address as the translated IP address and selects a random currently unused port for the new source port for the packet. This is step 2.

STEP 3 Translated request:

```
S: 72.254.149.76: 27409
D: 208.40.235.38: 80
```

Step 3 is the construction of the new packet with the translated source information, which is then transmitted over the Internet to the external server. The Web server receives a request whose source seems to be the proxy/firewall system.

STEP 4 Response from external server:

```
S: 208.40.235.38: 80
D: 72.254.149.76: 27409
```

Step 4 is the response generated and transmitted by the Web server.

STEP 5 Response sent to client by NAT:

```
S: 208.40.235.38:  80
D: 192.168.12.153: 13571
```

The proxy/firewall receives the response to the Web server's request. The NAT service uses the translation table to return the original client's information into the packet header as the destination. This is step 5. This process takes place at wirespeed. It is usually transparent to the client and server involved in the communication, because they are unaware that the translation took place.

Another purpose or use of NAT is to reduce the need for a significant number of public IP addresses you need to lease from an ISP. Without NAT, you'd need a single **public IP address** for each individual system that would ever connect to the Internet. With NAT, you can lease a smaller set of public IP addresses to serve a larger number of internal users.

This consolidation is possible for two reasons. First, most network communications are "bursty" rather than constant in nature. This means that computers typically transmit short, fast busts of data instead of a long, continuous stream of data. Some forms of network traffic, such as file transfer and video streaming, are more continuous in nature. But these tasks are generally less common on business networks than home networks.

Second, NAT does not reserve a specific public address for use by a single internal client. Instead, NAT randomly assigns an available public address to each subsequent internal client request. Once the client's communication session is over, the public address returns to the pool of available addresses for future communications.

Additionally, NAT often employs not just IP to IP address translation, but a more granular option known as **port address translation (PAT)**. With PAT, both the port and the IP address of the client convert into a random external port and public IP address. This allows for multiple simultaneous communications to take place over a single IP address. This process, in turn, allows you to support a greater number of communications from a single client or multiple clients on an even smaller number of leased public IP addresses.

NAT enables the use of the RFC 1918 **private IP address** ranges while still supporting Internet communications. The RFC 1918 addresses are:

- **Class A**—10.0.0.0–10.255.255.255 /8 (1 Class A network)
- **Class B**—172.16.0.0–172.31.255.255 /12 (16 Class B networks)
- **Class C**—192.168.0.0–192.168.255.255 /16 (256 Class C networks)

The addresses in **RFC 1918** are for use only in private networks. Internet routers drop any packet using one of these addresses. Without NAT, a network using these private IP addresses would be unable to communicate with the Internet. By using RFC 1918 addresses, networks create another barrier against Internet-based attacks and do not need to pay for leasing of internal addresses.

As briefly mentioned in the earlier section on IPSec, NAT is one of the technologies that have allowed the extended use of IPv4 even after the depletion of available public IP addresses. Now that the transition to IPv6 is underway, NAT is serving a new purpose in proving IPv4 to IPv6 translation. Many firewall and proxy devices may include IPv6 translation services. This feature is a worthwhile option that you might want to include on a feature list when researching a firewall purchase or deployment.

technical TIP

An interesting wrinkle on NAT and PAT is that most devices and software products that support PAT actually state in their documentation and in their configuration interfaces that they support NAT. It seems that NAT has been redefined to include the functionality of port address translation, even though an official acronym for that specific additional technology already exists. This combination is also true on most certification exams. Questions might use the NAT acronym but actually refer to port translation (PAT).

Routers, Switches, and Bridges

Routers, **switches**, and **bridges** are common network devices. While not directly or typically labeled as network security devices, you can deploy them to support security rather than hinder it.

A router's primary purpose is to direct traffic towards its stated destination along the best-known current available path (see Figure 1-11). Routing protocols such as RIP, OSPF, IGRP, EIGRP, BGP, and others dynamically manage route selection based on a variety of metrics. A router supports security by guiding traffic down preferred routes rather than routes that might not be as logically or physically secure. If a hacker can trick routers into altering the pathway of transmission, network traffic could traverse a segment where a hacker has positioned a "**sniffer**." A sniffer, also known as packet analyzer, network analyzer, and protocol analyzer, is a software utility or hardware device that captures network communications for investigation and analysis.

While this is an unlikely scenario, it's not an impossible one. Ensuring that routers are using authentication to exchange routing data and are protected against unauthorized physical access will prevent this and other infrastructure level attacks. Figure 1-11 depicts an example of a routed network deployment.

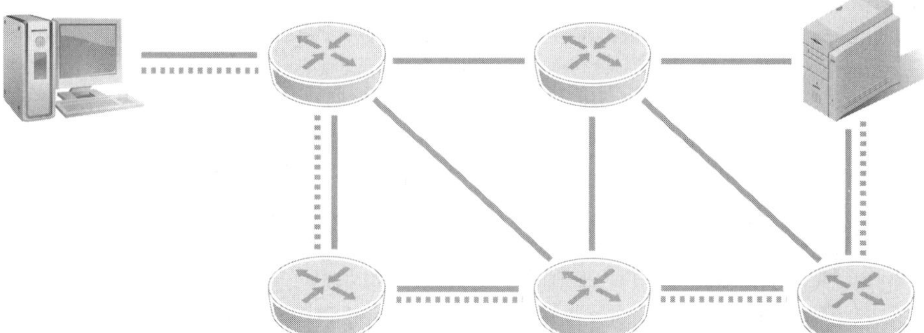

FIGURE 1-11 An example of router deployment.

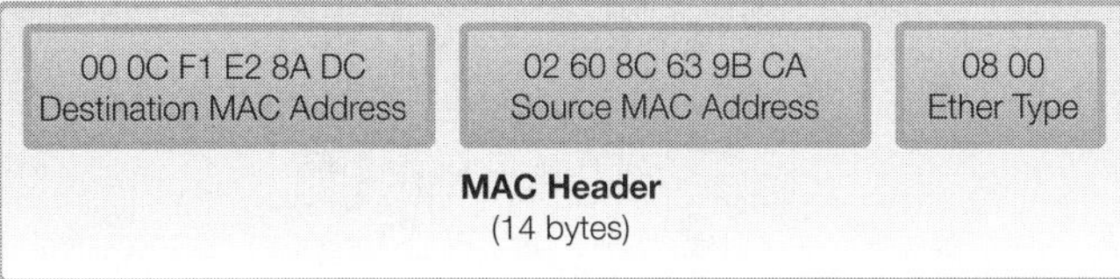

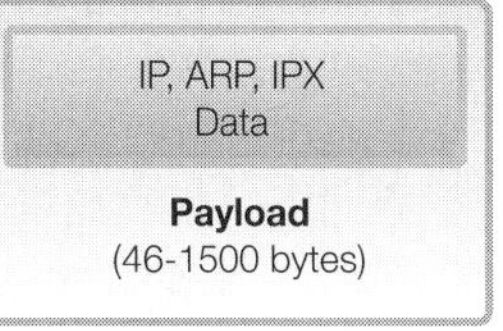

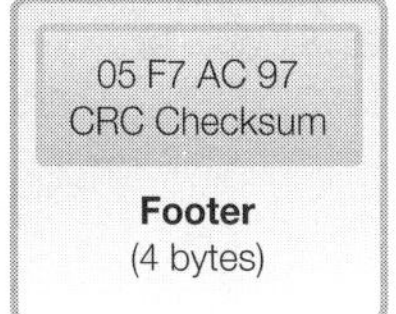

FIGURE 1-12

An example of switch deployment.

Switches provide network segmentation through hardware. Across a switch, temporary dedicated electronic communication pathways connect the endpoints of a session (such as a client and server). This switched pathway prevents collisions. Additionally, switches allow you to use the full potential throughput capacity of the network connection by the communication instead of 40 percent or more being wasted by collisions (as occurs with hubs). See Figure 1-12.

You can see this basic function of a switch as a security benefit once you examine how this process takes place. A switch operates at Layer 2, the Data Link layer, of the OSI model, where the MAC address is defined and used. Switches manage traffic through the use of the source and destination MAC address in an Ethernet frame. The Ethernet frame is a logical data set construction at the Data Link layer (layer 2) consisting of the payload from the Network layer (layer 3) with the addition of an Ethernet header and footer (Figure 1-13).

Switches employ four main procedures, labeled as "learn," "forward," "drop," and "flood." The learn procedure is the collection of MAC addresses from the source location in a frame header. The source MAC address goes into a mapping table along with the number of the port that received the frame. Forwarding occurs once a frame's destination MAC address appears in the mapping table. This table then guides the switch to transmit the frame out the port that originally discovered the MAC address in question.

If the frame goes on the same port that the mapping table indicates is the destination port, then the frame is dropped. The switch does not need to transmit the frame back onto the network segment from which it originated. Finally, if the destination MAC is not in the mapping table, the switch reverts to flooding—that is, a transmission of the frame out every port—to ensure that the frame has the best chance of reaching the destination.

By monitoring the activity of the switch, specifically watching the construction and modification of the mapping table and the variation of MAC addresses seen in frame headers, you can detect errors and malicious traffic. Intelligent or multi-layer switches themselves or external IDS/IPS services can perform this security monitoring function.

When the switch procedures fail, the network suffers. This could mean a reduction in throughput, a blockage causing a denial of service, or a redirection of traffic allowing a hacker to attempt to modify or eavesdrop. Fortunately, such attacks are "noisy" in terms of generating significant abnormal network traffic, and thus you can detect them with basic security sensors. This benefit alone is a significant reason to use switches rather than hubs.

FIGURE 1-13

An IEEE 802.3 Ethernet Type II frame.

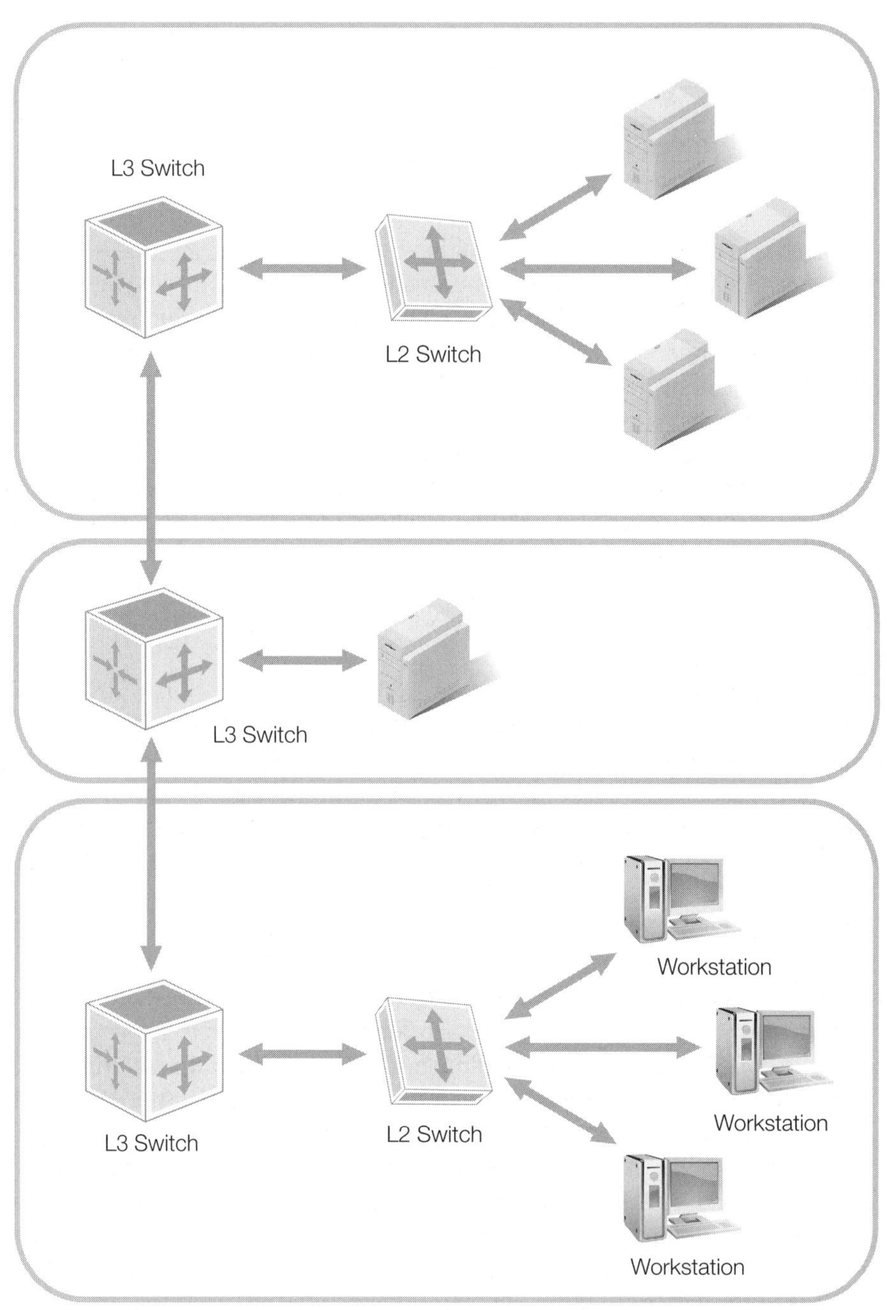

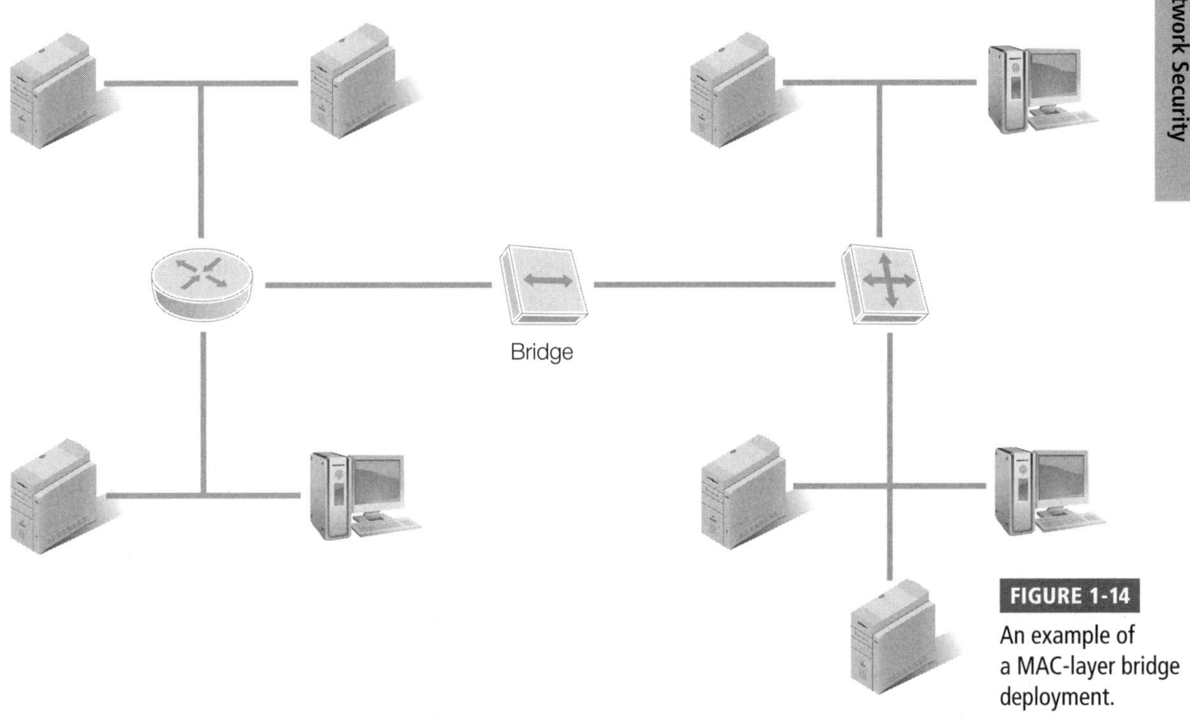

FIGURE 1-14
An example of a MAC-layer bridge deployment.

Bridges link between networks. Bridges create a path or route between networks only used when the destination of a communication actually resides across the bridge on the opposing network. An analogy of this would be a city split in two by a river. When a person traveling in that city wants to visit a specific location, if that location is on the same side of the river that they are, then they have no need to cross the bridge to get there.

The same is true of a network bridge. Bridges work in a similar manner to switches in that they use several basic procedures to manage traffic. Bridges use the process of learn, forward, and drop. Thus, with these processes, only traffic intended for a destination on the opposing network will go by the bridge to that network. All traffic intended for a destination on the same side of the bridge that received it will be dropped since the traffic is already on the correct network.

Bridges are used to connect networks, network segments, or subnets whenever you desire a simple use-only-if-needed link and the complexity of a router, switch, or firewall is neither specifically required nor desired. See Figure 1-14. Bridges can also link networks with variations in most aspects of the infrastructure barring protocol. This includes different topologies, cable types, transmission speeds, and even wired versus wireless.

You can use bridges to detect the same types of traffic abuses that switches do. In addition, both bridges and switches can impose filtering on MAC addresses. Here you can use a **black list** or white list concept, where you allow all traffic except for that on the black/block list or you block all traffic except for that on the white/allow list.

You can arrange to **log** activities across a router, switch, and bridge. You should review traffic logs regularly, typically on the same schedule as firewall and IDS/IPS logs. You will note the signs of abuse, intrusion, denial of service, network consumption, unauthorized traffic patterns, and more in these common network devices not typically considered to be security devices.

DNS

Domain name system (DNS) is an essential element of both Internet and private network resource access. Users do not keep track of the IP address of servers. So, to access the file server or social networking site, users rely upon DNS to resolve the **fully qualified domain names (FQDNs)** into the associated IP address.

Most users don't even realize that networks rely upon IP addresses to direct traffic towards a destination rather than the domain name that they typed into the address field of client software. However, without this essential but often transparent service, most of how the Internet works today would fail. In such a case, users would need to maintain a list of IP addresses of sites they wanted to visit or always go to a search engine for a site's IP address.

> **NOTE**
>
> A few Internet index sites still exist, but they are not as exhaustive (nor current) as most search engines. Think of the difference between the Yellow Pages dropped on your front porch each year versus dialing 411: one is more current and relevant than the other.

DNS is the foundation of most **directory services** in use today (such as Active Directory and LDAP) (see the following section). Thus, DNS is essential for internal networks, as much as it is for the external Internet.

DNS is vulnerable in several ways. First, DNS is a non-authentication-query-based system. This allows a false or "spoofed" response to a DNS query to appear valid. Second, anyone can request transfers of the DNS mapping data (called "the zone file"), including external entities if TCP port 53 allows inbound access. Third, DNS uses a plain text communication allowing for eavesdropping, interception, and modification.

> **technical TIP**
>
> Users also commonly do not know many server names or even domain names for resources they regularly access. This is both an expected consequence and a non-issue, as long as search engines exist. Search engines grant users the freedom from having to remember details, notably about system names, domain names, URLs, and especially IP addresses—as long as the user can remember how to access the search engine. As Einstein was reported to have said, "Why remember something when you can look it up?"

You can address some of the faults of DNS with local static DNS mapping in the **HOSTS file**, filtering DNS on network boundaries, and using IPSec for all communications between all hosts. However, these are defenses for DNS. Rather than providing a security to the network, DNS itself is an essential service that you need to protect.

Directory Services

A directory service is a network index. It helps users locate resources within a private network. A directory service is responsible for keeping track of which servers (as sometimes clients) are online, as well as the resources these hosts share with the network. A directory service operates much like a telephone book does for phone numbers and addresses.

Prior to directory services, less efficient methods of tracking or locating available resources were in service. These included local static or dynamic lists, which networks maintained using broadcast announcements. Only workgroup networks still use these outdated methods.

Directory services is another essential piece of modern networks that does not itself provide obvious security services. However, directory services needs the protection provided by other security services and devices. You should limit access to directory services to authorized and authenticated clients and users of the local network. Your network should ignore all external requests for information, with the exception of valid remote access or VPN links. If possible, you should deploy IPSec so that you protect every internal network communication.

IDS/IPS

Intrusion detection systems (IDS) and intrusion prevent systems (IPS) have become popular topics of discussion in the IT and security fields. The concept of an IDS is a system that watches over internal hosts or networks watching for symptoms of compromise or intrusion. Effectively an IDS is a form of burglar alarm that detects when an attack is occurring within the network.

An IDS serves as a companion mechanism to firewalls. Once an IDS detects an intruder, it can send commands or requests to the firewall to break a connection, block an IP address, or block a port/protocol. You must configure the firewall to receive these commands and authorize the IDS to send them. Not all IDSs and firewalls are compatible in this manner.

Eventually, the IPS concept appeared. The IPS strives to detect the attempt to attack or intrude before it has the opportunity to be successful. Once detected, the IPS can respond to prevent the success of the attempt, rather than waiting until after a successful breach to respond. IPSs do not necessarily replace IDSs. Instead, they are often used as a first or initial layer of proactive defense, relegating the IDS to a reactive measure against those events that the IPS misses or that internal personnel perform.

IDS and IPS are important components of a complete network security solution. However, they are not without fault. IDS/IPS solutions can create a false sense of security under certain conditions. Two commonly discussed conditions include unknown "zero-day" attacks and "false positives."

When unknown zero-day attacks threaten the network, an IDS or IPS might not have the mechanism to detect it. Thus, the lack of an alarm could cause administrators to assume that no attacks are occurring. In most cases, the lack of an alarm does mean that nothing malicious is happening. So this assumption is not completely unwarranted. But if an IDS never triggers an alarm, then you should suspect a poor detection system rather than the complete lack of compromise attempts or attacks.

False positives present the same result for the opposite reason, namely too many alarms from benign occurrences. After the first initial alarms turn out to be triggered by benign activity, the urgency of responding to alarms diminishes. After additional false positives, an administrator might put off investigating alarms. Eventually, you ignore the alarms altogether. Once this situation arises, you treat even alarms for malicious events as false positives, once again establishing a false sense of security.

NAC

Network access control (NAC) limits access or admission to the network based on the security compliance of a host. NAC is essentially an enforcement tool to make sure that all hosts connecting to the network have current and compliant security components. With NAC you can block or restrict access if a computer does not have the latest antivirus update, a certain security patch, or a host firewall.

NAC usually operates by placing an agent on each authorized host. When the host connects to the network, the agent contacts the master control program to find current host requirements. If the host fails to meet those requirements, then the NAC prevents the host from accessing the network. A non-compliant host may be granted access only to remediation servers. These remediation servers can provide the patches and updates needed to bring the host into full compliance.

Effectively, NAC is a method to enforce host-hardening rules through an automated systemwide mechanism. With NAC, systems must be in compliance or they are unable to access general network resources. Only after you update non-compliant systems are they allowed access to the network.

CHAPTER SUMMARY

Because of the complexities and difficult questions surrounding network security, you need to fully understand the fundamentals of network security. Once you have a firm grasp of these basic issues, you will be able to put security into practice on your own network.

A written security policy is the foundation of a successful security endeavor. Without a written policy, security will be chaotic and uncontrolled. A security policy defines and assigns roles and responsibilities to personnel within the organization. Network infrastructure design can have a significant impact on security. Administrators can employ numerous network components and devices to support a network security policy. These include firewalls, VPNs, and IDS/IPS.

KEY CONCEPTS AND TERMS

Access control
Appliance
Asset
Auditing
Auditor
Authentication
Authorization
Availability
Backdoor
Black list
Bottleneck
Breach
Bridge
Business task
Caching
Choke point
Client
Client/server network
Confidentiality
Defense in depth
Demilitarized zone (DMZ)
Denial of service (DoS)
Directory services
Domain
Domain name system (DNS)
Downtime
Egress filtering
Encapsulation
Encryption
Exploit
Extranet
Filtering
Firewall
Fully qualified domain name (FQDN)
Hacker
Hacking
Hardening
Hijacking
Host
HOSTS file
Ingress filtering
Integrity
Intrusion detection system (IDS)
Intrusion prevention system (IPS)
IPSec
Job description
Local area network (LAN)
Log
Logging
Malicious code (or **malware**)
Man-in-the-middle
Media Access Control (MAC) address
Monitor or **monitoring**
Network access control (NAC)
Network address translation (NAT)
Network security
Node
Open system interconnection reference model (OSI model)
Port address translation (PAT)
Permissions
Privacy
Private IP address
Privileges
Proxy

continued

KEY CONCEPTS AND TERMS, *continued*

Public IP address
Redundancy or **redundant**
Remote access
Remote access server (RAS)
Remote control
Replay attack
Resources
RFC (request for comment)
RFC 1918 addresses
Risk
Roles or **job roles**
Router
Security goals and **security objectives**
Security policy
Senior management
Server
Single point of failure
Single sign-on (SSO)
Sniffer
SOHO (small office, home office) network
Switch
Telco
Terminal server/services/session
Thin client
Threat
Trust
Tunneling
Virtual private network (VPN)
Vulnerability
White list
Wide area network (WAN)
Workgroup
Zero day exploits
Zeroization

CHAPTER 1 ASSESSMENT

1. An outsider needs access to a resource hosted in your extranet. The outside is a stranger to you, but one of your largest distributors vouches for them. If you allow them access to the resource, this is known as implementing what?

A. DMZ
B. Virtualization
C. Trusted third party
D. Remote control
E. Encapsulation

2. Which of the following are common security objectives?

A. Non-repudiation
B. Confidentiality
C. Integrity
D. Availability
E. All of the above

3. What is an asset?

A. Anything used in a business task
B. Only objects of monetary value
C. A business process
D. Job descriptions
E. Security policy

4. What is the benefit of learning to think like a hacker?

A. Exploiting weaknesses in targets
B. Protecting vulnerabilities before they are compromised
C. Committing crimes without getting caught
D. Increase in salary
E. Better network design

5. What is the most important part of an effective security goal?

A. That it is inexpensive
B. That it is possible with currently deployed technologies
C. That it is written down
D. That it is approved by all personnel
E. That it is a green initiative

6. What is true about every security component or device?

A. They are all interoperable.
B. They are all compatible with both IPv4 and IPv6.
C. They always enforce confidentiality, integrity, and availability.
D. They are sold with pre-defined security plans.
E. They all have flaws or limitations.

7. Who is responsible for network security?

A. Senior management
B. IT and security staff
C. End users
D. Everyone
E. Consultants

8. What is a distinguishing feature between workgroups and client/server networks? (In other words, what feature is common to one of these but not both?)

A. DNS
B. Centralized authentication
C. List of shared resources
D. User accounts
E. Encryption

9. Remote control is to thin clients as remote access is to?

A. NAC
B. VPN
C. DNS
D. IPS
E. ACL

10. What two terms are closely associated with VPNs?

A. Tunneling and encapsulation
B. Bridging and filtering
C. Path and network management
D. Encapsulation and decapsulation
E. Port forwarding and port blocking

11. What is a difference between a DMZ and an extranet?

A. VPN required for access
B. Hosted resources
C. External user access
D. Border or boundary network
E. Isolation from the private LAN

12. What is the primary security concern with wireless connections?

A. Encrypted traffic
B. Support for IPv6
C. Speed of connection
D. Filtering of content
E. Signal propagation

13. What are two elements of network design that have the greatest risk of causing a DoS? (select two)

A. Directory service
B. Single point of failure
C. Bottlenecks
D. Both A and B
E. Both B and C

14. For what type of threat are there no current defenses?

A. Information leakage
B. Flooding
C. Buffer overflow
D. Zero day
E. Hardware failure

15. Which of the following is true regarding a layer 2 address and layer 3 address?

A. MAC address is at layer 2 and is routable
B. Layer 2 address contains a network number
C. Layer 2 address can be filtered with MAC address filtering
D. Network layer address is at layer 3 and is routable
E. Both C and D are true

16. Which of the following are *not* benefits of IPv6?

A. Native communication encryption
B. RFC 1918 address
C. Simplified routing
D. Large address space
E. Smaller packet header

17. What is the most common default security stance employed on firewalls?

A. Allowing by default
B. Custom configuring of access based on user account
C. Caching Internet content
D. Denying by default, allowing by exception
E. Using best available path

18. What is egress filtering?

A. Investigating packets as they enter a subnet
B. Allowing by default, allowing by exception
C. Examining traffic as it leaves a network
D. Prioritizing access based on job description
E. Allowing all outbound communications without restriction

19. Which of the following is *not* a feature of a proxy server?

A. Caching Internet content
B. Filtering content
C. Hiding the identity of a requester
D. Offering NAT services
E. MAC address filtering

20. Which of the following is allowed under NAC if a host is lacking a security patch?

A. Access to the Internet
B. Access to e-mail
C. Access to Web-based technical support
D. Access to file servers
E. Access to remediation servers

CHAPTER 2

Firewall Fundamentals

TO SOME NETWORK ADMINISTRATORS, A FIREWALL is the key component of their infrastructure's security. To others, a firewall is a hassle and a barrier to accomplishing essential tasks. In most cases, the negative view of firewalls stems from a basic misunderstanding of the nature of firewalls and how they work. This chapter will help dispel this confusion.

This chapter clearly defines the fundamentals of firewalls. These include what a firewall is, what a firewall does, how it performs these tasks, why firewalls are necessary, the various firewall types, and filtering mechanisms. Once you understand these fundamentals of firewalls, you will able to look beyond the unschooled opinions, common mythology, and marketing hype surrounding them, and the crucial benefits of effective firewall architecture will become clear. Like any tool, firewalls are useful in solving a variety of particular problems and in supporting essential network security.

Chapter 2 Topics

This chapter will cover the following topics and concepts:

- What a firewall is
- Why you need a firewall
- How firewalls work and what they do
- What the basics of TCP/IP are
- What the types of firewalls are
- What ingress and egress filtering is
- What the types of firewall filtering are
- What the difference between software and hardware firewalls is
- What dual-homed and triple-homed firewalls are
- What the best placement of a firewall is

Chapter 2 Goals

After completing this chapter, you will be able to:

- Define firewalls
- Explain the need for firewalls
- Describe types of firewalls, including network router/interface firewall, hardware appliance firewall, and host software firewall
- Explain standard filtering methods, including static packet filtering, NAT services, application proxy filtering, circuit proxy filtering, dynamic packet filtering, stateful inspection filtering, and content filtering
- Define the meaning of ingress and egress filtering
- Compare and contrast software and hardware firewalls
- Illustrate on a typical business network diagram possible placements for a firewall
- Compare and contrast dual- and triple-homed firewalls

What Is a Firewall?

A **firewall** is like a **border sentry**. A firewall is like a **gateway**. A firewall is like a traffic control device. A firewall is a filtering device that enforces network security policy and protects the network against external attacks.

As a filtering device, a firewall watches for traffic that fails to comply with the **rules** defined by the firewall administrator. Firewalls can focus on **packet** header, packet **payload**, packet **header** and payload, the content of a **session**, the establishment of a **circuit**, and possibly other assets. Most firewalls focus on only one of these, rather than all of them. The most common filtering focus is on the header of the packet, with the payload of a packet a close second. Many firewall products focus on more than one aspect of communication filtering.

Filtering allows what you want on your network and denies what you do not. Filtering relies on filtering rules. Each rule has a pattern of concern and a response the firewall will make if an incoming element matches the pattern.

Firewalls follow a philosophy or stance of security known as deny by default, allow by exception. All the rules on a firewall are exceptions. Some exception rules define what you allow. Some exception rules define what you wish to deny. The final option, sometimes called the final rule, is anything that did not match one of the exceptions denied by default.

Firewall filtering compares each packet received to a set of exception rules. These rules state that content in the packet is either allowed or denied. If the packet matches an allow rule, it continues on to its destination. If the packet matches a deny rule, then the packet is dropped. Hence, a deny rule prevents the packet from reaching its destination. If a packet fails to match any rule, then the firewall drops the packet by default.

The filtering rules are the exceptions to the deny all rule that is the final and absolute rule of a firewall. In fact, if a deny by default rule didn't exist, the filtering device would not be a firewall at all. Instead, it would be more like a router or switch, allowing traffic to pass, even if it did not match an expected pattern or rule. So, keep in mind the security stance of deny by default, allow by exception. A firewall is a filtering device that helps support this stance.

Think of a firewall as a sentry along the borders of a country. The term firewall is not exactly the best term that could have been selected for this device or service that performs essential security filtering for hosts and networks. The term firewall comes from a building and automotive construction concept of a wall that is built to prevent the spread of a fire from one area into another. The firewall in a building or car engine compartment is a physical block against the spread of fire.

Network security administrators use the term firewall to refer to a device or service that allows some traffic but denies other traffic. This is not the same as a building's firewall, which only allows a fire to spread if the firewall fails. In network security, firewalls allow traffic through that's considered safe—or at least authorizes traffic without the entire firewall failing. Additionally, if a firewall does fail, it fails into a secured state. This means that when the firewall is offline, is locked/frozen, or otherwise experiences a problem, it stops all traffic, rather than allowing all traffic through. This is known as fail-safe or fail-secure.

Better ways to envision the job of the firewall are a sentry, doorman, or even border guard. These people positioned at the entrance or exit of a building watch for unauthorized attempts to enter the secured area. Some people are allowed to enter; others are prevented. In the event that the sentry isn't present, the doorway is locked, so only those with a key can enter. Think of a firewall as a border sentry.

A gateway is an entrance or exit point to access a controlled space. We all use gateways everyday in a variety of ways. An on-ramp is a gateway to the highway, a doorway is a gateway to a building, and a personal computer is a gateway to the Internet—and to your organization's network. You can also think of a firewall as the gate at a gateway. The firewall stands at the entrance of a network to block unwanted traffic.

Gateways are important because, typically, high levels of traffic pass through a gateway. Thus, positioning a firewall at a network gateway is an aspect of secure design. If the gateway already exists in the network infrastructure, then positioning the firewall at that point is an obvious security improvement. A firewall so positioned watches over all traffic crossing that gateway point.

If a network is still in its design phase, a network designer might make the secure choice to create a gateway in the network's layout. However, in this situation, the concentration point would be known as a choke point instead of a gateway. If a gateway is an access point to other areas of resources, a choke point is a specialized kind of gateway that focuses on traffic to a single concentrated pathway to simplify the process of filtering.

Whether labeled as a gateway for resource access or a choke point to control security, the result is the same. A firewall positioned at a gateway provides filtering services across all traffic. The choke point provides filtered access to resources. As a wise poet once said: "Good fences make good neighbors." So too, good gateways and well-positioned firewalls make secure networks.

You can also think of a firewall as a traffic control device. A significant amount of network security is little more than controlling traffic. Authorized traffic passes through the digital intersection, while unauthorized, unwanted, abnormal, or obviously malicious traffic is blocked.

The very basic and original form of the modern firewall was a **screening router**. Routers analyze traffic based on destination address. The best-known available route to the destination informs the Forwarding decision. However, screening routers added in additional rules that could discard traffic based on destination or source address. Once filtering expanded to address protocols and even ports, the screening router became the basic static packet filtering firewall.

In addition to filtering, firewalls can also offer routing functions, which are a holdover from this router ancestry. A multi-homed firewall can grant traffic access to one or another interface or **segment** based on the results of filtering. Traffic for a private LAN could traverse one segment, while traffic destined for the DMZ could follow another (see Figure 2-1). A firewall is an efficient, necessary traffic control device on the highway that is your network.

A firewall enforces your organization's network security policy. Specifically, a firewall enforces the network traffic access control security policy. A firewall is the physical embodiment of the security policy. It's the most obvious or direct enforcement of access

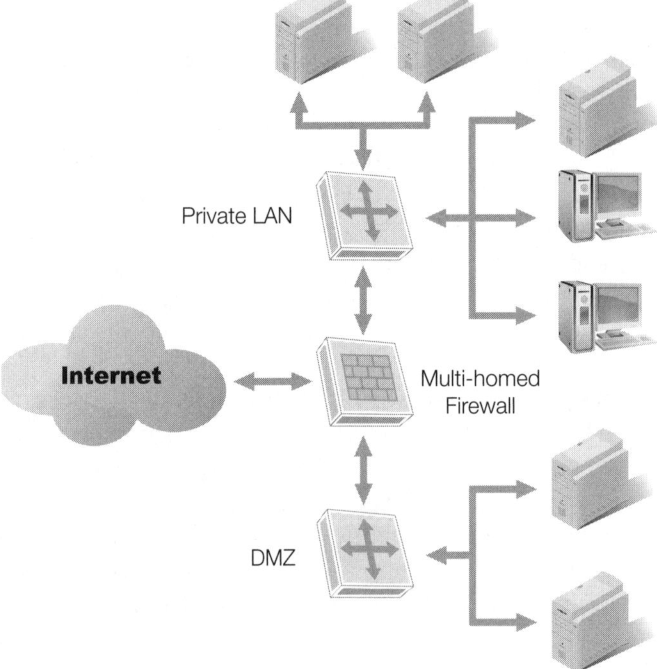

FIGURE 2-1
A basic multi-homed firewall filtering and routing for two network segments.

control on your network's traffic. No device more than your firewall is as directly involved in allowing authorized traffic and denying all else.

A security policy defines the goals, objectives, and procedures of security. Every security policy focusing on network security requires the deployment of a firewall. The firewall's job is to impose all restrictions and boundaries defined in the security policy on all network traffic. A firewall enforces your organization's network security policy just as a traffic policeman enforces the motor vehicle laws of a town or state.

A firewall's critical function is to protect your network against external attacks. It's no secret that threats from without are numerous. The onslaught of attacks is almost unbelievable, like a constant flood against every Internet-connected node. If it were not for vigilant hardening of hosts and the use of firewalls, the Internet and private networking as we know it could not exist.

It's no accident that some threats to computer networks are called viruses: external threats seem to continuously change and evolve. Some attacks are targeted specifically for your network or organization. Some attacks are untargeted and random. Instead, they are directed toward any host that happens to have a specific vulnerability. Malicious code relentlessly infects and compromises unprotected computer systems. Flooding attacks attempt to interrupt timely Internet communications. And these are only some of the external threats facing your organization's network.

A firewall stands as a sentry, as a front guard, as a defense against all attacks and attempts at system compromise. The good news is that many firewalls are well hardened against all known-to-date attacks. These firewalls can withstand the blitzkrieg of the attacks without faltering. A firewall protects the network against the substantial asset damage that external attacks can cause.

Understanding these definitions and distinctions are only the beginning of understanding firewalls. These topics are explored further in this chapter as well as in Chapters 7–11.

What Firewalls Cannot Do

A firewall is an essential part of network security. However, it's not the whole of network security. Don't make the mistake of deploying a firewall while ignoring other security management activities. A firewall is only one piece of the large complex puzzle of network security.

There are many things a firewall is not. Don't be fooled by the marketing. Some of these "deficiencies" can become cloudy as vendors sell combination or multi-function solutions. Often, these devices are designed for the SOHO or home user and thus were never intended to provide commercial-grade protections.

A firewall is primarily for network traffic filtering.

But it's not an authentication system. Firewalls aren't designed to check logon credentials, compare biometric scans, or even confirm the validity of digital certificates. These are the functions of an authentication service, typically hosted on a domain controller or primary network server.

That said, you might find it necessary for a firewall to allow authentication before granting access to a resource or allowing a session. Some firewalls can have enhancement features that provide for firewall-hosted authentication services. However, in many cases, a better solution would be to have the firewall offload that task to a dedicated authentication server or service, such as **802.1x, Public Key Infrastructure (PKI)**, or directory services. Most security experts do not recommend using a firewall to authenticate users, or at least not as a replacement for a network's directory service or centralized authentication solution. Firewalls are not authentication systems.

A firewall is not a remote access server. Connections from remote users do not have an endpoint at the firewall. Instead, the endpoint is a remote access server (RAS) or network access server (NAS). A firewall may function before or after the RAS/NAS to filter remote access traffic. However, that doesn't mean the firewall is the RAS/NAS itself.

Your firewall should of course filter all remote traffic. Especially since remote traffic is much more likely to be purposefully malicious or accidentally damaging than local traffic. Why? An organization has much more control over who can connect to their network locally than it does when it allows remote connectivity. Remember: A firewall does not replace a remote access server.

Like Superman, your firewall does not have x-ray vision into encrypted traffic; in other words, it cannot see the contents of encrypted traffic. A firewall can filter on the header of traffic using **transport mode encryption**, since the original header is in plain text form. However, a firewall cannot filter the original header of traffic using **tunnel mode encryption**, since the only plain text component is a temporary tunnel header that only includes information about the endpoints of the tunnel. It's like trying tell what's in the boxcars of a train, by observing only the locomotive and the caboose.

Position your firewall where it can be most effective. If the security design requires that all traffic content be examined by a firewall, then you need to position the firewall after encryption is removed from the traffic. If the security design only requires filtering on non-encrypted traffic, then positioning the firewall is not as critical.

Firewalls designed for use by Web e-commerce sites may have an additional ability to act as the endpoint of a **Secure Sockets Layer (SSL)** or **Transport Layer Security (TLS)** tunnel from an Internet client. This grants the client protection for their data as the information traverses the Internet. This allows a firewall to filter the content of the traffic before the Web server receives and processes the information.

Encryption is one method to evade filtering. Users and hackers can employ client-side encryption solutions that encode the data before transmission or create unauthorized encrypted encapsulation tunnels to prevent firewall filtering. In this situation, your network security policy may stipulate that the firewall needs to block encrypted transmission initiated by clients, especially if the destination is on the Internet. It's important to remember that firewalls are powerful, but they don't have x-ray vision into encrypted traffic.

A firewall is also not a malicious code scanner. Firewalls are traditionally rule-based filtering products. These **rule sets** usually have only a few dozen to at most a few hundred rules. To filter malicious code, the rule list would need millions of entries. As of Dec 2009, the AVG Anti-Virus definition database #270.14.88/2538 was tracking 24,303,360 malicious code infection definitions. That number of entries is simply impractical to include in a firewall rule set.

Some firewall products include an enhancement or add-on module for malicious code scanning. Such an enhancement is just an add-on component, not a core feature of a firewall. In most cases, it's more efficient and more secure to use separate anti-malware scanners than to add this function to your firewall.

Many firewall rules block traffic with spoofed addresses, uncommon ports, unauthorized protocols, invalid header constructions or values, etc. Such rules block a significant amount of traffic caused by malicious code, but these rules do not themselves directly block malware from entering or leaving a network. Keep in mind that your firewall can do many things, but it's not a malicious code scanner.

A firewall is also not an intrusion detection system. An intrusion detection system or IDS is a type of network burglar or intruder alarm that detects and responds to unauthorized activity inside your network. An IDS performs this task by monitoring all network traffic. While an IDS can be deployed on a network border or outside the network against the Internet, most IDSs operate inside private networks so that they can watch all internal network traffic.

A firewall can only detect malicious traffic when such traffic enters one of the firewall's interfaces. Firewalls generally don't watch over general interior network activity. Either firewalls are border devices for networks and subnets, or they are software products watching over a single host. In either case, they cannot see the same traffic nor perform the same tasks as an IDS. A firewall, therefore, is not interchangeable with a good intrusion detection system.

> **NOTE**
> IDSs can detect a plethora of unwanted activities, use several methods of detection, and can perform a wide range of responses, both passive and active. You'll find more on IDSs in Chapter 1 in the section, "Common Network Security Components" and in Chapter 15 in the section, "Intrusion Detection Systems (IDS) and Intrusion Prevention Systems (IPS)".

A common misconception is that firewalls protect against insider attacks; they cannot. A firewall can be a border device or a firewall can be software on a host. A border firewall can filter traffic entering or leaving a network or subnet. So a border firewall is unable to see any interior traffic (Figure 2-2). When an attacker from an inside client attacks a target that is also an internal host, a border firewall is not part of the communication and thus cannot detect nor block the attack.

A host software firewall can only see the traffic entering or leaving that one host. A host software firewall is unable to see any other interior traffic

Of course, if traffic does not pass through its interfaces, a firewall cannot filter the traffic. A firewall can only filter on what it sees. If malicious or unwanted traffic does not enter an interface of a firewall, the firewall will not be able to filter that traffic (see Figure 2-2). So you'll want to place firewalls on each host, on every border gateway or choke point, and between each significant subnet or interior network division. Another thing firewalls can't do is protect against social engineering. Social engineering is the category of attacks that focus on the personnel of an organization. These attacks get information from people just by asking for it in clever ways or convincing someone to perform an action that breaches

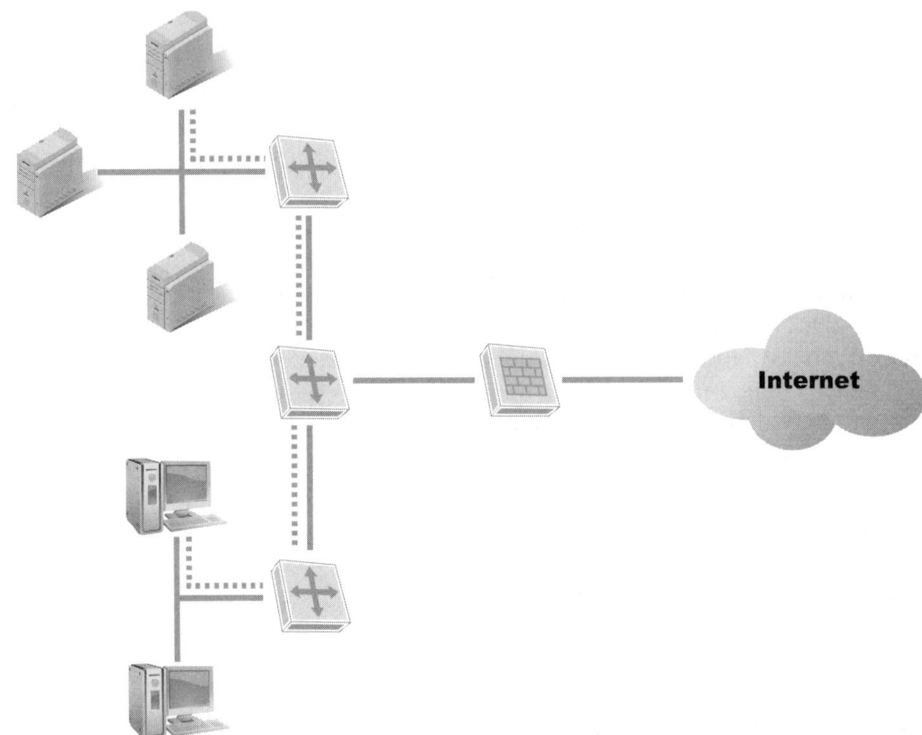

FIGURE 2-2
Border firewalls cannot filter internal communications.

network security. The only real protection against social engineering is worker training and awareness. A firewall cannot stop the attack stemming from social engineering.

A firewall can't protect against the threat posed by removable media. The widespread use of removable media has been a significant threat to every computer in existence, even those not connected to the Internet, an external network, or even a single other computer through a network link. Removable media include USB hard drives, USB thumb drives, CDs, DVDs, Blu-ray discs, HD-DVD discs, other optical discs, flash memory cards, firewire storage devices, tape media, e-mail attachments, and more. Removable media can leak information out of an organization or smuggle malicious code in. A firewall is not involved in the use of removable media nor any of the contents these devices may contain. A firewall cannot protect your network against the ongoing threat posed by removable media. Again, the best defense against this threat is good company policy, worker training, and awareness.

A firewall, of course, cannot protect against physical incursions or attacks. Physical attacks bypass any and all logical and electronic protection mechanisms. A firewall does not protect against theft of devices, planting of eavesdropping mechanisms, disconnection of cables, connecting a rogue notebook to an open node, destruction of equipment, dousing electronics with liquids, building fires, or any other form of physical attack. Only effective physical defenses can deter physical attacks. A firewall is not designed or intended to thwart physical attacks.

Firewalls aren't insurance against inept or ignorant administrators. Computer equipment and software can only do what it's designed and programmed to do. If an administrator mis-configures a security device, the device doesn't automatically compensate for that oversight. If a security administrator fails to learn about all the features and defaults of new equipment, the product cannot secure itself autonomously. Security requires training, research, careful planning, thoughtful implementation, and ongoing review and maintenance. This process is known as security management—and it takes work. The old expression was never more true than today: "Garbage in, garbage out." What you put into network security is precisely what you will get out of it. So remember that a firewall can't compensate for ineptitude or ignorance on the part of administrators.

In the same vein, firewalls can't compensate for poor security management. Proactive security management is essential for the success of any security endeavor. Security management is the process of reviewing, testing, tuning, and updating an organization's security policies and security infrastructure. This is an ongoing effort that requires knowledge, research, and vigilance. The threats and risks facing an organization are constantly evolving to become more persistent and virulent. Your security strategy should be just as rigorous and purposeful in defense. Keeping up to date on the most current threats to and trends in network security is a big part of this job. Networking, conferencing, and reading the latest industry literature are ways to keep yourself and your security efforts sharp.

Keep in mind that a firewall is a focal point of security. It's an embodiment—a physical representation—of your organization's security policy. When you use them well and wisely, firewalls provide reliable and consistent security from external threats. However, firewalls are a tool with limitations and are only part of the complete security strategy. By itself, a firewall cannot protect a network against every threat. A firewall cannot compensate for the lack of informed, state-of-the-art security management.

Furthermore, and this follows from everything we've discussed so far, firewalls are not a substitute for a solid, written security policy. A firewall is nothing but a reliable border sentry. It is not the complete security infrastructure and strategy. Even the decision to deploy a firewall is a significant strategic undertaking that shouldn't be taken for granted. Thorough research and planning will help design and deploy an effective firewall. A firewall policy ensures the success of your network's firewall. A company-wide security policy ensures the success of your organization's security infrastructure. Firewalls are in no way a substitute for such a security policy.

Finally, firewalls are not a perfect solution. As we've noted, a firewall is a border sentry, reliable but limited. A firewall can only filter what it sees. It can only perform filtering according to the rule sets defined by the security administrator. It cannot self-adjust to changing conditions or future threats. A firewall is only a part of a complete security infrastructure. Firewalls are mostly software, even when operating on dedicated hardware. They are software, written by fallible humans; they can, and do, therefore, have bugs and flaws. A firewall is never the perfect solution—but it is part of the solution.

Fortunately, in spite of all the things a firewall is not, a firewall is a solid filtering solution. A firewall can and should protect the borders of networks and individual hosts. No security strategy—or deployment—is complete without properly installed firewalls.

Why Do You Need a Firewall?

"Who needs a firewall?" Anyone who uses a computer to interact with and exchange resources with any other computer! Your personal computer needs a firewall. Your home network needs firewalls. Your company network needs firewalls. Every network needs firewalls. They are a fundamental of network communication.

High-speed Internet connectivity has become ubiquitous. Most computer users now have high-speed access at home, at work, and even on the go through mobile devices. Often, these broadband connections are always-on connections. This means computers and networks are online all the time—and exposed to attacks. A drawbridge is easy to cross if it's always down. When a system is always connected, it can be the focus of a concerted attempt to discover its vulnerabilities and breach its security.

How likely is it that a computer will be discovered and attacked over the Internet? Almost guaranteed. Most systems are detected, scanned, and probed within minutes of obtaining a public **IP address**. It is technical suicide to connect your system to the Internet before installing a firewall, as well as installing the latest vendor patches for the hardware, OS, and installed applications.

Does this mean that there are armies of hackers just waiting to find new targets to attack? Unfortunately, yes. Not, however, in the way you might think. Malicious programs perform most of the scanning and attacking automatically. These are commonly known as **agents**, robots, **zombies**, or just **'bots**. Groups of malicious code, known as **botnets**, scour the Internet for new victims constantly.

Another wrinkle in being constantly online over a broadband connection is the throughput speed. High-speed links to the Internet enable high-speed attacks against your system. On older, slower connections, the same risks existed, but the attacks were slower or fewer simply because the link to a targeted system throttled the speed of the attack. With 10 Mbps and faster connections common, attacks can occur at near-lightning speed.

This is not to suggest that only slow-speed Internet links are secure. On the contrary, you should take full advantage of high-speed Internet connections. However, you need to protect your systems with firewalls. A firewall will impose a significant barrier to most attacks that originate from the Internet.

With a firewall protecting your system from the Internet, hacker scans will be nearly worthless. Responses to probing packets will be filtered. An outsider will learn little about your infrastructure. This, in turn, means they will discover fewer vulnerabilities, thus wage fewer attacks. And even then, those attacks will more likely fail.

Firewalls are not only used for Internet protection. Don't forget that significant levels of threat exist internally. Firewalls stand guard against network segments inside your private network (Figure 2-3). Think of a firewall as a tool to prevent abuse or misuse of LAN resources. Each major department, subnet, or other relevant distinction within

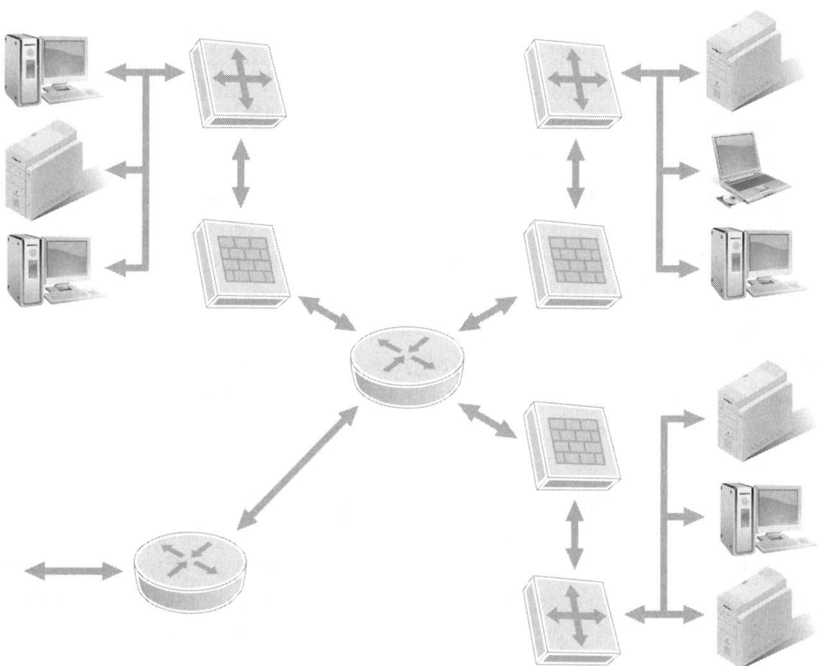

FIGURE 2-3
An example of a private network using firewalls to securely separate subnets.

an organization should have firewall protection. This will ensure that accidental compromises, as well as intentional abuses, are minimized internally. All networks protect against both internal threats as well as external ones.

Don't overlook that, while a firewall has its origins in routing, you still want to use a dedicated router for routing and a dedicated firewall for filtering. In many cases, the combination or multi-function devices offer lots of features, but not necessarily best of breed performance and efficiency. These may be money-savers for small networks, but they are often cause for expense for larger networks. If a device fails to perform at commercial levels when necessary, the repercussions can cost more than deploying the proper safeguards in the first place.

Firewalls should be used to protect a resource, no matter where that resource resides on your network. A **hardware firewall** can protect a single host or a network of hosts, while a software firewall can only protect a single host. Don't limit your definition of a firewall to just a border sentry device. Think of it, instead, as a sentry device in general, able to protect anything placed behind its filtering service.

Host firewalls protect a host and protect a network from the host. A host firewall's job is to filter traffic entering or leaving a single computer system. Attacks and malicious traffic can come from the Internet or the local network. A host firewall can protect the host against such threats. However, the host itself could be compromised by malicious code or be controlled by a malicious user. In this situation, the host firewall protects the network from the threats coming from the host.

Another way of looking at this is that a host firewall also protects the network from a user in general. A user is the most risky element in a network infrastructure. Even if every other component, hardware or software, does what it was programmed and configured to do, you can decide to violate security. Thus, the free will of human users is one of the biggest risks to every computing environment.

Users can be ignorant, make mistakes, be tricked by a Trojan horse, be the target of social engineering attacks, and perform malicious actions on purpose. The security of a host system, including general system hardening, anti-malware scanning, Internet client restrictions, blocking of non-approved software, and a host firewall, are all designed to protect the network from the risk of human users.

Firewalls protect against Internet threats, internal network threats, protect resources generally, and protect against the risk of users. These capabilities alone might make installing a firewall on every host and on every segment seem like the obvious follow through.

However, deploying firewalls everywhere has two significant drawbacks: cost and over-dependence. Most commercial grade firewalls are costly. Even if they have no purchase cost, due to promotions or being open source, the ongoing maintenance costs of firewalls add up significantly over time. With firewalls deployed on every host and on every segment, the overhead of firewall management would far exceed the total IT budget of most businesses.

A second drawback to ubiquitous deployment of firewalls is over-dependence. Firewalls are only part of a complete security solution, not a whole solution by themselves. By deploying firewalls on every host and every segment, other essential security endeavors might be overlooked or deemed unnecessary. This would be a disastrous security stance. Firewalls cannot compensate for poor security policy, poor security management, or a lack of proper system hardening.

With these concerns, how can your organization determine how many firewalls to deploy and where to deploy them? In most cases, this requires a process **risk assessment** and **risk management**. Risk assessment is a process of examining values, threat levels, likelihoods, and total cost of compromise versus the value of the resource and the cost of the protection. While many other factors affect risk assessment, this essential business and security process is as follows:

1. Determine the overall value of the resource or asset. Known as the **asset value (AV)**, this calculation should include both **tangible** and **intangible costs and value**.
2. Determine the threats that face that asset. For each threat, calculate the **exposure factor (EF)**, or the amount of potential harm expressed as a percentage. This will create a list of asset-threat pairs with a corresponding EF.
3. Calculate the **single loss expectancy (SLE)**: $SLE = AV \times EF$. This is the amount of potential loss that could be experienced due to a single occurrence of compromise against this asset for a specific threat. This will add an SLE value to each asset-threat pair.

4. For each threat, calculate the potential number of times the threat could be a realized attack within a year's time. This is known as the **annualized rate of occurrence (ARO)**.
5. Calculate the **annualized loss expectancy (ALE)**: ALE = SLE × ARO. This is the amount of potential loss that can be experienced due to any compromise of this asset for a specific threat within a year. This will add an ALE value to each asset-threat pair.
6. Sort the list of asset-threat pairs by the ALE. The highest ALE is the biggest risk for this specific asset/resource.
7. Take the asset-threat with the largest ALE and determine the possible counter–measures that could be used to protect against that threat. This creates asset-threat-countermeasure triplets.
8. For each asset-threat-countermeasure triplet, calculate a new ARO. The counter-measure should reduce the ARO. A perfect countermeasure would reduce the ARO to zero. There are few perfect countermeasures.
9. With the new ARO, calculate a new ALE for each asset-threat-countermeasure triplet.
10. For each asset-threat-countermeasure triplet, calculate the potential **cost/benefit**. The formula for this is: (Original ALE − New ALE) − cost of the countermeasure per year.
11. Sort the asset-threat-countermeasure triplets by their potential cost/benefit. The triplet with the greatest cost/benefit is the best choice.

In short, if the best cost/benefit for a particular asset-threat is for a firewall, then installing one is a good business, security, and budget decision. If some other countermeasure has a better cost/benefit, then that countermeasure is the better choice.

Performing detailed risk analysis is a complex task. Many small companies or home network enthusiasts might not want to spend the effort to perform a complex risk assessment. This is understandable, but failing to perform a full risk assessment doesn't mean that you have no risk or that you have no assets worth protecting.

At a minimum, you need to protect any and all data that is personally identifiable. This includes personal communications like e-mails, any custom crafted document, picture, video, or other file type, all medical information, all financial information, configuration settings, passwords and other credentials. Identity theft is one of the most frequent and devastating crimes of the interconnected world. Worrying only about your neighbors, the random home burglary, or the pickpocket on the street is nothing short of tunnel vision. Today, you must be concerned about all would-be criminals across the globe attempting to gain access to your electronic assets over the Internet.

Who needs a firewall? Everyone with a networked computer needs a firewall. Why are firewalls necessary? Firewalls are critical because threats and malicious entities lurk on the Internet, on private networks, and possibly within your own home!

What Are Zones of Risk?

A **zone of risk** is any segment, subnet, network, or collection of networks that represent a certain level of risk. The higher the risk, the more security you need to protect against that risk. The less of a risk associated with a zone, the less security is necessary because the threats of that zone pose less chance of harm.

The flipside of zones of risk is **zones of trust**. Highly trusted zones naturally require less security, while zones of low trust require more security.

Each zone of risk needs to be clearly and distinctly isolated from any other risk zone, especially if those zones have different levels of risk. The primary tool used to isolate zones from each other is the firewall.

FIGURE 2-4

An example of a private network with four risk or trust zones.

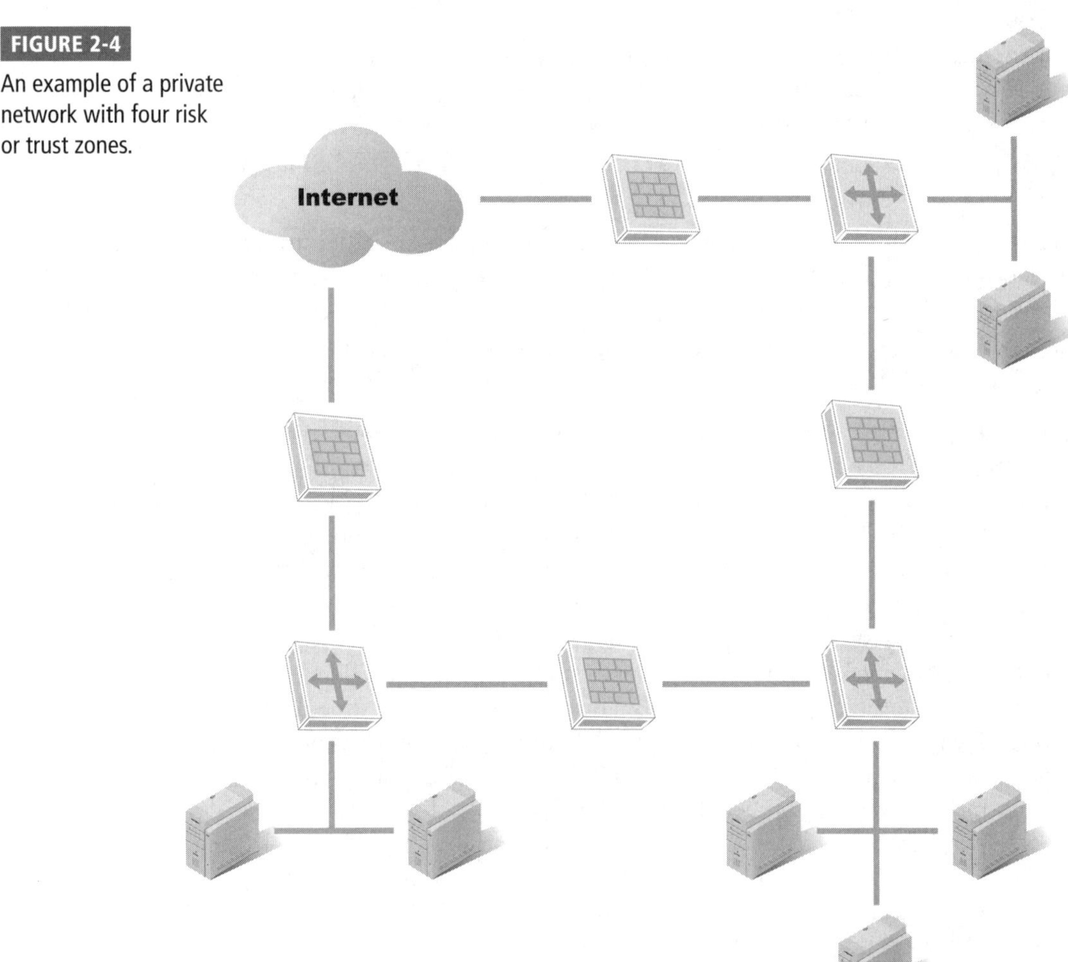

TABLE 2-1 Risk and trust levels of common network zones.

ZONE	RISK LEVEL	TRUST LEVEL
LAN	Low	High
Extranet	Medium–Low	Medium–High
DMZ	Medium–High	Medium–Low
Internet	High	Low

Most networks have two to four zones of risk. These include the private network, DMZ, extranet, and the Internet. See Figure 2-4. The private network zone has the lowest risk and is the zone of the highest trust. The Internet zone has the highest risk and is the zone with the least trust. A DMZ has less risk than the Internet, but is not as trusted as the private network. A DMZ zone has medium-high risk or medium-low trust. An extranet has more risk than the private network and more trust than the Internet. An extranet zone has medium-low risk or medium-high trust. See Table 2-1.

Your organization's written security policy should define where these zones exist and dictate the security requirements for each zone. Such requirements would include traffic management, use of firewalls, use of VPNs to cross the zone divisions, hardening of systems, malicious code scanning, and so on. Firewalls are likely found at risk zone divisions and may be the best cost/benefit security countermeasure in some circumstances. The next step is to understand what a firewall can do at these points and how it performs these tasks.

How Firewalls Work and What Firewalls Do

Firewalls work along a communication pathway. This can be the gateway point of a network, a choke point within a network, a point of zone transition, or on a host. In these locations, the firewall interrupts the traffic flow to inspect packets or sessions. If the contents are authorized, they continue to their destination. If the contents are not authorized, they are blocked and dropped.

Firewalls operate on a **bastion host** basis (Figure 2-5). This is most obvious in the case of hardware firewalls, but it's true of host software firewalls, as well. A bastion host firewall stands guard along the pathway of potential attack, positioned to take the brunt of any attack. A firewall acts as the vanguard, as the front line of defense against any attack. A bastion host can also be called a **sacrificial host**.

In the case of a host software firewall, the firewall will attempt to prevent all malicious interactions to and from the host. In the event that the firewall itself is compromised, it usually disconnects the system from the network. While this is a form of DoS, it's often a preferred **fail-safe/fail-secure** response over defaulting to an open unrestricted and unfiltered connection. This is especially true if the connection is directly to the Internet. Bastion host deployment is discussed further in Chapter 8.

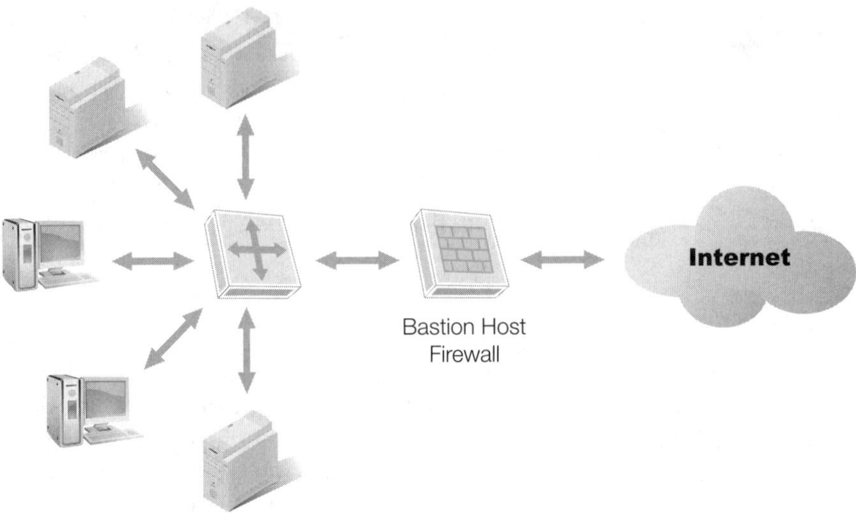

FIGURE 2-5
An example of a bastion host firewall deployment.

If the firewall is able to rebuff an attack, then the resources are secure. If the firewall falls due to the attack, it prevents any further communication with the resources behind it. Think of a firewall as a **dead-man switch**. If the firewall fails or goes offline, so does the connection it was filtering.

The most common function of a firewall is to screen or filter traffic. The firewall checks any packet received on its interface against its rule set to determine whether to forward or drop the packet. As we discovered earlier, firewalls typically function on a deny-by-default, allow-by-exception security policy.

The firewall performs most traffic filtering based on information in a packet or segment header. This can include the IP address of the source and destination, as well as the source and destination port. Some firewalls can also filter or block specific protocols or certain uses of protocols. For example, a firewall could block all streaming media protocols and block just the **Internet Control Message Protocol (ICMP)** type 3 (destination unreachable) and 11 (timeout exceeded).

Firewalls differentiate between networks or subnets. A firewall serves as a clear and distinct boundary between one network area and another. By positioning a firewall between network divisions or subnets, the network designer and security administrators are using traffic management and control for traffic attempting to cross that intersection. Firewalls serve as boundary devices both on the edge of networks facing the Internet, as well as internally between different divisions within an organization.

Open and unrestricted internal communications might sound like a good idea, but in practice such traffic causes severe degradation of overall infrastructure performance and stability. By preventing or at least limiting communications between certain divisions of an organization, traffic efficiency increases. Additionally, traffic control and management decreases risk.

For example, by blocking communications between the programming group's network and the production network, unapproved versions of software cannot leak out. Additionally, blocking general access to the accounting subnet, the research and development subnet, the DMZ, and the extranet from the production network protects against data leakage, spread of malicious code, and other forms of fraud and abuse.

Firewalls can act as a general filter for malicious activity or as a one-way sieve. As a general filter, a firewall will allow all normal benign traffic to pass through. This is the type of firewall used to protect a DMZ or differentiate subnets within a LAN. A general filter firewall works to stop malicious activities.

A general filter firewall can allow communication using any protocol on any port or to limit communications to specific protocols and ports (amongst other limitations). If only a few specific resources hosted behind the firewall are to be accessed by external users, the firewall can allow access to those specific internal systems based on IP address and port, but block all other inbound requests.

A sieve firewall will only allow traffic to originate from the private or trusted side. A sieve firewall will allow non-malicious responses to return from the public or less-trusted side, but it will generally block or prevent any initiation or inbound communication request from the outside. A sieve firewall typically protects a private LAN or an extranet.

Firewalls can support special inbound authorized connections with the LAN, such as VPN links from telecommuters. This is an important feature for an extranet, as well, since VPN access is often the only method to reach hosted resources through the Internet.

Firewalls can provide **port-forwarding** services. Port forwarding is a form of static reversal of network translation. In traditional or dynamic NAT or network address translation, external entities cannot initiate communications with internal systems because any packet received by the outside interface of the NAT system will not find a matching mapping in the translation table and therefore drops the packet as invalid.

With port forwarding or static NATing, a translation mapping is coded so that an external IP address and port combination are fixed and redirect traffic to a specific internal system, even if the internal system uses a private IP address. The combination of an IP address and a **port number** is known as a **socket**. In Figure 2-6, the external port 208.40.235.38:8081 is forwarded to an internal server's port at 192.168.5.74:80. Port forwarding can also be called **static NAT**, traffic forwarding, service redirection, **reverse proxy**, and "punching a hole through the firewall." Port forwarding and reverse proxy are discussed further in Chapter 8.

The alias "punching a hole through the firewall" points out a very important concern: namely, that using port forwarding reduces the effective security provided by the firewall. Without port forward or other similar services, a firewall can rebuff attempts to communicate with internal systems. Using port forwarding, you create a pathway across the primary border sentry. Several hacker exploits can take advantage of port forwarding to reach other internal systems on other ports than what was "allowed" by the port forwarding settings. These attacks are usually variations of fragmentation manipulation and are discussed in Chapter 4 "Network Security Threats and Issues."

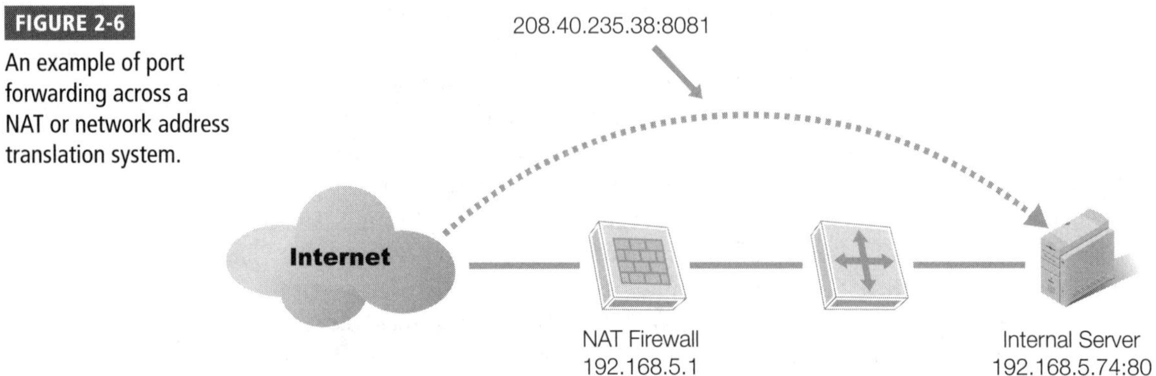

FIGURE 2-6

An example of port forwarding across a NAT or network address translation system.

Managing and controlling traffic is a primary concern and function of firewalls. Only authorized communications are allowed; everything else is blocked. The act of determining what to allow and what to block depends on the filtering features of the firewall. These include packet inspection, connection or **state** management, **stateful inspection**, and others. These filtering concepts are defined later in this chapter in the section, "Types of Filtering."

In addition, firewalls can block or filter outbound traffic. This function can block spoofed traffic or anything with an invalid IP address as the destination or source. Specific protocols or ports can be blocked, as well. And of course specific domain names or destination addresses can be blocked.

Firewalls can also filter based on content. The firewall can intercept specific content in a packet leaving the network before it reaches the outside. This could result in the packet being discarded, an entire connection being dropped, or the packet being edited to remove the blocked content and replace it with something else. **Content filtering** can focus on domain name, URL, filename, file extension, or keywords in the content.

Another capability of firewalls is the ability to filter based on encryption. A firewall can allow encryption without restriction. Or, a firewall can be set to block encryption on some ports and not others. Firewalls can also block encryption from and to all internal IP addresses except for servers, VPN devices, and RAS/NAS. The issue of firewalls and encryption is discussed further in Chapter 7.

Firewalls can perform intermediary functions between hosts where network administrators deem direct communication too risky. This is the basic function of a proxy. A proxy firewall positioned along a communication path can hide the identity of one or both endpoints of a communication from the participants. In most cases, proxy services hide the identities of internal systems from external entities.

Firewalls can perform address conservation through the use of an address conversion or translation system. NAT or network address translation is the most common translation service supported by networks. As discussed in Chapter 1, NAT translates between internal addresses and public external addresses. NAT allows a private network to use the RFC 1918 private IP addresses. This, in turn, provides additional security, since Internet hosts cannot address an RFC 1918 system directly.

Through the combination of all their features, functions, and capabilities, firewalls provide consistent, reliable protection for an organization's computer and electronic resources. But firewalls are not perfect and should not be the sole security component of a network infrastructure. They are only one element—although an essential one—of a network security strategy.

Firewalls can log events. Firewalls can be set to record any action into a log file. In addition, they can record the content of any malicious traffic into a log file. And they can record any abnormal network activity, performance levels, and traffic statistics into a log file. Logging events is an invaluable feature of a firewall. You can learn more about firewall logging and understanding those logs in Chapter 7.

Since perfect security products don't exist, you must rely on monitoring to watch for attempts (and any successes) to breach or violate security. Recall from Chapter 1 that security is locking things down to the best of your ability, and then watching for attempts to breach your defenses. Lock, then watch. A successful security strategy is not possible without both locking and watching. Additionally, most security components should include a locking and a watching aspect to them. Firewalls are no exception. If a proposed firewall product is unable to record a log of its actions and network activities, then you need to seek out a different firewall product. Remember the time-tested business adage: "You get what you inspect, not what you expect."

TCP/IP Basics

To fully understand the mechanisms of filtering employed by firewalls, you need a solid understanding of the TCP/IP protocol suite. Thorough knowledge of TCP/IP benefits a security administrator not just in the area of firewall management, but also in routing, switching, maintaining availability, improving network performance, managing network traffic, analyzing protocol, understanding vulnerabilities and exploits, and even performing penetration testing or ethical hacking.

Most networks, including the Internet, use the TCP/IP protocol. As discussed in Chapter 1, the most prevalent version in use is IPv4. However, IPv6 is gaining wider use across the globe. During this transitional period, you should learn about both versions of IP. If you need additional detailed information regarding TCP/IP, please consult:

- Stevens, W. Richard, and Gary R. Wright. *TCP/IP Illustrated, Volumes 1–3*. Addison-Wesley Professional, 1994.
- Kozierok, Charles. *The TCP/IP Guide: A Comprehensive, Illustrated Internet Protocols Reference*. No Starch Press, 2005.
- Comer, Douglas E. *Internetworking with TCP/IP, Vol 1 (5th Edition)*. Prentice Hall, 2005.
- The ARIN IPv6 Wiki at *http://www.getipv6.info*.

> **NOTE**
> The OSI model is the documented standard for discussing and describing network protocols. However, TCP/IP is the de facto or practical standard, as it was actually in use before the OSI model was developed into actual protocols. Few products can directly support the OSI model or its derived protocols. Instead, most products support TCP/IP, in spite of its not being the official, documented standard from the International Standards Organization.

OSI Model

Most protocol discussions begin with the **open system interconnection reference model (OSI model)**. The OSI model is a standard conceptual tool used to discuss protocols and their functions. The OSI model has seven layers (Figure 2-7). Each layer communicates with its peer layer on the other end of a communication session. While the OSI model is helpful in understanding protocols, most protocols are not in full compliance with it.

Below is a brief description of the OSI model's seven layers. Each layer has unique responsibilities, functions, and features. The OSI model defines what needs to take place at each layer and leaves the actual process of accomplishing those tasks to the protocols and, ultimately, to the protocol programmers.

- **Application layer (Layer 7)**—This layer enables communications with the host software, including the operating system. The application layer is the interface between host software and the network protocol stack. The sub-protocols of this layer support specific applications or types of data.
- **Presentation layer (Layer 6)**—This layer translates the data received from the host software into a format acceptable to the network. This layer also performs this task in reverse for data going from the network to the host software.
- **Session layer (Layer 5)**—This layer manages the communication channel, known as a session, between the endpoints of the network communication. A single transport layer connection between two systems can support multiple, simultaneous sessions.
- **Transport layer (Layer 4)**—This layer formats and handles data transportation. This transportation is independent of and transparent to the application.
- **Network layer (Layer 3)**—This layer handles logical addressing (IP addresses) and routing traffic.
- **Data link layer (Layer 2)**—This layer manages physical addressing (MAC addresses) and supports the network topology, such as Ethernet.
- **Physical layer (Layer 1)**—This layer converts data into transmitted bits over the physical network medium.

As data moves from a software application for transmission over the network, it traverses the layers of the protocol stack from top to bottom. As each layer receives data from the layer above it, that data becomes the payload with a layer specific header (Figure 2-7). At the Data link layer, where Ethernet resides, the data receives a footer, as well. This process is known as encapsulation. The inverse, known as **de-encapsulation**, occurs when a network communication is received. As this process takes place, the data set being manipulated receives unique names, depending on the layer it traverses. They are:

technical TIP

Logical addresses, such as IP addresses, create global distinction. At least for public IP addresses, all addresses used on the Internet are unique. **Logical address** assignment is independent of physical location. Logical addresses enable communications between two hosts, regardless of their physical proximity to each other.

Physical addresses, such as **MAC addresses**, create local distinction. MAC addresses must be unique only within the local subnet. This enables a distinction between physically proximate systems that are able to receive the same electronic signal. The manufacturer usually performs physical address assignment of the NIC and is thus dependent on the physical hardware component itself.

technical TIP

MAC addresses are dependent on the physical NIC; the manufacturer assigns these as a "permanent" **hardware address**. However, modifying or **spoofing** the effective MAC address is usually possible on most systems. MAC changes are possible using native commands, as with Linux, Unix, and Mac OS, or with third party utilities, such as required by Windows. Tools for this include MAC Spoof, MAC Makup, and MAC changer.

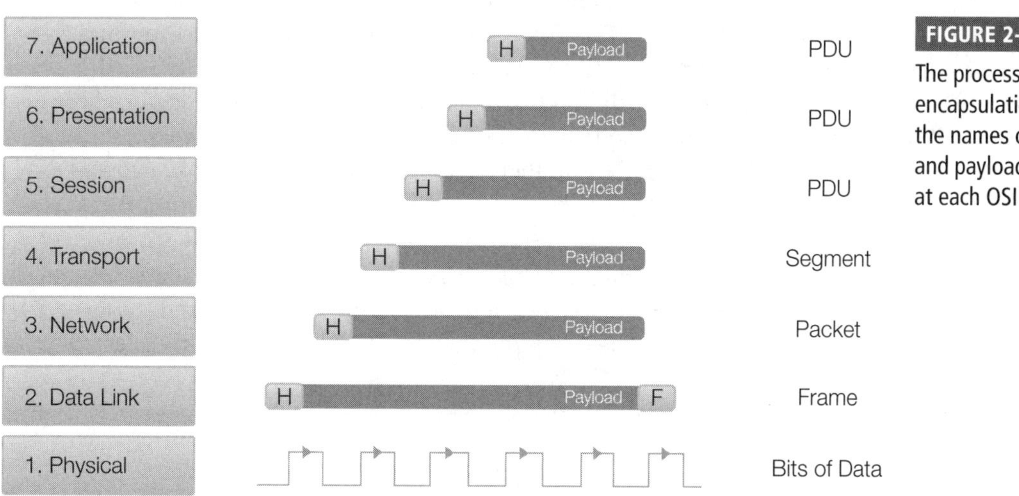

FIGURE 2-7 The process of encapsulation and the names of header and payload sets at each OSI layer.

- **Application layer (Layer 7)**—PDU (payload data unit) (data obtained from the host software application)
- **Presentation layer (Layer 6)**—PDU
- **Session layer (Layer 5)**—PDU
- **Transport layer (Layer 4)**—Segment
- **Network layer (Layer 3)**—Packet
- **Data link layer (Layer 2)—Frame**
- **Physical layer (Layer 1)**—Bits of data

The encapsulation process of adding headers (and a footer at the Data link layer) enables data exchange between layers on different systems. This is known as peer-to-peer communications. The content of a header includes information to be processed by the corresponding layer on the receiving end of a network link.

The content of the headers, mainly from layers 2–4, are the greatest concern and focus of a firewall. **Application proxy** firewalls and stateful inspection firewalls can also examine the headers and the payload content of layers 5–7. Learn more about the methods of filtering based on this layer information in the section, "Types of Filtering" later in this chapter.

Sub-Protocols

TCP/IP is not a single protocol, but a collection of protocols. Often referred to as the TCP/IP suite, this collection includes several core protocols, such as IP, **Transmission Control Protocol (TCP)**, and **User Datagram Protocol (UDP)**, as well as several commonly used protocols, such as ARP, ICMP, HTTP, and TLS. In addition to these, tens of thousands of other protocols can operate within the network infrastructure created by TCP/IP.

Since the focus and purpose of this book is an introduction to network security, firewalls, and VPNs, and not an introduction to networking or protocols, firm knowledge of these sub-protocols of TCP/IP is assumed, but not essential to grasping this book's scope.

Headers and Payloads

Firewalls, specifically packet-filtering firewalls, inspect the contents of headers to allow or deny frames, packets, or segments. Depending on the type of filtering and the layer or protocol focus of the filtering, the item examined and header it comes from can vary.

technical TIP

For a more complete list of the additional sub-protocols, along with their port assignments, please view the document hosted by IANA (Internet Assigned Numbers Authority) at: *http://www.iana.org/assignments/port-numbers*. Nearly every one of the 65,536 ports has one or more protocols and applications associated with it.

For a list of ports used by malicious software, visit: *http://www.glocksoft.com/trojan_port.htm* or *http://www.neohapsis.com/neolabs/neo-ports/neo-ports.html*.

Packet filtering often focuses on four main headers:

- The Ethernet header of the frame from the data link layer
- The IP header of the packet from the network layer
- The TCP header of the segment from the transport layer
- The UDP header of the segment from the transport layer

Each of these four headers has numerous details that affect a filtering action. These include MAC addresses, IP addresses, TCP header flags, port numbers, and more.

Addressing

You learned about the basic differences in IPv4 and IPv6 addressing in Chapter 1 in the section, "IPv4 Versus IPv6." The issue to focus on here is not the length of an address or subnet masks, both of which are important, but rather the issues of source and destination, public and private, known and unknown, benign and malicious, as well as real and spoofed addresses.

Many forms of filtering focus on IP address and/or port number to make an allow or deny decision. Such decisions or rules can focus on either the source address or the destination address found in the header of a segment, packet, or frame. In other words, port number, IP address, or MAC address can support filtering as either a source and/or destination concern.

Firewall filtering can focus on whether an address is public or private in both the source or destination position in the IP packet header. Generally, private addresses function on the private network and do not reach the outside. NAT will translate source-private addresses into a public address if the packet is heading towards an external destination. On the Internet, both routers and firewalls drop any IP packet that has an RFC 1918 address in the header. Firewalls can filter on whether an address is known or unknown. This function filters against addresses used for the source and/or the destination. Known addresses are usually trusted addresses. Packets with only trusted and known addresses are allowed to reach their destination. Unknown addresses are potentially not trusted. Packets with unknown addresses can be stopped in every case or further inspected before an allow or deny decision is made.

Firewalls can filter on whether an address is known to be benign or malicious, a variation of known and unknown filtering. However, instead of known addresses being trusted and unknowns not being trusted, this method twists the idea. A benign address is a known trusted address and a malicious address is a known, not trusted address. But in both cases here, the addresses are known. Any unknown address encountered using this form of filtering will require additional subsequent filtering that looks at other aspects of the traffic.

Firewalls can also filter on whether an address is real or spoofed. This form of filtering is not as clear and distinct as the previous types. Whether a segment, packet, or frame's address is the real correct address or a spoofed falsified address can be difficult to determine in every situation. When an address is a real address, in the sense that it's within the subnet ranges of a network, the methods for determining whether it's a spoofed address are few.

One method is to compare against a use table, such as that maintained by the DHCP, to see if the address is not currently assigned to any authorized system. Another method is to check the route, communication path, receipt vector, or receiving interface of the source address against what that aspect should be for a given address. For example, if a source address typically arrives on port 4 but it shows up on port 7, it's likely a spoofed source address.

Spoofed addresses can also be detected at border sentry points. When a source address comes from the opposite side of the firewall, then it's obviously a spoofed address. One clear example is when an internal LAN address appears as a source address in a packet on its way in to a network from outside. This form of spoof filtering can be part of ingress filtering.

Likewise, the same process can be used for packets leaving a network. Any packet whose source address is from the outside, such as an Internet address, but the packet is received by a firewall from an interface in the private LAN, must be from a spoofed address. This form of spoof filtering can be part of egress filtering.

These are most of the mechanisms that a firewall can use to filter or manage traffic based on addresses. The following sections examine the various types of firewalls and filtering methods.

Types of Firewalls

Listing the types of firewalls is almost like listing taxonomy of the animal kingdom in biology. The variations, models, and versions are so numerous. In addition, opinions vary about what is and is not a firewall. Many experts begin the discussion of firewall types by dividing the collective into two simple, main groupings: personal and commercial.

A **personal firewall** is designed to provide protection to a single system or a small network, such as a SOHO network. To take full advantage of their features, most personal firewalls do not require special training or certification. Most personal firewalls offer user-friendly interfaces that may be Web-based or graphical user interfaced (GUI) in nature.

A **commercial firewall** is designed to provide protection for a medium-to-large business network. Most commercial firewalls are quite complex and often require special training and certification to take full advantage of their features. Most commercial firewalls use a Unix-like command line interface (CLI) that, while powerful and efficient, is not intuitive.

These two groupings do not, however, represent the complete collective of firewalls properly, as several firewalls could easily fall into either or both categories. Another common grouping method, therefore, is to classify firewalls as either hardware or software.

A hardware firewall is a dedicated hardware device specifically built and hardened to support the functions of the firewall software running on it. A hardware firewall is also known as an **appliance firewall**. A hardware firewall does not require any additional hardware or software for its use. All it needs is one or more network connections and a power source.

A **software firewall** is an application installed on a host. A software firewall is also known as a host firewall. A software firewall depends upon the host's hardware and operating system. If the host's components are not properly hardened, the software firewall will be less effective, especially if there are other communication pathways or attack points on the host. Software firewalls must compete for resources among all other processes active on the host. A software firewall is only able to protect a single host from malicious network activity. A software firewall is only able to filter traffic that reaches the network interface of its host.

With these two types of divisions, four potential combinations exist:

- Personal hardware firewall
- Commercial hardware firewall
- Personal software firewall
- Commercial software firewall

A personal software firewall is a product used on individual home systems, on SOHO systems, and even on client/server network workstations and servers. Generally a personal software firewall is free or less expensive than commercial software firewall products. A personal software firewall operates on its own to protect a single host.

A commercial software firewall is a product used on client/server network workstations and servers. While they can be installed onto personal or SOHO systems, they are usually expensive and are part of an overall security management or NAC system. Most commercial software firewalls can be used in an agent/console infrastructure where each host's firewall can be remotely administered from a master management console.

A personal hardware firewall is part of an integrated firewall product, such as a wireless access point or a cable/DSL modem. Another variation of the personal hardware firewall is the re-purposing of a client or server computer into a home-crafted open-source firewall. One example of this is SmoothWall, a hardened bootable Linux-based firewall. You can read a case study of deploying SmoothWall in Chapter 11.

A commercial hardware firewall is usually a device that handles the complexity of larger organizational networks. A commercial hardware firewall is often very expensive, running in the range of $10,000 or more.

FYI

Two common but different dichotomies are: free versus paid and open source versus closed source. *Free* means you do not need to pay for the firewall to use it. *Paid* means you must pay either a purchasing fee and/or a licensing fee to use it. Many examples of both free and paid firewall products are available. **Open source** means the original source code is available for viewing and modification. **Closed source** means the distributed version is pre-compiled and the original source code is undisclosed.

Firewall products, as well as any other form of IT product, can be free and open sourced, free and closed sourced, paid and open sourced, and paid and closed sourced. You should not assume that, because something is free, it is open sourced, or that because something is commercial it must be purchased.

The personal and commercial versions of software and hardware firewalls might include different add-ons or enhancements than their commercial equivalents. These add-ons or enhancements include antivirus, password management, registry protection, driver protection, VPN gateways, remote access support, IDS, IPS, spam filtering, and more. Usually these add-ons make the firewall products more attractive to the potential individual buyer. However, most commercial entities would generally avoid integrated firewall solutions in favor of dedicated products to handle their distinct security or management functions. An integrated device might offer easier administration, but it represents a single point of failure for multiple services. Additionally, such bundled solutions are more difficult to troubleshoot due to the complexity of the communications they support.

Another variation of firewall, in fact the original variation, is a screening router. Most appliance routers and many software routers, such as the RRAS (Routing and Remote Access Service) of Windows Server, are able to perform firewall filtering services in addition to routing. Those screening routers that perform firewall filtering might provide enough sentry security for your needs. However, if you want more advanced features, a screening router is unlikely to be the best solution for your network.

Ingress and Egress Filtering

Ingress and egress filtering is a common tool for spoof filtering. A source address that comes from the opposite side of the firewall than where it is assigned is obviously a spoofed address. An example of this is when an internal LAN address appears as a source address in a packet on its way in to a network from outside. This form of spoof filtering can be part of ingress filtering.

Likewise, the same process can filter for packets leaving a network. If a packet with a source address from the outside such as an Internet address is received by a firewall from an interface inside the private LAN, this is also a spoofed address. This form of spoof filtering can be part of egress filtering.

Ingress and egress filtering can expand beyond spoofing protection and include a variety of investigations on inbound and outbound traffic. This can include black list and white list filtering, protocol and port blocking, and confirmation of authentication or authorization before communications continue.

Unfortunately, if a packet's spoofed addresses don't violate any of these concerns, the spoofed addresses might not be as easy to detect. For example, if a client spoofs an IP address to look like another client in the same subnet, the rules just described to catch spoofing would fail to notice this spoofed communication.

In addition to basic ingress and egress filtering, firewalls can support additional forms of packet examination and investigation.

Types of Filtering

Filtering is the primary function of a firewall. Through its filtering services, most of the other benefits and capabilities of firewalls apply. Firewalls can support many different forms of filtering. Additionally, the terms used for the type of filtering and the type of firewall are often used interchangeably. For example, a firewall that supports packet filtering is known as a packet filtering firewall.

Static Packet Filtering

The most common form of filtering is **static packet filtering**. Static packet filtering uses a static or fixed set of rules to filter network traffic. The rules can focus on source or destination IP address, source or destination port number, IP header protocol field value, ICMP types, fragmentation flags, and IP options. Static packet filtering is therefore mainly focused on the network layer (layer 3), but can also include transport layer (layer 4) elements. Static packet filtering focuses on header contents and does not examine the payload of packets or segments.

Static packet filtering is fast. Traffic matching a deny rule gets dropped, while traffic matching an allow rule gets to continue towards its destination. Static packet filters are invisible or transparent to hosts and users, unless their traffic is blocked, and then they will notice the actions of the firewall on their communications.

Static packet filtering requires the firewall administrator to define and tune the rule set. Most firewall rule sets, including static packet filtering rule sets, are a first-match ordered system. Static packet filtering can be problematic when the rule sets get too large. If the rules are in the wrong order or in a chaotic order, the rule set could create loopholes created or unintentionally discard authorized traffic.

The complexities of network communications, such as accepting query responses and port shifts, can be difficult to handle with static packet filtering. Static packet filtering may allow the subsequent packets of a fragmented message through, even though the lead packet was dropped. This can result in a DoS on the destination system, which would be waiting for the lead packet that never arrives.

Additionally, static packet filters perform their analysis on individual packets, regardless of the relationship or correlation between previous or future packets in a communication stream. This could allow complex multi-packet attacks to bypass the firewall if each individual packet is not recognized as malicious on its own.

Static packet filtering should still be used as a first line of defense, in spite of its shortcomings. By using static packet filtering as the first layer of defense, subsequent layers of filtering will have less bulk to address and thus can operate more efficiently.

Stateful Inspection and Dynamic Packet Filtering

Stateful inspection addresses the issue of complex malicious traffic. Stateful packet filtering determines whether or not a current packet is part of an existing session and allow/deny decisions are made based on this determination. A state is a session of communication. Often, state refers to the transport layer (layer 4) protocol TCP's virtual circuits established through the three-way handshake (using the SYN, SYN/ACK, and ACK flagged segments). However, stateful inspection systems can also track commutations in layers 5–7. A stateful inspection firewall will keep track of current sessions in a state table stored in memory.

> **NOTE**
>
> Stateful inspection is a form of dynamic packet filtering. Dynamic packet filtering is the process of automatically created temporary filters. In most cases, the filters allow inbound responses to previous outbound requests, but on a limited timeout basis. Both forms of state or session awareness, dynamic packet filtering and stateful inspection are usually interchangeable terms.

As the firewall encounters each packet, it is analyzed to determine whether the packet is part of an existing state or not. If not, it's likely to be dropped unless it's a packet used to help initiate a new authorized session. Such a stateful investigation can be considered a dynamic packet filter as well. With static packet filtering, rules had to be created to allow the outbound requests and the inbound replies. With **dynamic packet filtering**, once a session is established the filtering watches for packets that don't belong to authorized sessions. Using stateful inspection as dynamic packet filtering allows for simpler rule sets. A rule allows an outbound connection and the firewall's state management automatically allows the return traffic.

Unfortunately, stateful inspection can sometimes be fooled through manipulation of header contents that makes malicious traffic look like part of an existing valid session. More advanced stateful inspection filters keep track of not just the basic endpoints of a session, but additional details about the session, such as the sequencing and acknowledgement numbers. This reduces the risk, but does not fully eliminate it, as a hacker can eavesdrop on a session, learn the sequencing numbers, and predict future valid sequences.

Another issue with stateful inspection is that not all traffic uses states. Specifically, UDP and ICMP are connectionless protocols. So, state management won't apply to them. For these protocols, the firewall acts as if a state does exist for these protocols and keeps track of the source and destination from outbound packets. These are added to the state table with a timeout value. If the timeout occurs before a response is received, the state is removed from the table. A hacker can fool this mechanism in the same way as any stateful protocol like TCP.

Network Address Translation (NAT)

Network address translation (NAT) is not exactly a form of filtering, but is often included in lists of the filtering services or options provided by firewalls. NAT translates internal addresses into external addresses. NAT can perform this service against IP addresses as well as port numbers. Any firewall that supports NAT can be a NAT firewall. In most cases, NAT is an additional translation service to the core filtering functions of a firewall. NAT is a common, if not standard, feature of modern firewalls.

Application Proxy

An application proxy, **application firewall**, or **application gateway** is an application-specific version of a packet filter. However, unlike a static packet filter that is only able to inspect the header of a packet or segment, an application proxy is able to inspect traffic fully at any layer, including the application payload.

An **application proxy**, even if given the name firewall or gateway, acts as the go-between or middleman between a client and a server. All communications for the specific application are proxied. This grants the application firewall the ability to inspect application specific elements of the traffic. Application proxies are application-specific, so specific products for e-mail, Web, file transfer, database access, VoIP, and other TCP/IP sub-protocols are available.

When an application proxy is deployed, it usually requires that all client software be re-configured to point communications to the proxy server rather than the actual intended resource server. The application proxy will also re-build the request packet before sending it to the resource server. This can include NAT services, but in most cases, it's just a process of proxying the communication. The application proxy maintains two connections, one between itself and the requesting client and a second between itself and the resource server. Thus, application proxies are not transparent filters because a client is aware the proxy is in use. The client never establishes a direct connection between itself and the resource server when a proxy is involved.

Additionally, all other firewalls monitoring a network border must deny access for the application protocols to be managed by the application proxy. This prevents a user from attempting to bypass the application proxy.

Application firewalls can filter on the content of the application payload. This can include IP addresses, domain names, URLs, sub-protocols, attachments, keywords, and more. An application proxy can inspect every aspect of an application's communications. This is known as deep packet inspection.

Application proxies can also perform caching services to improve performance and reduce connection throughput consumption. See the Chapter 1 section, "Proxy" for a discussion of proxy services.

The primary limitation of application proxy firewalls is each unique application will need its own dedicated application proxy. Generic proxy systems are usually ineffective.

Circuit Proxy

A **circuit proxy** or **circuit firewall** focuses its filtering on the initial setup process of a session, state, or circuit. This form of filtering can focus on layers 3–5. It functions similarly to an application proxy, as it acts as a middleman between a client and server. A circuit proxy prevents a direct connection from existing between a client and server to protect the network.

A circuit proxy makes an allow or deny decision on the initiation of the session, state, or circuit. Once a circuit is created, no further filtering takes place. If a client is allowed to initiate communications with a resource server, then the content of their communication is unfiltered and unmonitored (at least not by the circuit proxy).

The filtering rules of circuit proxies are similar to those of static packet filtering, in that a list of rules of IP addresses, port numbers, domain names, networks, or even resource providers determines what circuits or connections are allowed and which are not. The filter set can be a deny all but allow exceptions stance, or an allow all but deny exceptions stance.

Content Filtering

Firewalls can also filter based on content. The firewall can intercept specific content in a packet leaving the network before it reaches the outside. This could result in the packet being discarded, an entire connection being dropped, or the packet being edited to remove the blocked content and replace it with something else. Content filtering can focus on domain name, URL, filename, file extension, or some other form of keyword.

Content filtering is often a feature of application proxy firewalls, stateful inspection firewalls, and dynamic packet filtering firewalls.

Software Versus Hardware Firewalls

A software firewall is an application installed on a host. A hardware firewall is a dedicated hardware device specifically built and hardened to support the functions of the firewall software running on it.

A software firewall is also known as a host firewall. A hardware firewall is also known as an appliance firewall.

A software firewall depends upon the host's hardware and operating system. If the host's components are not properly hardened, the software firewall will be less effective if other communication pathways or attack points on the host exist. A hardware firewall does not require any additional hardware or software for its deployment. All it needs is one or more network connections and a power source.

Software firewalls must compete for resources among all other processes active on the host. A hardware firewall has dedicated hardware resources not shared with any other service.

A software firewall is only able to protect a single host from malicious network activity. A hardware firewall can protect a single system or an entire network

A software firewall is only able to filter traffic that reaches the network interface of its host. A hardware firewall can also only filter traffic that reaches the network interfaces of its appliance. However, a hardware firewall can be positioned on a network at a choke point or gateway to analyze and filter all traffic.

A software firewall and a hardware firewall are both a form of software, but the hardware firewall has a dedicated appliance as its host, while the software firewall uses a standard client or server as its host. In either case, software flaws or bugs in programming can cause the firewall to fail.

A software firewall and a hardware firewall can both be targets of attack. Exploits can compromise their software component or physical attacks can harm their host/appliance.

A software firewall is often less expensive than a hardware firewall. A hardware firewall typically offers a wider range of features and capabilities than a software firewall.

Both software firewalls and hardware firewalls are options you can use throughout a network infrastructure.

IPv4 Versus IPv6 Firewalls

No real distinction between a firewall designed for IPv4 versus one for IPv6 exists. Many firewalls can already support both versions of IP. If you are planning on migrating to IPv6 or have already started the conversion process, be sure your firewalls support IPv6.

A small issue affects filtering between IPv6 and IPv4 subnets. You learned in Chapter 1 that a protocol translation tool can support interaction between network using different versions of IP. This translation tool is called Network Address Translation–Protocol Translation (NAT-PT) (and was defined in RFC 2766 by the IETF. Be sure your selected firewall supports NAT-PT if you plan on communicating across an IP version barrier.

If you would like to read more on this translation issue or gain further understanding about IPv6, please visit:

- The ARIN IPv6 Wiki at *http://www.getipv6.info*
- IPv6.com at *http://www.ipv6.com*

Dual-Homed and Triple-Homed Firewalls

Firewalls, specifically hardware appliance firewalls, typically have two or more network interfaces. A firewall with two interfaces is known as a **dual-homed firewall**, while a firewall with three interfaces is known as a **triple-homed firewall** or a three-legged firewall.

The benefits of multiple interfaces are that the segments, subnets, or networks connected to each firewall interface are electronically isolated from each other. This prevents unfiltered traffic from leaping from one segment to another in an attempt to bypass firewall filtering.

However, for software firewalls using multiple interfaces, you need to ensure that the TCP/IP protocol feature called IP Forwarding is disabled. IP Forwarding is actually a router rule that allows traffic from one interface to exit another interface without needing to move any further up the protocol static than where IP resides. In many cases, IP Forwarding allows packets to bypass filtering. If the system is to be a firewall, you should disable this feature.

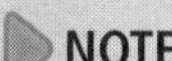

> **NOTE**
> If a system is to function as a router rather than a firewall, IP forwarding might be a desirable function.

Software host firewalls are most often single-homed firewalls since the host only has a single NIC. This is acceptable, since the software host firewall is not providing sentry services between network segments, but between the host and the network.

While firewalls with four or more interfaces are possible, they are rarely deployed. Such a configuration requires significantly more complex filtering and routing rules to operate effectively. It's also a significant single point of failure and a bottleneck to traffic flow between multiple network segments.

Placement of Firewalls

The placement of your network's firewalls depends on several key but subjective factors. No single correct answer or deployment strategy is perfect for everyone. However, several good general guidelines can be of help in planning firewall placement.

First, understand the structure of your network. Where are natural or organizational divisions on the network? Do they correspond to distinct subnets or geographic/physical locations? In many situations, placing a firewall between each division or physical location (even different floors of a building) can be beneficial. Do you have a DMZ or extranet? You will need to isolate these from the private LAN and from the Internet.

Second, know the traffic patterns of your network. What are the common vectors and pathways of communication, both between internal systems and between internal and external systems? Consider positioning firewalls so that they can filter all traffic. This may involve the creation of choke points.

Third, is Internet connectivity essential to business tasks? You should firewall-protect all Internet access points or gateways. In fact, any external gateway or portal should have a firewall.

Fourth, is any form of remote access in use, including wireless? You should position a firewall between each RAS or NAS and the private LAN. Assume all remote and wireless connections are potentially malicious.

Fifth, based on previous compromises, what are the most likely access pathways an internal or external hacker might use to breach your network? Place firewalls along these pathways.

Sixth, does any other unique aspect or feature of your IT infrastructure warrant consideration for firewall protection?

Placing a firewall everywhere mentioned in these guidelines may not be practical, cost effective, or secure. So before any deployment, conduct a risk assessment to determine whether a firewall is the best choice of countermeasure. Review the previous section, "Why Do You Need a Firewall?" for more information on conducting risk assessments.

CHAPTER SUMMARY

An essential element of network security, a firewall is a filtering service used to protect your network and hosts from a variety of threats, both internal and external. Several types of firewalls are available, including screening routers, hardware appliances, and host software products. Each of these firewalls can employ one or more features for ingress and egress filtering. The common filtering features include static packet filtering, stateful inspection or dynamic packet filtering, NAT, application proxy, and circuit proxy.

KEY CONCEPTS AND TERMS

802.1x
Agents
Annualized loss expectancy (ALE)
Annualized rate of occurrence (ARO)
Appliance firewall
Application layer (Layer 7)
Application proxy/firewall/gateway
Asset value (AV)
Bastion host
Border sentry
Botnets
'Bots
Circuit
Circuit proxy/firewall
Closed source
Commercial firewall
Content filtering
Cost/benefit
Data link layer (Layer 2)
Dead-man switch
De-encapsulation
Dual-homed firewall
Dynamic packet filtering
Exposure factor (EF)
Fail-safe/fail-secure
Filtering
Firewall
Frame
Gateway
Hardware address
Hardware firewall
Header
Host firewall
Intangible cost/value
Internet Control Message Protocol (ICMP)
IP address
Logical address
MAC address
Network layer (Layer 3)
Open source
Open system interconnection reference model (OSI model)
Packet
Payload
Personal firewall
Physical address
Physical layer (Layer 1)
Port forwarding
Port number
Public Key Infrastructure (PKI)
Presentation layer (Layer 6)
Reverse proxy
Risk assessment
Risk management
Rule set
Rules
Sacrificial host
Screening router
Secure Sockets Layer (SSL)
Segment
Session
Session layer (Layer 5)
Single loss expectancy (SLE)
Socket
Software firewall
Spoofing
State
Stateful inspection
Static NAT
Static packet filtering
Tangible cost/value
Transmission Control Protocol (TCP)
Transport layer (Layer 4)
Transport Layer Security (TLS)
Transport mode encryption
Triple-homed firewall
Tunnel mode encryption
User Datagram Protocol (UDP)
Zombies
Zone of risk
Zone of trust

CHAPTER 2 ASSESSMENT

1. What is another term for the individual rules in a firewall rule set?
   A. States
   B. Exceptions
   C. Policies
   D. Referrals
   E. Sentries

2. Which of the following is *not* associated with a firewall?
   A. Fail-secure
   B. Sentry device
   C. Fail-open
   D. Choke point
   E. Filtering service

3. A firewall is designed to allow what type of traffic to traverse its interfaces?
   A. Authorized
   B. Non-benign
   C. Unknown
   D. Abnormal
   E. Malicious

4. What is the first step in deploying a firewall?
   A. Determining the filtering process
   B. Defining rules
   C. Selecting a security stance
   D. Purchasing a license
   E. Writing a security policy

5. Which of the following is the best description of a firewall?
   A. An authentication service
   B. A remote access server
   C. Resource host
   D. A sentry device
   E. Malicious code scanner

6. A border firewall cannot protect against which of the following?
   A. Flooding attacks
   B. Insider attacking another internal target
   C. Protocol abuses
   D. Unauthorized inbound service requests
   E. Port scans

7. All of the following are mistakes in firewall security *except*:
   A. Managing security poorly
   B. Deploying too many firewalls
   C. Using firewalls to provide filtering for networks and hosts
   D. Not writing a security policy
   E. Failing to keep current with updates and patches

8. What is the primary reason a firewall is an essential security product?
   A. Low cost of deployment
   B. Threats exist
   C. High ROI
   D. Native protocol encryption
   E. Interoperability

9. What technique determines if a firewall is the best countermeasure choice for a particular threat against a specific asset?
   A. Conducting a risk assessment
   B. Reading blogs
   C. Buying the least expensive option
   D. Only using open-source products
   E. Using products from a single vendor

10. Which of the following is *not* a common zone of risk?
    A. An extranet
    B. A DMZ
    C. A private LAN
    D. The Internet
    E. Department subnets

11. Which of the following statements are true?

A. A firewall can be deployed as a bastion host.
B. Firewalls protect resources.
C. Firewalls are often the first line of defense for a network.
D. Firewalls are part of an overall security strategy.
E. All of the above

12. When a one-way or sieve firewall protecting your network allows external initiations of communications to occur over a specific socket, this is known as:

A. Static NAT
B. Traffic forwarding
C. Port forwarding
D. Reverse proxy
E. All of the above

13. What is ingress filtering?

A. Restricting traffic to a specific subnet
B. Preventing traffic from leaving a network
C. Limiting host activities to that host
D. Monitoring traffic on its way inbound
E. Blocking access to external resource sockets

14. Content filtering can focus on the following aspects of traffic *except*:

A. Source or destination IP address
B. Keywords in the payload
C. URLs
D. File extensions
E. Domain names

15. Which of the following will prevent firewall filtering from blocking malicious content?

A. Speed of the network
B. User permissions
C. Not being positioned at a choke point
D. Encrypted traffic
E. Cable type

16. Which of the following is *not* a valid method for determining whether a source address is spoofed?

A. Compare against a use table
B. Verify the route of reception
C. Check the DHCP logs
D. Check against RFC 1918
E. Perform ingress filtering

17. What form of filtering focuses on source or destination IP address and requires separate rules for inbound and outbound communications?

A. Stateful inspection
B. Static packet filtering
C. Application proxy
D. Circuit proxy
E. Dynamic packet filtering

18. Dynamic packet filtering is also known as:

A. Static packet filtering
B. Application proxy
C. Stateful inspection
D. Circuit proxy
E. Deep packet inspection

19. What method of filtering automatically keeps track of sessions on a limited timeout basis to allow responses to queries to reach internal clients?

A. Deep packet inspection
B. Static packet filtering
C. Application proxy
D. Dynamic packet filtering
E. Circuit proxy

20. What form of filtering allows communications regardless of content once the session is established?

A. Dynamic packet filtering
B. Circuit proxy
C. Stateful inspection
D. Application proxy
E. Deep packet inspection

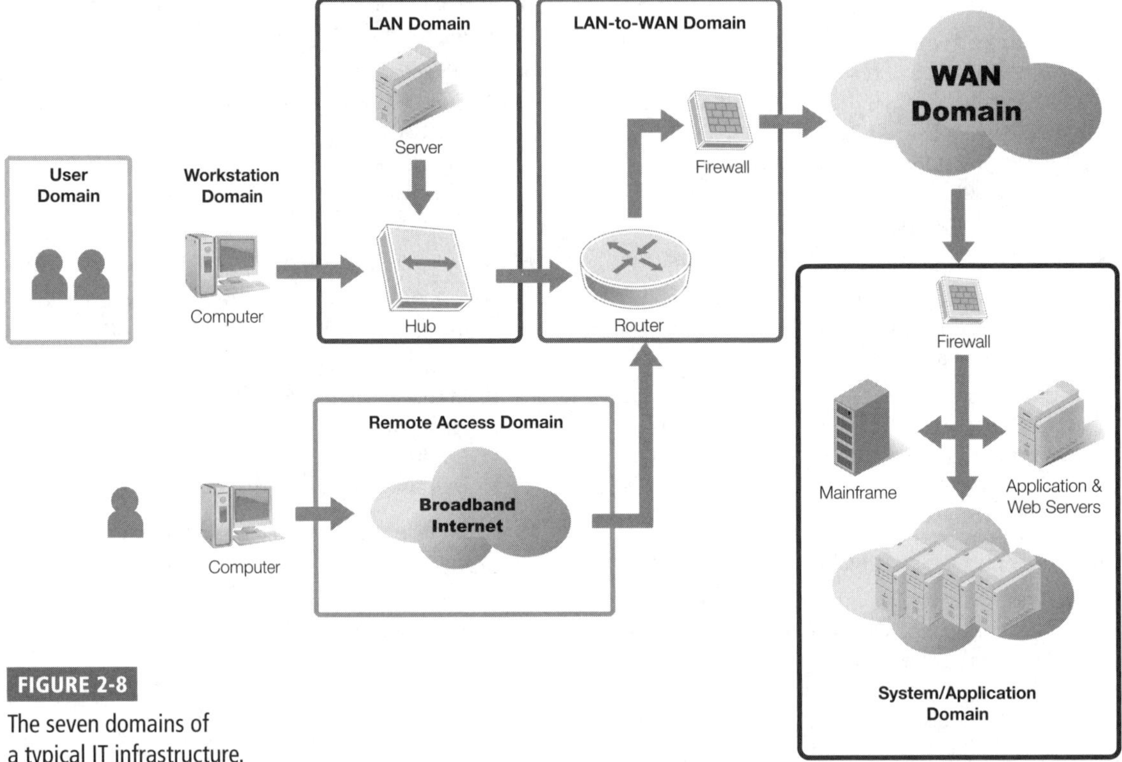

FIGURE 2-8

The seven domains of a typical IT infrastructure.

21. What type of firewall requires the presence of a host operating system?

A. Appliance firewall
B. Personal firewall
C. Software firewall
D. Commercial firewall
E. Screening router

22. Based on the seven domains of a typical IT infrastructure, all of the following locations (see Figure 2-8) are appropriate locations for firewall deployment *except*:

A. Between users and workstations
B. Between workstations and LAN
C. Between LAN and WAN
D. Between remote access and LAN
E. Between remote access and application servers

23. What activity performed by a triple-homed firewall cannot be performed by a dual-homed firewall?

A. Filter content
B. Physically isolate subnets
C. Support NAT proxy services
D. Be deployed as an appliance
E. Route traffic from the Internet to either an intranet or DMZ

CHAPTER 3

VPN Fundamentals

VIRTUAL PRIVATE NETWORKS (VPNS) allow organizations to transmit private and sensitive data securely over public intermediary networks. The Internet can serve as a cheap long-distance carrier for WAN connections established using VPNs. VPNs use native-operating system features or third-party software, as well as hardware devices, including edge routers, firewalls, and VPN appliances. Remote access for mobile users, linked multi-office intranets, and secured access into an extranet are common VPN architecture solutions.

The use of VPNs on small home networks to corporate global networks has dramatically expanded the ways people connect and do work. Through the use of VPNs, telecommuting employees, business partners, traveling workers, suppliers, distributors, and others can benefit from secured connectivity even while geographically distant. With a basic understanding of VPNs, you can begin designing and planning your own VPN solution.

Chapter 3 Topics

This chapter will cover the following topics and concepts:

- What a VPN is and what is it used for
- What the benefits of a VPN are and why would you deploy one
- What the limitations of a VPN are
- What the relationship between encryption and VPNs is
- What VPN authentication is and how is it implemented
- What VPN authorization is and why is it necessary

Chapter 3 Goals

When you've completed this chapter, you will be able to:

- Define VPNs
- Explain the business and personal uses of VPNs
- Describe the pros and cons of VPNs
- Illustrate deployment models or architectures of VPNs, including an edge router, a corporate firewall, a VPN appliance, a remote access server, a site-to-site VPN and supporting devices, and a host-to-host VPN and supporting devices
- Differentiate between a transport-mode VPN and a tunnel-mode VPN
- Describe the importance to VPNs of encryption, authentication, and authorization

What Is a VPN?

VPN is the acronym for "**virtual private network**." A short and direct definition is that a VPN is a mechanism to establish a secure remote access connection across an **intermediary network**, often the Internet. VPNs allow remote access, remote control, and highly secured communications within a private network. VPNs employ encryption and authentication to provide confidentiality, integrity, and privacy protection for network communications.

A more involved exploration of the phrase "virtual private networks," however, can reveal other import aspects that such a succinct definition overlooks. The term VPN has its origins in the telecommunications world. A telephone VPN created a PBX-like system for businesses without the need for deployment of true **private branch exchange (PBX)** hardware. Instead, the system used a public telephone service and the PBX services at the telco's central offices. This service/product sold under the name Centrex (a combination of the terms central and exchange) in the 1960s through the 1980s.

After the proliferation of computer networks and Internet connectivity, the term VPN evolved to refer to tunneling connections across network links. Early computer VPNs focused on the tunneling or encapsulation processes and rarely included encryption services. Today, VPNs are almost always secured using encryption. However, you should never assume anything is totally secure, especially connections over **public networks**. You should always confirm that a product performs encryption properly before depending on it for sensitive operations.

A VPN creates or simulates a network connection over an intermediary network. But, what makes a VPN private? At least three possible mechanisms can work:

- When the primary organization owns all of the network infrastructure components, including switches, routers, and cables. A true private VPN occurs when a single organization owns all of the hardware supporting their VPN. However, few organizations actually own all of the connections between their locations, so this is usually impractical or prohibitively expensive. This wholly owned and operated system constitutes a trusted VPN.
- When a dedicated set of **channels** is used across leased telco connections. This method provides physical isolation even on third-party equipment; hence privacy is maintained. This type of system is more practical, but is still expensive. This can also be called a trusted VPN, since you must be able to trust the owner of the hosting infrastructure to protect network communications against **eavesdropping**.
- When encryption ensures privacy even over public networks, such as the Internet. This method is the most reliable, as the other two options are still at risk to eavesdropping. Additionally, encryption to provide privacy is not only practical, it is the least expensive option as well. This system can be called a **secured VPN**.

A fourth type private VPN is possible, known as a **hybrid VPN**. This form of VPN establishes a secure VPN over trusted VPN connections. A **trusted VPN** allows an organization to know and control the pathway of their transmissions. However, a trusted VPN does not protect against eavesdropping or alteration. A secure VPN protects the confidentiality and integrity of data, but does not control or ensure the transmission path. When you combine these two VPN techniques, you create a potentially more secure and practical solution. Two possible layouts of hybrid VPNs are shown in Figures 3-1 and 3-2.

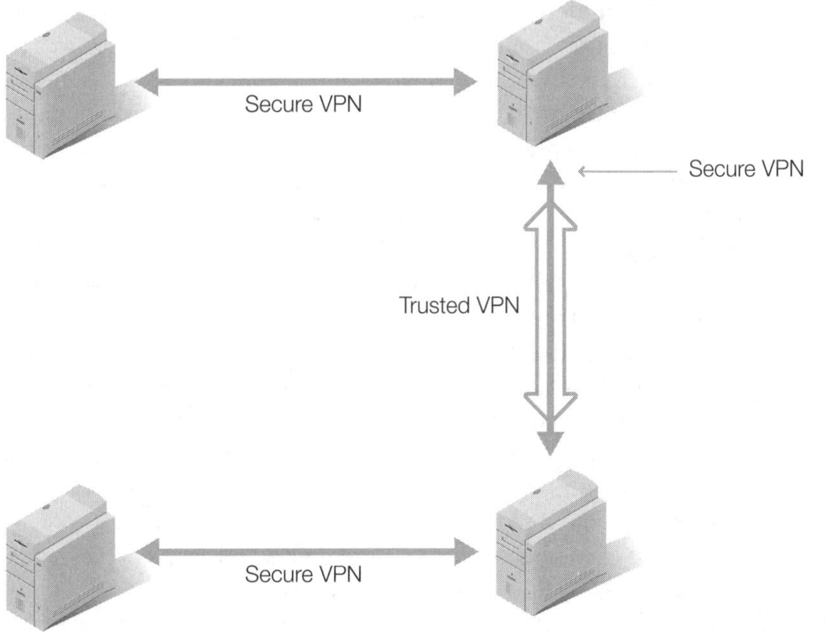

FIGURE 3-1 A hybrid VPN consisting of a secure VPN across an intermediary trusted VPN.

FIGURE 3-2

A hybrid VPN consisting of a secure VPN segment within a trusted VPN.

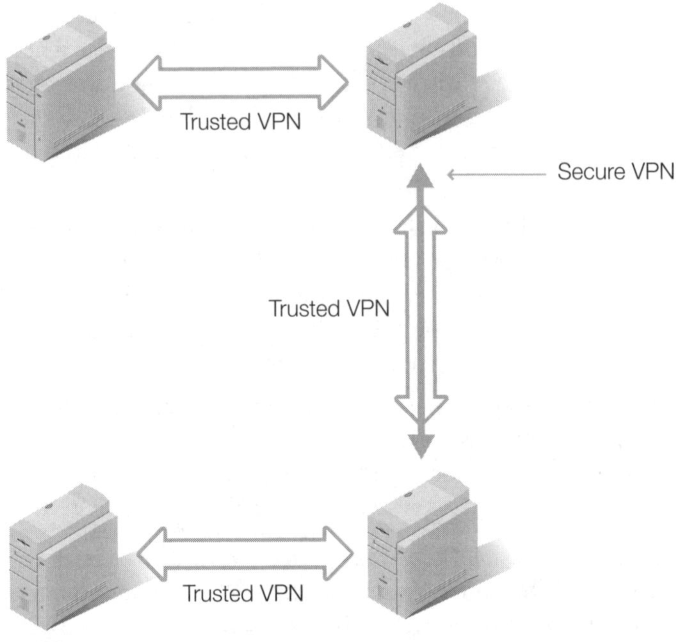

VPNs are often associated with remote access or remote control. However, these associations need clarification to have value. Remote control is the ability to use a local computer system to remotely take over control of another computer over a network connection. In a way, this process is the application of the thin client concept on a modern fully capable workstation to simulate working against a mainframe or to virtualize your physical presence. This application is generally the same as a VPN, which creates a remote network connection rather than a remote control session.

With a remote control connection in place, the local monitor, keyboard, and mouse control a remote system. This process looks and feels like you are physically present at the keyboard of the remote system, which could be located in another city or even on the other side of the world. Every action you perform locally acts as if you were physically present at that remote computer virtually via the remote control connection. The only limitations are the speed of the intermediary network link and inability to physically insert or remove media and peripherals.

You might think of remote control as a form of software-based thin client or terminal client. In fact, many thin client and terminal client products sell as remote control solutions. Many modern operating systems include remote control features, such as Remote Desktop found in most versions of Windows. Once enabled, a Remote Desktop Connection remotely controls another Windows system from across the network. You can learn more about Remote Desktop in Chapter 14 "Real World VPNs."

Remote access is different from remote control. A remote access link enables access to network resources using a WAN link to connect to the geographically distant network. In effect, remote access creates a local network link for a system not physically near the network. Over a remote access connection, a client system can technically perform all the same tasks as a locally connected client. Network administrators can impose restrictions on what resources and services a remote access VPN client can use.

Remote access and VPNs were originally supported over dial-up telephone links using **modems**. Today, remote access encompasses a variety of connection types including ISDN, DSL, cable modem, satellite, mobile broadband, and more. Due to the wide availability of high-speed Internet connections, VPNs and other remote access solutions have become very popular for both personal and business-purposes.

In many cases, a remote access connection is created from a remote client back to a primary network. If the remote client needs to connect directly to the LAN, such as over a dial-up connection, a RAS server will host a modem to accept the connection. If the remote client can use the Internet to access the LAN, then a local Internet connection is necessary. Once a normal LAN connection or Internet connection runs from the client, the VPN link is possible. Once the connection is established, the remote client now interacts with the network as if it were locally connected.

In Figure 3-3, a LAN and a remote client have a connection to the Internet. These two connections are independent of each other. The LAN's connection is usually a permanent or **dedicated connection** supporting both inbound and outbound activities with the Internet. The remote client's connection to the Internet can be dedicated or **non-dedicated**. In the latter case, the connection is established before a VPN can be created. Once both endpoints have a connection to the intermediary network, in this case the Internet, then the VPN can be created. In Figure 3-4, a new network connection is established from the remote client to the LAN across the intermediary network. This new network connection is the VPN.

VPNs can operate over standard Internet connections or dedicated business communication circuits, such as ATM and Frame Relay. However, the additional expense of a dedicated, isolated, and even secured business circuit isn't necessary with a VPN.

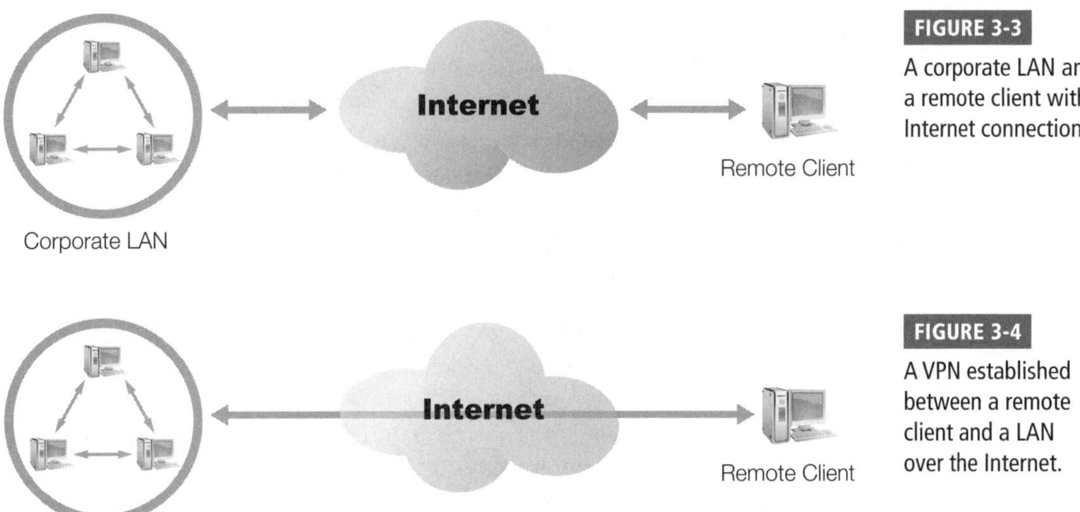

FIGURE 3-3 A corporate LAN and a remote client with Internet connections.

FIGURE 3-4 A VPN established between a remote client and a LAN over the Internet.

A VPN can operate securely over the Internet and still provide high levels of security through solid encryption. This allows inexpensive insecure links to replace expensive business-leased lines without sacrificing security.

VPNs are one of the most efficient and cost-effective means to provide secure remote connectivity. VPNs take advantage of cheap long distance connections when established over the Internet, since both endpoints only need a local Internet link. The Internet itself serves as a "free" long distance carrier. Because the speed of the VPN depends on the speed of the local Internet link, you still might want an **optical carrier (OC)** line (such as an OC-1 at 51.84 Mbps) for high-speed connectivity.

Connections from a LAN to an intermediary network, can support VPN traffic only or allow a combination of both VPN and normal non-VPN traffic. The latter configuration is less secure, but offers you flexibility as to whether all communications must be VPN-secured or not. An Internet connection reserved solely for VPN use, therefore, is not necessary. An OC-1 line is more than capable of supporting one or more VPN links in addition to numerous non-VPN Internet sessions with no difficulty or **latency**.

Setting up VPNs can require extensive knowledge and expertise on the part of the IT or security administrator. For example, some important concerns of secure VPNs include:

- All VPN traffic must be authenticated and encrypted. A VPN without authentication is not private, and a VPN without encryption is insecure.
- All VPN endpoints must abide by the same security parameters and algorithms. Each VPN tunnel must have corresponding **encryption key** sets to securely exchanged encrypted content. Additionally, the same security policy should govern all endpoints.
- Proper encryption protocols must ensure that no external third-party can affect the security of the VPN. Weak encryption makes a "secure" VPN worthless.

When you use a trusted VPN you need to consider its own unique concerns:

- Only the trusted VPN provider should be able to modify the channels or pathway of the VPN. A trusted VPN is based on the provider's ability to limit and control access to the VPN's content.
- Only the trusted VPN provider can add, remove, or change data in the trusted channel. Violating this violates the trust the client places in the provider.
- The addressing and routing performed within the trusted VPN must be defined before the VPN goes online. These services are usually pre-defined in the SLA (service level agreement), but may be dynamically modified for each VPN connection.

Even hybrid VPNs have an important focus for concern, namely that the segments of the VPN that are trusted vs. secured need clear definition. Mistaking security for trust—or vice versa—can have devastating results.

VPNs use tunneling or encapsulation protocols. Tunneling protocols encase the original network protocol so that it can traverse the intermediary network. In many cases, the tunneling protocol employs encryption so that the original data traverses the intermediary network securely. The protocols that create VPNs include IPSec, PPTP, L2TP,

SSL, and TLS. The dominant forms of secure VPNs use IPSec or SSL/TLS as the tunneling/encapsulation protocol. You can learn more about VPN protocols in Chapter 13.

Most VPNs use software that operates on top of the operating system of a host. However, some VPN appliances can support VPN connectivity without adding any software to the host. In much the same way that a host firewall only works on the host where it is installed, an appliance firewall provide security services for the entire network. A **host VPN** software product allows a single host access to VPN services, while a **VPN appliance** allows an entire network to access VPN services. Read more about VPN hardware devices in Chapter 13.

VPNs simplify many business networking problems by providing an easy and efficient means to securely connect headquarters, remote offices, traveling workers, and telecommuters.

What Are the Benefits of Deploying a VPN?

The reasons to deploy and use VPNs vary greatly among organizations. Many of the obvious reasons are based on the benefits of a VPN (discussed in the following section). Nevertheless, other reasons are based on business or personal factors needing the solutions VPNs readily provide.

Cost is always a significant factor in any business decision. Budgets are never unlimited (at least, not outside of Congress), so organizations must shepherd their limited funds to accomplish their missions and goals. One common goal is high productivity. Granting workers the ability to access and use resources in a timely and efficient manner assists in the completion of work. When those resources are computer files or network services, employees no longer need to be in the same building as those resources. Remote access to resources, therefore, is becoming more common than ever.

Secure remote access is essential. As the proliferation of access and connectivity spreads from work to home to portable/mobile devices, access to the Internet and private LANs is becoming ubiquitous. Companies must use security controls on resource access or suffer the consequences of insecure access methods. With the removal of physical limitations for access comes the loss of control over where and how workers connect back into the private LAN.

Workers connect into the company LAN from mobile phones, through Internet cafés, over hotel networks, and at random Wi-Fi hotspots. Many use personally owned laptop computers and hand-held mobile devices rather than officially issued company systems. All of these are outside the control of the company's IT and security department. The only option is to limit LAN connections to those that can be secured. Thus, VPNs have become a necessity in the brave new mobile and interconnected world.

VPNs support remote access from a wide variety of complex devices, reduce risk caused by insecure access locations, and enable interaction with all LAN resources. Furthermore, flexibility, **scalability**, ease of administration, reliability, and more make VPNs an obvious choice in the face of modern connectivity risks and challenges.

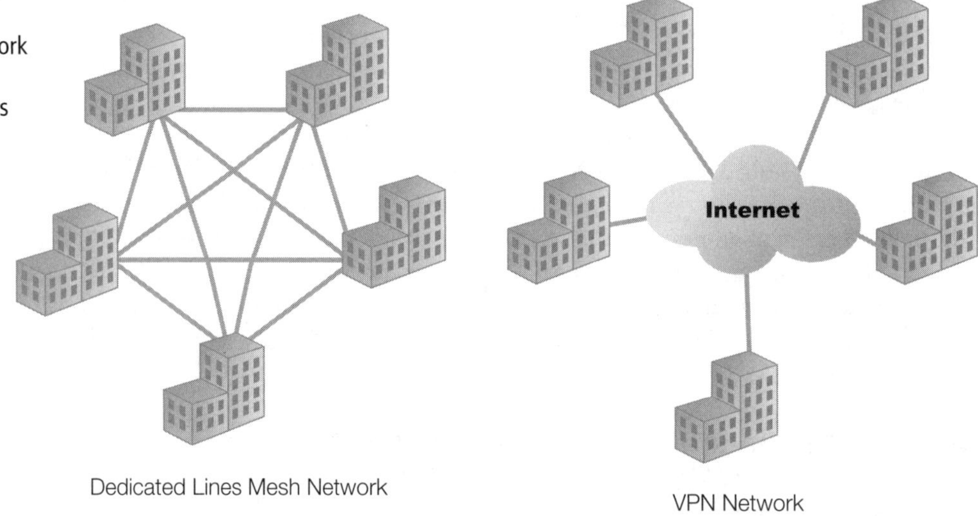

FIGURE 3-5
A corporate network using dedicated leased lines versus using VPNs over the Internet.

Does every worker and every organization need VPNs and remote access? No. Many worker situations exist where VPNs are not the correct solution. These include any form of work that requires special tools, physical access to equipment, or close supervision by managers.

Remote access, mobile connectivity, and secured communications are solid reasons to deploy and use a VPN. But are these the only positive aspects of a VPN?

The most often touted benefit of VPNs is cost savings. They are a great way to save on long distance charges for telecommuters and traveling workers. They also create huge savings for businesses that would only need local Internet links for a VPN rather than a dedicated **leased line** between each location (Figure 3-5). The farther away each business location is and the more locations a company has, the more of a cost savings a VPN can generate.

Additionally, to truly compare the connectivity that a VPN offers to dedicated leased lines, you need a **full mesh** of leased lines. A full mesh requires a line between each business location. This allows for a direct communication between one site and another. Since a VPN across the Internet would provide the equivalent site-to-site communication capabilities, only a mesh network of **dedicated lease lines** can truly compare. This solution is obviously very expensive compared to a VPN's significant cost savings.

As corporations seek to reduce IT infrastructure costs, a common technique is to allow employees to telecommute. **Telecommuting** allows workers to access corporate resources whether the employee works from home, while traveling, or while on-site with a customer. In the past, telecommuting clearly implied the use of dial-up connections to connect with the company LAN.

With the proliferation of high-speed broadband connections and WiFi, telecommuting has become more plausible and realistic. Through the use of VPNs, telecommuting enables a true remote office rather than just a file exchange and communication system.

VPNs make telecommuting not only possible, but also practical and secure. VPNs make expanding the workforce no longer a geographically limited proposition.

Extranets are often deployed as businesses establish new partnerships or seek more interaction with suppliers, distributors, and other external entities. Extranets are border networks, similar to a DMZ, where resources are hosted for access by external entities. However, unlike a DMZ, an extranet is not open for public use. Only a limited and specific set of users is allowed to connect into an extranet. Often, this limitation means that a specific VPN configuration is necessary to access the extranet's resources. With VPNs, extranets are both possible and practical.

VPNs allow for system administrators to remotely manage and control a network. VPNs allow employees to work from anywhere. VPNs allow friends to create WAN links to support multiplayer games. VPNs allow technical support to remotely repair client systems. A VPN is the solution anytime a network connection is needed between two systems or two networks, but installing a direct cable connection is unfeasible.

Often, the real benefits of a VPN are not from the VPN itself, but from all the new possibilities for work, research, learning, and play feasible because of a VPN. These benefits include:

- Reduced equipment costs
- Unlimited geographic connectivity
- Increased flexibility and versatility of worker location
- Improved privacy & confidentiality due to strong encryption
- Verified transmission integrity
- Fully scalable global infrastructure and architecture
- Rapid deployment options
- Flexible integration with existing networks and technologies
- Faster return on investment (ROI) than traditional WAN infrastructures
- Reduced dependence on long-distance carrier solutions
- Reduced support burden as ISP

Individuals and organizations that use VPNs and integrate them in new and unique ways are sure to reap additional benefits. History shows us that as new means of communication are created, they often change and are used in ways that were unpredictable at the beginning of their adoption. However, VPNs are not perfect, and some very real and challenging issues limit the use of VPNs.

What Are the Limitations of a VPN?

While the use of VPNs has many benefits, you need to evaluate the very real and distinct limitations before you put a VPN in place.

Although a VPN connection offers flexible secure communication options, it does not ensure quality of service. A VPN link is dependent upon the stability, throughput, and availability of the ISP connection as well as the intervening network connections between endpoints. VPNs over the Internet can easily suffer from latency, **fragmentation**,

technical TIP

Encrypted traffic does not compress. Compression reduces the size of a data set removing redundancies or repeated sections within the data set. Properly encrypted data produces **ciphertext** that does not contain redundancies or recognizable patterns. If ciphertext did have these characteristics, it would not be as secure. Thus, without these redundancies, it's not possible to compress encrypted data.

traffic congestion, and dropped packets. This also results in a lack of dedicated bandwidth between business sites, because of the volatility of the Internet.

While VPNs are excellent solutions over nearly every broadband connection option, over dial-up a VPN can be difficult to maintain. VPN traffic is encrypted and encrypted traffic does not compress. Most dial-up modem connections rely on **compression**—mainly hardware compression—to improve connection speed. When compression is not possible, a significant and noticeable speed reduction occurs. Additionally, VPN tunnel management can impose a significant increase in management overhead because of changes in protocol headers, potential authentication latency, and a prolonged connection establishment negotiation.

Another area of concern is the minor risk or potential of data exposure while in transit over the Internet. This is only a real concern if the VPN does not use encryption, uses poor encryption, or configures the encryption improperly. Proper security management will eliminate this as a serious concern.

Vulnerabilities exist at VPN endpoints. With a VPN, side attacks against the encrypted link are nearly eliminated. However, data entering or leaving the VPN is at risk. An end-user computer could be infected by malicious code that can traverse the VPN link into the company LAN. Also, private and confidential data from the company LAN can be copied across the VPN link to the end-user computer. On this computer, that data is less secure and subject to a wider range of threats.

You should also consider the increased difficulty in providing technical support remotely. This is especially true when the remote connection itself is not functioning. In addition, it's more difficult to keep remote systems in compliance with security settings, conduct training, allow supervisory oversight, enable HR management, and monitor user activities.

Not every person is a good candidate for a remote user. Those who are easily distracted, who are not motivated, or whose home environment is not conducive to work are prime examples of those who should stay in the office rather than work from home.

technical TIP

The latest generation of traditional telephone modems is often rated with a speed of 56 Kbps. Most of that speed is the result of hardware compression. Without compression, most modem speeds are significantly slower—at 24 Kbps or less.

An even larger concern is granting open or blanket unrestricted network-resource access to those connecting via VPN. You must enforce stronger authentication and authorization limitations on VPN users, especially on VPN telecommuters. Remote users should have access only to those resources necessary for their current tasks. Unlimited access to network resources can quickly result in exploitation and confidential data leakage, if the remote user or the remote computer is compromised.

If you understand these limitations and address them properly, you can help to avoid catastrophic mistakes when correctly installing and productively using VPNs. One of the primary tools to accomplish this is the VPN policy.

What Are Effective VPN Policies?

Effective VPN policies are those that clearly define security restrictions imposed on VPNs that align with the overall IT mission and goals of your organization. VPNs can offer numerous exciting possibilities of mobility and interconnection. However, VPNs can also be a risk to the confidentiality and stability of your organization's infrastructure.

Like all security policies, your VPN policy should derive from a thorough risk assessment and analysis. Without fully understanding the assets, processes, threats, and risks of VPNs, you can't effectively use or manage them.

Developing your VPN security policy is not a simple or straightforward task. You need to plan for time and effort to address a wide variety of issues and concerns. Some of the aspects of design and planning of a VPN policy include (but are not limited to):

- Consider the benefits and drawbacks of software and **hardware VPN** solutions
- Impose stringent **multi-factor authentication** on all VPN connections
- Implement strong access control (authorization) restrictions on all VPN connections
- Define how the VPN will be managed, through what interfaces, and by whom
- Explore the complexities of patch management over VPN
- Define the mechanisms of providing remote technical support for VPN telecommuters
- Enable detailed auditing on all activities occurring across or through a VPN
- Define distinct qualifications on granting user access to telecommuting VPNs
- Prescribe the user training requirements for all VPN activities

You can learn more about crafting a VPN policy in Chapter 12.

VPN Deployment Models and Architecture

One of the first decisions you face when deploying a VPN is: what device will serve as the termination point of the secured tunnel? You have several options, but often the decision rests on where in the network infrastructure you want to position the tunnel endpoint. Additionally, the features the VPN device provides may be a factor in the decision, as well.

Such factors include deciding which devices have sufficient processing power to maintain wirespeed even with heavy traffic and complex encryption. Another concern is whether NAT is present, as this can impose problems for tunnel mode encryption. (Learn more about this topic in Chapter 13 in the section, "VPNs and NAT.")

The three primary VPN device models are **edge router**, **corporate firewall**, and VPN appliance. In addition to the selection of the VPN device, you have several architectural decisions to make, as well. These focus on the intended purpose, function, or use of the VPN, such as remote access, host-to-host, site-to-site, and extranet access.

Edge Router

With edge routers as the VPN termination point, the VPN link exists only over the public intermediary networks, not within the private LAN(s). This does require that the edge router support VPN connectivity.

Edge router VPN termination ensures that a firewall can filter the traffic exiting the VPN on its way into the LAN. This method insures that all traffic, regardless of transportation means, complies with the firewall's filtering rules. If the VPN terminates inside the firewall, then traffic from the VPN could potentially violate security because it was not firewall-inspected.

VPN termination on edge routers is best suited for controlled access into the DMZ. Such a configuration grants business partners easy access to the DMZ without exposing their traffic to the Internet or granting them unnecessary access to the private LAN.

Corporate Firewall

Terminating the VPN at the corporate firewall is possible if the firewall supports VPN services. Not all firewalls provide this service, so this depends on your choice of make and model of the firewall product. With a firewall-to-firewall VPN across the public network, users from one network LAN can access resources in another network LAN without additional complexities. Primarily, this configuration treats the VPN link between the firewall endpoints as just another route in the LAN (actually WAN). The benefit here is that users don't need to re-authenticate or abide by additional firewall restrictions when the VPN terminates at the corporate firewall.

Corporate firewall termination of the VPN means that the traffic entering or leaving the VPN does not pass through the filtering restrictions of the firewall. Instead, the firewall simply serves as a tethering point for the VPN tunnel endpoint. Any traffic not associated with the VPN, however, is subject to firewall investigation.

This configuration has a potential limitation. As the number of VPN links increases or the traffic load of the VPNs increases, the resulting increase in cryptographic computations could interfere with the firewall's wirespeed filtering performance. In this case, perform a trend analysis to monitor for this condition and improve firewall performance before a bottleneck occurs.

VPN Appliance

A third device option is a dedicated VPN appliance. Unlike an edge router or firewall termination point, a dedicated VPN appliance specifically handles the load of a VPN, instead of VPN support being an add-on service.

You can position a VPN appliance outside the corporate firewall, in a similar location to an edge router, so that all VPN traffic passes through firewall filters. A VPN appliance

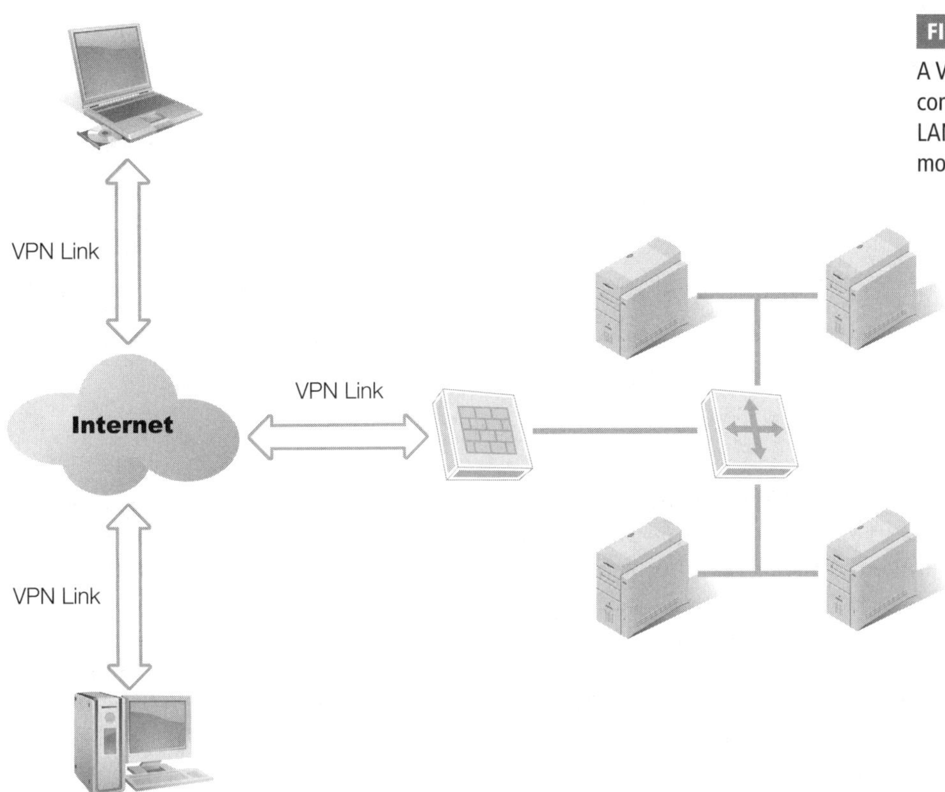

FIGURE 3-6
A VPN used to connect a single LAN with remote mobile users.

can also reside inside the corporate firewalls to prevent firewall filtration. This deployment is similar to the corporate firewall concept, at least in terms of not filtering VPN traffic. This second deployment method also ensures that no external entity can interfere with the endpoints of the VPN tunnel.

These techniques are useful when corporate firewalls already exist that do not support the VPN technology or architecture you want. So rather than replacing the firewalls, you install an additional dedicated VPN appliance.

Remote Access

The first VPN architecture is basic remote access (Figure 3-6). **Remote access VPN** is also known as **host-to-site VPN** since it supports single-host VPN connections into a LAN site. This design grants individual telecommuters or traveling workers easy access into the private LAN. A single LAN can support several remote users with any of the VPN endpoint concepts: edge router, corporate firewall, or VPN appliance.

Site-to-Site

A second VPN architecture is site-to-site (Figure 3-7). **Site-to-site VPNs** are also known as **LAN-to-LAN VPNs** or **WAN VPN** connections between LANs. Regardless of the name, a site-to-site VPN supports secure connections between LANs over intermediary

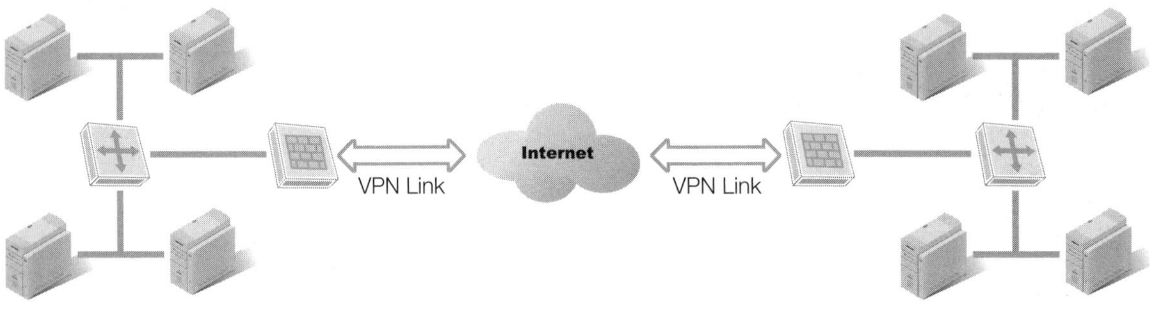

FIGURE 3-7

A VPN used to connect multiple LANs.

public networks. When you install it properly, a site-to-site VPN can be an inexpensive mechanism to create a single **distributed LAN** (also known as a WAN) for a multi-location organization. A site-to-site VPN uses any of the VPN endpoint concepts: edge router, corporate firewall, or VPN appliance.

A slight variation on the site-to-site VPN is the site-to-site VPN with remote mobile users. This is a combination of the site-to-site VPN concept with remote access VPNs (Figure 3-8). The benefit of this architecture is the ability to add new employees with secure connections to the LAN without needing additional corporate facilities to provide on-site workspaces.

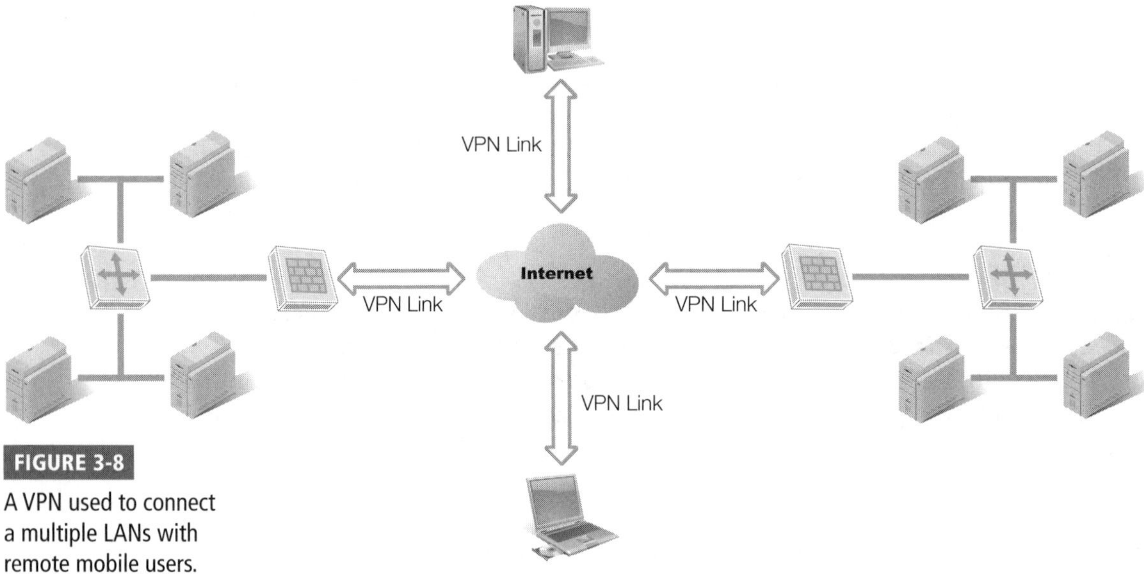

FIGURE 3-8

A VPN used to connect a multiple LANs with remote mobile users.

Host-to-Host

A third VPN architecture is host-to-host. Host-to-host VPNs are also known as client-to-server or remote-to-office or remote-to-home VPNs. A **host-to-host VPN** is a direct VPN connection between one host and another. This mechanism operates over a public network or within a private network. Over a public network, a host-to-host VPN provides a secure connection against the public. Over a private network, it provides an additional level of security for mission-critical or highly sensitive transactions.

Host-to-host VPNs labeled as **client-to-server VPNs** create secure client interaction with the services of a resource host. This is similar to, but not exactly the same as, a secure Web link between a Web browser and a Web server. SSL can be used for application protocol security, as it is with secure Web sessions, or as a VPN protocol. As a VPN protocol, SSL operates at the network layer; as a Web session security tool, it operates at the top of the transport layer. You can learn more about SSL operations in Chapter 13.

A **remote-to-office VPN** is a direct link between a portable or home system and an office workstation. This VPN link up allows a user to work from home or while traveling without sacrificing access to resources, services, or applications that might only be installed (or licensed) for use on the office workstation computer. This VPN can establish a remote control session as commonly as a remote access session.

A **remote-to-home VPN** connects a work computer or a portable computer back to a home system, effectively the opposite configuration of the remote-to-office. The remote-to-home VPN grants you access to a home computer while you are away from the house.

The host-to-host VPN variations usually depend on **software VPN** solutions native to the operating system or third-party applications installed on the host. However, some VPN appliances are adaptable to these simpler host-to-host connectivity architectures.

Extranet Access

A fourth VPN architecture is extranet access. With a VPN tunnel endpoint positioned at or inside the perimeter of an extranet, this option serves as a pathway for business partners, distributors, suppliers, and so forth to gain access to corporate resources without exposing their traffic to the Internet or granting them unnecessary access to the private LAN.

Additionally, a VPN linked into the extranet as opposed to the DMZ provides greater security to the remote entities. A VPN link to the DMZ exposes the remote entities to any threats found in the DMZ. Since the DMZ is publicly accessible, it's risky. An **extranet VPN** grants the remote entity secure communications without significant risks at the VPN termination point.

VPNs commonly serve as a choke point to control which external entities have access to the extranet. Only those granted specific access, assigned user accounts, and provided configuration details are able to configure and establish a VPN link with an extranet.

Tunnel Versus Transport Mode

VPNs can use two main types of encapsulation encryption. These are known as tunnel mode and transport mode encryption.

Tunnel mode encryption protects the entire original IP packet's header and payload. This encrypted packet becomes the payload of a new IP packet with a new IP header. This form of encryption ensures that the identities of the original endpoints of the communication are kept confidential while the traffic traverses the secured link. Tunnel mode encryption is commonly used by VPNs linking network sites together or providing secure remote access.

Transport mode encryption protects only the original IP packet's payload. The encrypted payload retains its original IP header. This form of encryption only protects the payload, not the identities of the endpoints. Transport mode encryption helps VPNs link individual computers together.

The Relationship Between Encryption and VPNs

Encryption and a secure VPN are virtually inseparable. A secure VPN exists only because its traffic is encrypted. But some trusted VPNs may or may not use encryption. To fully understand and appreciate the operations of VPNs, you need a reasonable understanding of encryption.

Encryption is just one aspect of the larger topic of **cryptography**. Cryptography is the art and science of hiding information from unauthorized third parties. Cryptography occurs through a complimentary and reversible process: encryption and decryption. Encryption is the process of converting original usable form data, called plain text, into unusable chaotic form, called ciphertext. **Decryption** is the process of converting ciphertext back into plain text. A real-world communication product must provide both encryption and decryption.

Modern cryptography is based on algorithms. An **algorithm** is a set of rules and procedures, usually mathematical in nature, that define how the encryption and decryption processes operate. Algorithms are often very complex. Many algorithms are publicly known and anyone can investigate and analyze the strengths and weaknesses of an algorithm.

technical TIP

Less than 10 years ago, 64 bits was considered strong encryption. Today, 128 bits is the smallest symmetric key length that can be considered strong. Is a key of twice the size of the previous key length stronger? Actually, while a 128-bit key is twice as long as a 64-bit key in that it has twice as many digits, the former creates a key space much more than twice the size of the latter. Every time an additional bit is added to a key length binary number, it doubles the size of the possible key space. A 128-bit key creates a key space that is doubled 64 times that of a 64-bit key. That is 2^64 or 1.8 × 10^19 times as large as that of a 64-bit key space.

Encryption algorithms use a key. The key is a unique and secret number that controls the encryption and decryption processes performed by the algorithm. A key is a very large binary number measured or defined in terms of its bit length. The bit length of the key is the number of binary digits that compose the key. For example, a key of 128 bits is 128 binary digits long.

The bit length of an algorithm's key defines that algorithm's **key space**. The key space is the range of keys that are valid for use for that specific algorithm. Any key created using the specific number of binary digits of the key length is part of that algorithm's key space. This key space includes every number between a key of all 0s to a key of all 1s (remember this is binary code with only 1s and 0s as digits). This means that 2^128 number of keys are available to an algorithm with a key length of 128 bits. 2^128 in decimal is over 3.4 × 10^38.

Three main types of algorithms operate within the realm of cryptography: symmetric, asymmetric, and hashing.

Symmetric Cryptography

Symmetric cryptography is based on algorithms that use a single, shared secret key. A common way to remember the type of key used by symmetric is to remember a synonym for symmetric: same. The same key must encrypt and decrypt data and the same key must be shared with all communication partners of the same session.

Symmetric cryptography is very fast in comparison to asymmetric cryptography, typically 10,000 times faster with similar key length and message size. Generally, the longer the length of a symmetric key, the stronger the encryption produced. Most algorithms have one or only a few key length options, so picking an algorithm with a longer key often ensures stronger encryption. Keys shorter than 128 bits are considered weak, keys of 128 to 256 bits are considered strong, and keys longer than 256 bits are considered very strong. That's why when you select a symmetric cryptography product, you should only use solutions employing 128 bit or longer keys.

Selecting a strong algorithm is more involved than just key length; you also need to consider other issues, such as use of random numbers, use of the **avalanche effect**, and resistance to reverse engineering attacks. Most weak algorithms do not survive long once released to the public, so most consumers do not need to focus as much on the details of the algorithm as to look for algorithms that support longer keys. The general rule (which does gloss over some of the details) is that longer keys are better. For more information on cryptography, selection of algorithms, and the internal workings of algorithms, please consult "Schneier's Cryptography Classics Library" or "Introduction to Modern Cryptography."

> **NOTE**
> Hypothetical communication partners Bob and Alice are commonly used to describe and discuss the functions of cryptography.

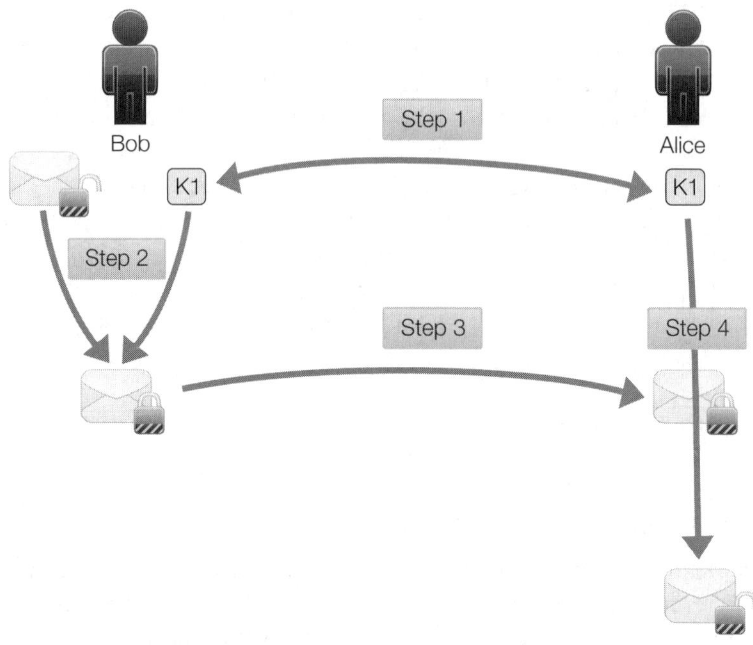

FIGURE 3-9
The symmetric cryptography process.

Symmetric cryptography works as follows (Figure 3-9):

1. Bob and Alice exchange a symmetric key (K1) (This process is normally performed by an asymmetric process or "**out of band**" communication).
2. Bob encrypts a message with the shared symmetric key.
3. Bob transmits the message to Alice.
4. Alice decrypts the message using the shared symmetric key.

The security service provided by symmetric cryptography is confidentiality. Symmetric encryption, with a reasonably long key, prevents unauthorized third parties from accessing or viewing the contents of communications or stored data files. Symmetric cryptography protects files on storage devices, as well as data in transit. In fact, due to its strength and efficiency, symmetric cryptography is the preferred method to secure data in storage or in transit of any size.

Some examples of symmetric cryptography algorithms or systems include: DES, 3DES, AES, CAST, RC4, RC5, RC6, RC7, IDEA, Twofish, and Blowfish.

VPN solutions employ symmetric cryptography to protect communications in transit. This protection prevents unauthorized eavesdropping or mid-stream modifications.

Asymmetric Cryptography

Asymmetric cryptography is based on algorithms that use either **key pairs** or some other special mathematical mechanism. Asymmetric cryptography that uses key pairs is commonly known as **public key cryptography**. All public key cryptography is asymmetric,

technical TIP

Keep in mind that an average 2048-bit asymmetric key is not just 8 times as long as a very strong 256 symmetric key; in fact, it has a key space that is doubled 1,792 times that of the key space of a 256-bit key, an astronomically large number: 2^1792 or 2.79 × 10^539 times that of a 256-bit key space. Numbers of this size are very hard to manage, much less run through complex mathematical computations.

but some asymmetric algorithms are not public key algorithms. A common way to remember the types of keys or non-keys that are used by asymmetric cryptography is to remember a synonym for asymmetric: different. Different keys are used for different purposes, different keys are used by different members of the communication session, and some systems use something different from keys altogether.

Asymmetric cryptography is very slow in comparison to symmetric cryptography. This is due to the complexity of the math used by these algorithms, as well as the length of asymmetric keys (when there are keys). Public key cryptography uses keys that are 1024 to 8192 bits long (and sometimes longer).

Asymmetric cryptography also uses math based on a concept known as one-way functions. A **one-way function** is a mathematical operation performed in one direction relatively easily, but impossible or nearly so to reverse. This type of math was formalized into cryptographic algorithms only in the late 1970s.

Asymmetric cryptography, therefore, is slow in comparison to symmetric due to its extremely long keys and its extraordinarily complex mathematical functions. Thus, asymmetric is generally not suitable for encrypting bulk data for storage or transmission; instead this type of encrypting is best suited for **identity proofing** and **key exchange**.

The protections provided by asymmetric cryptography are **authenticity** and **non-repudiation**. Authenticity is a term used to convey the combination of authentication and access control. Based on usage, especially with public key cryptography, asymmetric solutions can prove the identity of the source of a message (authentication) or control the destination or receiver of a message (access control). Additionally, when used properly, asymmetric cryptography may provide proof that a sender sent a message and prevent them from being able to credulously deny sending it. This is known as non-repudiation.

Public key cryptography, a sub-set of asymmetric cryptography, is based on key pairs. Each participant in a communication or community has a discrete key pair set. The key pair set consists of a **private key** and a **public key**. The private key is kept secure and private at all times. The public key is put out for open public access and use. The key pairs work together as opposites. The encryption or encoding that one of the keys performs can only be undone by the opposite key of the pair.

One mechanism afforded by asymmetric cryptography is a **digital envelope**. It works as follows (Figure 3-10):

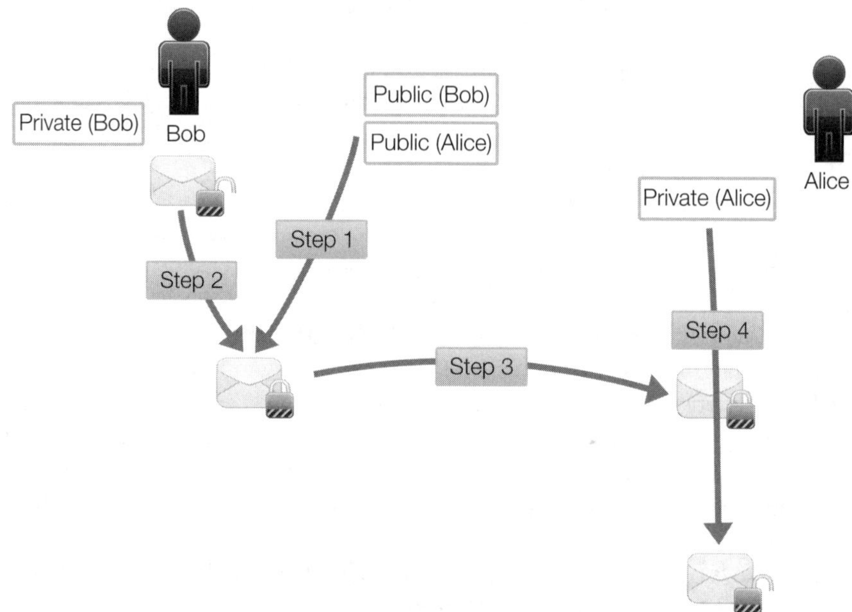

FIGURE 3-10
The asymmetric cryptography process of digital envelope.

1. Bob obtains Alice's public key.
2. Bob encodes a message with Alice's public key.
3. Bob sends the message to Alice.
4. Alice decodes the message using her private key.

The encoded message is only readable by Alice who has the corresponding private key. A digital envelope ensures that the message is only accessible by the intended recipient, namely the owner of the corresponding private key. The mechanism of digital envelope exchanges symmetric keys between communication partners. In this mechanism, one side of the conversation performs key generation, and then exchanges that key securely. This is the mechanism VPNs use to exchange keys securely.

Another mechanism afforded by asymmetric cryptography is a digital signature. A **digital signature** proves the identity of the sender. It works as follows (Figure 3-11):

1. Alice uses her private key to encode a message.
2. Alice sends the encoded message to Bob.
3. Bob accesses Alice's public key.
4. Bob uses Alice's public key to unlock the encoding.

This process proves to Bob that the message came from Alice. This is authenticity. A digital signature does not prevent others from viewing the message or confirming the source of the message. A digital signature is not encryption; it does not provide confidentiality protection. VPNs use digital signatures, but they usually employ the version that uses hashing as part of the process (see next example).

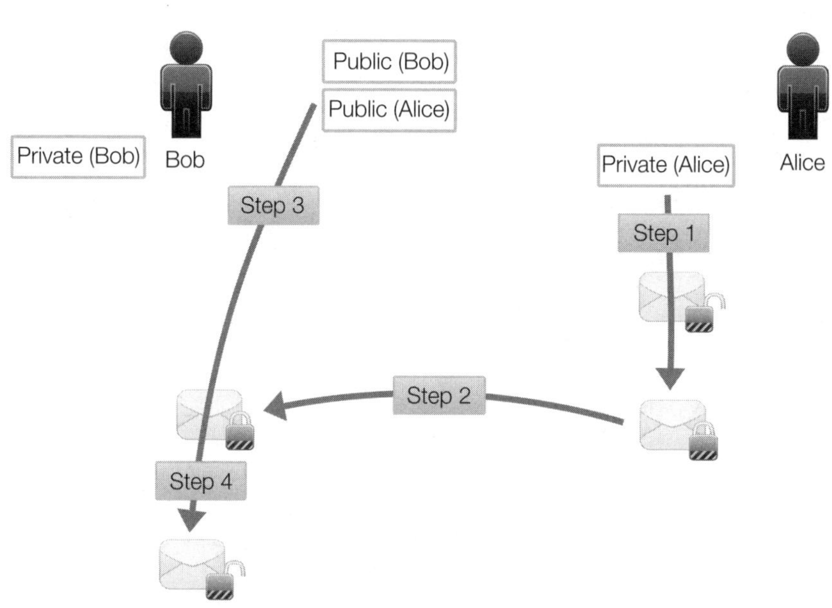

FIGURE 3-11
The asymmetric cryptography process of digital signature.

This mechanism of digital signatures improves through the addition of hashing. (Please see the discussion of hashing in the next section.) A digital signature using hashing is a bit more complex, and uses the following procedure:

1. Alice computes the hash value of a message.
2. Alice encodes the hash value with her private key.
   This encoded hash is the digital signature.
3. Alice adds the encoded hash to the message.
4. Alice transmits the message.
5. Bob strips off Alice's digital signature.
6. Bob hashes the original message to compute its hash.
7. Bob obtains Alice's public key.
8. Bob decodes Alice's digital signature to reveal Alice's original hash.
9. Bob compares Alice's original hash to the hash Bob calculated.

If the hashes are the same, Bob accepts the message as retaining its integrity. This has also proved that the message was from Alice (authenticity). Furthermore, this process ensures that Alice cannot deny having sent it (non-repudiation). VPNs commonly employ this form of digital signature to prove the identity of the endpoints and confirm the integrity of transmissions.

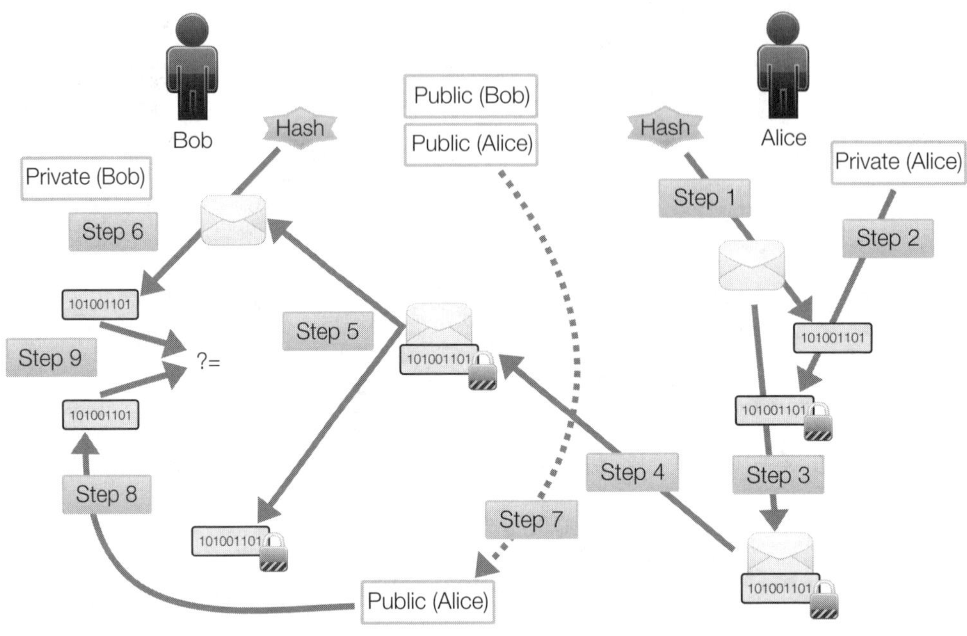

FIGURE 3-12 The asymmetric encryption process of digital signature with hashing.

Some examples of asymmetric cryptography algorithms or systems that are not-public key cryptography include: Diffie-Hellmann, El Gamal, and Elliptical curve cryptography (ECC). The most common example of an asymmetric cryptography algorithm or system that is public key cryptography is Rivest-Shamir-Adelman (RSA).

VPN solutions employ asymmetric cryptography to secure symmetric key exchange (via digital envelopes), authenticate VPN link endpoints or users (via digital signatures), and, when used in conjunction with hashing, verify source and integrity of transmitted messages (also digital signatures).

Hashing

> **NOTE**
> The output of a **hash algorithm** can be called a **hash**, a **hash value**, a message digest, a message authenticating code, a fingerprint, a digital value, or a checksum.

Hashing is the cryptographic function that takes the input of a file or message and creates a fixed length output. The input can be of any size, but the output is a fixed length based on the hashing algorithm used. Hashing does not modify or alter the original data in any way; it simply uses the original data to generate a hash value as a new data item. Common hash value output lengths include 128 bits (such as those produced by MD5), 160 bits (such as those produced by SHA-1), and even 512 bits or more (such as those produced by various members of the SHA-2 family).

Hashing checks integrity. Hashing computes a hash value upon storage or transmission of a file or message, then computes another hash value at the end of the storage period or upon receipt of the transmission. If the before and after hash values are the same, then the message retained its integrity. If the before and after hash values are different, then the message has lost its integrity and is no longer trustworthy or usable.

Hashing verifies integrity based on the complex mathematical functions used in the hashing algorithm itself. A central component or feature of these functions is the avalanche effect. This effect ensures that small changes in the input data produce large changes in the outputted hash value. A single binary digit change in a file should produce a clearly recognizable difference in the resultant hash value.

Hashes are a one-way function. A hash value cannot be reversed directly back into the original data file from which it was calculated. Thus, if an attack obtains a hash value, the data is not at significant risk of being extracted from the hash.

Some examples of hashing algorithms or systems include: MD5, HAVAL, SHA-1, and the SHA-2 variants (SHA-256, SHA-384, SHA-512, etc.).

VPNs employ hashing, often as part of digital signatures, as a method to confirm that transmitted data has retained its integrity. Any mis-matching of hash values discards the received data and requests a re-transmission. This ensures that either end of a VPN connection accepts only fully valid and true data.

Establishing VPN Connections with Cryptography

Now that you know about symmetric cryptography, asymmetric cryptography, and hashing, let's take a look at the overall process VPNs use to provide secure communications. A basic VPN setup process occurs as follows:

1. Bob computes the hash from a message (Figure 3-13).
2. Bob encodes the hash using his private key to create a digital signature.
3. Bob generates a random symmetric key (K1).
4. Bob uses K1 to encrypt the message.
5. Bob obtains Alice's public key.
6. Bob encodes K1 with Alice's public key to create a digital envelope.
7. Bob sends the digital signature, the encrypted message, and the digital envelope to Alice.
8. Alice uses her private key to decode the digital envelope to reveal K1 (Figure 3-14).
9. Alice uses K1 to decrypt the message.
10. Alice computes the hash of the message.
11. Alice obtains Bob's public key.
12. Alice decodes the digital signature with Bob's public key to obtain Bob's hash value.

Alice compares the pre- and post-hash values. If the hash values are the same, then the message has retained its integrity. Thus, the correct public key decoded the digital signature. Bob's identity is verified (authenticity and non-repudiation).

The result of this exchange now enables the symmetric key to secure subsequent messages from Bob to Alice or from Alice to Bob (Figure 3-15). Once a VPN has been established between Bob and Alice, an exchanged session key (K1) exists at both endpoints. Using this shared session key, Bob can encrypt messages (envelope #1) to send to Alice and Alice can encrypt messages (envelope #2) to send to Bob (Figure 3-15).

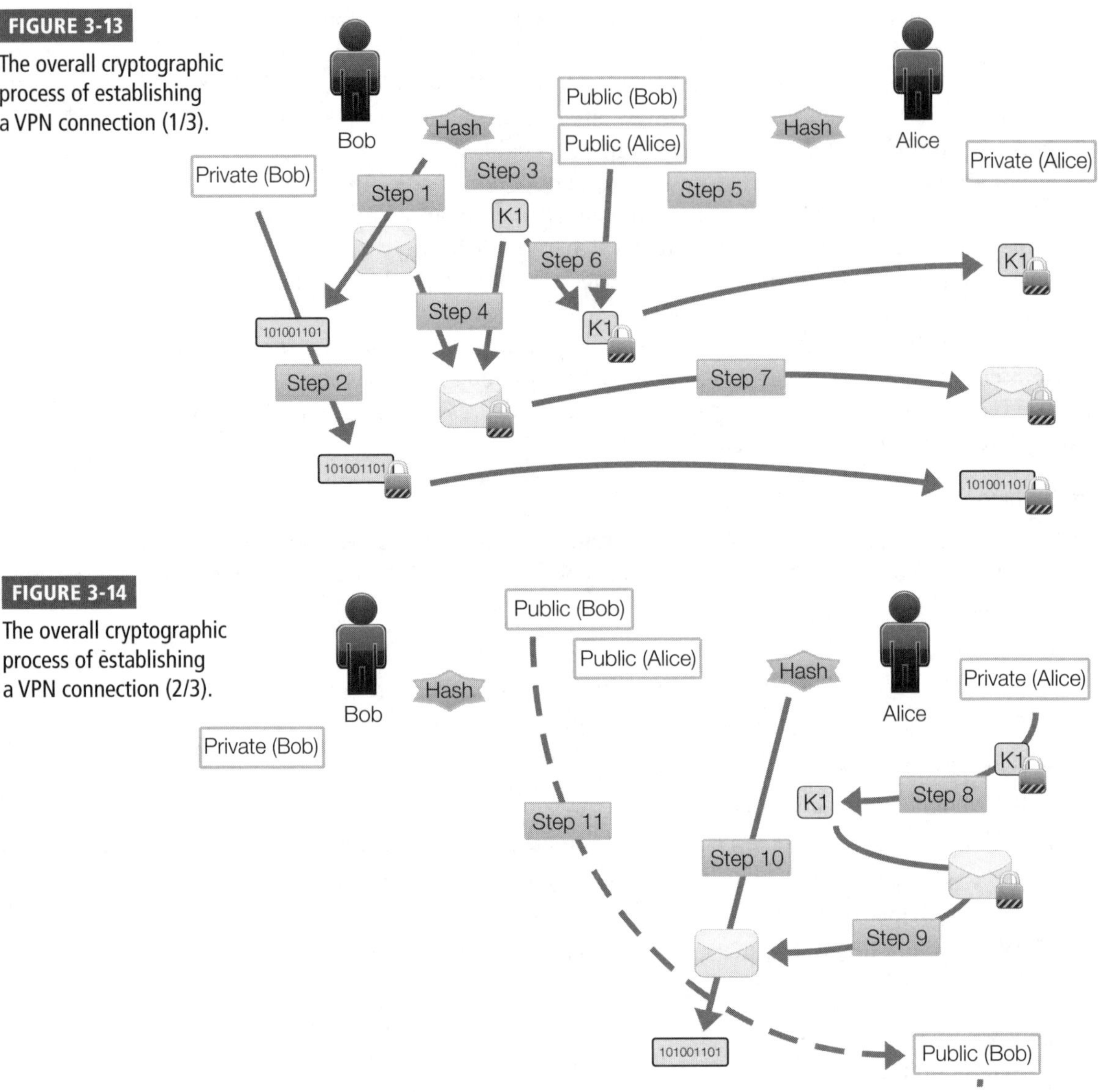

FIGURE 3-13

The overall cryptographic process of establishing a VPN connection (1/3).

FIGURE 3-14

The overall cryptographic process of establishing a VPN connection (2/3).

Variations on this basic VPN session establishment are possible. One variation would be to encrypt both the message and the digital signature with K1. Another variation would have Bob digitally sign K1 with his private key before using Alice's public key to encode it into a digital envelope.

This initial symmetric key exchange establishes the encryption that will protect all subsequent messages for the current communication session. When this session ends and a new VPN session begins, a new symmetric key will initiate the process. However, as long as the current session lasts, the same symmetric key applies.

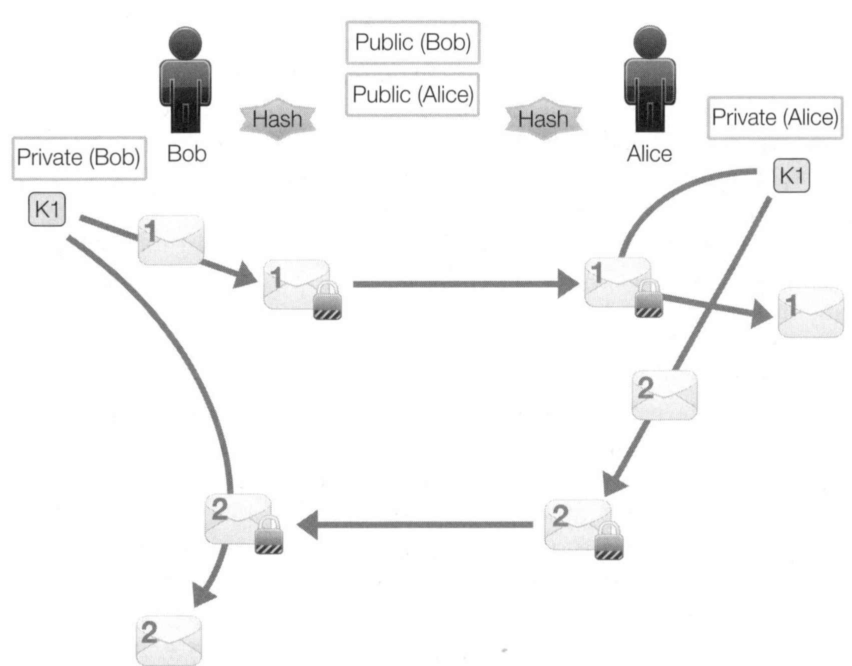

FIGURE 3-15

The overall cryptographic process of establishing a VPN connection (3/3).

Reusing a symmetric key poses a slight risk, even for multiple messages in the same session or conversation. To minimize or reduce this risk, some VPNs use **rekeying** processes. Rekeying discards the current in use key and generates and exchanges a new symmetric key. Rekeying comes in several types:

- **Time rekeying**—Rekeying triggers at a specific time.
- **Idle rekeying (lag or delay)**—Rekeying triggers when a specific amount of idle, lag, or delay in the conversation occurs.
- **Volume rekeying**—Rekeying triggers when a specific amount of traffic is transmitted.
- **Random rekeying**—Rekeying triggers at random time intervals.
- **Election rekeying**—Either member of a VPN session can elect to rekey at any time

If a VPN solution performs mid-session rekeying, you may or may not have an administrative configuration option to manage the rekeying processes. Rekeying may be imbedded in the encryption algorithms. **One-time pad** encryption systems are also possible. A one-time pad system uses a unique and random symmetric key for each segment of a communication. This is a more complex system, but offers greater security. Attempting to crack a multi-random-key encryption scheme is one of the most difficult attacks against encryption known.

NOTE

Technically, computers provide pseudo one-time pads, as they are currently unable to produce true random numbers. Instead, a **pseudo random number generator (PRNG)** is used. A PRNG uses a complex algorithm and the timing chip to produce seemingly random numbers. The result is very good, but not truly random.

Digital Certificates

You can increase the reliability of authenticity and non-repudiation by using **digital certificates** instead of plain public and private keys. A digital certificate is a public key and private key pair digitally signed by a **trusted third party**. This third party is a **Certificate Authority (CA)**. The CA first verifies the identity of the person or company, then crafts and issues the digital certificates.

In addition to improved reliability, certificates also resolve a scalability issue with public key cryptography systems. Without certificates, each system has to manage an ever-expanding library of public keys. With a third-party certificate-based system, each system no longer needs to retain public keys. Instead, they are exchanged at the beginning of each session with the assistance of the CA.

Each host stores only the trusted public keys of the CA. The CA's public keys are stored in the trusted roots list (TRL). Any certificate issued by a trusted CA is accepted as valid, providing the certificate is expired and has not been revoked.

The process is similar to the overall cryptographic process to establish a VPN connection. The primary difference is that instead of a sender's generic private key, the sender's digital certificate encodes the message. Then, the recipient uses the CA's public key to start the unpacking process. The CA's public key decodes the CA's private key encoding around the sender's public key (This is the sender's digital certificate). This confirms the identity of the sender through the CA's issued digital certificates. Then, the recipient uses the sender's public key to decode the sender's private key encoding on the message.

The use of digital certificates adds a few additional steps to the overall process, but this improves the identity verification of the participants in the secured communication. Once a communication session ends, the recipient can discard the sender's public key. Each time a new session starts, the sender's public key will be re-exchanged via the digital certificate process. This reduces the burden of public key management and makes any secure communication service, including VPNs, much more scalable.

What Is VPN Authentication?

Authentication is the process of confirming or proving the identity of a user and is of significant importance for VPNs. Since VPNs allow external entities to connect to and interact with a private network (or system), verifying the identity before granting access is paramount. VPN authentication takes place on two levels: connectivity and user.

When a VPN link starts, the hardware and software components at each endpoint must authenticate to establish the connection. Once the communication link begins, the user performs a separate and distinct authentication process. If either of these identity proofs fail, the VPN is severed.

The actual mechanism of authentication used in either case can vary. Options include username and password, smart cards, token devices, digital certificates, and even biometrics. As a rule of thumb, you should avoid username- and password-only solutions and lean toward multi-factor authentication options. Password-only based authentication is notoriously exploitable and is not reliably secure enough for a VPN.

The VPN services, whether software or hardware, may support authentication directly or indirectly when offloaded to dedicated authentication servers. Offloading can point to any number of widely used **AAA (authentication, authorization, and accounting) services** or technologies, including RADIUS, TACACS, 802.1x, LDAP, and Active Directory.

When selecting an authentication solution for a VPN, consider the strengths and weaknesses of the authentication factors independently of their VPN integration. If an authentication factor has weaknesses on its own, these are not relieved when used with a VPN.

VPN authentication should be scalable and support interoperability among potential connecting hosts. Don't use authentication that cannot support more than a few dozen users or hosts. Likewise, using a form of authentication that is only available on one platform or operating system will impose limitations difficult and expensive to resolve later.

VPN Authorization

Authorization is controlling what users are allowed and not allowed to do. Authorization is also known as access control. You must establish clearly defined policies as to what activities will and will not be supported for VPN connections.

An initial concern is defining who is and who is not allowed to establish a VPN connection. By considering VPN a resource rather than just a method of connectivity, clearly not all users should have access to all resources. If VPN connectivity is neither essential to nor conducive of a worker's assigned tasks and responsibilities, they should not be allowed to open or use VPN connections.

Authentication can help enforce this access control issue. Whenever a user account not VPN authorized attempts to authenticate across a VPN, that attempt should fail. In fact, automatically locking such an account is a reasonable security response. Users should have a clear understanding of whether or not they have been granted the privilege of VPN use. Any access of a non-VPN approved user across a VPN, therefore, is either a sign of a policy-violating employee or an outside intrusion attempt.

In addition to locking down use of the VPN itself, restrict access to resources across a VPN, even for authorized users. A VPN does establish a network connection indistinguishable except for speed from a local direct-wired connection, but that does not mean that the same level of authorization is necessary, required, or even recommended.

A stronger application of the principle of least privilege is needed with VPN connectivity. Not all of the tasks and resources employees use when on site are necessarily required for activities they perform remotely. A user should have one level or sphere of access when on-site and a different, smaller sphere of access when connecting through a VPN. This, of course, will depend upon the assignments of the worker and the sensitivity of the resources needed to carry out those assignments, but thoroughly consider this issue before granting default or wholesale access.

Mission-critical resources, processes, and information may be at risk if they're exposed to users connecting over a VPN. Since a remote user's computer is potentially less secure than workstations on-site, the additional risk may be significant. Does a telecommuter or traveling worker actually need access to a specific resource? If not, block access.

Should a remote VPN user be able to transfer sensitive, private, or valuable data to the remote host? This is the risk of information leakage. Once data leaves the LAN, the corporate security infrastructure loses its ability to fully control and protect the information. On a remote host, once the VPN disconnects, the LAN's security protections disappear. The only remaining security left is on the host and practiced by the user.

Remote access is inappropriate or just impractical for some resources. For example, consider preventing printer access by remote VPN users. Do traveling workers need to print documents they are unable to physically handle? Yes, in some situations, remote printing makes sense. But should you allow every local activity over a VPN just because it's possible?

Another authorization concern is whether or not to allow Internet communication for VPN users. If local LAN users are able to access the Internet, then technically so can VPN users. But should they? Is this an additional risk or just an additional bandwidth consumption burden?

If VPN users are unable to access the Internet from the LAN through the VPN, can they access the Internet simultaneously over the same ISP link as their VPN link to the LAN? This configuration is known as a **split tunnel**. Many organizations see this as a significant risk. This scenario enables the possibility that an Internet attack could breach the remote host, and then use the VPN to access the private LAN. This would be a nearly unrestricted pathway between the Internet and the LAN. Most organizations employ VPN connection solutions that prevent simultaneous local VPN and Internet connectivity on remote hosts.

Even with these VPN authentication issues, the overall process of enforcing access control is essentially the same for both local and remote hosts. In most cases, access control is defined on the resource itself, regardless of where the users are. Keep this in mind as you craft policies defining the parameters of VPN management and use.

CHAPTER SUMMARY

VPNs are mechanisms to remotely connect LANs and mobile hosts. VPNs save money and offer worker flexibility. VPNs secure communications over public intermediary networks. VPNs should be used whenever infrastructure costs are high or you need mobile access, and flexibility. VPNs can't guarantee quality of service over the Internet or protect against endpoint device/host vulnerabilities. You should deploy VPNs based on thoroughly researched VPN policies.

VPNs offer many advantages, including a wide range of implementation choices. Various devices and software products support VPN connections. VPNs' endpoints can be inside, on, or outside a firewall. VPNs can support remote access for mobile hosts, create links between individual systems, and support channels between networks. VPNs can employ either tunnel-mode or transport-mode encryption. They can use the same authentication and authorization techniques that you deploy elsewhere for general network security.

KEY CONCEPTS AND TERMS

Algorithm
Asymmetric cryptography
Authentication, authorization, and accounting (AAA) services
Authenticity
Avalanche effect
Certificate Authority (CA)
Channel
Ciphertext
Client-to-server VPN
Compression
Corporate firewall
Cryptography
Decryption
Dedicated connection
Dedicated leased line
Digital certificate
Digital envelope
Digital signature
Distributed LAN
Eavesdropping
Edge router
Extranet VPN
Fragmentation
Full mesh
Hardware VPN
Hash or hash value
Hash algorithm
Hashing
Host VPN
Host-to-host VPN
Host-to-site VPN
Hybrid VPN
Identity proofing
Intermediary network
Key or encryption key
Key exchange
Key pair
Key space
LAN-to-LAN VPN
Latency
Leased line
Modem
Multi-factor authentication
Non-dedicated connection
Non-repudiation
One-time pad
One-way function
Optical carrier (OC)
Out of band
Private branch exchange (PBX)
Private key
Pseudo random number generator (PRNG)
Public key
Public key cryptography
Public network
Rekeying
Remote access VPN
Remote-to-home VPN
Remote-to-office VPN
Scalability
Secured VPN
Site-to-site VPN
Software VPN
Split tunnel
Symmetric cryptography
Telecommuting
Traffic congestion
Trusted third party
Trusted VPN
Virtual private network (VPN)
VPN appliance
WAN VPN

CHAPTER 3 ASSESSMENT

1. Which of the following is *not* a valid example of a VPN?
   A. A host links to another host over an intermediary network
   B. A host connects to a network over an intermediary network
   C. A network communicates with another network over an intermediary network
   D. A host takes control over another remote host over an intermediary network
   E. A mobile device interacts with a network over an intermediary network

2. Which of the following is *not* ensured or provided by a secured VPN?
   A. Confidentiality
   B. Quality of service
   C. Integrity
   D. Privacy
   E. Authentication

3. Which of the following techniques make(s) a VPN private?
   A. A single organization owning all the supporting infrastructure components
   B. Leasing dedicated WAN channels from a telco
   C. Encrypting and encapsulating traffic
   D. Both A and B
   E. Items A, B, and C

4. What is the primary difference between a VPN connection and a local network connection?
   A. Speed
   B. Resource access
   C. Security
   D. Access control models
   E. Authentication factors

5. Which of the following is *not* a true statement?
   A. VPN traffic should be authenticated and encrypted.
   B. VPNs require dedicated leased lines.
   C. Endpoints of a VPN should abide by the same security policy.
   D. VPNs perform tunneling and encapsulation.
   E. VPNs can be implemented with software or hardware solutions.

6. What is a hybrid VPN?
   A. A VPN with a software endpoint and a hardware endpoint.
   B. A VPN supporting remote connectivity and remote control.
   C. A VPN consisting of trusted and secured segments.
   D. A VPN supporting both symmetric and asymmetric cryptography.
   E. A VPN using both tunneling and encapsulation.

7. What is the most commonly mentioned benefit of a VPN?
   A. Cost savings
   B. Remote access
   C. Secure transmissions
   D. Split tunnels
   E. Eavesdropping

8. Which of the following is a limitation or drawback of a VPN?
   A. Intermediary networks are insecure
   B. VPNs are not supported by Linux OSs
   C. VPNs are expensive
   D. VPNs reduce infrastructure costs
   E. Vulnerabilities exist at endpoints

9. On what is an effective VPN policy based?
   A. A thorough risk assessment
   B. Proper patch management
   C. Business finances
   D. Flexibility of worker local
   E. Training

10. What form of VPN deployment prevents VPN traffic from being filtered?
    A. Edge router
    B. Extranet VPN
    C. Corporate firewall
    D. Appliance VPN
    E. Host-to-Site VPN

11. What form of VPN deployment requires additional authentication for accessing resources across the VPN?

A. Site-to-Site VPN
B. Corporate firewall
C. Host-to-site VPN
D. Edge router
E. Remote access VPN

12. Which of the following is *not* a name for a VPN between individual systems?

A. Client-to-server
B. Host-to-host
C. Remote-to-home
D. Host-to-site
E. Remote-to-office

13. Which of the following is the primary distinction between tunnel mode and transport mode VPNs?

A. Whether or not it can support network to network links
B. Whether or not the payload is encrypted
C. Whether or not it can support host-to-host links
D. Whether or not the header is encrypted
E. Whether or not it supports integrity checking

14. What VPN implementation grants outside entities access to secured resources?

A. Edge router VPN
B. Corporate firewall VPN
C. Site-to-Site VPN
D. Extranet VPN
E. Remote control VPN

15. What form of cryptography encrypts the bulk of data transmitted between VPN endpoints?

A. Symmetric
B. Hashing
C. Public key
D. Transport mode
E. Asymmetric

16. What components create a digital signature that verifies authenticity and integrity?

A. Public key and session key
B. Private key and hashing
C. Hashing and shared key
D. Session key and public key
E. Shared key and hashing

17. By what mechanism do VPNs securely exchange session keys between endpoints?

A. Digital envelope
B. Digital forensics
C. Digital encapsulation
D. Digital certificate
E. Digital signature

18. What are the two most important features of VPN authentication?

A. Single factor and replayable
B. Scalability and interoperability
C. Transparent and efficient
D. Interoperability and single factor
E. Replayable and scalable

19. What VPN access control issue can be enforced through VPN authentication?

A. Blocking unauthorized VPN users
B. Restricting access to the Internet
C. Limiting access to files
D. Filtering access to network services
E. Controlling access to printers

20. When designing the authorization for VPNs and VPN users, what should be the primary security guideline?

A. Scalability
B. Multi-factor
C. Distributed trust
D. Principle of least privilege
E. Grant by default, deny by exception

21. All of the following statements about a host-to-host VPN are true *except*:

A. Are commonly supported by the host OS
B. Must be implemented with VPN appliances
C. Can be interoperable between different OS products
D. Usually employs transport mode encryption
E. Can be established within a private network

22. All of the following are commonly used in supporting a site-to-site VPN *except*:

A. VPN appliance
B. Commercial firewall
C. Client VPN software
D. Edge router
E. VPN gateway proxy

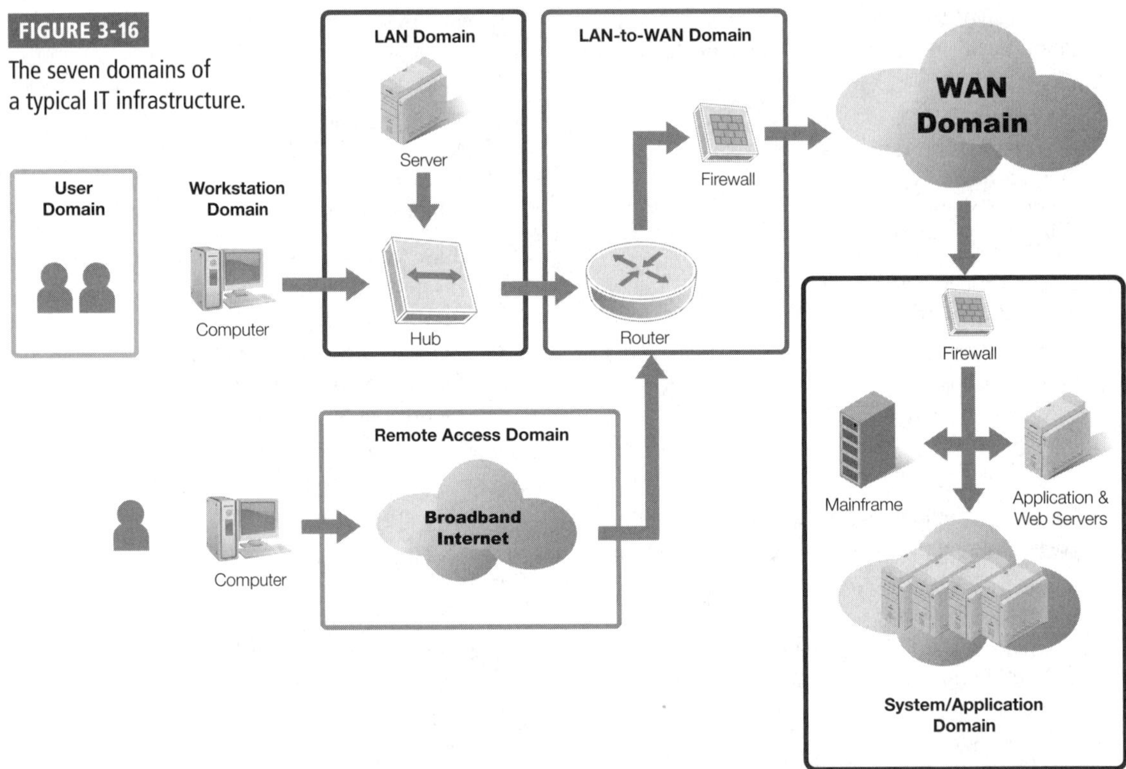

FIGURE 3-16
The seven domains of a typical IT infrastructure.

23. A VPN used to connect geographically distant users with the private network is located within which domain from the seven domains of a typical IT infrastructure (Figure 3-16)?

A. LAN Domain
B. User Domain
C. System/Application Domain
D. Remote Access Domain
E. LAN-to-WAN Domain

24. What feature or function in tunnel mode encryption is not supported in transport mode encryption?

A. The header is encrypted
B. The payload is encrypted
C. The source address is encrypted, but not the destination address
D. A footer is added to contain the hash value
E. Provides encryption protection from the source of a conversation to the destination

25. All of the following statements are true *except*:

A. Encryption ensures VPN traffic remains confidential
B. It is possible to have a private VPN without encryption
C. VPN authentication ensures only valid entities can access the secured connection
D. Authorization over a VPN consists exclusively of granting or denying access to file resources
E. VPN authentication can include multi-factor options

Network Security Threats and Issues

CHAPTER 4

NETWORK SECURITY IS UNDER CONSTANT ATTACK by threats both internal and external, ranging from disgruntled employees to world-wide hackers. There's no perfect defense because hackers are able to bypass, compromise, or evade almost every safeguard, countermeasure, and security control. Hackers are constantly developing new techniques of attack, writing new exploits, and discovering new vulnerabilities. Network security is a task of constant vigilance, not a project to complete. It's a job that's never done.

Why is understanding hacking, exploitation, vulnerabilities, and attacks critically important? As the sixth century B.C. Chinese general and author Sun Tzu stated in his famous military text *The Art of War*: "If you know the enemy and know yourself you need not fear the results of a hundred battles." Once you understand how hackers think, the tools they use, their exploits, and their attack techniques, you can then create effective defenses to protect against them. Understanding hacking not only improves network security; it also maintains security at a high level of readiness.

Chapter 4 Topics

This chapter will cover the following topics and concepts:

- What motivates hackers to attack computer networks
- Which assets attackers frequently target
- Which internal or external threats networks are vulnerable to
- What common IT infrastructure threats are
- What the various types of malicious code (malware) are and what the security concerns about them are
- What fast growth and overuse are

- What wireless and wired connections are
- What the risk of eavesdropping is
- What a replay attack is and how it is performed
- What an insertion attack is
- What fragmentation attacks, buffer overflows, and XSS attacks are
- What man-on-the-middle, session hijacking, and spoofing attacks are
- What covert channels are and how a hacker uses them
- What threats to network and resource availability are
- How a denial of service (DoS) functions
- What a distributed denial of service (DDoS) is
- What some common hacker tools are
- Who is at risk from social engineering

Chapter 4 Goals

Upon completion of this chapter, you will be able to:

- Describe the motivations of hackers and other malicious computer network intruders
- Compare and contrast threats from internal and external sources
- Describe how accidents, natural disasters, and ignorance affect network security
- Explain the risk posed by malicious code
- Express the effects of wired and wireless connectivity on network security
- Describe common network security exploits and attacks, including replay attacks, insertion attacks, fragmentation attacks, buffer overflow attacks, XSS attacks, man-in-the-middle attacks, hijacking attacks, spoofing attacks, covert channels, DoS, DDoS, botnet attacks, and social engineering attacks
- Demonstrate how hacker tools exploit vulnerable targets

Hacker Motivation

What motivates hackers to attack computer networks? Why does anyone get involved in illicit activity outside the mainstream? The motives are as numerous as there are ways of conducting the computer attacks: Many do it for the sheer thrill of hacking, for the sport of it. Some hackers consider hacking their hobby. Some love a challenge. Some are victims of peer pressure or are seeking social validation. To still others, hacking is a status trip. And finally, many hackers pursue their exploits for power and financial gain. Take a look at some of these motives in more detail to see if you can begin to understand the hacker mentality.

Many criminal hackers are in it simply for the money. There are many ways of gaining financially from attacking computer networks. These range from theft of credit cards and financial statements to blackmail and black markets. Some monetary gain is immediate. Hackers might be able to transfer funds out of a target account, for example. Other methods are more involved, such as stealing corporate documents and selling them to competitors or hijacking data using encryption and holding it for ransom. Hackers can become involved in selling their services, including distributing **spam**, **eavesdropping**, cracking passwords, and generating DoS events.

Demonstrating the ability to compromise a target, especially if the target is reasonably secure, is a way for a hacker to prove they are more powerful than the defenders. If you can control something, you have power over it. If a hacker can control your computer remotely, then the hacker has power over your computer, and in some ways has power over you as well. Hackers sometimes hack as an ego boost. If they can wage a successful attack, then they are showing dominance over their target.

For many hackers, it's an exciting challenge to find new vulnerabilities, develop new attack code, or discover new security breaches. Some hackers attack targets for the same reasons some people climb mountains - because it's there, because they can, and because they want to beat it. Some hackers continually seek out new more difficult targets to improve their skills and increase the level of the challenge.

Some hackers enjoy the sheer risk of attacking a network. As with any crime, the risk of being caught is always a possibility. A target network might have **honeypots**, IDS, IPS, firewalls, and other technical defenses that the hacker will need to detect and evade. Security professionals are always looking to discover new attack techniques and learn the identity of hackers. Every attack by a hacker, therefore, poses a risk of getting caught and prosecuted.

Hacking can be thrilling. Think of the way a treasure hunter on private property feels. The combination of power, challenge, risk, and potential pursuit along with discovering potentially valuable assets is a thrill for some hackers. The thrill of "getting away with it" motivates many hackers to continue their attacks once they figure out how to successfully hack into a network.

Some hackers have few exciting or engaging aspects of their life and they resort to hacking as an attempt to be entertained or distracted from their boredom. A successful system breach will usually initiate a response, often a cat-and-mouse game that is more entertaining for the hacker than anything else they can think of at the moment.

Hackers have peers and social groups just like everyone else. Peer pressure can be a powerful motivator to fit in, show off, or demonstrate loyalty to a group. Peer pressure is often a motivator for those in the lower levels or rankings of hacker communities. New or inexperienced hackers feel encouraged to perform attacks to maintain their membership in their peer group.

Hacking can also be a mechanism to validate someone socially, such as proving a qualification to join a group. Some attacks are performed as an initiation or rite of passage from a potential hacking group member to an actual full member.

Hacking can help the hacker achieve or maintain status. Hackers may be seeking to achieve status in the eyes of hacking peers, in the judgment of other hacking groups, or in the perspective of the world at large. Some hackers try to cause a media story and to get their name in the news. Other hacks are performed to instill fear and compliance in current and future targets.

Hackers perform hacks for many reasons, and this list is likely incomplete. These motivations drive them to do unethical activities. You might or might not completely understand the hacker mindset. It's important for you to try, however; the results, regardless of the motivation, can be devastating for companies and individuals alike.

Favorite Targets of Hackers

In terms of security, the things you want to protect are known as assets. An asset is anything used to conduct business over a computer network. Any object, computer, program, piece of data, or other logical or physical component employees need to accomplish a task is an asset.

Among a hacker's favorite targets are easy assets—ones that pay off quickly. Easy targets are IT infrastructures and elements not properly secured. Systems with well-known, exploitable holes exposed to the world are "easy pickin's" for hackers.

Targets that pay off quickly are those that earn the hacker some form of monetary or barter gain. Credit cards and bank accounts can be a solid monetary score. In other cases, access and control of networks, especially those with high-speed Internet links, are valuable targets. Such a network could be saddled with malicious code that transmits spam, eavesdropping, file exchange, encryption cracking, and so on. The hacker can then trade or sell these services to others.

Some hackers, however, do not seek the easy targets; instead they look for unique targets, new challenges, and complex infrastructures to test and improve their skills. Expert and highly experienced hackers often want to continue to improve their abilities, rather than waste their time on targets that any amateur hacker—or "**script kiddie**"—could compromise.

What valuable assets do attackers most frequently target? Every hacker is different, just as with any individual member of any sub-culture. While many agree on what is valuable, such as money and access, others might find corporate finances, secret formulas, medical history, credit reports, court records, accounting logs, and so on more preferable as their target of choice. For example, why do some people collect toys while others collect cars, or coke bottles, or pictures of Elvis?

To better understand of possible targets hackers might choose, review the seven domains of a typical IT infrastructure (Figure 4-1):

- **User Domain**—Any user, worker, employee, contractor, consultant, or individual can be a target. **Social engineering** is a hacker attack against people. This type of attack attempts to fool people through clever wording, lying, misdirection, relationship manipulation, fear, psychological tricks, and confidence games. The results of social engineering attacks can include users giving away private information or performing actions on a computer that causes a reduction in network security.
- **Workstation Domain**—The workstation, client, or standalone home system can be a target. These types of hosts are often less secure than LAN servers. This is not on purpose, because most security focuses on core components of the infrastructure, rather than those seemingly on the periphery. Many times the security measures on a workstation are often old, out-of-date, or improperly installed and configured.
- **LAN Domain**—The private LAN, from SOHOs to large corporations, is a common target. A LAN often consists of dozens to thousands of hosts. The odds that all individual systems are highly secure are unlikely. Once a hacker gains access to one system on the network, the rest of the LAN is vulnerable to attack. The compromise of a single host can lead to the compromise of the entire infrastructure.
- **LAN-to-WAN Domain**—The WAN connections between LAN locations, especially those controlled by third-party entities, are targets. Transition interfaces between a private LAN and a WAN connection can be potential weak points. If a compromise is successful against a WAN connection, the malicious traffic inbound across the WAN/LAN interface is unlikely to be filtered.
- **Remote Access Domain**—Remote access is always a popular target of hackers. Remote access removes the need for the hacker to be physically present to access and attack the LAN. Hackers anywhere in the world with an Internet or telephone connection can still reach out to attack any seemingly isolated target. Remote access is an invitation to hackers to try to breach your defenses.
- **WAN Domain**—WAN domains are networks, such as ATMs or Frame Relays, owned by a telco or a carrier network company that leases access to corporations. Often, the privacy of these WAN connections is electronic isolation rather than encryption. Hackers focusing on a specific target may attempt to breach the electronic isolation of the carrier network rather than focusing on the end-point LANs themselves.
- **Systems/Applications Domain**—Collections of servers hosting applications, virtualized systems, or databases are valuable targets. Sometimes the data hosted is the target. Sometimes the computing power of the servers is the resource the hacker wishes to seize.

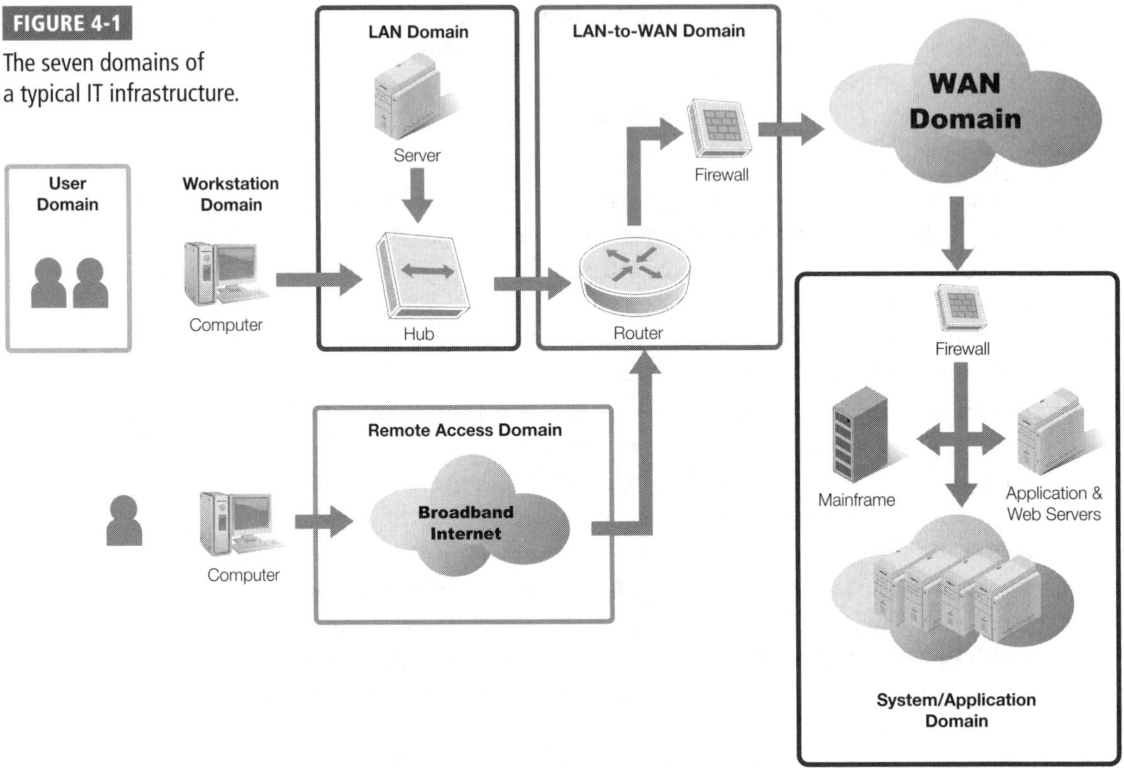

FIGURE 4-1
The seven domains of a typical IT infrastructure.

Assets do not have to be expensive, complicated, or large. In fact, many assets are relatively inexpensive, commonplace, and variable in size. For most organizations, including SOHOs (small office, home office) environments, the assets of most concern include business and personal data. If this information is lost, damaged, or stolen, serious complications can result. Businesses can fail. Individuals can lose money. Identities can be stolen. Even lives can be ruined.

Valuable resources abound on individual computers as well as on IT infrastructures comprised of interconnected LANs. Hackers seek out targets based on a variety of goals and motivations, as well as perceived value of a resource. But who are the hackers?

Threats from Internal Personnel and External Entities

What violates network security? The answer includes accidents, ignorance, oversight, and hackers. Accidents happen, including hardware failures and natural disasters. Poor training promotes ignorance. Workers with the best of intentions damage systems if they don't know proper procedures and lack the necessary skills. Overworked and rushed personnel overlook issues that can result in asset compromise or loss. Malicious hackers can launch attacks and exploits against the network, seeking to gain access or just to cause damage.

"Hacking" originally meant tinkering or modifying systems to learn and explore. However, the term has come to refer to malicious and possibly criminal intrusion into and manipulation of computers. In either case, a malicious hacker or criminal hacker is a serious threat. Every network administrator should be concerned about hacking.

Time and time again, research has shown that most of the security violations an organization experiences originate from within—from their own or **internal personnel**. Nearly 80 percent percent of breaches are caused by insiders, while only 20 percent are attributed to outsiders (source: 2001 CSI/FBI Computer Crime and Security Survey, *http://www.gocsi.com/*). This doesn't mean you should focus on employees and ignore outsiders. Instead, take a balanced approach, focusing on all vectors of compromise. Hackers can reside inside as well as outside the perceived boundaries of your organization or network.

Hackers are people. Misguided, unethical, ingenious, and criminal, but still people. The major threat to network security is mostly because of human intervention. While designing security, keep in mind that the threat is ultimately and mostly human. This awareness should lead to better selections of **deterrent**, detection, and response.

Employees and external entities represent differing levels of risk you need to address. An external entity does not start off intrusion attempts with physical or logical access. Initially the risk from an external attacker is low. Outside attackers must seek out and discover methods of gaining logical or physical access. Without access, hackers must resort to attacking external interfaces such as Web servers, VPN devices, firewalls, and RAS. If these are secure, then their default or fall-back position is to wage a DoS attack, attempt a burglary, or perform social engineering against insiders.

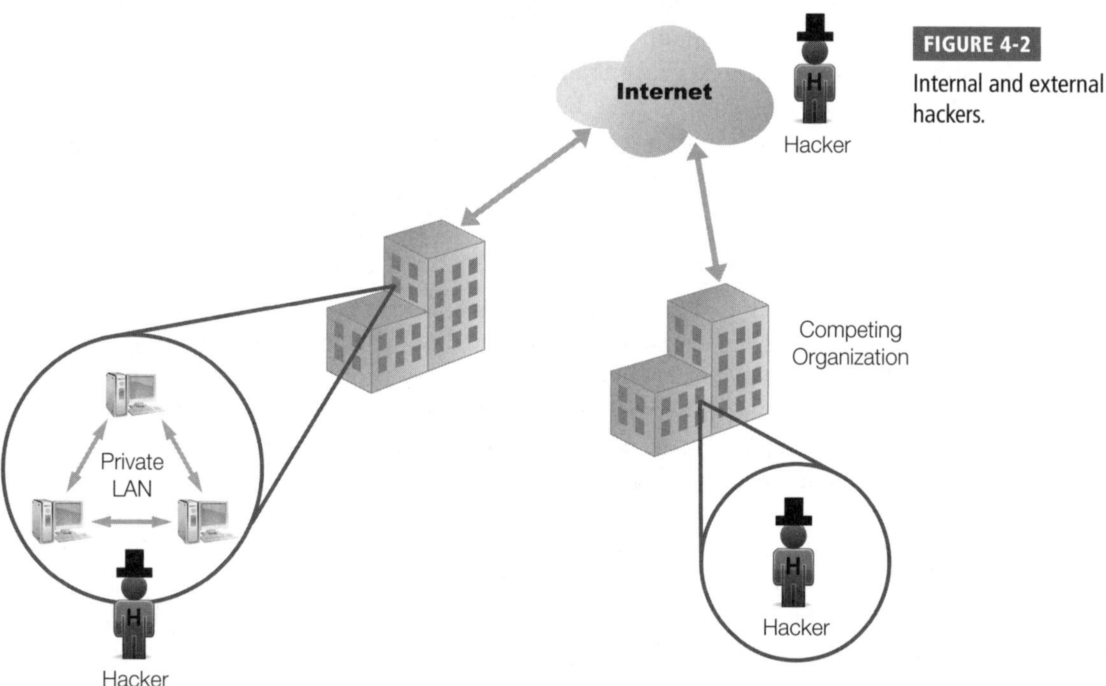

FIGURE 4-2

Internal and external hackers.

An on-site employee has physical access to the facility and logical access to the network. An employee may only have a standard or normal user account, but some level of logical access can be parlayed into greater levels of access (known as privilege escalation). Threats from insiders, whether physical or logical, are serious. You must address such threats in your security policy, network design, infrastructure deployment, and ongoing system and security management.

The people who represent the most common threats to an organization's network security include: **disgruntled employees**, **contract workers**, **recreational hackers**, **opportunistic hackers**, and **professional hackers**.

Disgruntled employees believe that they have been wronged somehow by the organization. Whether the wrong is real or perceived, their actions can cause severe disruption of mission-critical operations. Disgruntled employees may attempt to embezzle, steal supplies, waste time, deposit malicious code, leak confidential data, interrupt other workers, or derail projects. You can find a good example of this mindset in the movie *Office Space*.

Contract workers are outsiders brought in to perform work on a temporary basis. Contract workers can be consultants, temporary workers, seasonal workers, contractors, even day-laborers. Outsiders do not necessarily share the same loyalty to the organization that most full-time employees exhibit. Thus, if the opportunity affords itself to compromise the organization for personal gain, contract workers are more likely to act unethically. Such criminal outsiders don't worry about long-term stability or viability, or the fate of regular employees. Instead, they take advantage at the expense of others.

Recreational hackers are those who enjoy learning and exploring, especially with computing technology. However, they might make poor choices as to when to use their newfound skills. Bringing in unapproved software from home, experimenting on the company network, or just trying out an exploit to "see if it works" are all potential problems recreational hackers cause. Some hackers might not fully consider that their hobby can be dangerous and their actions are in violation of the company security policy.

Opportunistic hackers are hackers who are timid and not likely to initiate an attack. For whatever reason, they are unwilling to purposefully plan out and wage intrusions. However, if the circumstance presents itself for an attack that can be easily performed with little potential for discovery or consequence, the opportunistic hacker may take advantage of the fleeting moment. That moment could arrive when they happen to work late and end up being the only one left in the building. That moment could be when a fire drill that drives everyone else out of the facility. Or it could be when a random power outage occurs and half the workforce leaves for home. That moment could arrive when he or she notices a certain office door is left open and no-one else is watching ...

Professional hackers are criminals whose sole career objective is to compromise IT infrastructures. Whether operating as individuals, offering mercenary hacking services, or functioning as a member of a criminal ring, professional hackers focus all their time and energy on conducting the best security assault possible. When someone spends years learning and practicing in one primary area of interest, they can develop expertise and skills to rival all defenses. The perfect unbreachable security solution does not exist.

Professional hackers have the time, stamina, skill, patience, and backing to keep up an assault against a target until they succeed. They are to a network what termites are to a wooden building. You can deter them; you can keep them out most of the time. But they will always be nearby and eager to gnaw into the foundations if you drop your guard for a moment.

These descriptions are not meant to imply that all humans are by nature malicious. Instead, they offer a realistic perspective on who might be an unethical person, where potential human-based compromises exist, and what precautions you should take to protect your organization from both internal and external threats.

The Hacking Process

As much as IT professionals dislike the practice, hacking can be a fascinating process. Hackers' activities often appear chaotic and random, at least when observed from the mainstream IT industry. A hacker doesn't have to follow any fixed procedures or recognize any established boundaries. Instead, they are seeking out vulnerabilities on a selected target using any and all means at their disposal. For them chaos is both a methodology and a defense mechanism.

Generally, hacking falls into five main sub-groupings of events or activities. This categorization can represent hacking, but does not actually control or prevent hacking. These five categories are (Figure 4-3): **reconnaissance**, **scanning**, **enumeration**, attacking, and post-attack activities. This order of phases occurs if an attack is successful. If an attack is not successful, the hacker can instead attempt a fall-back position.

Reconnaissance

The initiation of the whole process of hacking is called reconnaissance. Reconnaissance means the act of inspecting or exploring and can also be called **footprinting**, discovery, research, and information gathering. This phase is the first of three pre-attack phases hackers use to learn as much as possible about a target before attempting the first actual attacks. Reconnaissance consists of collecting data about the target from all possible sources online and offline. The hacker is careful to avoid tipping off the target that it's being probed for information.

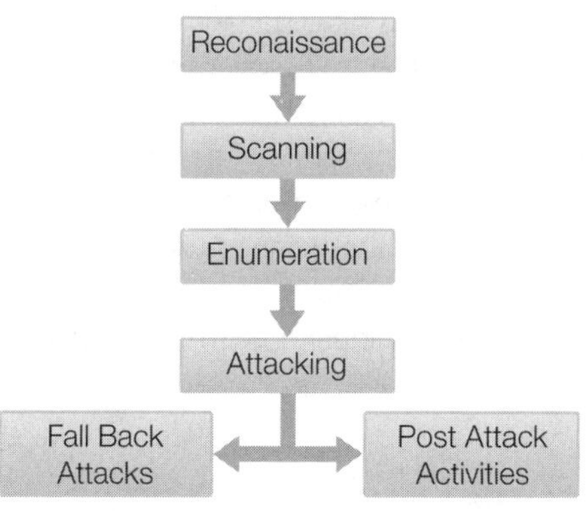

FIGURE 4-3 Five phases of hacking.

Reconnaissance can include:

- Researching old versions of a target organization's Web site at *archive.org*
- Examining search engine contents
- Reviewing the live Web site
- Investigating the background of personnel
- Performing location mapping
- Reading job postings
- Checking insider information leak sites
- Looking at newspaper and magazine articles or mentions
- Perusing press releases
- Searching **USENET newsgroups**, chat archives, **blogs**, and forums
- Auditing financial records or reviewing public filings
- Reviewing court cases and other public records
- Querying **whois**, **domain registrations**, and public IP assignments
- Eavesdropping on e-mail and other conversations
- Visiting a physical location

These are just a few of the possible reconnaissance activities a hacker can use. Information gathering is only limited by the time, resources, and imagination of the hacker. Once the hacker has built and organized a reasonable portfolio of information about the target, the next step is scanning.

Scanning

Scanning is the activity of using various tools to confirm information learned during reconnaissance and discover new details. Scanning is aimed at discovering live and active systems. Scanning can include **war dialing**, **war driving**, **ping sweeps**, and **port scanning**.

War dialing is an older tactic using the telephone system to locate any active and answering modems. Using a modem, a hacker's computer automatically dials target phone numbers. The hacker obtains phone numbers during reconnaissance, or by dialing all the numbers in an area code or prefix.

War driving is the technique of using a wireless detector to locate wireless networks. Originally derived from the term war dialing, as hackers used the early techniques to drive around a city with a laptop computer to discover wireless networks. Today, driving is not necessary and many smart phones can detect wireless networks. The presence of a wireless signal usually indicates the presence of computers or network access.

Ping sweeps are used to discover systems over network connections that will respond to Internet Control Messaging Protocol (ICMP) echo requests. Hackers commonly use ICMP for network health and testing. The ping command, or network mapping utilities, sends ICMP echo requests to all possible recipients within an IP address range or subnet. ICMP echo responses from system indicate their IP address and that they are up and running.

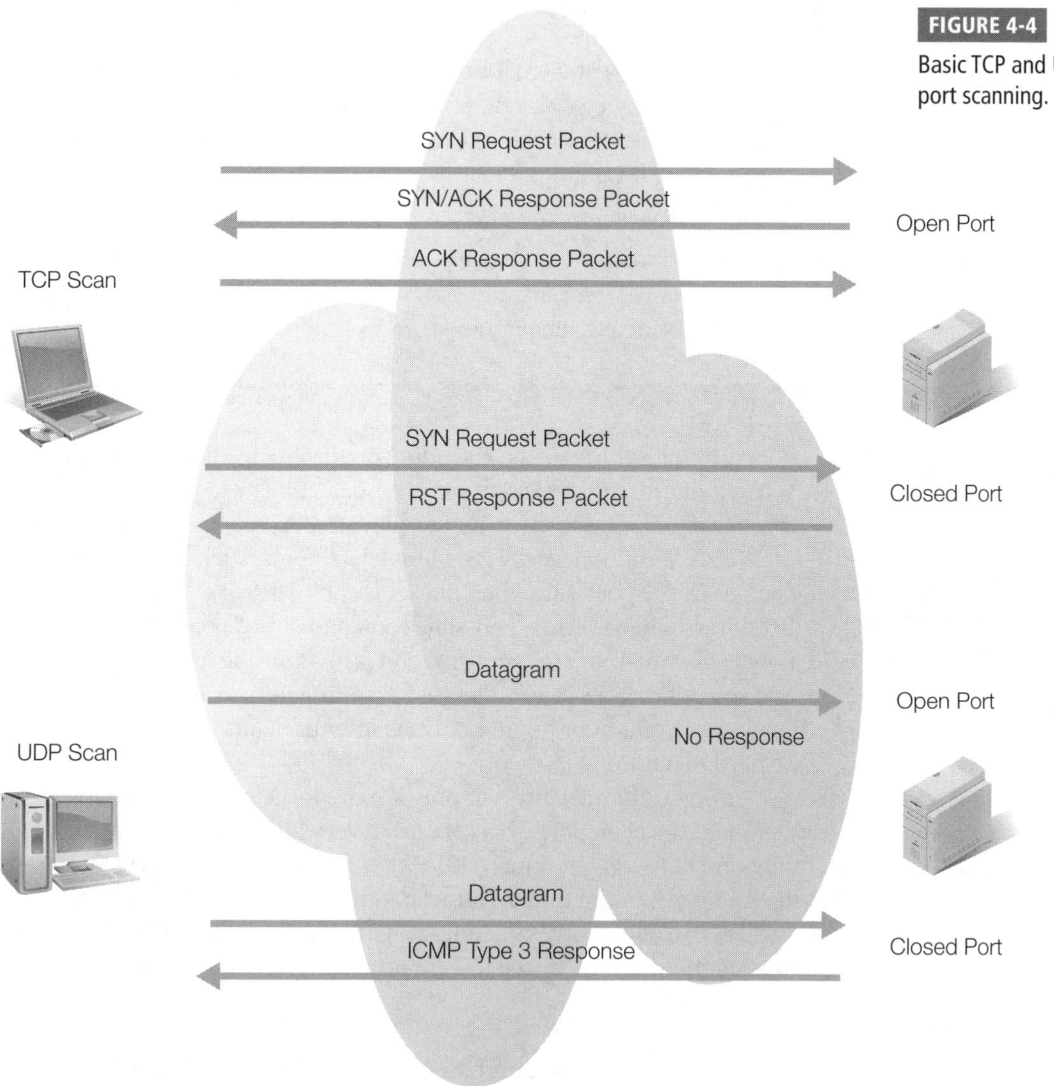

FIGURE 4-4
Basic TCP and UDP port scanning.

Hackers perform port scanning by sending various constructions of TCP or UDP packets to ports (Figure 4-4). If the system is not already known to exist, then a port scan can determine both the existence of a system at a specific IP address as well as whether a port is open, closed, or filtered. A TCP port is known to be open if a full TCP three-way handshake can establish a virtual circuit. A UDP port cannot be confirmed being open since the default response from an open port is always silence.

technical TIP

Ports exist at the Transport layer (layer 4) of the OSI model. TCP and UDP use ports to support multiple simultaneous communications, connections, or sessions over a single layer 3 IP address. There are 65,535 ports, but most systems can only support a few hundred concurrent transactions.

A port is open if an active service is ready to process data through the specific port. A port is closed if no service is associated with a specific port.

When communications elicit error messages or abnormal responses from a port, a firewall can filter out these responses. This will result in a port being visible for valid and normal communications. A firewall can block any attempt to elicit errors or abnormal responses.

NOTE

For more information on scanning, especially on advanced techniques, please consult the books listed in the references section at the end of the book.

Scanning is the process of sending out probes to elicit responses. When a hacker performs scanning, it's detectible. Reconnaissance is generally silent, secretive, and unobtrusive. You are also unlikely to detect scanning to verify individual data items, such as a single open or closed port. But when hackers scan to discover all possible IP addresses in use and all possible open and closed ports, it's very noticeable. Scanning for confirmation is to scanning for discovery as a sniper firing a single bullet is to a Gatling gun destroying a forest. One activity might or might not draw attention, but the other will be hard to ignore.

Hackers perform scanning until they discover one or more targets. Since scanning uncovers only a system and the open ports, hackers learn very little about the targets. Hackers stop scanning and move on to enumeration whenever they want, based on the purpose of their attacks. Keep in mind that an attacker only needs a single vulnerability to gain access. Once hackers can access one machine, moving on toward attacking it quickly is the most common escalation. The next step toward attacking is called enumeration.

Enumeration

The enumeration phase is the third pre-attack phase. Enumeration is the hackers' process of discovering sufficient details about a potential target to learn whether vulnerability exists that they can successfully attack. Enumeration often starts with operating system identification, followed by application identification, then extraction of information from discovered services. Enumeration, then, is the discovery and listing of potential attack targets.

Hackers perform OS identification by probing an open and closed port of a target. The responses from these ports identify the OS. This ID is possible because of the idiosyncrasies of different programmers writing interoperable code. Each OS uses a different group of programmers to write their network protocol stack. Even though the resultant protocol stack may be in compliance with IEEE standards, the defaults and reactions of the stack

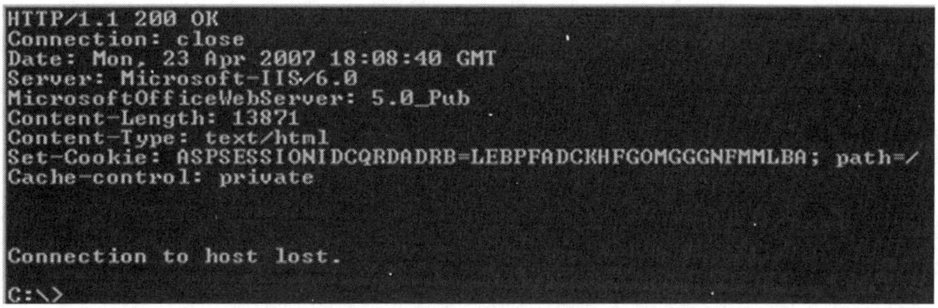

```
HTTP/1.1 200 OK
Connection: close
Date: Mon, 23 Apr 2007 18:08:40 GMT
Server: Microsoft-IIS/6.0
MicrosoftOfficeWebServer: 5.0_Pub
Content-Length: 13871
Content-Type: text/html
Set-Cookie: ASPSESSIONIDCQRDADRB=LEBPFADCKHFGOMGGGNFMMLBA; path=/
Cache-control: private


Connection to host lost.

C:\>
```

FIGURE 4-5
A banner grabbed from a Web server.

often differ from one OS to the next. These differences are known and maintained in a small database, which is coded into most network scanning and probing tools, such as **nmap**.

Each open port has a service running behind it. **Banner grabbing** is the activity of probing those services to obtain information (Figure 4-5). Once a connection has begun, a service may send an announcement of connection or communication confirmation. This announcement is called the banner. The **banner** may contain additional details such as the product name and version number of the service.

Once hackers have identified the service, they can request additional information. The information request may be secure and nothing goes out. But if insecure, the service may return volumes of data to the hacker. Depending upon the service and the queries the hacker performs, the extracted information could include system name, network name, user names, group names, share names, security settings, resources available, access control settings, and more.

Enumeration provides the hacker with identified, potential attack points. After reviewing vulnerability databases, such as **MITRE** (*http://cve.mitre.org*) or **National Institute of Standards and Technology (NIST)** (*http://nvd.nist.gov*), hackers evaluate the potential vulnerabilities. Once the hacker selects an attack target, he collects exploit tools and wages the attack.

Attacking

Attacking is the fourth phase of hacking. Although this seems to be the phase that attracts most of the hype about hackers, in fact, it's the briefest phase of the overall hacking process. A successful attack, based on solid research and preparation, can take just seconds.

If an initial attack fails, hackers can modify their exploits, tune their payloads, adjust their **shell code**, and reset their vectors, and re-launch the attack. Once hackers figure out that an assumed vulnerability doesn't exist or has been secured, they return to their enumeration results to select a new point of assault. Again, think of termites: if they can't get into the house structure through a door jamb, they will just as eagerly try to enter through a window sill. They are relentless.

Repeated attacks will either lead to an eventual successful breach or to the frustration of a successful defense by the target. If successful, the attacker moves on to post-attack activities. If unsuccessful, the attacker can elect to move to alternative fallback attacks.

Post-Attack Activities

In a successful attack, the hacker usually has breached the target's security to gain some level of logical access. This could be the credentials of a standard user account or a **command shell** accessed through a **buffer overflow** exploit. In any case, some common post-attack activities usually take place. These include **privilege escalation**, depositing additional hacker tools, pilfering data, and removing evidence.

Privilege escalation is the action of attempting to gain higher levels of access or privilege over the target. This can occur using a **keystroke logger**, known OS exploits to steal administrator or system access, manipulation of scheduled tasks, social engineering, Trojan horses, remote control programs, and potential other mechanisms. The result is that the hacker gains access to a user account or a command shell that operates as an administrator, root, or the system itself. With privileged access, the remaining post-attack activities are much easier.

Depositing additional hacker tools gives the hacker more power over the compromised system. Tools may enable additional abilities unavailable through the current connection method. Tools may assist in pilfering data. Tools may also assist in removing evidence. Or tools may assist in maintaining or regaining access in the future.

Pilfering data is just that: scouring storage devices looking for files of interest. Hackers look for anything they can turn into cash immediately. They also look for things that would be fun or interesting to disclose to the public. They look for items they can use to blackmail or coerce users. And, of course, they are on the lookout for potentially valuable information for bartering or trading with other hackers or criminals. Dumping the user account database and password hashes is often a priority as well. Cracking the passwords of other users will help in re-accessing the system in the future.

Removing evidence of the compromise and subsequent activities is an important step for the hacker. Failing to cover their tracks could lead to apprehension and prosecution. Allowing the IT and security staff to discover the intrusion will only lead to heightened levels security. Discovery makes future returns more difficult, if not impossible, depending on the hacker's skill set.

Once the hacker performs evidence cleanup, the attacker can claim to have owned (or "pwned," in **leetspeak**, hackers' secret code language) a system. He has demonstrated his skills through the discovery, tracking, and penetration of a target. This is often the goal of a hacker: to successfully penetrate a target. However, such successes are not always easy, or common. If the attacks fail, the hacker always has fall-back attack options.

Fall Back Attacks

Fall back attacks are the other options for mayhem a hacker can deploy after unsuccessful breach attempts against a target. Common alternatives to intrusion include DoS, eavesdropping, breaking and entering, social engineering, malicious code, **session hijacking**, man-in-the-middle attacks, wireless hacking, **SQL injection**, Web site attacks, and more. The following sections of this chapter discuss these and other attacks.

Common IT Infrastructure Threats

Some important aspects of security stem from understanding the techniques, methods, and motivations of hackers. Once you learn to think like a hacker, you may be able to anticipate future attacks. This enables you to devise new defenses before a hacker can successfully breach your organization's network.

So how do hackers think? Hackers think about manipulation or change. They look into the rules to create new ways of bending, breaking, or changing them. Many successful security breaches have been little more than slight variations or violations of network communication rules.

Hackers look for easy targets or overlooked vulnerabilities. They seek out targets that provide them the most gain, often financial rewards. Hackers turn things over, inside out, and in the wrong direction. They attempt to perform tasks in different orders, with incorrect values, outside the boundaries, and with a purpose to cause a reaction. Hackers learn from and exploit mistakes and anomalies, especially mistakes of network security professionals who fail to properly protect an organization's assets.

The more you understand about the various threats and risks to network security, the more defenses you can mount against attacks. Threats to network security include hacker exploits, as well as Mother Nature, device failures, and even normal business activities.

Hardware Failures and Other Physical Threats

Network security is not just about protection against hacking. Many other threats face computer systems on an ongoing basis. Computer equipment is complex and sometimes fragile. Hardware failures are the most common cause of unexpected downtime. Most equipment operates well beyond its expected lifetime in normal environments. Some forms of technology, however, are more prone to failure than others.

One of the most commonly discussed causes of unexpected downtime is hard drive failure. A hard drive is one of the few common computer components that has moving parts. While optical drives, tape drive, mice, and keyboards have moving parts, these devices seem to outlast hard drives by a significant margin. Hard drive failure can occur unexpectedly or with reasonable warning. The warning is usually a grinding, whining, or clicking noise coming from the drive as it begins to fail. These noises are clear signs that the end is near.

The best defense against hard drive failure, as well as hardware failure in general, is to be prepared. Being prepared includes consistent periodic backups, using **redundant array of independent disks (RAID)**, performing general cleaning and maintenance, and having spare parts on hand for the inevitable. Another method to avoid downtime and a loss of availability is to replace equipment before it fails. Most devices have a **mean time to failure (MTTF)** or **mean time between failures (MTBF)** that can determine the statistical likelihood of a failure. It is a good practice to replace the device before that period expires. While you will be replacing some devices long before their actual failure, this technique keeps the statistics on your side. When downtime is costly, preventing downtime, even at the expense of functioning hardware, is often worthwhile.

Another physical threat is heat. Too much heat damages computer equipment. Systems that experience severe temperature cycles, such as very hot to very cold, can have incidents of chip creep or warping and cracking of materials. **Chip creep** is caused by the expansion and contraction of metal because of temperature changes. Severe temperature cycling can even break soldered connections. The traditional debate about turning computers off at night or over weekends and leaving them in a running state speaks to the effects of these temperature changes. A running computer is at its optimum functioning temperature.

Static electricity discharge (SED) from dry conditions can destroy most circuits. Frayed wires caused by rubbing against sharp metal edges can cause a short circuit. Moisture due to high-humidity, weather, or liquid spills is always bad for electrical devices. Excessive vibration can be damaging to computer equipment. Vibrations caused by nearby heavy construction or regular passing of trains, subways, and airplanes can cause damage over time. Any obvious physical damage caused by devices falling, being knocked over, having heavy objects dropped on them, and so on can result in broken equipment.

You can eliminate or significantly reduce most physical risks and threats with reasonable precautions and common sense in proper handing, care, and storage of electronic equipment.

One final physical threat is theft. Physical facility protections ensure that an IT infrastructure is not threatened by unauthorized outsiders (or insiders) walking away with storage devices or other critical components.

Natural Disasters

Mother Nature is unpredictable and seemingly quite powerful. All sorts of serious weather events damage or destroy IT infrastructures. Knowing the types of severe weather common in your area will suggest the correct precautions, such as special insurance, structural reinforcements, lightning protection, surge protectors, bilge pumps, and so on. No matter what the potential disaster, the best protection for data is a reliable regular backup stored in a secured, offsite facility.

Accidents and Intentional Concerns

Accidents happen. Whenever humans are involved, things will go wrong. Murphy's Law states that "anything that can go wrong will."

An IT infrastructure is a large, complex, but fragile entity. And it is completely at the mercy of human beings. Accidental damage in the wrong location or at the wrong time can have devastating results. Accidents include spilling liquids on equipment, tripping over cables, pulling out the wrong power cord, tripping the building's circuit breaker, setting off the water sprinklers, placing candles on top of warm devices, knocking over a computer, turning off a system prematurely, installing the wrong driver, removing the wrong cable, and so on.

The best precautions and protections against accidents are backups, configuration documentation, and training. With some common sense adjustments to worker activity, paying closer attention to activities they perform, and watching out for precarious circumstances, you can avoid many "common" accidents.

Unfortunately, accidents are not the only concern when humans are around. Another threat to network security is intentional damage or sabotage. Disgruntled employees, dismissed contract workers, opportunistic janitorial staff, unhappy managers, and even careless visitors can wreak havoc in moments if they have access to sensitive equipment or information. Proper personnel screening, perceptive supervisory oversight, escorts, background checks, security cameras, training, paying attention to the corporate culture, giving in on some indulgences (such as an occasional long lunch or casual Fridays), and providing competitive pay scales can go a long way toward preventing intentional disruption or destruction of IT equipment and resources.

Malicious Code (Malware)

Malware is the shortened term for malicious software. Malware is unethical code hackers write to cause harm and destruction. Malware gains access to a system through a myriad of ways, usually without the consent or knowledge of the user. The most common vectors of this computer contaminant are portable storage devices and Internet communications. A wide range of types of malware exist, including **virus**, **worm**, **Trojan horse**, keystroke loggers, **spyware**, **adware**, **rootkit**, **logic bomb**, **trapdoor**, backdoor, **dialers**, **URL injectors**, and exploits. The number of unique malicious code examples is astounding. As of December 2009, AVG Anti-Virus reported 2,472,859 infection definitions (Figure 4-6).

Just like a biological virus, a computer virus needs a host object to infect. Most viruses infect files, such as executables, device drivers, DDLs, system files, and sometimes even document, audio, video, and image files. Some viruses infect the boot **sector** of a storage

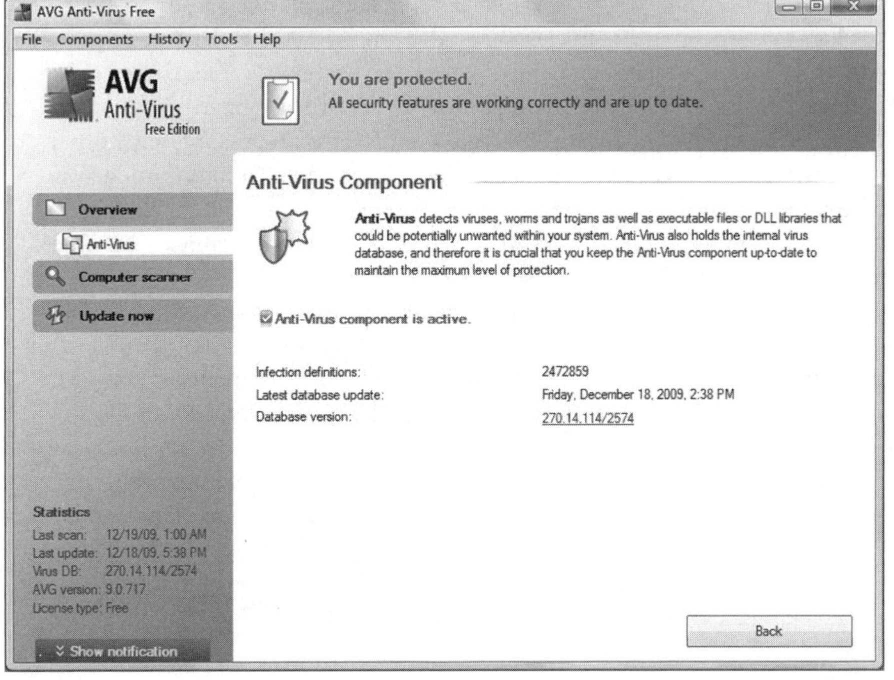

FIGURE 4-6

AVG Anti-Virus configuration pages showing current infection definitions count.

device, including hard drives, floppies, optical discs, and USB drives. Viruses spread through the actions of users. As users open infected files, the virus spreads to other files. As users send infected files to other systems, the virus spreads there, as well.

Unlike viruses, which spread from file to file, worms spread from system to system. Because human interaction isn't necessary for propagation, they can (and do) spread much more quickly than viruses. Today, nearly every threat described as a "virus" is really a "worm." Hackers design worms around specific system flaws. The worm scans other systems for this flaw, and then exploits the flaw to gain access to another victim. Once hosted on another system, the worm spreads itself by repeating the process. Worms can be carriers to deposit other forms of malicious code as they multiply and spread across networked hosts.

A Trojan horse is actually a mechanism of distribution or delivery more than a specific type of malware. During the Trojan War, the Greeks built a huge, hollow wooden horse, hid warriors inside, and seemingly departed the area. The Trojans took the horse into their citadel and were massacred overnight when the Greek warriors emerged from hiding. The concept now embeds a malicious payload within a seemingly benign carrier or host program. When the host program runs, the malware is delivered.

The gimmick of a Trojan horse is the act of fooling someone (a type of social engineering attack) into accepting the Trojan program as safe. Any program can be converted into a Trojan horse by embedding malware inside it, in the same way that any food can be poisoned by adding a toxic substance to it. In fact, hackers have specialized tools designed for the express purpose of building Trojan horses called **wrappers** or Trojan horse construction kits.

Keystroke loggers record the keyboard activity of a user. Hackers can deposit software keystroke loggers onto a victim's system through a variety of techniques, including a worm or a Trojan horse. Once a system is infected, the keystroke logger periodically transmits key logs to the originating hacker through e-mail, FTP, or **instant message (IM)**. Hardware keystroke logger attacks can come through the keyboard cable. These are hard to detect because they are so small and are a parasitic link to the keyboard cable.

Spyware is an advancement of keystroke logging to monitor and record many other user activities. Spyware varies greatly, but can collect a list of applications launched, URLs visited, e-mail sent and received, chats sent and received, names of all files opened, recording of network activity, periodic screen captures, and even recordings from a microphone or images from a Web cam.

Adware infiltrates advertisements. Spyware and adware are often linked together in a symbiosis, since the information learned about a target from spyware helps in selecting materials the adware will push through. Adware can push advertisements as pop-ups, as e-mail messages, or by replacing existing legitimate ads on Web sites as they display in the browser.

Rootkits are malicious camouflage that function as invisibility shields for anything a hacker wants to hide on a computer. A rootkit acts like a device driver and positions itself between the kernel (the core program of an operating system) and the hardware. From there, the rootkit can selectively hide files on storage devices and active process in memory from being viewable, accessible, or detectible by the OS. Rootkits hide other forms of malware or hacker tools. Rootkits can include other malware functions in addition to their stealth abilities.

A logic bomb is an electronic land mine. Once a hacker embeds a logic bomb in a system, it remains dormant until a triggering event takes place. The trigger could be a specific time and date, the launching of a program, the typing of a specific keyword, or accessing a specific URL. Once the trigger occurs, the logic bomb springs its malicious event on the unsuspecting user.

Trapdoor and backdoor malware are two terms for the same type of malware. A backdoor or trapdoor program opens an access pathway for a hacker to gain easy access into a compromised system. The access could be the creation of a new user account with credentials the hacker has defined; a rogue Web, telnet, or SSH server that gives the hacker remote command prompt access; or a source that enables full remote-control over the victim's machine (sometimes just by turning on Remote Desktop on a Windows host). Many other possible trapdoor or backdoor manipulations can grant access to external hackers.

A dialer is a rogue program that automatically dials a modem at a pre-defined number. Sometimes this process auto-downloads additional malware to the victim or uploads stolen data from the victim. In other cases, the dialer calls premium rate telephone numbers to rack up massive long distance charges. If the user normally connects to the Internet over a dial-up link, the dialer to could dial a rogue proxy site instead of the ISP. This site would act as a man-in-the-middle and be able to eavesdrop on all communications.

URL injectors replace URLs in HTTP GET requests for alternative addresses. These injected URLs cause a different Web page to appear in the browser than the one requested by the user's click. These replaced Web pages could present advertisement sites, generate traffic to falsify SEO, or lead to spoofed sites.

Exploits are any form of malware designed to take advantage of a flaw in programming, timing, communication, or storage. Hackers often embed exploits into other forms of malware to assist in their infection and distribution. Exploits also exist on their own, usually as tools employed by hackers to wage attacks, cause damage, and perform intrusions.

Spam is any unwanted and unsolicited message. Spam is not technically malicious software, but spam can have a series negative effect on IT infrastructures. Experts estimate that from 80 percent to 95 percent of e-mail Internet traffic is spam and other forms of malicious messages. Hackers can easily use spam to wage DoS attacks through **flooding** and commonly use it to wage social engineering attacks such as **phishing**.

Malware is spread through the same communication channels as legitimate, benign data. The difference is that hackers design malware to cause distress and destruction. A growing area of risk for the spread of malware is mobile code. **Mobile code** is software hackers write for easy distribution over communications networks, such as the Internet and mobile phone networks. Hackers design mobile code to download to a host, then execute on the host. Because of a lack of proper precautions and awareness by IT professionals, malware under the guise of mobile code is spreading more rapidly than ever.

Even with all the variations of malware that currently exist and those that will exist in the future, you can choose from few common defenses: antivirus software, anti-malware scanners, integrity checking scanners, and user awareness. Antivirus software actively searches for virus, worms, Trojan horses, and other similar infection and destruction forms of malware in memory and on storage devices. Anti-malware scanners look for spyware, adware, dialers, and so forth that an antivirus software might not address. An integrity checker keeps a database of hash values for all system and application files and reports when unauthorized changes occur to those files. You can improve user awareness by offering training that encourages security- responsible actions. Training will also encourage users take reasonable precautions against infection and attack both at work and at home.

Fast Growth and Overuse

Granted, network security is not always an organizational priority. Some organizations are more concerned with profits and rapid growth than spending time on network security. Security is sometimes viewed as an annoying overhead expense that consumes resources without actually any return to compensate for the outlay. While this mindset is common among senior management, it's a poor and incorrect understanding of the **return on investment (ROI)** of the crucial investment in network security.

Network security—in fact, most forms of security—protect the organization so that its profit centers can function without interruption or interference. Without network security, the capability and availability of the IT infrastructure would be unstable, especially during periods of accident, infection, attack, or hardware failure. Network security reduces the occurrences of downtime and damaged or lost resources. What could be more important to an organization's bottom line?

Organizations that fail to address security issues as they experience explosive growth are more likely to experience catastrophic failure. By failing to protect assets (communications, data stores, intellectual property, customer data, financial records, and private personnel data), any level of hacker breach could result in organizational implosion.

Racing to get ahead, without proper planning and preparation, usually ends in failure. When constructing a skyscraper, the top of the structure isn't built until each floor below it is properly erected. Growing a company too fast without adequate network security protections is like attempting to build the penthouse before the lower floors are completed. The rise to the top floor may be exhilarating, but the subsequent crash will be unavoidable. What goes up too fast will inevitably come down faster.

A slightly slower growth rate to build network security, concurrently with the expansion of the organization, is a much smarter plan. Such deliberate growth is more likely to provide sustained growth and longevity, than one based on an unbridled push for forward momentum without considering the risks.

Another potential oversight is an organization's pushing equipment, software, and connectivity beyond a reasonable load level. Trying to pull a yacht with a sports car comes to mind. It looks sexy, but what's at risk? Modern IT equipment is able to perform at astounding levels. But even the best equipment can only perform so far before it exceeds its peak operational limitations—and starts trending toward failure.

The growth of most organizations is predictable. Predictable growth can help plan for expansion of infrastructure before the infrastructure becomes a bottleneck. As growth passes 60 percent capacity of the current infrastructure, you should already be planning for expansion. As growth passes 80 percent capacity, take steps to implement expansion. As growth passes 90 percent, accelerate your efforts to complete the expansion.

If the company reaches 100 percent capacity before it completes expansion, a bottleneck inhibiting growth will result. This obstacle can create a bounce-back effect, in which interrupted growth could shrink the organization, making the return to growth more difficult. Equipment, storage space, memory capacity, backup capabilities, communication bandwidth, and processing capabilities should never reach maximum use or consumption. You should reserve sufficient overhead for the occasional spike above normal "maximum" activity.

Wireless Versus Wired

The security implications of a wireless network compared to a wired network are often exaggerated. The biggest difference is the mechanism and proximity of the attack. With wired networks, a hacker must gain physical proximity to a target to make direct contact with it. Once connected to the wired network, then the hacker can attempt various attack and exploits.

With wireless networks, the hacker doesn't have to be physically close. Hackers can attempt network breaches from a mile or more away from the access point (Figure 4-7). In most real-world situations, however, the range is often under a thousand feet with a small, but powerful directional antenna.

In either case, wired or wireless, the hacker must first obtain a network connection with the target network to attack, if the hacker's goal is to gain access to user accounts or data stored on the network. If the hacker is mainly interested in destruction and DoS, then logical network access isn't necessary.

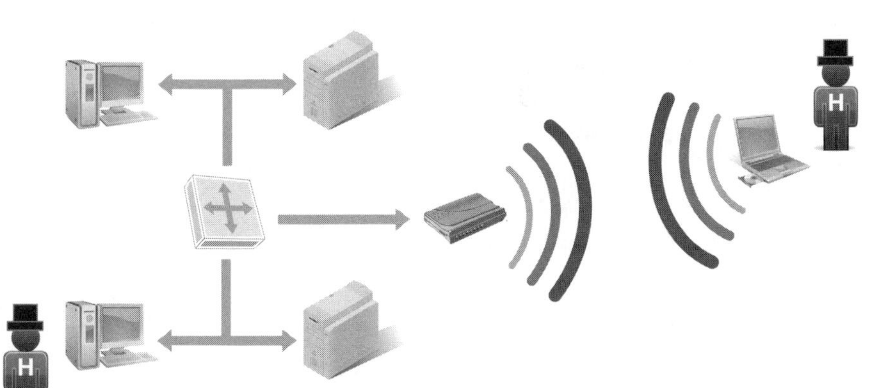

FIGURE 4-7
Wired networks require local attacks; wireless networks allow for remote attacks.

Eavesdropping

Eavesdropping is listening in on communications. Eavesdropping can be the recording of network traffic using a packet capturing tool, generically known as a sniffer (Figure 4-8). Hackers can eavesdrop against data packets or against voice traffic. Eavesdropping can occur over wired or wireless connections.

Any communication performed in plain and directly usable data forms is subject to interception and recording. You can prevent eavesdropping by using encrypted protocols. Only cryptographically encoded messages are safe from outsiders learning the content of the conversation.

Replay Attacks

Replay attacks are also known as **playback attacks**. A replay attack is the re-transmission of captured communications. The goal of a replay attack is to gain interactive or session access to a system. The traffic captured and re-transmitted for a replay attack is authentication packets (Figure 4-9). In this type of attack, the hacker captures traffic between a client and server, and then later re-transmits it against the same server as the original communication.

The goal of this attack is to replay the credential packets so that the hacker gains access to the user's account on the target host. Another type of replay attack is resending a transaction, such as "Send a $10 refund check."

Fortunately, you can thwart most replay attacks by using one of several common communication improvements. Many authentication transactions include a non-replayable random challenge-response dialog. This dialog consists of one endpoint generating a random seed value sent to the other endpoint. The second endpoint uses a mutual secret known by both endpoints to compute a response using a one-way computation. The response returns to the original endpoint, where the response was predicted. If the received and predicted responses match, the user is authenticated.

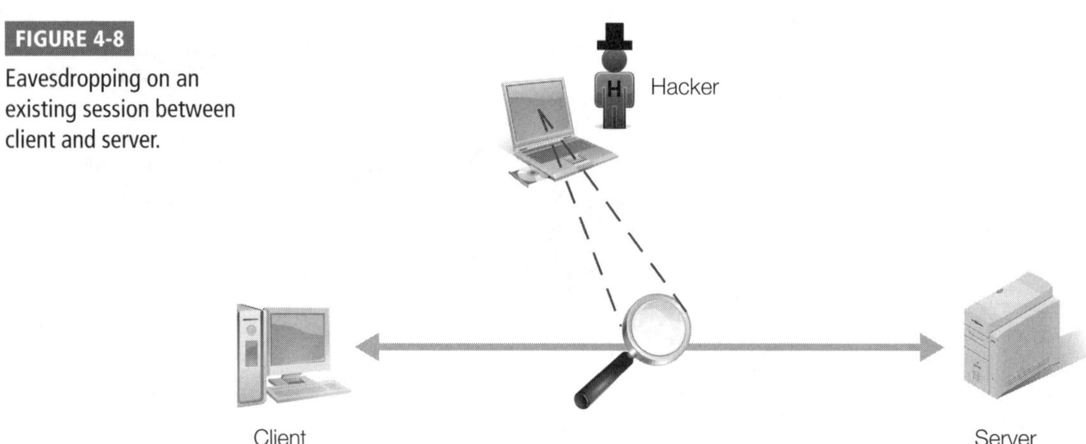

FIGURE 4-8
Eavesdropping on an existing session between client and server.

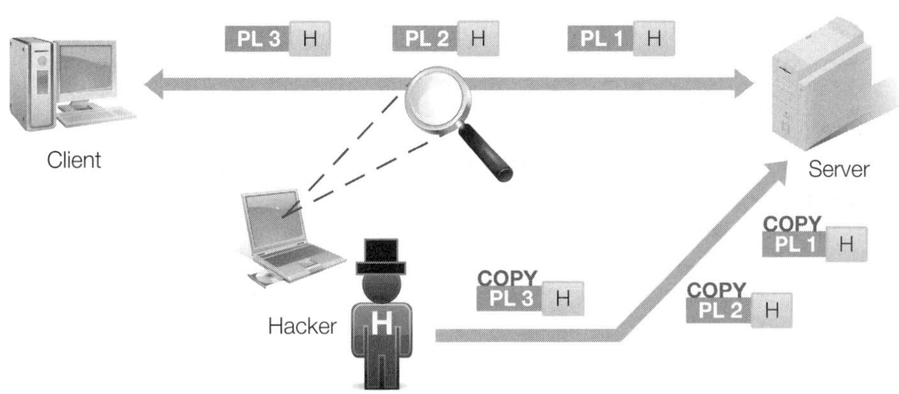

FIGURE 4-9
Replay attacks collect authentication packets, and then re-transmit them later.

Another defense against replay attacks is time stamps. Some authentication exchanges have encoded time details that are difficult to reproduce or modify without detection. Additionally, the use of one-time pad or session-based encryption can make replay attacks impossible.

Insertion Attacks

Insertion attacks come in many forms, all of them involve the introduction of unauthorized content or devices to an otherwise secured infrastructure. Three common insertion-based attacks include SQL injection, **IDS insertion**, and rogue devices.

SQL injection is an attack that inserts a hacker's code into a script hosted on a Web site. SQL injection attacks can give the hacker access to the back-end database of a Web application. The technique exploits a weakness in common Web communications that treats certain characters differently because they are assigned a special meaning or purpose rather than just treated as text. These are called **metacharacters** and act as programming markup. If you don't write a script defensively to block out or ignore metacharacters, then injection attacks can effectively re-write the script based on content a hacker submits. The injected code can perform just about any possible command line task imaginable.

IDS insertion is a form of attack that exploits the nature of a network-focused IDS to collect and analyze every packet to trick the IDS into thinking an attack took place when it really hasn't. The common purpose of IDS injection attacks is to trick signature- or pattern-matching detection of malicious network events. By interspersing attack traffic with packets that the target host will reject, but the IDS will view, the IDS fails to see the attack pattern, but the attack still takes place. For example, an attack is composed of four packets: A, B, C, and D and the IDS signature is a packet stream of ABCD. If the hacker transmits the attack as AXBCYD, where X and Y are invalid packets rejected by the target, then the IDS doesn't recognize the pattern. After X and Y are discarded, the ABCD attack occurs against the target.

Rogue device insertion is a physical form of insertion attack where a hacker inserts an imposter device into an infrastructure. The most common example of this is the insertion of a rogue wireless access point configured similarly to the real, authorized access point. Some users might be fooled into connecting to the rogue access point. This would constitute a man-in-the-middle attack where the hacker would intercept all transactions from the compromised system.

Each insertion attack method requires that you create a unique defense. You can prevent SQL injection attacks by defensive programming and filtering input. Squelch IDS insertion attacks by using modern IDS techniques such as anomaly, behavioral, and heuristic detection. You can derail a rogue device insertion through encrypted communications, pre-configured network access, prohibited wireless networking, user training, and regular site surveys.

Fragmentation Attacks, Buffer Overflows, and XSS Attacks

Fragmentation Attacks

Fragmentation attacks are an abuse of the fragmentation offset feature of IP packets. Fragmentation consists of many different network links connected to construct a global infrastructure. Some network segments support smaller datagrams (another term for packet or frame) than others, so larger datagrams are fragmented into the smaller, more compatible size. When the fragmented elements of the original datagram reassemble, manipulations of fragmentation can cause several potentially malicious reconstructions, such as overlapping and overrun. Think of the transporter on "Star Trek:" if anything gets in the way of the reassembly of the person being transported, you might end up with an evil Mr. Spock with a goatee.

Overlapping can cause full or partial overwriting of datagram components creating new datagrams out of parts of previous datagrams. Overrun can result in excessively large datagrams. Other fragmentation attacks cause DoS or confuse IDS detection and firewall filtering.

Protections against fragmentation attacks include modern IDS detection and firewall filtering features, as well as performing sender fragmentation. Sender fragmentation queries the network route to determine the smallest **maximum transmission unit (MTU)** or datagram size. The sender then pre-fragments the data to ensure that no in-route fragmentation needs to occur. "Beam me up, Mr. Scott-and make sure I get back all in one piece."

Buffer Overflows

A buffer is an area of memory designated to receive input. Buffers are of a specifically determined size set by the programmer, since only a finite amount of memory resides on a host. A buffer overflow is an attack against poor programming techniques and a lack of quality control. Hackers can inject more data into a buffer than it can hold, which may result in the additional data into the next area of memory.

This overflow could be totally ignored, could trigger an overflowing crash or freeze, or could result in **arbitrary code execution**. In the event of the latter situation, the hacker will craft the input stream so the overflowed data is a command-line code statement executed with system-level privileges. This process is known as arbitrary code execution.

Programmers can prevent buffer overflows. Using defensive programming techniques, such as input limit checks and avoiding programming language functions that do not check boundary limitations, buffer overflows become a useless form of attack.

XSS (Cross-Site Scripting) Attacks

Cross-site scripting (XSS) is similar to SQL injection, but the results attack future visitors to a Web page rather than grant the hacker access to the back-end database. An XSS attack submits script code to a Web site. XSS can result in persistent malicious modification of Web source files. This causes all future visitors to the site to receive compromised content.

XSS attacks can include e-mails to victims with falsified hyperlinks that point the script injection to a target site when the victim clicks on the e-mail's embedded links. Such an attack can grant the hacker access to the seemingly secured Web transaction of the victim. This form of attack is non-persistent since it only affects those who click on the links in the malicious e-mail.

XSS attacks are generally preventable if you use defensive coding techniques and metacharacter filtering. For end users, defenses include cookie management and disabling scripting support in browsers and e-mail clients.

Man-in-the-Middle, Session Hijacking, and Spoofing Attacks

Man-in-the-Middle Attacks

Man-in-the-middle (MitM) attacks occur when a hacker intervenes in a communication session between a client and a server. The attack usually involves fooling or tricking the client into initiating the session with the hacker's computer instead of with the intended server (Figure 4-10). This form of attack is also called **interception attack**, **proxy attack**, and **monkey-in-the-middle**.

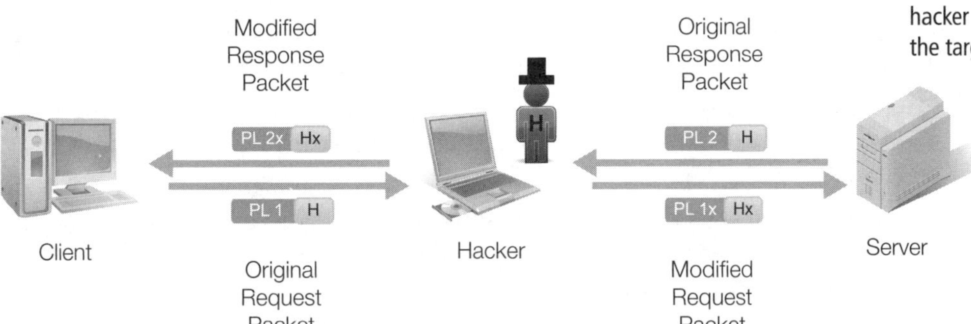

FIGURE 4-10 Man-in-the-middle attacks fool clients into initiating sessions with the hacker instead of the target server.

technical TIP

When a **non-authenticating query service** is in use, it does not confirm the source or the validity of any response received. Thus, if you receive a fake, spoofed, or rogue response, the system accepts it as genuine and the query session ends. If the real response arrives, the system rejects it as an invalid or stray packet because it will no longer correspond to any open query session.

MitM attacks involve a pre-attack element, in which the client is given false information that leads the client to request a session with the hacker's computer rather than the real server. The hacker can accomplish this using one of several methods:

- **ARP spoofing**—ARP is a non-authenticating broadcast query service that requests the MAC address from a system using a specific IP. If a hacker running an ARP spoofing tool sends a false response to the requester before the real response returns, then the sender will use the false MAC address. Subsequent frames go to the rogue MAC address, which the hacker's computer uses. ARP spoofing must occur within a subnet.
- **MAC spoofing**—The hacker's computer uses a server's MAC address; while the server is flooded, the hacker's system receives traffic instead of the intended server. MAC spoofing must occur within a subnet.
- **DNS poisoning**—A hacker compromises a DNS server and plants false FQDN to IP mapping records. The DNS source will feed subsequent user queries false data.
- **DNS spoofing**—DNS is a non-authenticating query service that requests the resolution of a FQDN into its related IP address. A hacker hosting a rogue DNS spoofing tool can send back false DNS responses.
- **ICMP redirect**—On subnets with multiple routers, ICMP redirects can cause a host to alter its routing table. This attack could redirect traffic along a different route than the default, expected, or optimal one.
- **Proxy manipulation**—A hacker re-configures a client's proxy configuration. Requests for services go to the hacker's system that acts as a MitM proxy.
- **Rogue DHCP**—A false DHCP server can provide IP address configuration leases for a unique subnet and define the default gateway since the hacker's computer acts as a MitM router/proxy.
- **Rogue access point**—A hacker configures a rogue wireless access point similarly to the real authorized access point that can fool users into connecting, which then serves as a MitM proxy.

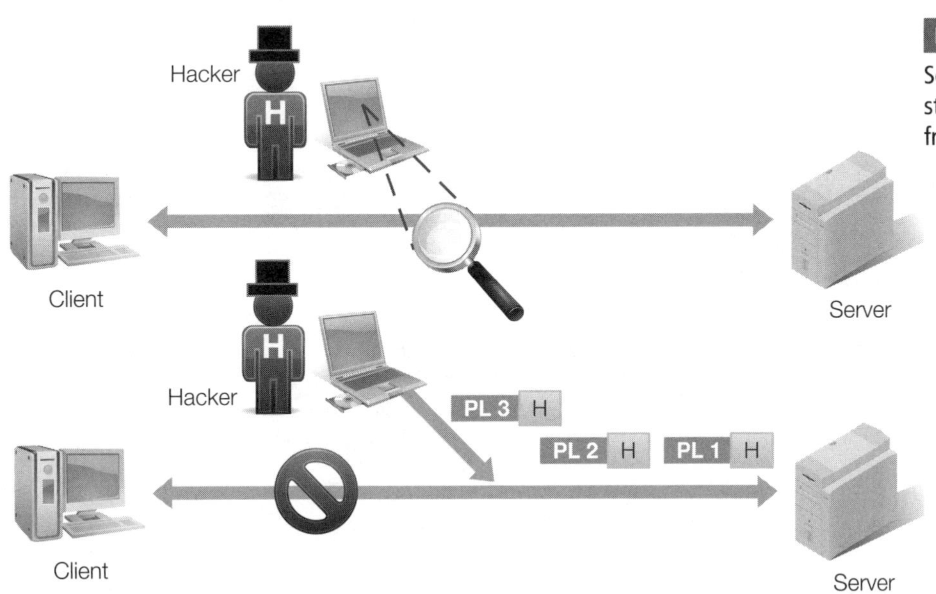

FIGURE 4-11
Session hijacking steals a connection from a client.

Defenses against MitM attacks include IDS and IPS solutions that monitor for common network abuses or abnormal network activity. Additionally, strong multifactor authentication and mutual authentication can reduce the success of MitM attacks.

Session Hijacking

Session hijacking occurs when a hacker is able to take over a connection after a client has authenticated with a server. To perform this attack, a hacker must eavesdrop on the session to learn details, such as the addresses of the session endpoints and the sequencing numbers. With this information, the hacker can desynchronize the client, take on the client's addresses, and then inject crafted packets into the data stream. If the server accepts the initial false packets as valid, then the session has been hijacked.

In a session hijack, the attacker does not directly learn the credentials of the client. If the hacker loses the connection, he will have to look for another session to hijack. The client who lost the session will be aware that the connection was lost, but will not necessarily be aware that the disconnect was a hijack attack.

Session hijacking sometimes employs DNS spoofing, poisoning, ARP spoofing, ICMP redirects, and rogue DHCP to alter the route or pathway of a session. The hacker uses this pathway alteration to make the session hijacking attack easier by forcing the target session to travel over a more accessible network segment.

Any host that uses TCP/IP without encryption is vulnerable to session hijacking. Even with complex or pseudo-randomized packet sequence numbering, a little eavesdropping is all that is necessary for hackers (or the hacker's tools) to predict future sequence values. The only true protection against session hijacking is encryption, such as a VPN.

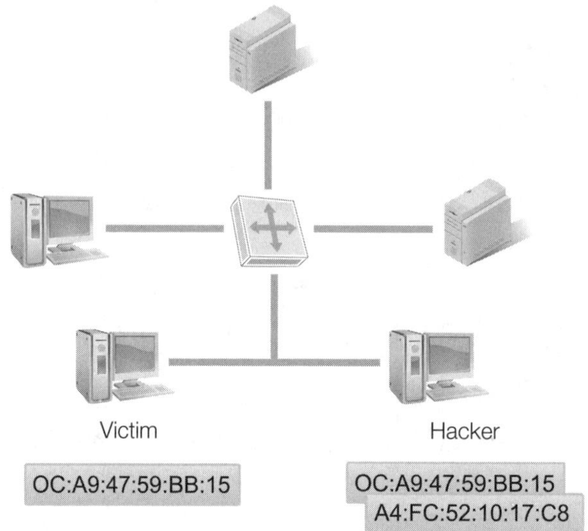

FIGURE 4-12
Spoofing of a client's MAC address by a hacker's computer.

Spoofing Attacks

Spoofing is falsification of information. Most spoofing is a falsification of the identity of a source. E-mail addresses, MAC addresses, and IP addresses are all easily spoofed. Spoofing tricks a user or a host into believing a communication originated from somewhere other than its real source. This is a common tactic in the transmission of spam. Spoofing impersonates an authorized entity, such as MAC spoofing to bypass wireless access-point MAC filtering.

Spoofing is difficult to prevent and only moderately detectible. Most spoofing detection occurs when you watch normal traffic and look for addressing anomalies. For example, if a switch sees that a specific MAC address as the source address for frames received on switch port #6, then that MAC address appears as the source address for frames received on switch port #9, that's a symptom of MAC spoofing (Figure 4-12). In another example, if a firewall receives a packet on its external interface and the source IP address is an internal LAN address, spoofing could be going on.

Spoofing is something to watch and filter for, but no real or direct prevention of spoofing exists. Additionally, hackers can intercept and modify data already in transit from a real source if it's not encrypted. Thus, spoofed data does not always originate as falsified communications.

Covert Channels

Covert channels are hidden, unknown, unique, atypical pathways of information transfer. The channel is covert because it is unknown and unseen. Hackers use covert channels for secretive communications, often to leak data out of a secured environment.

Covert channels are insecure pathways of transmission. If the pathway were known, it would be an overt channel and likely blocked, filtered, or otherwise secured.

Two main forms of covert channels exist: timing and storage. A timing channel conveys information through timed and synchronized activities. A few potential examples of timing covert channels include:

- Blinking lights to distribute information in Morse code.
- Manipulating a fan's speed so the higher and lower pitched noise creates binary transmission.
- Throttling the bandwidth consumption on an Internet link so that at a specific interval a utilization measurement reads a value below 60 percent as a zero and a value above as a one for binary communications.

A storage covert channel conveys information through unseen or undiscovered storage locations. A few potential examples of storage covert channels include:

- Using the **unpartitioned space** of a hard drive to store data written via a hex editor.
- Using a firmware flash memory on-board chip to store data.
- Using the alternate data streams of **new technology file system (NTFS)** to hide files.
- Using the **slack space** of a hard drive to store data.

The best defenses against covert channels include IDS and IPS, as well as thorough monitoring of all aspects of an IT infrastructure for aberrant or abnormal events of any type. Predicting covert channels is difficult because by their very nature they are unknown and unseen.

technical TIP

The **alternate data streams (ADS)** of NTFS are a feature added to this file system to support files from **POSIX**, **OS/2**, and Macintosh. This feature was added to NTFS in the mid-1990s to drive government purchase of Windows NT. However, even with POSIX and OS/2 support now dropped from Windows and Macintosh **hierarchical file system (HFS)** support no longer needed, NTFS has retained this feature. ADS is the ability of a file to contain multiple resource forks. The result of NTFS support for ADS is that not just additional resources, but complete additional files, can hide below any normal file object.

A normal file object, including directories, can contain numerous additional files underneath itself. The number of additional files is only limited by the total amount of free space on the drive and the size of the hidden files. Once a file stores as an ADS, it's no longer visible or easily accessible by the OS itself. Several hacking tools can create and manipulate ADS. A few scanning tools, such as Streams from sysinternals.com and only a handful of malware scanners can specifically explore a drive for ADS hidden code.

technical TIP

A hard drive contains segments known as sectors. A sector is the smallest fixed-size block of storage space of a drive and is 512 bytes. When a file system is applied to a **partition**, **clusters** are created out of one or more sectors. Slack space is the unused portion of the last cluster only partially consumed by a stored file. The cluster:sector ratio typically ranges from 1:1 to 1:128 for clusters of 512 bytes to 64 KB.

A file system has a fixed maximum number of addresses assigned to clusters. Larger drives have the same number of clusters as smaller drives, but the clusters are larger. It's a little like shoes: kids' shoes are one pair to a box, just like adult shoes, but the box containing adult shoes is bigger. A cluster is the smallest consumable element of storage space and can contain data from only a single file. No native mechanism addresses sub-cluster divisions in standard file system formats.

When a file writes to a drive, it consumes as many clusters as necessary to contain all of the data of the file. All clusters but the final or last cluster containing the file are filled. The last cluster is only fully consumed if the file happens to be an exact multiple of the cluster size (which is not very common). The unused portion of the last cluster is known as slack space (Figure 4-13). Slack space is effectively unusable, wasted storage space.

Hackers have developed special file manipulation tools that can locate and hijack the slack space and use it to create hidden volumes on a hard drive. These volumes are nearly impossible to detect because they are not contained, referenced, or addressed by the file system of the storage device. Instead, the slack space drive exists only because special software can address sub-cluster storage locations. The slack space drive software operates independently of the OS and the file system.

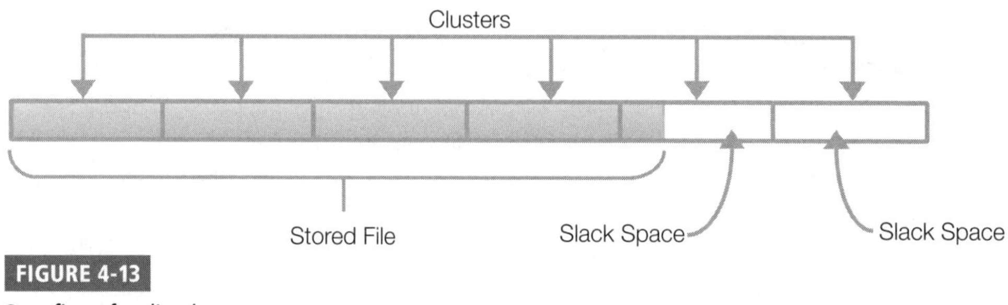

FIGURE 4-13

Spoofing of a client's MAC address by a hacker's computer.

technical TIP

Web servers, or at least Web sites, appear on the Internet in a least four different architectural deployment options: reverse proxy, DMZ, co-location, and hosting. Reverse proxy uses a static NAT mapping or port forwarding to allow outside visitors to initiate communications with an internal server. This is the poorest security choice because it could grant hackers access to the entire intranet if the Web server is compromised.

Hosting a Web server in a DMZ is a more secure solution. However, if compromised, a DMZ Web server gives the hacker a weapons platform just outside of the private network's front door. Co-location is placing a Web server host directly on an ISP network within a facility. Hosting is leasing access to space on an existing Web server owned and managed by the hosting entity (squarespace.com is a great example). These last two options are the most secure; if the Web server/site is compromised, the hacker gains no location benefit to breach the private network.

Network and Resource Availability Threats

To be successful, many exploits and attacks require special access on a private network. Some exploits will function against an Internet facing Web server, but such a server might not directly connect to a private network. If a hacker is unable to find an exploitable vulnerability that gains access or control over the targeted systems, a fall back or final resort option is to launch availability attacks.

An availability attack aims at preventing legitimate access or use of resources to delay or interrupt business. Generally, this is known as denial of service (DoS).

Denial of Service (DoS)

A denial of service (DoS) attack interrupts the normal patterns of traffic, communication, and response. A DoS interferes with timely processing and reply to legitimate requests for resources. A DoS can be of two primary forms: **flaw exploitation** or **traffic generation**.

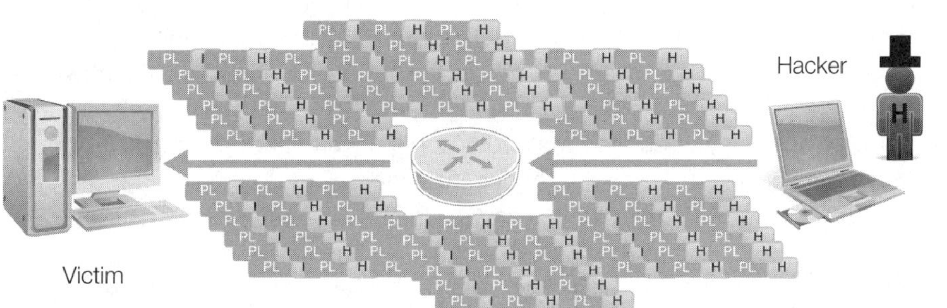

FIGURE 4-14
Denial of service flooding attack against a client.

Flaw exploitation DoS attacks take advantage of a programming bug, flaw, or convention. The DoS exploit results in the system freezing, crashing, rebooting, or failing to respond to external communications. You can mitigate flaw exploitation DoS attacks through the application of a patch and the use of an IDS or IPS system. Once you apply a patch, the DoS will no longer be effective. Flaw exploitation attacks are usually specific to a software version.

Traffic generation DoS attacks flood a target with traffic (Figure 4-14). The traffic consumes available bandwidth and processing, preventing legitimate communications. No patches exist to mitigate traffic generation DoS attacks. Instead, traffic filtering is the only effective response. **Upstream filtering**, however, is more effective than edge device filtering.

Upstream filtering occurs when a parent network, usually the ISP, provides filtering for traffic before it enters the child network to which individual and business customers connect. Edge device filtering will prevent malicious traffic from entering the private network, but not prevent a successful DoS. Only upstream filtering will reduce or eliminate the DoS traffic and allow legitimate communications to continue.

Distributed Denial of Service (DDoS)

Distributed denial of service (DDoS) attacks advance DoS attacks through massive distributed processing and sourcing. The foundation of DDoS is the agent, bot, or zombie. Agents, bots, and zombies are malicious code implanted on victim systems across the Internet. These mobile agents may create their own peer-network interaction or connect into a public communication medium, such as an **Internet relay chat (IRC)** channel. The resultant network is known as a **botnet army** or **zombie army**.

The hacker remotely controls the botnet and directs it to perform various malicious activities, including flooding attacks, against selected targets. Generally, the main targets of the botnet are known as primary victims, while the compromised systems hosting the botnet's agents are known as secondary victims. This form of DoS is distributed because the bots are disseminated across numerous secondary victims and the resulting attacks originate from a plethora of source vectors.

A hacker distributes the bots, agents, zombies to many secondary victims located throughout the Internet. The bots then connect back to some form of communication server, commonly a chat service like IRC, where they can receive instructions from the hacker. Once the hacker sends attack instructions, the bots launch attacks against the primary target (Figure 4-15).

A botnet can perform a wide range of malicious actions including flooding, spamming, eavesdropping, intercepting, MitM, session hijacking, spoofing, packet manipulating, malware distributing, phishing site hosting, passwords stealing, encryption cracking, and more.

Several botnets have appeared in the last few years, such as Storm and Conficker, which had an estimated secondary victim base of 75 to 100 million systems.

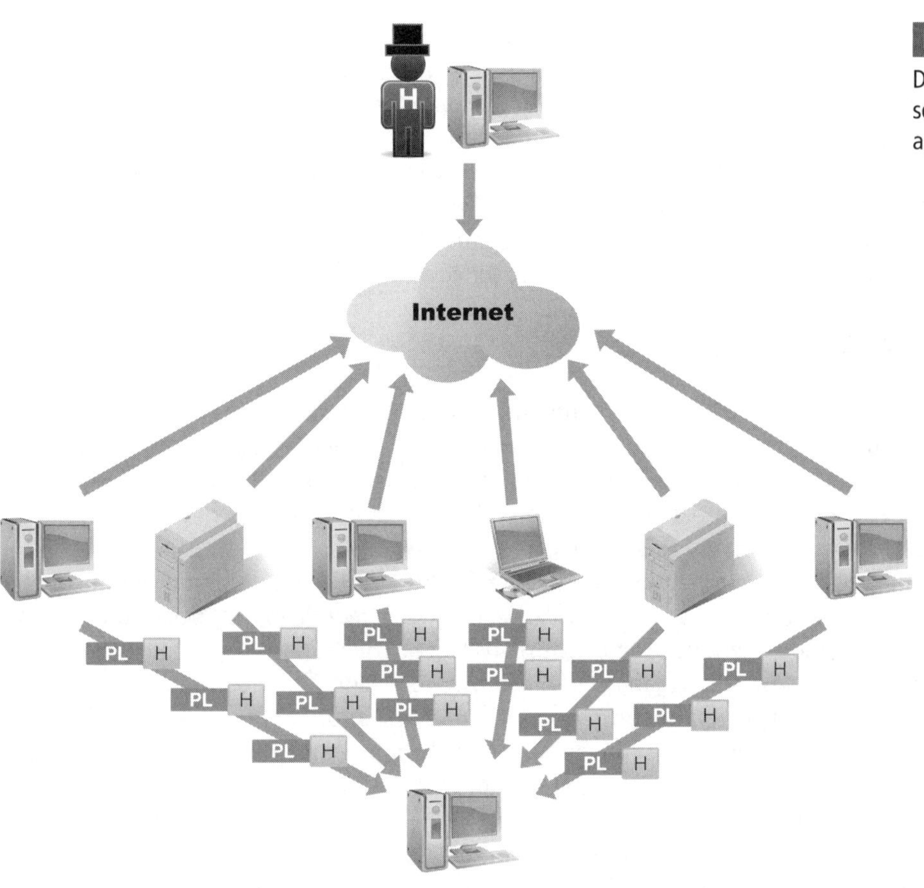

FIGURE 4-15
Distributed denial of service flooding attack against a primary target.

Defenses against DDoS focus on either avoiding becoming a secondary victim or protecting against primary victim onslaughts. To avoid becoming a secondary victim you should use measures including current antivirus and anti-malware scanning, user behavior modification, firewall filtering, and use of IDS/IPS solutions. Protection against primary victim onslaughts includes firewall filtering, honeypots, and use of IDS/IPS solutions.

Hacker Tools

Hacker tools include a wide variety of software from mundane native OS utilities to commercial applications to custom coded exploits. Generally, any software put to a malicious or unauthorized (according to company security policy) use is a hacking tool.

Hacking tools perform hacking activities. All of the exploit concepts mentioned in this chapter are possible through a wide variety of hacking tools and utilities.

No master list of hacker tools exists to search for or block access to protect IT systems. Just about every legitimate program can be put to some illicit task. To defend generally against hacker tools, consider using a white list restriction system.

A white list restriction system incorporates a list of software executables authorized for use. A user can launch any application on the list. You block from running all executables not on the list. A white list cannot focus on just authorized filenames; this process uses a hash value, as well, to prevent easy bypassing of the limitation through simple file renaming.

In addition to white listing, you can reduce the threat of hacking tools through limiting Internet downloads and file exchanges, controlling use of portable storage devices (especially those used on external systems), filtering e-mail attachments, installing IDS/IPS solutions, and providing user education.

Social Engineering

Social engineering is the art of manipulation and exploitation of human nature. Social engineering is the craft of manipulating people into performing tasks or releasing information that violates security. Social engineering is an exploit that can almost always be performed against a target organization. This is due to the presence of humans. Humans are the primary targets of social engineering.

Humans are the weakest link in most security solutions because humans are the only element in an organization with free will. Every other element can only perform within its programming and design. In addition, humans can be tricked or fooled, while hardware and software can only perform in accordance with its design and programming.

Social engineering can take place over any communication method, including face-to-face, telephone, e-mail, IM, and Web sites. Social engineering may focus on extracting information from a target or convincing the target to take action that alters the security status of a host or network.

Many social engineering attacks stem from some form of relationship, from initial and casual to business professional to long-term and highly developed. The more in-depth and long-term the relationship, the more leverage the hacker can exploit to turn, trick, or abuse the target.

Social engineering can employ a wide range of techniques, including impersonating a position of authority, reciprocating favors, using social validation, and creating urgency through scarcity. Often these attacks become more successful if the hacker can impersonate an insider.

Gaining access to inside information is often the first element of a social engineering attack. **Dumpster diving**, using reconnaissance, and **cold calling** are techniques to learn about the internal culture of the target. As a hacker learns more and more terminology, processes, organizational hierarchy, policies, events, gossip, social occurrences, calendars, project scheduling, and so on, the more he is able to simulate being an insider. Once a hacker fools a target into believing that he is just another employee, the initial attack is successful. With the standing gained, the hacker manipulates the target into revealing more internal information, reconfiguring systems, or downloading tools from questionable Internet locations.

Social engineering may be the first wave of hacker attacks or could be the last resort fallback plan if attempts to perform logical intrusion or physical burglary fail. Some hackers are naturally gifted at social engineering, while others must practice to obtain workable competency at the craft. These skills of social engineering are not unique to this unethical activity; instead they are the same skills most people use in normal social situations when trying to get their way, convince someone to go out on a date, ask for help, improve social status, get out of trouble, lead a group, sell and market, create advertising, and so on. The difference is that hackers have an unethical goal in their use of these skills.

Social engineering, primarily attacks against people, is invulnerable to typical IT countermeasures. Instead, the best defense against social engineering is thorough user training and awareness. Once personnel are aware that they are, have been, and will be targets of attack, they can adopt a slightly suspicious and cautious outlook. Employees should skeptically evaluate any activity, question, interaction, or relationship that seems odd or out of place.

You can help reduce the threat of social engineering by using security policies that employ information classification with related restrictions on communication methods. If you limit the communication channels that specific classes of information traverse, you will reduce information leakage caused by social engineering. For example, you restrict the use of passwords over the telephone or by e-mail, then anyone who requests a password will be obviously attempting to violate security. Employees should be trained to report all such requests to the network security staff.

CHAPTER SUMMARY

Hackers are consistently seeking to take advantage of anyone or any system not prepared or properly secured. Understanding the various means of attacks hackers commonly employ directly improves awareness and overall network security.

Hackers often seek monetary gain through attacks against individuals and organizations. Hackers can be employees or outsiders. Compromising situations are not limited to hacker attacks, but can also include accidents, oversights, hardware failure, rapid growth, and severe weather. Hacker tools and techniques include malicious software, exploiting wireless connections, eavesdropping, replay, insertion, fragmentation, buffer overflow, XSS, man-in-the-middle, session hijacking, spoofing, covert channels, and the availability attacks of DoS and DDOS. You should take action to restrict or limit hacker tools and use caution and training to avoid social engineering.

Other attacks and techniques than those listed here are likely by hackers. This chapter offers a generic description of the hacking process, not a definitive or exhaustive examination. However, from this foundation, you can develop a greater understanding of hacking and the threats posed by hackers (as well as other sources of threat and risk), leading to improved security design, policy, and implementation.

KEY CONCEPTS AND TERMS

Adware
Alternate data stream (ADS)
Arbitrary code execution
ARP spoofing
Banner
Banner grabbing
Blog
Botnet army
Buffer overflow
Chip creep
Cluster
Cold calling
Command shell
Contract workers
Covert channel
Cross-site scripting (XSS)
Deterrent
Dialer
Disgruntled employees
Distributed denial of service (DDoS)
DNS poisoning
DNS spoofing
Domain registration
Dumpster diving
Eavesdropping
Enumeration
Flaw exploitation
Flooding
Footprinting
Hierarchical file system (HFS)
Honeypot
ICMP redirect
IDS insertion
Insertion attack
Instant message (IM)
Interception attack
Internal personnel
Internet relay chat (IRC)
Keystroke logger
Leetspeak
Logic bomb
MAC spoofing
Maximum transmission unit (MTU)
Mean time between failures (MTBF)
Mean time to failure (MTTF)
Metacharacter
MITRE
Mobile code
Monkey-in-the-middle
National Institute of Standards and Technology (NIST)
New technology file system (NTFS)
Nmap
Non-authenticating query service
Opportunistic hackers
OS/2
Partition
Phishing
Ping sweep
Playback attack
Port scanning
POSIX
Privilege escalation
Professional hackers
Proxy attack
Proxy manipulation
Pwned
Reconnaissance
Recreational hackers
Redundant array of independent disks (RAID)
Replay attack
Return on investment (ROI)
Rogue access point
Rogue DHCP
Rootkit
Scanning
Script kiddie
Sector
Session hijacking
Shell code
Slack space
Social engineering
Spam
Spyware
SQL injection
Static electricity discharge (SED) or Electrostatic discharge (ESD)
Traffic generation
Trapdoor
Trojan horse
Unpartitioned space
Upstream filtering
URL injector
USENET newsgroups
Virus
War dialing
War driving
Whois
Worm
Wrapper
Zombie army

CHAPTER 4 ASSESSMENT

1. All of the following are common or likely motivations for a hacker *except* which?
   A. Ego boost
   B. Social validation
   C. College credit
   D. Challenge
   E. Adventure

2. Which of the following potential hackers represents the greatest threat because they likely already have physical and logical access to a target?
   A. Consultant
   B. Competitor
   C. Overseas black hat for hire
   D. Customer
   E. Recreational hackers under 16 years old

3. Which of the following is *not* a significant threat to availability?
   A. Natural disasters
   B. Hardware failure
   C. Accidental spills
   D. Stateful inspection filtering
   E. Lack of proper training

4. Which of the following is *not* a potential consequence of a malware infestation?
   A. Corruption of data
   B. Leaking of confidential information
   C. Crashing of systems
   D. Identity theft
   E. Improved throughput

5. What is the primary difference in network security between a wired connection and a wireless connection to a private LAN?
   A. Inability to access all network resources
   B. Lack of realistic throughput
   C. Needing to be inside the building to access the network
   D. Ability to support encrypted sessions
   E. Support for multi-factor authentication

6. Most exploits are based on the existence of which?
   A. Encryption
   B. Filtering
   C. Humans
   D. System anomalies
   E. Synchronization

7. What is the first stage or step in the hacking process?
   A. Scanning
   B. Penetration
   C. Enumeration
   D. Privilege escalation
   E. Reconnaissance

8. Which form of attack captures authentication packets to retransmit them later?
   A. Insertion
   B. Hijacking
   C. Replay
   D. Interruption
   E. Spoofing

9. Which form of attack can potentially evade an IDS?
   A. Virus
   B. Insertion
   C. Man-in-the-middle
   D. ARP poisoning
   E. Rogue DHCP

10. Which exploit takes advantage of variable MTUs?
    A. Spoofing
    B. Hijacking
    C. Covert channels
    D. DoS
    E. Fragmentation

11. Which form of attack submits excessive data to a target to cause arbitrary code execution?
    A. Buffer overflow
    B. DDoS
    C. Insertion
    D. Interruption
    E. Fragmentation

12. Which attack exploits a Web site to poison its dataset so future visitors receive corrupted content?

A. Cross-site scripting
B. Proxy manipulation
C. Rogue DHCP
D. SQL injection
E. Hijacking

13. Which attack uses rogue DHCP, ARP poisoning, or ICMP redirect?

A. Fragmentation
B. Injection
C. Man-in-the-middle
D. Social engineering
E. Buffer overflow

14. Which attack is preceded by eavesdropping?

A. SQL injection
B. Hijacking
C. IDS insertion
D. Covert channel
E. XSS

15. Which attack is based on the impersonation of a legitimate host?

A. DoS
B. Replay
C. Fragmentation
D. Spoofing
E. Hijacking

16. Which method of communication is unseen, unfiltered, and based on timed manipulations?

A. Buffer overflow
B. Man-in-the-middle
C. DDoS
D. Covert channel
E. IDS insertion

17. Which form of attack is based on malware distributed by Trojan horse or worm and that can generate massive levels of traffic toward a primary target from numerous source vectors?

A. Fragmentation
B. Hijacking
C. DDoS
D. Playback
E. XSS

18. Which attack uses non-technical means to achieve results?

A. Spoofing
B. SQL injection
C. Buffer overflow
D. Covert channels
E. Social engineering

19. A hacker writes an exploit to compromise targets due to the presence of which?

A. A vulnerability
B. Multi-factor authentication
C. Sufficient throughput
D. A bot army
E. Traffic filtering

20. What is the primary benefit to network security of knowing hacker attacks and exploits?

A. Training contract workers
B. Improved antivirus detection mechanisms
C. Defending against specific threats
D. Alterations of network subnet organization
E. Reduced infrastructure cost

PART TWO

Technical Overview of Network Security, Firewalls, and VPNs

CHAPTER 5

Network Security Implementation

IMPLEMENTATION is the act of designing, installing, deploying, and configuring network security. This chapter focuses on the foundations of network security essential to every organization, from an individual computer at home to a multinational corporation's network. The foundations of security apply universally no matter the size, purpose, or function of computers and networking.

The foundations of network security include layered defenses, proper use of protocols, communication management, system hardening, and more. Based on some common, often simple, principles, you can significantly improve your organization's computer systems. Following the suggestions in this chapter will reduce the risk of system compromise from accident, oversight, Mother Nature, or malicious intent.

Chapter 5 Topics

This chapter will cover the following topics and concepts:

- What the seven domains of a typical IT infrastructure are
- What network design and "defense-in-depth" is
- What protocols and topologies are
- What common types of addressing are
- How to control communication pathways
- How to harden systems
- Which method to use for selecting equipment
- What authentication, authorization, and accounting are
- What communication encryption is
- What the best architecture is: local hosts only or remote and mobile hosts
- What redundancy is
- What node security is

Chapter 5 Goals

Upon completion of this chapter, you will be able to:

- Describe elements of network security design.
- Compare and contrast public and private addressing as well as static and dynamic addressing.
- State the importance of system hardening.
- Describe why authentication, authorization, accounting, and encryption are essential for network security.
- Identify the security concerns of local hosts as well as remote and mobile hosts.
- Define the elements of node security.

Seven Domains of a Typical IT Infrastructure

Seven domains are commonly found in the typical IT infrastructure (Figure 5-1) of moderate- to large-sized organizations. These seven domains were introduced in the first chapter, but in the context of network security implementation, they require more detail and focus.

Hackers look for every opportunity to exploit a target. No aspect of an IT infrastructure is without risk or immune to the scrutiny of hackers. When designing and implementing network security, you need to analyze every one of the seven domains of a typical IT infrastructure for potential vulnerabilities and weaknesses. Security measures must be detailed, focused, and exhaustive. You must consider every possible avenue of attack, assess risk, and if the risk is sufficient, apply a countermeasure. Failing to do so will leave an open pathway for a hacker. A hacker only needs one crack in your defenses to begin chipping away at the security of the entire network.

Each of the seven domains of a typical IT infrastructure has unique aspects that need security improvements. Later chapters will expand on these topics, but a quick list of important foundational network security issues related to these seven domains is pertinent here:

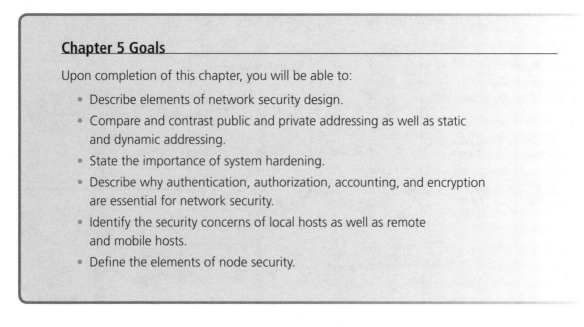

- **User Domain**—This domain refers to the actual user whether they be employees, consultants, contractors, or other third parties. Any user who accesses and uses the organization's IT infrastructure should review and sign an acceptable use policy (AUP) prior to being granted access to the organization's IT resources and infrastructure. This domain should also be the focus of training, strong authentication, granular authorization, and detailed accounting. Additionally,

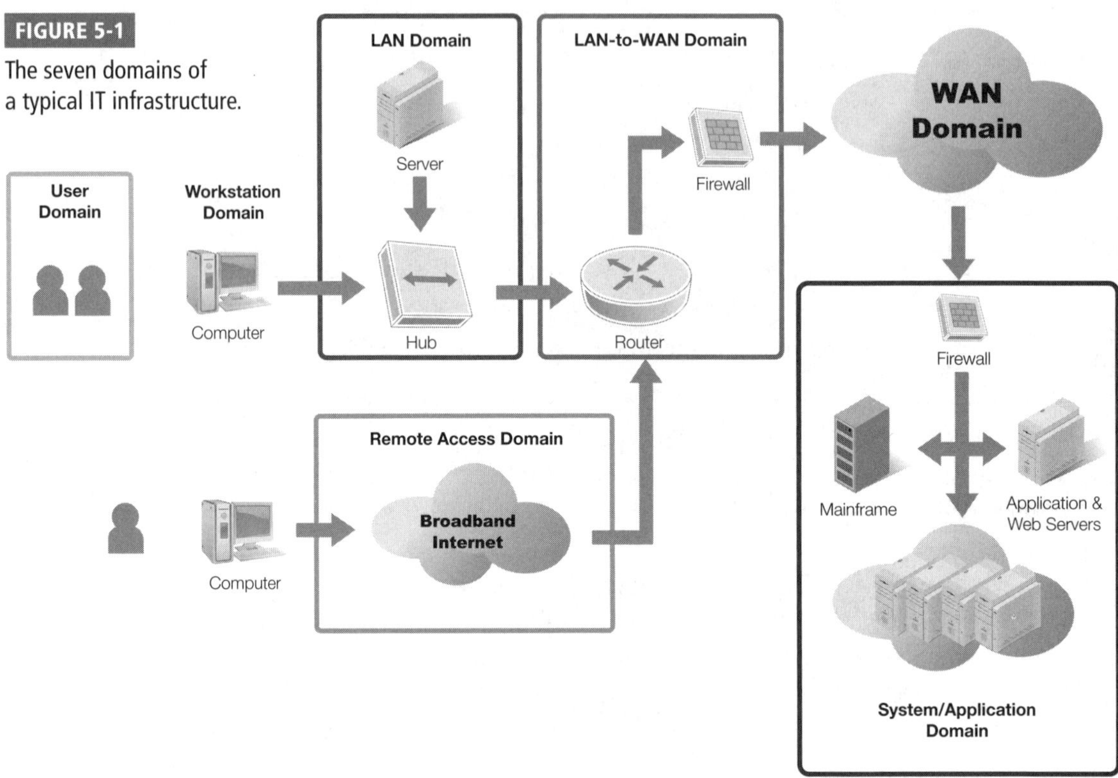

FIGURE 5-1
The seven domains of a typical IT infrastructure.

many of the protections added to other domains provide additional protections for and against the user domain.

- **Workstation Domain**—This domain refers to the end user's desktop devices such as a desktop computer, laptop, VoIP telephone, or other end-point device. Workstation devices typically require security countermeasures such as antivirus, anti-spyware, and vulnerability software patch management to maintain the integrity of the device. System **hardening**, communication protection, and positioning of workstations are critical to security.
- **Local Area Network (LAN) Domain**—This domain refers to the physical and logical local area network technologies used to support workstation connectivity to the organization's network infrastructure. Protocols, addressing, topology, and communication encryption provide security for this domain.
- **LAN-to-Wide Area Network (WAN) Domain**—This domain refers to the organization's internetworking and inter-connectivity point between the LAN and the WAN network infrastructures. Switches, routers, firewalls, proxies, and communication encryption are important aspects of security for this domain.

- **Remote Access Domain**—This domain refers to the authorized and authenticated remote access procedures for users to remotely access the organization's IT infrastructure, systems, and data. Remote access solutions typically involve SSL 128-bit encrypted remote browser access or encrypted VPN tunnels for secure remote communications. Knowing where a host is located helps determine the types of security necessary on that host.
- **WAN Domain**—Organizations with remote locations require a wide area network to interconnect them. Protocol selection, addressing schemes, and communication encryption are elements of securing this domain.
- **Systems/Applications Domain**—This domain refers to the hardware, operating system software, database software, client-server applications, and data that are typically housed in the organization's data center and/or computer rooms. Network design, authentication, authorization, accounting, and node security are important security concerns for this domain.

Network administrators need to recognize that the potential for compromise exists throughout an organization. This recognition leads the need for adequate network security throughout an organization. Starting from the knowledge that risk exists and threats loom, network security administrators can design and implement appropriate countermeasures and safeguards.

Network Design and Defense-in-Depth

Every network is different. However, common security principles apply to every network, regardless of its unique elements. One of these common principles is secure network design. Secure network design embeds core protections and improvements into an IT infrastructure before it is implemented. Design comes from planning. Planning comes from sufficient knowledge and understanding.

Common security goals include confidentiality, integrity, availability, privacy, authentication, authorization, non-repudiation, and accounting. To efficiently accomplish these goals, informed planning assists you in designing the network before deployment.

An underlying fundamental of network security design is that no security solution is perfect. Any single security protection, countermeasure, and safeguard is insufficient. Hackers will use some method, technique, or exploit to bypass, evade, or render useless a security protection. The potential concerns include placement, programming flaws, default settings, maximum values, processing capabilities, memory capacity, backdoors, malicious code, social engineering, and physical attacks. This list is not exhaustive, but represents the key issues. In theory, no security solutions are sufficient and complete.

Thus, you need to use multiple security components. This is known as defense-in-depth or multiple layers of defense (Figure 5-2). By following a defense-in-depth design concept, numerous safeguards will protect each asset. As one defense tool interlocks with another, they overlap and improve the overall security. The strengths and benefits of one countermeasure supplement or compensate for the weaknesses and limitations of another.

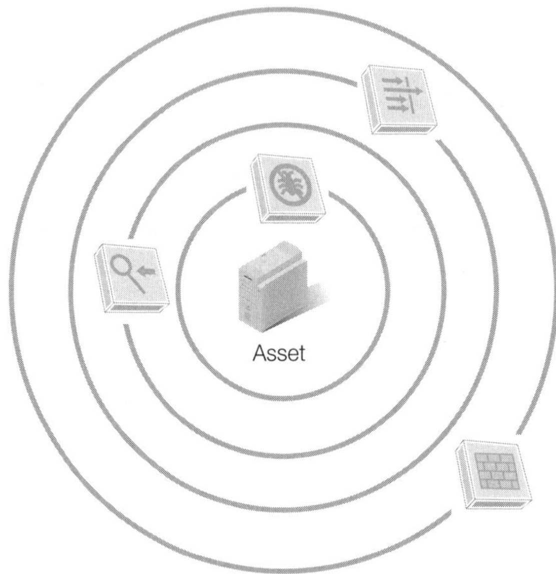

FIGURE 5-2
An example of defense-in-depth around an asset.

Defense-in-depth leads many security professionals to two additional guidelines: 1) avoid single points of failure; and 2) divide and conquer. A single point of failure is any element, component, or aspect of a system that could lead to failure or compromise of the entire system. Divide and conquer is the process of separating a large project into multiple, smaller, and manageable pieces.

Avoiding single point of failure must take place on multiple fronts. A hacker only needs a single flaw or weakness to exploit a target. Efforts should focus on finding and eliminating as many vulnerabilities as possible to remove the single points hackers seek to exploit.

Good design filters every user interaction with an asset multiple times. This filtering should include authentication, authorization, content filtering, and context filtering. Only relying upon a single filter or check system is a form of a single point of failure. Always assume that any one service or function is flawed or will fail.

Effective network design monitors and examines all activities against an asset using multiple techniques. This could include object auditing, server monitoring, client monitoring, network monitoring, and so on. Only using a single monitoring viewpoint could be a single point of failure. Everyone has seen video footage from a single perspective that guides the viewer into seeing or believing one thing, but from another camera angle the truth, the trick, or an alternate explanation becomes clear.

Divide and conquer is not just a tactic for waging actual war; it is also a tactic in the war against network security breaches. By dividing up a larger project or task into manageable components, you can focus on and care for each component to ensure accuracy and completeness in addressing network security concerns. Attempting to tackle the security of a network as a whole is often a recipe for disaster. Evaluating the big picture is always a good idea, but working exclusively on the whole may lead to overlooking details or missing subtle nuances only perceived upon close detailed inspection.

A layered security approach throughout the IT infrastructure works best: slow, methodical, compartmentalized, and thorough. Properly designed network security should support timely delivery of information and adequate response of transactions. A properly secured network provides reliable and stable communications. Well-designed security adapts to changing conditions. Well-designed security anticipates future growth and expansion.

Designing network security is neither a simple nor short-term task. Thorough network security design must include adequate research, thorough planning, and extensive **modeling** and testing. The process of security design must evaluate a wide range of technologies performing an astounding number of functions.

Ultimately, good network security design produces a blueprint to guide the construction of a securely functioning network infrastructure. The blueprint is the foundation for your organization's security policy. Most network designs have limitations. These limitations include budget, internal politics, regulations, standards, and industry practices. Network design should focus on providing the best security possible within prescribed budgetary boundaries.

One method to reduce compromise by hackers is to keep them from finding your network as a target. By staying offline and only using trusted communication pathways, your organization can avoid significant level of risk. However, this form of technological hide and seek is not perfect nor does it eliminate all issues. External hackers might not be able to hack a non-Internet-connected intranet from the outside; however the risk from disgruntled employees and other internal users is still present.

The idea of hiding from danger is commonly known as **security through obscurity**. While it's true that if you are not found then you cannot be attacked, the issue is often a false hope if obscurity rather than actual countermeasures and safeguards protect the network. Being obscure or difficult to locate may be a good thing, but it's not itself a form of reliable security. Use only direct and real security defenses when you are designing network security.

Security is essential to the long-term survival of any modern organization. Without security, logical, physical, and social breaches would render most companies vulnerable to failure. But security cannot work without balance. You can over-secure an infrastructure to the point where security interferes with work tasks. Usability and security must be in balance. Usability will not survive long without security, and too much security can cripple usability. Good network security design balances security and usability.

One goal of most organizations is to expand and grow. They often seek to attract new customers, support more clients, sell more products, offer more services, make more money, and so forth. But growth can be a two-edged sword. While growth can lead to a more reliable and assured future, it can also cause growing pains. For any organization, growing pains occur when the existing infrastructure, facilities, and even personnel are pushed to the limit or beyond to support the additional workload caused by growth.

Growth can be expected, unexpected, gradual, or abrupt. A proper network design process evaluates and predicts potential growth scenarios and plans contingencies for each. One contingency for growth is to build additional capacity into the current infrastructure. If slow growth is expected, then 20 percent additional capacity may be sufficient, while rapid growth may consume 50 percent additional capacity in a short time (Figure 5-3).

Growing too fast is as much of a burden as shrinking. By stretching beyond an organization's capacity to support, sell, create, maintain, respond, produce, and so forth, small problems quickly snowball into avalanches. Steady, controlled, limited growth is often a method to ensure long-term viability and stability. This is true in general business management and it's true in network security design.

During the network design phase, consider the scalability of all technologies you select for deployment. Does a component or system have a maximum value or limitation it will quickly reach? Can the component or system expand without compromising efficiency, cost effectiveness, and security? Will the component or system need replacement by a scalable solution once moderate growth occurs? If so, why not use the scalable solution now? Planning for growth will reduce problems associated with outgrowing function and security capacity.

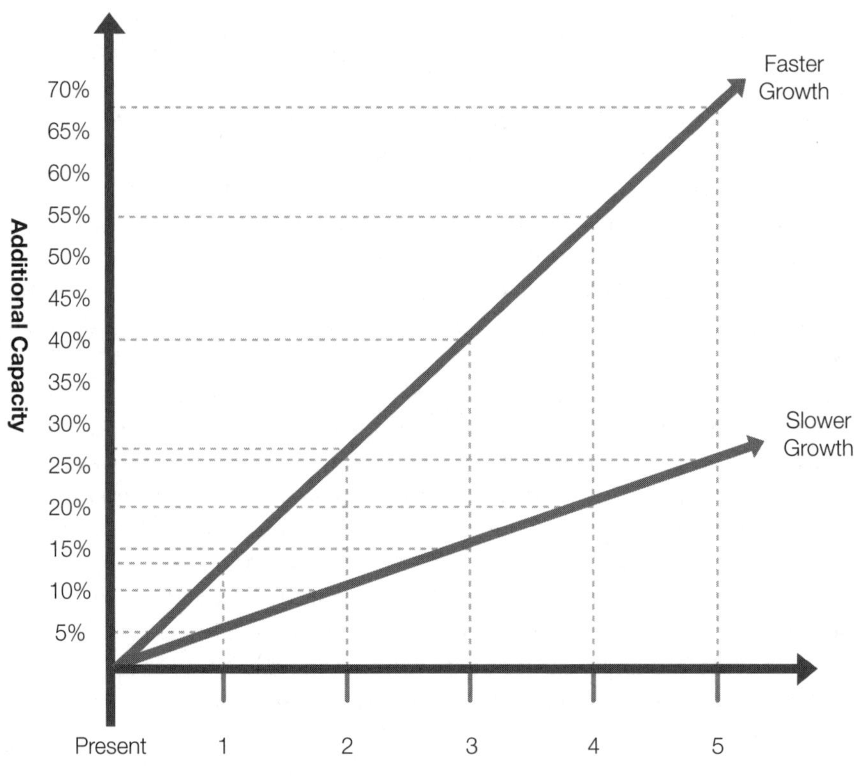

FIGURE 5-3

Rate of growth used to predict needed additional capacity.

No security endeavor will succeed without the active involvement of senior management. In fact, without their explicit approval and support, any security effort is likely doomed to fail. Senior management has the responsibility to dictate the strategic goals and plans of the organizations and, hence, its IT infrastructure and integrated security. Senior management must approve budgetary funding, encourage compliance, and support security, even when problems occur.

Throughout the entire design and implementation process for network security, senior management monitors and approves progress reports. Senior management steers the organization and its security planning through the changing business environment. But secure network design isn't only about following the leader; it's also about integrating every employee into the overall security design process. Security is the responsibility of everyone in the organization, not just managers and executives.

The elements of secure network design touch on every aspect of an IT infrastructure. This includes hosts, nodes, communications, encryption, local and remote systems, **redundancy**, and more. Often, the process of designing security starts by focusing a central or core element found throughout the infrastructure. Examples of distributed core components are networking protocols and topologies.

Protocols and Topologies

A significant portion of network security is about making the right technology choices without falling into easy traps or defaults. One common trap is to continue doing the same thing or using the same product. You need to re-evaluate old technologies and existing solutions on a regular basis. Most organizations choose to perform a security design evaluation annually. When performing a security evaluation, re-think every aspect of the infrastructure, including network protocols and topologies.

Most networks use Transmission Control Protocol/Internet Protocol (TCP/IP) as their primary network protocol. Specifically, most networks in 2010 still use IPv4 as opposed to IPv6. Using IPv4 is not an open invitation for hackers, but it does have numerous commonly exploited weaknesses and concerns. IPv4 typically defaults to a plaintext form of transmission, while IPv6 can be set by default to encrypt transmissions. IPv4 can be encrypted using IP Security (IPSec) or other virtual private network (VPN) protocols.

Other issues to consider include:

- Is the current protocol easy to compromise?
- Are there numerous exploits for this protocol available for novice hackers?
- Can encryption be applied?
- Is the process of adding encryption complex or costly?
- Will encryption interfere with other technologies?
(such as IPSec and network address translation [NAT])
- Is there an alternative or replacement available?
- Is the alternative backwards compatible?
- Is the alternative supported by all current hosts and nodes?

This is only a partial and not exhaustive list of questions you need to consider when assessing the currently deployed networking protocol for possible replacement. The point is to give serious consideration to this issue on a regular basis. Most of the elements of a network's security are based on the protocol in use. If the protocol has changed or improved, this could cause sweeping changes throughout the production environment, most important in the security of that environment.

As a general rule of thumb, if most hosts and software are less than five years old, then upgrading to IPv6 is likely possible with minimal complication. However, if IPv4 with IPSec or other forms of encryption are functioning well within performance and security parameters, there's no strong need to upgrade to IPv6.

When you consider a protocol upgrade, you'll need to thoroughly research and test every aspect of the production and security environment to confirm compatibility with IPv6. Any transition is going to have some hurdles, and certainly switching the main network protocol is a candidate for major hurdles. Perform the rollout of a protocol change in stages, only after **piloting** in a lab and consider running dual protocols for a transition period.

TCP/IP, or at least IP itself, is not the only protocol in use on most networks. Every single protocol across every theoretical layer of the OSI model network protocol stack needs re-evaluation on a regular basis. Do you still want to continue using **Simple Mail Transfer Protocol (SMTP)** and **Post Office Protocol (POP)**? What about **File Transfer Protocol (FTP)**, **Network News Transfer Protocol (NNTP)**, and **telnet**?

If a protocol operates in plaintext, consider using a protocol with native encryption or investigate the possibility of encapsulating it inside an encrypting tunneling protocol, such as IPSec or SSL/TLS.

Are **AppleTalk**, **Internetwork Packet Exchange/Sequenced Packet Exchange (IPX/SPX)**, **Systems Network Architecture (SNA)**, **NetBios Extended User Interface (NetBEUI)**, or other protocols still present on the network? Are they still necessary? Have the older systems requiring them been replaced or removed? Can newer secure alternatives replace these older and insecure protocols? Can any system still using a legacy protocol be replaced to gain host security and remove the protocol?

Don't let tradition, personal bias, or **sunk cost** get in the way of making a smart security design decision. Just because something has always been done a certain way doesn't mean it should continue that way, especially if the old way was insecure. Personal bias in terms of likes, dislikes, comfort, and familiarity are not good business reasons to avoid moving on to more secure solutions.

Sunk cost is the money or investment already made in the past, as opposed to prospective costs that are investments likely in the future. Often those managers overly concerned with wasting resources already invested will make poor decisions. Avoiding loss is a good principle of business, but just because you have already spent some money, time, and effort does not mean you should continue on a set path. Often, throwing good money after bad is compounding the loss due to sunk cost. If the future benefit of an existing system, solution, or product is not assured, then no amount of sunk cost justifies its continued use. In most cases, you should only analyze future costs and benefits in making a decision. Already incurred expense (sunk cost) should influence future choices.

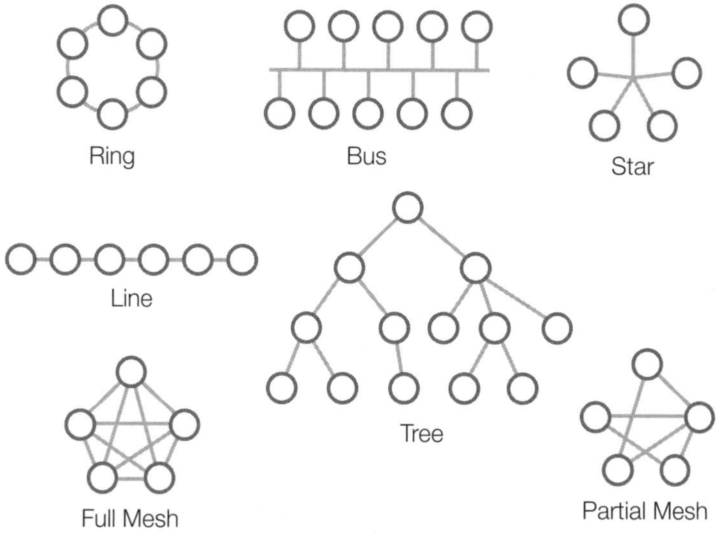

Ring Bus Star Line Tree Full Mesh Partial Mesh

FIGURE 5-4 Seven basic network topologies.

In addition to reevaluating protocol choices, you should reconsider your network's topology, as well. A network's **topology** is the physical interconnections between hosts and nodes. Several common or foundational topologies (Figure 5-4) are:

- Ring topology
- Bus topology
- Star topology
- Line topology
- Tree topology
- Full Mesh topology
- Partial Mesh topology

technical TIP

Ring topology is a network design where host segments are attached to a central cable ring. **Bus topology** is a network design based on a single backbone cable to which all host segments connect. Ethernet is logically a bus topology-based technology, although it can operate in numerous other physical topologies. **Star topology** is a network design in which host segments radiate from a central node. **Line topology** is a network design in which hosts are connected end-to-end, each system being connected to no more than two others. **Tree topology** is a network design that organizes hosts into a hierarchy. Each host is connected upstream to a single parent, but can be connected downstream to none, one, or many hosts. **Full Mesh topology** is a network design that establishes all possible connections between hosts. A full mesh topology is the most fault tolerant topology possible, but is also the least resistant to propagation of malware. **Partial Mesh topology** is a mesh network design that establishes many but not all possible host-to-host links. This is not as fault tolerant as a full-mesh topology.

While some network topologies are designed before deployment, others grow organically as growth occurs. In either case, periodically re-assess your network's topology as well as every other aspect of your IT infrastructure.

On face value, a network topology seems like little more than a physical cabling solution. But, when you realize that a cable is a communication conduit for electronic transmissions, the security concerns become more apparent. The main concern is traffic management. A network administrator should know the pathways that mission-critical data traverse. You need to secure these pathways in relation to the value of the data traveling over them.

When dealing with cabling layouts and topologies, you must also be concerned with single points of failure. A single cable is just one fault away from a lost connection. While multiple links to every client may not be essential, it's reasonable to have two or more connections between every server and mandatory to have multiple connections to every essential service host (such as authentication, domain resolution, security assessment, and backup).

Designed topologies are more likely to provide long term security and performance benefits, but even the best planning cannot predict all possible occurrences in reality. Changes may occur that are outside the scope of the original plan, or maybe growth comes faster or more chaotically than expected. Organically produced topologies are nearly guaranteed to have flaws in terms of a lack of redundancy or poor traffic management.

A secure network design includes a topology appropriate for the organization, its communications, and the value of its resources. Short or direct pathways should exist between servers that commonly interact. Departments that do not share resources should use network paths that have little intersection. Position clients with a minimum number of segments away from the resource servers most appropriate for getting work done.

Topology is both a logical and a physical concern. **Physical topology** concerns include the amount of cabling consumed and the actual physical pathway through the building a cable takes. Secure physical topologies minimize access or exposure of cabling to outsiders, unauthorized personnel, or those with limited or lower access.

Logical topology concerns include networking technologies (such as Ethernet), signal propagation, **latency**, and addressing. Ethernet is a logical bus topology-based technology deployed over a wide range of non-bus physical topologies, such as star, mesh, and tree.

Each time a communication signal crosses a node or host, some amount of delay occurs between reception on one interface and transmission on another interface. The accumulation of this delay is called latency. Too much latency between end-points or within a round-trip, two-way communication can result in communication failures. Too many segments crossed by a signal, especially with sub-grade nodes, can result in unacceptable latency.

Logical topology also affects addressing. When IPv4 is in use, you need to manage subnets. A subnet is a logical collect of hosts, typically within a limited physical distance.

Often a subnet consists of hosts interconnected through a hub or switch. **Subnetting** controls traffic. Communication between hosts within the same subnet is unhindered, but a router handles communications between hosts in different subnets. A router will make decisions on whether or not to route traffic and which pathway to use when traffic is forwarded. A router can perform basic filtering functions (As discussed previously, routers are the predecessors of firewalls).

Certain topologies encourage or discourage the use of routers, switches, hubs, repeaters, bridges, and other networking nodes and devices. Some of these devices impose subnetting restrictions or requirements. Thus, when selecting a topology, consider the implications on the desired addressing scheme, as well.

Most networks employ layered, mixed, or hybrid topologies. Mixing and matching the basic topologies into larger, more complex topologies is not necessarily a straightforward endeavor. You need to thoroughly investigate and analyze network and system requirements to ensure that your communication, production, and security needs are supported by the deployed topologies.

Common Types of Addressing

Addressing is the assignment of a logical numbering system to the hosts on a network for the purposes of efficient traffic routing. Addressing is more than just a system imposed by a network topology; it's often a means to control traffic. Traffic managing through routing and traffic filtering are possible through the use of logical addresses.

The most common protocol in use worldwide is TCP/IP and this network protocol dictates the most common addressing scheme. You learned in Chapter 1 that the addressing schemes of IPv4 and IPv6 are quite different. Some common elements, security concerns, and management techniques remain consistent, however.

Internal IP addresses can be public addresses, private addresses, or a mixture of both. A public address is an address issued by the IANA, monitored by RIRs, and leased directly through ISPs. The **Internet Assigned Numbers Authority (IANA)** (*http://www.iana.org/*) is the entity responsible for global coordination of IP addressing, DNS root, and other Internet protocol resources. A **Regional Internet Registry (RIR)** is one of five regional organizations that oversee and monitor the use and assignment of IP addresses (both IPv4 and IPv6). An ISP (Internet service provider) may randomly assign or semi-permanently lease an IP address to an individual or organization. Public addresses are those obtained from an ISP.

 **NOTE**

In the past, it was possible to purchase or own IP addresses, specifically large groups or an entire class of addresses. However, this practice is mostly no longer possible, not because ownership of IP addresses is prohibited, but because of the lack of available IP addresses to sell. Many of the original Class A and Class B subnet owners still own, control, and use their purchased address. Some of these are actually ISPs that now lease out sub-sets of their owned IP address ranges. Today, most public IP addresses are leased rather than sold or owned.

A public address also implies that it communicates directly with resources on the Internet. The Internet itself only uses public addresses. Without a public address, it's impossible to communicate to or receive responses from an Internet-hosted resource.

Public addresses are assigned from Class A, B, and C ranges of the IPv4 address spectrum (as Class D and E are reserved for multicasting and experimentation respectively). Public addresses for IPv6 are most of the 2^128 addresses, except for the fc00::/7 address block.

In Request for Comments (RFC) 4193, IANA set aside the fc00::/7 address block for use as private addresses for IPv6 similar to that of RFC 1918 for IPv4. Private IPv4 addresses herald from RFC 1918 that sets aside three class ranges for private use:

- **Class A**—10.0.0.0–10.255.255.255/8 (1 Class A network)
- **Class B**—172.16.0.0–172.31.255.255/12 (16 Class B networks)
- **Class C**—192.168.0.0–192.168.255.255/16 (256 Class C networks)

A private address is used only within a private network. Individuals and organizations without approval or fee from an outside entity can use private addresses. However, using private addresses requires NAT services to communicate with Internet resources. All Internet routers automatically drop any packet with a private address in its header.

Private addresses serve as a basic isolation security measure as external entities with public addresses cannot directly communicate with internal privately addressed hosts. But a NAT server allows communication with Internet resources.

You should review your organization's choice to use private or public addresses internally. The issue is not only about saving money. Private addresses are free while public addresses are usually leased. Private addresses require translation, while public addresses do not. Private addresses are natively isolated from the Internet, while public addresses are not. It's even possible to mix private and public addresses on an intranet.

Another addressing concern is whether to employ static or dynamic addressing. Static addressing pre-assigns a specific IP address to each host, while dynamic addressing hands out IP addresses to hosts from a pool. Dynamic addressing does not guarantee that a host will always have the same address assigned to it, unless a reservation is created for the host.

technical TIP

A DHCP reservation is the pre-assignment of a specific IP address to a host by reserving it using the target host's MAC address. Reservations ensure that the same address is always issued to a specific host. It can also simulate static addressing, but retain centralized control of address assignment.

Static addressing typically requires that the IP address be configured on each individual host. This ensures that a host always uses the same IP address. However, if changes to the network configuration or topology arise, manual changes to IP addresses on a host-by-host basis are a significant amount of additional administrative overhead.

Because of this, most organizations use dynamic assignment, typically using a Dynamic Host Configuration Protocol (DHCP) system. If static addressing is preferred, then DHCP reservations can simulate static addressing while maintaining centralized control. With reservation based static addressing, changes can be made by editing the reservations on the DHCP server, without needing to manually adjust each host individually.

When addresses are assigned dynamically, it's possible for a rogue system to come online and receive a valid IP address just by asking. If addresses are assigned statically, then the attacker will need to discover a valid but unused IP address and manually configure his system to use it. Similarly, if DHCP reservations are used, the attacker will either manually statically assign his own address or spoof a Media Access Control (MAC) address to "borrow" an IP address from another offline system.

Address management is an important concern of network security. Another concern is the management of communication pathways.

Controlling Communication Pathways

Controlling the flow of information is a key element of network security. This involves ensuring that data travels along pathways isolated, secured, and controlled, and not along pathways that are public, insecure, and uncontrolled. Part of communication pathway control is about topology selection, but it's also about router configuration, encrypted protocols, physical access management, and filtering.

Routers are the primary network devices administrators use to control the pathways that communications traverse. Failing to design router configuration and deployment with security in mind is a serious oversight. Routers make real-time determinations of the best available path to a destination. However, the information available to a router to make those decisions can be true and accurate or incorrect, falsified, and misleading.

Secure network design includes protections for routers, routing protocols, and routing information. Physical isolation of a router is important to ensure that only authorized router administrators can access the device itself. Failing to protect routers physically means that the logical activities and the resulting routes selected will not be trustworthy.

Routers employ routing protocols to exchange information about routes and connected pathways. This information calculates the best path to guide a packet towards its destination. Depending upon the make and model of router, the routing protocol, and the related configurations, routing data, a hacker can spoof or manipulate through false Internet Control Message Protocol (ICMP) type 5 Redirect messages. Configure routers to only accept routing information from other known routers through authentication of the source. Consider also encrypting all communications between routers.

Encrypted protocols are another important aspect of communication pathway security. Even the best design, proper installation, and reasonable physical isolation are not guarantees that a wired or wireless communication channel will not be the target of an eavesdropping, interception, or man-in-the-middle attack. Assuming that physical access is under your control all the time is naive. The possibility of an internal malicious entity or the planting of a socially engineered listening device always exists.

To thwart eavesdropping and related attacks based on eavesdropping, you should encrypt all traffic over a network communication link. This especially applies to any traffic traversing a network segment physically accessible from outside your organization's facilities. But it also applies to physically isolated and internal connections, as well. Compromise of every physical connection is always possible, so the best defense against content eavesdropping is encryption.

Physical access management should always be a part of communication pathway security. Even with encrypted protocols, hackers can gain significant information by eavesdropping on a network segment. Even if you encrypt every single packet (which is often not the case), eavesdropping can still glean a wide variety of information about the protected communications.

Such gleaned information can include a count of the number and size of packets. This can estimate the size of the payload delivered which in turn can extrapolate the likely type of data, such as e-mail transmission, Web surfing, file exchange, or database synchronization.

Eavesdropping can also glean the identity of the endpoints of the secured communication. If the transaction is using transport mode encryption, then the endpoints are the actual sending and receiving hosts. If the transaction is using tunnel mode encryption, then the endpoints are either both VPN gateways or one end is a remote host.

Eavesdroppings can also glean the general identity or purpose of each endpoint discovered, based on the timing of and volume of traffic sent to and from each discovered endpoint. This can allow an outside user to reliably predict which endpoint is a server, a client, or a VPN gateway.

Generally, data gathering through eavesdropping on communications, whether encrypted or not, is known as traffic and trend analysis. Such analysis can reveal many important details about internal processes and the importance, value, or criticality of systems. Thus, even with encryption, prevention of physical access to communication cables and wireless signals is paramount.

Filtering is another important part of communication pathway security. The movement of data between departments, subnets, WAN connect LANs, and the Internet requires that you monitor and filter communications to prevent violations of disclosure, intrusion, and malicious code infection.

Covert channels are a risk for many organizations in communication pathway security and control. As discussed in Chapter 4, covert channels are pathways of communication unknown to or uncontrolled by security systems or personnel. Covert channels, whether timing- or storage-based, can leak information out or bring malicious content in.

The best defenses against covert channels include IDS and intrusion prevention system (IPS), as well as thoroughly watching all aspects of an IT infrastructure for aberrant or abnormal events of any type. Predicting covert channels is difficult because their very nature is to remain unknown and unseen.

While planning and designing communication pathway security, evaluate the protections you'll need for inbound and outbound traffic and how to manage internal-only, external-only, or border-crossing communications.

You'll need to examine inbound traffic by asking several key questions. Is the inbound communication a response to a previous request from an internal entity or is it a communication that originates from an outside source? Responses are often allowed, unless the initial request itself was for a resource that's off limits. Restrictions along these lines include blocked protocols, IP address or domain name, unauthorized services and applications, or users without sufficient or correct authorization.

If the communication has external origins, rather than being a response, is the communication generally allowed or not? If the communication is for a resource offered to the public, then the communication could be allowed. However, if no public resources exist, the communication is more likely unauthorized.

Is the source address in the communication from a known or unknown location, and if known is it known to be malicious or questionable? If the latter, then blocking the traffic is more likely the proper security stance. Is the traffic obviously spoofed? Does the traffic match any known malicious patterns, have any construction anomalies, or have questionable content? Can it otherwise be classified as abnormal or atypical? In most of these cases, the packet should be dropped rather than allowed to continue on to its claimed destination.

You should subject outbound traffic to the same investigations and analysis as inbound. Does the outbound communication take place over an abnormal protocol or port? Does it attempt to communicate with a blocked or prohibited host or service? Is the traffic spoofed, does it have abnormal time stamps, is it a clone of another packet, or is it part of a flood?

Fortunately, inbound and outbound traffic filtering is the primary function and purpose of firewalls using ingress- and egress-focused filters. Secure communications pathway management often requires the use of firewalls. Firewalls are an essential element in secure network design. For more on firewalls, see Chapter 2.

One final area of concern for communication pathway security is the difference between traffic management based on whether the traffic is internal-only, external-only, or border- crossing. Generally, internal only traffic is more trustworthy than any other form of traffic. In most cases, internal traffic originates from a trusted internal host and terminates at a trusted internal host. However, because the possibility always exists of a rogue internal host or a malicious insider, blindly trusting internal traffic just because it originates internally is a security blunder.

A good practice is to treat all traffic with caution. Trust nothing until it's proven to comply with security policy and not to match any known malicious patterns. Monitoring and filtering of internal communications is as important as monitoring external and border crossing communications.

Naturally, external only communications are more likely to be malicious, but since they do not end or originate from an internal source, there's usually little need for concern. Malicious activity that does not attempt to breach your network borders is not really your problem. However, if external only communications are defined as those that do not interact with your intranet but which may interact with your DMZ or extranet, then you should be concerned.

With this definition of external only communications, you must filter, monitor, and block the most obvious malicious packets and events, but still allow any conforming communication request even if the origin or source is unfamiliar.

Border-crossing communications are those that either leave the intranet heading to the Internet or enter the intranet from the Internet. In either case, an increased risk of compromise exists. Inbound communications could be carrying malicious code or an intrusion attempt. Outbound communications could be revealing internal secrets or distributing confidential files. While these are extreme examples, they're not uncommon. Most border-crossing traffic is benign, but since the risk of malicious traffic is greater at border crossings, you need additional filtering, monitoring, and blocking.

Controlling communication pathways is an important part of managing and designing network security. But another important piece of the security puzzle is management of hardened systems between which the secured communications take place.

Hardening Systems

Hardening systems focuses on improving security of hosts and nodes. Hardening is the process of reducing the **attack surface** of a potential target by removing unnecessary components and adding in protections. While each organization usually creates its own custom and internal hardening processes and procedures, most hardening guidelines have common elements and components.

Some of the common recommendations to improve the security or harden a host include:

- Remove all unnecessary protocols.
- Uninstall all unnecessary applications and services.
- Define a complex password for all accounts; do not leave any account with a default password or a blank password.
- Configure account lockout and define a logon warning banner.
- Install all available final release updates, patches, fixes, service packs, and so on for the operating system and every remaining application and service.
- Update all hardware device firmware or BIOS with the lasted final release from the vendor.
- Install the latest final releases of all device drivers.
- Install and update antivirus and anti-malware scanners.

- Configure communication encryption.
- Install and configure a host firewall.
- Use a file system that supports file level permissions and auditing.
- Configure system monitoring and auditing.
- Synchronize the clock.
- Run vulnerability assessment tools against the host, such as HFNetChkPro and Nessus.
- Configure regular backups.
- Impose any organization-specific security limitations, such as blocking USB drives or using white list execution management; this is often performed using a security template file.
- In Windows, disable the guest account, and rename the Administrator account. In Unix, establish policies whereby the root account is never used directly, but administrators must "SU" to obtain root access (thus creating a log of their events).

In addition to these hardening suggestions, organizations add additional steps to their securing procedures based on the purpose of the system, the criticality of the system, and the risk present in the environment.

Once you've hardened your system, you must maintain it over time. On a regular schedule, re-examine every host against your organization's hardening policies to ensure compliance. Remove from service any system out of compliance with hardening policies until you are able to bring it into compliance. Then investigate the cause of the security noncompliance and take countermeasures to prevent a re-occurrence.

Equipment Selection

Equipment selection is a commonly overlooked aspect of secure network design. The general belief that any hardware capable of performing an IT function is suitable for deployment is, unfortunately, not the case. Both cheap and expensive products may have well-known or not-yet-discovered security flaws.

Arbitrarily or automatically choosing the least expensive or the most expensive products isn't a winning security strategy. You should carefully evaluate each piece of computer equipment, from network device to host system for its native security defenses or lack thereof, regardless of its cost.

As you select, purchase, and deploy equipment, consider the vulnerabilities introduced and any protections or improvements to the infrastructure's security stance. Every piece of equipment will either improve security or reduce it in some way. Some equipment adds new weak points or expands the organization's attack surface, while other equipment will act as a countermeasure, protecting weak points of other components and reducing the attack surface.

Whenever possible, select equipment providing greater improvement to security rather than acting as a detriment. This seems an obvious guideline, but you can only follow it if you are conscientious about evaluating the security profile of each device. Failing to evaluate the security of a new device properly could mean that you inadvertently introduce new vulnerabilities into the organization's network and systems.

Some of the security concerns regarding equipment include:

- **Electricity consumption**—Excessive energy use can cause not only increased electric bills, but also increased temperature within the device and on electrical distribution systems. A circuit drawing too much power can cause a breaker overload. A tripped breaker causes downtime and may cause data loss and equipment damage.
- **Heat produced**—The more heat a device produces, the more the heating, ventilation, and cooling (HVAC) system must work to keep the temperature of the room within acceptable boundaries. Excessive heat-producing devices can also increase the risk of fire.
- **Reset button**—A reset button is used to return a device to the default factory settings. Any defined security configuration on the device is lost if someone presses the reset button. When possible, select equipment without a reset button or a button that can be disabled to provide physical security for the device.
- **Easy access power switch**—If the power switch is easily accessed or triggered, casual contact with the device could cause power interruption. Additionally, an easy-access power switch allows a malicious person to power off equipment or trigger a reboot.
- **Easy access management console port or interface**—If device can be reconfigured through an LCD screen and a few buttons (such as a printer) or if a console or terminal port allows quick access to a configuration or management interface (such as a wireless access point, router, or switch), then use caution when deploying the device and assess the level of physical access security.
- **Removable media**—Equipment with removable media bays (such as tapes, optical discs, floppies, and so on) or external peripheral ports (such as Universal Serial Bus USB, firewall, Ethernet, and so on) may be easier to compromise than those with fewer or none of these access points.
- **Removable case**—The easier it is to remove or open the case of a device, the easier it is to hack into the device, plant a listener, or modify its functions.
- **Portability**—Is the device small enough to fit into a pocket, purse, or backpack making it easy to steal?
- **Rack mountable**—A rack-mounted device is less likely to be stolen once screwed into a rack case, which can be locked.

- **BIOS/firmware flashing**—Being able to change the embedded software of a device is both a benefit and a problem. Flashing to an updated more secure version of firmware is a positive benefit. However, being able to replace firmware with a third-party version or an older version with flaws could be a problem if a hacker can perform this easily.
- **Remote connection**—If remote connectivity to a device is possible, then risk increases. Limit, encrypt, and monitor remote connections.
- **Plaintext protocols**—The more a device defaults to or only supports plaintext protocols, the less secure it is. Choose equipment than supports encryption.

Many other aspects of equipment security are important when evaluating the deployment of a new device. Whether a high-end server, a user's notebook, a smart phone, a network router, or anything else, consider the security of equipment thoroughly and don't just make purchasing recommendations based on equipment cost.

Keep in mind those devices that are cheap or free up front may cost considerably more to manage and secure over time than a more expensive device. However, just because something has a high cost doesn't ensure that it has a low security management requirement. Money alone is rarely the true measure of the security of anything.

Authentication, Authorization, and Accounting

Security ultimately is supported and enforced by authentication, authorization, and accounting. Without all three of these security fundamentals properly implemented, real security cannot exist.

Authentication is the verification or proof of someone or something's identity. The most common form of authentication is the use of a password. While passwords are the most common, they are also one of the weakest forms of authentication. People typically often pick passwords that are easy to guess or that are somehow predictable. They often re-use the same passwords on multiple systems.

Passwords reside in account databases in hashed form, which means the original password can't be recovered from the hash value. However, by hashing large numbers of potential passwords, password-cracking techniques can potentially match a password hash to the target hash. Password cracking techniques including **dictionary attacks**, brute force attacks, and hybrid attacks can often reveal poorly constructed passwords.

Multifactor authentication is significantly more secure than any single factor form of authentication. Passwords are but one example of the first type of authentication factor. Three commonly recognized authentication factors are:

- **Type 1**—Something you know
- **Type 2**—Something you have
- **Type 3**—Something you are/do

technical TIP

Password cracking typically focuses on generating and hashing large numbers of passwords with the goal of matching a stolen or captured password hash. Dictionary password cracking uses a pre-created list of potential passwords. Each password from the list is hashed using the same hashing algorithm as the target/stolen password. If a match is found before the list is exhausted, the attack is successful.

A **brute force attack** builds potential passwords out of a selected character set, creating ever longer and longer passwords using every possible valid combination of characters. The hacker hashes each crafted password and compares it to the target hash until a match is found or the attack is abandoned. Given enough time and the right character set, a brute force attack will eventually be successful.

A **hybrid attack** uses a dictionary list as seed passwords that are then brute-force-modified. First the hacker makes all possible one-character modifications, then two, then three. This technique is often more successful, since many people pick an easy-to-remember word and then make only a few character modifications, such as changing an "a" to a "@" or an "l" to a "1" or just adding one or two characters.

The best defense against password cracking techniques is to select a long password. For example, using at least 15 character passwords on Windows systems avoids the weakness of the backward-compatible (and vulnerable to brute-force cracking) LANMAN hash of passwords 14 character or less. Adding complexity (mixing multiple character types: uppercase, lowercase, numbers, and symbols) and using multiple words or phrases instead of a single base word also improve password strength.

Something you know can be anything you memorize so that you can type, write, or speak it when asked to authenticate. Passwords are the most common example of a Type 1 authentication factor.

Something you have can be anything you must physically carry with you, such as a device or token. These can include metal keys, smart cards, radio-frequency identification (RFID) chips, ID badges, or electronic devices known as dynamic password tokens.

technical TIP

A dynamic password token is a device with a display screen that shows a seemingly random non-repeating one-time use password. The password displayed on the token must be included in the logon process, usually with a separate Type 1 PIN or password. This two-part mechanism is a form of multi-factor authentication.

Something you are or do is commonly known as biometrics. Some part of the human body is used as an element in an authentication process. This can include fingerprints, retina scans, facial geometric, palm scans, signature dynamics, keystroke dynamics, and voice-pattern analysis.

A mixture of two or more authentication factors is multifactor authentication. Multifactor- authentication is much more secured than single-factor. With single factor authentication, an attacker only needs to have a single skill or exploit to successfully log on with a compromised user account. With multifactor authentication, an attacker needs to have multiple skills or exploits to successfully log on with a compromised user account.

Strong authentication prevents unauthorized entities from gaining easy access to the internal workings of an organization's infrastructure. Apply strong authentication to the logical environment as well as the physical environment.

Authorization, commonly known as access control, defines what actions a user can and can't perform. Proper granular use of authorization ensures that authorized users perform only authorized activities.

The principle of least privilege is often a good guideline on which are the most appropriate authorization settings to make. This principle states that you should grant users the fewest capabilities, permissions, and privileges possible to complete their assigned work, without additional capabilities. In other words, you grant users enough power and access to perform their assigned work but no additional capabilities beyond their job descriptions are necessary.

Accounting is the activity of logging, monitoring, and auditing the environment, focusing both on users as well as system activities, to check for security policy compliance. Accounting is the process of holding users and systems accountable for their actions and activities. Through the use of thorough accounting and detailed auditing, you can detect and respond to any violations, attempt to violate, or trends towards violations.

Remember, security is locking things down then watching for attempts to breach the lock. Authentication and authorization are a form of locking, and accounting is the watching. However, these are not the only forms of locking and watching on a secure network. Another important area of network security is communication encryption.

Communication Encryption

Communication encryption is the use of encryption protocols to secure the contents of communications. Use encryption anytime a transaction occurs with an outside entity. Use encryption when a communication crosses a segment that is at risk to eavesdropping. You should also use encryption internally whenever the potential for loss or compromise, even by internal personnel, would cause significant harm to the organization.

You can protect transactions by encryption in two main ways. One is to use encapsulating intermediary protocols that provide encryption, such as IPSec and SSL/TLS; another is to encrypt data before goes to a network protocol.

Protocol encryption ensures that all or most data sent over the network is safe from eavesdropping, modification, and other forms of compromise. A widely used mechanism of protocol encryption is that of a VPN. VPNs can function between individual systems or between entire networks or any other combination of endpoints.

Data encryption, performed either by the client or server software, ensures that even if the protocol encryption fails or is compromised, the data itself is safe by its own encryption. Software or data encryption is not as interoperable as protocol or VPN encryption, but it can be a viable option when both endpoints of the transaction are using compatible software components.

When in doubt, always encrypt. While not a perfect solution, since no perfect security solution exists, encryption offers significant protections from outside eavesdropping and modification. However, encryption fails if the selected algorithm is poor, insecure key management exists, if either endpoint of the communication has been compromised (such as by hacker intrusion or planting of malicious code), or if intermediary network nodes that decrypt and reencrypt fail.

Choosing to encrypt by default is an excellent network security rule of thumb. This guideline does not imply that the same encryption protects both internal only–communications as well as those that cross the network's boundaries. In deciding what encryption to use, it's important to consider where the hosts are located.

Hosts: Local Only or Remote and Mobile

When designing network security, focus on the function of each device as well as the physical and logical location of the device. When a host is local and communicates with only other local hosts, then you can use slightly less stringent application of security on internal communications. However, when a host is remote or mobile or otherwise outside of the private network, use significant additional precautions.

Once you allow remote access, you lose the benefit of the physical access controls. Once you support remote connectivity, a hacker or intruder need no longer be physically present in a facility to launch an attack. Thus, remote access itself is a risk, and it lowers the overall security of an environment. To compensate for this security reduction, you should impose more rigid limitations in terms of authentication, authorization, and accounting.

As security is designed and deployed, consider the purpose or function of each device, especially clients and servers, as well as its location in one (or more) of the seven domains of a typical IT infrastructure (see Figure 5-1). Then, consider what other devices will need to communicate with it. The more vulnerable the communications pathways, the more security you will need to impose.

If both endpoints are physically located in the same facility, but the network pathway linking them involves any exterior segments, then the transaction demands greater security than a local-only communication. If the endpoints are geographically distant, then you need to use encrypted communications.

Remote and mobile devices are inherently more risky as they are exposed to a greater number of potential threats. Inside the office, most threats are known, controlled,

technical TIP

Location-aware anti-theft software periodically collects IP information and any available location data and uploads it to a centralized site. If the owner of a system reports the item lost or stolen, this automatically posted data might help recover the device. However, if the thief reformats the hard drive, then the anti-theft software might be removed.

and monitored. But mobile and remote devices are potentially exposed to unknown, uncontrolled, and unmonitored situations, data, software, and users. Being outside of the organization's facility also means less strictly controlled physical access to the device.

These changes to security and potential exposure to risks require additional protections on remote and mobile devices. These devices should continue to host antivirus scanners, anti-malware scanners, and host firewalls. But they can also benefit from whole hard drive encryption, multifactor authentication, and location-aware anti-theft software.

Remote and mobile devices are most likely to be out of compliance with security requirements, such as patch levels or application of security templates. A Network Access Control (NAC) system can isolate and quarantine devices until they have installed all the necessary patches and updates.

Even with good host management, whether local, remote, or mobile, consider redundancy requirements. Is one of something enough or just enough to cause a significant problem when it goes offline?

Redundancy

Security is not complete without adequately addressing preparedness. **Redundancy** is at the heart of preparedness. Can your organization survive downtime, blackouts, communication loss, server crashes, hard drive failure, floods, building eviction, virus infection, or any other potential threat? In most cases the ability to answer, "yes, the organization can survive" is dependent upon the level of preparedness of that organization.

Preparedness is also known as business continuity planning or disaster recovery planning. The purpose of such planning is to ensure a plan exists to recover from any realistic threat. Assess each serious threat to the stability and function of the organization. Then, develop procedures to respond to the threat. The procedure can focus on prevention or recovery (or a combination of both).

A core element throughout this form of planning is redundancy. Redundancy is the act of avoiding single points of failure by building in multiple elements, pathways, or methods of accomplishing each mission-critical task.

Redundancy works in many ways. Redundant Array of Inexpensive Disks (RAID) is a form of redundancy for hard drives. RAID protects against drive failure. Uninterruptible Power Supply (UPS) is a form of redundancy for power. UPS devices provide temporary power in the event of a brownout or blackout. A UPS can trigger a graceful shutdown to prevent loss of data if facility power is not restored promptly.

Redundancy can apply to communication pathways. Good network design requires at least two pathways to every important resource. Redundant links to and from clients may not be a strong need in most cases, but having multiple pathways to reach resources is often essential.

Redundant communication links for voice and data are also important considerations. Construction workers could accidentally dig in the wrong location and sever the primary wire bundle supporting the organization. Redundant lines to service providers could make the difference between a nuisance and a company-ending event. Do you want to leave the power of terminating your organization in the hands of outsiders?

Redundant firewalls, proxies, routers, switches, servers, and databases begin to make security and financial sense once they become an essential or mission-critical element of the IT infrastructure. Don't entrust the viability of an organization to any single component. Always have a secondary option or back-up plan.

Failing to plan is planning to fail. Hardware failures, mistakes, accidents, or intentional damage will occur in every system in an organization at some point. No organization is immune. The difference is whether an organization is prepared for the problem with a ready-to-use response solution, or will be caught off guard, scrambling to recover in a panic.

Node Security

Implementing network security is about both the big picture and the granular details. Infrastructure design, topology, and redundancy are all important big-picture items. But do not overlook the details that need attention on a node-by-node basis.

A node is any device on the network, even those without an IP address. Node security focuses on the tasks for each type of networking device to improve its security. Node security or node hardening takes the generic recommendations of system hardening and expands them with additional node/host specific improvements.

Clients

Clients are the devices directly controlled by people. Thus, clients must protect the network from the user and vice versa. Thinking of clients as two-way interfaces can assist in proper security design and implementation for this command and essential IT infrastructure component.

Every client needs the following security elements:

- Antivirus and anti-malware scanners
- Host firewall
- Secured Internet client software—browser, e-mail, file transfer, chat, and so on.
- Password-protected screen saver with auto timeout
- Ability to encrypt network communications
- Ability to encrypt storage devices
- Auditing of all user activity
- An integrity checking system that monitors for unauthorized file changes using hash value comparison

Clients should be subject to NAC procedures to prevent an insecure client from compromising the rest of the network. Use multifactor authentication whenever possible to minimize the risk of an unauthorized person gaining access to the client and hence the entire network.

Servers

Servers are the backbone of any IT infrastructure. Whether a file server, database host, e-mail server, proxy server, or authentication server, a server is usually supporting an essential or mission-critical function for the organization. Servers need protection against downtime. This can include redundancy in terms of RAID, duplicate servers, and/or clustering.

Duplicate servers means having two identically configured systems running side by side, but only one is performing services live for the network. The second system is acting as a backup and receives all data changes as they occur. In the event of the primary server failure, the secondary server can take over supporting the services for the network.

Clustering is having two or more identically configured systems running as a collective. All the systems share in supporting the live service to the network. If any member of the cluster goes offline, the remaining members continue supporting the service. Clustering allows for a service to be available consistently while still allowing for scheduled maintenance and occasional individual server downtime.

Servers need strong multifactor authentication to ensure that only administrators ever have the ability to log into them at the keyboard. You should sequester servers in a dedicated room or vault to prevent casual or intentional access by unauthorized users. Lock and monitor the server vault at all times.

Routers

Routers are an essential traffic-management device of any network. Network router security is primarily about preventing unauthorized access. First and foremost, a router should be physically inaccessible to any non-administrator. All router configuration or management interfaces must require strong authentication. Some environments have elected to eliminate local accounts on the routers themselves and rely upon Terminal Access Controller Access-Control System Plus (TACACS+) for router authentication and access.

Limit management interface access to a direct console or terminal cable connection only, rather than allowing in-network access. Require that all management interface communications and router-to-router communications be encrypted.

If a password is stored in a configuration file for the router, be sure to use an encoding scheme that is not easily cracked or reverse engineered. For example, the Cisco IOS password 7 hashing method uses a weak reversible algorithm and can be cracked easily using software tools dating back to 1997.

Generally, configure the following on the router:

- Block all directed IP broadcasts.
- Drop all packets from the Internet using an RFC 1918 source address or any other internal address.
- Disable the TCP and UDP small services of echo, chargen, discard, and daytime.
- Enable a warning banner for all attempted connections to the router, especially to the management interface.

If SNMP is used on the network, require the use of SNMP v3 that allows for encrypted transactions and authentication of SNMP sessions. Then, use custom community names rather than the default public or private communities.

Consider the software or firmware of the router. Only install full final releases, never beta or partial firmware. If you are concerned that the latest release has not been thoroughly tested in the real world, sticking with a previous release is acceptable, provided there are no published reports of critical security flaws.

Try to limit the use of a router as a filtering device. Keep the router table focused on traffic routing and implement firewalls to provide content filtering and blocking of suspicious or malicious traffic. Protect any router considered a border router with a firewall.

Switches

Switch security is similar to that of router security. Maintain control over who can physically reach the switch. Limit access to management consoles and require strong authentication to access the management interface. If a password is stored in a configuration file for the switch, be sure to use an encoding scheme not easily cracked or reverse engineered.

If SNMP is used on the network, require the use of SNMP v3 that allows for encrypted transactions and authentication of SNMP sessions. Then, use custom community names rather than the default public or private communities.

Consider the software or firmware of the switch. Only install full final releases, never beta or partial firmware. If you are concerned that the latest release has not been thoroughly tested in the real world, sticking with a previous release is acceptable, provided there are no published reports of critical security flaws.

Consider deploying switches that support IDS-like features such as watching for MAC spoofing and ARP flooding. MAC spoofing tricks a switch into thinking a hacker's computer is actually a legitimate host. The hacker steals or spoofs a legitimate MAC address. If a switch is monitoring for MAC addresses that change ports, then MAC spoofing ceases to be a serious threat, unless a hacker can physically access the port connection of the MAC he is trying to spoof.

ARP flooding overloads a switch's mapping table, so that instead of forwarding packets out the correct port the switch will default into flooding mode and transmit packets out all ports. This type of attack is part of active sniffing. Active sniffing is an attempt to eavesdrop on switched networks.

Use switch features such as Virtual Local Area Network (VLAN) support and auditing port. VLANs are hardware-imposed network segmentation. VLANs control traffic. Using VLANs to manage traffic is often cost-effective, since it does not require re-cabling or changing of IP addresses; as all of the VLAN configuration takes place within the switch.

The audit, mirror, or IDS port on a switch connects an IDS or IPS to monitor all the traffic traversing the switch. Since a switch only transmits data out the port where its intended destination resides, attempting to monitor all traffic on a switched network is not possible without the use of the auditing port.

Also, disable all unused switch ports. This prevents the easiest method of adding rogue devices to a network—namely just plugging into an open port.

Firewalls and Proxies

Firewalls and proxies defend the network, but you need to secure them, as well. Otherwise, if a hacker can compromise the firewall, then the security it provides is unreliable.

Firewalls and proxies, as with routers and switches, need physical access protection. No non-administrative user should be able to gain direct physical contact with a firewall or proxy. Limit access to management consoles and require strong authentication to access the management interface. If a password is stored in a configuration file for the firewall or proxy, be sure to use an encoding scheme not easily cracked or reverse engineered.

If simple network management protocol (SNMP) is used on the network, require the use of SNMP v3 that allows for encrypted transactions and authentication of SNMP sessions. Then, use custom community names rather than the default public or private communities.

Consider the software or firmware of the firewall or proxy. As noted earlier, only install full final releases, never beta or partial firmware. If you are concerned that the latest release has not been thoroughly tested in the real world, sticking with a previous release is acceptable, provided there are no published reports of critical security flaws.

A firewall should drop all packets addressed directly to the firewall, as the firewall does not host traditional services accessed in this manner. The same is generally true of a proxy server, but some instances apply where the proxy server is either directly communicated with or that hosts additional accessible resources.

Make a final security evaluation of any device, including firewalls, proxies, switches, routers, servers, and clients. You can perform this evaluation using an automated vulnerability scanning tool or a custom manual penetration test. The goal is to find any remaining vulnerabilities in these devices so they can be made as secure as possible, as quickly as possible.

CHAPTER SUMMARY

Network security implementation relies on a thorough understanding of your organization, its goals, its risks, and the technologies employed within your IT infrastructure. Before you can properly deploy network security, you must first design it. Most network security designs include layers of defense as well as sufficient capacity for growth.

Network security includes an evaluation of the protocols and topologies your organization uses. If the current design is insufficient, replace it with a design that addresses productivity and security. You need to assess the addressing schemes in use, whether public or private, static or dynamic, in light of how they improve or detract from security.

Other important components of network security design and deployment include controlling communication pathways; hardening systems; and selecting proper equipment, authentication, authorization, accounting, communication encryption, types of hosts, redundancy, and node security specifics.

KEY CONCEPTS AND TERMS

AppleTalk
Attack Surface
Brute force attack
Bus topology
Dictionary attack
File Transfer Protocol (FTP)
Full Mesh topology
Hybrid attack
Internet Assigned Numbers Authority (IANA)
Internetwork Packet Exchange/Sequenced Packet Exchange (IPX/SPX)
Latency
Line topology
Logical topology
Modeling
NetBIOS
NetBIOS Extended User Interface (NetBEUI)
Network News Transfer Protocol (NNTP)
Partial Mesh topology
Physical topology
Piloting
Post Office Protocol (POP)
Redundancy
Regional Internet Registry (RIR)
Ring topology
Security through obscurity
Simple Mail Transfer Protocol (SMTP)
Star topology
Subnetting
Sunk cost
Systems Network Architecture (SNA)
Telnet
Topology
Tree topology

CHAPTER 5 ASSESSMENT

1. Which of the following is *not* an important factor when included as part of network design?
   A. Usability
   B. Capacity
   C. Obscurity
   D. Growth
   E. Defense-in-depth

2. All of the following are elements of network design *except*:
   A. Satisfying security goals
   B. Understanding of the seven domains of IT infrastructure
   C. Implementing multiple layers of defense
   D. Thorough research and planning
   E. Utilizing a single vendor

3. Which IT infrastructure domain does *not* require firewalls to be included as part of its network design?
   A. Workstation domain
   B. LAN domain
   C. User domain
   D. Remote Access domain
   E. System/Application domain

4. Which of the following is a benefit of private addressing that is not present in public addressing?
   A. Isolation from the Internet
   B. Subnetting
   C. Use of IPv6
   D. Routing traffic
   E. Filtering by source and designation address

5. Why would a network implement public addresses internally instead of private addresses?
   A. Avoid the use of NAT
   B. Be able to custom subnet
   C. Maintain isolation from the Internet
   D. Prevent external initiation of communications with internal hosts
   E. Reduce costs

6. How can static addresses be simulated with DHCP?
   A. Round robin assignment
   B. Manual configuration on each host
   C. Duplicate MAC addresses
   D. Reservations
   E. DNS reverse lookup

7. Which of the following is a flaw or weakness that both static and dynamic addressing share?
   A. Assignment server can go offline
   B. Changes required manual modification on each host
   C. Public queries will fail
   D. Hackers can spoof valid addresses
   E. The first half of the address identifies the NIC vendor

8. What is a primary benefit of system hardening?
   A. It reduces user performance
   B. It increases network throughput
   C. It decreases the attack surface
   D. It improves host ROI
   E. It tracks attempted intrusions

9. All of the following are elements of system hardening *except*:
   A. Removing unnecessary protocols, services, and applications
   B. Implement ingress and egress filtering against spoofed addresses
   C. Installing patches and updates
   D. Configure encryption for storage and communication
   E. Installing antivirus and a host firewall

10. All of the following are true statements about system hardening *except*:
    A. System hardening is a one-time process that does not need to be repeated on the same host.
    B. System hardening removes or reduces many known vulnerabilities.
    C. System hardening is different for each system with a unique function.
    D. System hardening is dependent on the location or placement of a host within the seven common domains of an IT infrastructure.
    E. Any system discovered to be out of compliance with system hardening guidelines should be quarantined until it can be repaired.

11. System hardening should be applied to all of the following *except*:
    A. Clients
    B. Servers
    C. Switches
    D. Routers
    E. Cable adapters

12. Which of the following is *not* usually part of the system hardening process?
    A. Update hardware firmware or BIOS
    B. Install additional RAM
    C. Configure a backup process
    D. Configure account lockout
    E. Replace outdated device drivers

13. What is the essential purpose or function of authentication?
    A. Control access to resources
    B. Monitor for security compliance
    C. Watch levels of performance
    D. Verify entity identity
    E. Prevent distribution of malware

14. What is the essential purpose or function of authorization?
    A. Grant or deny access to resources
    B. Check policy compliance
    C. Identify entities
    D. Monitor levels of utilization
    E. Detect spoofed content

15. What is the essential purpose or function of accounting?
    A. Detect intrusions
    B. Prove identity
    C. Control access to assets
    D. Record the activities and events within a system
    E. Throttle transactions

16. What is the essential purpose or function of encryption?
    A. Verify integrity
    B. Prove the identity of endpoints
    C. Protect content from unauthorized third parties
    D. Maintain performance
    E. Validate parking

17. A remote host has all of the following additional security issues or concerns in comparison with a local host *except*:
    A. Potential exposure to unfiltered Internet
    B. Poor end user training
    C. Greater risk of physical theft
    D. Possible lack of patches and updates
    E. Additional interaction with external entities

18. Which of the following is a protection against a single point of failure?
    A. Encryption
    B. Filtering
    C. Auditing
    D. Redundancy
    E. VPNs

19. When performing node security on a router, all of the following are important concerns, *except*:
    A. Block all directed IP broadcasts
    B. Disable echo, chargen, discard, and daytime
    C. Watch for MAC spoofing
    D. Drop RFC 1918 addressed packets from the Internet
    E. Enable a warning banner for all attempted connections

20. When configuring node security on a switch, all of the following are important elements *except*:
    A. Enable keystroke logging
    B. Limit access to management interfaces
    C. Monitor for ARP flooding
    D. Upgrade to SNMP v3
    E. Use a final version of firmware

CHAPTER 6

Network Security Management

COMPUTER NETWORK SECURITY is not a final solution or a task to be completed. Security is a continuous journey. Safeguards and infrastructures that worked before might offer little or no protection against future attacks. You must constantly develop and deploy new defenses against new exploits. This vigilance is the essence of network security management.

Network security management strives to maintain established security, adjust the infrastructure to future threats, and respond to breaches in a timely manner. Using a variety of techniques and tools, including incident response, host security, backup and recovery, checklists, and security assessment, network security management is a complex, but essential component of long-term, reliable security.

Chapter 6 Topics

This chapter will cover the following topics and concepts:

- What best practices for network security management are
- What fail-secure, fail-open, or fail-close options are
- What the important elements of physical security are
- Why is it essential to watch for compromise
- What incident response is
- How to trap intruders and violators
- What containment is
- How to impose compartmentalization
- How to use honeypots, honeynets, and padded cells
- What some essential host security controls are
- How to properly implement backup and recovery
- What the importance of user training and awareness is

- What some important network security management tools are
- How to create and use a security checklist
- What the basics of network security troubleshooting are
- What compliance auditing is
- What security assessment is
- What a configuration scan is
- What vulnerability scanning is
- What the purpose of penetration testing is
- Why post-mortem assessment review is important

Chapter 6 Goals

Upon completion of this chapter, you will be able to:

- List examples of network security "best practices."
- Describe the importance of physical security.
- Compose a procedure for incident response.
- Enumerate key components of an effective network security installation.
- Describe the methods of network security assessment.

Network Security Management Best Practices

Network security management "best practices" are recommendations, guidelines, or standard operating procedures for obtaining reasonable security on a real-world budget. Best practices are usually not specific recommendations for products or tools; instead, they are recommendations for philosophies, stances, or concepts to use. The following items are suggested "best practices." These might not apply to every environment, although you should consider, adapt, or adopt each when appropriate.

The foundation of any security endeavor and the start of security best practices is having a written plan. A written security policy has no substitute. Any other method, any other process, and other attempted procedure for defining, implementing, and managing security will fail. Only a written security policy has the potential to succeed.

To have a plan, you must thoroughly understand your organization's infrastructure, its mission and goals, and the processes necessary to produce its products and services. This means understanding what technology your co-workers need and use, what assets are involved, what resources are consumed, where everything resides, and how users access the infrastructure. Consider larger and more complex environments in light of the typical IT infrastructure.

A written security policy establishes a documentation trail that everyone in the organization can subscribe to. To write a comprehensive security policy, you must first thoroughly inventory and examine every component of the IT infrastructure. Only once you fully understand the environment can you create a comprehensive and effective security policy.

To create a useful and relevant security policy, perform a risk assessment. The process of understanding assets, vulnerabilities, threats, and likelihoods is the heart of risk assessment. You learned about some of the basic formulas of risk assessment in Chapter 2.

Once you have designed and deployed a written security policy, regularly review the policy. Investigate whether the overall quality and reliability of the existing security is sufficient or in need of improvement. Verify that assets are still properly protected. Evaluate whether prevention, deterrence, and response have been adequate and effective. Wherever you discover a deficiency, act to improve and rectify the situation immediately.

Security cannot succeed without the solid endorsement and support of senior management. Executives should support the security policy, follow the limitations themselves, and stand behind the decisions made by you and the IT staff. When the security staff and the executives are focused on the same goal, solutions will follow. When these two groups are not working in concert, time, money, and effort go to waste, and network security fails.

Establish a no-exceptions policy. Every device connecting to the company network must be in full compliance with the security policy and current with approved patches and updates. Block any device not in compliance with these restrictions from interacting with the network. This effectively is the function of a NAC (network access/admission control) service. But it should also be a written element of the security policy. Define "no exceptions" in writing, and then use technology to enforce this element of the plan.

Maintain physical security control over all personnel access to IT equipment. Block access to all servers or networking equipment to all non-administrative users. Limit access to client systems to authorized personnel within each department. Ensure that departments are separated by locked doors. Limit visitor, consultant, and other authorized non-employee access primarily through a mandatory escort system. More suggestions about physical security are included in a later section in this chapter.

Limit and filter Internet connectivity. In spite of many users' desire for an unrestricted, unmonitored Internet connection for personal use, the Internet poses a significant risk for most organizations. An unrestricted or unfiltered Internet connection is a pathway for malicious code, social engineering attacks, and intrusion attempts. If an Internet service, protocol, domain, or IP address is not essential to a necessary business task, block it. Computer access to the organization's network and assets is for work tasks, not personal activities.

Install antivirus scanners, anti-malware scanners, and firewalls on every host. Every portable device, every desktop workstation, and every server should have these malicious code and malicious traffic protections. No system is immune to malware and malicious communications; basic filters and barriers to known issues prevent easily avoidable compromises and downtime. Antivirus and other host essentials are discussed further later in this chapter.

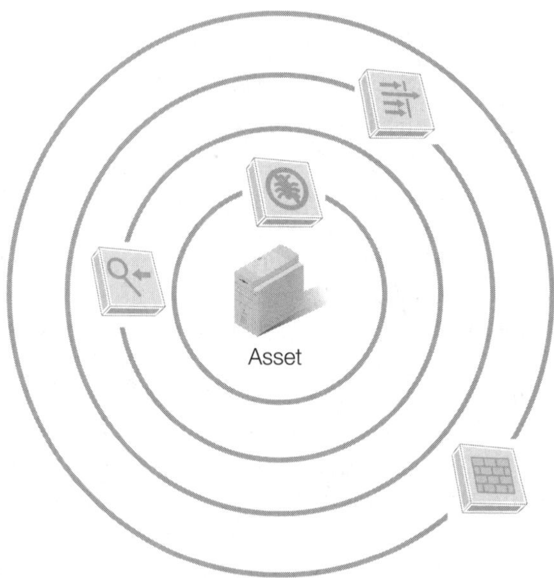

FIGURE 6-1
An example of defense in depth around an asset.

Do not rely upon single or individual defenses. Attempt to interlock and layer defenses. Implement defense-in-depth or a multiple-layered defense wherever possible (Figure 6-1). By following a defense-in-depth design concept, you will protect each asset with numerous safeguards. As one defense tool interlocks with another, they overlap—like medieval armor plate—and improve the overall security. The strengths and benefits of one countermeasure can supplement or compensate for the weaknesses and limitations of another.

When possible, avoid remote access. Limit access to local direct connections only. When remote access is necessary, require a virtual private network (VPN). Once you allow remote connectivity, you allow the possibility of remote hacking. Remote hacking attempts to breach security without the need to be physically at or within the target's facilities. Requiring VPNs for all remote connections reduces this threat by preventing open connections or communications vulnerable to eavesdropping.

Any device that is portable or easily accessible by a non-employee should use **whole hard drive encryption** or at least **file encryption**. While not absolutely foolproof, encrypting an entire hard drive makes accessing the data on a portable device much more complex. If a system is stolen when powered off, the hard drive's encryption typically presents an insurmountable barrier. If the equipment is running when stolen, a hacker might bypass the hard drive encryption by hacking the encryption key out of active memory. However, this is an unlikely attack.

Require encryption of all internal network communications. Use Internet Protocol Security (IPSec) to secure all intranet communications. This is often an easy and cost-effective means to quickly reduce the risk of eavesdropping, man-in-the-middle, replay, and many other forms of network attacks. Well-encrypted data is much less likely to fall into the hands of hackers, thieves, and unauthorized personnel.

Harden both internal hosts as well as border devices. Do not focus exclusively on one area or issue of security to the exclusion of all others. Provide consistent and thorough security throughout the IT infrastructure. All networked devices are at risk, perhaps from different threats, but still at risk.

Always test new code before deployment onto a production system. No matter what the source of new code, you must test it. Even if an internal programmer wrote the code, you must test it. Even if the code addresses a **mission-critical** issue, you must test it. Test all new code without exceptions. Any and all untested code is unauthorized and you should block it from all production systems.

Implement multi-factor authentication whenever possible. **Single-factor authentication**, especially password-based authentication, is no longer a truly secure or sufficient method of protecting the logon process. Adding at least one additional factor significantly increases the authentication security of the environment. Once multi-factor authentication begins, allow no exceptions that fall back on single-factor solutions. Otherwise, intrusion efforts will focus on the single-factor pathway.

Backup, backup, backup. Backups are the best form of insurance against data loss. Don't store backups on the same system or even in the same locale as your other assets. Store backups on separate storage devices. While you can store backups both onsite and offsite, offsite is the preferred secure location in the event of natural or manmade disasters. Backup and recovery are covered in more detail later in this chapter.

If an asset is worth the time and effort to secure, then it's worth monitoring as well. Lock each asset as necessary, and then watch for attempted breaches of that security. No perfect security solutions exist; thus, to improve security, prepare to respond immediately when you detect breaches. Lock, then watch. Failing to watch a secured asset means that when a compromise occurs, you won't notice immediately. Watching for compromise is discussed further later in this chapter.

Have an intrusion and **incident response plan**. Bad things and failures will happen. Breaches will take place. Be prepared. Evaluate and examine the realistic threats facing your assets. But plan for the worst. Define procedures to respond to any situation. Incident response is addressed further later in this chapter.

Do not overlook making a **business continuity plan** and a **disaster recovery plan**. Above and beyond security breaches are business-terminating events in the form of natural and manmade disasters. Building collapse, flooding, earthquakes, hurricanes, fire, sabotage, blackouts, malware infection, criminal activities, and so on can end your organization's operations. If alternate means of accomplishing mission-critical tasks are not available, your organization will cease to exist. Plan to recover from disasters and do business in the future.

KISS—Keep It Simple: Security. Security is complex enough without purposefully imposing additional complexity. Focus on designing security that the average user can comply with easily and simply. The more arcane and cryptic procedures become, the greater chance that users will misunderstand, fail to comply, or purposefully subvert. Simplicity encourages compliance.

Focus on balancing security and usability. Security does not need to make all work difficult. Likewise, essential work functions need not compromise security. Finding a balance between these two extremes is important. The focus should be on reducing risk to the infrastructure, while enabling users to perform authorized work with a minimum of hassle.

Prioritize. Security concerns will always seem to be ready to overwhelm available time, effort, or budget. Focus on the big impact and big result issues first, rather than attempting to swat every minor annoyance that arises. Security is constantly changing; the goal is to maintain reasonable rather than perfect security. (Remember, this is an unattainable goal anyway!)

Always be fully and truly aware of the state of the organizational security. Don't make assumptions. If you are not positive that an aspect of the organization is secure, find out. Assuming security exists leads to a false sense of safety. A lack of knowledge about the security status can lead to complacency. By assuming nothing is wrong, you feel no urgency to investigate and rectify problems. Do not fall into the "I thought it was protected" trap; if you do not know or are not sure, take the time to investigate and be sure.

Look for the weakest link. Every system or structure has a weak point and a security structure is no different. It might be power; it could be humans; it might be a coding issue; it could be processing capacity, or any number of other potential culprits. In any case, some weakest link exists in the security chain. Think like a hacker and look for it. Find it. Improve it. Then, go looking for the next weakest link.

Focus on known, real, probable threats rather than on unknown, imagined, or possible threats. You don't have enough time, energy, or budget to protect against everything. Perform a risk assessment and focus on current, significant issues.

Develop a standardized, procedural-based process for hardening new systems. You should subject every new piece of host equipment, including switches, routers, firewalls, servers, and clients to a rigorous and thorough hardening process before it is deployed onto the production network. In fact, having a dedicated isolated new system-testing network will protect both the existing production network from new systems, as well as protect new systems from threats from the existing production network.

Develop and implement an efficient **patch management** system. You need to analyze, evaluate, and install promptly every new patch released from your vendors, whether for hardware or software. Never short-circuit the test-all-code-before deployment policy and never implement code based on fear. Instead, have a focused and efficient process for testing and approving new updates so that they can be rolled out to production systems quickly. Keep every system current on patches; remember, however, that pushing out a patch too soon and without proper testing is just as bad as delaying patch approval because you lack the time to examine it.

User training and behavior modification is essential. Technology cannot solve or remedy all security concerns. Technology cannot compensate for the human factor. Be sure to train all authorized personnel on general security concepts as well as task-specific security concerns. Train users on what policy expects, define what policy prohibits, and encourage buy-in and support of the overall organizational security effort. User training is addressed further later in this chapter.

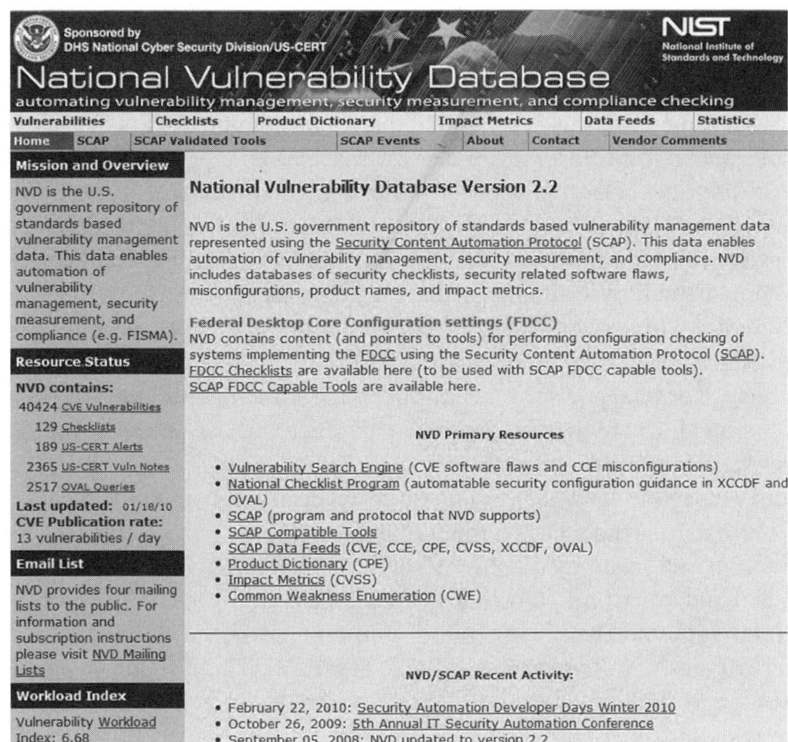

FIGURE 6-2

National Institute of Standards and Technology (NIST): National Vulnerability Database.

Stay current on security and vulnerability research. You can't protect against existing, new, and upcoming threats unless you know what they are. You need to seek out this information, because most general news sources, even those focusing on technology, don't address most of the security vulnerabilities, exploits, or compromises that arise daily. Find good resources-related security and vulnerability research (Figure 6-2) and consult it religiously. Knowledge is often one of the best weapons in the fight for security.

Develop a security checklist. Review it for completeness and accuracy periodically, such as every quarter. Confirm every element on the checklist on a regular and frequent basis, such as once a week or once a day. You can automate this to an extent, but checking often requires human effort to test and confirm that every security mechanism is in place, active, armed, and effective. Security checklists are discussed further later in this chapter.

Perform regular self-assessments. Numerous security groups and government/military agencies post security implementation guidelines, manuals, and checklists. Commonly known as **Security Technical Implementation Guides (STIGs)**, you can use these documents to review and assess your organization's status and state of security. A self-assessment attempts to take an external, unique, or independent viewpoint in evaluating security. This is why using external security guidelines, standards, and measurements can reveal oversights in an existing security infrastructure.

Perform internal **compliance audits**. Thinking you are secure isn't enough; the law in many industries such as financial and medical now require compliance. Ensuring that you are in full compliance with all federal and state laws and regulations is not only good security management; it will keep your company officials out of jail. Using external auditors is often a poor substitute for internal self-verification.

Implement the **principle of least privilege**. All users, including administrators, only need the necessary privileges, access, and permissions to accomplish their assigned work. Any abilities beyond this minimum increase the potential for compromise and abuse.

Isolate and compartmentalize administrative privileges through the implementation of **separation of duties**. This is also known as split knowledge. Administrators are given limited administrative power over a limited area of the IT infrastructure. No single administrator has full or total power over the entire environment. This limits the scope of potential abuse and harm both by disgruntled administrators, as well as by hackers who compromise administrative accounts.

Test all security measures for sufficiency. Perform verification scans of all deployed countermeasures to ensure their correct functioning. Improper installation or misconfiguration can render a well-meaning safeguard worthless. Test every new security control when you install it and every time you reconfigure it.

Perform regular vulnerability assessments. Use automated tools with updated databases of security tests and exploit simulations. These tools should confirm patches and updates, verify security configurations, and probe for known vulnerabilities and exploit weaknesses. Quickly resolve any issues discovered by the scans.

After you have improved and fine-tuned your security infrastructure, put it to the ultimate test: perform penetration testing. Hire or develop an ethical hacking team to test the strength and weaknesses of the IT security as well as the security of the facilities and the employees. Ethical hackers use the same tools and attack techniques as criminals, but without the intention to cause actual damage. Professional security assessors can customize attacks, modify exploits, and react in real-time to fully stress security defenses.

Focus on the core security services when designing security: confidentiality, integrity, availability. Failing to properly and adequately buttress these essential security services will result in damage, data loss, and downtime. Confidentiality is the prevention of unauthorized access, but supports authorized access. Integrity is the protection against unauthorized modifications. Availability is the assurance that resources are accessible in a timely manner.

Consider designing security, especially physical security, around three central functions: deter, detect, and delay. Deterrence is the use of security to convince the potential attacker that the efforts to compromise a system are not worth it. The attack may be perceived as too hard or too complex, the attempt too easy to detect, and the consequences too severe. Detection is to watch for the attempts at breaching security so as to respond promptly. Delay is to slow down the attack so that even successful breaches give the defenders time to respond in order to apprehend or prevent further intrusion.

Another common trio of parameters for security design and implementation is prevention, detection, and response. Prevention is the use of safeguards to thwart exploitation or compromise. It is usually more efficient, easier, and cost effective to prevent intrusions and breaches rather than react to them. Immediate detection of attempted and successful security breaches is important. The longer the time span between a malicious action and authoritative response, the greater the likelihood the perpetrator will get away without consequence. Response means being prepared to contain damage, restrict further compromise, and effect repairs to return the system to normal.

Don't overlook the importance of authentication, authorization, and accounting. These services are essential to a secured infrastructure. You must control who is allowed into a facility and onto the network. Place limitations on what authorized users can do. Hold all entities—even upper level management—accountable for their actions, activities, and results.

Focus on establishing a philosophy of **default deny** rather than **default permit.** By blocking everything as a starting point, only those features, services, protocols, ports, applications, users, and so on that you judge and deem safe and appropriate can be enabled by exception. A default-permit stance means you must create a never-ending stream of explicit denials as you detect new compromises or malicious events. Deny by default, allow by exception is always the preferred security stance.

Implement white-list application control. A white list is a list of allowed exceptions against a background of default deny. By configuring a system with a white list, you block all executables unless they are on the list of allowed exceptions. A white list consists of the application name, its file name, and the file's hash value. This prevents spoofing by malicious or unapproved applications that simply rename the executable.

This collection of network security management "best practices" should serve as a starting point for the development of your effective security endeavors. Other valid and useful guidelines exist, so don't assume this list of recommendations—or any other list from any other source—is exhaustive. You always have new lessons to learn, new challenges to face, and new wisdom to obtain.

Fail-Secure, Fail-Open, Fail-Close Options

Failure is not an option, it's a certainty. At some point in the life of your organization, failure will happen. Will you be prepared to handle it properly, and how much harm will the failure cause?

Failures can be hardware ceasing to operate properly due to an unknown flaw in materials or construction. Failures can be the accidental discharge of static that damages circuits. Failures can be atypical weather that floods the building. Failures can be malware infection that crashes a server. Failures can be a zero-day exploit that compromises security from outside.

Failure means problems, downtime, loss, consequences. However, failures do not have to mean bankruptcy, going-out-of-business, jail time, or catastrophic loss. The difference between calamity and mere inconvenience is planning. As with most aspects of security, proper and extensive planning can assist in designing an infrastructure that can avoid or effectively survive any issue or concern.

Planning for failure is planning how to respond to and recover from failures. The goal is to fail into a state of security or safety rather than into a state of insecurity or chaos. This is known as fail-secure. A fail-secure state reverts to a condition where little or no harm, or at least no further harm, is likely to happen. Depending on the situation, a fail-secure state could be fail-open or fail-close.

To fail-open is to revert to a state of being open, available, or unlocked. In the case of the physical world, fail-open is important for the safety of personnel. Fail-open doors allow people to leave a building easily. However, such easily opened doors might represent a weakness that an intruder could exploit to access secured internal areas. In the case of IT, fail-open is to revert to a state of unfiltered communication or data access.

To fail-close is to revert to a state of being closed, unavailable, or locked. In the case of the physical world, to fail-close is to prevent a doorway or container from being opened during an emergency or compromise. In the case of IT, fail-close blocks access to communications and other digital resources.

Either state, fail-open or fail-close, can be the fail-secure or fail-safe option depending on the circumstances. In any case, you should carefully consider and plan the type of default response you will use, especially during an emergency, intrusion, compromise, or system failure.

Physical Security

There is no security without physical security. Logical protections can only protect against logical attacks. Physical protections protect against physical attacks. With just a few moments of physical contact, a hacker can overcome or bypass most logical security.

Physical security is the prevention of direct physical contact, access, or influence of an unauthorized person to a sensitive component of an IT infrastructure. Any well-designed network security solution will include physical security components. If you fail to address physical security adequately, you fail to understand the threats facing your organization.

Physical security includes a facility that resists forcible entry. Select, improve, or build facilities that prevent and deter unauthorized physical intrusion. If physical breaking and entering is possible and potentially profitable for a thief, it's more likely to take place.

Physical security should include the monitoring of all personnel activity. Solid physical access control includes keeping track of when an employee enters and exits every secured or sensitive area. Good physical access control blocks outsider access and enforces escorts for visitors.

Physical security should include card key entry, burglar alarms, motion detectors, and security cameras. Use the best available technology to both deter and detect physical security violations.

Watching for Compromise

Everyone in your organization is part of the physical security effort. Every individual is responsible for staying within the security boundaries themselves. They are also responsible for reporting violations or suspicious activity. Security is about locking and watching. Not every employee can assist in the process of locking things down, but they can and should all assist with watching for violations and suspicious behaviors.

Use all available technologies in addition to human eyes to look for security violations. Use auditing, IDS/IPS systems, security cameras, motion detectors, and so on when appropriate. Proper network security management includes proper design to watch for violations.

Violations can occur both in the physical world as well as within the logical world of computers, networking, and the Internet. Don't assume that just because a violation causes no direct physical harm that the issue is not worth knowing about or pursuing. A crime is still a crime whether it's a physical crime or a logical one. Design and implement detection mechanisms to notice, log, and monitor suspicious or abnormal activities.

Incident Response

Incident response is the planned reaction to negative situations or events. Inevitably, security breaches, or at least attempts to breach security, are going to occur. When those events affect the organization or its abilities to perform its tasks in any way, incident response is triggered. The goals of incident response are to minimize downtime, minimize loss, and restore the environment back to a secured normal state as quickly as possible.

Most incident response solutions include six primary steps or phases:

- **Preparation**—Select and train IRT (incident response team) members, allocate resources
- **Detection**—Confirm actual breaches
- **Containment**—Restrain further escalation
- **Eradication**—Resolve the compromise
- **Recovery**—Return to normal operation
- **Follow-up**—Review the process and improve future responses

An incident response plan is an important element of network security management.

Trapping Intruders and Violators

Security often aims at prevention and deterrence. When an intrusion or security violation takes place in spite of the precautions, the next stage or level of security must respond. The next stage of security is detection. Knowing if and when a security violation occurs is essential to a timely and adequate response to a breach.

Once you detect a breach, you must immediately initiate a response. The first stage of response is containment. The goal of containment is to prevent further spread of a known malicious event. Containment is a mind-set, a plan of action, and an element of design. As a mind-set, containment is the focus of first responders or members of the IRT. Their goal is to prevent any expansion or spread of the compromise to other systems.

Why Containment Is Important

Using containment can be as simple as unplugging a network cable from a compromised system. This effectively cuts off any communication to and from the suspect host. You can also impose containment through disabling user accounts, stopping services, adding entries to filtering devices, and so on. Whatever the vector or source of the malicious event, its source or target should be cut off from causing continued harm.

The act of containment should interrupt or interfere with the continued spread or operation of the unwanted event. This type of initial response is often effective against malicious code, remote access, backdoor control, compromised user account, social engineering, and many other forms of network or system compromise.

Containment is often considered a form of response. Containment is the action taken by a first responder. However, even before you experience a security breach, you can employ another preventative measure similar to containment known as compartmentalization.

Imposing Compartmentalization

Compartmentalization is the element of infrastructure design that takes into account the likelihood of a security breach by malicious code or other intruder. Compartmentalization distinctly separates a network into areas or zones of access. Often these zones are around departments or entities that commonly interact over the network. Any entity that does not commonly interact is separated by default using network security access control devices, such as routers, switches, and firewalls.

The purpose of compartmentalization is to create small collectives of systems that support work tasks while minimizing risk. The typical risk is that if one system is compromised, the breach can quickly lead to other systems being compromised. This is especially true of malicious code, which distributes rapidly. But it can also apply to remote hacker intrusion as they attempt to leap from system to system searching out valuable resources.

Network compartmentalization is similar to the bulkheads on ships. In the event of a hull leak, the bulkhead doors of the affected compartment close and seal. This prevents the entire ship from being sunk by a single breach. The same is true for computer network compartmentalization. When you detect a breach, you can sever the links between network compartments to prevent any further malicious communication to or from the affected sections.

Using Honeypots, Honeynets, and Padded Cells

Another specific intruder trap you can add to a security infrastructure is a honeypot. A honeypot is a hacker or intruder trap. A honeypot is a system or network that appears to contain valuable information, and appears to be part of legitimate organizational network, but, in fact, it's a specially designed trap. The purpose of a honeypot is to trap hackers/intruders, detect new attacks, or simply serve as a decoy to deflect attacks from reaching the actual primary network.

A honeypot can be a single system or a network of many systems constructed to look, act, and operate like a real network environment, but that contains seemingly attractive but actually fake resources. For a honeypot to be effective, it must look and act just like a real target. Otherwise, hackers will quickly uncover the fake and search harder to find the real targets. A honeypot often includes extensive focus auditing and recording capabilities to thoroughly capture all activities that take place within it.

Honeypots can be single systems or multiple networked systems. A network of honeypots is sometimes called a **honeynet**. Both honeypots and honeynets are decoy systems that are always operating in the hopes of attracting would-be hackers and intruders. Another form of honeypot is the **padded cell**. The padded cell is turned on only after you detect an intruder, and then lure the intruder into entering the padded cell.

Configure and situate honeypots so that they do not interfere with authorized users performing authorized activities. However, you need to position them along common pathways of access that an outsider or intruder might take, in much the same way a hunter will hide along a trail in the forest. A honeypot should be attractive and interesting enough to persuade a hacker to attack it, but not too attractive as to trigger that voice in the back of the hacker's mind that says, "It's a trap."

A honeypot has value in two primary circumstances. First, if the organization's primary goal is to learn about new hacking exploits, then a honeypot can serve as a laboratory for that purpose. Second, if the organization's primary goal is to prosecute criminals, then a honeypot may assist in the discovery, identification, and apprehension of suspects. However, if neither of these two purposes is a primary goal of the organization, then deploying a honeypot is generally not a worthwhile endeavor.

Essential Host Security Controls

Every host needs protections from its users as well as from the network it communicates with. There are always risks, even within a private network, from authorized users. Precautions include equipping host devices with reasonable defenses against known potential avenues of compromise.

Every host needs an antivirus scanner. While in a few operating systems malicious code is not as serious a threat as in others, hackers create malware for every platform. You can no longer safely claim immunity based on your operating system selection alone.

An antivirus scanner needs to be current. The scanner engine, the core mechanisms for malware detection, should be less than a year old. Typically, a deployed antivirus should have the current year in its name or as its build date. Any antivirus scanner more than a year old is too out of date with new and current scanning technologies, malicious embedding techniques, and cleanup or removal procedures.

An antivirus scanner needs to have its database of definitions updated at least once per day. This should be an automated process so that as soon as the vendor releases a new update, it is downloaded and applied. Using a scanner with an old database is just as bad as using an old scanner. An antivirus product only provides protection against known threats, so don't allow your antivirus software to develop amnesia from delayed updates.

An antivirus scanner must be configured to perform constant, consistent, and automatic scans. Monitor the memory, processing stack, and any other active element of a computer system in real-time for symptoms of malicious code compromise. When malware reaches a host, it can infect that host and distribute its spawn in moments. Without real-time monitoring for infections, serious damage can take place long before a periodic scan notices the breach.

An antivirus scanner should be configured to perform complete, systemwide, low-level scans across all memory and storage devices on a periodic basis, every day or at least once a week. By scanning the entire system on a regular basis, you can detect and remove malware that was able to gain access through some unmonitored or covert channel.

In addition to an antivirus scanner, hosts should benefit from an anti-malware scanner. An anti-malware scanner is also known as a spyware or adware scanner. These are companion scanning products to antivirus software in that they find other forms of malicious, nuisance, or suspicious code that might not qualify as a virus or worm. Their targets include spyware, adware, keystroke loggers, rootkits, hacker tools, backdoors, Trojan horses, malicious/abnormal cookies, suspicious mobile code, bots, zombies, and so on. Don't let the names fool you. All of these things represent the potential for real network damage.

Every host should be equipped with a software host firewall. A host firewall provides filtering services for data entering and leaving the local box. A host firewall can limit network connectivity for local applications as well as allow or deny access to resources from external entities. Please review chapters 2, 7 through 10, and 13 for more details on the benefits of host firewalls.

Most hosts can benefit from the added security of whole hard drive encryption. This ensures that all data on the drive is secured. Depending on the product and technology you employ, whole hard drive encryption can be unlocked through a boot password or the use of a hardware device, such as a USB drive or a **Trusted Platform Module (TPM)** chip. Whole hard drive encryption essentially prevents a hard drive from being stolen and easily read by another system.

Some forms of system and file damage occur from activities that are not malware related. Using a hash integrity checking mechanism to watch for unauthorized file changes can assist in tracking down abnormal sources of compromise. Monitor every system file and device driver. Any change not associated with installation of a valid update is likely a symptom of malicious activity.

You should configure and review auditing on all hosts, not just servers. Malicious activities and communications can take place on any system. Configure every host to audit, monitor, and log local and network events. Then, using an intrusion detection system (IDS) or other form of security auditing tool, scan the log files for symptoms of concern. What you do not know can harm you, so arm yourself with as much knowledge as possible.

Backup and Recovery

Backup, backup, backup. There is no excuse for lacking a backup solution. Backups are the only insurance against data loss. Failing to make a backup is planning for failure and data loss. A single data loss incident, such as a failed hard drive, could be enough to cause the failure of an organization. Do not lose data because of carelessness; implement a backup process immediately.

Backups are not difficult. They just take a bit of planning. First, plan where you want to store the backups. The three main choices are online, offsite, or onsite.

Online or cloud backup storage is growing in popularity, availability, and cost effectiveness. Online backups offer access to your data from any Internet connection, making recovery possible from anywhere. However, online backups put your data on someone else's hardware and you are dependent on their security, confidentiality assurance, and reliability. Plus, backup transfer speeds are dependent on the local Internet link speed, which is usually much slower than most local media backup options.

Offsite and onsite storage employ the use of backup media. Backup media can be tapes, optical disks, hard drives, and solid state drives/cards. Physical media require space for storage and are subject to the threats of physical existence, namely theft, damage, and destruction. Offsite storage is the better option when faced with major catastrophes. This protects your backup media from damage by problems occurring at your primary work location. Onsite storage provides for quick recoveries around minor issues.

Mid- to large-sized organizations often elect a multi-staged backup solution that provides both onsite and offsite storage benefits. One possible configuration is to use banks of re-writable high-speed optical storage devices to host a live online onsite backup. Then perform periodic backups from the optical storage set to portable media, such as tapes, for secure storage offsite.

This configuration provides for fast backup from the original systems to the optical media, then provides a convenient process for creating tape copies quickly. It also allows for fast restoration of data from the online onsite optical backup, while providing major disaster protection with the offsite secure storage of tapes.

As much as possible, automate the backup process to ensure that it happens. If the act of backing up the network's data interferes with production, then install a secondary network to exclusively support data transfer for backups. This will require a second network interface in every system protected through the backup process.

The offsite storage location for backup media should be secure and reasonably protected from disasters, especially severe weather. If your organization is large enough to have multiple locations, rather than the same building or even buildings within a few blocks of each other, then offsite storage can switch from third party storage to internal storage at distant branch locations.

User Training and Awareness

User **training** is an essential part of any security endeavor. Not every worker in an organization is automatically an IT or technology expert, nor should you expect them to be. Security training and **awareness** aims at providing all users with basic security knowledge as well as job-specific security information.

To hold users accountable for their actions, first clearly define the network security policy boundaries and limitations. Having a set of rules and restrictions without informing personnel of their existence won't enforce policy and can lead to employee grievances. Training and awareness is necessary to educate users on their responsibilities and the consequences for violating organizational policy.

Without adequate security education for users, maintaining a secured environment is difficult, if not impossible. However, many organizations fail to support end-user training adequately. This results in users not understanding the importance, need, and benefits of security. Additionally, it will result in an increase in violations, most of which are benign and accidental, but incidents that nonetheless you will need to investigate and resolve.

A few common end-user security mistakes or problems caused by a lack of security training include:

- Opening e-mail attachments from unknown sources or from a known source with an unexpected or unusual attachment
- Preventing updates and patches from installing, even when approved and recommended by the security staff
- Installing unapproved software on work computers, including games, screensavers, utilities, instant messaging clients, and browser plug-ins
- Installing software on work computers that you have not verified as safe and free from malicious code
- Failing to make backups of personal data or work data on work computers
- Using a modem or wireless connection from a desktop or notebook work computer while still connected to the company LAN
- Using a password storage/tracking utility that does not encrypt its database
- Walking away from computers while still logged in

- Connecting unknown and unapproved devices to a work computer
- Using portable media and storage devices on a work computer from an external source
- Installing remote control or remote access software on work computers without obtaining approval
- Using the same password on multiple systems
- Leaving portable devices in locations outside of work where they could be easily stolen, such as in a car's backseat

These are just some examples of common security problems caused by untutored users. You can avoid or at least minimize most of these issues with reasonable user security education. However, it's also common for IT staff to make security mistakes, even though they are much more knowledgeable about technology. Just because someone is a "tech guy" or might be considered a computer geek does not necessarily imply he or she is security smart as well.

Some mistakes made by technology experts (who really should know better) include:

- Using the same password on multiple systems
- Allowing new systems to go online before they are properly hardened and/or tested
- Failing to keep current with available patches and upgrades, especially those related to security
- Using remote system and device management mechanisms that are convenient but not secure, such as telnet, http, and ftp
- Discussing passwords over the phone, including changing passwords based on over-the-phone requests
- Failing to properly check identity, authority, and permission before giving out information or access to resources
- Failing to implement a proper backup solution
- Not verifying and testing backups are working properly
- Assuming something is secured or properly configured without specifically checking and verifying
- Allowing unnecessary and potentially insecure applications, services, and protocols to remain on a system
- Using security and network devices with their default settings, such as firewalls, proxies, routers, and so on.
- Failing to understand all of the security configuration options on a new software or hardware product
- Putting new software or hardware into production before thoroughly testing and gaining approval
- Allowing anti-malware defenses to become out of date or go stale
- Allowing sensitive information to be communicated without an encrypted channel

Even a knowledgeable technical professional can learn how to be more secure through proper training and awareness **education**. Every single person throughout an organization has security responsibilities. These need to be defined, explained, and taught. Users will improve their behaviors once they understand what the risks are, what is at stake, and how their behavior will affect them if they fail to support security.

The goal of security-related training is user behavior modification. Users need to take steps to change their regular activities from those that place themselves and their workplace at risk to those that avoid risk. Risk is easy for most people to understand, but they need to be made aware of risk to trigger a change in their actions.

Good user training will cause an improvement in user compliance with the standards, policies, procedures, and guidelines of your organization. Often, the beginning of security training is awareness. Awareness is introductory, foundational, and ubiquitous security information that applies to all employees. Awareness aims at establishing a common baseline of security understanding for the entire organization.

The principal means of awareness training is in a classroom setting. It should, however, include a wide variety of communications, including online videos, interactive Web sites, posters, e-mail reminders, regular memos or newsletters, wall banners, coffee mugs, post-it notes, manager review meetings, loudspeaker announcements, screen savers, mouse pads, and even voice mail messages. The point is to inform users about basic security essentials, then reinforce those basics while they are at work.

Awareness is important for all personnel, in all job positions, at every level of access, from top to bottom of an organization. Everyone should understand and comprehend basic security issues. These often focus on general responsibilities, liability, seeking to avoid waste and fraud, reduction of unauthorized activities, and looking out for abnormal or suspicious events.

It's important for employees to see through both words and deeds that security is important. This means that even top executives must be held accountable to the same basic principles enforced throughout the general employee population. If employees see evidence of compromise or compliance avoidance by senior management, then they get the impression that the rules are not important enough for anyone to follow. You don't want employees to be frustrated and confused by a "Do as I say, not as I do" management model.

After awareness comes training. Training focuses on security issues and topics more closely related to specific job tasks. Training consists therefore of job-specific security information. Security training of this type assists users in accomplishing their individual work tasks while staying within the boundaries of the security infrastructure.

Most organizations offer in-house awareness and training. This is common because such training directly reduces incidents and the associated costs of handling and responding to internal accidental and ignorance-based breaches.

Beyond training is security education. This form of learning has a broader scope than just a job description or even the organization as a whole. The purpose of security education is to obtain extensive knowledge about security and related subjects, even if they don't directly apply to current work responsibilities or tasks. Education is for the advancement of the individual, perhaps to improve their career outlook.

Education is usually obtained outside of an organization. A company might perceive education as either a threat to employee retention or a benefit to keep employees happy. Most organizations want to improve the skills of their personnel. Either way, security education improves the knowledge and skill of the individual.

Security awareness, training, and education are beneficial for any security endeavor. Including and funding it in your organization's overall security solution will improve your odds of success.

Network Security Management Tools

The best network security management tools are neither commercial nor open-source products or solutions. Instead, the best network security management tools are quite simple and obvious. The best tools are:

- A written security policy
- Complete inventory of all hardware and software
- Physical cabling layout and device location map
- Logical organization, addressing, and subnetting map
- Complete configuration documentation for every device
- Change documentation and log
- Backup and restoration procedures
- Business continuity and disaster recovery strategy
- Troubleshooting guidelines
- Hardware and software documentation
- Personal knowledge and skill
- Access to online resources

Security management is not about having the most expensive products or the most automated configuration. Instead, good security management is rooted in a solid understanding of the infrastructure and having the tools to improve, respond, and repair as necessary. Focusing on the glitz of shiny products can even distract from the basics of security management.

Security management should always center on protecting assets, supporting authorized activities, and responding to threats as you discover them. It may be more efficient or cost-effective to use off-the-shelf security management products, but using them is no substitute for addressing the organization's core security concerns.

Security Checklist

Security is fragile. Hackers only need to discover a single flaw in your defenses to mount an attack. Changes to the infrastructure, whether physical or logical, could open new holes not previously present. Additionally, users and personnel may intentionally or accidentally breach security.

One method to maintain the efficacy of security is through regular verification and validation checks of every single countermeasure, safeguard, security control, deterrent, prevention, and defense. This requires an inventory of all security measures. This inventory can then become a checklist.

Physical security and logical security each need a separate list focusing on their respective areas of concern. A security guard or a security tech investigates every physical security measure to ensure that it is still in effect, active, and un-modified. Such tasks at the level of logical security are best left to security techs with proper administrative access.

A security checklist shakedown should occur regularly and often, once a day at most to once a week at least. Every single item on the checklist should be physically visited and inspected. If any issues or concerns arise, document them and immediately bring them to the attention of the security team. Employ remedial measures promptly and investigate to track down the root cause of the concern.

A physical security checklist should include every security control deployed for facility control, these include:

- Checking every window lock
- Checking every door lock
- Checking every external wall
- Inspecting access points to raised floor areas
- Inspecting access points to drop ceilings
- Ensuring that cabinets or containers are locked
- Verifying that security cameras are pointed in the correct direction
- Verifying that all light bulbs are of the correct type and are functioning
- Checking motion detectors
- Testing alarm systems
- Interviewing security guards and confirming compliance with procedures

Depending on the industry and specialization, many more components can make up the physical security of organizations; this list is just a sample of what the typical physical security checklist should contain. Look for any modification, destruction, or general failure of every element of physical security. A single bad window lock or a door that does not fully close automatically can result in easy access for a burglar intent on computer mischief.

A logical security checklist should include every security control deployed for computer and network control. These include:

- Checking authentication
- Checking authorization and access control
- Auditing systems
- Verifying firewalls and other filters
- Checking proxies and other communication management solutions
- Verifying encryption, including key management
- Updating antivirus software and scanners
- Backing up and storing archival information securely

Many more elements exist in well-designed security infrastructure for an exhaustive logical security checklist. Again, this list is just a sample of some common elements found in most secure organizations. Poor configurations, overlooked defaults, and out-of-date systems can leave gaps that a probing hacker will discover and exploit.

Never assume you are secure. Check and verify everything regularly. No one else will do it for you.

Use the security checklist with the intention of maintaining effective security over time, in spite of change, accidents, and human nature. However, even a complete checklist cannot resolve problems caused by poor design and implementation. To ensure that your checklist is truly a benefit and not just re-organizing deck chairs on a sinking ship, consider the following common oversights or issues:

- Do not assume that a service or protocol is secured by some other layer or service. Verify that the data traversing a network segment is encrypted or otherwise secured.
- Know the limitations of security products. Each security mechanism addresses a single or small set of issues within a specific context. The presence of security in one location does not cause a magical blanket of security to exist in other locations. Be sure specific and relevant security solutions are in place where necessary. For example, use of IPSec for network encryption does not imply that data stored on clients is encrypted.
- Do not rely on authentication at session initiation alone. Session hijacking is a serious threat on most commonly used protocols. Use solutions that support periodic mid-stream re-authentication, as well as communications encryption.
- Assume programs are inherently insecure. Security is not often a priority or a requirement in programming. When possible, use secure programming quality assurance.
- Plan for handling failures, errors, intrusions, and downtime. Focus on what to do when bad things occur. The goal should be a fast and efficient recovery. Failing to plan is planning to fail.

- Assume you may become a victim of a denial of service (DoS) attack. Every communications system is vulnerable to DoS. Do not forget that physical damage can be an effective DoS.
- Learn from your mistakes. When a problem is uncovered, when a design flaw is revealed, when a process is shown to be ineffective, lean in, take the hit, own up to the responsibility, and then deal with it. Improve the environment to resolve the issue. Review the process and learn from it.

A security checklist can be an effective tool in managing and maintaining network security. Make it a point to start your list now and use it in real-world review immediately.

Network Security Troubleshooting

Security troubleshooting aims at recovering from problems related to the countermeasures themselves. Problems will occur with the defense mechanisms themselves. Downtime of a security control is as critical as downtime of a core business process or asset. Troubleshooting failures of security controls is an important part of network security management.

As with most concerns, prevention is always preferable to repair or response. By working to ensure that failures do not occur, or at least do not occur as often, maintaining effective security will be easier and less costly in terms of both budget and manpower.

Network security troubleshooting is often about triage—deciding which issues or problems are of the most imminent concern. The more a security component affects a mission-critical process, the more important rapid response and repair becomes. When security is down, the previously protected assets are put at greater risk for compromise. Minimizing the length of time consumed by the response is important to minimizing long-term losses.

One of the most effective preventative techniques in network security troubleshooting is installing patches and updates. As with patches and updates to production systems, always test the new code thoroughly before deployment. Once tested and approved for application, apply updates when downtime would cause the least number of problems. Always be prepared with a redundant option if the updating process itself causes further security control problems.

Possible complications from the application of patches and updates include resetting to factory defaults, loss of some but not all configuration settings, and "bricking" (i.e., making it non-functional) the control. If the security control resets back to factory defaults, then it will need to be fully reconfigured. If a recent configuration backup is available, restoration might be a swift repair. Otherwise, manual resetting will be necessary. To facilitate this process, always have complete documentation of all settings of all security controls.

If you lose some but not all configuration settings, then the security control is unlikely to operate as you expect. Restore or reconfigure the settings promptly. The update itself may have added or modified settings that need testing and verification for function and compatibility. If a new feature interferes with a business task, you might find it necessary to disable the feature or rollback the update.

If the update process causes a complete failure of the security control, the real possibility exists that the product is useless. This is known as bricking—turning a useful device into a worthless brick. In some cases, a hard reset can revive a seemingly bricked device, while there may be more esoteric repair and recovery options for other devices. If the vendor does not provide an unbricking solution, search the Internet for user groups or discussion forums for a home-grown solution.

Configuration errors might be the cause of a security control malfunction. Configuration errors may be caused by human error, oversight, or ignorance as well as by updates, power fluctuations, and physical damage. When a security control is improperly configured, it does not provide the expected security. Troubleshooting this situation can be as simple as reverting to a previously saved configuration or manually reapplying the settings.

However, a more serious concern arises when configuration errors are not easily fixed. A recent patch or update may have rendered the product unstable, or a patch or update might be needed to stabilize it. If the configuration error reappears after every power cycle, then the device might be defective, it might need additional memory (or need defective memory replaced), or be attached to an uninterruptable power supply (UPS) to reduce the number of unplanned power fluctuations.

Physical damage should be repaired expeditiously. If unrepairable, you may need to replace the device. Install preventative measures that will prevent the reoccurrence of the physical damage.

In some situations, the problems with security are not with the security components themselves, but with the overall infrastructure design. Perform a re-assessment of the design on a periodic basis, such as once a year, to judge whether the current infrastructure continues to meet the security needs of your organization. Since security changes over time, the security design might need to evolve to meet the demands of new risks, threats, and concerns.

Power faults can take place for many reasons. If the building's power grid is not reliable, if sags and spikes occur on a regular basis, the focus of the long-term repair should be on improving the building's power distribution systems. Short-term responses can include surge protectors, UPSs, and generators.

If a device encounters a power fluctuation due to overheating, investigate whether the room where the device is operating has adequate HVAC service. The average temperature for a room dedicated to housing computer equipment should be at or below 70 degrees Fahrenheit with moderate relative humidity to avoid generating static electricity. In rooms where people work with computers, the temperature should remain below 80 degrees Fahrenheit. Also, check the device to see if it has sufficient internal airflow to maintain appropriate internal operating temperatures. Don't forget to check filters and vents for accumulation of dirt or dust.

Power faults can include power supply or power grid variances. In this situation, the only responses are surge protectors, UPSs, and generators as customers are unable to affect the quality of the power company's electricity by themselves. If switching power suppliers is an option, investigate this to determine the reliability of other providers, as well as the expense and hassle of switching. Sometimes actively and publicly "shopping" power suppliers can result in improved service from your present supplier.

Static electricity is also a concern. Electrostatic discharge (ESD) or static-electric discharge (SED) can easily damage equipment, including security equipment. The amount of electricity discharged between someone's finger and a doorknob when you can see the spark jump is more than enough voltage to destroy most computer chips. Take precautions to prevent static damage.

Physical damage can be a concern requiring troubleshooting. Damage might be caused through intentional destruction, accidents, and Mother Nature. If the damage is superficial or cosmetic, the device can be returned to service. However, if the damage prevents the security device from operating properly, then in most cases you need to replace it. Address the cause of the physical damage to reduce the likelihood of a reoccurrence.

Network security troubleshooting focuses on whether an intruder can bypass a security defense or restriction. A security control that can be bypassed is worthless. Once you discover that a security control can be bypassed, you need to investigate the method or mechanism of the bypass. Then if possible, remove or block the method of bypass. If the flaw is a design or infrastructure concern, consider revising the design to remove the loophole.

From time to time hackers find flaws in the programming of a security control. Once an exploit is written, the security control can be rendered useless through taking advantage of the flawed code. Vigilance in reviewing vulnerability databases and research, paying attention to vendor information, and watching the log files of the organization's network should alert you when an exploit succeeds.

Defending against an exploitation focusing on a security control is the same as when one focuses on any other aspect of a network. If possible, reconfigure the control to minimize the effectiveness of the exploitation. Consider removing the component until you can implement a new defense. Apply a patch or update from the vendor as soon as it becomes available.

A final concern in relation to network security troubleshooting is hardware failure. While not a common occurrence, hardware can fail. Over the life of an organization, you are almost guaranteed downtime caused by hardware failure. When that hardware is a security control, the downtime is more severe in that it places the rest of the environment at greater risk.

Manage hardware failure by having replacements on hand or being able to obtain them quickly. Reduce downtime through redundant infrastructure design. Monitoring ongoing performance metrics might enable the detection of a future hardware failure as performance degrades. However, abrupt hardware failures are difficult to predict. Thus, being prepared with alternatives and replacement parts is often the best troubleshooting solution.

Compliance Auditing

Compliance auditing is a type of assessment that judges how well an organization is accomplishing set goals or requirements. These goals and requirements can be internal or set by government, industry, and other regulatory agencies. Compliance auditing is an important part of maintaining a business, especially growing businesses, as it ensures that the organization is following all necessary security guidelines.

Compliance auditing may be a legal requirement for some industries, such as financial and medical. Independent external auditors perform compliance audits to ensure that a target organization is fully abiding by the rules and regulations imposed by the government. This audit is a comprehensive investigation and review of the ongoing business processes. The audit requires a review of the security policy, access controls, risk management processes, and historical log files.

The focus of compliance audits varies based on industry, information type, and whether the organization is public or private. Auditors investigate an organization through documentation analysis, interviewing personnel, and combing through audit logs. Compliance auditing can examine recent security breaches, evaluate incident response, interview ex-employees, judge user access levels, interview executives over critical security concerns, and more.

Organizations are usually distinctly aware when compliance auditing is a mandated periodic occurrence. In those cases, companies should prepare for audits by collecting the various types of information and creating the appropriate records as needed by the auditor. In fact, establishing a standard practice of producing and archiving the necessary information is prudent. The goals of these actions are not to manipulate the data, but to provide adequate access to the facts and historical activities.

Organizations that do not have mandated compliance audits should consider self-imposed audits. The processes of thoroughly investigating the compliance level with the stated security policy can improve the long-term stability and security of every organization. The act of self-assessment and improvement is a common characteristic of most successful IT organizations.

Security Assessment

Security assessment is the judging, testing, and evaluation of a deployed security solution. The state of the world, in terms of security, is constantly changing. The hacking community is actively developing new techniques, methodologies, and exploits to compromise targets. The defenses and strategies that worked yesterday might not be as effective tomorrow.

Security assessment is the ongoing process of evaluating security so that you can improve it. As discussed in previous sections of this book, security is established through the act of performing a risk assessment. The results of the assessment are formulated into a policy that guides the implementation of the initial security infrastructure. From that point forward, security management takes over.

Security management is the process of watching for breaches, tuning existing security, and evaluating the need for improvements to security. It is this latter area of concern that is the focus of security assessment. Security assessment employs several techniques to appraise the effectiveness of deployed security.

Configuration Scans

A configuration scan probes a system to determine the current state of configuration and settings. This scan determines which available vendor patches are installed or missing. This scan also evaluates numerous system configuration settings against a database of recommendations. Depending on the tool you use to perform the configuration scan, you may find different levels of recommendations based on the function of the system or the general level of desired security.

One well-known example of a configuration scan tool is Microsoft Baseline Security Analyzer (MBSA). The MBSA scans a Windows system and produces an easy to read report (Figure 6-3). This tool provides a fast evaluation of the overall security stance of a single system.

MBSA is a great tool for small offices and end users to employ to quickly check their systems for well-known patch and security setting configuration compliance. However, this is just a first step; it should not be the only tool you employ. You'll need other tools, especially non-Microsoft software, that focus on broader issues to obtain a complete and thorough configuration scan.

> **NOTE**
> The MBSA tool does not seem to have a dedicated home page within the Microsoft Web site; however, it is easily located performing a Microsoft or general Internet search.

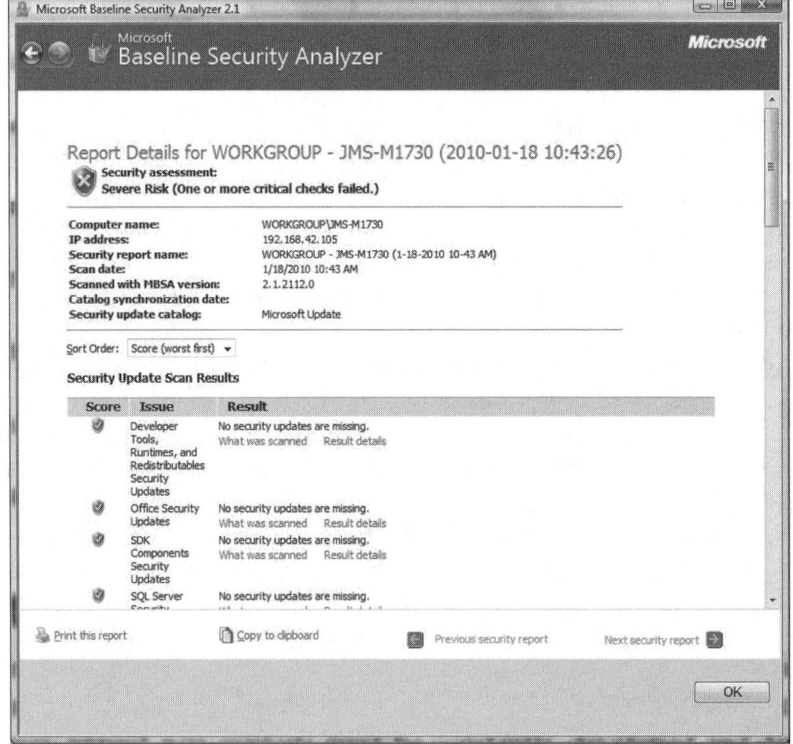

FIGURE 6-3
An MBSA scan report example.

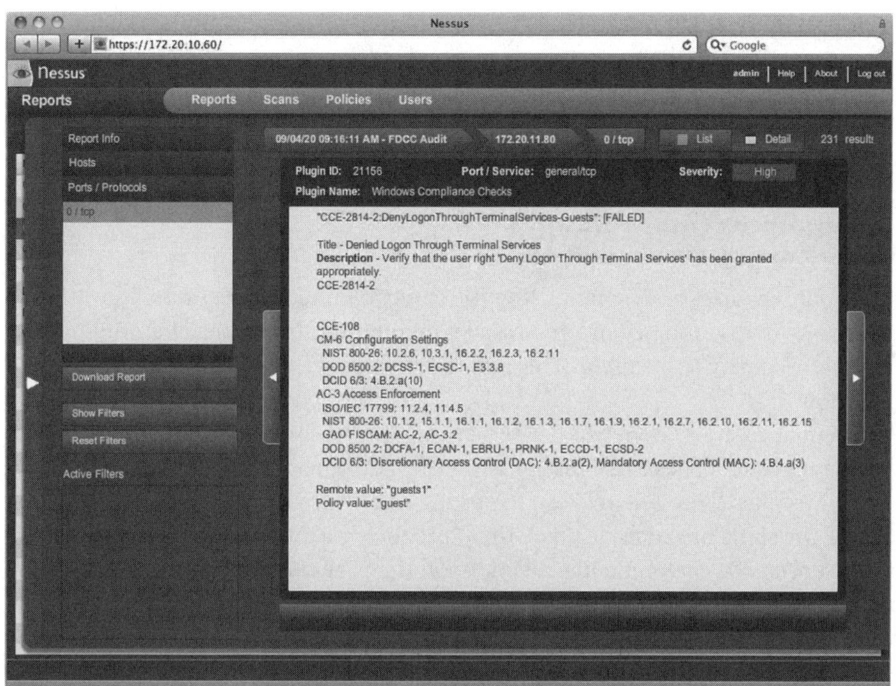

FIGURE 6-4

A Nessus scan report example.

Vulnerability Scanning

The next step or stage in security assessment is **vulnerability scanning**. Vulnerability scanning focuses on locating known exploitable weaknesses or vulnerabilities in deployed systems. You perform this type of scanning by using an automated tool with an updatable database of exploitations and test scripts. A vulnerability scan will reveal problems with configuration, installation, and product code. A scan of this type is only as reliable as the product itself and the currency of its testing database.

A popular and well-known vulnerability scanning product is Tenable Network Security's Nessus. Nessus is available in a free version for home use and a paid version for commercial use. Nessus is a powerful scanning engine with a massive database of exploitation plug-ins that offers excellent reporting capabilities (Figure 6-4).

> **NOTE**
> Nessus can be found online at *http://www.nessus.org/*.

Penetration Testing

The third and final step or stage in security assessment is penetration testing. Also known as ethical hacking, this process is the application of hacking techniques, methodology, and tools in the hands of trusted ethical security experts. The purpose of penetration testing is to evaluate the resiliency of current security infrastructure and recommend improvements. Penetration testing is performed by a team of professionals who can customize and adapt exploits on-the-fly.

Penetration testing typically consists of five main phases or steps: reconnaissance, scanning, enumeration, attacking, and post-attack activities. These were discussed in Chapter 4. The steps or components of criminal hacking and ethical hacking are the same. The difference is the goal and abiding by ethical restrictions and contractual boundaries.

Post-Mortem Assessment Review

Even with adequate security assessment using the three main techniques (configuration scans, vulnerability scans, and penetration tests) you may still have a need for one additional form of security assessment. This additional form is the port-mortem assessment review.

A port-mortem assessment review is the self-evaluation performed by individuals and organizations after each security assessment task. The purpose of a port-mortem is to learn from mistakes. This will improve the process in future events and avoid the reoccurrence of the same mistakes. It's true that "practice makes perfect." If you practice the same tasks repeatedly, each time improving upon the previous performance, you'll eventually master the task.

Port-mortem reviews provide incremental improvements on a consistent basis along with the rare revolutionary improvement. A review of this type can include numerous elements of appraisal focus, including:

- The process as a whole
- Each performed step
- The order of the steps
- Whether steps might be missing
- What other actions could be taken
- Were participants properly trained
- Were additional resources needed
- Were resources wasted
- Were additional people needed
- Were too many people involved
- Was reporting sufficient or insufficient
- What was missing
- What could be improved next time

Many other queries could be posed as long as the goal aims at improving future application of the assessment processes and tools. A post-mortem review is a beneficial process when used consistently.

CHAPTER SUMMARY

Network security management focuses on vigilance. Vigilance to remain current in terms of technology. Vigilance to remain knowledgeable about new threats and exploits. Vigilance to respond promptly to downtime and compromise. Vigilance to restore, repair, and update security on a regular, consistent basis.

A wide number of activities make up the realm of network security management, including fail-secure responses, maintaining physical security, detecting compromise, preparing for incident response, trapping intruders, host security components, backup procedures, user training, management tools, checklists, troubleshooting, compliance auditing, and security assessment.

KEY CONCEPTS AND TERMS

- Awareness
- Backup
- Business continuity plan
- Compliance audit
- Default deny
- Default permit
- Disaster recovery plan
- Education
- File encryption
- Honeynet
- Incident response plan
- Mission-critical
- Padded cell
- Patch management
- Principle of least privilege
- Security Technical Implementation Guides (STIGS)
- Separation of duties
- Single-factor authentication
- Training
- Trusted Platform Module (TPM)
- Vulnerability scanning
- Whole hard drive encryption

CHAPTER 6 ASSESSMENT

1. All of the following are examples of network security management best practices *except*:
   A. Write a security policy
   B. Obtain senior management endorsement
   C. Filter Internet connectivity
   D. Provide fast response time to customers
   E. Implement defense-in-depth

2. All of the following are examples of network security management best practices *except*:
   A. Avoid remote access
   B. Purchase equipment from a single vendor
   C. Use whole hard drive encryption
   D. Implement IPSec
   E. Harden internal and border devices

3. All of the following are examples of network security management best practices *except*:
   A. Use multi-factor authentication
   B. Backup
   C. Have a business continuity plan
   D. Prioritize
   E. Spend each year's budget in full

4. A firewall host that fails and reverts to a state where all communication between the Internet and the DMZ is cut off displays a type of defense known as:
   A. Default permit
   B. Explicit deny
   C. Fail-close
   D. Egress filtering
   E. Security through obscurity

5. The purpose of physical security access control is to:
   A. Grant access to external entities
   B. Prevent external attacks from coming through the firewall
   C. Provide teachable scenarios for training
   D. Limit interaction between people and devices
   E. Protect against authorized communications over external devices

6. A complete and comprehensive security approach needs to address or perform two main functions, the first is to secure assets and the second is:
   A. Watch for violation attempts
   B. Prevent downtime
   C. Verify identity
   D. Control access to resources
   E. Design the infrastructure based on the organization's mission

7. Incident response is the planned reaction to negative situations or events. Which of the following is not a common step or phase in an incident response?
   A. Containment
   B. Recovery
   C. Eradication
   D. Detection
   E. Assessment

8. All of the following are elements of an effective network security installation *except*:
   A. Backup and restoration
   B. User training and awareness
   C. Compliance auditing
   D. Security checklist
   E. Unplanned downtime

9. The task of compartmentalization is focused on assisting with what overarching security concern?
   A. Limiting damage caused by intruders
   B. Filtering traffic based on volume
   C. Controlling access based on location
   D. Supporting transactions through utilization
   E. Assessing security

10. Which of the following types of security components are important to install on all hosts?
   A. firewall
   B. antivirus
   C. whole hard drive encryption
   D. spyware defenses
   E. All of the above

11. What is the only protection against data loss?

A. Integrity checking
B. Encryption
C. Traffic filtering
D. Backup and recovery
E. Auditing

12. All of the following are common mistakes or security problems that should be addressed in awareness training *except*:

A. Opening e-mail attachments from unknown sources
B. Using resources from other subnets of which the host is not a member
C. Installing unapproved software on work computers
D. Failing to make backups of personal data
E. Walking away from a computer while still logged in

13. The best network security management tools include all of the following *except*:

A. Complete inventory of equipment
B. Written security policy
C. Expensive commercial products
D. Logical organization map
E. Change documentation

14. The purpose of a security checklist is:

A. To keep an inventory of equipment in the event of a disaster
B. To create shopping list for replacement parts
C. To ensure that all security elements are still effective
D. To complete the security documentation for the organization
E. To assess the completeness of the infrastructure

15. Which of the following is *not* a potential hazard when installing patches or updates?

A. Resetting configuration back to factory defaults
B. Reducing security
C. Bricking the device
D. Installing untested code
E. Improving resiliency against exploits

16. Which of the following is a true statement in regards to compliance auditing?

A. Compliance auditing is a legally mandated task for every organization.
B. Compliance auditing ensures that all best practices are followed.
C. Compliance auditing creates a security policy.
D. Compliance auditing is an optional function for the financial and medical industries.
E. Compliance auditing verifies that industry specific regulations and laws are followed.

17. Which of the following is not typically considered a form of network security assessment in terms of how well existing security stands up to current threats?

A. Configuration scan
B. Compliance audit
C. Vulnerability assessment
D. Ethical hacking
E. Penetration testing

18. Which of the following cannot be performed adequately using an automated tool?

A. Checking for current patches
B. Confirming configuration settings
C. Vulnerability assessment
D. Scanning for known weaknesses
E. Ethical hacking

19. What is the key factor that determines how valuable and relevant a vulnerability assessment's report is?

A. Timeliness of the database
B. Whether the product is open sourced
C. The platform hosting the scanning engine
D. The time of day the scan is performed
E. The available bandwidth on the network

20. What is the primary purpose of a post-mortem assessment review?

A. Reducing costs
B. Adding new tools and resources
C. Placing blame on an individual
D. Learning from mistakes
E. Extending the length of time consumed by a task

CHAPTER

7

Exploring the Depths of Firewalls

A FIREWALL IS A KEY COMPONENT of a complete security infrastructure. And while common, a firewall is by far not a simple security measure. You must understand the complexities of a firewall to design a firewall's security policy, build the firewall, and configure it properly.

This chapter builds on the firewall information previously presented by discussing the foundations of firewall rules, authentication, and authorization. You will learn how these relate to monitoring and logging, interpreting firewall logs and alerts, intrusion detection, firewall limitations, improving firewall performance, how encryption relates to firewalls, various firewall enhancements, and security concerns related to firewall management interfaces.

Chapter 7 Topics

This chapter will cover the following topics and concepts:

- What good firewall rules are
- What authentication and authorization are
- What monitoring and logging are
- How to understand and interpret firewall logs and alerts
- What intrusion detection is
- What the limitations of firewalls are
- How to improve firewall performance
- What the downside of encryption is with firewalls
- What firewall enhancements are
- How to use firewall management interfaces

Chapter 7 Goals

Upon completion of this chapter, you will be able to:

- Construct examples of common firewall rules
- Design a policy to guide effective firewall monitoring and logging
- Discuss the limitations and weaknesses of firewalls
- Describe methods to manage firewall performance
- Define the concerns of encryption related to firewalls
- Evaluate the benefits and drawbacks of firewall enhancements
- Demonstrate how to access and use firewall management interfaces

Firewall Rules

Firewalls filter traffic using **rules** or **filters**. Whether static packet filtering, stateful inspection, application proxy, circuit proxy, or content filtering, all firewalls use rules to filter traffic. Rules are lines of code or instructions that evaluate and take action on network traffic.

Generally, two main philosophies or security stances govern the use of rules: default deny or default permit. Default deny is also known as deny by default or deny all. **Default allow** is also known as **allow by default** or allow all. These two rules define the foundation for rules governing traffic crossing the firewall.

A default deny stance assumes that all traffic is potentially malicious or at least unwanted or unauthorized. Thus, everything is prohibited by default. Then, as benign, desired, and authorized traffic is identified, an exception rule grants it access. This is known as **deny by default**, allow by exception. This method of rule creation allows security administrators to focus on what is wanted or needed, rather than having to watch out for all possible forms of unwanted or malicious activity.

A default allow stance assumes that most traffic is benign. Thus, everything is allowed by default. Then, as malicious, unwanted, or unauthorized traffic is identified, an exception rule blocks it. This is known as allow by default, deny by exception. This method of rule creation forces the security administrator to be on constant watch for new and different forms of unwanted, unauthorized, and malicious activity.

Most security experts agree that a deny by default philosophy is the more secure stance to adopt. This stance automatically prevents most malicious communications by default, while the opposite allow by default stance allows most malicious communications by default. In most situations, fewer exceptions are required for a default deny solution than for a default allow system.

Firewall rules are used to control what traffic enters or leaves a secured network area. Depending on where the firewall is positioned, this mechanism can protect the private network from the public Internet or filter traffic between internal subnets or departments. The security administrator or the dedicated firewall administrator configures firewall rules in accordance with the organization's security policy.

Most firewalls, both hardware and software varieties, usually come pre-configured with rules above and beyond their default rule. Firewalls are normally factory-configured in a deny by default stance with some common exception rules thrown in for end-user/customer convenience (Figure 7-1). Often these rules allow the most common forms of communication to occur across a new firewall without your needing to fully configure the firewall upon initial installation. Some of the more common factory default rules allow for Web, e-mail, IM, and file transfer through common Internet services on default ports.

While this can be a convenience, it's not in your best long-term security interest to ever rely upon a third party's assumptions about your environment or their guesses as to what types of traffic you do or do not want to cross your firewalled boundaries. Always take the time to review any factory-installed rules before deploying them in the production environment. Delete or disable any rule that you do not need or want. Any rule that you do want or need, double-check to make sure it's in line with your security policy. If you need rules that are not present by default, add them carefully and double-check your work as you go.

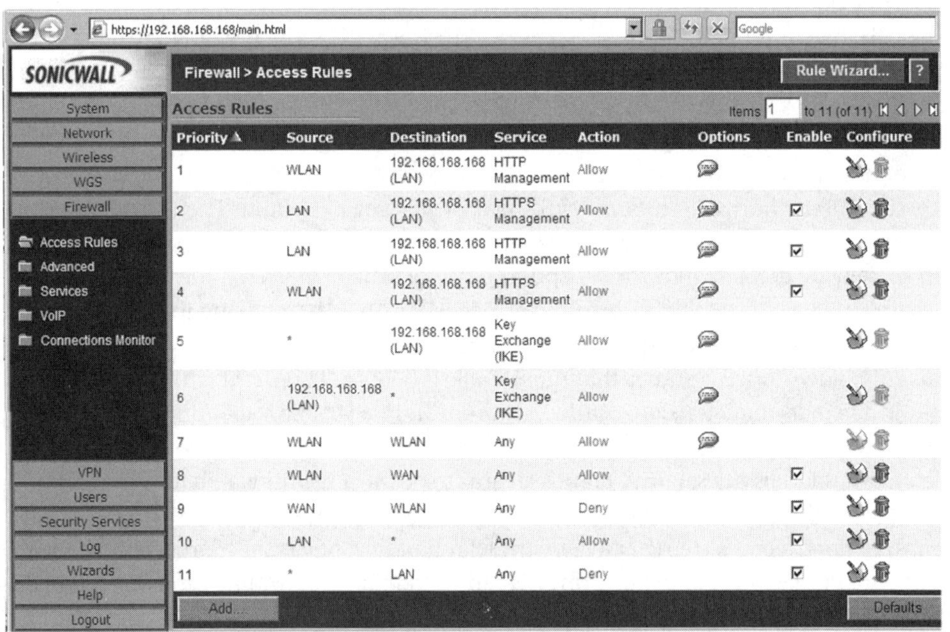

FIGURE 7-1

SonicWall's default rule configuration interface, showing a default deny as the last rule (rule 11).

Deciding which rules to define is subject to the organization's security policy. If the appropriate sections related to firewalls do not pre-define what rules to define on a new firewall, then perform the following procedure:

- Inventory all essential business processes and communications that will cross the checkpoint
- Determine the protocol, ports, and IP addresses of valid traffic for both internal and external hosts
- Write out the rules on paper or using a firewall rule designer/simulator
- Test the rules in a laboratory environment
- Obtain written approval for the rule sets from a change approval board
- Document the rules into a security policy procedure amendment and submit the amendment to the security policy management team for inclusion in the official document

Ultimately, this is the basic process for creating any new element of security. The goal always is to have a written security policy for every security component. If no current policy or procedure defining the steps to take for the deployment of a new security element exists, then you must write, test, and get approval for a new policy or procedure. Once a procedure exists, use it to judge successful deployment.

The exact rules to add to a new firewall are completely dependent upon the business processes that are unique to every organization. However, some common types of rules are found on most firewalls. These include:

- Access to insecure Internet Web sites (HTTP)
- Access to secure Internet Web sites (HTTP over SSL or TLS)
- Access to other Internet Web site protocols (SQL, Java, and so on)
- Inbound Internet e-mail
- Outbound Internet e-mail

Obviously, if other Internet services are essential to a business task, rules allowing or enabling such communications would be needed. Try to keep the number of rules to a minimum, however. Grant access only to traffic that is essential. For each additional rule added to a firewall, you are increasing its attack surface—and therefore its security vulnerability.

Keep in mind that most network communications are two-way transactions, exchanges, or sessions. Often an internal client makes an initiation request to an external server. The server responds and sets up a communication channel, often called a virtual circuit (at the Transport layer based on TCP) or generically "a session." Traffic can traverse the session in either direction. Thus, most rules should allow inbound responses to initial outbound requests.

Depending upon the firewall, sometimes a single rule can define both the outbound and inbound communication parameters. Other firewalls need two separate rules—one rule for the initial outbound request and a second rule to handle the resultant inbound response. In either case, each desired session-based communication service must be supported or allowed through proper two-way rule construction.

In addition to rules that allow traffic based on internal user initiation, consider rules that manage inbound communications for externally initiated communications. When a firewall is to allow an external host to request access to internal resources, you need to create an inbound rule or ingress filter. Only define rules that allow inbound initiations if external entities need to access services and resources hosted internally.

Otherwise, allow the firewall to serve its primary purpose and to prevent outsiders from gaining easy access to internal systems. Most firewalls deny by default all access to internal resources from external entities. This is done either by ignoring all requests received on a specific interface (such as on dual-homed or triple-homed firewalls) or by having a specific rule (or a set of rules) that filter out all traffic originating from non-internal IP addresses.

A firewall rule can also be called a filter or an **access control list (ACL)**. These terms are often used interchangeably in documentation, books (such as this one), and in the firewall's own configuration or **management interfaces**. Don't be confused by this. A rule is a written expression of an item of concern (protocol, port, service, application, user, IP address) and one or more actions to take when the item of concern appears in traffic. A filter is the same thing as a rule, but the point or purpose of using this term is to stress the intention to block or deny unwanted items of concern. The use of the term ACL stresses the intention to grant or deny traffic on an access control/authentication basis. An ACL focuses on controlling a specific user or client's access to a protocol or port.

Rules allow traffic to pass unhindered or block/deny traffic to prevent it from reaching its intended destination. A rule can also include a logging element so the traffic can be logged whether allowed or denied. The concept of firewall logging and monitoring is discussed later in this chapter.

technical TIP

Use your firewall to ensure that only properly originated communications are authorized. Unless you are running internal services (such as a Web server), external entities should never be able to initiate a connection.

technical TIP

Most session-based communications will use a well-known default port for the destination port where the service or resource resides. They will use a randomly selected higher order port (any port above 1023) for the client source port. Most firewalls, especially stateful inspection capable firewalls, will automatically handle and adjust for the random source port when establishing a session. If this is not the case with a specific firewall, you may need a custom rule or consider replacing the firewall with a better product.

Setting up or defining rules for a home, a portable host, or a SOHO environment can be fairly easy if the number of different types of access is minimal. But, as the number of controls, limitations, restrictions, and exceptions increases, defining rules properly can become more complex. Obviously, larger networks with more advanced infrastructures and communications require more intricate sets of rules to effectively manage sophisticated communications.

The basics of defining or crafting rules are the same (or at least similar) across all firewall products. However, some firewalls support editing or writing the rules directly while others employ a graphical interface or use a design wizard to accomplish the task. Software host firewalls, especially those designed for end-users, typically use a graphical wizard-based system, while hardware firewalls typically expose the raw rule itself.

NOTE

Ingress and egress filtering and spoofing filtering are discussed in Chapter 2.

Most rules have six main elements or components (Figure 7-2):

- **Base Protocol**—Set as TCP, UDP, ICMP, and potentially other layer 2, 3, or 4 protocols
- **Source Address**—Set as a specific IP address, a subnet, a range of addresses, or ANY for all possible addresses
- **Source Port**—Set as a specific port, a set of ports, a range of ports, ports less or greater than, or ANY for all possible ports
- **Target Address**—Set as a specific IP address, a subnet, a range of addresses, or ANY for all possible addresses
- **Target Port**—Set as a specific port, a set of ports, a range of ports, or ANY for all possible ports
- **Action**—The two standard actions are: Allow and Deny. Some firewalls include Log and Alert actions that allow additional actions in a single rule.

FYI

Some firewall rule systems include application protocol designations in the rule set. This is usually a human-friendly naming convention pointing out the application layer protocol rather than an element of the filter used to select traffic. However, some firewall interfaces will substitute a common protocol name for the destination port. For example, port 80 would be displayed as HTTP and port 25 as SMTP. However, these are usually for human viewing; the port number itself is still used in the actual protocol-level filtering activity.

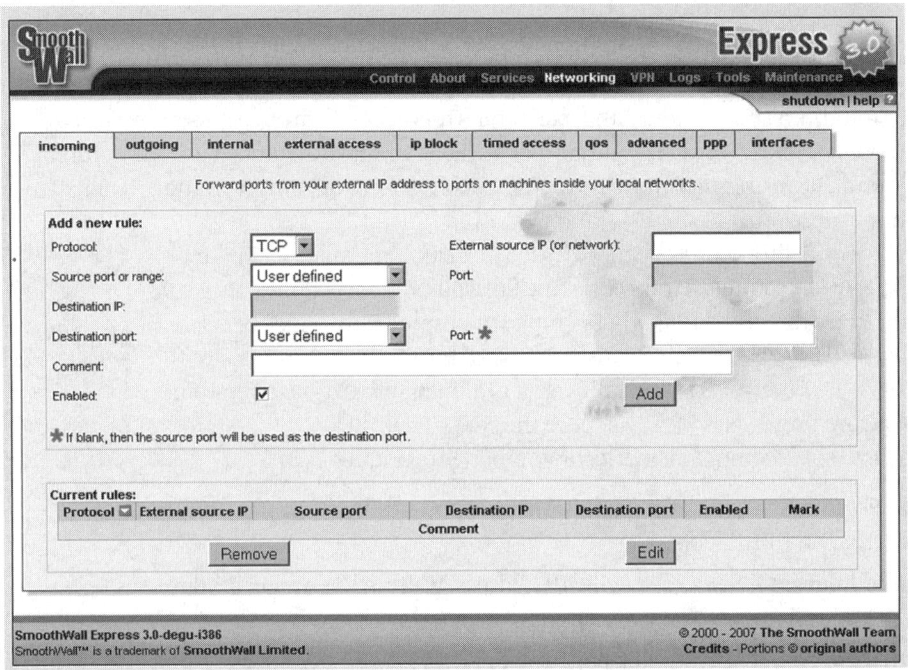

FIGURE 7-2

SmoothWall's rule configuration interface.

Depending upon the firewall, TCP and UDP rules (as well as ICMP, IGMP, ARP, and other OSI Layer 2, 3, or 4 protocols) may be defined in the same place or within different interfaces, pages, or **rule sets**. When all rules are defined in the same place, use an additional rule element designating TCP, UDP, ICMP, and so on. All of the following examples of rules assume TCP-based communications, unless otherwise noted.

The common rule structure is:

[Protocol]	[Source Address]	[Source Port]	[Target Address]	[Target Port]	[Action]

When defining outbound rules, the source address and port are often set as ANY unless the rule is to apply to a specific system(s) or port(s). For example, a rule that allows any internal client on the 192.168.42.0/24 subnet to access any insecure Internet Web site would be:

TCP	192.168.42.0/24	ANY	ANY	80	Allow

A rule to allow access to any secured Internet Web site would change the destination port 80 to 443:

TCP	192.168.42.0/24	ANY	ANY	443	Allow

A rule to block internal clients from accessing Internet based FTP sites would be:

TCP	192.168.42.0/24	ANY	ANY	21	Deny

FYI

Keep in mind that firewall vendors may have crafted unique management interfaces that display firewall rules differently than the basic line form discussed here. For example, some firewalls have a configuration page for allow rules and a separate page for deny rules. In that example, the rules on each page would not include an Allow or Deny action, as the page they are defined on implies the action.

When defining inbound rules, the source address and port address are often ANY unless the rule is to apply to a specific system(s) or port(s). For example, a rule that allows any external host client to access an insecure Web site hosted on the 192.168.42.98 would be:

TCP	ANY	ANY	192.168.42.98	80	Allow

An inbound rule to deny external hosts access to a Telnet server hosted on the same internal system as the Web server would be:

TCP	ANY	ANY	192.168.42.98	23	Deny

Generally, inbound rules are only needed when an internal resource is specifically hosted for the purposes of being accessed by external entities. This type of rule is commonly found on DMZ and extranet firewalls, but shouldn't be used on intranet border firewalls. The only common inbound rule that might be required is one that allows responses to previous internal client requests to resources outside of the network.

A stateful inspection firewall usually allows response traffic automatically, but static filtering firewalls might require a specific respond rule set, such as:

TCP	ANY	ANY	192.168.42.0/24	>1023	Allow

When a UDP rule set needs to be defined, you must either switch to a different rule set interface on the firewall, or change the protocol designation from TCP to UDP. Assuming a firewall interface with a leading protocol designation for each rule, a rule set allowing user queries with an internal DNS server at 192.168.42.104 by external entities, but blocking attempts to perform DNS zone transfers could be:

TCP	ANY	ANY	192.168.42.104	53	Deny
UDP	ANY	ANY	192.168.42.104	53	Allow

To write a firewall rule controlling ICMP, change the protocol designation to ICMP (or change interfaces) and define an ICMP type. The port designations are dropped completely (as they are not used by ICMP at OSI Layer 2) Multiple ICMP rules can be defined for various sub-types to allow some ICMP traffic and a Deny all "catch-all" rule for everything else. For example, to block only inbound ICMP Echo_request packets use the following filter:

ICMP	ANY	192.168.42.0/24	Type 8	Deny	Allow

technical TIP

The ICMP protocol's header defines the purpose of the protocols control message through the use of numbered types. There are dozens of defined types. The most commonly used are Type 8 Echo Request, Type 0 Echo Reply, Type 3 Destination Unreachable, and Type 11 Time Exceeded. Many types are further specified with the use of a numbered code. For example, Type 3 Code 3 is destination port unreachable.

For a more exhaustive presentation of the ICMP Types and Codes, please read RFC2939 at *http://www.iana.org/assignments/icmp-parameters*.

When defining firewall rules, keep a few basic guidelines in mind:

- Keep the rule set as simple as possible.
- Document every rule.
- Use a change control mechanism to track rule modifications.
- Always confirm the Default Deny before using changed/updated rule sets.

A simple rule set is a set with as few rules as possible. Fewer rules mean fewer complications. Fewer rules mean less chance for a loophole. Fewer rules are easier to test. Fewer rules are harder to attack and compromise.

Every rule enforced by a firewall should be written in the security policy. Only rules in the written security policy should be enforced by a firewall. Anytime you need to change a firewall rule, first update the security policy, then reconfigure the firewall to match the settings defined in the security policy. Always fully document the rules actively filtering traffic.

Do not just document that a rule exists and what the basic rule structure is; also include a description of the intention or purpose of the rule. Sometimes a rule written in a way that appears straightforward may not perform the intended purpose. When other security administrators review the documentation and examine the rules, they may see the discrepancy and correct it. Get in the habit of making notes about intentions, thoughts, and concerns. Often these stray comments will lead to solutions or assist in future troubleshooting.

A change control mechanism tracks and monitors the changes to a system. It does this by recording every change, modification, or adjustment. Often, a change management solution requires manual change logging; thus, it must be an enforced and followed by a written component of the security policy. The change control process produces historical documentation of the state of security components. Change documentation is often essential in troubleshooting and repair.

Most firewalls operate on a default deny stance, but it may be possible to modify this stance. Stance modification may be a general setting in the overall configuration of the firewall, or it might just be the last rule in the rule set. If it's just a rule, be sure that the final rule is always default deny and that the default deny rule is never edited or modified. A default deny rule should look like or enforce filtering as follows:

TCP	ANY	ANY	ANY	ANY	Deny

Since a firewall is a first-match-apply rule-based system, rules are ordered on the firewall. Traffic is compared with each rule starting from the top rule. If a rule matches the traffic, the rule's action is applied. Once a matching rule's action is applied to the traffic, no further rule matching is attempted. If the traffic does not match any rule except the final rule, then it will be denied by default. All rules previous to the default deny can be either exception allows or specific denials. No matter what the structure of the rules or the number of rules in the set, always ensure that there is a default rule.

Here is an example of a basic TCP rule set:

TCP	ANY	ANY	192.168.42.0/24	>1023	Allow
TCP	192.168.42.1	ANY	ANY	ANY	Deny
TCP	ANY	ANY	192.168.42.1	ANY	Deny
TCP	192.168.42.0/24	ANY	ANY	ANY	Allow
TCP	ANY	ANY	192.168.42.55	25	Allow
TCP	ANY	ANY	192.168.42.98	80	Allow
TCP	ANY	ANY	ANY	ANY	Deny

FYI

All of the firewall rule examples are using the default common port for common services as defined by: *http://www.iana.org/assignments/port-numbers*

This collection of seven rules performs the following filtering functions:

- Allow response TCP Connections to internal hosts
- Prevent the firewall (192.168.42.1) from directly connecting to anything
- Prevent external hosts from directly accessing the firewall
- Allow internal hosts to access external resources
- Allow external hosts to send e-mail inbound to the e-mail server at 192.168.42.55
- Allow external hosts to access an internal Web server at 192.168.42.98
- Apply a default deny rule to all traffic not matching a previous exception

Building a rule set is not complex, but it does take focus on the details. Be sure to use a single IP address for a single host and the correct subnet or range designation for a collection of hosts. Specify the port when possible, otherwise use a valid port range. Include specific deny rules when needed. Remember that in the first-match-apply based system that is a firewall, order matters.

To grant every system but a few specific ones access to a resource, you need a rule to block the few and allow the rest. Position the Deny rule of this set before the Allow rule of the rest since the Allow rule will likely be an ANY-based rule instead of naming all of the many that are granted access.

When the wrong rule is positioned first, this creates a potential loophole. A loophole is a flaw in the logic of filtering that will allow an unwanted action to occur. A firewall can only perform the operations for which it is programmed and the specifics of and the order of the rules are a form of programming. Take the time to evaluate, test, and verify that you have defined all firewall rules correctly and placed them in the best order.

If getting the rules in the right order seems daunting, the following general rule of thumb usually results in less access rather than greater access. The general rule of thumb to firewall rule set order is to list specific deny rules first, then the allow exceptions, and always keeping the default deny rule last. At best, this will result in exactly what you want and expect. At worst, more things will be blocked than you intended, but that is usually a better security stance than allowing more things than you intended.

As rule sets get larger, they become more complex. Often the complexity stems from having explicit allows with additional deny specifications. This results in rules that overlap. Overlapping is acceptable when you understand it and use it on purpose. When overlapping occurs accidentally, it can result in undesired loopholes. Again, the solution is to keep the rule set as simple as possible, document every rule with its intentions, and test the rule thoroughly before deployment.

> **NOTE**
> For the discussion on testing firewalls, please see Chapter 9 "Firewall Tests."

With this basic understanding of rules, your next step in understanding and deploying firewalls is to consider the options for authentication and authorization across the firewall.

Authentication and Authorization

Authentication is the process of verifying the identity of an electronic entity. Authentication is also commonly called logging on. Authorization is the process of defining which resources can be accessed by an electronic entity and what level or type of access is granted. Authorization is also commonly called access control.

Authentication can take place at the firewall itself or be passed through the firewall to take place beyond the firewall. Authentication at the firewall takes place when the allow/deny decision is dependent upon the identity of the host or user. Authentication beyond the firewall happens when the allow/deny decision is not dependent upon the identity of the host or user; instead, the firewall filters for traffic characteristics and leaves authentication up to the internal host receiving the connection.

When authentication takes place at the firewall, the firewall itself serves as the gatekeeper allowing communication beyond the firewall. Whenever different types or levels of port, protocol, or circuit access are granted based on individual user identity or membership in specific groups, authentication at the firewall takes place.

When authentication takes place at the firewall, the firewall itself can perform the logon process or it can forward the task to a dedicated authentication service. Native firewall authentication methods can be basic, such as supporting username and password online, or complex, such as supporting credit card payments or use of smart cards. However, most firewalls have a limited number of authentication options.

Generally, authentication on or at a firewall supports only one—or at best a few—options. "At-firewall" authentication often requires defining credentials on the firewall separately and distinctly from any identity on the network. Thus, most at-firewall authentication solutions do not integrate into a network's single sign-on system. For this reason, large organizations rarely employ at-firewall authentication.

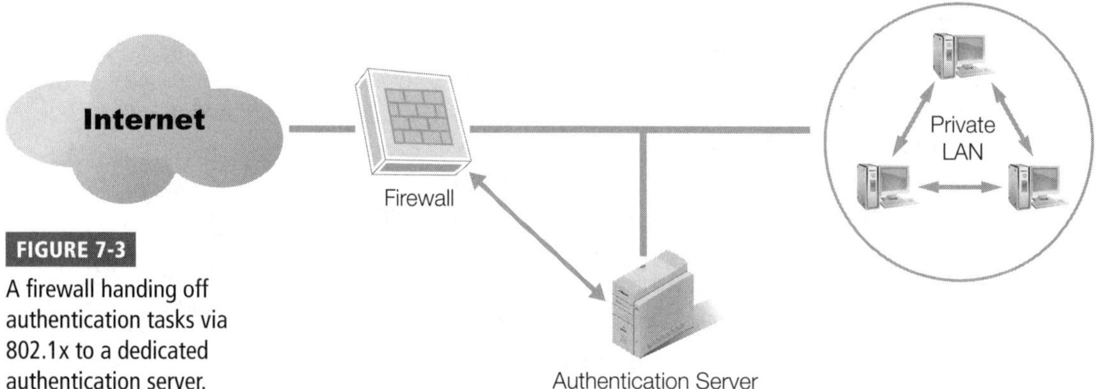

FIGURE 7-3

A firewall handing off authentication tasks via 802.1x to a dedicated authentication server.

When a firewall hands off the authentication task to a dedicated authentication service that performs the logon process on behalf of the firewall (Figure 7-3), a much wider assortment of authentication options becomes available. A common use of this mechanism is **IEEE 802.1x**. IEEE 802.1x is known as **port-based network access (admission) control (PNAC)**. In this term, port is not referring to a port number in OSI layer 4, instead it refers to a more generic reference of a connection point to a network infrastructure.

IEEE 802.1x is commonly found on many network devices, including firewalls, switches, routers, and wireless access points. It also has the nickname of "portal authentication." An 802.1x device establishes the initial electronic connection or virtual circuit between the requesting host and itself, but before communication to a host beyond the portal device takes place, authentication must occur. 802.1x can support RADIUS, TACACS, Kerberos, certificates, passwords, smart cards, biometrics, special access codes, and even credit cards as means of authentication.

Hand off authentication, such as when 802.1x is used, is a fully scalable architecture. Use it to manage at-firewall authentication for any number of users or hosts. The only limitation to 802.1x is the scalability of the authentication server that takes over the responsibility of managing logons on behalf of the firewall.

When authentication takes place beyond the firewall, the firewall makes allow/deny decisions based on traffic factors rather than user- or host-identification factors. In this configuration, the firewall is not involved in the authentication process. Instead, the host beyond the firewall that receives the communication handles any necessary authentication.

For example, a firewall can protect a DMZ. Most DMZ firewalls do not perform at-firewall authentication. Instead, the Web servers hosted in the DMZ can provide both anonymous content and authenticated content to visitors. Visitors log on using any means of authentication supported by the Web server, the protocols in use, and the visiting client. Commonly this is forms-based authentication secured through an SSL or TLS encrypted session.

When any form of authentication takes place, whether at or through the firewall, always encrypt all authentication-related communications. Non-encrypted or plain text authentication traffic is subject to eavesdropping and thus theft of credentials. Encrypted authentication traffic is resistant to eavesdropping as well as replay attacks and in some circumstances even man-in-the-middle attacks.

Many different authentication protocols, both encrypted and plaintext, can be employed by at-firewall or beyond-firewall authentication. Whatever the solution, evaluate all authentication options in light of its native security and inherent risks. If you are using authentication encryption, realize this does not ensure that subsequent data exchanges are automatically encrypted. Select solutions that provide protection for both authentication traffic as well as data traffic.

You can avoid authentication completely with anonymous connectivity. In an anonymous connection, the user and/or host identity is unknown and access is granted or denied based exclusively on the traffic content and the proper formation of resource requests. For example, public Web site access can be anonymous, such as at Wikipedia (*http://www.wikipedia.org*), which supports mostly anonymous connections to its online community encyclopedia.

Authorization takes place after authentication. Authorization, as with authentication, can take place either at the firewall or beyond the firewall. When authorization takes place at the firewall, the firewall itself makes a decision on allowing subsequent communications across the firewall. This is sometimes known as controlling the circuit. If the authenticated user does not have access to a resource, the firewall will block or drop the connection. If the authenticated user does have access to a resource, then the firewall allows and supports the connection.

Usually, the firewall is only involved in authorization of the connection or circuit. Any content within the subsequent communication might be subject to content filtering, but that's a distinct and separate service and function of the firewall. This form of authorization control is the same as a circuit proxy.

When authorization takes place beyond a firewall, just as with beyond the firewall authentication, the destination host controls what is and is not accessible to users. The firewall is only involved in monitoring for abuses or potentially filtering content. When the firewall performs content filtering on a communication not managed by the at-firewall authorization, this is the same as an application proxy.

While authentication and authorization are commonly used together to control users' access based on their identity, they can be employed independently. For example, a firewall performing at-firewall authentication does not need to also provide separate authorization. If users authenticate, then they have access to whatever is beyond the firewall. If users fail to authenticate, then they do not have access. In this example, the authentication process itself is a form of authorization.

Similarly, a firewall can perform at-firewall authorization without authentication. This is the basic or normal function of firewall rules. Authentication is assumed when addresses and ports in traffic headers "identify" the communications; the rule sets themselves provide authorization restrictions. If a port is closed, access is denied. If a source address is blocked, then access is denied.

Authentication and authorization are important components of a complete network security structure. Use these services on a firewall or beyond the firewall as necessary. Additional important services related to firewall security are monitoring and logging of traffic and events that occur on or across a firewall.

> **NOTE**
>
> One example of a device able to record all traffic within a sliding period is the Solera DS series of network forensic appliances. For more information on this type of advanced network monitoring product, visit their Web site at: *http://www.soleranetworks.com/*.

Monitoring and Logging

Monitoring and logging are the recording of events and traffic that take place on or across a firewall. While in theory you can record every packet traversing a firewall, this is usually impractical because the storage space required would be immense. Certain products can maintain a sliding window of recorded traffic encompassing hours of communications using multiple terabytes of storage. However, these devices are for advanced security management and beyond the scope of this book.

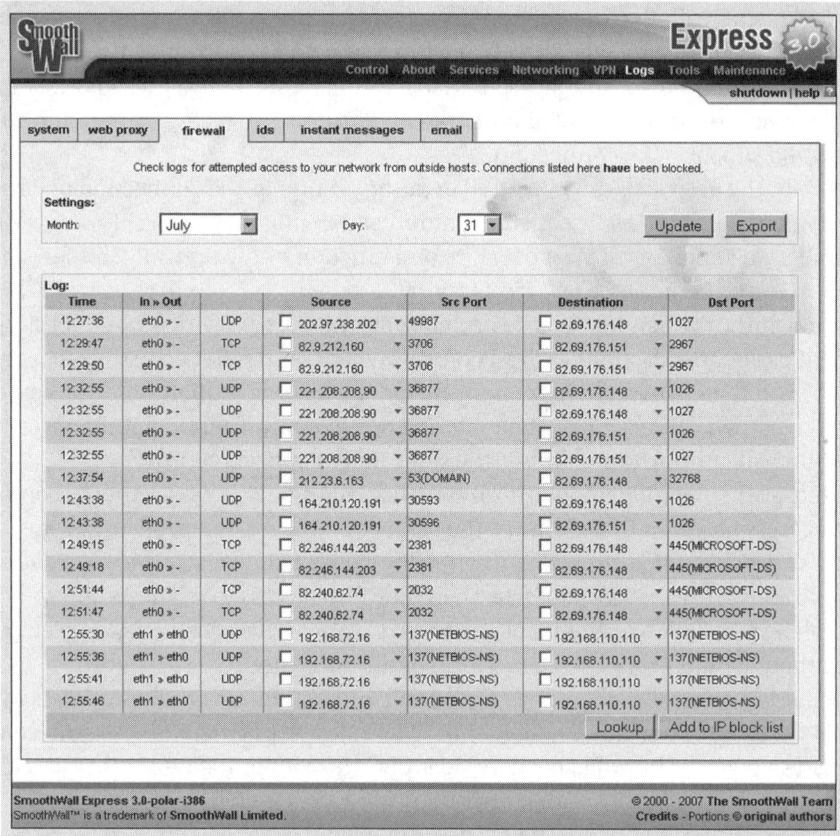

Time	In » Out		Source	Src Port	Destination	Dst Port
12:27:36	eth0 » -	UDP	202.97.238.202	49987	82.69.176.148	1027
12:29:47	eth0 » -	TCP	82.9.212.160	3706	82.69.176.151	2967
12:29:50	eth0 » -	TCP	82.9.212.160	3706	82.69.176.151	2967
12:32:55	eth0 » -	UDP	221.208.208.90	36877	82.69.176.148	1026
12:32:55	eth0 » -	UDP	221.208.208.90	36877	82.69.176.148	1027
12:32:55	eth0 » -	UDP	221.208.208.90	36877	82.69.176.151	1026
12:32:55	eth0 » -	UDP	221.208.208.90	36877	82.69.176.151	1027
12:37:54	eth0 » -	UDP	212.23.6.163	53(DOMAIN)	82.69.176.148	32768
12:43:38	eth0 » -	UDP	164.210.120.191	30593	82.69.176.148	1026
12:43:38	eth0 » -	UDP	164.210.120.191	30596	82.69.176.151	1026
12:49:15	eth0 » -	TCP	82.246.144.203	2381	82.69.176.148	445(MICROSOFT-DS)
12:49:18	eth0 » -	TCP	82.246.144.203	2381	82.69.176.148	445(MICROSOFT-DS)
12:51:44	eth0 » -	TCP	82.240.62.74	2032	82.69.176.148	445(MICROSOFT-DS)
12:51:47	eth0 » -	TCP	82.240.62.74	2032	82.69.176.148	445(MICROSOFT-DS)
12:55:30	eth1 » eth0	UDP	192.168.72.16	137(NETBIOS-NS)	192.168.110.110	137(NETBIOS-NS)
12:55:36	eth1 » eth0	UDP	192.168.72.16	137(NETBIOS-NS)	192.168.110.110	137(NETBIOS-NS)
12:55:41	eth1 » eth0	UDP	192.168.72.16	137(NETBIOS-NS)	192.168.110.110	137(NETBIOS-NS)
12:55:46	eth1 » eth0	UDP	192.168.72.16	137(NETBIOS-NS)	192.168.110.110	137(NETBIOS-NS)

FIGURE 7-4
An example of SmoothWall's firewall logging display interface.

Firewall monitoring and logging are about recording events that take place on or across a firewall (Figure 7-4). You can use various approaches to logging, such as log everything to log only events of seeming importance. Generally, you will fine-tune logging through real-world experience over time. Most security professionals recommend capturing everything initially. Later, you can tune logging and reduce it once you've identified specific types of information, traffic, or events as having no forensic, evidentiary, or historical value.

Firewall logging ensures that the defined filters or rules are sufficient and functioning as you expect. By watching traffic coming through a firewall's filtering scheme, you can discover traffic the firewall should have blocked, but for which an effective rule was not defined (or properly defined). Firewall logging helps to confirm that the restrictions imposed by the firewall are functioning as you expect and the security you assumed the firewall would provide is actually present.

Generally, record every connection allowed by the firewall as well as every packet dropped or blocked. This stance of "log and monitor everything" ensures that nothing goes unnoticed and that future investigations of log file contents will reveal complete data. You can always throw out extra and unnecessary data later, but you can't recover important data not recorded during the actual event.

Firewall logging can take place on the firewall itself or offload to a dedicated logging system. In either case, the firewall itself collects the event and/or packet you want to record. The difference is whether the information goes into a log file stored locally on the firewall or moves across a network connection to a dedicated logging server.

One well-known and widely used **centralized logging system** is syslog. Syslog is a standard for forwarding log messages from a client device (the firewall in this situation) to a centralized server. Linux and Unix systems have supported syslog capabilities for decades. Windows systems prior to Windows 7 required third-party products to interact with syslog services. Most network devices, including firewalls, switches, proxies, and so on, natively support syslog.

Firewall logging:

- Creates a historical record of activity for traffic and trend analysis as well as growth prediction
- Tracks usage levels and times for load balancing, account, or even back-charging users
- Discovers new methods or techniques of attack, especially those based on network packet manipulation
- Detects intrusions or attempts to breach security
- Creates legally admissible evidence for use in prosecution

Having a firewall log of all events produces a significant amount of recorded information. Always track available remaining storage capacity to ensure sufficient space remains to store new logged events. As a current storage device reaches capacity, back up and move the records into long-term archival storage. In a future investigation, you can never know how far back you'll need to look to discover evidence of a security breach. Your organization's written document retention policy should define how long you will retain logs.

In addition to juggling the storage requirements, you will need to be able to analyze logged data. Log file analysis is not usually an exciting proposition for most people. Long and tedious, it can be mind-bendingly boring. Fortunately, a growing field of automated analysis tools can reduce the time and burden of log file investigation. First-hand knowledge, understanding, and experience are always the best tools for interpreting and understanding firewall log contents.

If a hacker finds a way to infiltrate your network, one of the first steps most experienced hackers take is to remove all evidence of their activities. They normally do this by deleting log files or surgically editing log files with specialized tools. For example, WinZapper is a tool that edits Windows log files and removes only those entries matching a keyword such as an IP address or username. To combat this potential threat, use a **write-once read-many (WORM)** storage device to save all log files. Intruders cannot edit data written to a WORM device.

If you make the decision not to record everything taking place across the firewall, here's a short list of essential things to log:

- All connection attempts rejected by the firewall
- All traffic directed at the firewall
- Any access to internal resources by external hosts
- Any access to external resources by internal hosts
- Any modification or disabling of firewall rules and filters
- All firewall reboots, storage device shortages, or other abnormal operational events

Every firewall management interface is different. Thus, the methods and mechanisms you employ to configure your specific logging and monitoring will be different as well. Always be sure to consult the firewall's documentation about the type of logging and what types of events are logged before deploying a firewall.

Define firewall logging in the firewall security policy included in your organization's written network security policy. The logging and monitoring features of a firewall are as essential as the rule and filter mechanism you use to allow or deny traffic. Configuring and recording logs is important, but understanding how to interpret firewall logs is more important.

Understanding and Interpreting Firewall Logs and Alerts

Enabling firewall logging is often a fairly simple task. Recording traffic and events into a file is not really a complex task. But deciding which events warrant the triggering of an alert and what the contents of a log file actually mean is not always so straightforward.

An **alert** is the automated notification of an administrator when a specific event affects the firewall. Some software host firewalls are preconfigured with a wide number of pop-up messages triggered each time one of the all-too-common activities occurs. For example, each time a new application attempts to communicate with the network, a firewall pop-up alert might notify the user of this event and prompt an action (Figure 7-5).

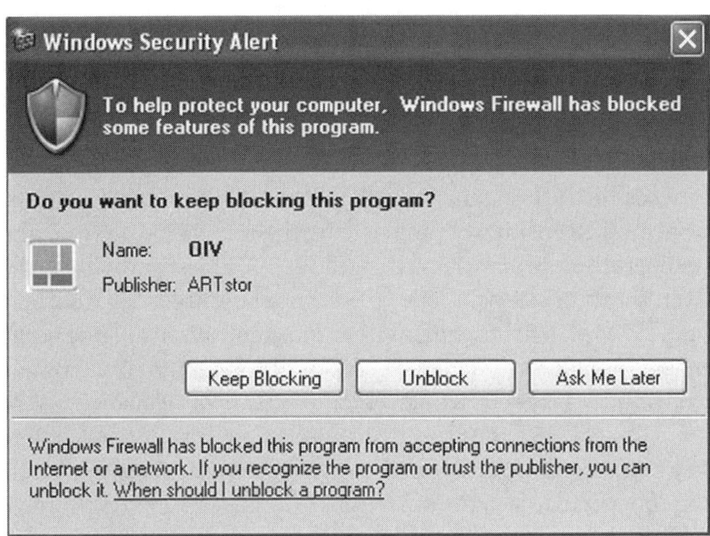

FIGURE 7-5
An example of a Windows Firewall pop-up alert.

Appliance firewalls and those generally designed to protect a network rather than a single host are usually not as commonly configured with pre-set default alerts. Instead, the firewall administrator makes choices about what events actually need alerts. Some common events that usually warrant alerts include:

- Firewall reboot
- A connection attempt with the firewall host itself.
- Communications to or from a pre-identified IP address or subnet
- Detection of some or all attack attempts
- Detection of any successful intrusion or security breach

Ultimately, the organization's security stance and the level of risk determine which events require alerts, as opposed to simply recording them in a log file. A common recommendation is to alert only on those events likely to require an administrator's immediate response or action. Everything, or nearly so, should go into a log, but not everything warrants an alert.

With or without alerts, a firewall's logging system creates a massive amount of raw data that isn't useful. You can perform analysis of a log file either in real-time or in periodic batches. You can hire a large staff of professionals whose primary task is to perform real-time log file analysis, or you can use an automated analysis or IDS/IPS tool. In most cases, automated log file analysis tools both reduce the strain on manpower and leverage the power of high-speed computing against the massive volumes of information collected by network firewalls.

Through careful analysis of firewall logs, you can detect several different types of unwanted or malicious activities, including worms, Trojan horses, remote control tools, port scans, and directed intrusion attempts. When you perform manual log analysis, the first hurdle is to gain access to the log file content.

Many firewalls record their log files in binary or obfuscated form so that they are difficult for external or unauthorized users to access. Such log files require administrators to access the log contents through a firewall-log reading interface. Some third-party products function as alternative management interfaces and can also interpret the log file format for viewing.

Once you obtain access to the log contents, either directly or through an interpretation interface, the next hurdle is to ensure you are viewing the correct log. Several different types of log files can operate on your system, including traffic logs, audit logs, alert logs, console logs, and even a host device's OS logs for software host firewalls. Another nuance is that the firewall device itself, a management host, or a centralized logging server might store its own logs. Finally, several dated versions of a log might exist. Be sure to open or access the most recent log—or whatever date range is of relevance to a specific investigation.

Of course, the key to interpreting and understanding the contents of a firewall log lies in understanding how network communications function. Every communication session involves two hosts, each with its own IP address and port number. Some forms of communications have less information, such as blocked connection attempts, connectionless traffic, and layer-3 protocols such as ICMP and IGMP.

By examining each established session to evaluate the source and destination IP addresses and the port numbers in use, you can quickly determine whether the transaction was valid or invalid. If the addresses are known—or at least not known to be malicious—and the ports are for acceptable services, then the communication is most likely benign. However, if an address is a known malicious host or an invalid address (such as an unassigned internal address) or you discover a known malware port, these are signs of unwanted and potentially malicious communications (or at least attempts to communicate).

IANA and some security vendors maintain a list of well-known port numbers and the associated applications. They often list known malicious software and their commonly used port numbers. Search for "malicious ports" or "Trojan ports" to find current lists.

General guidelines for examining and interpreting firewall logs might include:

1. Identify and discard all packets involved in benign sessions between valid hosts and valid ports.
2. Identify and discard all valid UDP transmissions from and to valid hosts and ports.
3. Identify and discard all valid ICMP (and other authorized protocols) to and from valid hosts.
4. Identify any communication from known malicious addresses. (This is a symptom of communications from known malicious hosts).
5. Identify any communication from unauthorized or unassigned internal addresses. (This is a symptom of rouge internal hosts).

6. Identify any communication to an unknown or unauthorized port on an internal host.
(This is a symptom of rouge internal services).
7. Identify any patterns of serial communication attempts across a sequential or randomized set of addresses and/or ports.
(This is a symptom of scanning and probing).
8. Identify significant volumes of non-session traffic of the same or similar construction to one or a small group of internal addresses.
(This is a symptom of flooding).
9. Identify any packet of invalid size or invalid header construction.
(This is a symptom of scanning, probing, and exploitation attempt).
10. Identify any packet with configured source routing.
(This is a symptom of attempted intrusion or traffic shaping).
11. Identify packets destined to non-resource sharing systems, such as firewalls or routers.
(This is a symptom of probing, network scanning, and exploitation attempt).

This is just the start of a firewall log file analysis procedure. For each and every threat, exploit, attack, or concern that an organization wishes to identify, add a step to search log contents for the appropriate symptoms. Remember that many symptoms are shared across a wide variety of malicious activities.

Keep in mind that hackers can perform malicious activities within seemingly benign traffic. This is especially true when the payload of traffic is the malicious content itself. Firewalls can detect malicious or abnormal characteristics based on header information and packet construction oddities, but many types of malicious payloads are not firewall filterable. For example, password guessing against a logon prompt is typically not a filterable activity. An Intrusion Detection System (IDS) or an Intrusion Prevent System (IPS) could potentially detect online password guessing, but not a firewall.

This brings up an important issue discussed previously, but it bears repeating: firewalls are not perfect. Firewalls are only part of a security infrastructure; they are not the totality of security in and of themselves. Even when you use them properly, firewalls have limitations. For example, they are of no help in protecting against an insider attack. You can learn more about firewall limitations in a later section in this chapter.

The best tool for interpreting the contents of a firewall log is solid and thorough familiarity with the normal and expected traffic that occurs across a network. By knowing what is normal and expected, you are much better prepared to detect and identify the abnormal and unexpected. Keep complete configuration documentation and actively seek direct, hands-on knowledge and experience to improve your ability as a firewall administrator to examine, interpret, and take action on the contents of log files.

Intrusion Detection

A firewall is a border sentry device. A controlled network border sentry device filters any traffic attempting to cross. However, not all traffic that needs monitoring crosses a network border guarded by a firewall. That's where an intrusion detection system comes into play. An IDS or an IPS monitors internal hosts or networks watching for symptoms of compromise or intrusion. Effectively, an IDS is a form of burglar alarm that detects when an attack is occurring within the network.

An IDS serves as a companion mechanism to a firewall. Once an IDS detects an intruder, it can send commands or requests to the firewall to break a connection, block an IP address, or block a port/protocol. You must configure the firewall to receive these commands and authorize the IDS to send them. However, not all IDSs and firewalls are compatible in this manner.

Eventually, security professionals developed the IPS concept. The IPS strives to detect the attempt to attack or intrusion before it can be successful. Once detected, the IPS can respond preventing the success of the attempt, rather than waiting until after a successful breach to respond. IPSs do not replace IDSs. Instead, they are often used as a first or initial layer of pro-active defense and relegating the IDS to a reactive measure against those events that the IPS misses or that internal personnel perform.

IDS and IPS are important components of a complete network security solution. However, they are not without fault. IDS/IPS solutions can create a false sense of security under certain conditions. Two commonly discussed conditions include unknown "zero-day" attacks and "**false positives**."

When unknown zero-day attacks threaten the network, an IDS or IPS might not have the mechanism to detect them. Thus, the lack of an alarm could cause administrators to assume that no attacks are occurring. In most cases, the lack of an alarm does mean that nothing malicious is happening. So this assumption is not completely unwarranted. But if an IDS never triggers an alarm, then suspect a poor detection system, rather than the complete lack of compromise attempts, or attacks.

When an IDS fails to detect an attack, whether it's a zero-day or a known attack that was simply overlooked, this is called a **false negative**. A false negative is one of the most problematic issues with an IDS, as it can lull the organization into a false sense of security. When alarms are not going off, it's common to assume that no malicious events are taking place. If that's a false assumption, then real attacks are occurring and the security staff is unaware. This is the worst type of security breach.

False positives may create a false sense of security for the opposite reason, namely too many alarms from benign occurrences. Remember the story of the little boy who cried, "Wolf!"? After the first initial alarms turn out to be benign activity, the urgency of responding to alarms diminishes. After additional false positives, an administrator might put off investigating the alarms. Eventually, you ignore the alarms altogether. Once this situation arises, you treat even alarms for malicious events as false positives, once again reinforcing a false sense of security.

IDS and IPS can use rule-based detection mechanisms similar to those of a firewall, but they can also employ detection mechanisms borrowed from antivirus technology. For example, some IDS/IPS have a database of signatures or patterns of known malicious activity. This is known as **signature-**, **database-**, or **knowledge-based detection**. Any attack within the database can be detected in live activity by the IDS.

Another form of detection is anomaly based. **Anomaly-based detection** systems look for abnormalities. To do that, you have to first define "normal." Normal can be defined by rules or filters that prescribe all of the valid packet constructions and header contents. Then, anything that fails to match the definition of normal is an anomaly. Since mistakes, errors, and poor network application programming can occur, an anomaly is not necessarily malicious or an intentional attack.

Yet another detection mechanism is behavioral based. **Behavioral-based detection** looks for differences from normal-based on a recording of real-world traffic that establishes a baseline. A normal baseline can be recorded over hours or days. Once recorded, it's the yardstick to measure all future activities. Any future event not similar to behaviors in the baseline set represents a possible violation.

As with anomaly detection, behavioral-based detection has its own limitations. For example, all forms of benign behavior may not have occurred during the behavior recording time. Or, during the recording period, malicious events might have taken place. In either case, future situations can generate false positives (mistaking benign behavior as malicious) or false negatives (mistaking malicious behavior as benign).

Some IDS/IPSs can import and interpret firewall logs as another source of information in their efforts to detect unwanted activity. Thus, in addition to reviewing log files manually or with separate investigation tools, they can also benefit IDS/IPS and improve their scope and effectiveness.

IDS and IPS are not substitutes for firewalls, but potential supplemental or companion solutions that might expand the effective detection methods already available. When you are considering an IDS and/or IPS to improve the filtering already provided by a firewall, carefully consider deployment options and thoroughly plan out the improved infrastructure. Compare the plan to a typical IT infrastructure and consider within where the placement of an IDS/IPS makes the most sense for your organization.

Limitations of Firewalls

Firewalls are essential components of security. Standalone home systems to global IT infrastructures all need firewalls as part of their overall security solution. However, firewalls are not perfect solutions. In fact, you need to account for several well-known limitations in the design and management of network security.

Firewalls are ultimately software code written by humans. In either a host firewall or an appliance firewall, the logic and controlling mechanisms of the firewall are software code. Software code is designed and written by people. Whenever people are involved, the possibility exists that they made mistakes or oversights. Fortunately, most firewall products are rigorously and thoroughly tested as a counterbalance to this threat. But nobody should assume that the firewall software code is inherently perfect.

It doesn't happen often, but it has happened—and will happen again—that administrators and hackers discover software coding bugs or flaws in real-time use. Hackers are constantly using scanning, testing, and probing tools to discover exploitable weaknesses. Once a vulnerability appears, a hacker will create an exploit that takes advantage of the flaw. Some exploits have caused firewalls to freeze or crash while others have given hackers the ability to read or adjust filtering rules.

Some exploits are based on buffer overflows. A buffer overflow is a condition whereby a memory buffer exceeds its capacity and extends its contents into adjacent memory. Hackers often use this as an attack against poor programming techniques or poor software quality control. Hackers can inject more data into a memory buffer than it can hold, which may result in the additional data overflowing into the next area of memory. If the overflow extends to the next memory segment designated for code execution, a skilled attacker can insert arbitrary code that will execute with the same privileges as the current program. Improperly formatted overflow data may also result in a system crash.

Once the firewall vendors become aware of an exploit in the field, they quickly develop and release a patch. By having an effective security management and patch management system, you can quickly test and install such new updates for the firewalls protecting your production environment. If the release of a patch or the application of a patch is delayed, the window of opportunity for hackers to compromise your environment remains open.

Firewalls can sometimes be vulnerable to fragmentation attacks. Fragmentation attacks are an abuse of the fragmentation-offset feature of IP packets. Fragmentation may occur in a network where many different network links join to construct a global infrastructure. Some network segments support smaller datagrams (another term for packet or frame) than others, so larger datagrams fragment into the smaller size. When the fragmented elements of the original datagram reassemble, reassembly of the fragments can cause several potentially malicious reconstructions, such as overlapping and overrun.

Overlapping can cause full or partial overwriting of datagram components creating new datagrams out of parts of previous datagrams (Figure 7-6). Overrun can cause excessively large datagrams to be constructed. Other fragmentation attacks are designed to cause DoS or attempt to confuse IDS detection or firewall filtering.

Protections against fragmentation attacks include using modern IDS detection and firewall filtering features, as well as performing sender fragmentation. Sender fragmentation queries the network route to determine the smallest maximum transmission unit (MTU) or datagram size. Then the sender pre-fragments the data to ensure that no in-route fragmentation will occur.

Firewalking is another known firewall limitation. Firewalking is a technique to learn the configuration of a firewall from the outside. The technique uses a valid IP address of an internal host. Then, from an external system, a hacker attempts to establish a communication session with the internal host over a multitude of different ports. Effectively, this is a form of port scanning, but with the addition of the known internal host, the hacker can learn not only which ports are open, but also which ports actually allow communications with an internal system. Effectively, firewalking discovers the rules or filters on a basic packet filtering firewall. Modern stateful inspection firewalls are usually not as vulnerable to firewalking as they can detect this mechanistic activity.

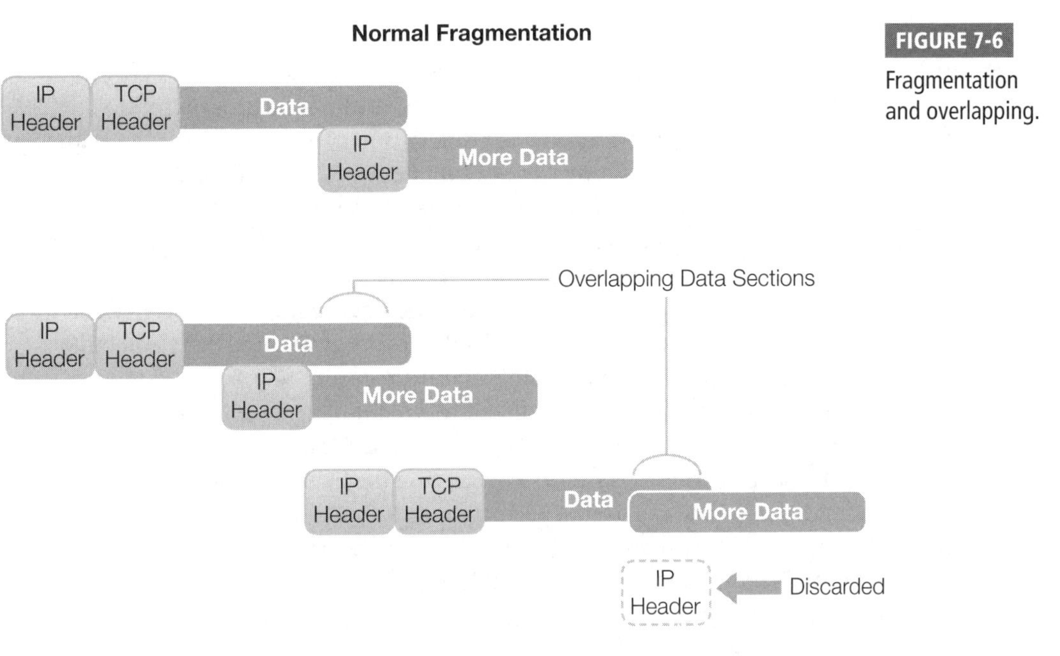

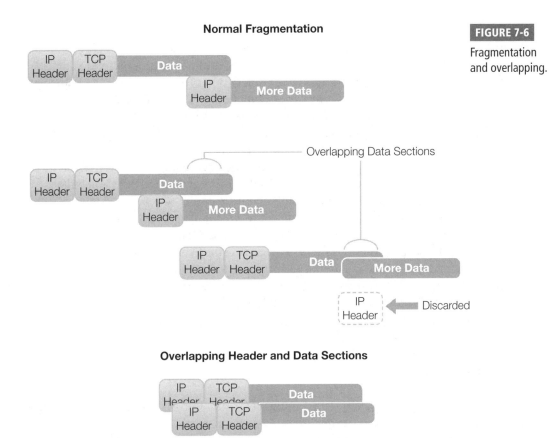

FIGURE 7-6
Fragmentation and overlapping.

Internal code planting is another known firewall limitation. Firewalls are often deployed as border sentries. They are intended to protect internal systems from communications that originate from external entities. Unfortunately, some security administrators only use inbound firewall filtering that leaves outbound traffic uncontrolled and unfiltered.

In this situation, if a hacker can plant code internally, trick a user into running code, or an employee brings in code of his own, the possibility exists that outbound connections to malicious external entities could occur. Many hacker tools are based on this technique, such as Loki, Back Orifice, NetBus, and event netcat. A hacker creates a server of sorts that is hosted on an external host. The automatic connection client utility executes on an internal host. The client utility establishes the connection, and then the external host is able to send data or commands back to the internal client. Often this form of attack results in a hacker gaining modest to complete remote control over the compromised internal host.

Denial of service (DoS) is another common problem that reveals a limitation of a firewall. A denial of service, specifically a flooding- or traffic-based DoS, sends massive amounts of data to a target victim. If that victim has a firewall, then the firewall can detect and discard the potential DoS traffic. The firewall's filtering service can usually prevent the DoS traffic from breaching the network's perimeter and affecting internal systems.

However, since the firewall has to collect, analyze, and respond to every packet received on its interfaces, a well-organized DoS can consume all available bandwidth of the connecting segment to the firewall as well as consume all of the processing capabilities of the firewall. This in turn prevents any legitimate traffic from reaching the network. Thus, even with a firewall protecting the internal network, a DoS flooding attack can still successfully disconnect or interfere with external communications.

The vulnerability to DoS flooding is the one limitation or weakness of firewalls that you cannot fix, improve, or repair by either upgrading the firewall or applying a patch. Upgrading to a stateful inspection firewall addresses fragmentation, firewalking, and even internal planting of code. Patching will address programming bugs and buffer overflows. Upstream filtering is one possible countermeasure to prevent flooding attacks from reaching an Internet-facing firewall, but this technology requires cooperation from Internet service providers (ISP) and other third parties.

Knowing these limitations, as well as recognizing the likelihood of others, brings the security administrator back to basics. Security management is mandatory to maintain any semblance of security in any environment. Keep systems current with patches, use a hardened configuration, stay knowledgeable about new exploitations, and monitor the environment for successful and attempted compromise. These are the essential long-term strategies for maintaining security.

Improving Performance

Using a firewall is mainly about establishing and maintaining border security, but security managers must also look into other areas of importance and concern beyond just security. One of these additional non-security areas is performance. Since the goal of security is to protect the production environment, installing security measures that severely hinder capabilities necessary to accomplish work is counterproductive.

One of the most common concerns with the use of firewalls is network communication speed. When selected and installed properly, a firewall should function at **wirespeed**. Functioning at wirespeed means the firewall does not introduce any delay or latency in communications because it operates at the same speed as the network. If there is a 1000 Mbps network, then a 100 Mbps capable firewall is too slow.

Two primary means can help you to improve firewall performance above and beyond purchasing a firewall suitable for the network's known transmission speed. These two means are caching and **load balancing**.

Caching is a technique to seemingly improve performance borrowed from proxy servers. In fact, adding caching to a firewall effectively transforms it into a proxy server for whatever service you configure the caching to supplement. Caching is the holding of often-accessed content in storage or memory on the firewall, so that when a future request for the same content is received, the cached copy goes into service rather than the original external source. This does require that the content be relatively static and that a staleness value be used to trigger a content refresh.

technical TIP

Router load balancing traffic management can use a variety of scheduling algorithms, such as **round robin** or **fair queuing**. Round robin simply hands out tasks in a non-priority sequence. For example, with three firewalls and five transactions, transaction one is sent to firewall one, transaction two to firewall two, transaction three to firewall three, transaction four to firewall one, and transaction five to firewall two. Fair queuing operates by sending the next transaction to the firewall with the least current workload.

Unfortunately, caching is only beneficial on two main services: Web and file transfer. If the potential or actual bottlenecks to performance across a firewall are not due to these two types of communication, then caching is not a good solution.

Load balancing is the distribution of the firewall filtering workload across multiple parallel firewalls. You can use this as shown in Figure 7-7 using a phalanx of two or more firewalls deployed in parallel between routers that perform load balancing traffic management on both inbound and outbound communications. Load balancing allows for deeper-packet inspection while maintaining wirespeed performance using parallel-distributed firewall processing.

The use of load balancing often has additional benefits, such as redundancy and fault tolerance. Both of these improve the availability of the firewall filtering service for network communications. Having a fail-safe or fail-secure plan to disconnect communications if the firewall is compromised is essential. However, a more secure and productivity-friendly solution is to maintain continued communication with filtering by having redundant pathways with duplicate firewalls.

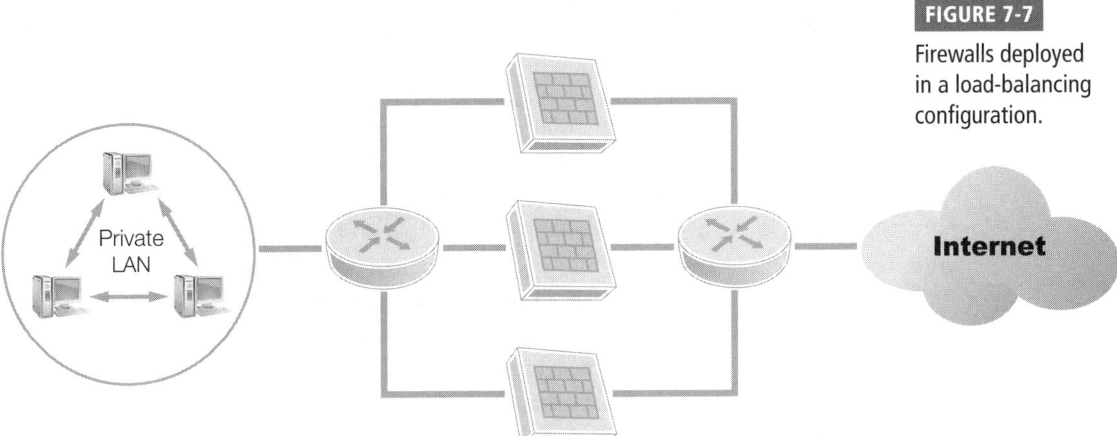

FIGURE 7-7

Firewalls deployed in a load-balancing configuration.

The Downside of Encryption with Firewalls

Encryption is a common security mechanism you can employ to protect data in storage and in transit. When used properly, encryption provides confidentiality protection. Encryption prevents unauthorized third parties from gaining access to secured content. With the risk of eavesdropping and data theft constantly increasing, the use of encryption is becoming not just a good idea, but also an essential element of storage and transaction security.

However, encryption does have a downside relative to firewalls. A firewall is typically not the intended destination or direct communication partner of a communication, especially encrypted communications. Thus, any encrypted data cannot be filtered by a firewall. However, just because packets are encrypted does not automatically mean that nothing about the packet remains in plain text.

As discussed in Chapter 3 about VPNs, two main forms of transaction or communication encryption apply: tunnel mode and transport mode. Tunnel mode encrypts the entire original payload and header, while transport mode only encrypts the payload. In tunnel mode, a temporary header goes with the encrypted packet to guide its path across the VPN tunnel. In transport mode, the original header remains in plain text.

A firewall can still view and filter on the contents of the tunnel mode header or the transport mode header. However, the tunnel mode header only contains details about the end-points of the tunnel, not the endpoints of the actual communication itself. So, tunnel mode header filtering is not very useful as a filter against malicious traffic.

Filtering on the transport mode header is a viable option, as this is the same filtering and the same header in the packet was not transport mode encrypted. Thus, any header-only filtering rules could still apply to transport mode-encrypted communications. However, any filtering that required an examination of the payload will be rendered null.

When building or designing firewall filtering rules, you must make a choice about how to handle encrypted content. Consider both the valid and invalid reasons for content encryption. The organization can choose to support or allow encryption of specific types over specific protocols or ports, but disallow and prevent encrypted communications elsewhere. Encryption for Web communications and e-mail exchanges are often acceptable, while other transactions with the Internet might not be encrypted.

When designing the firewall rules, the management of encrypted traffic can range from full allowance to full denial. Whether to allow encryption over a specific port but not another and whether to allow encryption all the time, for only certain users, or for no one are common issues your organization needs to address and plan for.

No ultimate right or wrong decision about whether to allow encryption across a network border is possible. Decide based on the security stance of your organization, the risk presented by both encrypted and plain text transactions, and the types of communications essential for your particular business's tasks.

A growing trend in secure deployments, especially for DMZ or other hosted resources designated for public access, is to support encrypted communications, but have the encrypted tunnel end at or on a firewall. This allows you to examine the contents of the communications before they reach the actual destination. This is becoming

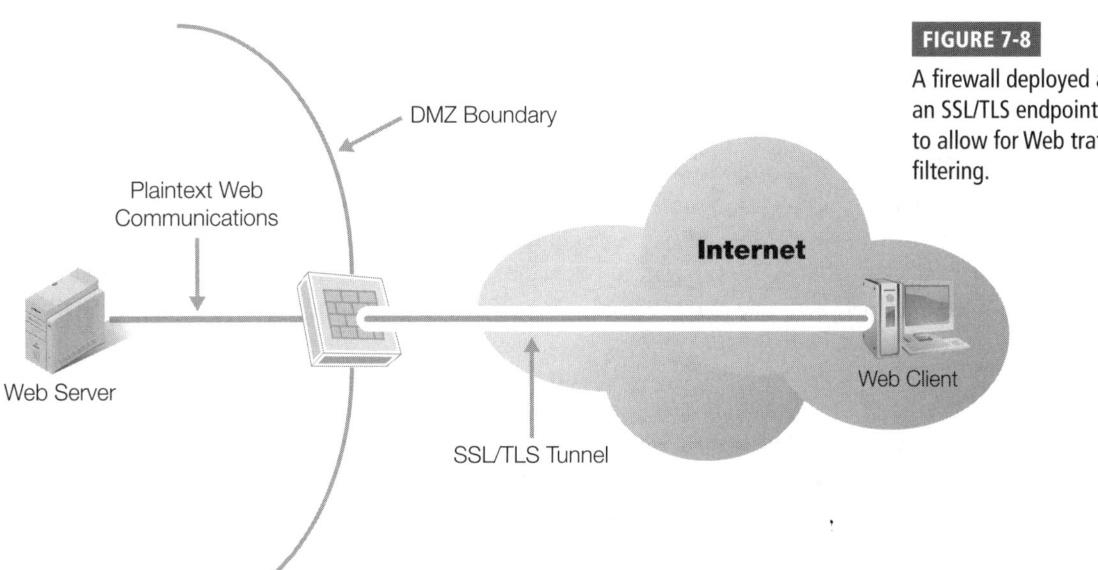

FIGURE 7-8
A firewall deployed as an SSL/TLS endpoint to allow for Web traffic filtering.

a common infrastructure design component for public facing Web sites. Figure 7-8 shows an example configuration where SSL or TLS links from external Internet clients end at the firewall; then, they traverse the last segment in the clear to reach the destination Web server.

Another concern is that when encrypted traffic crosses a firewall, the firewall is usually unable to perform NAT. This is dependent on the encryption system in use, but it's worth investigating before deployment. If the encryption mechanism hashes the header, even if it remains in plain text, the modification to the header by NAT will cause the hash verification process to fail, thus rendering the transmission void. With an encrypted header, NAT will be unable to modify the addresses. Be sure to select encryption protocols that are NAT-compatible if this is a necessary function of the network's infrastructure.

Firewall Enhancements

Firewalls emerged from basic router traffic control systems into full-featured content filters. However, throughout this evolution, firewalls have remained focused on their primary purpose—namely detecting unwanted, unknown, or malicious traffic and blocking it. The filtering mechanisms have typically been identification-based. Whether IP address, port, protocol service, MAC address, content keywords or even user authentication, the allow and deny decisions relied directly on easily definable elements.

Modern firewalls now offer a variety of enhancements, improvements, or add-on features some organizations might find attractive. As mentioned in Chapter 2, consider the value of these enhancements in light of the ability of the device to continue to perform the essential core services of firewall filtering. Do not let the snazzy up-sell add-ons distract from obtaining and deploying a reliable border sentry-filtering device.

It seems that all vendors dream up new enhancements to add to their product line each time they refresh, update, or make a product revision. So, be sure to thoroughly research any newly offered enhancement before making a purchase. Just because the bumpers are shiny does not mean the engine runs.

A common or popular firewall enhancement is malware scanning. Adding an antivirus, anti-spyware, anti-Trojan, anti-whatever scanner to a firewall is not a significant stretch of the core firewall's capabilities, especially for application proxies and stateful inspection firewalls. The main concerns should be whether such an enhancement can maintain wirespeed performance and the firewall's anti-malware abilities are on par with existing standalone malware protections.

If you are considering a firewall malware scanning enhancement, pay attention to the details. Important considerations are the detection engine and the mechanism of periodically updating virus signature definitions.

Firewalls can also offer IDS and IPS features. In fact, the merging of intrusion detection and prevention is a logical combination. The ability of a single device that can filter traffic as well as watch for and defend against intrusions is attractive. But the caveat remains: does the combination device perform both tasks at a level of excellence at least as good as common independent products? If not, then the combination is more of a detriment than a benefit. Also, does the firewall maintain its ability to operate at wirespeed?

Some firewalls are equipped to function as a VPN endpoint. You learned about this type of firewall device in Chapter 3. When designing a firewall and VPN architecture, this might be an attractive option, but as with every firewall enhancement, evaluate its features and performance against that of standalone solutions.

Unified threat management (UTM) is the deployment of a firewall as an all-encompassing primary gateway security solution. The idea behind UTM is that you can use a single device to perform firewall filtering, IPS, antivirus scanning, anti-spam filtering, VPN end-point hosting, content filtering, load-balancing, detailed logging, and potentially other security services, performance enhancements, or extended capabilities. UTM has its advantages, mainly in the ability to deploy a single product and manage multiple security services from a single interface.

UTMs can be a jack-of-all-trades product and a master of none. With many of the larger firewall and security product vendors developing product lines supporting UTM, however, it's possible to deploy a reliable single-device solution. But even a reliable UTM product remains a single-point of failure.

UTMs are obvious improvements to environments that use simple or outdated firewalls and those that lack independent coverage in the non-firewall security categories. An all-in-one UTM device can quickly and effectively improve your organization's security.

As the trend toward virtualized networks, hosts, and applications continues to expand, the need for security within virtualized networking environments increases as well. Just because the virtual hosts exist in memory alone does not imply that they are immune to hacking or exploitation. In fact, they may be at even greater risk. Include firewalls in the construction of virtualized networks.

You can still use a hardware firewall when traffic between virtual hosts crosses a physical network segment. However, when virtual host communications occur within memory alone, a virtualized firewall is necessary. A virtualized firewall is really the same as a virtualized host; it's a software construct of a hardware environment that hosts the operating system so it can function in memory, rather than on actual physical devices. You can install a software firewall into a virtual host to act as a firewall for virtual network connections. When designing and using a virtualized network, make the effort to include virtual firewalls as part of the infrastructure.

Management Interfaces

You must configure firewalls for them to perform the security functions you expect of them. Every firewall has a **management interface** used to configure its functions and features. Through the management interface, you can control and define all aspects of a firewall.

A firewall's management interface may be command-line-based (Figure 7-9) or graphical based (Figure 7-10). A graphical user interface(GUI)-based interface might be a standalone client application you must install onto a host, or it may be a Web interface hosted on the firewall's own internal mini-Web server.

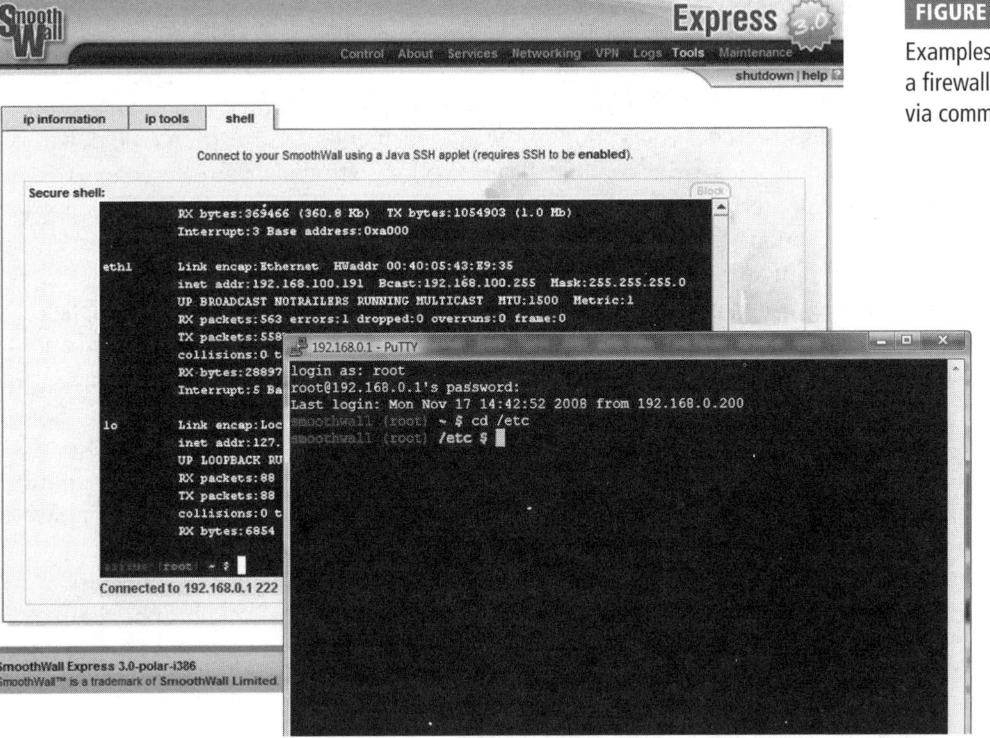

FIGURE 7-9
Examples of accessing a firewall (SmoothWall) via command line (SSH).

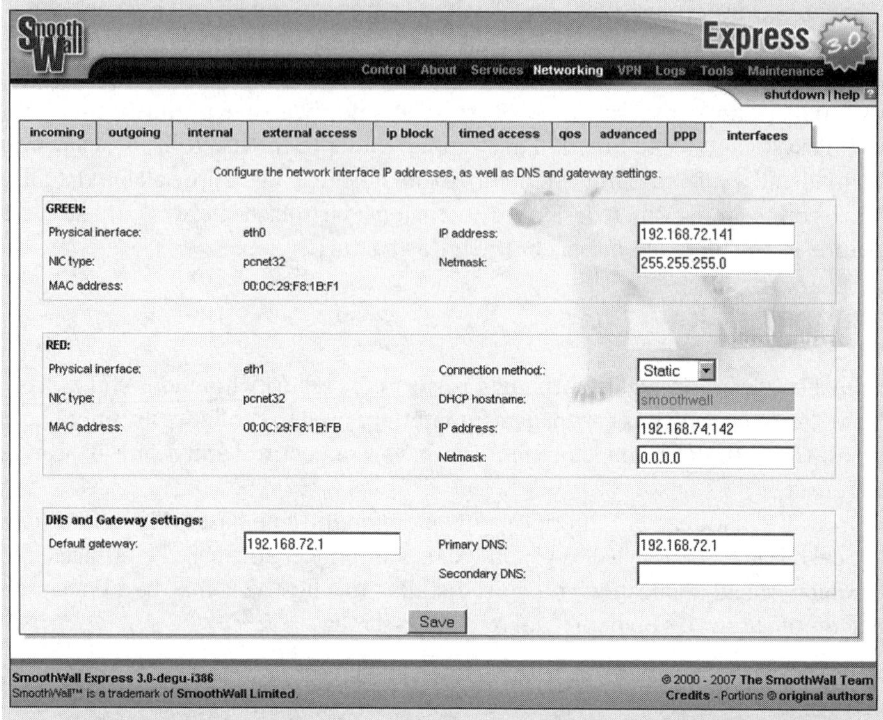

FIGURE 7-10

An example of a GUI firewall interface (SmoothWall).

A firewall's management interface may or may not offer encrypted access by default. If the firewall does not offer encryption of the management interface, then replace it with a firewall that does. Always enable the encryption so that all future accesses to the management interface are protected from eavesdropping, interception, and session hijacking. Encryption of the session accessing a firewall's management interface is the most important and critical aspect of management interface configuration.

Secure a firewall's management interface both physically and logically. This implies that direct physical contact with the firewall device (or firewall host) will be limited and restricted to authorized administrative personnel only. Prohibit any physical contact or proximity to external or unauthorized entities.

Secure all logical access to the firewall's management interface through a strong authentication process. If multifactor authentication is supported, use it. If not, require long and complex passwords. Ensure that administrators do not re-use the same password on any other system. Administrators, as well as all users, should never re-use an old password on any system once it expires. Think of passwords like milk, they only last so long, even with proper care and storage, but once expired, they can never be re-used.

Limit the methods to access a firewall's management interface. Upon initial deployment, the manufacturer likely enabled all possible avenues of access to ensure ease of installation. However, disable all methods of accessing the management interface except for the sole secure mechanism selected for use by your organization. Potentially available avenues of access include telnet, encrypted telnet, Web, encrypted Web, SSH, and other proprietary options. Select one of the secure options and disable the rest.

Also, consider the communication pathways for accessing the management interface. Usually the physical cable connection port, often labeled as CON for console, TER for terminal, or ADM for administration, cannot be disabled through software. This port is a dedicated port used for direct physical connection management and not for any other purpose (in most cases). A crossover cable or a special console cable (often RS-232 based) is necessary to connect a computer directly to the firewall to gain access to the management interface.

However, most in-network or over-the-network logical access pathways can be disabled. Be sure to disable access to the management interface on every physical network interface or port that faces outward. In other words, the less-secure NIC ports should not support access to the management interface.

If more than one NIC port exists on the secure side, then limit access to only one of those two ports. If the firewall is a multi-functional device that also supports wireless connectivity, disable management interface access over a wireless connection. The resulting configuration should allow management interface access only via the physical CON connection and one logical pathway. Disable all other methods of access.

Configure the firewall to record every attempted and successful connection to the management interface into a log file. It might also be a good idea to record all subsequent configuration changes made via the management interface. This log can serve as a component of change documentation and will assist with future troubleshooting, investigations, and reconfiguration.

CHAPTER SUMMARY

Firewalls are essential to maintaining security, such as supporting valid communications and blocking malicious traffic. However, firewalls are often more than just simple filtering tools. The standard and enhanced features of firewall products require knowledge and skill if you are to properly employ them.

This chapter discussed building firewall rules, ordering rule sets, configuring authentication and authorization based on the presence of a firewall, confiuring firewall logging, making sense of the contents of firewall logs, expanding firewall functions with intrusion detection, dealing with the limitations of firewalls, maintaining high-speed network performance with a firewall, managing encryption across a firewall, evaluating firewall enhancements, and handling firewall management interfaces.

KEY CONCEPTS AND TERMS

Access control list (ACL)
Alert
Allow by default
Anomaly-based detection
Behavioral-based detection
Caching
Centralized logging system
Database-based detection
Default allow
Deny by default
Fair queuing
False negative
False positive
Filters
Firewalking
IEEE 802.1x
Knowledge-based detection
Load balancing
Management interface
Port-based network access (admission) control (PNAC)
Round robin
Rule sets
Rule(s)
Signature-based detection
Unified threat management (UTM)
Wirespeed
Write-once read-many (WORM)

CHAPTER 7 ASSESSMENT

1. Which of the following is a firewall rule that prevents internal users from accessing public FTP sites?
   A. TCP ANY ANY ANY FTP Deny
   B. TCP 192.168.42.0/24 ANY ANY 21 Deny
   C. TCP 21 192.168.42.0/24 ANY ANY Deny
   D. TCP ANY ANY 192.168.42.0/24 21 Deny
   E. TCP FTP ANY ANY Deny

2. Which of the following is a default deny rule?
   A. TCP ANY ANY ANY ANY Deny
   B. TCP 192.168.42.0/24 ANY ANY ANY Deny
   C. TCP ANY 192.168.42.0/24 ANY ANY Deny
   D. TCP ANY ANY 192.168.42.0/24 ANY Deny
   E. DENY TCP ANY ANY ANY ANY

3. The default deny rule appears where in the rule set?
   A. First
   B. After any explicit allows
   C. Anywhere
   D. Last
   E. After any explicit denies

4. What mechanism allows a firewall to hand off authentication to a dedicated service hosted on a different system?
   A. IEEE 802.11
   B. RFC 1918
   C. IEEE 802.1x
   D. RFC 1492
   E. IEE 802.3

5. When an organization first deploys a firewall and chooses to begin logging activity, what should you include in the log file?
   A. Only malicious traffic
   B. Only DoS traffic
   C. Only dropped packets
   D. Only allowed packets
   E. All events

6. You can use firewall logging to perform all of the following activities *except*:
   A. Discover new methods or techniques of attack
   B. Create a historical record of activity used for traffic and trend analysis
   C. Track usage levels and times for load balancing
   D. Stop intrusions
   E. Create legally admissible evidence for use in prosecution

7. All of the following events appearing in a firewall log warrant investigation by an administrator *except*:
   A. Firewall host reboot
   B. A connection attempt to the firewall host
   C. Detection of an attack attempt
   D. Inbound packets with spoofed internal source addresses
   E. An internal user accessing a public Web site

8. Which of the following is a highly recommended method or technique for keeping firewall logs secure and uncorrupted?
   A. Storing them in binary form
   B. Using 15,000 RPM hard drives
   C. Recording only important events
   D. Centralized logging
   E. Using timestamps

9. Which of the following is an event found in a firewall log file that is a symptom of a rogue host operating within the private network?
   A. Packets from a known malicious address
   B. Packets from an unassigned internal address
   C. Packets to an unknown port on an internal host
   D. Packet in a serial grouping that attempt to access a sequential sequence of ports
   E. Packets in a very large grouping that are all exactly the same directed toward a single target

10. What is the biggest issue or problem with an IDS?
   A. False positive
   B. Failing to operate at wirespeed
   C. False negative
   D. Keeping the pattern database current
   E. Using anomaly detection

11. Which of the following is *not* a limitation or potential weakness of a firewall?
    A. Firewalking
    B. Software bugs or flaws
    C. Using first match apply rule systems
    D. Fragmentation attacks
    E. Internal code connecting to an external service

12. When a firewall is able to process packets, filtering malicious code, and transmit authorized communications onward to their destination without introducing latency or lag, this is known as operating at ________.

13. Which of the following is not related to improving or maintaining performing of a firewall?
    A. Native antivirus scanning
    B. Round-robin task assignment
    C. caching
    D. fair queuing session management
    E. Load balancing

14. What form of encryption allows a firewall to filter based on original source and destination address (assume the firewall is located along the path between session endpoints)?
    A. Tunnel mode
    B. VPN remote access encryption
    C. Transport mode
    D. VPN LAN to LAN encryption
    E. Header encryption

15. What type of communication session can be performance improved using caching on a firewall?
    A. Instant messaging
    B. Remote access
    C. E-mail
    D. Time synchronization
    E. Web

16. Which of the following limitations or potential weaknesses of a firewall cannot be fixed or corrected with the application of an update or patch?
    A. Programming bug or flaw
    B. Firewalking
    C. Buffer overflow vulnerability
    D. Fragmentation
    E. Denial of service due to traffic from external sources

17. What is the primary factor used to distinguish a great firewall enhancement from a marketing gimmick used to drive up sales?
    A. Does the enhanced firewall cost the same or less than separate products
    B. Does the enhancement affect the operating speed of the firewall
    C. Does the enhancement operate as good as or better than the original firewall
    D. Does the enhancement require the purchase of a new firewall, or can it be added to existing products already deployed
    E. Does the enhancement have a reoccurring license or subscription fee

18. What is the name of a single device that is based on a firewall but which has been expanded and improved to perform a wide variety of services, such as filtering, IPS, antivirus scanning, anti-spam filtering, VPN end-point hosting, content filtering, load-balancing, and detailed logging?
    A. Load balanced filtering
    B. Port based network access (admission) control
    C. Unified threat management
    D. Multi-factor authentication
    E. IEEE 802.1x

19. The most important configuration element in related to a firewall's management interface is:
    A. Access over wireless is prevented
    B. Access through a network interface is enabled
    C. Access is encrypted
    D. Access through a CON port is allowed
    E. Access to the device physically is controlled

20. All of the following avenues of accessing a firewall's management interface should be limited, restricted, or disabled *except*:
    A. wireless
    B. telnet
    C. Public facing NIC interface
    D. Port 80 Web
    E. Private network NIC interface

CHAPTER

8

Firewall Deployment Considerations

FIREWALLS CAN BE COMPLEX security solutions. Plan the deployment of a firewall carefully, whether it's for a small home office or a large corporation. Evaluate as many firewall deployment considerations as possible before ramping up.

Make a clear determination as to what types of traffic you will allow to cross the network border and which types you want to block. Evaluate common security strategies. They include security through obscurity, principle of least privilege, simplicity, defense-in-depth, defense diversity, choke point, weakest link, fail safe, and forced universal participation. Determine which strategies you want to use and integrate them into the organization's security policy and its firewall deployment.

Evaluate the purpose and content of the firewall policy. Clearly define the software and hardware firewall options you will use when adopting the firewall policy. Determine whether features such as reverse proxy and port forwarding are necessary to the infrastructure's network communications. Weigh the benefits of bastion host OSs before using new firewalls. Make sure to order firewall rules properly and use the least number of rules possible to enforce security goals.

Every organization is different and must evaluate its own business and security needs. Determine which tasks are essential, optional, personal, or malicious. Use firewalls and other controls to support what's necessary and block everything else. Security administrators are responsible for evaluating needs and solutions and for preparing a response when security and business interfere with each other.

Chapter 8 Topics

This chapter will cover the following topics and concepts:

- What should you allow and what you should block when using a firewall
- What common security strategies for firewall deployments are
- What essential elements of a firewall policy are
- What the software and hardware options for firewalls are
- What the benefit and purpose of reverse proxy are
- What the use and benefit of port-forwarding are
- Which considerations aid in selecting a bastion host operation system (OS)
- How to construct and order firewall rules
- How to evaluate needs and solutions in designing security
- What happens when security gets in the way of doing business

Chapter 8 Goals

Upon completion of this chapter, you will be able to:

- Compose a firewall policy defining what to allow and what to block.
- Describe various firewall security strategies.
- Define the pros and cons of reverse proxy and port forwarding.
- Explain the important of a bastion host.
- Assess the business impact of security over availability and performance.

What Should You Allow and What Should You Block?

The most commonly asked question when installing a firewall is "What should be allowed and what should be blocked?" This question assumes a distinct and definitive answer. The answer, however, is subjective and variable.

A single **security stance** or filtering configuration that works for every situation, every organization, or every system doesn't exist. Network security managers must investigate the needs and threats to make informed decisions about what traffic to allow and what traffic to block.

The first stage in making this determination is to perform a complete inventory of all needed or desired communications. This should include every transaction between internal systems, as well as any interaction with external systems. As part of this inventory, indicate the protocol in use, the port(s) in use, and the likely source and destination addresses.

A possible inventory of network communications could look like Table 8-1.

This is not an exhaustive table, but it shows the basic idea of an inventory of network communications. Notice that some communications are internal only, while others cross the network boundary. Based on a complete and exhaustive inventory of your network's communications, you can establish a potential rule base.

From the inventory, block from crossing the network border all communications that should only be internal. In most cases, the default-deny rule of a rule set will block those communications from doing so. However, when a port or protocol is in common, it's possible that an allow rule for a valid external communication would also allow external entities access to an internal-only communication.

In Table 8-1, an example of this issue is the e-mail protocol SMTP operating over port 25. By defining an allow-exception rule, you could create a loophole that threatens the internal communication on this same port. Reduce or eliminate this risk by using a very specific rule or by adding an additional deny exception.

A very specific rule in this example would allow external communication over port 25 only if it originated from the internal e-mail server at 192.168.42.115. With this rule defined, if any other internal host attempted an external SMTP communication on port 25, it would not be allowed—as the IP address would not match this specific rule and instead be blocked by the default-deny.

TABLE 8-1 A partial list of communications occurring on a network.

TRANSPORT LAYER PROTOCOL	PORT	PROTOCOL	SOURCE	DESTINATION
TCP	8080	HTTP	Internal Clients	192.168.42.101 (Internal Web site)
TCP	8081	HTTPS	Internal Clients	192.168.42.101 (Internal Web site)
TCP	80	HTTP	Internal Clients	Numerous Internet Web sites
TCP	443	HTTPS	Internal Clients	Numerous Internet Web sites
TCP	110	POP	Internet Clients	192.168.42.115 (Internal Email Server)
TCP	25	SMTP	Internet Clients	192.168.42.115 (Internal Email Server)
TCP	25	SMTP	192.168.42.115	External E-mail Server (ISP based)
TCP	22	SSH	Internal Clients	Numerous internal servers

If an allow-exception rule for external communications also applies to internal communications, you can add a specific deny exception rule just prior to the allow rule. The deny exception can specifically block internal communications from crossing the network border, but still allow the subsequent allow-exception to grant access to the valid transactions.

Once you complete a thorough inventory of network communications, determine which communications are mission-critical, important, optional, for personal recreational use, or actually malicious. Block any traffic you deem malicious or just unwanted, whether through an explicit deny or via the catchall default-deny.

Evaluate all other forms or types of traffic against several factors, including policy. If it's not in support of the business, is it really needed? Are communications for personal entertainment or nonbusiness function permitted by policy, or considered a waste of resources? Are any communications duplicated or redundant? Is this a waste of resources, an expansion of the attack surface, a valid redundancy, or avoidance of a single point of failure? Are any of the communications no longer necessary and should you disable or remove them?

Base your evaluation of the many other possible questions or issues on your organization's policy statements, including mission and goals. Take the time to understand the communication needs of your network, then design the filtering rule set accordingly. Remember that the firewall is often the front sentry or the first line of defense against malicious communications originating from outside networks. Leaning towards caution and locking things down is a more effective security stance than leaving communications open and hoping detection mechanisms will notice malicious events.

While some exceptions to these suggestions will arise from your organization's business model or strategies, the following items are commonly considered communications to block in most, if not all, circumstances:

- All Internet control message protocol (ICMP) traffic originating from the Internet
- Any traffic directed specifically to the firewall
- Any traffic to known closed ports
- Any traffic to known ports of known malware, such as 31337 used by Back Orifice
- Inbound Transmission Control Protocol (TCP) 53 to block external domain name system (DNS) zone transfer requests
- Inbound (User Datagram Protocol) UDP 53 to block external DNS user queries
- Any traffic from IP addresses on a black list
- Any traffic from internal IP addresses that are not assigned

As an organization manages its security over time, especially as it reacts to intrusion attempts, experiences scanning, and becomes the target of hacking and flooding, it must create additional communication filtering rules to respond to real-world conditions. Security does not stand still, because the hacker attacks are constantly changing. Thus, the filtering rules that work well today may be insufficient in the near future.

Networks can be very large and very complex. Be fully aware of the communications taking place across your network to know what to allow and what to block. In addition to this knowledge, having established a security strategy through a written security policy will direct and guide the deployment of firewall rules, as well as other aspects of your security infrastructure.

Common Security Strategies for Firewall Deployments

A security strategy is a guideline, philosophy, or approach to using security for firewalls, as well as the entire organizational security infrastructure. Many different strategies are available. Some organizations focus on a single strategy, while others combine several strategies into a custom policy.

Security Through Obscurity

Security through obscurity is the idea of gaining protection by using abnormal configurations. This is both a positive security action and a poor one. It simply depends on the type of obscurity involved. A poor choice for security through obscurity would be to use alternative configurations for standard products.

With a network environment based on standard products, whether operating system, network service, or security solution, just modifying basic configuration settings does not actually provide true security. For example, a service typically operating on one port that's reconfigured to use a different port is not good security. Also changing names, addresses, network size, subnetting, bandwidth consumption, or even spoofing banners, headers, or identity does not provide true security.

Some common mistaken examples of obscurity-based security include:

- Hiding your front door key under a rock in a flower bed
- Connecting to the Internet assuming your system is one in 300 million and therefore won't be noticed
- Hiding money in a mattress
- Keeping an encryption algorithm secret
- Hiding your car keys behind your bumper while at the park or beach
- Changing the default service port of a network service
- Hiding your financial records among the audio files on your MP3 player

All attempts to provide network security based on hide-and-seek can be overcome or bypassed with basic network scanning techniques. When a hacker can discover or breach a host, service, or network just by looking hard enough, no real security exists. Hiding might work for keeping colored eggs and candy secure, but a security solution employed by bunnies has no place in a modern IT environment.

Security through obscurity is problematic for several reasons. First, if it's the only form of security employed, no real security exists. Second, the obscurity method employed might not actually be as obscure as you think. Hiding a key under a flowerpot is not as obscure as burying it in an unmarked location in the middle of a field. Third, it often distracts from accurately assessing the true state of security provided by other measures. Fourth, obscurity can instill a false sense of confidence.

True security through obscurity relies on using obscure and non-standard technologies. If everyone knows the most common or most popular operating system or software product is insecure, it can be a security improvement to use a more obscure product instead. This doesn't guarantee that other flaws or vulnerabilities won't be present on the alternative system, but usually the exact same exploit or compromise won't be a risk.

However, switching to an alternative technology is a security improvement only if the same flaw does not also exist there. It must provide actual security in and of itself. Switching technologies, such as changing operating systems, does not eliminate the need for security management. It simply moves the security concerns to other areas.

Generally, the only security obtained through obscurity is when hackers are unable to determine which technologies you are using. The less hackers know about your software, configuration, deployment, addressing, infrastructure design, patching schemes, and so on, the less successful their attempts to compromise security will be. Obscuring information about the internal IT environment itself is a primary defense against their hide-and-seek mentality.

Least Privilege

The principle of least privilege is one of the basic concepts of network security. The idea behind the principle of least privilege is that users have the minimum level of access to resources needed to complete assigned tasks. Any abilities, access, or privileges beyond that necessary minimum increase the risk of compromise and lead to wasted time, effort, and focus.

In most environments, most users need not access every host, every system, every resource, every file, every network service, and every Internet resource. Within a default-deny environment, you block all access to all resources, internal and external, by default. You use the principle of least privilege by adding in explicit and specific allow-exceptions only when necessary based on job descriptions.

However, the drawback to least privilege is the need to control every user's access individually. Each worker will need individually defined resource and activity permissions. This represents a significant increase in user administration. Because of this extra overhead, many organizations only partially use least privilege.

A common practice is to group users into collections of similar job functions or security levels, granting permissions to the group as a whole. This gives users additional privileges beyond what is strictly necessary for their work, but not enough to present a serious risk to the organization's security, stability, or confidentiality. Instead, this small security tradeoff considerably cuts down on administration overhead.

An extension of the principle of least privilege known as separation of duties specifically addresses administrative users. A lazy and insecure approach to network security is to grant some high-end users full administrative privileges across the entire IT infrastructure. This is a recipe for disaster. If an administrator makes a mistake, then he or she can accidentally harm the entire organization. If an administrator becomes disgruntled, feels wronged by the company, is marked for layoff or forced retirement, he or she can deliberately harm the organization and would have the systemwide power to do it. If another user or an external intruder compromised such an administrator's account, a hacker could use the administrator's advanced access to cause significant havoc.

A safer approach is to apply the principle of least privilege to all users, especially administrators. Under the label of separation of duties, divide the collection of all administrative tasks into small sets of privileges, focusing on a single task, system, service, or issue. Then, assign administrators subtasks within one of these focused areas and permissions only within the scope of their assigned tasks. This compartmentalizes administrative functions and provides a type of firewall or blockage against accidents, sabotage, and intrusion.

The result of applying separation of duties is that you eliminate godlike, systemwide administrators. Instead, each administrator has sufficient privileges only within a limited scope of responsibility. Some areas may have multiple administrators and some administrators may have powers in multiple areas, but overall the compartmentalization of administrative privileges significantly increases security and decreases risk.

Keep in mind that the principle of least privilege applies to both users and systems alike. Controlling which resources and communication pathways a service or device can touch will directly reduce the potential for abnormalities, abuse, and compromise.

Simplicity

Keeping things simple is an important part of security. It makes them easier to understand, manage, and troubleshoot. When things are too complex, they are much more difficult to understand, harder to manage, and much more complicated to troubleshoot. Furthermore, it's harder to verify that a complex system is providing adequate security.

The more complex a solution, the more room for mistakes, bugs, flaws, or oversights to creep in undetected by security administrators. The more complex the system, the more likely a hacker can find a vulnerability unseen by the system designers and network managers.

Simple is not always possible, however, especially when it comes to software and network infrastructures. But when you have a choice between a simpler solution and a more complex one, the simpler option may provide a more realistic and verifiable level of security. The 20th century physicist Albert Einstein once said, "Keep things as simple as possible, but no simpler." Keep in mind that too simple has the same flaws as too complex. Avoid sacrificing security for the sake of simplicity.

Defense-in-Depth

Installing a security infrastructure requires numerous systems to interact and interlock. The goal of any security solution is to prevent unwanted events while supporting authorized and necessary ones. A reliable security infrastructure is typically not a single control, a single defense, or a single countermeasure. Instead, multiple security safeguards provide complete and exhaustive coverage.

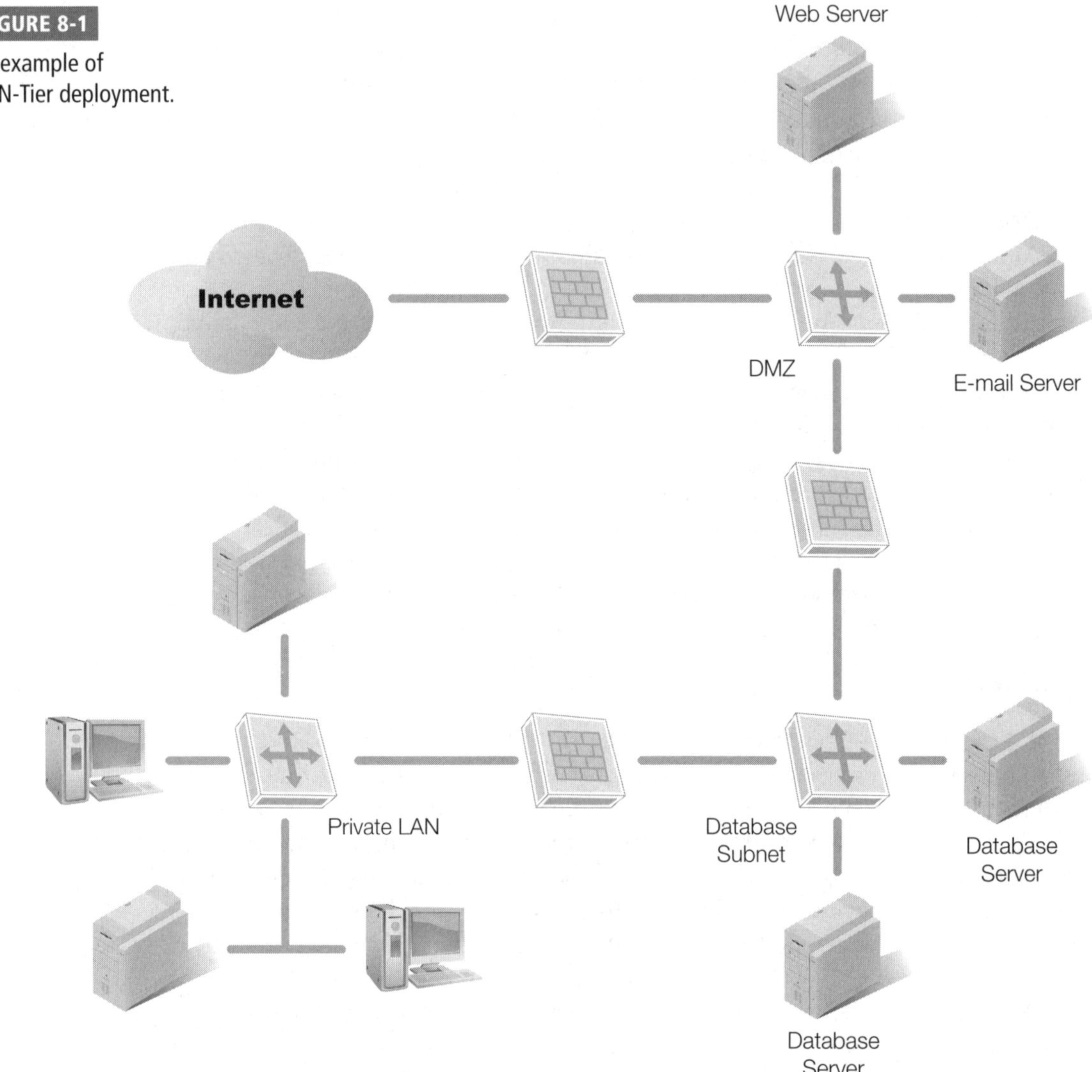

FIGURE 8-1
An example of an N-Tier deployment.

One aspect of infrastructure security design is to think of the defenses as multiple layers or barriers to access secured resources. This is known as layered defenses or defense-in-depth. When designing security, consider the net result if any component of the security system were to fail. If a single component failing results in a compromise or intrusion, the environment has a single layer of protection. When defense-in-depth is used, a single component failure does not result in compromise or intrusion. Instead, each component has a backup, an alternative, or a supplemental component. Depending on a single security product as the sole component of a security solution is a bad idea. Firewalls are great products, but firewalls alone cannot provide complete security. They are only one component, one piece of a complete security infrastructure. A proper security infrastructure has numerous components interlocked and deployed in layers or levels.

Another aspect of defense-in-depth is to deploy multiple subnets in series to separate private resources from public. This is known as an **N-Tier** deployment. N represents the number of subnets under private control. Figure 8-1 shows a common construction of a three-tiered deployment using a demilitarized zone (DMZ), a database subnet, and the private local area network (LAN).

When properly implemented, defense-in-depth ensures that multiple security controls are involved in every communication, connection, and transaction, regardless of its source or destination. Through the use of multiple or redundant security systems, any attempt to compromise or breach security becomes substantially more difficult, not only for the external intruder, but for the internal saboteur as well.

Diversity of Defense

Diversity of defense is similar to defense-in-depth—it supports multiple layers of security. The difference is that each (or at least most) of the layers uses a different security mechanism. Thus, the diversity of defense comes from using a collection of diverse security solutions.

Multiple firewalls in a series is defense-in-depth, but not defense diversity. Adding tools such as an intrusion detection system (IDS), antivirus, strong authentication, virtual private network (VPN) support, and granular access control converts a monolithic defense-in-depth to a more substantial multilayered diversity of security.

It might be tempting to claim that multiple firewalls from different vendors (or any security mechanism from different vendors) constitute diversity of defense. While using different products from different vendors will reduce some forms of risk, it's not as beneficial as true diversity—not just of vendors but also of security component types.

Using a variety of vendors will reduce the likelihood that a single flaw in one product is present in every other product from different vendors. For example, using three different vendor antivirus products is a reasonable idea. Having one vendor for clients, one vendor for internal servers, and a third vendor for border devices will increase the likelihood of detecting malicious code and decrease the threat from undetected malware. However, relying exclusively on antivirus and using no other type of security mechanism is a poor security solution.

Proper defense-in-depth will include diversity in both vendor selection and security component types. Be aware though that focusing too heavily on vendor diversity can increase management and administration complexity. It's difficult enough to manage single-vendor solutions, but when two, three, or more different vendor products of the same product type are involved, the complexity of management increases significantly.

When selecting products, whether by type or vendor, keep in mind the overall infrastructure design, such as parallel versus serial connections, as well as redundancy options. In some circumstances, using two different defenses can result in a larger rather than reduced attack surface. For example, if two different products each have a different vulnerability when they are deployed in parallel, then both weaknesses are vulnerable simultaneously, giving the hacker the option of one or the other. Were they to be deployed in series, the hacker would have to compromise the first layer of defense successfully before attempting to breach the second. Consider whether the planned diversity is truly a security improvement, since poor design can lead to reduced security when you employ diversity improperly.

When investigating and designing an infrastructure to include diversity of defense elements, keep the following concerns in mind:

- Some companies re-sell their products, technology, or intellectual property through other vendors. Private-label or re-labeled products from company B might be the same product from company A, with a different name or packaging.
- Security systems configured by the same security administrator can potentially have the same misconfiguration or design weakness. Consider using a team of security administrators or at least have several security experts review and check all configurations.
- Many products come from a single original code base or standard. Product version 2.0 from company A and product version 5.0 from company B might both include the same protocol stack code borrowed from an open-source or creative commons licensed code base. Don't automatically assume that products from different vendors, even with different build versions, represent 100 percent different programming.
- Many systems of the same type will all have the same inherent weaknesses in the underlying technology, design, and security concept.

When implementing diversity, ensure that you are using actual diversity-improving security, rather than false or misguided diversity that reduces security. All security designs and perceptions should withstand the scrutiny of evaluation and testing.

Choke Point

A choke point forces all traffic, communications, and activities through a single pathway or channel. This pathway can be used to control bandwidth consumption, filter content, provide authentication services, or enforce authorization. The purpose of a choke point is to ensure that the security device at the control location controls everything. No traffic, user, or data passes unchecked.

Other names for a choke point include checkpoint, filter pathway, or bottleneck. A choke point can be used to force network traffic along a single pathway monitored or filtered using security devices, including routers, switches, firewalls, IDS/intrusion prevention system (IPS), antivirus, network access control (NAC), and so on. A choke point can also control user activity, such as requiring authentication and enforcing access control.

As a security measure, a choke point has value only if it's hard to bypass or avoid the bottleneck itself. If a hacker can interact with a target without going through a choke point's filtering system, then the choke point is worthless.

If the security of a network has choke-point infrastructure components as a central part of the infrastructure, be sure to evaluate and consider all possible alternative pathways a hacker might employ. For example, a firewall is less effective as a choke point if outsiders can access wireless access points, physical connection ports, or dial-up modems.

In many cases, a single choke point won't be enough. Using multiple choke points may be the only effective means of ensuring that your network evaluates and filters all traffic. Some potential choke points can include any crossing of a network domain boundary into another. By using choke points across the boundaries of a typical IT infrastructure, you filter most pathways of communications that could host malicious interactions.

Consider potential indirect routes that might bypass "standard" choke points. For example, if a VPN link is established between two sites, whether branch offices or business partners, the Internet connection of one site could be an alternate pathway into the second site. This breach is possible if one site uses strong choke point security while the other does not.

Weakest Link

Any chain is only as strong as its weakest link. A security infrastructure is only as strong as its weakest component. You must know your security infrastructure thoroughly to have an understanding of where the weakest point lies. Once you've identified the weakest link, replace or remove it.

The **weakest link** security stance is an ongoing process of locating the least secure element of an infrastructure and securing it. Once you've secured the current weakest link, it's no longer the weakest link, and therefore a new weakest link exists. Repeat the cycle by seeking out the next weak point and improving it.

The idea behind this security stance or process is that hackers are performing this exact task as they seek out vulnerabilities to compromise. Ultimately, hackers discover and break the weakest links to gain access and entry into a secured environment. By actively and consistently seeking out vulnerabilities and weak points to secure them, you reduce the potential of a hacker finding and exploiting a weak link.

Weakest links are inevitable. But a strong weakest link is always better than a frail weakest link. Using a find-it-then-secure-it mentality helps build security that can withstand most common exploitation and intrusion attempts.

Fail-Safe

Chapter 6 discussed fail-safe, fail-secure, fail-open, and fail-closed as design elements of firewalls and other security controls. Fail-safe is also an overarching security stance to drive an organization's security. The fail-safe security stance is not just about using fail-safe security devices, but about designing the overall infrastructure with fail-safe as a core focus.

When any aspect of security fails, the best result of that failure is to fail into a state that supports or maintains essential security protections. Generally, this means to maintain confidentiality and integrity protections. However, most fail-safe solutions will sacrifice availability protection to retain confidentiality and integrity.

Fail-safe does not need to be a standalone security stance. You can integrate fail-safe notions into any security perspective. Keep in mind the ultimate goals and policies of your organization. If availability is top priority, then fail-safe may not be as viable an option as for environments where you can sacrifice availability to support other security protections.

Forced Universal Participation

It almost goes without saying that for security to be effective, everyone must work within the limitations established by your organization's written security policy. If you make exceptions—for upper level managers, for instance, who see themselves above the rules, able to do whatever they want without consequences—then you only have an assumption of security. No true security is present. Security only works when you employ forced **universal participation**.

Every worker, every manager, every senior executive, every temporary worker, every consultant, every vendor, every customer, every business partner, and every outsider must be forced to work within the security policy's limitations. Yes, exceptions often are necessary in the real world, but when exceptions become the norm, security is lost. When it easy to bypass, avoid, or even ignore security controls, an attacker can use that same pathway to compromise the entire security environment.

Universal participation is not just about official configurations and designations. Every enterprise that cares enough about security to write a security policy has official configurations and designs that assume everyone follows the same rules. When it's unwritten policy to violate security to accomplish work tasks, an obvious disconnect exists between security and productivity. In this situation, re-examine both security and productivity goals. Security should support productivity, not impede it.

Universal participation is not just about paying lip service to the rules, however. It's also about ensuring that everyone abides by security limitations. Potentially, users have many ways to purposefully violate security. This often occurs in environments where workers perceive the security limitations as too restrictive or when newly imposed rules strongly limit freedoms they enjoyed previously. The less workers believe in and buy into the organization's security policy, the more likely they are to violate rules they perceive as unfair.

Examples of users purposefully avoiding or violating security, i.e. not actively supporting and participating in security, include:

- Choosing poor passwords
- Sharing accounts with others
- Using personal computer equipment on the company LAN
- Installing an unauthorized wireless access point
- Using personal removable media on company equipment
- Using proxy tools to bypass firewall filtering
- Configuring a dial-out modem connection to establish unfiltered Internet access
- Using Internet based remote-access/remote-control tools to access their workstation from an external system without authorization
- Installing unapproved software

To achieve universal participation in the security efforts, workers must believe either that compliance is in their best interests, or you must force compliance through consequences for violations. In most cases, voluntary compliance is better because it causes workers to support the security effort, rather than setting up employees to be adversaries pitted against the security infrastructure.

Essential Elements of a Firewall Policy

A firewall policy is a security policy that focuses on the deployment of firewalls within the organization's IT infrastructure. The first step in deploying a firewall is constructing a firewall policy. Once you've established a firewall policy, deploy subsequently installed firewalls in full compliance with the firewall.

A written firewall policy provides several benefits and serves several purposes, such as:

- A guide for installation
- A guide for configuration
- A tool to assist in troubleshooting
- A guideline to detect changes and differences
- A mechanism to ensure consistent filtering across all firewalls

A firewall policy should address several specific issues and contain specific configuration details. One of the first important elements of a firewall policy is defining and designating security zones. Every network has different zones of risk and zones of trust (see Chapters 1 and 2). Often zones are differentiated along the same lines as a typical IT infrastructure. Create clear descriptions of what each subnet does, its level of risk, and its level of trust. Based on this information, you can formulate a basic firewall deployment strategy.

A firewall policy should define specifically what type of firewall you need. It may even prescribe the specific vendor, make, and models of firewalls at each zone transition or interface. Firewall types include static packet filtering, proxy, and stateful inspection.

For each prescribed firewall, define a complete firewall rule set. Define each rule in full detail, not just the configuration settings to make on the firewall's interface. Support each rule with justifications and reasons why you defined or selected it. Give a clear indication of the orders of the rules.

A firewall policy should also prescribe host software firewalls for deployment on clients and servers. This should include configuration settings and rule sets as well. Design and configure host firewalls to complement appliance firewall security.

The firewall policy should also address:

- What to log
- How logging happens
- Where to store log files
- How often to review log files
- What add-ons or enhancements to use
- Who is responsible for firewall administration
- How to access firewall configuration interfaces
- Where to physically and logically locate the firewall
- What level of physical access control is necessary
- What form of backup or redundancy option is present
- How to manage encryption and where to use or disallow it
- How to deploy and configure IDS/IPS to interact with firewalls

As with every security policy, the firewall policy must be as exhaustive as possible. It should address and define every aspect of firewall design, deployment, implementation, management, tuning, repairing, recovery, troubleshooting, and monitoring. A firewall policy should be the first and last authority on all things firewall within the organization.

The first draft of a firewall policy will probably not be exhaustive or accurate. So, review and improve your firewall policy periodically, just as you do with the rest of your organization's security policy. Each review period should assess whether the firewall is meeting the security needs and how to improve it so it continues to provide sufficient security. Work all improvements into the written security policy. Then adjust the deployed infrastructure to comply with the written security policy.

Software and Hardware Options for Firewalls

> **NOTE**
>
> Chapters 10 and 13 examine specific firewall products in detail for demonstration purposes. They aren't intended as product recommendations.

You learned about software firewall solutions and hardware firewall products in Chapter 2. Remember that most real-world solutions include a combination of software and hardware firewall options.

Since technology changes and advances so swiftly, it's not wise to make specific product recommendations here—many products can go through significant upgrade or generational change in as little as six months. So, this discussion will focus on software and hardware options in more generic terms.

Many operating systems include host software firewalls as part of their standard installation build. Microsoft Windows XP is one well-known example. Beginning with Service Pack 2, Windows XP has included the Windows Firewall as a standard security component. Other operating systems may offer optional firewall products. A software host-based firewall has benefits on both client systems and servers.

You can usually replace a native or default software firewall product found within a general-purpose operating system (OS) with a third-party option. Many open-source, free, and commercial host software firewalls are easily available. When considering third-party options, especially when replacing the native firewall, consider whether investing time, effort, or money in an alternative host software firewall is as effective an investment as using an appliance firewall to enhance or supplement a host firewall.

> **technical TIP**
>
> It's often possible to replace an appliance or device firewall's OS with a third-party alternative; this can even apply to ISP devices and wireless access points. Some of the better-known device firmware replacement options are DD-WRT, Open WRT, and Tomato.

Home users, SOHO environments, and small companies may benefit from a firewall on their Internet connection devices. Most DSL and **cable modem** devices include basic to moderately capable firewall options. Evaluate the included firewall in an Internet connection device rather than automatically discarding it as insufficient or inferior. Many current Internet service provider (ISP) devices include firewalls that are more than adequate for small network environments.

Most **wireless access points**, both consumer and commercial grade, include some form of firewall to provide filtering services for wireless clients and physical cable connections, as well. Many wireless access points could be accurately labeled as routers and/or switches, especially when they include two to six extra-wired connection ports. IPS device and wireless access point firewalls are discussed further in Chapter 10.

If a separate, dedicated firewall device is necessary in addition to an ISP device or a wireless access point, consider building a firewall using leftover hardware. Chapter 13 explores this idea in a case study of the SmoothWall product. Building your own hardware firewall can be a way to obtain firewall appliance control and security on a shoestring budget.

The final step up in terms of firewall options is the appliance firewall, which is a dedicated hardware device functioning as a black-box sentry. Appliance firewalls can range from low-end consumer-grade to very expensive high-end, commercial-grade solutions. In most mid-sized and larger organizations, a dedicated hardware firewall is a necessity. Whether you buy that firewall as a pre-built component, or build it, is based on your organization's knowledge, skill, and budget.

Keep in mind that security is not about always purchasing the most expensive, the best-known, the most efficient, or even the most-secure option. Budgets are not infinite. Your goal should be to deploy security that is adequate and effective for the environment within the confines and limitations of your budget, knowledge, and skill. Getting sufficient security at the best price possible is usually everyone's priority.

Benefit and Purpose of Reverse Proxy

Reverse proxy is a firewall service that allows external users access to internally hosted Web resources. This service takes the traditional proxy function and inverts it. Instead of hiding the identity of the client reaching out to the Internet, reverse proxy hides the identity of the Web server accessed by the Internet (or external) client.

External users direct their queries to a public Internet IP address and a default or assigned port number as when accessing any service. However, the IP address is the address of a proxy server, not the actual Web server hosting the requested resource. The proxy server then performs network address translation (NAT) on the request to convert the destination address to the internal (likely private) address of the resource host.

You can deploy reverse proxy to support load balancing or load distribution across multiple internal resource hosts. This allows clients to use a single public address to access a cluster of internal Web servers.

Other common reasons to deploy reverse proxy include:

- **Reverse caching**—**reverse caching** allows static content to be cached and served by the proxy rather than requiring that each request for the same content be served by the Web server itself.
- **Security**—using a reverse proxy adds an additional layer of protection and control between Internet-based users and internally hosted servers. Proxying allows the real identities of the internal servers to remain unknown or at least obfuscated.
- **Encryption**—the proxy server itself can serve as the end-point for Secure Socket Layer (SSL) or Transport Layer Security (TLS) encryption tunnels. This can allow a firewall or IDS to monitor and filter the contents of the traffic before it reaches the Web servers. Proxy-based encryption can also benefit from hardware and software acceleration to maintain high-performance communications.

Reverse proxy does not have to function solely on the private network's borders. It can also operate internally between subnets or departments, especially within IT infrastructures of very large corporations. Reverse proxy is also useful in an extranet or a DMZ. Just because a Web site is hosted for public access does not mean security precautions should vanish. Indirect access by reverse proxy can often be a significant security benefit when you deploy and manage it properly.

Use and Benefit of Port-Forwarding

Port forwarding is the firewall, proxy, and routing service that can receive a resource request on an interface at one port, then forward the request to another address on the same or different port. Port forwarding is used in reverse proxy, but only for Web traffic. Port forwarding itself can support any service on any port.

Port forwarding is a variation or enhancement of NAT. When a request reaches an outward-facing interface to a specific port, the request goes to an internal host. The routing is controlled by a static NAT mapping that defines which internal IP address and port will receive communications sent to an external IP address and port.

Port forwarding does not support caching, encryption end-point, or load balancing. Only a single internal machine can use a forwarded port at a time. The internal receiving (destination) host will perceive the source of the communications as the port-forwarding device because the translation service will rewrite the source address as its own. Thus, the destination system will not know the real originator of a communication.

You can find port forwarding services on almost any service or device that supports NAT. This includes most firewalls (hardware and software), wireless access points, and Internet connection devices (such as DSL and cable modems). Port forwarding is also an essential element in the Internet Connection Sharing (ICS) service of Windows that allows multiple systems to share a single Internet connection through the primary connected computer.

Considerations for Selecting a Bastion Host OS

A **bastion host OS** is a system designed, built, and deployed specifically to serve as a front-line defense for a network. A bastion host is the first (or nearly so) host accessed by external entities on their way to access DMZ, extranet, or private network resources. The bastion host withstands the brunt of any attack attempt to provide protection for hosts behind it.

A bastion was the highly fortified sections of medieval castles designed to assist with defense. The bastion was located along the castle perimeter wherever access attempts were likely, such as around the main gateway or entrance, any side or back entrances, or natural landscape pathways of approach. The bastion areas usually had thicker, stronger walls, room for additional warriors, and special defensive features. These special defensive features might have included slits for shooting arrows, holes for ramming spears or pushing away ladders, and pots of boiling oil to pour on attackers.

On modern computer networks, a bastion is a fortified computer device, possibly a host, firewall, or router, placed in the line of fire between privately owned and controlled networks and the public Internet. The purpose of a bastion host is to provide front-line filtering and defense against typical or common attacks. Most firewalls, especially appliance, hardware, or device firewalls operate as bastion hosts. Software firewalls can also be bastion hosts if the host is properly locked down and hardened.

Knowing that firewalls are commonly deployed as bastion hosts raises the question of what type of operating system (OS) you should use as the host OS on a bastion host firewall. Two main categories or divisions of bastion host OS are **proprietary OSs** and **general purpose OSs**.

Proprietary OSs are operating systems built exclusively to run on a bastion host device. Most appliance firewalls employ a proprietary operating system. This includes commercial firewall devices as well as many ISP connection devices and wireless access points. These proprietary bastion-host OSs support the functions or services critical to security (or their other primary purposes) and little else. An example of a proprietary bastion host OS is Cisco IOS.

A firewall device's bastion host OS supports only firewall functions. An ISP connection device's bastion host OS supports firewall services and connectivity services. A wireless access point's bastion host OS supports firewall services, wired connectivity services, wireless connectivity services, and possibly other services, such as 802.1x.

General-purpose OSs include Windows, Linux, Mac OS, UNIX, and others. These are operating systems that support a wide variety of purposes and functions, including serving as client or server host OSs. When used as a bastion host OS, they must be hardened and locked down. Otherwise, an insecure host OS can render the security provided by a firewall worthless. If an attacker can crash the firewall host or bypass the firewall filtering, then the firewall is not providing effective security.

It's possible to reasonably harden a general purpose OS for use as a bastion host OS, but this takes specific and detailed modifications. Most software firewall products include a guide to perform OS hardening to improve the security of the bastion host and reduce the vulnerabilities and backdoors that might permit firewall compromise.

The hardening guidelines discussed in Chapter 5 can also help if you are working independently of vendor-provided suggestions.

Some firewalls include a prehardened version of a general purpose OS as the bastion host OS. This is the case for many Linux-based firewalls, such as SmoothWall (discussed in detail in Chapter 13).

The benefit of using a general-purpose OS as a bastion host OS is that such OSs are widely available. Some are free—mostly Linux variations. Also, you can leverage your current knowledge and skill with a general-purpose OS when you are using it as a bastion host OS. Keep in mind, however, that general-purpose OSs are much more widely attacked and the risk of new exploits is high.

The benefits of a proprietary OS as a bastion host OS are fewer known attacks and less risk of future exploits. However, proprietary OSs might be significantly different from other OSs in the environment and may require learning a completely new system to properly and securely administer the firewall. Also, most proprietary OSs are officially released only on the bastion host hardware. This makes them more difficult to obtain and more expensive in most cases (at least in comparison to free- and open-source alternatives).

Constructing and Ordering Firewall Rules

You learned about the basics of firewall rules in Chapter 7. As you begin to seriously consider the options for firewall deployment, a closer examination of firewall rules is critical to success. The most important aspect of a firewall rule set is its order.

Getting rules out of order causes unexpected and unwanted consequences. This can include traffic you want to block and other unwanted traffic crossing the checkpoint. Rule-set ordering is critical to the successful operation of firewall security.

The first and most basic rule-set-ordering convention is that the universal denial rule should be the last and final rule. The use of deny by default or default denial rests on the premise that the last rule is the catchall rule to block all traffic not allowed access due to a previous rule-based exception.

Another common guideline to rule-set ordering is to place critical denial exceptions first or early in the rule set. When specific internal or external IP addresses or ports, or even entire protocols, are to be absolutely blocked, you may need a denial exception rather than relying upon the default-deny final rule. Some of the previous allow-exceptions might inadvertently permit communications due to universal application (with the use of ANY). By using a preemptive specific enforced denial before any of the allow-exceptions, you eliminate the possibility of accidentally allowing a known malicious or unwanted communication.

Whenever possible, use fewer rules rather than more rules. Even with proper ordering, the more rules you have, the greater the likelihood of configuring something incorrectly or creating a loophole. One issue that causes more rules rather than fewer is infrastructure design specifically related to addressing. A need for more rules arises if a range of IP addresses is allowed access, but within that range, some addresses are refused access. For example, compare two scenarios.

First, a network has a host address range of 192.168.42.140–190. All hosts except for 188, 189, and 190 are allowed access to a certain port. A single rule allowing hosts 140–187 is all that is necessary because the default-deny rule takes care of blocking the remaining non-included hosts.

Second, a network has a host address range of 192.168.42.140–190. All hosts except for 165, 171, and 188 are allowed access to a certain port. You need multiple rules to use this configuration. One or more rules must define deny exceptions for 165, 171, and 188, followed by the allow rule of the 140–190 range. If the firewall only allows a single address or a range of addresses per rule, rather than allowing a list of nonsequential addresses, then three deny rules would be necessary in this scenario.

In this example, network design and addressing can be used to make firewall rule-set construction either larger and more complex or shorter and more distinct and compact. The latter is preferred both for administrative purposes as well as security and efficiency. If the process of creating rules requires a significant number of special exceptions to modify or adjust ranges of addresses or ports, consider re-configuring the network rather than using a too complex or too long rule set. When designing or writing firewall rules, especially when writing pairs or sets of rules, consider using a single rule or a simpler rule set if the network's addressing scheme, infrastructure design, or subnet layout is adjusted.

As another guideline to ordering rule sets, consider placing rules related to more common traffic earlier in the set, rather than later. Comparing traffic to the rule sets takes time; each check of each rule takes some finite amount of time. The fewer rules you need to check before you grant an allow, the less delay to the traffic stream. Prioritize in the rule-set list the more commonly used forms of traffic, whether by IP address, port, or protocol. Put the less commonly used forms of traffic further down in the rule-set list.

Ultimately, rule sets are about enforcing security relevant to the organization. The rule set should reflect the guidelines prescribed in your written security policy, specifically the firewall policy. The goal of designing, writing, and ordering rules for a firewall should be to focus on obtaining the necessary security. Elegance and speed are dividends, but not as essential as blocking the bad and allowing the good. Never lose focus on the primary goal: filtering traffic in accordance with your security policy.

Evaluating Needs and Solutions in Designing Security

Any organization larger than a single person will generate multiple opinions about what should and should not be allowed across the firewall. Almost everyone would agree on allowing (at some level) the necessary protocols, applications, and services essential for mission-critical or at least operationally necessary business tasks to cross the firewall-secured network boundaries.

Opinions may differ about what constitutes a necessary business task, but if it's a necessary task, the organization's security solution should make the task possible. Restrictions, limitations, filtering, and logging of even necessary business communications must occur. The point, however, is making a determination about what should and should not cross a firewall.

Generally four main types of communications take place within a business environment: business-essential, business-wanted, personal, and malicious. Business-essential communications must take place or the business itself will suffer. Blocking critical transactions will directly cause problems for the business by impeding the production and distribution of products, inhibiting customer service, reducing profits, and so on. The security infrastructure must support business-essential communications.

Business-wanted communications are not essential to the core function or purpose of the organization. The failure of these business communications might be inconvenient or reduce quantity or quality, but the essential business functions go on. Business-wanted communications help the business do what it does better, faster, cheaper, cleaner, more efficiently, or in a flashier way. But when those wants are not available for whatever reason, the business's core activities still function sufficiently.

Personal communications are those transactions between individuals inside the company and with external entities not directly related to business tasks. If you eliminated personal communications, all business functions would continue unhindered. However, that's in a perfect world. In the real world, stifling human communications can lead to low job satisfaction, feelings of isolation, and even worker disaffection. This, in turn, causes a reduction in productivity and quality.

Most organizations must strike a balance between allowing only business communications and allowing all communications. Obviously, allowing every communication is a bad idea from both a security standpoint as well as a productivity one. Often a modest level of Web site access, filtered e-mail access, and potentially other nonthreatening services as forms of personal communications can travel on and over company equipment during work hours with a reasonable amount of security.

But no clear or distinct boundaries define what level of personal communication will maintain worker morale and job satisfaction. It's often fairly obvious when restrictions are too tight because job performance suffers or breaches of security increase. Part of the solution to this problem is educating users or workers about what is acceptable and unacceptable behavior on the company's network. This includes defining what types of communications to allow or block, whether for business or personal use.

Malicious traffic, the fourth common type of network traffic, should always be blocked. This is a widely held security stance and the whole point of using security in the first place. However, it's not easy to identify all malicious traffic, and it can sometimes appear to be one of the other three common forms of communications. Improving security over time is essential to maximize protections against malicious communications while at the same time supporting necessary, desired, or benign personal communications.

Every organization must define its own parameters and justifications for each type of transaction allowed across any security perimeter, whether network traffic or physical access. Whatever the determination, clearly spell out the designations for valid versus invalid transactions in your organization's written security policy, and then implement them in the security infrastructure.

Once you've defined necessary transactions and prescribed the desired security, use these concepts in actual security-enforcing software and hardware solutions.

This is where your understanding of the goals of security, the organization's mission, and the budget is critical. There is always a product that costs more, but more expensive does not always mean better security. In fact, in many cases cheap or free solutions can offer equivalent or better security than the most expensive product available.

Using security is an essential part of the risk assessment and management process. As discussed in previous chapters, part of evaluating security is to understand the threats, attacks, and risks as well as the available countermeasures. One aspect of understanding countermeasures is performing a cost/benefit analysis to obtain the best security solution for the invested dollar. Don't just purchase the most expensive solution; that's never a reliable measure of security quality.

Also, don't automatically purchase the product your cost/benefit analysis says is the best option. You must also evaluate each proposed solution in light of all other elements of the security infrastructure as well as the size of your budget. It's usually not the right choice to spend 50 percent or more of the budget on a single security component. Instead, devise a spending plan or ratio tool to guide security solution procurement.

One possible method is to allocate 10 percent of the budget to each of the ten major sections or divisions of security addressed. This assumes you can divide the overall security of your organization into just ten compartments—you might need thirty sections or maybe you can get by with just four. Whatever the number of divisions you use, grant each an equal or weighted portion of the budget based on risk. When a solution costs more than is available within a certain section, you can then shift funds between sections as needed.

The purpose of this system is to make security administrators and designers more aware of the cost of security and to prevent overspending in one area and underspending in another. You should spend security funds somewhat evenly to secure the overall organization, rather than over-securing one area and neglecting another. If a hacker or intruder encounters a highly fortified defense, he is likely to go looking for a less secure backdoor.

Ultimately, you should treat your security budget just like any other budget. Categorize and prioritize expenses. Outline spending on paper before writing the first check or swiping the plastic. Allocating funds based on needs and importance, then adjusting those allocations based on market conditions or changing threats is all part of proper security management (as well as security budget management).

What Happens When Security Gets in the Way of Doing Business?

Organizations exist to perform tasks such as producing products or providing services. When the security infrastructure interferes with essential business tasks, something has to change. Security should prevent compromise while supporting and allowing business functions. When security changes or when business tasks change, the security policy and the business should adjust.

Absent this adjustment, security can interfere with business operations. Many organizations will never face this situation, but every business must have a response plan in place in case it does. When business tasks are at odds with security protections, what should you do?

A few short term options are available, none of them optimal. One short-term option is disabling security so the business tasks go forward. When the security is disabled for a short period or "permanently," you provide the opportunity for compromise, intrusion, or sabotage. Using this shortsighted solution might not immediately cause harm to the infrastructure, but it establishes a pattern and mindset that security is not important.

Organizations might get away with turning off security defenses. Hackers might not ever notice the reduction of defense or might not happen to time their probing or attacks to correspond to the period of disabled security. However, even if no actual attacks occur due to the security reduction, the real damage is done.

The real damage is the change in mentality towards security-shifting from viewing security as essential and mandatory to optional and nonessential. Once an organization believes that security can be turned off when inconvenient, then security suffers, and it's only a matter of time before a catastrophic compromise occurs. Security depends on vigilance. Once the commitment to vigilance is lost, so is real security.

Another short-term option is not to perform the task that security is blocking. If the task is not essential, it might be possible to move forward as an organization without performing that specific task again. However, if it's an essential or critical task, failing to support it will negatively impact the organization.

There is another way. The preferred and secure long-term response is to re-evaluate the business task in the light of the security infrastructure. Design a new security solution or modify how the task is accomplished. Support both security and business functions. They are both essential to the long-term stability and vitality of an organization.

CHAPTER SUMMARY

Never deploy firewalls hastily. Instead, use careful investigation and planning in the design and use of firewalls. Consider numerous firewall deployment issues.

Some important concerns include deciding:

- What to allow and block
- Which security strategies to integrate
- Whether the firewall policy is sufficient
- Which hardware or software options to use
- Whether you need reverse proxy
- Whether to configure port forwarding
- Which bastion host OS to use
- How to order the firewall rule sets
- What the essential firewall needs are
- How will the firewall interact or interfere with business processes

KEY CONCEPTS AND TERMS

Bastion host OS
Cable modem
Diversity of defense
General purpose OS
N-tier
Proprietary OS
Reverse caching
Security stance
Universal participation
Weakest link
Wireless access point

CHAPTER 8 ASSESSMENT

1. When crafting firewall rules, determining what to allow versus what to block is primarily dependent on what factor?

A. Traffic levels
B. Business tasks
C. Bandwidth
D. User preferences
E. Timing

2. The first step in determining what to allow and what to block in a firewall's rule set is:

A. Review vulnerability watch lists
B. Poll users for what services they want
C. Read blogs about best practices for firewall rules
D. Record traffic for 24 hours
E. Create an inventory of business communications

3. What is the purpose of including rules that block ports, such as 31337?

A. Prevent users from accessing social networking sites
B. To prevent DNS zone transfers
C. To stop ICMP traffic
D. Block known remote access and remote control malware
E. Allow users to employ cloud backup solutions

4. What security strategy is based on the concept of locking the environment down so users can perform their assigned tasks but little else?

A. Simplicity
B. Principle of least privilege
C. Diversity of defense
D. Choke point
E. Weakest link

5. What security strategy reverts to a secure position in the event of a compromise?

A. Fail-safe
B. Universal participation
C. Defense-in-depth
D. Security through obscurity
E. N-tier deployment

6. Which security stance most directly focuses on the use of firewalls or other filtering devices as its primary means of controlling communications?

A. Universal participation
B. Weakest link
C. Fail-safe
D. Choke point
E. Simplicity

7. A firewall policy performs all of the following functions *except*:

A. Assist in troubleshooting
B. Placing blame for intrusions
C. Guiding installation
D. Ensuring consistent filtering across the infrastructure
E. Detect changes in deployed settings

8. Which of the following is *not* a viable option for an enterprise network that needs to control and filter network traffic?

A. Virtual firewall
B. Appliance firewall
C. Physical firewall
D. Host firewall
E. Software firewall

9. A reverse proxy is useful in which of the following scenarios?

A. Grant outside users access to internal e-mail servers
B. Support internal users accessing the public Internet
C. Allow private hosts to access external Web servers
D. Offer external entities access to an internal Web server
E. Cache file transfers for peer-to-peer exchange protocols

10. All of the following are true statements in regards to port forwarding *except*:

A. Is a variation of NAT
B. Limited to Web traffic only
C. Hides the identity of internal hosts
D. Allows the use of non-standard ports for publicly accessed services
E. Internal servers do not see the identity of the real source of a communication

11. Which of the following statements is true with respect to reverse proxy?

A. Reverse proxy cannot be used in conjunction with secured Web sites.
B. Reverse proxy can be used with tunnel mode IPSec VPNs.
C. Reverse proxy can only support SSL tunnels.
D. Reverse proxy caches client requests and archives them for load balancing purposes.
E. The reverse proxy server can act as the end-point for a TLS tunnel.

12. Which of the following is *not* a true statement in regards to port forwarding?

A. Port forwarding services can be found on almost any service or device that supports NAT.
B. Port forwarding is an essential element in the Internet Connection Sharing (ICS) service of Windows.
C. Port forward is used in reverse proxy, but only for Web traffic.
D. Port forwarding supports caching, encryption endpoint, and load balancing.
E. Port forwarding is a variation or enhancement of NAT.

13. Which of the following is *not* considered a viable option as a bastion host OS?

A. UNIX
B. Linux
C. Android
D. Mac OS
E. Windows 7

14. You are selecting a new appliance firewall for deployment in the company network. You are concerned with OS flaws and exploits appearing not only on your hosts but also on the firewall. To minimize that risk, what bastion host OS should you choose?

A. Cisco IOS
B. Windows 7
C. UNIX
D. Mac OS
E. Linux

15. What is the most important aspect or feature of a bastion host OS?

A. Leveraging existing OS administrative knowledge
B. Ease of use
C. Remote administration
D. Resistance to attacks and compromise attempts
E. Support of a wide range of services

16. What is always the most important element within a firewall rule set?

A. Using specific addresses instead of ANY
B. Listed deny-exceptions after allow-exceptions
C. List inbound exceptions before outbound exceptions
D. Final rule of default-deny
E. Blocking every known malicious port

17. Which of the following examples of complete firewall rule sets is the most valid?

A.

TCP	ANY	ANY	ANY	ANY	Deny
TCP	192.168.42.0/24	ANY	ANY	80	Allow
TCP	192.168.42.115	ANY	ANY	80	Deny

B.

TCP	192.168.42.115	ANY	ANY	80	Deny
TCP	192.168.42.0/24	ANY	ANY	80	Allow
TCP	ANY	ANY	ANY	ANY	Deny

C.

TCP	192.168.42.115	ANY	ANY	80	Deny
TCP	192.168.42.116	ANY	ANY	80	Deny
TCP	192.168.42.119	ANY	ANY	80	Deny

D.

TCP	192.168.42.0/24	ANY	ANY	80	Allow
TCP	ANY	ANY	ANY	80	Deny
TCP	ANY	ANY	ANY	ANY	Deny

E.

TCP	ANY	ANY	ANY	ANY	Deny

18. Which of the following guidelines is most important?

A. Include all specific denials for known malicious remote control tools after explicit allows.
B. Include every possible address and port in a rule within the set to ensure an explicit callout exists for every type of communication.
C. There should be more inbound rules than outbound rules.
D. Place explicit denials for individual systems before explicit allows for ranges that include those individual systems.
E. Place universal allows before universal denies.

19. When considering the security response triggered by a firewall detecting unwanted traffic, what is the main factor in choosing between 1) a response that protects confidentiality and integrity and 2) a response that protects availability?

A. Traffic load
B. Number of external clients
C. Port in use
D. Business mission and goals
E. Whether the breach takes place during non-business hours

20. When security mechanisms and business communications are at odds, what is the best and most secure response?

A. Disable security to allow the business communication.
B. Modify the security policy to protect the business communication.
C. Disable both security and the offending business communication.
D. Disable business communication to maintain security.
E. Do nothing.

CHAPTER 9

Firewall Management and Security Concerns

FIREWALL MANAGEMENT is about focusing on the essential security goals of the environment and making sure the deployed firewalls assist in fulfilling those goals. Following general best practices will help ensure compliance with care and due diligence. Realize that while a firewall is very important, even essential, firewalls are not the totality of security; you'll need other security safeguards to create a complete solution.

When selecting a firewall, focus on the purpose and needs of your organization. Find a product that meets the real needs of your organization's network environment, not the most popular or cheapest solution. Consider whether building your own firewall device rather than purchasing a ready-made appliance makes better sense.

But even with an appropriate, properly configured firewall, ongoing security concerns will invariably arise. Plan on the inevitable attacks, exploits, and threats to the security provided by a firewall. Hackers might attempt to use tunneling or virtual private network (VPN) services as a mechanism to bypass firewall filters. Be aware of these issues and be prepared to deal with them. Have an incident response plan in place.

Firewall management also includes testing, monitoring, and troubleshooting. Many excellent tools can help simplify or automate these processes. But even the best tools require solid information and a working knowledge of your environment. Detailed implementation plans can also be a significant benefit to maintaining reliable security.

Chapter 9 Topics

In this chapter, the following topics and concepts will be covered:

- What best practices for firewall management are
- What some security measures in addition to a firewall are
- How to select the right firewall for your needs
- What the difference is between buying and building a firewall
- How to mitigate firewall threats and exploits
- What the concerns related to tunneling through or across a firewall are
- How to test a firewall's security
- What some important tools are for managing and monitoring a firewall
- How to troubleshoot firewalls
- What the procedure is for proper firewall implementation
- How to respond to incidents

Chapter 9 Goals

Upon completion of this chapter, you will be able to:

- Describe firewall management "best practices."
- Select the best firewall for a given network scenario.
- Demonstrate the use of tools for managing and monitoring a firewall.
- Troubleshoot common firewall problems.
- Write a firewall installation plan.

Best Practices for Firewall Management

Firewall management "best practices" are recommendations, guidelines, or standard operating procedures for obtaining reliable firewall security on a real-world budget. Best practices are usually not specific recommendations for products or tools. Rather, they are recommendations for philosophies, stances, or concepts on how to proceed. The following items are suggested "best practices." These might not apply to every environment, although you should consider each and adapt or adopt when appropriate.

NOTE

The foundation of every firewall implementation is to *have a plan*. There is no substitute for a written firewall policy. Any other method, process, or procedure for configuring, using, and managing a firewall will fail. Only a written firewall policy can guide you toward a successful and reliable firewall deployment.

A *written firewall policy* establishes a documentation trail that everyone in the organization can read, consider, and follow. To write a firewall policy, learn about and thoroughly examine every communication, transaction, and service within, across, and through the IT infrastructure. You can write a comprehensive and effective firewall policy only once you know and understand your operating environment.

To have a plan, you must *thoroughly understand your organization's infrastructure*, its mission and goals, and the processes necessary to produce its products and services. This means understanding your organization's technology use, assets availability, and resources consumption, in addition to where everything resides and how users work with the infrastructure. Consider larger and more complex needs in light of the typical IT infrastructure.

Once you understand your operating environment thoroughly, you can then *decide where a firewall is necessary*. In most cases, every host should have a local software firewall, every border communication point should have a firewall, and every transition between subnets of different trust, risk, or purpose should have a firewall. Firewalls provide communications control; deploy them liberally.

To create a useful and relevant firewall policy, *perform a risk assessment*. The process of understanding assets, vulnerabilities, threats, and likelihoods is risk assessment. Only though a proper risk assessment can you be sure to know the threats and risks facing your environment and its communications. This in turn will guide the configuration of a firewall for maximum benefit.

Once a firewall policy is in place, *regularly review the policy*. Investigate whether the overall quality and reliability of the existing firewall security is sufficient or needs improving. Verify that all services are still properly protected. Evaluate whether prevention, deterrence, and response have been adequate and effective. Wherever you discover deficiencies, strive to improve and rectify the situation immediately.

Establish a *no-exceptions policy*. Every service, every transaction, every communication must pass through one or more firewalls, filtered according to the guidelines of the firewall policy. Terminate any communication found to take place without firewall filtering immediately.

Maintain physical security control over all personnel access to firewalls. No one except the firewall administrator should have physical access to the firewall devices. Firewalls are concentrations of security and often the main embodiment of communications security. The risk of compromise from unauthorized access is significant.

Limit and filter Internet connectivity. In spite of a user's desire for an unrestricted, unmonitored Internet connection for "personal use," the Internet is a significant risk for most organizations. An unrestricted or unfiltered Internet connection is a highway for malicious code, social engineering attacks, and intrusion attempts. If an Internet service, protocol, domain, or IP address is not essential to a necessary business task, block it. Work assets are for work tasks, not personal activities. Configure the firewall accordingly.

Install antivirus scanners, anti-malware scanners, and firewalls on every host. Every portable device, every desktop workstation, and every server should have these malicious code and malicious traffic protections. No system is immune to malware and malicious communications; prevent easily avoidable compromises and downtime with basic filters and barriers to known issues.

Don't rely upon a single or individual firewall. Attempt to interlock and layer firewalls along the pathways of communication and transactions. *Use defense-in-depth* or a multiple-layered defense wherever possible. By following a defense-in-depth design concept, numerous filtering events will shield each asset.

When possible, *avoid remote access*. Limit access to local direct connections only. When remote access is necessary, require a VPN. Remote connectivity enables remote hacking. Remote hacking attempts to breach security without the need to be physically at or within the target's facilities. Requiring VPNs for all remote connections reduces this threat somewhat by preventing open connections or communications vulnerable to eavesdropping. All communications crossing the firewall are potential vulnerabilities.

Require encryption of all internal network communications. Use Internet Protocol Security (IPSec) to secure all intranet communications. This is often an easy and cost-effective means to quickly reduce the risk of eavesdropping, man-in-the-middle, replay, and many other forms of network attacks. Well-encrypted data is much less likely to fall into the hands of hackers, thieves, and unauthorized personnel. Configure firewalls to allow IPSec, VPNs, and other forms of encrypted communications where appropriate, but don't universally allow encrypted communications. Encryption can obfuscate malicious activities. Strongly authenticated endpoints are less likely to be sources of malicious actions.

Harden both internal firewall hosts and border firewalls. Use hardened firewalls against compromise regardless of their network location. Provide consistent and thorough security throughout the IT infrastructure. Protecting the stability and reliability of firewalls will, in turn, protect the security of the network as a whole.

Always test new code before you deploy it onto a firewall. No matter who the source of new code, test it. Even if the code addresses a mission-critical issue, test it. Test all new code without exception. All untested code is unauthorized and you should block it from all production firewalls.

Backup, backup, backup. Security includes the guarantee of availability. Failing to have a backup increases the risk that that if data is lost, damaged, or corrupted, it will never be available. Backups are the best form of insurance against data loss. Don't store backups on the same system or even in the same locale. Store them on separate storage device, both onsite and offsite. Remember that offsite is more secure in the face of larger disasters. Don't allow the only copy of a firewall configuration to be in memory on the firewall. Always make a backup.

If an asset is worth the time and effort to secure, then it's worth monitoring as well. Configure each firewall as you deem necessary, and then watch for attempted breaches of that security. Perfect security doesn't exist. To improve security, be prepared to respond when breaches happen—and they will. *Lock, then watch.* Failing to watch a secured asset just means that when the compromise occurs, you won't notice it immediately.

Firewalls can be the focus of an attack, just as much as any other host. Being aware of and prepared for such an attack gives you the edge to respond promptly.

Have an intrusion and incident response plan. Bad things will occur. Failures will happen. Breaches will take place. Firewalls can fail. Malicious traffic goes overlooked. But be prepared, nevertheless. Evaluate and examine the realistic threats facing your environment. Plan for the worst. Define procedures to respond to any and all situations.

Don't overlook *business continuity planning and disaster recovery planning*. The greatest threats to organizations are not necessarily security breaches, but threats that represent business-terminating events. Building collapse, flooding, fire, sabotage, blackouts, malware infection, criminal activities, and so on shut down an organization's operations. If alternate means of accomplishing mission-critical tasks aren't available, then the organization will soon cease to exist. Plan to recover from disasters so that your organization survives to do business in the future. Recovering a business process does not mean leaving it unprotected; redeploying firewalls is just as essential as restarting business processes themselves.

KISS—*Keep It Simple: Security*. Firewalls are complex enough without purposefully imposing additional complexity. Focus on designing and configuring firewalls that use simple and direct rule sets. The greater the complexity involved, the greater the chance for mis-configuring, incorrectly ordering rules, or creating loopholes in protection.

Focus on *balancing security and usability*. Firewall filtering does not need to make all work tasks difficult. Likewise, essential work functions need not compromise security. Finding a balance between these two extremes is important. Focus on reducing the risk to the infrastructure while enabling users to perform authorized tasks with minimal hassle.

Prioritize. Security concerns always threaten to overwhelm available time, effort, and budget. Focus on the big impact and big result issues first, rather than attempting to swat at every minor annoyance that arises. Security is constantly changing; the goal is to maintain reasonable security rather than keep perfect security (remember, this is unattainable anyway!). The deny-by-default, allow-by-exception philosophy should keep minor nuisances to a minimum.

Always be fully and truly aware of the state of the organizational security, especially in regard to firewall performance and function. *Don't make assumptions*. If you are not positive that an aspect of the organization is secure, find out. Assuming security exists is a false sense of safety. A lack of knowledge about the security status could lead to complacency. Assuming nothing wrong, removes the urgency to investigate and rectify problems. Don't fall into the "I thought it was protected" trap; if you don't know or are not sure, take the time to investigate and know. Testing is relatively cheap; recovering from intrusion damage can be disastrously expensive.

Develop a firewall checklist. Review it for completeness and accuracy on a periodic basis, such as every quarter. Confirm every element on the checklist on a frequent regular basis, such as once a week or once a day. You can automate this to an extent, but it often requires human effort to test and confirm that every security mechanism is in place, active, armed, and effective.

Perform regular self-assessments. Numerous security groups, government, and military agencies post security implementation guidelines, manuals, and checklists.

Commonly known as STIGs (Security Technical Implementation Guides), these documents can help you to review and assess your organization's status and state of security. A self-assessment attempts to take an external, unique, or independent viewpoint in evaluating security. This is why using external guidelines, standards, and measurements of security can reveal oversights in an existing security infrastructure.

Perform internal compliance audits. It's no longer sufficient to think you are secure; compliance audits are now the law in many industries, such as the financial and medical sectors. Ensuring that you are in full compliance with all federal and state laws and regulations is not only good security management; it keeps company officials out of jail. Using external auditors is often a poor substitute for internal self-verification.

Test all uses of the firewall for sufficiency. Perform verification scans of all deployed firewall settings to ensure they are functioning. Improper installation or mis-configuration can render even well meaning safeguards worthless. Test every new security setting or rule on installation and at every reconfiguration.

Perform regular vulnerability assessments. Use automated tools with updated databases of security tests and exploit simulations. These tools should confirm patch and updates, verify security configurations, and probe for known vulnerabilities and exploit weaknesses. Quickly resolve any issues the scans uncover.

After you've improved and tuned firewall security, put it to the ultimate test: *perform penetration testing*. Hire or develop an ethical hacking team to test the strengths and weaknesses of the firewalls. Ethical hackers use the same tools and attack techniques as criminals, but without the intention to cause actual damage. Professional security assessment teams can customize attacks, modify exploits, and react in real-time to fully stress security defenses.

Focus on establishing a philosophy of *default deny rather than default permit*. By blocking everything as a starting point, only those features, services, protocols, ports, applications, users, and so on you judge and deem safe and appropriate can proceed by an exception. Using a default permit stance forces a never-ending stream of explicit denials as new compromises or malicious events arise. Deny by default, allow by exception is always the preferred security stance.

This collection of firewall management "best practices" should serve as a starting point for the development of an effective firewall deployment. Other valid and useful guidelines deserve consideration, so don't assume this list of recommendations, or any other list from any other source, is exhaustive. There are always new lessons to learn, new challenges to face, and new wisdom to obtain.

Security Measures in Addition to a Firewall

A firewall is an essential part of any security infrastructure. Every single host needs a firewall. Every single network needs border firewalls. Firewalls are concentrations of security, and are easily recognizable embodiments of an organization's security policy. A firewall is an incomplete security solution on its own, however.

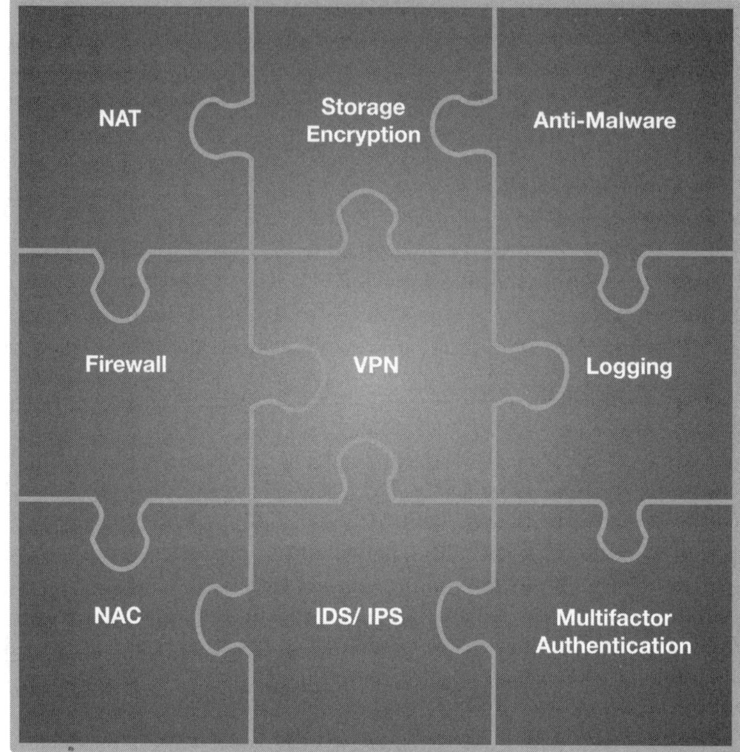

FIGURE 9-1
Firewalls: Only part of the security puzzle.

A complete security solution requires many more components (Figure 9-1) than just a firewall. Proper understanding of the organization's essential processes, threats, and goals will guide you toward the creation an effective security plan. Without a proper risk assessment, however, recommendations for safeguards and countermeasures are just guesses.

Several common elements characterize most properly designed security systems. These include:

- Multifactor authentication
- Anti-malware scanning
- Full hard drive encryption
- Communications encryption
- Detailed logging and auditing of events
- Intrusion detection and prevention systems
- Network segmentation and traffic management
- Private IP addresses and NAT proxies
- VPNs for remote access
- Network access control

You learned about these and other important elements of a security solution in Chapter 1. While these are often excellent security components, they are not all necessarily applicable and required in every environment. Addressing your environment's specific risks is always more preferable than deploying a security product just because it seems like a good idea.

Selecting the Right Firewall for Your Needs

Choosing the best firewall for your specific environment requires knowledge of firewall options and understanding of the security needs of your network environment. Automatically selecting the most expensive option, or the cheapest one, or an open-source solution fails to properly assess the situation. Firewalls are essential elements of security. They are concentrated security. It would be careless to select a product without due diligence.

> **NOTE**
> Selecting and purchasing the right firewall for your organization's situation requires careful evaluation. As with any big decision, first find "the longest poles in the tent": Always resolve important aspects of the process sooner rather than later. For example, first familiarize yourself with the budget for the purchase.

Knowing the amount of money available for firewall protection helps you quickly eliminate those products clearly outside your price range. Don't automatically discard every product above the budget limit, but realize that anything more than about 15 percent of your maximum allowance is probably out of reach.

Next, consider whether an open-source solution is a viable option for your corporate culture. Some organizations are philosophically opposed to open-source solutions, while others embrace and encourage such endeavors.

Do you want to include the option to build your own or only focus on off-the-shelf, ready-to-deploy options? Making this decision early will help guide you toward a viable choice.

Familiarize yourself with the wirespeed of the network, general traffic levels, the types of filtering desired, types/forms of recent attacks, and future growth and expansion plans. Armed with these pieces of information, you can begin a serious hunt for the most appropriate firewall solutions.

The firewall technology advances quickly. Often new attacks and exploits crafted by hackers drive these advancements and upgrades. A specific recommendation for a specific model, product line, or even a vendor has a finite life. Suggestions you hear today are likely to be out of date, superseded, or compromised in the next few short months. Products at the top of the market one year might not even place in the next.

Seek out current firewall reviews both online and in technical publications and trade journals. Find firewall options that fall within the parameters you laid out based on your understanding of the network and known threats.

Some general guidelines will assist you in this process:

- If speed, flexibility, and simplicity are priorities, then select a packet filtering firewall or a stateful inspection firewall.
- If real-time applications and high-bandwidth communications are priorities, then select a dedicated application-specific proxy firewall.

- If strong authentication is a priority, then select an application gateway firewall or a dedicated application-specific proxy firewall.
- If detailed logging is a priority, then select an application proxy firewall.
- If customized, unique, or complicated filtering options are a priority, then select a dedicated application-specific proxy firewall or a stateful inspection firewall.
- If stopping internal attacks is a priority, then select a dedicated application-specific proxy firewall or a personal host firewall.

A single firewall product rarely satisfies every need. However, you should be able to find one or more firewall solutions that address the primary security concerns of your organization.

The Difference Between Buying and Building a Firewall

Carefully consider the choice of whether to buy a ready-to-deploy firewall versus building it yourself. An off-the-shelf firewall that you simply plug in can be an attractive solution. However, an out-of-the-box product will generally cost more than an equivalent self-constructed system. In addition, most pre-configured systems are not as flexible or expandable as a custom-built version.

That's not to say that a do-it-yourself firewall is always the best answer, either. A self-constructed firewall can be less expensive and provide a wider variety of features and options. However, when an in-house, custom firewall experiences a problem, you can usually find little formal technical support beyond a user-community discussion forum.

If you are prepared to fully research and understand a firewall product to install, configure, and manage it yourself, then a do-it-yourself firewall can be a great cost-saving solution. However, if your organization's IT staff is already stretched and overworked, then home-built solutions will likely cause more problems than they solve.

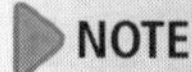
NOTE

Build-it-yourself firewalls are usually less costly because they usually don't include dedicated hardware and often use open-source (free) source code. However, the tradeoff for the savings to successfully deploy a reliable border sentry solution is that you need to know more about firewalls generally and the product specifically.

A pre-built, off-the-shelf firewall is more likely to work right out the box by plugging it in, setting the configuration, and connecting network cables. A build-it-yourself firewall may require additional hardware manipulation, juggling device drivers, hardening a host OS, and so on. Ask yourself: Is custom-built worth the hassle?

Don't automatically reject either buy or build firewall options before you research and assess the options. You might be surprised at the low cost and feature richness of a boxed product or caught off guard by the complexity, instability, or high-cost of a do-it-yourself product. Always look for the best firewall solution for your specific needs and current threats.

Mitigating Firewall Threats and Exploits

Firewalls are one of the most important components of a complete security solution. However, they are not without their own issues, threats, and concerns. Exploits will cause a firewall to fail. Remember that a firewall is software that sometimes includes dedicated hardware and a host operating system. Any software product is prone to flaws and errors in programming. Simply calling it a firewall does not eliminate this concern.

Ultimately, firewalls are software code written by human beings. In either a host firewall or an appliance firewall, the logic and controlling mechanisms of the firewall are software code. Software code is designed and written by people. And whenever people are involved, there's a high probability that mistakes or oversights are possible.

Although coding errors are not as common in firewall products as they are in operating system or other forms of software, don't think coding errors are nonexistent. Most firewall programmers and vendors take extra care to comb through and test every line of code to exacting quality control and security standards. Standard industry practice requires considerable pilot testing of firewall code before release into the commercial environment.

In spite of these precautions, firewalls have in the past been released to market with software coding errors later discovered and exploited. Hackers are constantly using scanning, testing, and probing tools to discover exploitable weaknesses. Once vulnerability appears, hackers take advantage of the flaw. Historical firewall exploits have caused firewalls to freeze or crash and others have given the hacker the ability to read or adjust filtering rules. In most cases, vendors quickly release updates and patches to correct these problems. When selecting a firewall, check the version and patching history. Firewall products with lots of patches might not be as reliable in the future as a product with fewer patches.

How long does the vendor typically take to release a patch once a flaw or exploit for the product becomes public knowledge? The longer the vendor takes to release a fix, the longer you will be left insecure waiting for the update.

Some exploits cause buffer overflows. In a buffer overflow, a memory buffer exceeds its capacity and extends its contents into adjacent memory. Hackers often use this attack against poor programming techniques or poor software quality control. Hackers inject more data into a memory buffer than it can hold, which results in the additional data flowing over into the next area of memory. If the overflow extends to the next memory segment designated for code execution, a skilled attacker can insert arbitrary code that will execute with the same privileges as the current program. Improperly formatted overflow data may also cause a system crash.

Once the firewall vendor becomes aware of an exploit in the wild, they quickly develop and release a patch. An effective security management and patch management system will enable you to quickly test and update the firewalls protecting your production environment. A delay in the release of a patch or its application keeps the window of opportunity for hackers to compromise your environment wide open.

A good rule of thumb is to avoid the first generation or first release of a firewall product. Version 1.0 is bound to be more prone to programming errors than later releases.

If the first version of a product seems better than any other product from any other vendor, then wait at least six months after its initial release before deployment. This gives other people, good and bad, a reasonable time to find flaws, test exploits, and trigger release updates by the vendor.

Once you've chosen a firewall product, always install every available patch and update from the vendor. Always test updates first—no exceptions—but then get them installed as quickly as your testing process will allow. Install only full and final releases of a firewall patch. Never deploy alpha, beta, pre-release, release candidate, or test-build patches on a production firewall.

Another potential concern of firewall security is the filtering it uses. Understand that no perfect security measures exist. Each form of firewall filtering or traffic management is vulnerable in some way. The easiest is basic packet filtering.

Basic packet filtering uses a simple and static rule set. Numerous allow- and deny-explicit exceptions compromise the rule set's final deny-all rule. Rules can focus on IP address and port number of the source and/or destination, as well as the protocol in use. A firewall testing and probing technique known as firewalking can potentially discover some or all of the rules on a static packet filtering firewall.

Firewalking sends basic Transmission Control Protocol (TCP) virtual circuit initiation packets (synchronization-flagged packets) to a known internal target system. The firewalking tool manipulates the parameters of the IP and TCP headers using a brute force technique. This process sends a wide variety of packets toward the internal target in hopes of discovering a packet configuration that succeeds in passing the restrictions of the firewall rule set.

Once a hacker knows the packet constructions that make it past the firewall, he or she can use that knowledge to attack the known internal target or discover and attack other internal targets.

Other forms of firewall filtering are vulnerable if they do not perform content filtering or deep packet inspection. Non-content filtering firewalls do not examine the contents of packet payloads. Thus, once an attack establishes what seems like a benign connection to an internal target, subsequent communications can contain malicious payloads.

Even when stateful inspection, content inspection, and deep packet inspection are present, hackers can employ fragmentation and overlapping attacks. These attacks use packets crafted to seem benign when analyzed individually, but once received by the destination, the fragmentation offset values cause an abnormal re-assembly that overlaps packets to craft new payload and/or new header content. Such attacks can change target ports or deliver a malicious payload past a filtering sentry.

Fragmentation attacks are an abuse of the fragmentation offset feature of IP packets. Fragmentation may occur in a network where many different network links join to construct a global infrastructure. Some network segments support smaller datagrams (another term for packet or frame) than others, so larger datagrams fragment into the smaller size. When the fragmented elements of the original datagram reassemble, manipulations of fragmentation can cause several potentially malicious reconstructions such as overlapping and overrun.

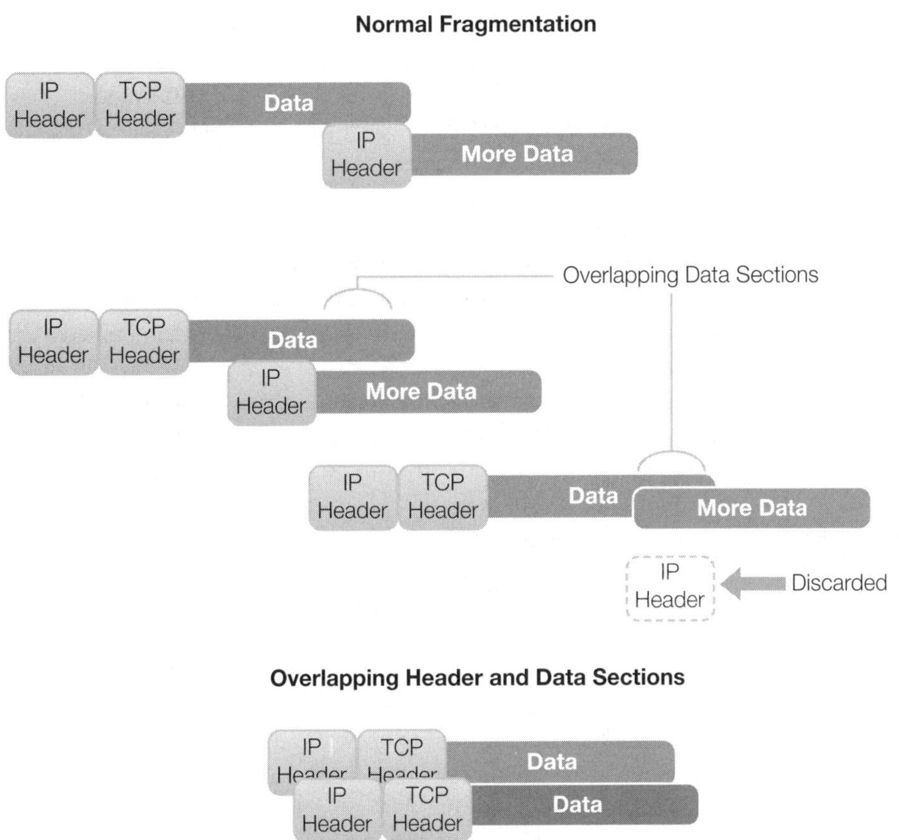

FIGURE 9-2
Fragmentation and overlapping.

Overlapping can cause full or partial overwriting of datagram components creating new datagrams out parts of previous datagrams (Figure 9-2). Overrun can create excessively large datagrams. These and other forms of fragmentation attacks cause DoS or attempt to confuse IDS detection or firewall filtering.

Fragmentation is a supported function of IP packets. Packets fragment when they encounter network segments that support smaller MTU (maximum transmission unit). When packets reassemble, the fragments usually return the data to its original configuration. However, overlapping attacks can abuse the fragmentation offset value in the IP header causing reassembly overlap. Reassembly overlap can create new payloads or headers. For example, if a payload of "EVIL PAYS BLUE LOAD" fragments into "EVIL PAYS BLUE " and "LOAD," an overlap reassembly could result in the creation of "EVIL PAYLOAD."

Protections against fragmentation attacks include using modern IDS detection and firewall filtering features as well as performing sender fragmentation. Sender fragmentation queries the network route to determine the smallest maximum transmission unit (MTU) or datagram size. Then the sender pre-fragments the data to ensure that no in-route fragmentation needs to occur.

The only reliable method of stopping these attacks is to deploy a dynamic filtering system that performs virtual reassembly. Virtual reassembly will piece together both fragmented packets and the original payload. The reassembled payload is analyzed, and then only if it is deemed non-malicious are the original packets transmitted to the internal network. Virtual reassembly is not a completely foolproof technique, but it does greatly reduce the risk of these exploits.

The most common method of exploiting and/or bypassing a firewall is internal code planting. Firewalls are often border sentries. They protect internal systems from communications that originate from external entities. Unfortunately, some security administrators use only inbound firewall filtering, which leaves outbound traffic uncontrolled and unfiltered.

In this situation, if a hacker can plant code internally or trick a user into running code, or if an employee brings in code of his or her own, outbound connections to malicious external entities might be possible. Frequently, laptops that pick up malware connect to the internal network, placing the malware behind the firewall. Many hacker tools rely on this technique, such as Loki, Back Orifice, NetBus, and even netcat. A server of sorts is hosted on an external host and the automatic connection client utility runs on an internal host. The client utility establishes the initial connection as an outbound connection (thus allowed by the firewall), and then the external host is able to send data or commands back to the internal client through this connection. Often this form of attack results in a hacker gaining modest to complete remote control over the compromised internal host.

Denial of service (DoS) is another common threat to firewalls and networks as a whole. A denial of service attack, specifically a flooding or traffic based DoS, sends massive amounts of data to a target victim. If that victim has a firewall, then it will detect and discard the DoS. The firewall's filtering service can usually prevent the DoS traffic from breaching the network's perimeter and affecting internal systems.

However, since the firewall has to collect, analyze, and respond to each and every packet received on its interfaces, well-managed DoS can consume all available bandwidth of the connecting segment to the firewall, as well as consume all of the processing capabilities of the firewall. This, in turn, prevents any legitimate traffic from reaching the network. Thus, even with a firewall protecting the internal network, a DoS flooding attack can still successfully disconnect or interfere with external communications.

A firewall's vulnerability to DoS flooding is the one limitation or weakness that you can't fix, improve, or repair by either upgrading the firewall or applying a patch. Upgrading to a stateful inspection firewall addresses fragmentation, firewalking, and even internal planting of code. Patching will address programming bugs and buffer overflows. Although highly specialized tools are available that can perform partial upstream DoS detection and filtering, in general no fixes to prevent flooding attacks from reaching an Internet-facing firewall exist.

Knowing these threats and exploits, as well as realizing the probability of others, should remind the security administrators to be proficient at the basics. Security management is mandatory to maintain any semblance of security in any environment.

Your essential long-term strategies for maintaining security include keeping systems current with patches, using a hardened configuration, staying knowledgeable about new exploitations, and monitoring the environment for successful and attempted compromise.

Concerns Related to Tunneling Through or Across a Firewall

Hackers tunneling through or across your firewall deployments are a serious threat to your organization's network security. Tunneling is the creation of a communication channel similar to the creation of a VPN. In some cases, it uses actual VPN solutions and protocols. Tunneling can create either a covert channel or a known channel that's unfiltered.

Tunneling uses two techniques. One method is installing a server component on an internal system, and then an external client component initiates the connection. This technique requires the firewall to allow inbound initiation connections to internal systems. A second method is to install a server component on an external system, then use an internal client component to initiate the connection. This technique requires the firewall to allow outbound connections.

Most firewall deployments strictly limit or restrict inbound initiation of communications to specific ports and services. Thus, a tunneling setup using an inbound connection must "hijack" an existing open port or reconfigure the firewall to open another port for use by the tunnel. If the perpetrator of this security violation has the ability to reconfigure the firewall, you have much more serious security concerns to address than tunneling.

Firewalls commonly allow most outbound communications with little or no restrictions. While not the best security stance, it is convenient and easy. Proper use of a deny-by-default stance should limit both inbound and outbound connections to those explicitly allowed. If the firewall freely allows outbound connections, then internally initiated tunnels are extremely easy to establish.

Tunnels can potentially use almost any protocol, including IP, ICMP, TCP, UDP, and most application protocols. Specialized tunneling server/client applications can replace traditional payload content with whatever content the hacker wishes. Effectively, this can convert almost any protocol at any layer of the OSI model into an encapsulation or tunneling protocol.

Tunneling is an obvious abuse and violation of protocol rules. However, if a firewall is not investigating the payload of a frame, packet, segment, and so on, then a hacker can set up a tunnel using a protocol not designed to perform encapsulation.

FYI

Once a tunnel is open, data can move in either direction. The directionality of the connection has little to do with which end of the tunnel is the controller and which is the ultimate target or victim.

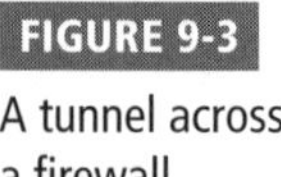

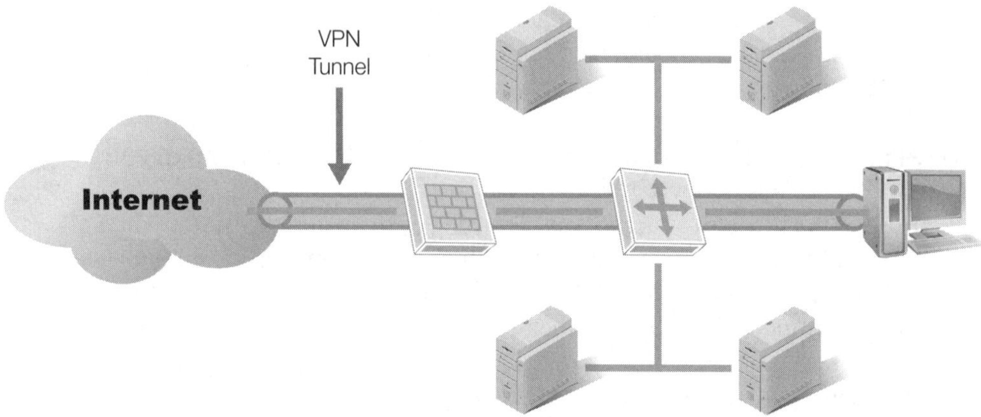

FIGURE 9-3
A tunnel across a firewall.

The problem gets worse when the tunneling system employs encryption. This makes payload investigations more difficult because the firewall will be unable to decipher the content or purpose of the encoded payload. To combat this complexity, set the firewall to either block all encryption, allow only encryption that originates or terminates at the firewall, or allow encryption only on certain ports (potentially limit communications to and from specific IP addresses as well).

Encrypted tunnels across a firewall are not inherently or automatically malicious in nature. VPNs are encrypted tunnels that commonly and widely create security for personal and business communications across the Internet and within private networks. However, most VPNs use well-known VPN protocols, such as IPSec and SSL, on standardized ports, with predictable header constructions and characteristics. Unauthorized or rogue tunneling mechanisms often use odd protocols for encapsulation and can operate on any port, use invalid packet constructions, and violate to communication standards.

In addition to the standard VPN protocols used for this purpose, such as IPSec, SSL, TLS, OpenVPN, PPTP, L2F, L2TP, and so on, several other legitimate and subversive services/products/protocols can configure unauthorized tunnels. These include:

- **Loki**—uses ICMP as a tunneling protocol.
- **Netcat**—can create TCP and UDP network connections to or from any port.
- **Cryptcat**—a version of netcat that creates encrypted connections.
- **NetBus**—a malicious remote control tool.
- **Back Orifice**—a malicious remote control tool.
- **SubSeven**—a malicious remote control tool.
- **Remote Desktop Protocol (RDP) & Remote Assistance**—native features of Windows OS; RDP is disabled by default, and Remote Assistance requires an invitation (see Chapter 14).
- **TOR (The Onion Router)**—a double-blind encapsulation system enabling anonymous, but not encrypted, Internet communications (see Chapter 14).

- **JanusVM**—a Linux VMWare VM that creates SSH encrypted tunnels used in combination with TOR (see Chapter 14).
- **PacketiX VPN**—An encrypted Web proxy service (see Chapter 14).
- **HotSpotShield**—An encrypted Web proxy service (see Chapter 14).
- **HTTP Proxy**—A Web proxy service.
- **GoToMyPC, GoToAssist, LogMeIn, and other similar services**—third-party remote desktop control services (see Chapter 14).

This list of products, services, solutions, and protocols used to create illicit tunnels across a firewall is not exhaustive. Several of these are legitimate services with valid uses, but when a hacker employs them without permission, especially across nonstandard ports, they represent a serious threat. Any ability to breach a firewall to allow unfiltered, full-duplex communications is cause for concern and response.

The best defense against these tunneling exploitations is to strictly enforce deny-by-default for both inbound and outbound communications. Clearly define in the acceptable use policy (AUP) which tools are unauthorized and are considered security breaches. Use network and host IDS/IPS monitoring. Deploy white-list controls to prevent the installation of unapproved software. Limit mobile code, such as ActiveX, Java, Flash, Silverlight, and JavaScript in browsers to minimize the possibility that a Web-only form of tunneling might use an authorized Web client.

Testing Firewall Security

Firewall tests are an important and integral part of the build and management process. Standard security management practice is to test security to confirm proper configuration, performance, and strength against attacks and exploits. Failing to test a firewall is a serious breach of this best practice.

Because a firewall is one of the most important parts of your security infrastructure, is a concentration of security controls, and is your first line of defense against inbound attacks, failing to test a firewall thoroughly practically ensures you will have a breach or intrusion.

Every update, change, or alteration to any aspect of your firewall or the network segments connecting to a firewall should trigger another round of firewall testing. Test a firewall as if you were practicing for the Olympics. Repeat the testing again and again, striving to push the limits and improve with each drill. Strive to ensure your firewall deployment is the best it can possibly be.

technical TIP

Testing a firewall involves the use of several tools and techniques. These include automated vulnerability assessment tools, exploitation frameworks, and rogue hacker attack tools.

One type of firewall testing is simulated. A simulated firewall test uses an attack simulator to transmit attack packets to the firewall. You can locate the attack simulator inside or outside the firewall to simulate an internal attack or an external attack. An attack simulator can verify that a specific weakness is present on a firewall, without actually causing damage or interrupting production. Most simulator tests are secure by design.

Creating a virtualized network environment using a virtualization tool, such as VMware, performs virtual firewall tests. A virtual intranet is created, a virtual firewall bastion host goes up, and virtual external systems become active. The administrator then works through a variety of scenarios of attack, both from internal attackers and external ones. Logically the virtualized environment functions like the real one, but you can test it using techniques that might otherwise damage or interrupt the production network.

Laboratory tests run in non-production subnets where you've configured a duplicate of the production environment. The laboratory setup mirrors each system, including the firewall. Test-run in the lab environment anything that might interfere with production or might cause data loss or system damage.

Laboratory tests and virtualized testing are similar, but both are useful mechanisms; use them both rather than forgoing laboratory tests in favor of using virtual testing exclusively. The actual physical devices of firewall and systems might reveal weaknesses not present in the virtualized versions.

Any of these testing configurations can benefit from the use of **fuzzing tools**. Fuzzing tools use a brute force technique to craft packets and other forms of input directed toward the target. Fuzzing tools stress a system to discover if it will react improperly, fail, or reveal unknown vulnerabilities. Fuzzing tools can discover coding errors, buffer overflows, race conditions, remote exploit flaws, injection weaknesses, and so on. The downside to using fuzzing tools is that they can take a significant amount of time to discover anything interesting.

Using a variety of testing methods to put a firewall thoroughly through its paces is an important part of security management. To maximize your network's security effectiveness, plan, design, deploy, test, and then fine-tune. .

Important Tools for Managing and Monitoring a Firewall

Proper security management requires that you manage and monitor the firewalls in your infrastructure. As with every type of security, you can't just install them and forget them. Every security safeguard must be locked down, tuned, and monitored over time. Once it has been installed and configured, the work of managing the firewall begins.

Firewall management is about understanding that new threats are coming from hackers on a constant basis, and the defenses and settings that work successfully today might not be the best defense against new attacks tomorrow. Firewall management is the essential task of maintaining a firewall in spite of these new threats.

Firewall management includes verifying that the configuration settings of the firewall remain in place and don't change without authorization. Device failures, electrical fluctuations, and unexpected reboots can delete or corrupt firewall configurations. So, regularly verify that the desired settings remain active on the firewall.

Firewall management includes applying updates and patches to the firewall. Always test updates before deployment. Back up firewall configurations before applying new and tested updates. Once you apply an update, confirm that the application of the update didn't reset the configuration to the default settings.

Firewall management includes testing the resistance of the firewall to attacks. This can include the use of a variety of automated and manual attack tools and techniques. Effectively, firewall testing is the application of penetration testing or ethical hacking against the firewall as the primary target. Using the tools and methodology of criminal hackers in an ethical and boundary-limited manner is an excellent way to verify the ability of a firewall to withstand known attacks.

Firewall management includes the use of monitoring tools to watch over the performance and reliability of a firewall over time. Properly use any valid tool in this endeavor. Some recommended tools to consider include:

- **Nmap**—a network mapper, port scanner, and OS fingerprinting tool. Can check the state of ports, identify targets, and probe services.
- **Netstat**—a simple command line tool to list the current open, listening, and connection sockets on a system.
- **Tcpview**—a GUI tool to list the current open, listening, and connection sockets on a system as well as the service/program related to each socket.
- **Fport**—a command line tool to list the current open, listening, and connection sockets on a system as well as the service/program related to each socket.
- **Snort**—an open-source, rule-based IDS that can detect firewall breaches.
- **Nessus**—an open-source vulnerability assessment engine that can scan for known vulnerabilities.
- **Wireshark**—a free packet capture/protocol analyzer/sniffer that can analyze packets/frames (Figure 9-4) as the enter or leave a firewall.
- **Netcat**—a hacker tool that creates network communication links using UDP or TCP ports that support the transmission of standard input and output. Commonly creates covert channels to control a target system remotely or bypass a firewall. Can test a firewall's ability to detect and block covert channels. Cryptcat offers similar capabilities using encryption.
- **Backtrack**—a Linux distribution that includes hundreds of security and hacking tools, including Nessus and Metasploit. Can perform attacks against or through a firewall for testing purposes.
- **Syslog**—a centralized logging service that hosts a duplicate copy of log files. Provides real-time backup of every log on every participating host.

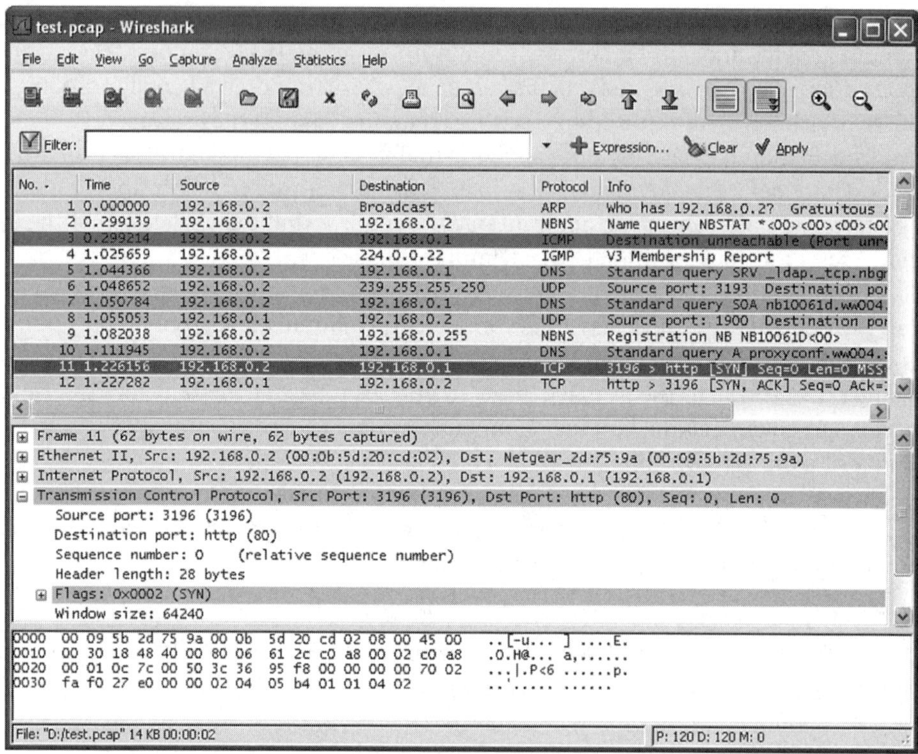

FIGURE 9-4

Wireshark.

These are only a few of the excellent tools to manage and monitor a firewall. But more important than the tools you use is ensuring that the careful management, monitoring, and tuning of your firewalls actually take place.

Troubleshooting Firewalls

Firewall troubleshooting, like any form of troubleshooting, is about the process more than the actual result. Most firewall problems can be relatively easy to troubleshoot if you've planned a detailed troubleshooting procedure with extensive documentation. The foundation of successful troubleshooting is preparation.

When trouble arises in or around the security of the network, especially in regard to the firewall, act promptly to resolve the issues at hand. Troubleshooting is both an art and skill set to systematically diagnose and eliminate problems whatever the source. Although troubleshooting might sometimes sound exciting, in reality it's a fairly lengthy and tedious process. Knowing a few procedures and commonsense guidelines can improve your troubleshooting skills and help keep downtime and security breaches to a minimum.

You can never have too much useful troubleshooting information. Information, data, documentation, resources, and so on are the primary tools you can use to find and resolve problems. Useful troubleshooting information includes:

- Complete hardware and software inventory (relative to firewalls)
- Written and electronic copies of configuration settings
- Firewall policy
- Change documentation
- Previous troubleshooting logs
- Activity, error, and alert logs
- Maintenance logs
- Any information about the current problem

Once you have this information in hand, you can begin the overall troubleshooting process. Don't wait until a problem occurs to collect this essential information, however. Instead, maintain this collection of documentation as a normal, regular, essential element of system maintenance and management. The best time to document the environment and configuration is when you do not urgently need it. When problems do arise, you want to be able to focus on deliberately resolving the issue, not collecting resources and tools. Pre-assemble the tools and resources you'll need for troubleshooting so that you will be ready for action.

Murphy's Law dictates that when things go wrong, and they will, they will go bad at the least convenient time. To combat this, be prepared before the problems arise. So, when the firewall fails, locks up, freezes, lets through unwanted traffic, or falls to a hacker, then you can focus on dealing with the stress, time crunch, data loss, and downtime ramifications without also having to deal with collecting the essential materials to resolve the problem.

Being prepared is always a solid first step. Next, develop a troubleshooting plan, technique, or procedure. While some problems are predicable and have a known method of resolution, many situations will require off-the-cuff brainstorming to craft a new solution. Most solutions come from a liberal application of common sense. Below are several commonsense elements you need to integrate into your troubleshooting planning:

- **Have patience**—Keeping your cool and taking your time will pay off by allowing you to find a solution quickly without making mistakes, overlooking essential details, or intensifying the problem further.
- **Know your firewall thoroughly**—The more you already know about the firewall, hardware and software, the more you will know how it functions and can immediately use that knowledge to seeking out a solution.
- **Isolate the problem**—Whenever possible, isolate elements or components of the firewall system that are functioning correctly to narrow the range of suspects of potential problem sources.
- **Simplify**—Disable or disconnect software and hardware not essential to the function of the firewall. This will reduce the complexity of the situation and may assist in discovering the cause.
- **Focus**—Seek to find a solution to the current most critical problem. Don't waste time fixing, repairing, upgrading, resetting, or configuring any other problem or aspect of the firewall system until you've resolved the primary problem. You can become distracted by minor details that "only take a second" to address; make a list of these smaller issues and come back to them later.

- **Review change documentation**—Could a recent change be responsible for the unwanted activity? If so, try to undo the change to see if the problem stops.
- **Review previous troubleshooting logs**—Consider whether the current problem is the same as or similar to recent problems already in the log. Try repeating successful solutions.
- **Update the troubleshooting log**—Record every action attempted, whether successful or not. Record it into the troubleshooting log and use it as a journal. Think of something, then write it down and try the solution; write it down, then test for effectiveness; write it down, then repeat the failure fix; write it down, then repeat until resolved; write down the successful solution and make note of any other thoughts, ideas, or observations.
- **Try the quick and easy fixes first**—Try the fast and easy stuff before the hard and complicated options. You might be lucky, but if not, undoing easily attempted failed solutions will be simpler than undoing more complex options.
- **Avoid destructive or irreversible solutions until last**—Attempts to use an irreversible fix is a poor idea early in the troubleshooting process; only after reversible and/or safe solutions have failed should you attempt more drastic measures.
- **Try the free options before the costly ones**—Always try to perform repairs and fixes in-house using tools and resources that you already own or can obtain free. Hold off on purchasing new resources or hiring technical support until you've exhausted other options.
- **Let the problem guide and direct you**—The more you understand how your firewall operates and what the problem is, the more the problem directs you toward the affected area or the source of the issue.
- **Make fixes one at a time**—Try only one fix or repair option at a time; attempting multiple fixes at once is more complex and might mask the successful resolution.
- **Test after each attempt**—After each fix is made, test the repair to see if it was successful.
- **Reverse or undo solution failures**—If a fix does not resolve the issue, undo it to return to the previous state. Leaving failed fixes in place may cause other problems or may intensify the main problem.
- **Repeat the failure**—Sometimes causing the failure to repeat can assist in identifying the cause. However, do so only when the repetition will not cause further harm or loss.
- **Perform post-mortem review**—The most valuable result of a problem, especially a resolved problem, is your ability to learn something from the event. Always review the entire troubleshooting response process. Look for ways to improve the response to future problems.

Use these commonsense highlights to create an official how-to procedure that your IT and security staff can follow when a firewall problem arises. Firewall problems won't wait; strive to understand and resolve them fast. Otherwise, your network will be at risk or productivity can suffer; neither is beneficial to the long-term viability of your organization.

Proper Firewall Implementation Procedure

Successful firewall implementation comes from a written plan. As with every aspect of security, a written procedure is essential for a reliable and trustworthy deployment. If a firewall policy does not exist in your organization, then your first step should be to craft one.

A firewall implementation procedure should prescribe the systematic process to properly install and configure a firewall. Since each firewall product is different and each type of deployment is likely different (a border firewall versus an internal host firewall, for instance). You may even find that you need several firewall implementation guides.

The specifics of an implementation guide are different for each organization. Customizing a plan for your specific environment is essential to obtain the best security from the deployed firewall. However, every plan should have certain common elements. Whether you are developing your own firewall implementation policy or revising an existing one, use the following plan components to make yours is the best possible policy for your organization.

Every firewall procedure should clearly define the requirements for the firewall. A generic description of a firewall is insufficient. Don't just indicate that you need a software firewall or an appliance firewall. Instead, dictate the specific capabilities, features, and requires to accomplish the tasks and security goals. You can include a specific example of a vendor's exact make and model. However, products change, are revised, replaced, and retired by vendors on a rather frequent basis. So, include an inventory of features and specifications, even if you focus on a certain off-the-shelf product.

Specify the network design that the firewall will complement. To be effective, network firewalls (as opposed to host firewalls) must be at choke points or transition points. The design of the network is an essential element of effective firewall deployment. Define and even map out the network structure that should exist along with pinpointing exactly where the firewall is, down to the logical configuration and the physical cables connecting to it. Your network design will change over time, but this can always change in the future when you perform change documentation and guidelines revision.

Write the plan down. Write out step by step, point by point, every action to take from the moment the firewall arrives on site through the point of enabling the filtering of production traffic. Include hardening of the bastion host, applying patches, updating firmware, changing defaults (especially passwords), locking down management interfaces, changing configuration settings, defining the rule sets, configuring interfaces, installing the physical components, backing up the configuration, testing at start up, testing for stress and load, documenting performance and stability, obtaining approval from senior management, and initiating filtering of production traffic.

Prescribe the process of shopping for and purchasing (or otherwise obtaining) the firewall. Not all firewalls have a purchase cost, such as those which are free, open source, or obtained through bartering options. Nonetheless, document a procurement process. Consider purchase price, whether the product is new, used, or reconditioned; understand the return policy; look for discounts; investigate the warranty; and know what levels of technical support are free or available for a fee. If the product gets shipped to you, either verify that it's in stock or determine the backlog waiting period. Consider overnight shipping and insuring the package against shipping damage and loss. Don't spend hundreds or thousands of dollars on a product that may arrive damaged without having recourse to a claim with the shipping company.

Document, document, document. Write down every aspect of firewall use before deployment. Journal every step performed from start to finish of deployment, and then record into the documentation every action in managing, administering, monitoring, and troubleshooting the firewall for the remainder of its deployment life. No action or event is too insignificant to record relative to your firewall deployment. This comprehensive firewall documentation is essential to management, troubleshooting, recovery, and incident response.

Responding to Incidents

Incident response is a key part of every security infrastructure. Incident response is the planned reaction to negative situations or events. Security breaches, or at least attempts to breach security, will occur. When those events affect the organization or its abilities to perform its tasks in any way, incident response triggers. The goals of incident response are to minimize downtime, minimize loss, and restore the environment to a secure, normal state as quickly as possible. This applies to breaches of a firewall as well as every other aspect of security.

Most incident response solutions include six primary steps or phases:

- **Preparation**—Select and train IRT (incident response team) members and allocate resources.
- **Detection**—Confirm actual breaches.
- **Containment**—Restrain further escalation.
- **Eradication**—Resolve the compromise.
- **Recovery**—Return to normal operation.
- **Follow-up**—Review the process and improve future responses.

Incident response is an important element of firewall management.

CHAPTER SUMMARY

Firewall management involves addressing all security concerns related to the security provided by a firewall. This includes following recommended best practices, knowing that a firewall is only part of a complete security infrastructure, picking the right firewall for the environment, considering the options of building versus buying a firewall, being prepared to mitigate firewall threats and risks, dealing with tunneling across a firewall, firewall testing, using tools for management and monitoring, troubleshooting problems, planning out use, and being prepared with an incident response policy.

KEY CONCEPTS AND TERMS

Fuzzing tools

CHAPTER 9 ASSESSMENT

1. All of the following are considered firewall management best practices *except*:

A. Have a written policy
B. Provide open communications
C. Maintain physical access control
D. Don't make assumptions
E. Develop a checklist

2. All of the following are firewall management best practices *except*:

A. Lock, then watch
B. Backup, backup, backup
C. Keep it simple
D. Perform penetration testing
E. Implement fail-open response

3. You are the security administrator for a small medical facility. To be in compliance with federal HIPAA regulations, you need to deploy a firewall to protect the entire office network. You are concerned that a firewall failure could result in compliance violations as well as legal costs due to client court cases. Which of the following is the best choice of firewall for this situation?

A. Deploy a client system with a native OS firewall
B. Select any open-source firewall product
C. Use the firewall provided by the ISP connection device
D. Deploy a well-known commercial firewall from the approved products list
E. Use a multi-function device, such as a wireless access point

4. From the following options, what is the most important factor in selecting a firewall?

A. Biometric authentication
B. Types of traffic to be filtered
C. Sales or discounts
D. Bastion host OS
E. Built-in antivirus scanning

5. A well-designed and configured firewall provides more than sufficient security protection without any additional safeguards.

A. True
B. False

6. Which of the following is a benefit of buying a ready-to-deploy firewall over using a build-it-yourself firewall?

A. Minimal setup time
B. Less expensive
C. Repurpose existing hardware
D. Use open-source software
E. More complex troubleshooting

7. Which of the following is a benefit of using a build-it-yourself firewall over buying a ready-to-deploy firewall?

A. More costly
B. On-site technical support
C. Greater flexibility and customization
D. Product warranty
E. Requires skill and knowledge to deploy

8. Which of the following is *not* one of the possible but rare attacks or exploits against a firewall?

A. Coding flaw exploitation
B. SMB share exploitation
C. Buffer overflow attacks
D. Firewalking
E. Fragmentation

9. The exploit or attack known as ________ can be used to cause a DoS, confuse an IDS, or bypass firewall filtering.

A. Obfuscation
B. Trojan horse
C. SQL injection
D. Fragmentation overlapping
E. Spoofing

10. Although successful attacks and exploits against firewalls are rare, what is the best response or resolution to such compromises?

A. Deploy anti-malware scanning
B. Add additional rules to the set
C. Position the firewall on a non-choke point
D. Increase the transmission frequency
E. Patching and updating

11. Tunneling across or through a firewall can be used to perform all of the following tasks *except*:

A. Use a closed port for covert communications
B. Bypass filtering restrictions
C. Use any open port to support communication sessions
D. Allow external users access to internal resources
E. Support secure authorized remote access

12. Which of the following statements is false?

A. ICMP can be used as a tunneling protocol.
B. Encryption prevents filtering on content.
C. Outbound communications don't need to be filtered.
D. Tunnels can be created using almost any protocol.
E. Tunnels can enable communications to bypass firewall filters.

13. Which of the following provides anonymous, but not encrypted, tunneling services?

A. Cryptcat
B. JanusVM
C. TOR
D. PacketIX VPN
E. HotSpotShield

14. What is the best way to know that a firewall is functioning as expected?

A. Review the documentation
B. Presume it is until a patch is received from the vendor
C. Test it
D. Check the configuration
E. Watch the log files

15. Which method of testing a firewall grants the tester the greatest range of freedom to perform tests that might cause physical or logical damage to a firewall?

A. Live firewall tests
B. Virtual firewall tests
C. Laboratory test
D. Simulation tests
E. Production firewall tests

16. Which of the following tools tests and probes whether a port is open or closed?

A. nmap
B. netstat
C. tcpview
D. fport
E. wireshark

17. Which of the following testing tools is an open-source vulnerability assessment engine that scans for known vulnerabilities?

A. Snort
B. Nessus
C. Wireshark
D. Netcat
E. Syslog

18. What is always the best tool for firewall troubleshooting?

A. Source code
B. Crimping tool
C. Vulnerability scanner
D. Information
E. Fuzzing tool

19. Which of the following is *not* a recommended commonsense element of troubleshooting?

A. Isolate the problem
B. Set it aside and return to it later
C. Review change documentation
D. Make fixes one at a time
E. Have patience

20. Which of the following is *not* part of a successful firewall use?

A. Written plan
B. Specific requirements
C. Purchasing guidelines
D. User survey of preferences
E. Documentation

CHAPTER

10 Using Common Firewalls

THE ACTUAL DEPLOYMENT of a firewall is a fairly straightforward process. This process begins with understanding the network environment, includes selecting a product that satisfies security needs, and ends with a more secured network infrastructure. Toward that end, this chapter examines a few of the remaining concepts that are often part of the decision-making process.

Firewalls are useful in many different situations. Every network infrastructure can benefit from proper use of a firewall. This chapter presents additional concerns and decision points for small and large network environments, host software firewalls, native operating system (OS) firewalls, third-party OS firewall alternatives, internet service provider (ISP) connection device firewalls, commercial firewall options, open-source firewalls, hardware firewalls, and virtual firewalls.

Chapter 10 Topics

This chapter covers the following topics and concepts:

- What some options are for individual and small office/ home office (SOHO) firewalls
- What common uses for a host software firewall are
- How to use Windows 7's host software firewall
- How to use a Linux host software firewall
- How to manage the firewall on a connection device from an Internet service provider (ISP)
- What commercial software network firewalls are
- What open-source software network firewalls are
- What appliance firewalls are
- What virtual firewalls are
- What some simple firewall techniques are

Chapter 10 Goals

When you complete this chapter, you will be able to:

- Configure the Windows Firewall on Windows 7
- Set up a broadband connection device firewall

Individual and Small Office/Home Office (SOHO) Firewall Options

Firewall options for the individual or for those running a small office range from native OS firewalls to special-purpose devices. Most individuals and small office/home office (SOHO) users are concerned about security but don't want to spend more than really necessary. Obtaining a reasonable level of security for most home or small office environments is actually quite easy and cost effective.

First, understanding the common threats facing such an environment suggests that firewall options can be simple and inexpensive. While the Internet is not a safe place, interacting with Internet resources is not an automatic recipe for damage and destruction. Common sense and use of basic security tools greatly reduces the likelihood that a significant compromise from the Internet will take place.

Generally, Internet threats fall into two main categories: passive and active. **Passive threats** are those you must seek out to be harmed. For example, you have to visit a Web site to be harmed by malicious code embedded in that site. Likewise, downloading infected content occurs only when you elect to click on a download link. Most users can avoid most passive threats by making good and safe choices as to where to go and what to do on the Internet.

To address passive threats, modern Web browsers include **pop-up blockers**, **cookie filters** (Figure 10-1), and malicious site managers to limit exposure. The use of antivirus scanning, an anti-spyware scanner, and anti-SPAM filters addresses other common threats. Adding a firewall to your security stance protects against most of the passive threats on the Internet that might be casually triggered. While it's still possible to go looking and find trouble, most well-known and popular sites take security seriously and strive to make accessing their resources as secure as possible.

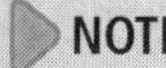

NOTE

Installing a handful of security tools doesn't mean that you can throw caution to the wind and randomly explore the entire Internet safely. Instead, by using simple security tools along with common sense, most threats are either blocked or avoided. Potential exceptions can always affect this rule, of course, such as when a trusted site is compromised and your next visit results in the transfer of malware to your hard drive.

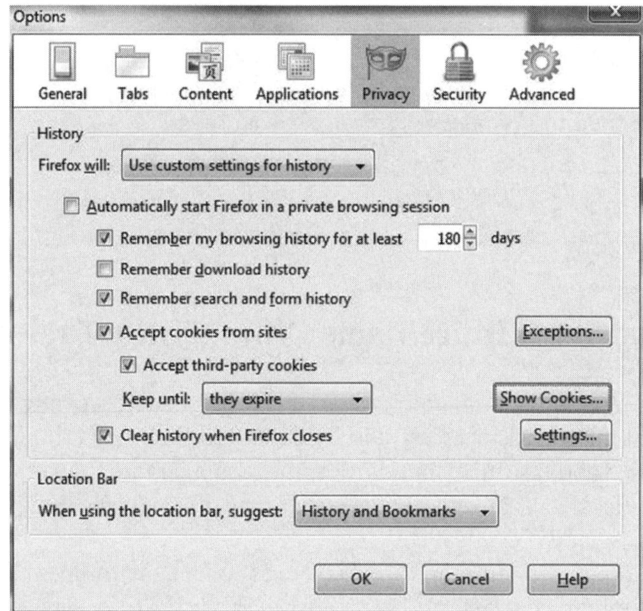

FIGURE 10-1

The Privacy section of Firefox's Options dialog; note cookie settings.

The other category of Internet threat is active. An **active threat** is one that takes some type of initiative to seek out a target to compromise. These can be hackers, intruders, or automated worms. In any case, an active threat seeks out vulnerable targets. If you do not have reasonable security deployed and an active threat discovers your system, you might be at risk for a compromise.

Fortunately, most individuals and small office environments are not significant or primary targets of most hacker activity. There just isn't enough value or benefit in spending the time and effort to compromise a moderately secured single computer or small network. If your business is getting lots of traffic and orders or you happen to be hosting hundreds of systems, then you naturally become a more valuable target to hackers.

In most circumstances, the average home user and most small offices (such as those operating a dozen or fewer computers in a network) can obtain reasonable security protection from very simple and inexpensive firewall options.

The first firewall option to consider is any **native firewall** of the operating system. Most OSs include a default or native firewall. If so, investigate its features and options before automatically tossing it aside. Many of the firewalls found in the latest releases of operating systems are as good as or better than most commercially available third-party host software firewall options.

One of the most well-known examples of a native operating system firewall is Windows Firewall. The Windows Firewall made its debut in the Windows OS as part of Service Pack 2 for Windows XP. Initially, Windows Firewall was panned because it imposed security, restrictions, and control on the Windows OS where none existed before. Many applications and services failed to function with the Windows Firewall. Ironically, many of these "failures" were caused not by Windows Firewall, but by a service performing insecure and unfiltered activities blocked by the security provided by the new OS firewall.

Since its initial release, Windows Firewall has matured. It appeared as a standard native feature in Windows Vista and Windows 7 (Figure 10-2). The measure is likely to remain a key OS component in future versions of Windows. The feature set and uses of Windows 7 Firewall are discussed in a later section in this chapter.

Other OSs may or may not have a firewall as well recognized as Windows Firewall, but you should still investigate the standard options and feature set provided natively before seeking out alternatives. After all, you'd never custom turbo-charge a brand new car until you've driven it and road tested its standard features.

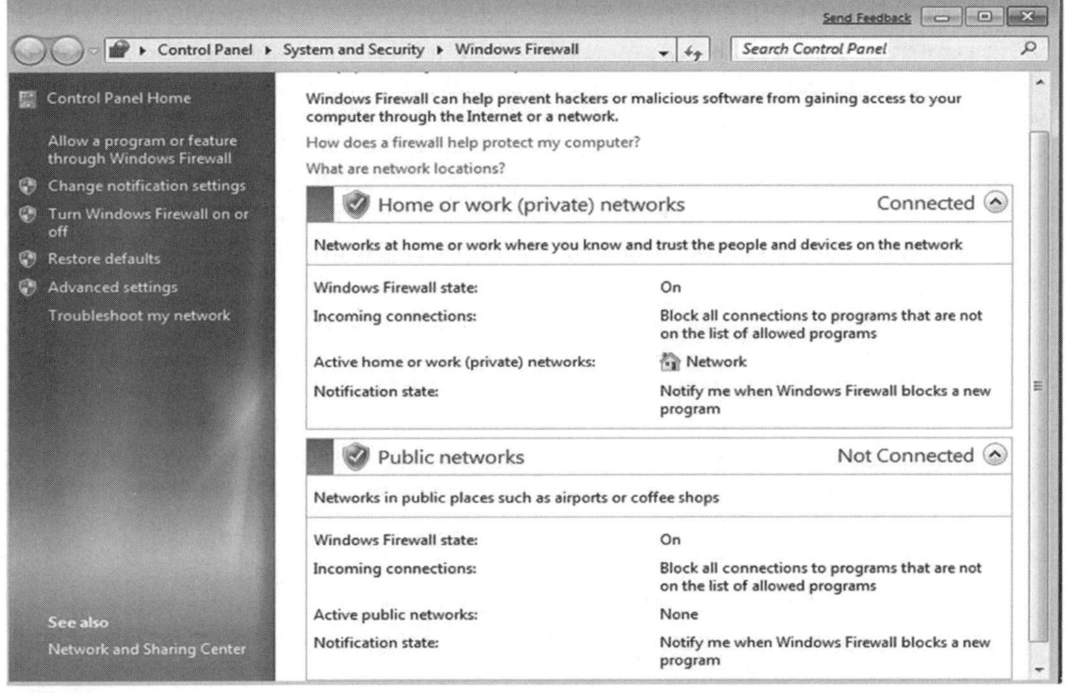

FIGURE 10-2

Windows 7's Windows Firewall Control Panel status dialog.

FYI

Current industry nomenclature gives most ISP connection devices a name that includes the word "modem." Don't be fooled by this label; the term modem comes from the function of a device that *mod*ulates and *dem*odulates (hence, *mod-dem*) digital information into analog signals. Most ISP connections, including cable, DSL, satellite, and long-range wireless, are digital signaling systems that don't employ analog signals or information of any type. So, the use of the term "modem" is a merchandising ploy to make the device sound familiar and comfortable, rather than complex and scary.

Linux distributions do not automatically come with a native software firewall. And even when Linux provides a native firewall, it's not likely to be enabled or configured by default. Due to the wide range of variations in Linux distributions, Linux provides a range of firewalls. Linux firewalls include older products such as ipchains and iptables, as well as newer options such as PF, Netfilter, and Vyatta.

In addition to the free or native OS firewall options, another simple and easy firewall that individuals and SOHOs can use is firewalls hosted by ISP connection devices or wireless access points. Most ISP connection devices, including cable modems, digital subscriber line (DSL) modems, satellite modems, and wireless modems include firewall features. A firewall feature may or may not represent a fully functional firewall. Some are basic filtering tools that block IP addresses, ports, or protocols using a simple blacklist technique.

If the ISP connection device provides firewall services, obtain a copy of the original manufacturer's user manual for the device. This will provide the best initial information on accessing and configuring the device's firewall, since your ISP has probably chosen to lock down access to the connection device. For more on the use of an ISP connection device firewall, please see the section later in this chapter.

An ISP connection device may or may not offer wireless connectivity. If the provider does not offer a wireless option or requires you to pay extra for wireless via their equipment, you should consider deploying your own wireless access point. Most wireless access points for consumers and SOHO environments cost under $100 and offer firewall services as well as wireless connectivity.

The use of native host OS firewalls and a hardware firewall provided by an ISP connection device or wireless access point is usually more than sufficient filtering security for a home user or a small office network. However, if you want to explore other options or you have a larger, riskier, or more sensitive environment, consider the other firewall alternatives.

Uses for a Host Software Firewall

The next step up from a native OS firewall (or even an OS without a firewall) is a third-party host software firewall. These options include both open-source and commercial software firewalls for most operating systems.

You can use a host software firewall in several situations. The first and most obvious use is simply to protect a client system. This is the original and intended purpose of a host software firewall. Keep in mind that a host software firewall provides protections for both inbound and outbound communications. A host software firewall protects the client from compromises on the network and protects the network from compromises on the client.

Use a host software firewall as an additional layer of protection on a server system. Most server operating systems do not include a host software firewall. Therefore, often a dedicated firewall appliance deploys on the network. A host software firewall on a server is never a substitute for an appliance firewall. However, it can be a supplement.

A host software firewall can provide firewall filtering services in relation to a virtual private network (VPN). Just because the VPN link itself may be encrypted does not guarantee that the other end of the VPN connection is as secure as you might desire. Using a host software firewall in conjunction with either a software host VPN (such as a transport mode VPN or a remote access VPN) or an appliance VPN adds an additional layer of protection against compromises that could traverse the VPN connection.

A host software firewall can provide modest protection for small networks. Home networks, gaming networks, and small office networks are sometimes constructed using a primary system connected to the Internet that shares that connection with a small network off of a secondary network interface. On a Windows system, this Internet Connection Sharing service makes this type of network configuration simple. Use a host software firewall and provide the secondary network with modest firewall filtering services.

A host software firewall likely has many other uses. Don't limit your imagination or deployment options to those discussed in books, described in manuals, or prescribed by the vendor. Use host software firewalls in any network configuration. The goal is to establish additional layers of security, not conform to static notions of design and implementation.

NOTE

Before installing any third-party software firewall, always double-check for full compatibility with your current operating system version and patch level. If the firewall's documentation does not specifically list your operating system as being fully compatible, don't assume that the measure will work properly. Firewall security is not something to leave to chance.

NOTE

When installing a third-party software firewall, make sure all native or other firewalls are disabled or uninstalled. Do not attempt to run two software firewalls simultaneously on the same computer system. It's acceptable to run different software firewalls on different systems and to even use one or more appliance hardware firewalls. Just do not attempt to use two software firewalls on one system.

Examples of Software Firewall Products

Software firewall products are important options to consider when designing and deploying a security solution for home environments as well as corporate IT infrastructures. However, as with any type of software, the available products change constantly. Updated versions of software firewalls are released frequently; some products disappear from the marketplace, while new firewall products appear on the scene all the time.

Before selecting a specific firewall product, do research to confirm that the firewall is still a fully supported and maintained solution. You don't want to "buy into" a product that has already been marked for retirement or phase-out, or be invested in the installation of a version imminently at risk of being superseded. Verify that the vendor is still supporting the firewall product. Check on the revision history and, based on previous time frames, estimate if the current version release is it a bit stale or a bit tardy for a revision.

Beware the textbook answer. Most authors are reluctant to recommend specific current products. Books typically take six to twelve months to reach the hands of readers once the author completes the manuscript; coincidentally, six to twelve months is often the lifespan of many product versions. A product an author recommends might no longer be the best option by the time that recommendation reaches readers.

So, take caution when following any specific "textbook" advice about a specific product, especially a specific version of a product. Question a product's shelf life. Gather fresh information. Always double-check the facts, reviews, and suggestions via current Internet search resources, vendor Web sites, IT association blogs and discussion forums, industry journals, and the mass market computing magazines available. Like milk and cheese, most computer software products have an effective "use by" date that you should be familiar with.

A host of third-party software firewalls are worth considering. Here are just a few of the more widely known options:

- Checkpoint ZoneAlarm Pro (free and retail)
- Comodo Firewall Pro (free)
- eConceal Pro (retail)
- Injoy Firewall (retail)
- Jetico Personal Firewall (retail)
- Lavasoft Personal Firewall (retail)
- Look'n'Stop (retail)
- Norman Personal Firewall (retail)
- Outpost Firewall Pro (free and retail)
- PC Tools Firewall Plus (free)
- Prevention (retail)
- PrivateFirewall (free)
- Sphinx Software Windows 7 Firewall Control (free and retail)
- Tall Emu Online Armor Personal Firewall (free and retail)

In addition to standalone, third-party firewalls, some firewalls come packaged as part of a security suite. These suite-member firewalls are not available as standalone products. However, the collection of security applications might be a worthwhile collection if you don't already have existing solutions. Some security suites to consider include:

- Bullguard Internet Security
- Computer Associates Internet Security
- F-Secure Internet Security
- Kaspersky Internet Security
- McAfee Personal Firewall Plus
- MicroWorld eScan Internet Security Suite
- Norton Internet Security and Norton 360
- Panda Internet Security
- Trend Micro Internet Security
- Webroot Internet Security Essentials

How fresh are *these* lists? These products were current and available as of summer 2010. The lists are not exhaustive and include only well-known products. As you read this, new firewall options might now be available and some of the listed products might have been terminated. If you want to search for more or current options, search using keywords such as *software firewall*, and *review*.

Using Windows 7's Host Software Firewall

The native Windows Firewall of Windows 7 (Figure 10-3) is a sufficient security measure for many situations. Before rushing to replace this free security component, take the time to evaluate the benefits of this capable firewall option. The Windows 7 firewall is available only on Windows 7 and is a host software firewall. However, it can be used in a variety of situations and network configurations for most home and SOHO environments.

Windows 7 Firewall includes configuration profiles, so you can create custom firewall configuration settings for Work, Home, and Public connections. This allows strict limitations in public, modest settings at work, and more options available when accessing from home (or whatever your preferences). The benefit is that, once configured, the firewall will adjust its settings based upon the network connection each time you're connected to a known, previously accessed network.

Windows 7 Firewall creates a password-protected homegroup or workgroup that allows file and printer sharing between systems authorized by a password. This is an improvement over previous versions of the Windows Firewall, which often encouraged users just to turn off the whole firewall rather than properly configure file and printer sharing access rules. In addition, this applies not just to Windows systems, but any devices or computers recognized as media sharing devices (such as an Xbox 360).

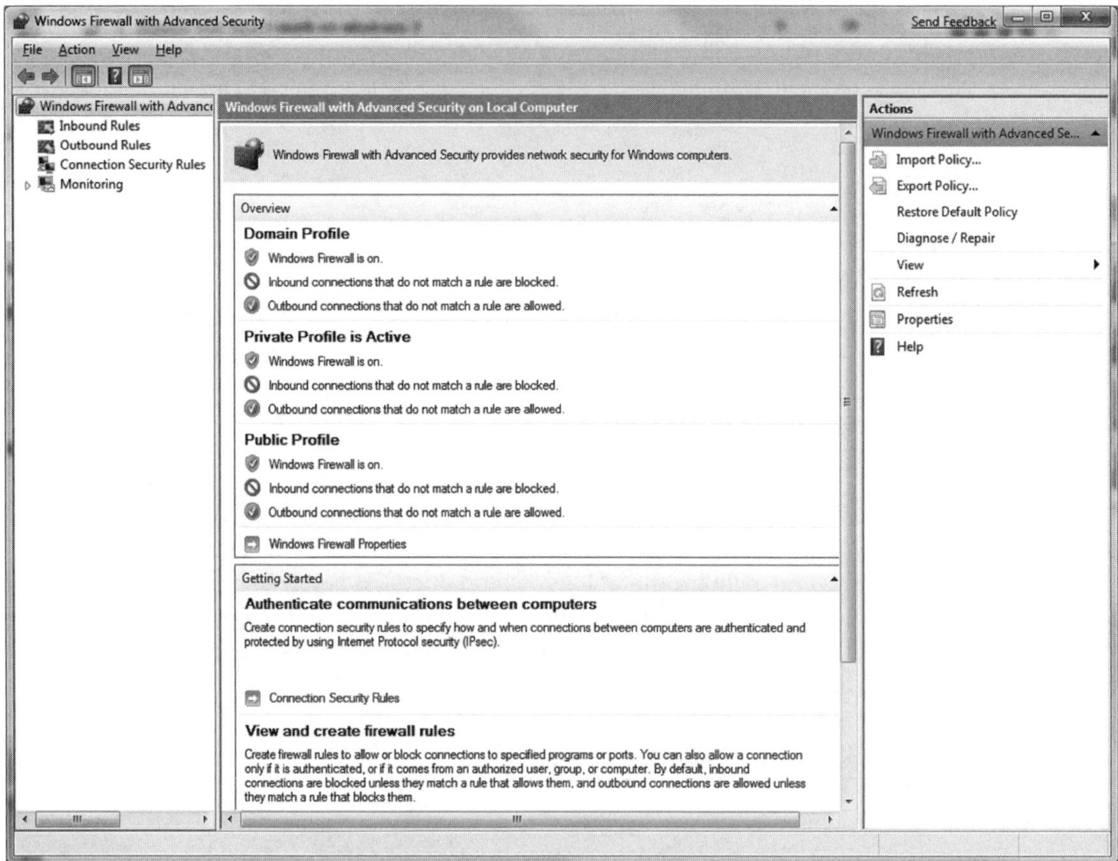

FIGURE 10-3

Windows 7's Windows Firewall with Advanced Security configuration dialog.

Other Windows Firewall improvements in the Windows 7 version include a more granular control and configuration management interface, more extensive logging, and extended ability to be managed from a command line (using "netsh advfirewall firewall" command instead of the previous "netsh firewall" command).

While not revolutionary, and still lacking a few features such as being a true two-way personal firewall with program control, Windows 7 Firewall is a worthwhile host software firewall for most clients in most network situations. That said, you should still explore how this product fits your own computing environment and security needs.

Using a Linux Host Software Firewall

A Linux system can benefit from a host software firewall or can support a software firewall for a network. The first idea is simply to install a host software firewall for the benefit of the local user. This is the same idea as the Windows Firewall on client versions of Windows. A variety of host firewall options are available for Linux, including both open-source and commercial options including:

- IPCop
- SmoothWall (Figure 10-4)
- IPFire
- pfSense
- m0n0wall

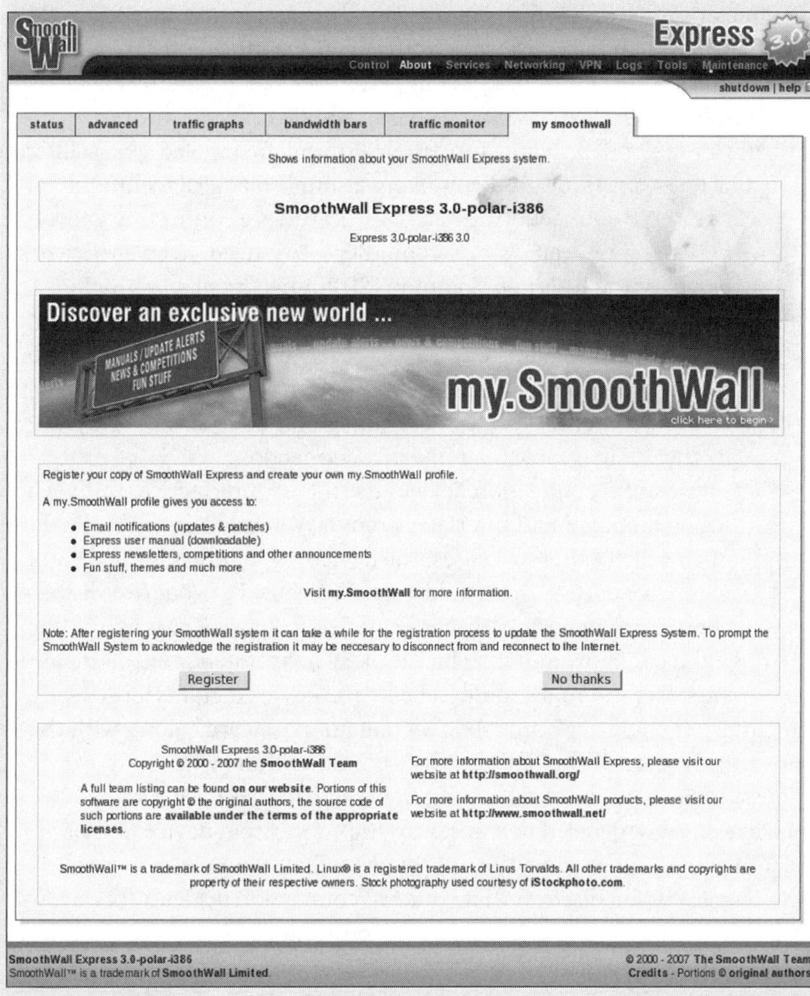

FIGURE 10-4

SmoothWall, a Linux host software firewall.

If you selected Linux for its low cost of entry, then selecting an equally low-cost host software firewall is often an attractive option. However, paying for commercial host firewall products might offer a greater range of functions or services, along with better technical support.

Using a Linux software firewall as a replacement for a commercial firewall appliance can be a very cost-effective solution. Linux often can repurpose computer hardware that's no longer sufficient to support larger, bulkier, more resource-intensive operating systems, such as Windows. Linux can often extend the useful lifetime of computer hardware by several years. A repurposed computer system running Linux is a great option for use as a software firewall host. For a more complete examination of the use of Linux as a host OS for a software firewall, see Chapter 13, Firewall Implementation: A Thorough Case Study.

Managing the Firewall on an ISP Connection Device

In addition to the free or native OS firewall options, another simple and easy firewall that individuals and SOHOs can use is firewalls hosted by ISP connection devices, routers, or wireless access points. Most of ISP connection devices, including cable modems, DSL modems, satellite modems, and routers, include firewall features. A firewall feature may or may not be a fully functional firewall. It could be a basic filtering tool that blocks IP addresses, ports, or protocols using a simple blacklist technique.

TIP

If the ISP connection device provides firewall services, obtain a copy of the original manufacturer's user manual for the device. This documentation will provide the best initial information on accessing and configuring the device's firewall.

An ISP connection device is any hardware connecting a local network—or even a single computer—to a telco's carrier network to access the Internet. Common ISP connection devices include DSL modems and cable modems (remember that these are modems in merchandising-name only; they are really routers). This definition can also include a wide range of other broadband devices, including routers, switches, and wireless access points, especially when required by the ISP to establish an Internet connection.

Most ISP connection devices use a Web interface. To initiate access to the management interface, point a Web browser to the IP address of the device. In most cases, the device's IP address is the default gateway address, DHCP address, or possibly DNS address of the client's interface directly connected to a physical port on the device.

Attempting to open the configuration interface is likely to prompt for authentication credentials. The vendor's user manual should indicate the device defaults for these. If not, search the Internet using keywords such as "default password" along with the device name, make, and model. If that fails, try username "admin" with a password of "admin" or "password." It's shocking how often these are correct.

Your ISP has likely chosen to lock down access to the connection device. This is sometimes done as a precaution against the uninitiated, who might cause increased technical support hassles. If you discover that your ISP connection device is locked down, try calling your ISP and asking them to grant you access (often by their revealing the credentials to log into the device).

If they refuse to offer this information, then you have four choices. First, you can accept their refusal as "just how it is" and employ some other device as a hardware firewall. Second, you can change ISP or service provider to a carrier that will grant you access to configure the device. Third, see if you can replace the carrier's device with one that you own and fully control. Fourth, you can seek out ISP and device-specific information on the Internet, which might include bypass or hacking details. However, be very cautious when choosing this latter route; it's often unproductive, is probably a violation of the ISP terms of service, is unethical, and may even be illegal.

> **NOTE**
> Whatever their reasons, cable providers are generally less likely to allow you access into their connection device, while most DSL providers seem willing to grant at least partial access.

> **NOTE**
> Be careful about searching for Web sites that offer information on how to hack or bypass ISP equipment. Often the sites are "booby trapped" with malware to trap the unsuspecting visitor. In addition, some ISP equipment may be leased, not sold, and attempting to access internal features may violate the contract, if not the law.

If you are unable to find a legitimate path to accessing the configuration interface of your ISP connection device, hacking the device should be your last and final option. Hacking an ISP-provided device will void your contract and could make you liable for the cost of the device plus fines and possible legal action. A more ethical solution would be to replace the device with one you own and control, or switch ISPs altogether.

If all else fails, add your own firewall between the ISP connection device and your first networked system. With this configuration, you are still gaining the benefit of an in-line firewall without violating any contracts or flirting with legal troubles. In most cases, you'll want to supplement or disable an ISP connection device's firewall anyway. Thus if your ISP blocks access to it, just design your security as if the device offered no firewall protection to begin with.

Converting a Home Router into a Firewall

Many home routers have sufficiently robust features that you can configure them to function as firewalls. To ensure ease of use (and minimize product returns), these devices are usually shipped with all security features turned off. Because "plug 'n' play" results in immediate connectivity, many users never go back to configure their equipment for security. Thus, hackers and malware often are able to intrude easily into home networks. You can prevent that by understanding what is available in this class of products.

To access a home router, type into your browser the IP address of your gateway. To determine that on a Windows machine, type Start > Run > Command, and at the `C:\>` prompt, type `ipconfig`. Most routers ship with a default address of 192.168.1.1. If you remember, 192.168.X.X is a non-routable range of IP addresses, which means that traffic inside that address range will not be shared with addresses outside that range.

Once logged in, consider changing a number of settings (Figure 10-5). First, if the router is a wireless device, change the Service Set Identifier (SSID) from the default setting. You do not want to be one of eight "Linksys" access points in your neighborhood. Why is this important? Most PCs will grab the strongest wireless signal from a known SSID. If you have standard SSIDs such as "Linksys" in your wireless access table, you may

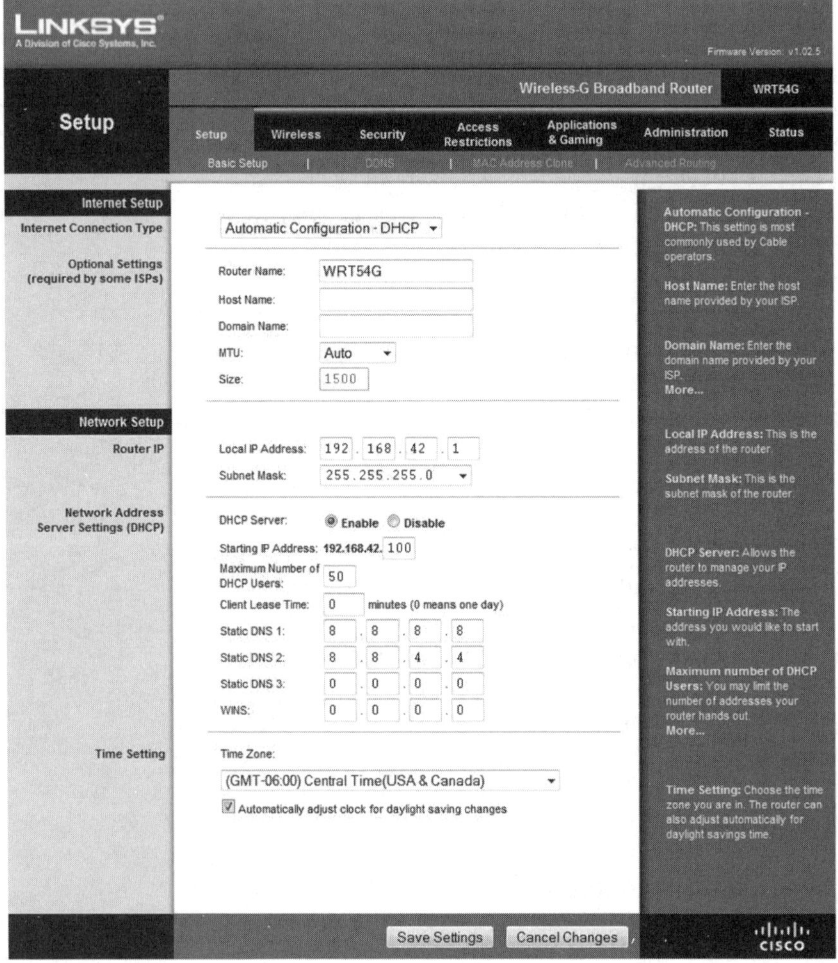

FIGURE 10-5

The initial configuration screen on a Cisco Linksys wireless router.

> **NOTE**
>
> Don't forget to change the default administrator password of your device.

find yourself on a neighbor's (or hacker's) system some day without realizing it. Another good idea is to change the default IP address range to something else other than 192.168.1.X. This creates a custom range for your own network. If you hard-code your internal network range to something like 10.20.30.X, you're less likely to stumble into that situation.

Most routers enable dynamic host configuration protocol (DHCP) by default. You could lock down your network by either hard-coding IP addresses into each authorized machine (and turning off DHCP), or by setting a strict upper limit on the number of devices permitted to have DHCP leases (most default settings are 100). If you have five devices, limit the number of connections to five. (Don't forget about the Xbox 360 or PS3—they need IP addresses too)!

For firewall settings, most routers will have a configuration page to block services or control port access. Determine what ports you need to access the Internet, and then block all of the rest. Note this setting restricts OUTBOUND traffic. So why block it if it originates from within? Malware, zombies, bots, and other hostile applications usually have to connect to the outside to do their damage. If you accidentally download dangerous malware onto your laptop at your favorite coffee bar, and then connect to your home or office network behind the firewall, that malware may have access to all of your peer systems. However, if you are blocking all nonessential outbound traffic, then most malware won't be able to exfiltrate your sensitive information or ask for evil instructions. Only those applications that use a common port (like 80) will be able to get through.

Which outbound ports should you block? First, consult your policy, or determine what programs you are using. For the most part, you'll want to PERMIT the following outbound ports open at all times:

- **Port 25**—SMTP (outbound mail)
- **Port 53**—DNS
- **Port 80**—http
- **Port 110**—POP (initiate request for inbound mail)
- **Port 443**—https
- **Ports 465 and 995**—SMTP and POP (if you're using Gmail)
- **Port 1024–1035**—DCOM ports for downloading files (increase number of ports based on number of systems protected; ten is usually sufficient for a home network)

Beyond port 1035, you may not need to allow outbound traffic, unless you are using cPanel to access an externally hosted Web site on port 2083, or port 11371 if you're looking up PGP keys. By blocking all other high ports, you'll also quickly hear from people who may have been using some of these ports, which are dedicated to gaming software. At home, you might want to allow (or set time limits); at work, you probably want to block these ports.

In general, you should not accept any connections that originate from outside your firewall. Your policy may permit exceptions, such as remote access tools, so be careful about blocking everything. Some home firewalls don't provide a direct way to block specific incoming ports, but most allow you to do "port forwarding." A clever way to use this to thwart external attacks is to forward to a nonexistent port. So, for example, if your local network range goes from 10.20.30.40 to 10.20.30.49, forward incoming connection requests to port 10.20.30.99—where no one is listening! Ports you might consider forwarding are:

- **Ports 20 and 21**—ftp-data and ftp. Prevent external connections from downloading your files.
- **Port 23**—telnet. Prevent external connections from insecurely logging into your internal systems.
- **Port 53**—DNS. Prevent external entities from poisoning your DNS cache.
- **Port 80**—http (unless you are running a Web server from behind your firewall, which is a bad idea).
- **Ports 81 and 82**—often used as "overflow" for port 80. No valid use, so block them.

- **Ports 137, 138, 139**—netbios. Often exploited by malware, this provides access into Windows systems.
- **Port 443**—https (unless you are running a secure Web server from behind your firewall, which is still a bad idea).
- **Port 445**—netbios for Windows 2000 and later.
- **Port 3074**—Xbox game port. Don't allow strangers to connect to your Xbox while you're away. Remember—it "lives" on your internal network.

An excellent way to test your configuration is to go to Steve Gibson's *http://www.grc.com* Web site and run his free ShieldsUP! port scanning tool (Figure 10-6). Most people end up scoring poorly. If you can achieve 100 percent stealth, you've done a great job.

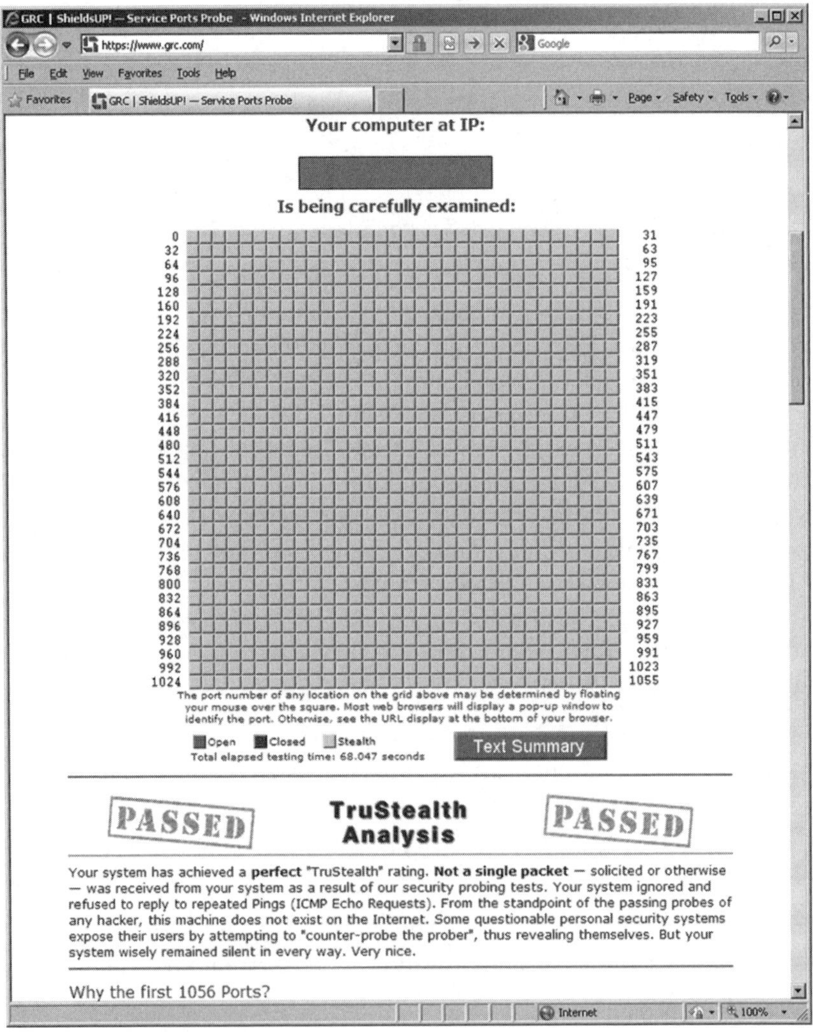

FIGURE 10-6

ShieldsUP! port scan result confirming a well-configured set of home router firewall rules.

FYI

A "commercial" product is simply one that's for sale rather than given away without cost. Commercial is not necessarily the antonym of open-source or a synonym of closed-source. Additionally, commercial is not necessarily the opposite of "free."

An open-source product is one where the source code can be obtained and viewed by anyone. A closed-source product has its source code protected so that the public cannot view it. A commercial product can be either open-source or closed-source. However, most commercial software is closed-source. This is viewed as a means to protect intellectual property and allow the vendor to continue to charge for the product.

"Free" can mean both no price or having liberty. Free software can have no cost, which makes it non-commercial. Free software can also be commercial software that grants liberties to its users.

For further discussion on free software, please visit GNU organization's site at *www.gnu.org*.

Commercial Software Network Firewalls

Commercial software network firewalls install onto your own hardware and provide network-level security services. Some commercial software network firewalls install on top of existing operating systems, such as Windows. Others are complete OS replacements, many of which are Linux-based.

As with any firewall selection, know your environment and understand your security needs before shopping for a firewall solution. It's bad security to purchase a product because it's on sale, is prominently advertised, or is recommended by a salesperson (or even an author). Instead, match your security needs with the product that best suits, fulfills, or satisfies those needs.

Open-Source Software Network Firewalls

An open-source software network firewall is a product that is usually available at no monetary cost and whose source code is available for review. An open-source solution often can be a cost-effective option. However, just because a product is free does not ensure its reliability or trustworthiness. Additionally, being able to review the source code doesn't warrant the reliability of a product.

You should thoroughly review and test every security product, including firewalls, before purchase and deployment. Seek out a product that meets your specific organizational security needs, rather than selecting something just because it's open source or free of charge.

Appliance Firewalls

Appliance firewalls, whether called device or hardware firewalls, are common and nearly essential elements of every moderate to large network infrastructure. A hardware firewall is a dedicated hardware device that has been specifically built and hardened to support the functions of the firewall software running on it. A hardware firewall is also known as an appliance firewall.

A hardware firewall does not require any additional hardware or software for its deployment. All it needs is network connections and a power connection. A hardware firewall has dedicated hardware resources not shared with any other service. A hardware firewall can protect a single system or an entire network.

A hardware firewall can filter only traffic that reaches the network interfaces of its appliance. However, you can position a hardware firewall on a network at a choke point or gateway to analyze and filter all traffic.

Firewalls, specifically hardware appliance firewalls, typically have two or more network interfaces. A firewall with two interfaces is known as a dual-homed firewall, while a firewall with three interfaces is known as a triple-homed firewall or a three-legged firewall.

The benefit of multiple interfaces is that the segments, subnets, or networks connected to each firewall interface are electronically isolated from each other. This prevents unfiltered traffic from leaping from one segment to another in an attempt to bypass firewall filtering.

However, for firewalls using multiple interfaces, ensure that you disable the TCP/IP protocol feature IP Forwarding. IP forwarding is actually a router rule that allows traffic from one interface to traverse to another interface without needing to move any further up the protocol stack than where IP resides. In many cases, IP forwarding allows packets to bypass filtering. If you're using the system as a firewall, be sure to disable this feature.

A personal hardware firewall can be part of an integrated firewall product, such as a wireless access point or a cable/DSL modem. Another variation of the personal hardware firewall is the repurposing of a client or server computer into a home-crafted, open-source firewall. One example of this is SmoothWall, a hardened bootable Linux-based firewall. A case study of deploying SmoothWall is found in Chapter 11, Firewall Deployment: A Case Study.

A commercial hardware firewall usually handles the complexity of larger organizational networks. A commercial hardware firewall is often very expensive—$10,000 or more is not uncommon.

The personal and commercial variants of software and hardware firewalls might include different add-ons or enhancements than their commercial equivalents. These add-ons or enhancements include antivirus, password management, registry protection, driver protection, VPN gateways, remote access support, IDS, IPS, spam filtering, and more. Usually these add-ons make the firewall products more attractive to the potential individual buyer. However, most commercial entities would generally avoid integrated firewall solutions in favor of dedicated products to handle the distinct security or management functions. An integrated device might offer easier administration, but represents a single point of failure for multiple services. Additionally, such devices are more difficult to troubleshoot due to the complexity of the communications supported.

A variety of manufacturers and vendors make and service appliance firewalls. The specific products in this category change constantly, so including a list of exact make and models would be outdated within months. (Remember the "sell by" date on that carton of milk?) Instead, to find the best products available for either SOHO or enterprise-sized environments, visit the vendor's technical review sites for updated product discussions, blogs and discussion forums, and buyer's guides. Some of the major vendors/brands to consider include:

- Barracuda
- Cisco
- D-Link
- Fortinet
- Juniper Networks
- Linksys (now owned by Cisco)
- NetGear
- SonicWall
- WatchGuard
- ZyXEL

When selecting a hardware or appliance firewall, keep a few important points in mind. Commonsense or basic concerns include ease of use, secured management interfaces, port filtering support, stateful inspection filtering, and the ability to be firmware/ software upgraded.

Never skimp on throughput. Firewalls often represent bottlenecks to network bandwidth and thus should be selected to maintain wirespeed. Be sure a hardware firewall can more than handle the current network speeds and allow for future growth. If you are currently pushing a 1 Gbps network, consider a firewall capable of filtering at 2.5 Gbps wirespeed or higher.

For larger networks, centralized and remote management options are often essential. If firewall management requires direct physical contact or if you can configure only a single firewall at a time, you may find these significant hindrances to managing very large networks. An important part of a realistic firewall solution for enterprise networks can be multiple device management, including simultaneous configuration synchronization features.

Consider whether add-ons, upgrades, or extras are available and whether that's important to your decision. Some firewall devices convert to firewall-plus devices or true multifunctional devices. Additional features may include e-mail scanning, message quarantine, attachment stripping, virus scanning, mobile code filtering, anti-spyware, intrusion detection system (IDS) and intrusion prevention system (IPS) features, spam filtering, compliance monitoring, and network access control. Products that support expansion or firewall additions are known as unified threat management tools or may fall under the heading of advanced intrusion detection and prevention systems.

Whatever the options presented by a vendor, always consider them in light of your actual current and future network needs. Just because a product is expensive does not guarantee it will work better than a free, build-it-yourself alternative.

Virtual Firewalls

The term "virtual firewall" describes a variety of firewall and firewall-like concepts. This can include virtualized software firewalls that provide filtering services for a standard physical network, as well as firewalls running virtualized between virtualized client and server operating systems. In theory, the use of a virtualized software firewall as a replacement for a network appliance could work as long as the host OSs network communication is routed through the virtual firewall before leaving the host's network interface controller (NIC).

This is a relatively new and growing area for firewall deployment. Virtualization offers numerous benefits over traditional a single OS to a single hardware box deployment. Virtualization allows for rapid development, quick prototyping, isolation, traffic management, quick recoveries, testing, and so on. By virtualizing firewalls along with operating systems, you can craft new network architectures that do not or could not exist in the traditional network architectural concepts.

For example, with a virtualized firewall, you could route every communication between every virtualized OS through the filtering services. This would be the equivalent of deploying an appliance firewall between every system, but without the hassle, expense, or complexity.

Most of the content discussed in this book applies to software, hardware, and virtualized firewall solutions alike. Virtual firewalls are not a universal panacea. Virtual firewalls will not be useful in every situation, but they are an interesting new option for deployment to monitor, manage, and filter network traffic over traditional or virtualized network segments.

Simple Firewall Techniques

A few mundane concerns affect every firewall user when employing a firewall of any type. In most cases, these issues are common sense or at least "well known," but they are often overlooked, forgotten, or discounted. To avoid this, they are included here.

After writing a firewall security policy, obtaining approval, and obtaining the firewall to install, the first step in deploying a new firewall is to change the default password of the administrator account. Better yet, modify every pre-defined user account and every default access code of any type. Use something unique, original, and difficult to predict.

Testing is essential. No change or alteration of configuration is so minuscule that testing is inappropriate. Every change should trigger a test to confirm that the change took effect and caused no unintended consequences.

Many firewall appliances can be quickly reset to factory defaults with the simple press of a button. Some devices have a reset button prominently located and labeled so that anyone with a finger can casually revert to default status. However, such an obvious button has disadvantages, such as accidental or innocent hand movements.

Fortunately, a growing number of devices that still offer button-based reset options have receded the button behind a tiny pinhole. A straightened paper clip (or an expensive tiny screwdriver) depresses the reset button. Often a single quick press is insufficient to reset the device; a series of presses or a prolonged 10- or 30-second depress may be necessary to trigger a reset. This feature makes accidental depression impossible but also makes intentional resetting a bit of a challenge. Be sure to consult the user manual for instructions that may not be obvious or intuitive.

Keep a printed or written copy of all rule sets and settings on hand. Periodically, verify manually that all settings remain as you want them. This is done by viewing the configuration or management interfaces and comparing the live settings to those defined in your documentation. Whenever you discover a discrepancy, investigate and repair it at once.

Finally, regularly visit the vendor's Web site and discussion forums (including non-vendor supported ones) for news and information about your firewall product. Keep current with announcements of updates, problems with updates, newly discovered holes or exploits, alternative configuration ideas, troubleshooting options, and more.

CHAPTER SUMMARY

Firewalls are useful in many different situations. Every network infrastructure can benefit from proper use of a firewall. When making a choice about what firewall to deploy, consider a breadth of options, including the needs of both small and large network environments, host software firewalls, native OS firewalls, third-party OS firewall alternatives, ISP connection device firewalls, commercial firewall options, open-source firewalls, hardware firewalls, and virtual firewalls.

KEY CONCEPTS AND TERMS

Active threats
Cookie filter
Native firewall
Passive threats
Pop-up blocker

CHAPTER 10 ASSESSMENT

1. What types of Internet threats are considered passive, in the sense that the user must seek them out to be harmed? (Select all that apply)

A. Malicious Web sites
B. Worms
C. Downloaded content
D. SPAM
E. Trojan Horse

2. Average home users and workers at a large corporation can both benefit from which of the following:

A. Open-source hardware firewall
B. Gateway server firewall
C. Commercial appliance firewall
D. Host firewall
E. Proprietary device firewall

3. What are the two locations that a home or SOHO user is likely to find a firewall by default? (Select all that apply)

A. A self-installed software firewall
B. Hosted by the operating system
C. A build-it yourself appliance firewall
D. Hosted by the ISP connection device
E. A commercial firewall device

4. Windows operating systems are the only operating systems that include a native or default host firewall.

A. True
B. False

5. What is the maximum number of host software firewalls that should be operating on a single computer at any point in time?

A. One
B. Two
C. Three
D. Four
E. None

6. Firewalls are design to provide protection for both ________ and ________ communications.

7. An organization should consider purchasing last year's model firewall instead of this year if they receive a significant discount.

A. True
B. False

8. When considering the deployment of a firewall, which of the following should be considered? (Select all that apply)

A. Commercial firewalls
B. Legacy firewalls
C. Open-source firewalls
D. Beta firewalls
E. Do-it-yourself (DIY) firewalls

9. The Windows 7 firewall includes a new easy-to-configure feature that allows file and printer sharing between systems authorized by a password. This feature no longer encourages users to just turn off the whole firewall rather than figure out how to properly configure file and printer sharing access rules. What is this feature called?
   A. Internet connection sharing
   B. Quick config
   C. Homegroup
   D. Shared computing
   E. Microsoft Easy Access Firewall

10. What is the command line tool used to configure the Windows 7 firewall?
   A. route firewall
   B. netsh advfirewall firewall
   C. new use firewall
   D. firewall config
   E. netsh firewall

11. Using a Linux software firewall as a replacement for a commercial firewall appliance can be a very cost-effective solution. Linux often can repurpose computer hardware that is no longer sufficient to support larger, bulkier, more resource-intensive operating systems.
   A. True
   B. False

12. The firewall configuration on an ISP connection device is most commonly accessed through what type of management interface?
   A. SMTP
   B. HTTP/HTTPS
   C. SSH
   D. FTP
   E. RSH

13. If your ISP refuses to grant access to configure their connection device, what legal options are available to you as alternatives? (Select all that apply)
   A. Live without configuring it
   B. Hack into it
   C. Deploy your own hardware firewall alternative
   D. Purchase your own connection device
   E. Change ISPs

14. What is the command line utility used to display the IP configuration of your Windows computer?
   A. ifconfig
   B. net use network
   C. netconfig
   D. ipconfig
   E. netstat

15. When configuring a wireless access point to provide firewall services, which of the following are important configuration actions to take? (Select all that apply)
   A. Change the default administrator password
   B. Block unwanted ports
   C. Change the SSID
   D. Turn off SSID broadcasting
   E. Change the default IP address range

16. In general, you should not accept any connections that originate from ________ your firewall.

17. If your home firewall device is unable to block ports, use ________ instead to route data to nonexistent hosts.

18. It is best to pick a firewall based on:
   A. Actual network security needs
   B. Recommendations of a salesperson
   C. The list of awards given the product
   D. The price
   E. Prominent advertisement

19. Appliance firewalls are only and always commercial firewalls.
   A. True
   B. False

20. When selecting a firewall, especially a hardware firewall, never skimp on ________.

CHAPTER

11 VPN Management

VIRTUAL PRIVATE NETWORK (VPN) MANAGEMENT is a critical component in your organization's computer security. VPNs extend the internal network beyond the perimeter secured by firewalls and other security technologies. Proper management of a VPN requires an understanding not only of VPN technologies, but also the business requirements driving VPN implementation.

Using the wrong type of VPN or a VPN that doesn't meet your organization's requirements can create security problems where none previously existed. Before selecting a VPN product or technology for your organization, create a detailed requirements document. This should factor in not only the security requirements for the VPN, but business requirements as well. Although security is important, keep in mind that security exists to support your organization's goals, not the other way around.

As soon as you have a set of prioritized requirements, start looking for a solution that meets as many of these requirements as possible. You may not be able to find a single product that meets all requirements. When that occurs, choose the solution that best fits the highest priority requirements. In some cases, using multiple solutions to meet all the requirements may be the right solution.

Good research is crucial to selecting the appropriate VPN. Don't rely solely on Web sites, technical magazine reviews, or an attractive sales pitch. Depending on your requirements, you may want to explore robust public domain solutions rather than an off-the-shelf commercial product.

Keep in mind that VPNs are a security technology, but they may also degrade the security perimeter discussed in earlier chapters. Putting the VPN in place is just the beginning of the project; you'll need to address a number of additional factors for a successful VPN deployment.

Chapter 11 Topics

In this chapter, the following topics and concepts will be discussed:

- What VPN management best practices are
- How to develop a VPN policy
- How to develop a VPN deployment plan
- What common VPN threats and exploits are
- What the tradeoffs are between commercial or open-source VPNs
- What the differences are between personal VPNs and network VPNs
- How to balance anonymity and privacy
- How to protect VPN security to support availability
- What the importance of VPN user training is
- How to troubleshoot VPN issues

Chapter 11 Goals

Upon completion of this chapter, you will be able to:

- Describe VPN "best practices"
- Write a VPN policy
- Describe the issues involved with deployment, placement, and implementation of a VPN
- Appraise the threats and attacks against VPNs
- Contrast the needs and features of personal and enterprise or network VPNs
- Compare anonymity and privacy
- Compose an introductory VPN training program for users
- Formulate a procedure for troubleshooting VPNs

VPN Management Best Practices

First, familiarize yourself with the recommendations, guidelines, and procedures that will allow you to manage your VPN securely, efficiently, and as cost effectively as possible. These techniques and recommendations are known collectively as "best practices" and are generally developed and published or shared by experts in the field. VPNs have been around since the late 1990s. That means a significant amount of "real world" experience is available in the industry for your reference.

A "best practice" is generally not a tool, but rather the collected wisdom of fellow security practitioners sharing what they have learned. One of the great things about working in the information security field is that a large pool of experts are generally willing to share their experience. Be warned, however: Security experts tend to have very strong opinions, so any time you are reviewing a best practice, be sure to keep the needs and requirements of your own environment in mind. A process that works great in a 25,000-person global manufacturing company may not work nearly as well in a 50-employee medical records processing company.

That said, you might well be able to adapt a process from another company to fit your environment. The key to getting the most out of best practices is to consider them with your specific environment and requirements in mind. Keep what works, modify what you can adapt, and ignore what doesn't make sense. After some time in the business, you will be the person other people come to for advice.

Provide redundancy, because everything, including VPNs, can break. If your organization will be relying on your VPN for remote access, encrypting, and securing data, or for providing a business partner access to your extranet, you will find out quickly how critical your VPN has become on the day it breaks. Most commercial VPN products offer a fail-over or load-balancing capability, so that in the event one device fails, the other will pick up the traffic.

Alternatively, keep a spare VPN product on your shelf, configured and ready to go live in the event of a failure. Generally, waiting for tech support or ordering a spare part can take more time than your organization is willing to wait for restored service. You'll learn more on this later in the chapter.

Choosing the right VPN product is critical to the long-term success of your VPN deployment. Take your time, document your requirements, carefully evaluate the capabilities of each VPN product you review, check with peers if available, and review appropriate industry literature. A security magazine review of VPN products is a valuable tool for starting your search—or even narrowing the field once you have your requirements documented—but don't select your solution solely based on who won last year's Editor's Choice Award from your favorite industry magazine. While the editors and reviewers at most industry magazines, Web sites, and blogs are technically capable and spend a lot of time looking at products, they don't have to support the product in your environment. Ultimately, you will be responsible for meeting your organization's requirements and maintaining support.

Beware the vendor with the slick PowerPoint presentation offering a free lunch. **"Slideware"** is not reality; avoid purchasing products based on promises rather than proven capabilities. Slideware, also sometimes known as "vaporware," is any product that appears in a vendor's PowerPoint presentation, but is not yet available as one of their products. When possible, road-test a product in your environment before purchasing. It's always a good idea to see what a product can do first hand.

Finally, when looking for a product, consider using resellers and consultants. A good reseller can do some of the legwork for you by narrowing the search to a smaller pool of products. While some resellers work much like a standard department store, selling whatever is on the shelves, many will go the extra mile to ensure you get a product that will work in your environment. This saves them the challenge of trying to support a poor product after they've sold it, and if you like the solution, they have the opportunity to sell you additional products in the future.

A VPN policy (often referred to as a Remote Access Policy) documents your organization's rules for using the VPN. We will discuss creating a VPN policy at length later in the chapter; recognize, however, that proper policy framework is a key best practice when dealing with security technologies, especially one offering remote access to your computing environment.

The client is a critical component of your VPN solution. For the most part, VPN technology is both mature and secure. VPNs are subject to Denial of Service (DoS) attacks, but VPN servers are rarely hacked. Nevertheless, VPNs remain a viable vector for someone who wants to attack your network. The target of these attacks is typically the weakest link of the VPN chain—the client. A typical VPN client runs an operating system that needs to be patched at least once a month, runs applications that may need to be patched almost as often, and is vulnerable to viruses, spyware, and other attacks. Be sure to install antivirus software, anti-malware software, and a software firewall on every client that will be connecting to your network through the VPN.

Split tunneling is a configuration setting that allows simultaneous access to both an untrustworthy network (like the Internet) and a secured VPN network connection. This may not sound like a bad idea at first—after all, why wouldn't you want someone connected to the VPN to access the Internet or their home network (or another network) at the same time? The reason split tunneling is a bad idea is that it potentially opens a door into your network that you can't control.

If the client machine is compromised by a virus that permits remote control of the system by an attacker, and that client machine connects to the VPN, the attacker now has access to your internal network from anywhere on the Internet. If you prohibit split tunneling, then, even if the attacker can compromise the client, as soon as the VPN connects, the external connections terminate, ensuring your network is secure, even if the client is not.

If it doesn't belong to the company, it shouldn't connect to the company's network. One of the challenges of working with Remote Access VPNs is making sure that the client at the other end of the connection is secure. Remote Access VPNs permit access to a secure network from a remote location across an untrustworthy network. If the client system is not secure, you run the risk of compromising your secure network.

Fortunately, you have some control over your organization's computers. You can require antivirus, anti-malware, IDS, and firewall software on any computers your company owns. With systems not owned by the organization, you cannot require anything.

As a result, if you don't prohibit non-company systems from connecting to the network, you cannot control whether those systems are secure, meaning you can't ensure that your network remains secure. It's very easy for an end user to load a VPN client on a home PC and connect to your network. While some VPN solutions offer techniques to prevent uncontrolled systems from successfully connecting, it's important that you lay the groundwork by prohibiting the practice.

Effective **vulnerability management** can help manage your remote clients. These are the technology and business processes used to identify, track, and mitigate known weaknesses on hosts within a computing environment.

Remember, everything is vulnerable to attack. UNIX, Windows, routers, network printers, and even your VPN solution will have vulnerabilities. Examples of vulnerabilities include software coding errors, improper configurations, and poor password choices. The danger with a VPN is that it expands your network from systems you can closely control to include systems in a home office, a branch office, a hotel, a Starbucks, or even a business partner's network.

Vulnerability management is a combination of tools and processes that allow you to reduce risk in your computing environment, including VPN-connected systems and networks. Use tools that periodically test your environment, including the VPN systems, for missing patches, configuration issues, known exploits, and other vulnerabilities. This will ensure that your remote systems as well as your local systems are secure. Scan often and address issues when you find them.

Your VPN is only as secure as your authentication method. One of the easiest ways to compromise a VPN is by compromising the authentication credentials. All it takes is one user with a password of "password" to open a direct connection to your network. A best practice is to use **two-factor authentication** for VPN access. This is a method of proving identity using two different authentication factors. Authentication factors are something you know, something you have, or something you are. Examples include a smart card (something you have) with a PIN (something you know); a biometric device

technical TIP

When addressing vulnerabilities in your environment, be efficient. If you are using a tool that ranks vulnerabilities from Level 1 to Level 5, where Level 1 is informational and Level 5 is critical, you might be tempted to address the Level 5s first, and then come back and address Level 4s next, then Level 3s, and so on. But this would be similar to having a keyboard with several broken keys: You wouldn't fix the "e" key first, then come back later to fix the "u" key because it's less critical—you'd fix them all at once. Take a similar approach with vulnerabilities. Determine what level of vulnerabilities you want to address in your environment (all Level 3 and above, for example), then tackle them, system by system. While this approach may leave some Level 5s in the environment a little longer, it will take a lot less time to secure the entire environment, since you will not need to touch the systems multiple times.

(something you are) coupled with a password (something you know); or a proximity card (something you have) that activates a fingerprint reader (something you are).

If you fail to plan, you plan to fail. Document your implementation plan! You can't simply find an open rack in the data center, run a cable, plug in a device and keep your fingers crossed that it will work. Document your implementation and support plans. You'll learn more on this later in the chapter.

Monitoring the availability of the VPN can be a lifesaver. The typical (and worst) method to discover issues with your VPN is when users start calling for help. This can be particularly challenging when the callers include members of your organization's senior management team. A corollary of Murphy's Law may be, "The likelihood that a senior management team member will be trying to access the network over the VPN is directly proportional to the likelihood that the VPN will fail." Better to alert senior management of temporary problems than to be informed by them that something isn't working. Since VPNs are network components, you can generally use the same monitoring equipment that you use to monitor routers, switches, and other network gear.

NOTE

Vendors can be very helpful when your equipment is down. Many technical and information security professionals believe they can fix anything, and sometimes they will work on a problem for long hours before finally reaching out to tech support. While tech support can be problematic, especially when wading through the first level of support, the vendor can be invaluable when the problem is in the VPN equipment or software.

Once you have your VPN deployed, regularly review usage. When you notice employees who are not using the VPN, you may want to remove their access. If you see employees who have multiple concurrent connections, you may have a security issue, and should investigate further.

Backup your VPN configuration regularly. This is a good practice for any network equipment, but in the event your VPN hardware fails and needs replacement, you'll want to be able to restore your known working configuration quickly. Rebuilding a VPN configuration from the default settings can be a long and challenging task—not to mention making post-incident review meetings an unpleasant experience.

Patch regularly. Vendors typically release patches and updates to VPN code throughout the life of the product. These patches address security issues, fix bugs, or provide additional functionality. In an ideal environment, you will have a development VPN that you can use to test patches and updates. In most environments, you will not have the luxury of a development VPN and will have to test when you implement in production. In either circumstance, work closely with your vendor to make sure you receive prompt notice of patches and updates, and establish an operational process and maintenance window to apply patches and updates in a timely fashion.

Your VPN solution may end up being a critical component of the organization's business continuity planning and disaster recovery planning. In the event of an incident that prevents employees from getting to their work location, a VPN that provides work-from-home is a key component of many recovery plans. Events such as earthquakes, snowstorms, tornadoes, flooding, and other natural disasters can make working remotely a viable alternative to standard operations.

This collection of VPN management best practices is meant to serve as the starting point for your successful VPN deployment. It's not meant to be comprehensive, but instead to offer some common practices and processes to help you with your VPN deployment. Depending on your VPN solution, your environment, your business requirements, and your experiences, you may find that you will use every one of these—or use only a few. The key is to ensure that you are doing what works in your environment. If you need help, don't be afraid to reach out to your peers for advice and suggestions. You will find, over time, that you will develop your own set of best practices as you gain more experience as a security practitioner, and soon others may be asking you for advice.

Developing a VPN Policy

If you are implementing or supporting a VPN solution, use a VPN policy to ensure your users understand the requirements for computing on the VPN. A VPN policy is sometimes called a Remote Access policy, a term used when dial-up lines and modems were the primary means to access the network remotely. Keep in mind that a VPN policy should be a part of your overall policy framework, and not a standalone. If you try to develop your VPN policy in isolation from the overall policy framework, you may find that you are duplicating information, or potentially writing VPN policy that conflicts with other aspects of your overall policy framework. For example, if you put a requirement in your VPN policy that user passwords must be 10 characters long and the password policy says they have to be eight characters long, you will confuse end users.

The components of a solid VPN policy include:

- **Introduction**—State the policy by name and tell how it fits in the organization's policy framework.
- **Purpose**—Describe the issues the policy addresses, and how it should be used. Include references to any applicable governance, risk, or compliance issues, as well as any specific legal or regulatory requirements supported by the document.
- **Scope/Binding Nature Statement**—Describe the systems, networks, or people covered by the policy. Describe penalties associated with not following the policy. The phrase "disciplinary action up to and including termination" is common in security policies.
- **Definitions/Acronyms**—Define technical terms or acronyms used in the policy.
- **Document**—Include the document creator, creation date, version, document status (for example, draft, template, policy, and guidelines), as well as any version tracking information.
- **Policy**—The actual policy language. Be very clear in this section and leave as little open to interpretation as possible.

- **Optional Elements**
  - **Summary**—If your policy is very long, you may want to summarize in a bulleted list at either the beginning or end of the policy. This provides employees a quick method to check for policy statements.
  - **Roles and Responsibilities**—If your document is lengthy, or you need to document who does what under the policy, include Roles and Responsibilities. For example, a policy dealing with infrastructure might include roles for the system manager, system architect, end user, developer, or other key people within the organization.

Some specific topics to include in your VPN policy are:

- Restrict remote access to the organization's VPN solution.
- Prohibit split tunneling.
- Define what classes of employee can access the network by VPN. This could include regular employees, vendors, contractors and temps, or it could be restricted to only home office workers, depending on business requirements.
- Define what types of VPN connections will be permitted.
- Define authentication methods permitted.
- Prohibit sharing of VPN credentials.
- List the configuration requirements for remote hosts, including current virus protection, anti-malware, host-based intrusion detection system (HIDS) and a personal firewall. Some VPN solutions include the ability to check for these types of configurations.
- Prohibit the use of non-company equipment, or if personal systems may connect to the VPN, define the minimum standards for those connections.
- Define required encryption levels for VPN connections.
- If you will be using your VPN for network-to-network connections, define the approval process and criteria for establishing a network-to-network connection.

Have your policy reviewed and approved by your Communications, Legal, and Human Resources Departments before release. Document the appropriate approvals in the document status portion of the policy, then communicate the policy to your employees. Posting the policy to an information security or security policy intranet Web site is a common practice. Once it's available on the intranet, you can use standard communications methods to make employees aware of the policy requirements. These methods can include e-mail, a structured awareness program, inclusion in new-hire training, or even Web-based or in-person policy training. The method you select will be based on your organizational size, locations, and requirements. They key with any type of awareness training is to structure your communications to the correct audience. A group of engineers will require a very different introduction to a technical policy than a sales team might.

FYI

Before selecting and purchasing a VPN solution, consider a number of factors before making your selection. One that is too frequently ignored is the budget for the solution. Carefully consider your criteria and evaluate your options, always keeping in mind that you need to live within your budget. When budgeting, be sure to look at not only acquisition costs, but also the ongoing support and maintenance costs for at least the first three years.

These are just some of the factors in developing a VPN policy for your organization. While they should form the basis for the development of your organization's policy, be sure to cover all applicable requirements. One sure way to alienate your employees is by releasing a policy that either makes no sense to them, or that you have to revise too soon to cover things you didn't think of the first time through. Take your time, consider all the requirements, and you will end up with a usable VPN Policy.

Developing a VPN Deployment Plan

NOTE

With proper negotiating, you generally will not have to pay list price for a VPN product. Many vendors will readily discount their products anywhere from 15 to 40 percent depending on the volume of product you buy.

Now that you have an understanding of best practices and VPN policy, you'll look at how to select, place, and use a VPN.

The pros and cons of the different types of VPNs will be discussed in more detail in Chapter 12.

Consider these criteria during your search:

- What types of VPN connections does the solution support (user access, site-to-site, or both)?
- What is the encryption protocol(s) supported (IPSec, SSL, SSH, etc.) to encrypt the data?
- How many VPN connections are supported?
- How well does the VPN perform compared with a high-speed network?
- How well does the VPN interoperate with your existing network infrastructure?
- What are the support options available from the vendor?
- How easy or difficult is the VPN to setup?
- What are the management capabilities available with the VPN?
- What additional features does the VPN offer?
- Does the VPN support failover or high availability configurations?
- How scalable is the VPN?

Once you have gathered this information, you can start to narrow your selection based on how well these features meet your criteria.

Next, consider where you will deploy the VPN on your network. Three common architectures typically accompany VPN solution deployments.

Bypass Deployment

A bypass architecture (see Figure 11-1) deploys the VPN so that traffic to the VPN and from the VPN to the internal network is not firewalled in any way.

This was a common architecture when VPNs were first introduced to the market. The logic behind this deployment architecture is that the since the VPN will accept only encrypted connections on a specific port, the security is adequate without additional firewalling. An additional consideration is that the since the traffic is encrypted, it doesn't require additional protection. Even if you did place a firewall on the Internet-facing VPN connection, the firewall would not be able to analyze the encrypted VPN traffic. This architecture also considers anyone connected to the VPN as a trusted host. Finally, passing traffic across a firewall always causes concerns about performance impacts and justifiably so..

Two significant issues arise with this implementation model. First, VPNs are like any network device—they can have a variety of vulnerabilities. As a result, they are still vulnerable to an attack against the device itself. The second issue is that the uses for VPN have expanded greatly since the technology first appeared, and it's not uncommon in today's environment to leverage a VPN to provide untrustworthy hosts access to portions of the network. These could be customers accessing an order management portal, vendors supporting systems on the internal network, or suppliers who are transferring invoices to your internal systems. While some controls (usually routing table-related) are available in most VPN solutions, terminating a VPN directly on your internal network is a very dangerous practice. As a result, the circumstances where a bypass VPN architecture is still a viable solution are limited, unless your risk tolerance is pretty high.

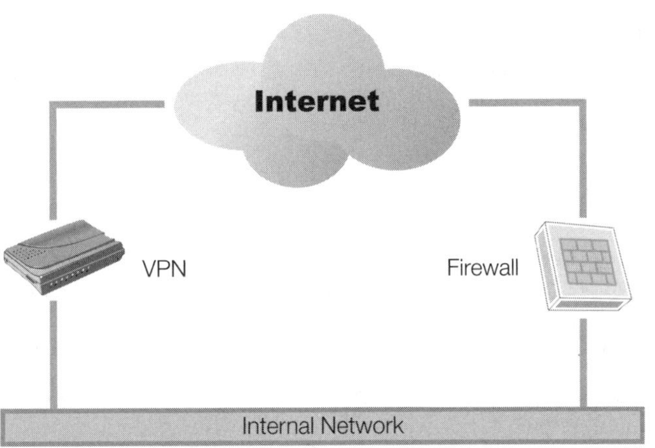

FIGURE 11-1
A bypass VPN implementation.

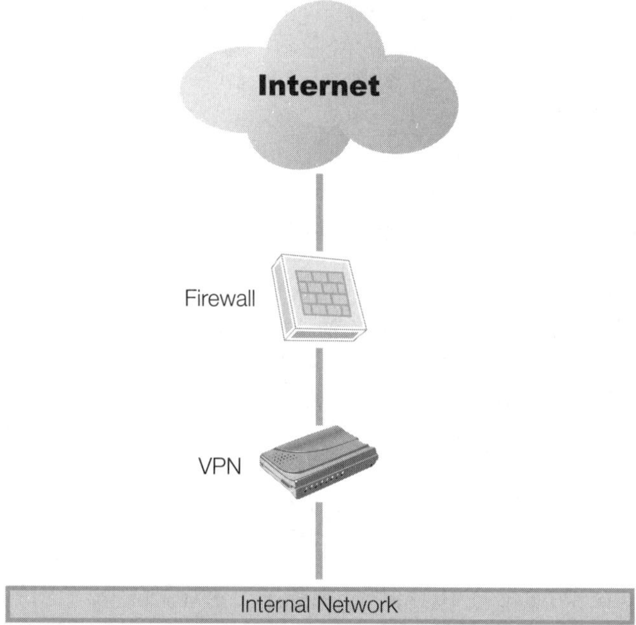

FIGURE 11-2
An internally connected VPN.

Internally Connected Deployment

An internally connected architecture (see Figure 11-2) deploys the VPN so that traffic to the VPN and from the VPN to the internal network is not firewalled in any way.

An internally connected VPN architecture recognizes that the VPN is vulnerable to attack if placed directly on the Internet, so it places the Internet-facing VPN connection behind a firewall. As we discussed in Chapter 9, Firewall Management and Security Concerns, selecting the appropriate firewall for this solution is critical to a successful implementation. The VPN then connects any remote users or site-to-site connections directly to the internal network.

While this is an improvement over the bypass architecture, it still doesn't address the potential security issues associated with untrustworthy VPN connections. This architecture is not recommended, although it will work if the only hosts connecting are trusted hosts.

DMZ-Based Implementation

A demilitarized zone (DMZ)-based implementation (see Figure 11-3) addresses the main shortcomings of the previous two architectures.

This architecture features a firewall both in front of the VPN to protect it from Internet-based attacks, as well as a firewall behind to protect the internal network. The firewall on the inside can be configured to protect important infrastructure like financial or research servers, restrict business partners to only the systems they need access to, or even limit vendor access to only those systems that they support.

The largest negative in this design is the cost of deploying multiple firewalls for the implementation. However, many companies already have DMZs set up in this configuration, so it may be just a matter of leveraging the existing infrastructure for your needs.

After selecting the ideal VPN and determining where you're going to place it in your infrastructure, it's time to work up your deployment plan.

> **NOTE**
>
> You can use a project management application to plan your VPN rollout, or use something as simple as a word processing application. The purpose of this plan is to allow you to structure your deployment more formally than a plan written on the back of a cocktail napkin.

Before we look at the components of a successful deployment plan, keep in mind that your environment is unique to your organization. Some elements we will discuss won't apply to your deployment. These are, rather, just some common elements found in most typical VPN deployment plans. Just as with the other topics we've discussed, review these while thinking of the requirements of your organization.

To deploy your VPN successfully, you need to:

- Plan the physical location of the VPN. This is commonly rack space in your data center.
- Ensure your selected location meets power and cooling requirements. Get information on power and cooling requirements from your VPN's technical specifications.

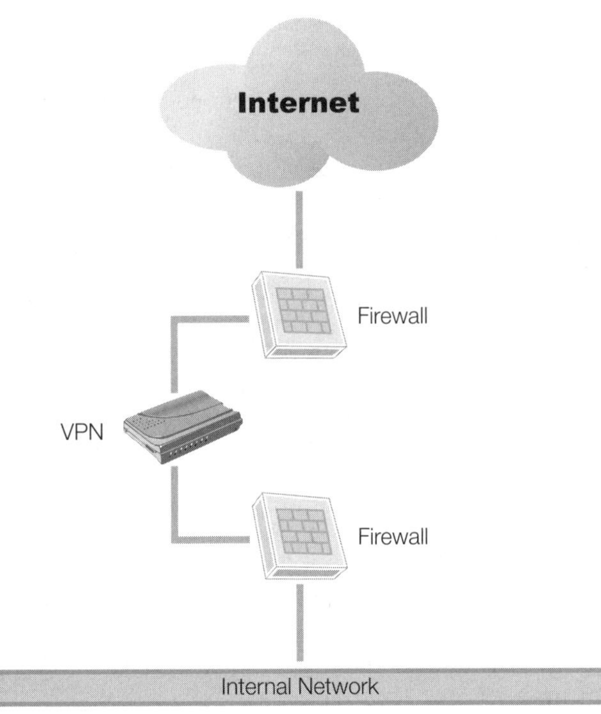

FIGURE 11-3
A VPN implemented in a DMZ.

- Plan your IP addressing for the external and internal network connections on the VPN, as well as a pool(s) of addresses assigned to clients when they connect to the VPN. Plan for peak usage when assigning these pools to the VPN—while an average number of users is an excellent use benchmark, peak use determines the maximum number of IP addresses to ensure that all users can connect. If this is a site-to-site connection, your IP addressing plan will not be as complex, but will still be important when setting up the tunnel.
- If you are using firewalls as discussed in the previous section, plan the rules you'll need on the firewalls to permit the VPN to work. Generally IPSec VPNs will require UDP port 500 for the IKE packets, and TCP port 443 for the IPSec traffic. SSL VPNs use port 443 exclusively. We will discuss this in more detail in Chapter 12, VPN Technologies. Most VPN rule sets permit ICMP packets from the Internet. If you are experiencing issues with the VPN, it's frequently useful during troubleshooting to determine if the user can reach the VPN server using tools like *ping* or *traceroute*.
- Configure the VPN server by setting up the IP address pools, assigning IP addresses to the interfaces, establishing your banner message, and disabling split tunneling. It's also a good idea to have the vendor review your configuration before going live to ensure you haven't missed anything in your planning. In some cases, you might even want to have the vendor install the VPN for you while you concentrate on client rollouts, policy communications, and other rollout tasks.
- Setup the authentication mechanism. Ideally a token-based authentication solution, it could also be RADIUS-based authentication, or in some smaller environments, user accounts set up on the VPN itself.
- Follow your organization's change management policies when deploying the VPN. If your organization doesn't have a formal change management process, be sure to inform management of your planning schedule to avoid no surprises. The last thing you want is to bring the VPN online during the same weekend Accounting is doing a major upgrade to your organization's financial systems. If there's a problem with their upgrade, you can count on at least one person blaming it on your VPN rollout.
- Once the VPN is up and on the network, create a pilot group to test the deployment. Address any issues before you roll out to a larger user pool. Minimize any issues that the employees might face with the new solution. The best way to doom a new solution is to deploy it with lots of problems. You may find some employees will have a low tolerance for issues.
- Develop your operations manual, which will document the configuration, the operations procedures, change planning processes, and change history.
- Develop your user documentation. Include how to install the client (if a manual install is required), how to login, whom to call for support, frequently asked questions, and any other information you think will make the user's experience with the VPN easier.

- Develop your support processes. Who gets the first call when there's an issue? What is the escalation path if the issue can't be resolved?
- Communicate the rollout plan to management and affected employees. Let them know the timing, benefits of the new solution, and anything else that you believe will help you have a successful deployment.
- Install the VPN client for any remote access users. If this is a site-to-site deployment, configure the tunnel connection.
- Distribute authentication credentials, tokens, and so on.
- Train your users.
- Go live—and enjoy a successful VPN rollout.

You now should be able to select, plan, and successfully deploy a VPN for your organization.

VPN Threats and Exploits

Consider the threats and attacks against your VPN, and how to mitigate them. A VPN can be a critical component of your information security infrastructure. A properly implemented VPN addresses a number of common attacks against your infrastructure, including eavesdropping, man-in-the-middle, replay, and others. However, while your VPN can mitigate attacks, it can also opens up an entirely new set of security issues.

Remember VPNs are essentially network devices and subject to many of the same security issues you would find in a router or a switch. If you are running a software VPN, then your VPN can have many of the issues you find on your network's servers.

A hardware VPN solution can suffer from a number of security vulnerabilities, including:

- Weak default password
- Insecure default configuration or mis-configuration by the installer

One of the most common and easily exploited vulnerabilities on any hardware network device is the default password. Vendors set an initial password on their equipment and usually all it takes to discover this password is a quick search on the Internet. Usually it's not even particularly hard to guess. Try the vendor name, "admin," or "password," and your odds are good that you'll be able to login. It seems like a sensible mechanism—the vendor doesn't want to distribute their equipment without a password, so they set a standard password that's easy for the installer to remember.

The potential problem occurs when the installer forgets to change that password. It's not uncommon for an installer to leave the password in place for the duration of the installation. Typing in "admin" after each reboot is much easier than typing in "$$Th!s!sAS3cur3P@ssw0rd!!" every time after making a change requiring a reboot. The problem occurs when either the installer forgets to change the password when the work is done, or an attack occurs while the installer is in the middle of the installation.

Imagine the installer has a couple of additional settings to change, but it's 6:00 p.m. on a Friday and he's ready for the weekend. He decides to come in early Monday to finish up the configuration. So for the entire weekend, the VPN you're counting on to provide secure access to your network is on the Internet with the password "admin." The best way to address this type of vulnerability is through stringent system configuration procedures and strong awareness training for your support staff or contractors. Disciplinary action when an installer fails to follow the instructions is remarkably effective at getting the message across.

The second common issue with hardware VPNs is a device that is installed in the default configuration. Very few network devices will come out of the box in a fully secure configuration. For example, important configuration setting we discussed was disabling split-tunneling. A default VPN configuration might not disable that setting without modifying the configuration. If you are completing your first install, it's very tempting to just change enough of the configuration to get the VPN up and running and stay away from any unfamiliar settings.

A related issue occurs when an inexperienced installer modifies the configuration without understanding the impact of the changes. For example, an installer with a limited understanding of encryption protocols might decide that using the DES algorithm for VPN encryption would be "good enough" and would improve performance over a higher encryption algorithm like 3DES. The installer probably read somewhere that the longer the key length used for encryption, the higher the impact on performance. This is often true, but longer key lengths usually mean more secure communications. Installer-induced security threats are some of the hardest to track down. Since they were caused by someone with a limited understanding of what he or she is doing, the installer's ability to help you track down the issues is equally limited.

To mitigate the risk of these issues, make sure that you train your installer (or yourself) before installing the VPN. If you do not have the time or justification for training on the product, then engage a vendor or systems integrator to either assist with the install, or even complete it for you. Once the installation goes online, it pays to have an expert perform a vulnerability or penetration test against your VPN. It never hurts to have an expert check your work.

A software VPN solution can suffer from the following vulnerabilities:

- Operating system vulnerabilities
- Operating system mis-configuration
- Application conflicts
- Stability
- Viruses and malware

While software VPN solutions are not typical in corporate environments, they are not uncommon in smaller organizations, academic environments, and other areas where a hardware VPN did not meet the business requirements. The main threats to software VPN solutions arise in the operating system. Operating systems like UNIX or Microsoft Windows consist of highly complex coding. They are designed to support a number of business-related tasks, and are more highly complex than the operating systems found on hardware-based VPNs. As a result, the software-related threats can also be much more complex.

Operating systems contain millions of lines of software code, and as with anything written by people, they always contain mistakes. Those mistakes are what attackers seek to exploit when attacking an operating system. Exploits may include buffer overflows, privilege escalation, or any number of other issues. As a result, if you run your VPN on a general-purpose operating system, your VPN becomes susceptible to the same software vulnerabilities as your operating system. In addition, software VPNs have many more possible operating system configuration errors than hardware VPNs.

Some organizations run VPN software on a server that supports multiple applications. For example, the VPN server might also be a SQL server, a Web server, or a file server. If this is the case in your environment, be aware of potential vulnerabilities created by application conflicts. This could be a matter of two applications that contend for resources on the servers causing issues, but it could also be the chance that one of the applications opens a new vulnerability in the VPN software. Think about a VPN server that is also a Web server. If the Web server is configured incorrectly, you could expose VPN configuration files to an attacker through the Web server interface. In that event, you could configure your VPN server securely just to have an attacker pull a copy of your configuration files out of a Web directory, bypassing your security.

Another potential threat associated with software VPNs is stability. Many information security professionals are reluctant to run software VPNs due to the challenges of the operating system crashing and taking the VPN with it. Many security professionals wouldn't ever want to run a VPN that could be taken out by a "Blue Screen of Death"—the nickname for the Microsoft server crash screen.

Finally, operating systems are vulnerable to viruses and other forms of malware. These would include Trojan horses, rootkits, or any of the other destructive malware currently active on the Internet. Any of these infections could compromise the security of your VPN, as well as your internal network.

If you are planning to run a software VPN, be sure to run it on a dedicated server, double-check both the operating system configuration, as well as the VPN configuration, and keep the operating system fully patched and up-to-date. When your VPN is fully configured, run a vulnerability management tool against it, or have a professional come in and conduct a penetration test. Moreover, be sure to install and maintain current antivirus and anti-malware software on the server. It's a good idea to install a firewall application and an intrusion detection/prevention application to ensure that your VPN remains secure.

Vulnerabilities common to both hardware and software VPN implementations include:

- Denial of service attack
- Missing patches
- Backdoor attack
- Unpublished vulnerability in the code
- Weak client security
- Weak authentication

In a Denial of Service (DoS) attack, the attacker is trying to crash or overload the VPN, essentially, to deny access to the VPN service. Attackers use specially crafted packets designed to crash the VPN, or more likely, direct a flood of traffic at the VPN in an attempt to overload it. This is not a very common attack because of the large amounts of traffic required to overload most companies' network infrastructures. Generally, you will not see a VPN targeted with a DoS, as attacks against VPNs are typically designed to allow the attacker access to the internal network. DoS is more common is against popular Web sites like Twitter or Facebook, where there is significant publicity, or against online merchants, who are subject to blackmail. When your Web site is a significant source of revenue, a DoS attack can be very expensive.

Any hardware or software platform that can run VPN software is vulnerable. That's the nature of any computer technology. When these vulnerabilities are discovered, the vendor will typically develop a patch or an update to address the issue. If you do not keep your VPN current, you leave your network open to these issues, and attackers will try to exploit known vulnerabilities with your VPN.

A backdoor account attack is pretty rare, but can happen in some instances. An example of the traditional backdoor attack was featured in the movie *War Games*, where the system developer left a user account and password on a secure system in case he needed to get back in. This account was exploited by an attacker (in the movie, a kid just looking to play games)—nearly causing the end of the world. Needless to say, the issues in your environment will not be quite as dramatic, but they are still of concern. Code running on VPNs and operating systems is closely scrutinized, so system developers are less likely to be a threat, but what about a system administrator who thinks he's about to be fired? Or a vendor who comes in to support your VPN and creates an account for support that he or she forgets to delete before leaving? The best way to mitigate this type of attack is through scheduled auditing of all accounts on your VPN, as well as strong, documented procedures for how and when accounts are created and deleted. This particularly applies to accounts with elevated privileges or on systems accessible from the Internet.

One of the trickiest (and fortunately rarest) security threats is an unpublished vulnerability in the VPN code. Researchers or potential attackers can discover an unpublished vulnerability. If it's unpublished, it means the vendor is not yet aware of it, and thus has not yet developed a patch or an update. These are probably the most difficult threats you will face because there isn't a lot you can do beyond following security best practices, creating a layered security environment, and monitoring the behavior of your environment for anomalies. Should you encounter this issue, be sure to follow your incident response process and work with the vendor to identify the issue and create a patch.

Another vulnerability is not directly on the VPN, but is vulnerability in the devices connecting to the VPN. VPNs offer significant security advantages, but if the client at the other end of the connection is not secure, then your network is at risk. To mitigate this risk, have a standard client configuration, which includes antivirus, anti-malware, firewall, and maybe even intrusion-detection software. Also make sure that the only clients connecting to the VPN are company-owned. Permitting personal assets to connect to your network opens a number of additional issues, since you are not able to supervise the configuration of those systems. All it takes is one employee whose daughter clicks on the video link that her friend sent her (generally with a comment like "check out this video I took of you") and you could end up with a virus on your network when Dad connects to the VPN using the same system.

A final vulnerability to consider is the challenge of weak authentication. Your VPN is really only as secure as your authentication mechanism. If you are authenticating with user ID and password, you run the risk of someone guessing or stealing those credentials and accessing your network without permission. To mitigate this risk, rely on either token-based or biometric authentication methods instead of—or in addition to—a user ID and password. If you must use user ID and password for authentication, be sure to coach users in the use of strong passwords.

A familiarity with the various threats, attacks, and mitigations is critical to the long-term support of your VPN and your total network. Be aware that no list of threats and attacks can be all-inclusive, because the attackers are constantly contriving for new methods for compromising your network. In the absence of specific threats and attacks, rely on good security practices to keep things safe.

Commercial or Open-Source VPNs

When looking at VPN solutions, decide if you want to include the option to leverage open-source VPNs. If so, be aware of some of the tradeoffs you will encounter when leveraging an open-source VPN product.

A commercial solution offers the following benefits:

- Ease of installation and management
- Available management tools
- Access to vendor support
- Available hardware maintenance

The benefits of an open-source solution include the following:

- Low cost
- Flexibility
- Ability to run on existing hardware
- Access to Internet-based support

Both commercial and open-source solutions pose some challenges. Commercial solutions are typically easier to implement, but that ease of installation comes at a cost. Not only are commercial solutions more expensive than open-source solutions, but also they are typically less flexible. Open-source solutions like OpenVPN (*www.openvpn.net*) offer significant flexibility, but generally require significantly higher skill in installation and support of the product. You rarely have access to vendor support, as open-source solutions usually rely on the knowledge of the user and the development community. When you have an issue, you can normally post it on a discussion board, and the community will assist you in resolution of your issue.

While weighing the pros and cons of open-source VPN solutions, take into account a couple of other factors. First, many organizations have policies about the use of open-source software. These policies derive from the company's tolerance for risk, the open-source licensing agreements, and intellectual property implications of open source. If your organization embraces open source, an open-source VPN is probably worth considering.

The best VPN application still comes down to identifying your requirements and finding the best solution for your organization. If you're on a low budget or have access to solid technical resources, an open-source solution could be the best choice for your needs.

Differences Between Personal and Network VPNs

Much of the information in this chapter has dealt with VPNs deployed in support of an enterprise or at least a moderate-to-large network. Another class of VPN applications—the personal or individual VPN—is sometimes referred to as the small-office or home-office VPN solution. Many home routers will include support for VPN connections, and open-source VPNs are also very popular in this space. Shrew Soft (*www.shrew.net*) offers an open-source VPN client that will connect to many of the standards-based VPN gateways like OpenSWAN (www.openswan.org). The value of these personal VPNs is twofold. First, implementing a personal VPN provides you secure access to your home network. Even better, implementing a personal VPN provides you with some valuable experience with VPNs that you can then transfer to your organization's enterprise VPN.

Balancing Anonymity and Privacy

A key concept to understand about VPN technologies is the difference between anonymity and privacy. **Anonymity** is the ability for a network or system user to remain unknown. Some tools that support anonymous access include Tor (*www.torproject.org*), an open software and network to anonymously surf the Web. A hardware solution that leverages the Tor network for anonymity is JanusVM (*www.janusvm.com*). The problem with solutions for anonymity is that they don't always protect your privacy. In many cases, the traffic carried anonymously by these applications is unencrypted, which means an attacker can read it with access to the right part of the network. If you are passing user IDs and passwords, credit card numbers, or other information that you would like to keep private, these are not the correct solutions for you.

Privacy, on the other hand, is keeping information about a network or system user from being disclosed to unauthorized people. If you want to protect your information, a VPN connection does an excellent job of this by encrypting the data that it carries. Leverage VPNs whenever you are connected to an untrustworthy network and want to send sensitive information. Wireless networks are a particularly ripe environment for attackers trying to get private information from a public network. VPNs do not offer any anonymity, however, as you are always able to track the endpoints of a VPN connection—that information is needed to maintain the VPN connection.

technical TIP

When considering VPN availability, don't overlook the little things. Put your VPNs in separate racks, connected to separate power supplies. Nothing's more embarrassing than explaining to your manager that the VPN was down for two hours because someone accidentally switched off a power strip.

Protecting VPN Security to Support Availability

One of the design decisions you made when selecting your VPN was whether you needed a highly available solution. Once your users expect to access the network from a hotel, a customer location, or Starbucks, or from home when they have a sick child, you will find they have little tolerance for outages. A VPN down means none of your remote workers can do much work, and in some organizations that can mean a majority of the company could be off the network until the VPN is back up and running. A highly available solution makes a lot of sense.

The most common method for implementing a highly available VPN is pretty simple. You buy two VPN hardware units (or implement two open-source VPNs) and then configure them as a highly available pair using the vendor's high-availability mechanisms. Cisco offers the Hot Standby Router Protocol (HSRP) for example, which allows configuration of a pair of Cisco VPNs so that in the event that the primary VPN fails, the backup takes over seamlessly. If configured correctly, end users don't even notice the cutover. A more industry-standard protocol that offers similar functionality is the Virtual Router Redundancy Protocol (VRRP). You also have the option to use a third-party solution. Many of today's load balancers offer the ability to load-balance VPNs. When one VPN fails, the load balancer automatically directs all traffic to the remaining gateway.

In addition to ensuring your VPN is highly available, also ensure that your Internet circuits have similar redundancy. You don't want to end up with your VPN up, and your one Internet connection down. The net result is still unhappy users who cannot access the network. In the event of circuit outages, the user will typically need to reconnect to the VPN. This is still better than not being able to connect at all.

When you are considering a highly available VPN solution, be sure to consider not only the acquisition costs, but also the ongoing maintenance costs over the following three to five years. It's important to capture the full cost of the solution, rather than just the purchase price.

The Importance of User Training

Now that your VPN is up and running, train your users on how to use the VPN. One of the most common challenges with IT infrastructure deployments, especially with security infrastructure like a VPN, is for the IT team to assume that, since they understand how the solution works, their end users understand it as well. That's almost always a bad assumption. It can turn a successful rollout into an unsuccessful one.

To develop good user training, start by setting appropriate training goals. One of the first mistakes security practitioners make when developing training is jumping past any planning and starting with taking screen shots, typing up documentation, and scheduling meetings. However, much like a successful VPN deployment, the first part of successful training is planning. Determine the following before designing your user training:

- Who is your target audience for the training? Before you start writing your training, understand who will be learning.
- What is the technical awareness level of your audience? Are you training tech-savvy IT professionals, or salespeople who just want to turn on their PCs and start working?
- Where is your audience? Is your audience in one central location, or spread out regionally—or even nationally? This will impact the choice of media you use to train users.
- What level of training are you trying to deliver? Will users need to install the client software? Do you want to include basic troubleshooting in the training? Are you trying to sell features or do you just want to train them on how to login? Should you include additional security issues in this training?

Once you gather the appropriate information, determine the best mechanism for delivering the training. You may distribute some written instructions, have a conference call, or even a Web conference. For high-profile users, or users who require significant support, hold classroom training. If you decide to go with live training, definitely plan to do additional information security training. After all, you have their attention for the period of the training—maximize the benefit not only to your users, but also to your company. Remember that well-trained employees tend to be the most secure computer network users.

Other things to keep in mind as you do user training: Make sure your training plan includes how you will train new employees. Will your training post to an intranet Web site, or load onto a DVD that new hires can watch? Will you offer new-hire training at a regular interval to ensure everyone understands how to use the VPN?

Finally, don't forget your support staff. If a user with VPN issues is supposed to call the Help Desk, make sure the Help Desk knows how to help.

VPN Troubleshooting

To successfully troubleshoot and resolve VPN issues, be organized, methodical, and prepared. Like anything else on your network, your VPN at some point will experience an issue. The preparations you undertake during installation and maintenance will prove to be critical components of your troubleshooting process.

technical TIP

When troubleshooting issues with a VPN, or any network equipment, be sure to review all recent changes to the environment, not just changes to the VPN. An update to a DNS server, the replacement of a router, or changes to IP addressing can impact your VPN.

Before you start troubleshooting your VPN issue, have access to the following information:

- A network diagram showing the placement of the VPN and other key network components like firewalls, routers, and switches.
- A copy of the current VPN configuration.
- Any error, system, or alert logs.
- Operations guide.
- Maintenance logs and change management records.

Now that you have your basic information, you can start troubleshooting. There's no one way to troubleshoot an issue, particularly a VPN issue. What you can do is determine what works best for you, and stick with that process. Some people like to start at the far end and work back to the local VPN server. Others will start at the network layer and work their way up to the application. The actual process is not as critical as having an established process and sticking with it. One way to tackle this process is the following:

- **Identify the symptoms**—Frequently when dealing with a user-reported issue, the reported item will bear little resemblance to the actual problem. Users tend to generalize with statements like "No one can get on the VPN" or "The intranet is down from the VPN." You need more specifics before you start correcting an issue. Ideally you will receive an automated alert from your monitoring system, which generally permits you to track down issues much more quickly than a Help Desk ticket.
- **Determine the scope of the problem**—Know whether your problem is bigger than a breadbox or a 747. Do you have one user who cannot connect, one hundred users, or the entire company? Not only will this help you get a handle on the urgency of the issue, but it also gives you valuable clues to what the problem might be. If it's one user, the odds are pretty good that it's a client issue, or possibly a network issue on the user's end, and the Help Desk can probably assist with the issue. If a large group but not everyone is affected, you can look for commonalities. Do all the users belong to the same VPN group? Do they all connect from the same part of the country (could be an ISP issue)? If you have multiple VPNs, are the problems all on one VPN?

- **Look for changes**—Before you assume something is broken, see if anything has changed. If the issue is with a single user, did he or she install a new application like Skype or Tor that could be interfering with the VPN? If the VPN is unreachable from the Internet, was someone working on your Internet connection? Did you do a code upgrade over the weekend? The importance of formal change management is critical to successfully maintaining a production computing environment. When you are troubleshooting, determine what has changed. Be aware that sometimes the toughest part of chasing down change-related issues in a complex environment is figuring out which of the 20 or 30 changes performed during a weekend change window is causing your problem.
- **Call the vendor**—It's never a bad idea to call the vendor and see if they have seen your issue before. If you don't have phone support with the vendor, visit their Web site and check their knowledge base. The Internet is an invaluable tool for helping with troubleshooting.
- **Try the most likely solution**—As the resident expert, once you have gathered all the information and reviewed the likely issues, try a fix. Record these fixes not only in your Operations Guide, but also in your change control process.
- **Test it**—You made a change; test to see if it worked. If not, back out the change you made and repeat the previous step with the next most likely fix. Repeat the process until the problem is solved. Do not keep trying fix after fix without backing out previous fixes; you could end up making so many changes that you won't be able to easily get back to a stable configuration.
- **Check to see if you broke anything else**—This is a critical step. Changes to the environment—even if you are trying to fix something—can have unpredictable impacts. The last thing you want is to assume the problem is solved, just to get a call later saying no one can get to the Internet.
- **Document, document, document**—This is probably the most important part of the process. If you don't write processes and procedures down, it's as if you didn't even do them. When the next expert comes along to troubleshoot, and your changes aren't documented, he or she has to start with incorrect information or guesswork. And if you encounter the same problem twelve months later, you'll be glad you can refer to your previous process to speed up the second recovery. Create be a section in your Operations Guide just for this kind of documentation.

Now that you have a general troubleshooting process, consider some other things when troubleshooting a situation:

- **Don't panic**—During a major outage, people tend to panic. They will start sending e-mails to large distribution lists, sending alerts, escalating issues, and doing a variety of other things that are not particularly helpful to you while you're troubleshooting an issue. Keep your cool, work the problem at hand, and keep management informed of the progress you make.

- **Don't over commit or make promises you can't keep**—If you don't know what the issue is, don't tell your manager that the network will be back up in an hour.
- **Focus on the problem at hand**—Getting sidetracked when troubleshooting a complex issue is easy. Be sure that the problem at hand is the one you are working to address. If you identify other potential issues unrelated to the current outage, document them and handle them under your change control process. But don't go off on a tangent and delay addressing the immediate issue.

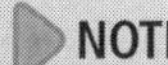

NOTE

When you are troubleshooting a VPN issue, management will often require frequent status updates. The worst place for you to be when the VPN is down is spending all your time on conference calls fielding questions like "When will it be fixed?" Management needs to be educated to the concept that things won't be fixed until you get off the phone and back to working the problem.

You can do a couple of quick and easy tests if you are having a major VPN outage and you just want to be sure that your VPN is still on the network. Generally your VPN will have two interfaces. One will be accessible from the Internet, and the other will be the connection to your internal network (possibly through a firewall). In the event of a major outage, start by verifying that both of those ports are functioning.

To verify the internal port is available, you can use the ping command from the Windows command prompt, or from a UNIX command line. See Figure 11-4 for a sample successful PING response.

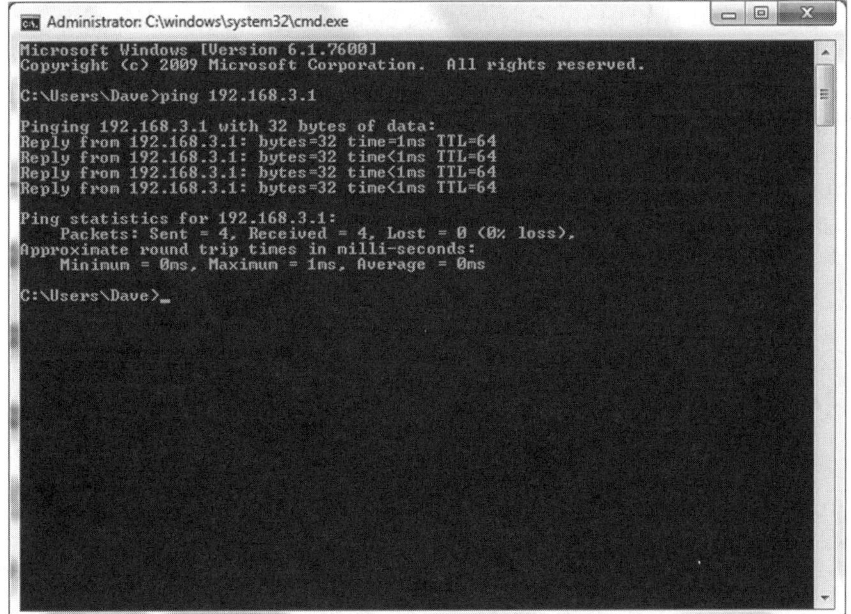

FIGURE 11-4

Troubleshooting a VPN issue using PING.

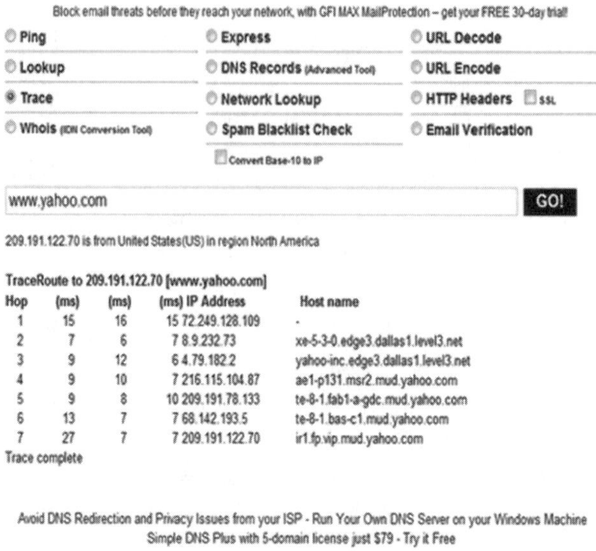

FIGURE 11-5

Using Internet-based Traceroute tools to determine if your VPN is accessible from the Internet.

Block email threats before they reach your network, with GFI MAX MailProtection – get your FREE 30-day trial!

Ping	Express	URL Decode
Lookup	DNS Records (Advanced Tool)	URL Encode
Trace	Network Lookup	HTTP Headers SSL
WhoIs (IDN Conversion Tool)	Spam Blacklist Check	Email Verification
	Convert Base-10 to IP	

www.yahoo.com GO!

209.191.122.70 is from United States(US) in region North America

TraceRoute to 209.191.122.70 [www.yahoo.com]

Hop	(ms)	(ms)	(ms)	IP Address	Host name
1	15	16	15	72.249.128.109	-
2	7	6	7	8.9.232.73	xe-5-3-0.edge3.dallas1.level3.net
3	9	12	6	4.79.182.2	yahoo-inc.edge3.dallas1.level3.net
4	9	10	7	216.115.104.87	ae1-p131.msr2.mud.yahoo.com
5	9	8	10	209.191.78.133	te-8-1.fab1-a-gdc.mud.yahoo.com
6	13	7	7	68.142.193.5	te-8-1.bas-c1.mud.yahoo.com
7	27	7	7	209.191.122.70	ir1.fp.vip.mud.yahoo.com

Trace complete

Avoid DNS Redirection and Privacy Issues from your ISP - Run Your Own DNS Server on your Windows Machine
Simple DNS Plus with 5-domain license just $79 - Try it Free

Once you've validated the internal port, also validate the external port. This is frequently a challenge because in most organizations a direct connection to the outside of the network is not readily available. In some larger organizations you may have a DSL Internet connection dedicated for testing, but if you don't have that type of access, a number of Internet sites will let you run network diagnostics from their Web sites. See Figure 11.5 for a sample Internet Traceroute command from *www.network-tools.com*. If you do an Internet search on "Network Tools," you can find a number of sites that offer a similar capability.

You now have the tools to create your own troubleshooting process for your VPN, using some or all of the steps and tips discussed. You just need to determine what works best in your environment. Be methodical, don't panic, keep focused on the issue, and you will be very successful in quickly addressing VPN issues in your environment.

CHAPTER SUMMARY

VPN management is a complex activity that requires attention to detail and good documentation. A variety of best practices may assist you in your VPN deployment and ongoing support. Selecting and deploying a VPN solution that meets your business requirements is essential. This includes deciding between open-source and commercial VPN solutions when selecting your product. Understanding the threats, attacks, and mitigations, and ensuring your VPN is available are key components of success. In addition, understand the difference between privacy and anonymity, know the difference between personal/individual and enterprise/network solutions and, finally, be able to train your users well. Once you have mastered all these facets of successful VPN rollout and support, you'll be ready to move on to other security topics.

KEY CONCEPTS AND TERMS

Anonymity
Privacy
Slideware
Two-factor authentication
Vulnerability management

CHAPTER 11 ASSESSMENT

1. Which response contains the three most common VPN deployment architectures?

A. Bypass, encrypted, OpenVPN
B. DMZ, OpenVPN, internally connected
C. DMZ, Encrypted, OpenVPN
D. Encrypted, OpenVPN, internally connected
E. Bypass, DMZ, internally connected

2. All of the following are considered VPN management best practices except:

A. If one is good, two is better
B. Patch regularly
C. Permit split tunneling
D. Do not allow employee-owned computers to connect
E. Review usage

3. Three of the threats common to both software and hardware VPNs include ________, ________, and ________.

4. The two different types of VPN commonly used for remote access VPN are ________ and ________.

5. Pick *two* advantages of using an open-source VPN solution instead of a commercial solution.

A. Low cost
B. Good vendor support
C. Minimize installation and configuration time
D. Use existing hardware
E. Easier to troubleshoot.

6. The ability for a network or system user to remain unknown to adversaries is ________.

7. Which of the following are benefits of using a commercial VPN instead of an open-source VPN solution? (Multiple answers may be correct.)
   A. More costly
   B. Less flexible
   C. Product support
   D. Requires higher skill set to deploy and support.
   E. Dedicated hardware

8. A document that details the requirements for using the VPN is called a ________.

9. Which of the following are vulnerabilities common to both software and hardware VPN solutions? (Multiple answers may be correct.)
   A. Default password
   B. Unpublished vulnerability in the code
   C. Weak client security
   D. Weak authentication
   E. Blue Screen of Death

10. Which of the following are components of a VPN Policy? (Multiple answers may be correct.)
    A. Introduction
    B. Scope
    C. VPN Configuration Settings
    D. Definitions
    E. Backup Strategy

11. Keeping information about a network or system user from being disclosed to unauthorized people is known as ________.

12. Recognizing that vulnerabilities will be found with both hardware and software VPNs, be sure to ________ frequently.

13. Which of the following are not VPN best practices? (Multiple answers may be correct.)
    A. Backup your configuration
    B. Pick the solution that gets the best reviews
    C. Don't permit split tunneling
    D. Use vulnerability management
    E. Secure your endpoints

14. The best authentication method for client VPNs is ________.

15. When protecting the availability of your VPN, it is a good practice to have ________ VPN gateways in your environment.

16. Which of the following are protocols that can be used for high availability with VPNs? (Multiple answers may be correct.)
    A. IPSec
    B. 3DES
    C. HSRP
    D. VRRP
    E. SSL

17. If you want to verify that the VPN is on the network, what is the simplest tool you can use?
    A. Snort
    B. Ping
    C. Traceroute
    D. VPN Monitor
    E. Syslog

18. When troubleshooting a VPN issue, which of the following are valid troubleshooting steps? (multiple answers may be correct)
    A. Don't panic
    B. Gather the symptoms
    C. Run a vulnerability scan
    D. Review changes to the environment
    E. Upgrade the VPN software

19. Your VPN policy should address which of the following topics? (multiple answers may be correct)
    A. Define authentication methods permitted.
    B. Define the VPN platform
    C. Define required encryption levels for VPN connections
    D. Define the troubleshooting process
    E. Define how to respond to incidents

20. In addition to redundant VPNs, also make sure to have redundant ________ for your VPN to be truly available.

CHAPTER

12

VPN Technologies

VIRTUAL PRIVATE NETWORK (VPN) is a general industry term that actually covers a many different technologies. Ask anyone who works in a large company and needs to access a corporate network remotely and he or she will probably confirm using a VPN to connect to the network and get to his or her e-mail, intranet, and other corporate applications. Ask him or her how that VPN works, however, and you will almost always get a blank stare. End users are typically interested only in the result of a solution, not in how it works. For you the information security practitioner, however, just how a VPN works is as important as what benefits aVPN provides your organization.

VPNs deploy in a number of different ways, leveraging a variety of technologies, platforms and protocols. Determining which VPN is the right fit for your organization requires successfully gathering and interpreting your business requirements. Once you've documented those requirements, it's up to you as the security practitioner to understand those different options and capabilities to fit the VPN technology to the appropriate business requirements.

A variety of technical factors affect the selection and installation a VPN solution. Some VPNs are available as software installed on a workstation or a server. Other VPNs are software components of other devices, like a router or a firewall. Finally, dedicated VPN hardware appliances provide secure remote connectivity.

You need to know that a variety of underlying protocols can provide different functions, features, and levels of encryption. When a vendor starts talking about L2TP, IPv6, SSL and SSH, or IPSec, you'll need to speak the lingo and make the right technology decision for your organization.

Finally, other infrastructure considerations you need to take into account when working with VPN technologies include how things like network address translation (NAT), Internet Protocol version, and the use of virtualization can affect how you deploy, maintain, and troubleshoot a VPN.

Chapter 12 Topics

This chapter will cover the following topics:

- What the differences are between software and hardware solutions
- What the differences are between Layer 2 and Layer 3 VPNs
- What Internet Protocol Security (IPSec) is
- What Layer 2 Tunneling Protocol (L2TP) is
- What the Secure Sockets Layer (SSL)/Transport Layer Security (TLS) is
- What the Secure Shell (SSH) protocol is
- How to establish performance and stability for VPNs
- How to use VPNs with network address translation (NAT)
- What some types of virtualization are
- What the differences are between Internet Protocol (IP) versions 4 and 6

Chapter 12 Goals

Upon completion of this chapter, you will be able to:

- Contrast hardware and software VPN solutions
- Describe VPN protocols, their uses, features, and problems
- Explain the problem of using VPNs with NAT
- Evaluate hardware VPN devices

Differences Between Software and Hardware Solutions

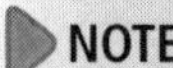

NOTE

In the early days of VPNs, VPN software commonly ran on a Windows or UNIX server. Today, server-based implementations show up mostly in small environments because of the poor scalability and reliability of the operating system. Most software VPNs act as a component of a firewall or router, not as an add-on to a server.

A key topic in discussing VPN technologies is the differences between software and hardware solutions. The following definitions help reveal those differences:

- **Software VPN**—Software-based VPNs are sold either as part of a server operating system, as part of an appliance operating system, or as a third-party add-on software solution.
- **Hardware VPN**—A hardware VPN is a standalone device, dedicated to managing VPN functions such as authentication, encapsulation, encryption, and filtering.

While the functionality of software and hardware VPN solutions are essentially the same, providing a secure remote connection on demand points out some important differences.

Software VPNs

When evaluating whether or not to deploy a software VPN, consider two types of software VPNs:

- **Operating System-based VPN**—An operating system-based VPN solution is an application that runs on a Windows or UNIX operating system. These are generally used in smaller companies, as they tend to be less scalable and less stable than other VPN solutions. They are generally less expensive, especially as they are running on a shared server, which may be running other applications. Many of these solutions are open source, which further reduces the cost, although it can increase the complexity of the solution.

  One potential security issue with this solution is that the server communicates with the public network (generally the Internet) for the connections to occur. Any time you connect a server and the associated operating system to a public network, you increase the security risk, since you are exposing it to a much larger pool of attackers. You can mitigate this risk by limiting the ports open to the server, and, if you are doing just site-to-site VPN connections, you can sometimes restrict the connections to specified IP addresses. You can also add a firewall to the VPN server, which adds to the overhead on the server, but will provide additional protection to offset the increased exposure.
- **Module-based VPN**—A module-based VPN runs as a component on a larger system. These are sometimes included as part of the overall feature set, or in other cases may require the purchase of additional licenses to use the VPN. An example of this would be the VPN capability included with many firewalls. Many routers also offer this type of capability, which permits the easy encryption of WAN links for security-conscious companies. The benefit of this type of VPN solution is reduced complexity of the environment, since you have fewer discrete devices to manage. VPN modules are also typically less expensive than hardware VPN solutions. Some vendors also offer hardware accelerators for improving overall performance of this solution.

Hardware VPNs

Hardware VPNs are dedicated appliance-based solutions, generally based on a router-type platform. Hardware VPNs are the most common type of VPN deployed in corporations today. While hardware VPNs can be complex to deploy, they are typically more scalable than their software counterparts, and can be easily deployed in a redundant manner. Hardware VPNs can increase the complexity of an environment, because you are deploying additional equipment. The good news is that you can usually manage this additional hardware with the same types of network management tools you use to manage the routers and switches in an environment.

NOTE

You must make a risk-based decision on whether to accept the possibility of undiscovered bugs in a new version of hardware or to live with the known bugs in a previous version. If an upgrade is issued primarily for fixing security flaws, you may be better off with the new version, surprises and all.

Hardware VPNs can create some security issues, largely related to potential vulnerabilities in the VPN software code on the appliance itself. A number of security alerts related to VPN vulnerabilities have appeared in recent years. Fortunately, you can manage this issue fairly easily by keeping current on your vendor's security alerts and by upgrading VPN code in a timely fashion. A good rule of thumb is to run the N-1 version of code, where N is the current version of code, unless a known issue with that previous version of the code has been published.

Ultimately, the requirements of your business will drive your selection of a software or hardware VPN. The good news is many options are available to you in your search for the best solution.

Differences Between Layer 2 and Layer 3 VPNs

One facile component of current VPNs is that they use a variety of transport protocols to establish their connections. This is helpful not only because the protocols have different capabilities, encryption strengths, and authentication mechanisms, but they also can run at different layers of the OSI (open systems interconnection) model. The OSI model is the standard seven-layer conceptual tool that describes protocols and their functions. Each layer communicates with its peer layer on the other end of a communication session. While the OSI model is helpful in discussing protocols, most protocols are not in full compliance with it.

In the case of VPNs, the protocols used by the vast majority of solutions work at Layers 2 and 3 of the OSI model.

Layer 2 of the OSI model is the Data Link layer. The Data Link layer is the protocol layer that transfers data between adjacent network nodes. In the case of a VPN, this protocol transfers data from one VPN endpoint to the other.

An example of a protocol that communicates using Layer 2 would be Layer 2 Transport Protocol (L2TP).

Layer 3 of the OSI model is the Network layer. The Network layer is responsible for end-to-end packet delivery and includes the ability to route packets through intermediate hosts.

An example of a VPN protocol that communicates at Layer 3 is IPSec.

technical TIP

SSL/TLS and SSH are protocols that operate at Layer 7 of the OSI model, the Application layer.

technical TIP

An RFC is Request for Comments, which is published by the **Internet Engineering Task Force (IETF)**. The IETF is the standards body for Internet-related engineering specifications. The IETF uses RFCs as a mechanism to define Internet-related standards. (See *www.ietf.org* for more information.)

Internet Protocol Security (IPSec)

Internet Protocol Security (IPSec) is a standards-based protocol suite designed specifically for securing Internet Protocol (IP) communications. IPSec authenticates and encrypts each IP packet in an IP data stream. In addition, IPSec has protocols that can establish mutual authentication and cryptographic key negotiation during a session. IPSec operates at the Network layer of the OSI model.

The IPSec standard utilizes three major components:

- The Authentication Header (AH)
- Encapsulating Security Payload (ESP)
- Internet Key Exchange (IKE)

According to the National Institute for Standards and Technology (NIST), **authentication header (AH)** provides integrity protection for packet headers and data, as well as user authentication. It can optionally provide replay protection and access protection. AH cannot encrypt any portion of a packet. In the initial version of IPSec, the ESP protocol could provide only encryption, not authentication, so AH and ESP were often used together to provide both confidentiality and integrity protection for communications. Because authentication capabilities were added to ESP in the second version of IPSec, AH has become less significant; in fact, some IPSec software no longer supports AH. However, AH is still of value because AH can authenticate portions of packets that ESP cannot. Also, many existing IPSec implementations use AH.

Encapsulating Security Payload (ESP) is the second core IPSec security protocol, NIST's *Guide to IPsec VPNs* notes. In the initial version of IPSec, ESP provided only encryption for packet payload data. Integrity protection was provided by the AH protocol if needed. In the second version of IPSec, ESP became more flexible. It can perform authentication to

technical TIP

Why does the layer matter? Because IPSec operates at Layer 3 of the OSI model, it can encrypt any traffic in Layers 4 through 7 of the OSI model. That means IPSec can be used to encrypt any application traffic.

> **NOTE**
> IPSec supports the Data Encryption Standard (DES), a 56-bit encryption protocol and 3DES (data is encrypted three times using DES), which effectively yields a 168-bit encryption protocol.

provide integrity protection, although not for the outermost IP header. Therefore, in all but the oldest IPSec implementations, ESP can provide encryption only, encryption and integrity protection, or integrity protection only. This chapter mainly addresses the features and characteristics of the second version of ESP.

Internet key exchange (IKE) negotiates, creates, and manages security associations. Security association (SA) is a generic term for a set of values that define the IPSec features and protections applied to a connection. You can also create SAs manually, using values agreed upon in advance by both parties, but because these SAs cannot be updated, this method does not scale for real-life large-scale VPNs. In IPSec, IKE provides a secure mechanism for establishing IPSec-protected connections.

IPSec supports two different modes:

- **Transport mode (host-to-host)**—In transport mode, only the data packet payload is encapsulated, while the packet header is left intact. In this mode, the destination host decapsulates the packet. This is the mode used in a Microsoft Windows environment to secure a client-to-server connection using IPSec.
- **Tunnel Mode (gateway-to-gateway or gateway-to-host)**—In the tunnel mode, the IP packet is entirely encapsulated and given a new header. The host/gateway specified in the new IP header, decapsulates the packet. This is the mode used to secure traffic for a remote access VPN connection from the remote host to the VPN concentrator on the internal network.

IPSec is a little different from some of the other protocols. It provides high-quality interoperable, cryptographically based security for IPv4 and IPv6. As a result, the protocol supports a comprehensive set of security services, including:

- Access control
- Connectionless data integrity checking
- Data origin authentication
- Replay detection and rejection
- Confidentiality using encryption
- Traffic flow confidentiality

IPSec-based VPNs have been the dominant VPN platform for many years, although in recent years SSL-based VPNs have been making significant inroads. IPSec is so popular for three reasons:

- It supports all operating system platforms.
- It provides secure, node-on-the-network connectivity.
- It offers a standards-based solution, permitting easier interoperability between different devices and vendors.

For more information on IPSec, see *http://tools.ietf.org/html/rfc4301*. While RFC4301 provides the main IPSec standard definitions, separate RFCs exist for some IPSec features. The full set of RFCs defines the entire standard.

Layer 2 Tunneling Protocol (L2TP)

Layer 2 Tunneling Protocol (L2TP) is an older protocol largely replaced by IPSec and SSL/TLS-based VPNs in production environments. You will still encounter references to the protocol in current VPN literature, and it may still be in use in some older environments, where backwards compatibility could still be an issue. L2TP was used extensively in the early VPN solutions, but lost its popularity as other protocols proved to be more usable as industry standards developed.

L2TP is a combination of the best features of **Point-to-Point Tunneling Protocol (PPTP)**, a Microsoft proprietary protocol and the **Layer 2 Forwarding (L2F)** protocol, which was an early competing protocol for PPTP, developed by Cisco Systems. Like PPTP, L2TP was an extension of **Point-to-Point Protocol (PPP)** to allow PPP to be tunneled through an IP network. L2TP support was first included in a Microsoft server product with the release of Windows 2000 Server. Prior to Windows 2000, PPTP was the only supported protocol. A number of hardware VPN vendors, including Cisco, also supported it.

One of the challenges with L2TP is that it only provides a mechanism for creating tunnels through an IP network. It doesn't provide a mechanism for encrypting the data being tunneled. As a result, L2TP was typically used in conjunction with IPSec protocol's ESP (Encapsulating Security Payload) for encryption. For this reason, you may sometimes see L2TP referred to as L2TP/IPSec.

RFC 3193 defines the use of IPSec to secure an L2TP implementation.

For more information on IPSec, see *http://tools.ietf.org/html/rfc2661*. While RFC2661 provides the main L2TP standard definitions, separate RFCs for some other implementations and features exist. The full set of RFCs defines the entire standard.

Remember that you may never encounter L2TP in a production environment, but you should know the basic aspects of this protocol when looking at tunneling and VPN protocols in general.

technical TIP

PPP, the Point-to-Point Protocol, was a protocol defined in the late 1990s to provide a standard transport mechanism for point-to-point data connections. This was used largely in conjunction with modem connections and has been phased out as high-speed Internet connections have replaced modem connections.

Secure Sockets Layer (SSL)/Transport Layer Security (TLS)

One of the key VPN protocols today is SSL/TLS, which is the main alternative for a VPN solution if you don't want to leverage an IPSec solution. However, before you consider this protocol in conjunction with VPNs, it's important to understand the origin of this protocol.

> **NOTE**
> SSL supports 128-bit encryption, while TLS will support the Advanced Encryption Standard (AES) with keys up to 256 bits.

If you have ever surfed the World Wide Web, you have used the Hypertext Transfer Protocol (HTTP) to connect to a Web site. One of the drawbacks of HTTP is that is does not include the ability to encrypt or otherwise protect the data stream between the client and server. This wasn't an issue until the early 1990s, when the need to protect against eavesdropping on communications became critical to the ultimate success of the World Wide Web. While several technologies have addressed this need, one solution has rapidly become the industry standard: Secure Sockets Layer (SSL).

HTTPS is the Web protocol that utilizes SSL to encrypt HTTP, and is used worldwide today for secure Web communications. (See Figure 12.1)

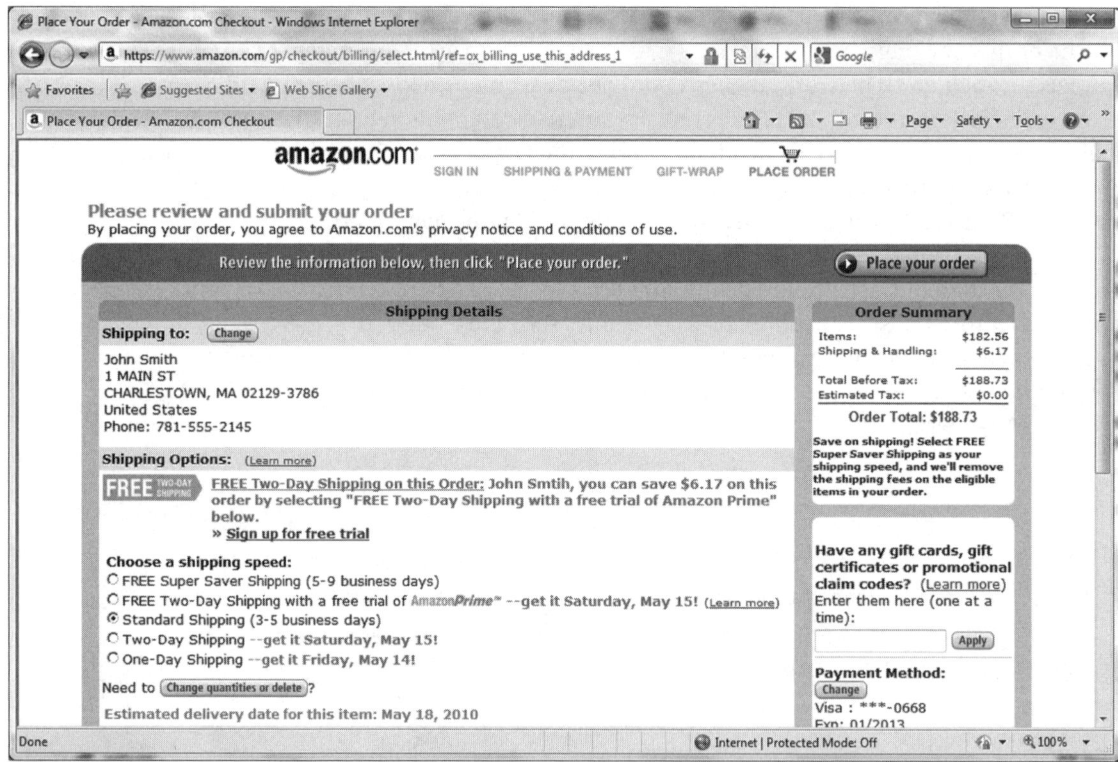

FIGURE 12-1

A secure browser session using SSL.

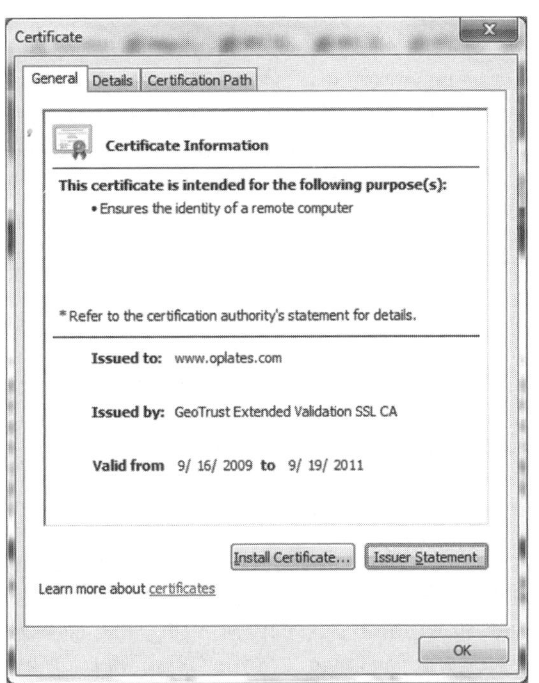

FIGURE 12-2

A certificate used to authenticate a server in an HTTPS connection.

SSL was originally proposed as a standard by Netscape. Version 1.0 had serious security flaws, which were corrected in versions 2.0 and 3.0. As this protocol has become more widely used, it has been formalized in the IETF standard known as Transport Layer Security (TLS). The SSL/TLS protocol provides a method for secure client/server communications across a network. SSL/TLS prevents eavesdropping and tampering with data in transit. SSL/TLS also provides endpoint authentication and communications confidentiality through encryption.

In typical end-user/browser usage, SSL/TLS authentication is one-way. Only the server is authenticated when the client compares the information entered to access a server to information on the SSL certificate on the server. The client knows the server's identity, but not vice versa; the client remains unauthenticated or anonymous. See Figure 12-2 for an example of the information in a server certificate.

technical TIP

The terms SSL and TLS sometimes confuse people. In practical terms, they are the same thing. While the IETF standard refers to the protocol as TLS, the industry still uses the acronym SSL when referring to the protocol used to secure browser communications.

FYI

While SSL/TLS is supposed to authenticate servers, it hasn't been as robust as originally planned. Phishing attacks, that is, attacks that direct a user's browser to a counterfeit Web site, are a major problem for security professionals. Users typically do not check to see if a site is encrypted or if the certificate information matches their destination Web site. Newer versions of browsers (Internet Explorer 8, for example) check encryption status for the user and warn of a mismatch between a certificate and the domain presenting it.

SSL/TLS can also perform bidirectional authentication by using client-based certificates. This is particularly helpful when using this protocol to access a protected network, as it adds an additional layer of authentication to the access.

SSL/TLS and VPNs

As you learned in the section on IPSec, a VPN creates a secure tunnel through a public network like the Internet. While SSL VPNs still leverage the concept of tunneling, they create their tunnels differently than IPSec. An SSL VPN establishes connectivity using the SSL protocol. IPSec works at the Layer 3 of the OSI model, while SSH functions at Layers 4 and 5. SSL VPNs can also encapsulate information at Layers 6 and 7, which makes SSL VPNs some of the most flexible available.

On additional function of an SSL VPN is that it usually connects using a Web browser, whereas an IPSec VPN generally requires client software on the remote system.

SSL VPNs create predominantly remote access VPN connections, where a client connects to applications on an internal network. This is different from a site-to-site connection, where two gateways connect disparate private networks across the Internet.

SSL/TLS VPNs benefits over IPSec VPNs include:

- **Less expensive**—Since an SSL VPN is typically clientless, you don't have the costs of rolling out, supporting, and updating client software.
- **Platform independent**—Since the access to an SSL VPN comes through the standard SSL interface, which is a component of virtually every Web browser, virtually any OS that runs a browser is supported. While the operating system (OS) support for VPN clients is good for common OSs, a significant lag can exist in client development following the release of a new OS or the release of a new client version. You may see a Windows client 90 to 180 days earlier than the Mac version.
- **Client flexibility**—As a general rule, IPSec clients are generally installed only on corporate systems, as you learned in Chapter 11, VPN Management. Due to the additional configuration flexibility, SSL VPNs allow access from a variety of clients including corporate systems, home systems, customer or supplier systems or even a kiosk machine in a library or an Internet cafe. This wider accessibility tends to increase employee satisfaction with the technology.

- **Network Address Translation (NAT) is not a problem**—Historically, NAT caused issues with IPSec VPNs. As a result, virtually all IPSec vendors have created workarounds for this issue. With an SSL VPN, you don't have these issues because SSL works at a higher layer than IPSec, and, as a result, is not affected by NAT.
- **Granular access control**—A benefit or a drawback, depending on your environment. SSL VPNs require a greater granularity of access than a typical IPSec VPN because instead of creating a tunnel from the host to the internal network, SSL VPNs require explicit definition of each resource accessed. The upside is that, unless you have defined it explicitly, an SSL VPN user cannot access the resource. Although this barrier has significant security benefits, in a complex environment this could add significant overhead to your VPN support.
- **Fewer firewall rules required**—To access an IPSec gateway across a firewall, you need to open several ports to support the individual protocols for authentication and the tunnel. With an SSL VPN, you need to open only port 443, which is easy because of the prevalence of the HTTPS protocol.

For more information on TLS, see *http://tools.ietf.org/html/rfc5246*.

Secure Shell (SSH) Protocol

The **Secure Shell (SSH)** protocol is a method for secure remote login and other secure network services over a public network such as the Internet. SSH service a number of applications across multiple platforms including UNIX, Microsoft Windows, Apple Mac, and Linux.

You can use SSH:

- For login to a shell on a remote host (replacing Telnet and rlogin) (See Figure 12.3 for an example of an application that uses SSH for this application)
- For executing a single command on a remote host (replacing rsh)
- For file transfers to a remote host
- In combination with rsync to back up, copy, and mirror files securely
- In conjunction with the OpenSSH server and client to create a full VPN connection.

The SSH protocol consists of three major components:

- Transport Layer Protocol, which provides server authentication, confidentiality, and integrity with perfect forward secrecy.
- User Authentication Protocol, which authenticates the client to the server.
- Connection Protocol, which multiplexes the encrypted tunnel into several logical channels.

For more information on SSH, see *http://tools.ietf.org/html/rfc4251*.

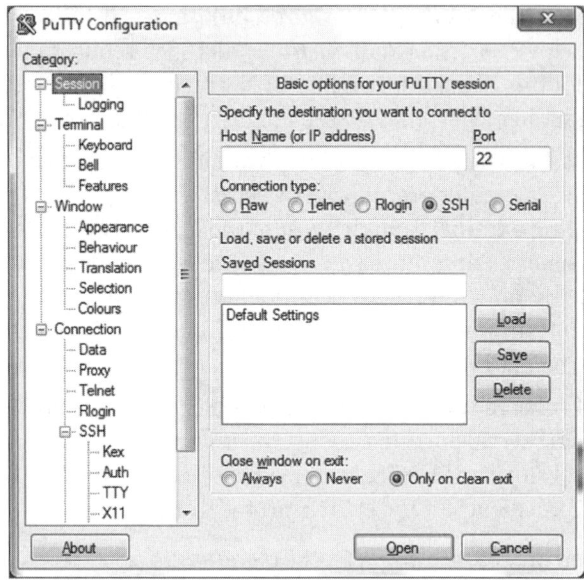

FIGURE 12-3

PuTTY is an application that leverages SSH to provide secure connections to hosts.

Establishing Performance and Stability for VPNs

Now that you have an in-depth understanding of the many options available to you for both VPN as well as other secure access protocols, it's time to discuss some of the challenges you might encounter when supporting your VPN. For your VPN rollout to be successful, consider two factors: performance and stability.

Performance

Some critical factors can affect the performance of your VPN:

- **VPN type**—When considering the performance of your VPN, consider the type of VPN you've chosen. The performance characteristics of a VPN supporting remote clients can be very different from the performance characteristics of a VPN supporting site-to-site connections, or even a mixed remote client and site-to-site connections.
- **Protocol**—The performance characteristics associated with an IPSec VPN can be very different from what you may find with an SSL VPN implementation. How you apply IPSec and SSL/TLS in a VPN solution can affect your VPN's performance. Validating the performance specifications of the solution before you rollout should allow you to address any performance issues associated with the protocol start-up.
- **Load**—The number of remote access or site-to-site VPNs will affect the overall performance of your VPN rollout. The challenge in addressing this issue, particularly in an environment supporting a large pool of remote clients, is that the performance issues will tend to crop up during peak use. To appropriately diagnose these issues,

you'll need to be able to report on use in a way that tracks the peaks. Many of the current reporting tools available for VPNs tend to show averages over time, which can hide peaks and valleys in your use numbers. Be sure you fully understand these performance reports.

- **Client Configuration**—In a remote VPN connection, much of the performance is actually related to the client's capabilities. If the remote client is running on old hardware with limited memory and an underpowered processor, the overhead associated with encrypting the traffic will affect performance of the VPN connection. Another factor contributing to overhead is: what else is being done with the remote PC? If the user is running a memory-intensive application such a photo editing suite, you may find that this resource impact reduces the performance of the VPN.

NOTE

Don't forget time-of-day considerations when investigating load-related performance issues. You will generally find your peak times for VPN use will be first thing in the morning, as employees get started for the day; after lunch, when everyone comes back from the break; and at the end of the business day. Be sure to note the times of day if performance issues arise, to help correlate the data and identify root causes or at least a common factors.

- **Bandwidth**—The bandwidth available to your VPN can have a significant impact on its performance and can vary widely among the remote hosts and gateways. If your VPN is supporting site-to-site VPNs connecting two locations, the bandwidth allocated at either (or both) ends of the connection may affect performance. You may find, for example, that an unreliable DSL connection at a remote client location creates unacceptable delays for the user.
- **Topology**—Depending on the location of your VPN endpoints, the topology may affect performance. For example, if your VPN connection has to traverse a firewall or a proxy server you may find reduced performance, depending on how well those devices handle the VPN traffic.
- **Encryption Level**—The higher the encryption level, the greater impact on the memory and processor of the endpoint devices. That being said, you should always run the highest available encryption available. If you suspect encryption is causing performance issues, you can look into either a dedicated processor for handling encryption or upgrading the processing capabilities of the central processor.
- **Traffic**—An issue related to bandwidth is traffic loads. If, for example, the Sales Department likes to watch streaming video baseball games on Wednesday afternoon, and you have VPN performance issues during that time, increasing bandwidth may fix the problem, but does not really address the root cause, which is a traffic spike rather than too little bandwidth. To diagnose a performance issue related to traffic, devise some way to look at the traffic on your network. Another facet of this issue is: what does the traffic load look like across the VPN? Do your remote users store their documents on servers in the core network? Since you are running your VPN with split tunneling disabled, are remote users doing Web browsing through the VPN connection? Optimizing traffic both within the VPN as well as outside network traffic can go a long way to ensuring you don't encounter performance issues.

- **Client version**—Sometimes the version of the client can impact the performance. Managing older versions on remote devices can be very difficult, depending on how your organization manages those devices. Keep your clients up-to-date and you should be able to avoid any performance issues related to client versions.

Stability

To ensure a successful VPN deployment, the implementation must be stable. Some factors that can affect VPN stability include:

- **Configuration**—Ultimately how you configure your VPN will have an major impact on your VPN deployment. Not only should you check your internal VPN configuration, but also factor stability into your initial design. If access to the network through the VPN is mission-critical, you should ensure you use a configuration that includes some level of high availability or failover.
- **Location**—Consider where you have placed your VPN in the network. If the VPN connection has to traverse three firewalls, multiple local routers, and a proxy server, you may find that the connections are not as stable as you need them to be.
- **Software version**—The version of VPN software (or in the case of a hardware VPN, the concentrator code) can have a significant impact on the stability of your rollout. Be sure to keep your VPN software up to date. Updating too quickly can also be a source of stability issues, so a good rule of thumb is to keep your software version one less than the latest version number of the VPN software. That model allows you to keep your VPN relatively current, so you avoid any issues contained in older versions of code, but also keeps you from being the vendor's beta tester for new code, which is never a good idea in a production environment.
- **Underlying OS**—The OS on which you run your VPN can definitely impact the stability of your VPN implementation. A VPN running on an old Windows operating system might have issues with the dreaded "Blue Screen of Death." A hardware-based VPN could run into challenges if there are firmware or OS issues, although those problems are typically less common than an OS-based solution. The number of lines of software code needed to run a hardware VPN are quite a bit less than the current OS coding. The leaner the software, the less risk you run of issues with the OS.

While these lists contains many of the most common sources of performance issues you may encounter, be sure to reference your troubleshooting processes and procedures when diagnosing VPN performance and stability issues.

Using VPNs with Network Address Translation (NAT)

VPNs and network address translation (NAT) have historically suffered from some conflicts when used together. NAT is an Internet standard that allows you to use one set of IP addresses on your internal LAN, and a second set of IP addresses for the Internet connection. A device (usually a router or firewall) stands in between the two connections that provides NAT services, managing the translation of internal addresses to external addresses. This allows companies to use large numbers of unregistered internal addresses while needing only a fraction of that number of addresses on the Internet, thus conserving the addresses. This is similar to a company that may have hundreds of phones in a building, but only pays for a small number of connections to the phone switch, as it is unlikely that every employee would pick up the phone at the exact same time.

NAT was created as a workaround to IP addressing issues. Since the Internet relies on the TCP/IP protocol for communications, it also relies on the IPv4 addressing that is an integral part of the TCP/IP protocol suite. The explosive growth of the Internet threatened to exhaust the pool of IPv4 IP addresses. Without unique addresses, the Internet would be unable to successfully route TCP/IP traffic. This was clearly unacceptable because the Internet was fueling the explosive growth of many businesses. As a result, NAT was proposed and adopted widely as a way to conserve critical IPv4 addresses.

In the early days of the Internet, when IP addressing was being created, developers believed the 32-bit addressing scheme (known as IPv4) to be more than adequate for any potential network growth. Theoretically 4,294,967,296 unique addresses were available using 32-bit addressing, and, even discounting the reserved ranges, more than 3 billion addresses were possible. At the time, that was enough addresses to provide one for every person on the planet.

Unfortunately, the designers of the addressing scheme dramatically underestimated the explosive growth of the Internet, as well as the popularity of TCP/IP in business and home networks. There are no longer enough addresses to go around. IPv6 is contains an addressing scheme that allows for a dramatically larger pool of addresses, but is receiving very limited deployment in corporate networks or on the Internet today. This is due in large part to the use of NAT. For more information on NAT, see RFC 3022, Traditional IP Network Address Translator (traditional NAT), at *http://tools.ietf.org/html/rfc3022*.

Two main types of NAT are available:

- **Static NAT**—This version of NAT maps an unregistered IP address on the private network to a registered IP address on the public network on a one-to-one basis. This is used when the translated device needs to be accessible from the public network. For example, a Web server on your private network might have an unregistered address of 10.10.10.10, but a NAT address of 12.2.2.123. A user trying to connect to that Web site can enter 12.2.2.123, and the router or firewall at the other end will translate that address to 10.10.10.10 when the packet reaches it.
- **Dynamic NAT**—This version of NAT maps an unregistered IP address to a registered IP address from a group of registered IP addresses. This is more commonly used when large pools of systems on the internal network need to access the Internet and don't have a requirement for a static address. The workstation's address is translated to the next available registered address as soon as it initiates a connection to the public network.

The critical thing to remember about NAT is that due to limitations in the IPSec standard, IPSec has issues traversing a translated network. VPN vendors have addressed this issue, but the workaround they have put in place can create challenges when troubleshooting issues. If possible, run your IPSec VPNs on untranslated addresses. Or deploy an SSL VPN. Because SSL runs at a higher level in the OSI model, it's not affected by NAT.

NAT traversal is a general term for techniques that establish and maintain TCP/IP network and/or UDP connections traversing NAT gateways.

For IPSec to work through NAT, configure the firewall to permit the following protocols and ports:

- **Internet Key Exchange (IKE)**—User Datagram Protocol (UDP) port 500
- **Encapsulating Security Payload (ESP)**—IP protocol number 50
- **Authentication Header (AH)**—IP protocol number 51

Types of Virtualization

A number of definitions and types of virtualization are available to businesses today. Operating system virtualization is the emulation of an operating system environment hosted on another operating system. A virtual machine exists logically, but does not have an associated, dedicated physical device. Thus, a single physical machine can host multiple virtual machines. Virtualization of storage allows a storage manager to abstract the underlying physical storage technologies and manage storage at a logical level. Network virtualization allows you to run multiple logical switches within a single physical switch chassis. Some SSL VPNs support VPN virtualization.

All of these technologies can potentially affect your VPN environment.

Desktop Virtualization

Desktop virtualization (sometimes called client virtualization) is a concept that separates the personal computer desktop environment from the physical desktop machine by using a client-server model of computing. This model is reminiscent of the thin client client-server architectures of years ago, where the operating system was run centrally. This generation of the model offers significantly more business benefits. A virtualized desktop is hosted on a remote central server instead of on the local hardware of the remote client. This allows users to work from their remote desktop client, while all of the programs, applications, processes, and data used are kept and run centrally.

Where this has an immediate impact on your VPN is ensuring the compatibility of your VPN client with the virtualized desktop. The possibility always exists that the virtualization of the client might cause issues with the client or complicate troubleshooting any issues with the VPN. The best approach to working in a virtualized desktop environment is to test your VPN applications carefully before the virtual implementation goes into production.

Another issue that can come up in conjunction with the VPN is how you publish the virtual desktop to a remote client that is not connected to the network. One model would be to make the VPN connection first, then publish the virtual desktop across the VPN connection. This is an environment that lends itself well to SSL VPNs, due to the lack of dedicated client software. With an IPSec VPN deployment, you need to get a working VPN client on the remote desktops before publishing the virtual desktop, adding to the complexity of your VPN environment. The other model is to publish the virtual desktops natively from a DMZ environment across the Internet, and then connect back to the network via VPN, publishing the VPN client (if using IPSec) as part of the virtual desktop image.

Some limitations of desktop virtualization include:

- Additional security risks associated with the complex network and desktop image environments used when working with remote virtual desktops.
- Loss of employee privacy as all storage and processing is centralized.
- Maintaining your VPN clients in the virtual images.
- Increased downtime in the event of network failures. Outages can also affect a greater number of employees.

The concept of virtualization is becoming more popular among enterprise customers. For SSL VPNs, the need for virtualization is natural. Enterprises like to provide different remote access VPN presences to different user groups, such as partners and different departments of employees. The following section covers some of the basic capabilities you should consider for a "virtualized" SSL VPN deployment.

SSL VPN Virtualization

Virtualized SSL VPNs provide a unique virtual VPN configuration for each individual user group. Much like other types of virtualization, a virtualized SSL VPN allows you to separate the physical and logical sides of the VPN.

Some benefits of a virtualized SSL VPN environment include:

- **Greater flexibility**—The ability to create custom authentication methods and VPN group policies for different user groups.
- **Delegation of management**—Virtual VPNs allows the delegation of management roles for each virtual instance. If one virtual VPN instance allows a business partner to connect to an internal application, the management of that virtual VPN can go to someone supporting that business partner.
- **Added security when working in a multi-group environment**—Virtual VPNs provide a total logical separation of the VPNs instances in terms of system resources, routing tables, user databases, and policy management interfaces.

The use of virtualized VPNs is especially attractive to companies that provide VPNs as a service. Being able to create completely separate environments and resource pools is critical to a successful service provider. Setting up dedicated hardware environments for each customer does not allow a service provider to take advantage of the economies of scale offered by a single implementation.

Differences Between Internet Protocol (IP) Version 4 and Internet Protocol (IP) Version 6

One of the critical topics associated with today's VPN implementations has to do with IPv4 vs. IPv6. A quick look at the history of the Internet Protocol (IP) will be helpful first.

The Internet has driven the development of the TCP/IP protocol suite, and the two remain tightly coupled. TCP/IP has always been at the root of the Internet; today you are using TCP/IP in your corporate network because of the success of both the Internet and the TCP/IP protocol. In the early days of computing, multiple protocols ran on corporate networks, and you had to worry about how to tunnel other protocols across the VPN. Today, most networks run TCP/IP exclusively.

The TCP/IP Protocol Suite

> **TIP**
>
> IANA—The assignment of both IPv4 and IPv6 addresses is the domain of suborganizations of a global organization called the Internet Assigned Numbers Authority (IANA). To find out more about IANA, go to *www.iana.org*. In the U.S., the suborganization is ARIN (the American Registry for Internet Numbers)—*www.arin.net*.

The TCP/IP suite comprises a large number of protocols, defined in a series of RFCs. Each of the protocols in the TCP/IP suite provides a different function, and together they provide the functionality known as TCP/IP.

The TCP/IP protocol suite got its name from the two main protocols in the suite: TCP (Transmission Control Protocol) and IP (Internet Protocol). TCP is responsible for providing reliable transmissions from one system to another, and IP is responsible for addressing and route selection. IP defines how computers communicate over a network. IP version 4 (IPv4), the currently prevalent version (defined at *http://tools.ietf.org/html/rfc791*), contains just over four billion unique IP addresses. IPv6 offers a newer numbering system that provides a much larger address pool than IPv4, among other features.

IPv4 Challenges

The largest challenge with IPv4 is address exhaustion. While the IPv4 addressing has kept the Internet and corporate networks running since the early years of the Internet, the industry is running out of addresses. The judicious use of NAT has extended the life of IPv4 far beyond its expected lifespan, however currently less than 10 percent of total IPv4 address space remains. Organizations will soon need to start adopting IPv6 to support applications that require ongoing availability of contiguous IP addresses.

FIGURE 12-4
Comparison of IPv4 and IPv6 addresses.

10.200.19.4

IPv4 Address—Dotted Decimal Notation.
Address Space supports approximately 4.3 billion addresses.

4334:ab8:85a3:4:8a2e:277:7445:ae

IPv6 Address—Hexadecimal digits, colon separating notation.
Address Space supports approximately 340 trillion trillion trillion addresses.

IPv6

IPv6 is the next-generation IP version and has been designated as the successor to IPv4, the first implementation used in the Internet. The main driving force for the redesign of Internet Protocol is the foreseeable IPv4 address exhaustion. IPv6 was defined in December 1998 by the IETF with the publication RFC 2460. IPv6 is documented in several **requests for comment (RFCs)** starting from RFC 2460.

While IPv6 is a relatively mature protocol, having been defined in 1998, adoption has been very slow thus far. According to ARIN, users requested only 395 IPv6 address blocks during 2009.

Based on the latest statistics, Europe has been requesting the highest percentage of IPv6 addresses, at 45.9 percent in the past 18 months, followed by Asia Pacific at 33.2 percent and the United States trailing with just 20.4 percent of the requests.

Some benefits of IPv6 include:

- **Increased address space**—IPv6 supports 340 undecillion (3.40282E38) IP addresses for network devices.
- **More efficient routing**—The routing functionality of IPv6 has been enhanced.
- **Reduced management requirement**—more robust protocol requires less management. Original IPv4 required significant add-on management capabilities due to new requirements after introduction of the protocol.
- **Better Quality of Service (QoS) support for all types of applications**—Support for QoS is built into the protocol, whereas it was an add-on in IPv4.
- **Security**—IPv6 includes a native information security framework (IPSec) that provides for both data and control packets.
- **Plug and Play configuration with or without DHCP**—IPv6 permits hosts to automatically configure themselves when they connect to an IPv6 network by querying the local routers with a multicast message. If the routers are configured correctly, they will respond with the appropriate configuration information. If this mechanism is not appropriate for a specific environment or application, support is available for an IPv6 version of DHCP. It also supports static configurations.

Three mechanisms currently exist for the transition from IPv4 to IPv6. It's important to understand that when the IPv6 standard appeared, the expectation was that the two protocols would need to co-exist in the network for 20 to 30 years, allowing for a gradual transition period. Three of the proposed migration strategies are:

- **Dual-stack**—A transition solution where both IPv4 and IPv6 protocol stacks coexist in the same terminal or network equipment. This would allow the network to communicate using both protocols, but adds significant overhead to the network infrastructure.
- **Tunneling**—Allows two IPv6 hosts to create a tunnel for traffic between two IPv6 hosts through an IPv4 network, or vice-versa, as IPv4 starts to phase out. This could add significant configuration overhead.

- **Translation**—Enables an IPv4 host to talk to an IPv6 host. This solution will require additional development, as currently IPv6 does not include this capability.

IPSec and IPv6

IPSec is a mandatory component for IPv6, and is used to natively protect IPv6 data as it is sent over the network. The components of IPSec in IPv6 are not dramatically different from the IPSec that industry has been using since the 1990s. In IPv6, IPSec uses the AH authentication header and the ESP extension header.

The IPv6 IPSec is a set of Internet standards that uses cryptographic security services to provide the following:

- **Confidentiality**—IPSec traffic is encrypted and cannot be deciphered without the appropriate encryption key. This should be easier to use in conjunction with IPv6, since it's a native component of the protocol.
- **Data origin authentication**—Ipv6 IPSec uses a cryptographic checksum that incorporates a shared encryption key so that the receiver can verify that it was actually sent by the apparent sender. This prevents spoofing of transactions.
- **Data integrity**—The cryptographic checksum can also be used by the receiver to verify that the packet was not modified in transit.

You can find more information about IPv6 in RFC2460 at *http://tools.ietf.org/html/rfc2460*.

CHAPTER SUMMARY

You should now be familiar with the different VPN and related protocols and their uses, such as IPSec, Layer 2 Tunneling Protocol (L2TP), Secure Sockets Layer (SSL)/ Transport Layer Security (TLS) and SSH. You should also understand the advantages and disadvantages of hardware and software solutions, and be able to determine which solution would be appropriate in your environment.

You learned how some of the challenges associated with establishing performance and stability for VPNs can impact the performance and stability of your VPN.

You learned about the issues network address translation (NAT) can present when rolling out a VPN, as well as the impact of both client and VPN virtualization on your VPN.

You took a detailed look at Internet Protocol version 4 (IPv4) and Internet Protocol version 6 (IPv6), including challenges and benefits associated with the rapidly approaching migration to IPv6.

KEY CONCEPTS AND TERMS

Authentication Header (AH)
Encapsulating Security Payload (ESP)
Internet Engineering Task Force (IETF)
Internet Key Exchange (IKE)
Request for Comment (RFC)
Layer 2 Forwarding (L2F)
Layer 2 Tunneling Protocol (L2TP)
Point-to-Point Protocol (PPP)
Point-to-Point Tunneling Protocol (PPTP)
Secure Shell (SSH)

CHAPTER 12 ASSESSMENT

1. What are the two modes supported by IPSec? (Multiple answers are correct.)

A. Transition
B. Tunnel
C. Encrypted
D. Transport
E. Internally connected

2. All of the following are considered IPSec services (multiple answers may be correct) *except*:

A. Access Control
B. Encryption
C. NAT interoperability
D. Replay rejection
E. Support for AES encryption

3. The strongest encryption protocol currently supported by IPSec is ________.

4. The two different protocols commonly used for remote access VPN are ________ and ________.

5. Pick two advantages of using an IPSec-based VPN solution instead of an SSL-based solution. (Multiple answers are correct.)

A. Provides direct connection to the network.
B. Since IPSec works at Layer 3, it can support virtually all network applications.
C. Requires configuration of each application being accessed via the VPN.
D. Clientless solution.

6. A solution that permitted industry to extend the life of IPv4 addresses is ________.

7. Which of the following are benefits of using an SSL VPN? (Multiple answers may be correct.)

A. More costly
B. Less flexible
C. Support for NAT
D. Fewer firewall rules required
E. Used for secure logins

8. SSL VPNs are considered ________ because access is granted through SSL, which is supported by Web browsers on virtually all platforms.

9. Which of the following are areas that can impact the stability of your VPN? (Multiple answers may be correct.)

A. Number of users
B. VPN Configuration
C. Code Revision Level
D. Operating System
E. Encryption Level

10. Which of the following are types of Network Address Translation? (Multiple answers may be correct.)

A. On Demand
B. Dynamic
C. Secure
D. Static
E. Encrypted

11. The mechanism used by the IETF to document Internet standards is the ________.

12. Separating the physical devices from the logical devices is known as ________.

13. Which of the following are uses for the SSH protocol? (Multiple answers may be correct.)

A. Secure Remote Login
B. Secure File Transfers
C. Secure access to a Web site
D. Encrypting data on backup tapes
E. Creating a VPN connection

14. The L2TP protocol was created by the combination of these two protocols: ________ and ________.

15. When you need to securely connect to a router for remote login, ________ would be the recommended protocol.

16. Which of the following are protocols that can be used for a VPN connection? (Multiple answers may be correct.)

A. IPSec
B. 3DES
C. SSH
D. IETF
E. SSL

17. When working with IPSec in an environment using network address translation, which protocols and ports need to be open for IPSec to communicate? (Multiple answers may be correct.)

A. (IKE)—User Datagram Protocol (UDP) port 500
B. Internet Key Exchange—UDP port 500
C. Encapsulating Security Payload—IP port 50
D. Secure Sockets Layer—TCP port 443
F. Authentication Header—IP protocol number 51

18. When designing a VPN solution, which of the following areas could impact VPN performance? (Multiple answers may be correct.)

A. Available bandwidth
B. Client configuration
C. Client patch level
D. Traffic
E. Topology

19. Which of the following are benefits of IPv6? (Multiple answers may be correct.)

A. IPSec is defined as a native protocol.
B. Support for SSL included in the standard.
C. Ability to address a limit of 4.3 billion hosts
D. Plug and Play configuration with or without DHCP
E. Define how to respond to incidents.

20. The ability to traverse a firewall using Network Address Translation on port 443 is a component of which VPN protocol ________?

PART THREE

Implementation, Resources, and the Future

CHAPTER

13 Firewall Implementation

THE LOCAL AREA NETWORK (LAN) ADMINISTRATOR oversees all aspects of Internet and Web security administration. This chapter is for those professionals who don't have enough time to dig into the more technical aspects of Internet and Web security, but need reliable options for Internet protection. Here are practical instructions to get a firewall up and running at your organization.

Chapter 13 Topics

This chapter will cover the following topics:

- How to construct, configure, and manage a firewall
- What SmoothWall is
- How to examine your network and its security needs
- What the hardware requirements for SmoothWall are
- How to plan a firewall implementation with SmoothWall
- How to install a firewall with SmoothWall
- How to configure a firewall
- What the elements of firewall deployment are
- How to perform testing with SmoothWall
- How to troubleshoot a firewall with SmoothWall
- What some additional SmoothWall features are
- What firewall implementation best practices are

Chapter 13 Goals

Upon completion of this chapter, you will be able to:

- Install a host software firewall

Constructing, Configuring, and Managing a Firewall

Say you want to protect the small office/home office (SOHO) network of about 25 computers. Many firewall products are available for small businesses and those working from home. SOHO VPN hardware firewalls are often built on a secure virtual private network (VPN) connection to the company network to transfer e-mail and sensitive files. (For more information about VPNs and how a VPN connection works, see Chapter 14, Fundamentals of Network Security, Firewalls, and VPNs.)

In many cases the SOHO firewalls have additional features such as an antivirus tool, IP filtering, Web content filtering, router options (router/firewall combinations), intrusion detection, and DDoS/DOS attack detection. Some of the firewalls come with a Linux or Linux-like operating system and use ipchains to manage their filter rules.

A SOHO VPN hardware firewall is the best solution when you already have a working network and want to provide remote access. For example, you may already connect your personal computers within your office. If you want to open a new office in another location, you could connect both offices with a SOHO VPN firewall at each office. It will create a secure connection to transfer sensitive data (bank information, customer information, or company-related information) from one office to the other. Another example is a mobile worker such as a salesperson working in the field. The salesperson could use the VPN's secure connection to access company files and presentations or customer-related information directly from the company office, even when working in the field.

Recall that firewall allows you to restrict unauthorized access between the Internet and an internal network. It exists to block unauthorized connections and keep outside attackers from penetrating the internal network. It also prevents inside connections from reaching out to the Internet without authorization. By monitoring inside users, firewalls can prevent them from sending out to the Internet sensitive information, such as personally identifiable information or sensitive corporate data.

SmoothWall

You have many choices for firewall applications. This section discusses one possible choice: SmoothWall, which supports many different network types and is a practical solution for just about any organization. SmoothWall uses colors to differentiate networks. A *green* network interface card (NIC) is a private, trusted segment of the network, while an (optional) *orange* NIC is not trusted, but does share the Internet connection. A *red* interface is a connection to the Internet. This could be a conventional Ethernet adapter, a dial-up modem, **Integrated Services Digital Network (ISDN)**, or a USB **Asymmetrical Digital Subscriber Line (ADSL)** or a conventional Ethernet adapter. Figure 13.1 illustrates this scenario. A *purple* interface indicates a wireless connection.

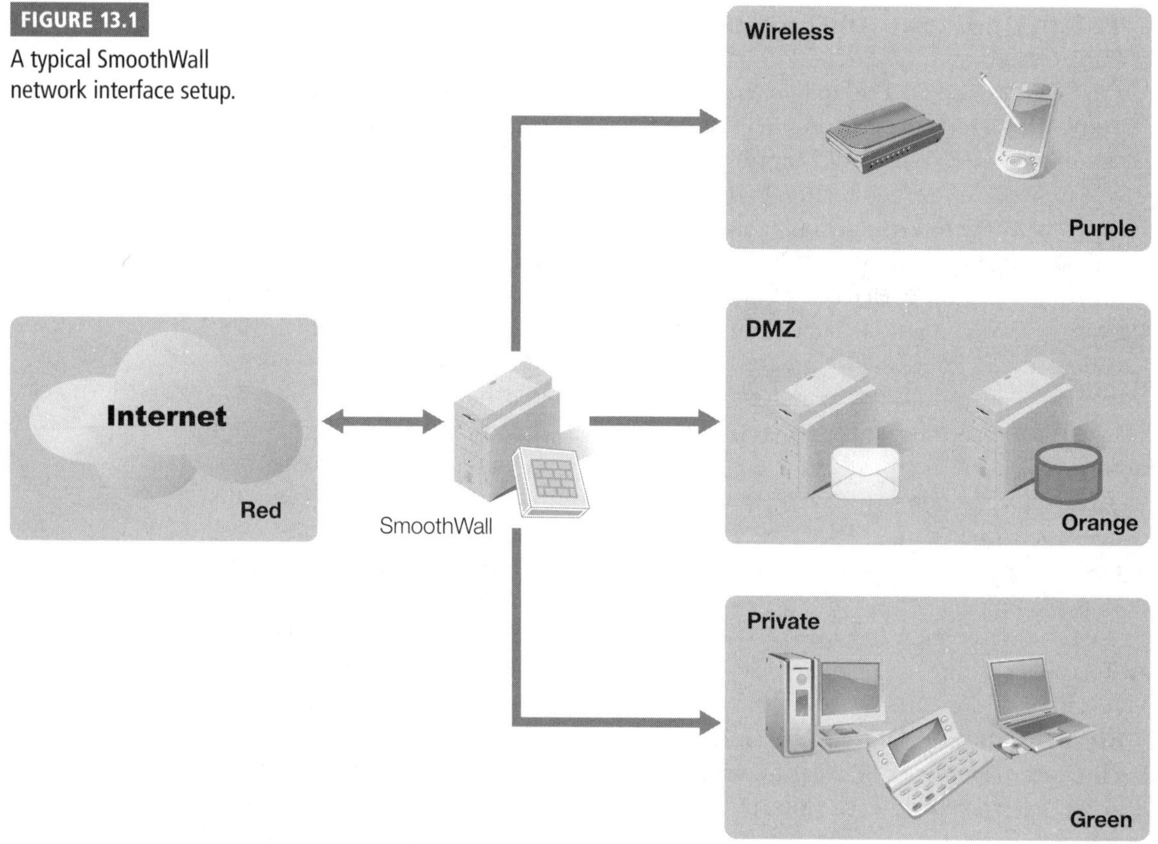

FIGURE 13.1
A typical SmoothWall network interface setup.

Key features of the SmoothWall firewall include:

- Compatible with wide range of hardware and systems
- Flexible and easy to use
- Multiple network zones—Client local network (green), demilitarized zone (DMZ) for hosting servers (orange), wireless client (purple), and external (red).
- Comprehensive reporting and logging capabilities
- POP3 e-mail antivirus proxy
- Web proxy support
- Snort IDS support
- Static and dynamic **Domain Name System (DNS)** support
- Remote access and VPN support
- DHCP and network time server support
- Powerful traffic graphs and bandwidth bars
- Inline proxy support for Instant Messaging (MSN, ICQ, Yahoo!, AOL) and VoIP with logging capabilities

- Universal plug 'n' play support (UPnP)
- Bandwidth management
- Real-time graphs and traffic stats per IP
- System update
- Outbound traffic blocking with time-based controls

Examining Your Network and Its Security Needs

According to the **National Security Agency (NSA)**, attacks to systems connected to the Internet are becoming more and more complex and more dangerous. For instance, hackers can penetrate computer systems using a variety of techniques to exploit weaknesses hidden in the complex code of many operating systems and applications.

> **NOTE**
>
> Tim Berners-Lee started the World Wide Web while at CERN (the European Laboratory for Particle Physics). The project sought to build a "distributed hypermedia system." The Web is a large collection of interconnected Web pages providing dynamic content documents, accessible throughout the world. Berners-Lee is still working on this project, now under the auspices of the W3 Consortium at MIT.

What to Protect and Why

Internet-facing servers are accessible to people anywhere in the world that have Internet access, and these servers are often targets of attacks. This includes Web servers, e-mail servers, File Transfer Protocol (FTP) servers, and more. If a server has a public IP address, it's a potential target for hacker attack. Firewalls provide protection for Internet-facing servers. Firewalls also provide protection for internal clients. They provide a layer of protection to limit the ability of attackers to exploit system weaknesses—both hardware and software.

Imagine an organization that sells products over the Internet and processes credit card transactions. Customers insist that the merchant protect their credit card data. To do this, organizations need to address two distinct security areas:

- **Network security**—Computers, hard disks, databases, and other computer equipment attached directly or indirectly to the Internet need protection. Firewalls serve an important role in this aspect of network security.
- **Transaction security**—Web servers must be able to securely complete private transactions with other entities in databases accessible on the Internet. Hypertext Transfer Protocol Secure (HTTPS) is an important tool used to encrypt the transactions. Additionally, firewalls provide protection for the data. For example, it's common for a Web server stand behind one firewall. The database server stands behind a second firewall that restricts access to the database to only the Web server. When the Web server stands between two firewalls like this, the area where the Web server operates is called a demilitarized zone (DMZ).

Network security and transaction security have four overlapping types of risk:

1. Risk that unauthorized individuals can breach the server's document tree. Depending on what data resides on the server, this threat can compromise the confidentiality of documents stored there.
2. Risk that transaction data can be intercepted. This threat can include personal data, financial data, or credit card information.
3. Risk that information about the server can be accessed. If attackers learn details about the server, such as type of server and its operating system, they may be able to identify and exploit its known vulnerabilities.
4. Risk of denial of service (DoS) attacks. Many different types of DoS attacks are possible. A simple SYN-flood attack withholds the third packet in the TCP three-way handshake, for example. Hundreds of these incomplete sessions in a short time can consume substantial resources on a server and even crash it.

If your organization conducts business on the Internet, you need to take steps to protect those transactions. E-commerce requires a zero tolerance for failure. Protection is not optional.

Protecting Information and Resources

An organization must protect against attackers trying to access information and resources within the internal network, such as servers and workstations. Servers can host massive amounts of data that's invaluable to attackers. Database servers may host personally identifiable information (PII) about customers including their credit card data. Domain Name System (DNS) servers host information such as the IP addresses and names of all systems in the network.

Protecting Clients and Users

Most organizations have a written security policy that outlines specific security requirements. A firewall can be useful in upholding the security policy by providing perimeter security. In other words, the firewall limits the risk of attack from hackers outside the internal network.

However, if you want to guarantee the security of an organization's network and protect its clients' and users' interests, you should do the following as well:

- **Treat private messages as confidential**—Private messages should be encrypted to ensure the message remains confidential. Encryption prevents the unauthorized disclosure of the private message.
- **Maintain integrity of information**—Integrity methods verify that data has not changed. For example, hashing is often used to verify integrity of messages. A hash is simply a number calculated using an algorithm on a message. No matter how many times you calculate the hash, it will always be the same as long as the data has not changed. The hash is calculated at the source and sent with the message. The hash is recalculated at the destination on the received message and compared with the hash sent with the message. If they're both the same, the integrity of the message is assured.

- **Use strong authentication and non-repudiation methods for all transactions**—Digital signatures commonly accompany both authentication and non-repudiation. For example, a sender can sign a message with a digital signature. The receiver can use this signature to verify the identity of the sender. In other words, the digital signature provides authentication. Additionally, since it was digitally signed, the sender can't later deny sending it. In other words, the digital signature also provides non-repudiation.

Preserving Privacy

It's more difficult to preserve a user's privacy on the Internet than in the physical world. Usually, you can close your door when seeking privacy or whisper something, so that others can't hear you. But the digital era has changed things. There's no such thing as whispering on the Internet.

When data is sent or received by a user surfing the Internet, that information can be intercepted and collected. Much of this data is stored in databases and can be made available for sale to others. Data mining methods are then used to help build customer preference profiles. From the perspective of an organization selling products, this data is valuable for identifying an individual's buying habits and targeting advertising. However, this data can be easily misused.

The **Electronic Privacy Information Center (EPIC)** was established in 1994, in Washington, DC. It's goal is to alert the public on emerging privacy issues relating to the **National Information Infrastructure (NII)**, such as the **Clipper Chip**, the Digital Telephony Proposal, medical record privacy, and the sale of consumer data. EPIC's mission is to preserve the right of privacy in the electronic age as well as to give individuals greater control over personal information, and to encourage the development of new technologies that protect privacy rights. EPIC can provide valuable information to IT Professionals on emerging cyber laws and other privacy threats.

TIP

If you want to know more about EPIC, you can check out its Web page at *http://epic.org/*

Preserving privacy on a corporate network may require more stringent security if you have users accessing resources from all over the world. While administrators have the responsibility for setting up security policies to guarantee users' privacy, each user accessing the company's network is responsible for browsing the Web with ethical regard for others. They also should be aware of information they may reveal while accessing resources from outside of the network. This will be discussed in Chapter 14, which focuses on VPNs.

Typically, most network servers (and Web servers) log all the hits they receive. This log usually includes the IP address and/or the host name. If the site uses any form of authentication, the server will also log the username. If the user filled out any form during the session, all the values of any variable from that form will be also recorded. Status of the request, size of data transmitted, user's e-mail address and so on can also be logged. Moreover, Web servers can make all this information available to **Common Gateway Interface (CGI)** scripts. Since the majority of the Web browsers are running on single-user PCs, very likely all the transactions can be attributed to the individual using the PC.

Revealing any of this information can harm the user. This is especially true if the user has logged any PII. Attackers can use PII for identity theft. Some PII may allow an attacker to access bank accounts or fraudulently charge credit cards. As a subtler example, if a user researches a job opening opportunity at a site, it may indicate that the user is searching for a new job. Browser lists, hotlists, and caches can also reveal certain patterns about the user.

A proxy server, for instance, will track every single connection outside the Web by IP address and the URL requested. If you install a proxy server within an organization, data needs to be protected so that only authorized individuals have access to it.

Firewall Design and Implementation Guidelines

When deciding to install a firewall, you should consider several basic decisions before going ahead with the project.

Before you start thinking about the type of firewall you want to use, where to install it, and how to deploy it, you should make sure you have a guideline in hand. You need a policy that will set the security standards for the network including the rules users and system administrators will follow, and the security strategy configuration you plan to deploy.

Many security policies have a special section just for the firewall, outlining how to configure and use it. For example, many organizations recognize that every service and protocol allowed through the firewall represents a risk. By blocking traffic that isn't needed to support the organization, these risks are eliminated. A simpler route is to just monitor the activity at the network and Web server, but it may subject the network to risks you can easily avoid.

Be prepared to face a situation where the final design of the firewall may involve political issues from upper management and other departments of the company. For example, the security policy may state that the Network News Transfer Protocol (NNTP) is not essential for the organization. You would then design the firewall to block all NNTP traffic. Even though it may not be essential, upper management may decide to allow the traffic.

Once you decide on the design, then you need to identify a firewall that can meet your needs. You'll need to consider several items including:

- **Suitability**—Can the firewall implement the policy?
- **Flexibility**—Is it easily reconfigurable?
- **Training**—Is training required and if so, what is the cost?
- **Need**—Make a list of traffic you want to allow, filter, or block. This is often derived from the organization's security policy.
- **Risk**—Make a separate list of all the risks in the network based on the traffic allowed.

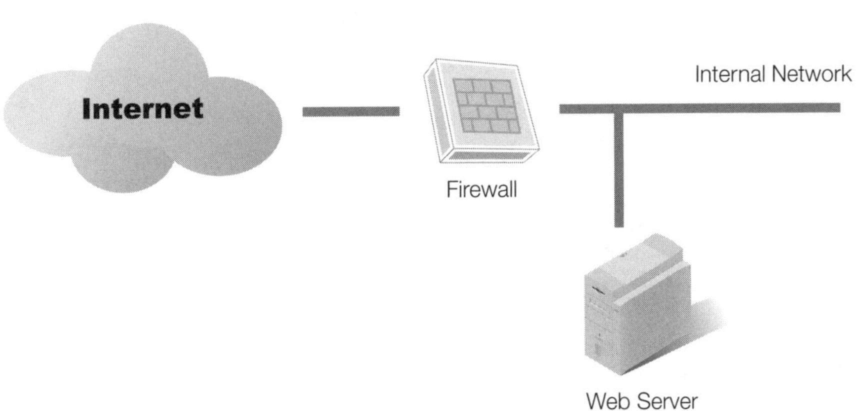

FIGURE 13.2
Simple firewall solution.

- **Cost**—Last, you need to add the two lists up and find out how much it will cost to provide everything. You then need to divide this result by available financial resources and you will have a clear picture of how much it will cost to implement your ideal firewall system. The result may even point out the likely type of firewall you must purchase. Many times, you'll find you need to re-evaluate your needs so that the plan is more realistic, from both the security and financial perspectives.

You can recommend a firewall solution that costs almost nothing or a solution that may cost hundreds of thousands of dollars. You need to balance the security needs with the resources within your organization.

On the technical side, you need to decide how you to configure the firewall and what strategy you'll use. Figure 13-2 shows a simple firewall solution with one network firewall and all resources placed behind it.

This method is generally not recommended for organizations that host Internet-facing servers such as e-mail servers or Web servers. These servers can go behind this single firewall and you can configure the firewall to direct Internet traffic to the servers using port forwarding. However, this exposes the internal network to potential threats from the Internet. If you instead put your Internet-facing servers directly on the Internet, you expose them to threats of attack from anywhere in the world.

An alternative for organizations that have Internet-facing servers is to use a perimeter network. Figure 13.3 shows one example. The firewall has three connections: one to the Internet, one to the internal network, and one to the perimeter network. This is also known as a bastion host.

In this solution, the firewall will direct traffic destined for the Internet-facing servers to the servers on the perimeter network. Unrequested traffic from the Internet will be blocked from entering the internal network.

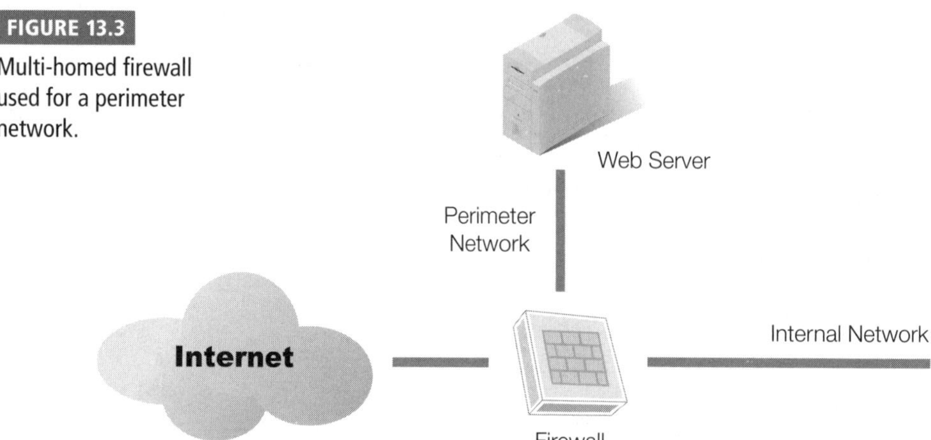

FIGURE 13.3

Multi-homed firewall used for a perimeter network.

The third solution uses two firewalls to create a DMZ as shown in Figure 13.4. This provides several benefits. The two firewalls provide an additional layer of security for the internal network. If the Web server accesses a database, the database server can go in the internal server for better protection. Internet users won't be able to access the database server directly.

Many organizations use two different brands for their different firewalls. If a flaw or vulnerability appears in one, it's unlikely the second firewall will be vulnerable at the same time. Additionally, an attacker may be an expert on one brand of firewall, but it's less likely that the attacker has the same level of expertise for two separate brands.

Remember, though, you need to balance the needs of the organization with the security requirements. While it's a true a DMZ provides more protection than a single firewall, it also costs more.

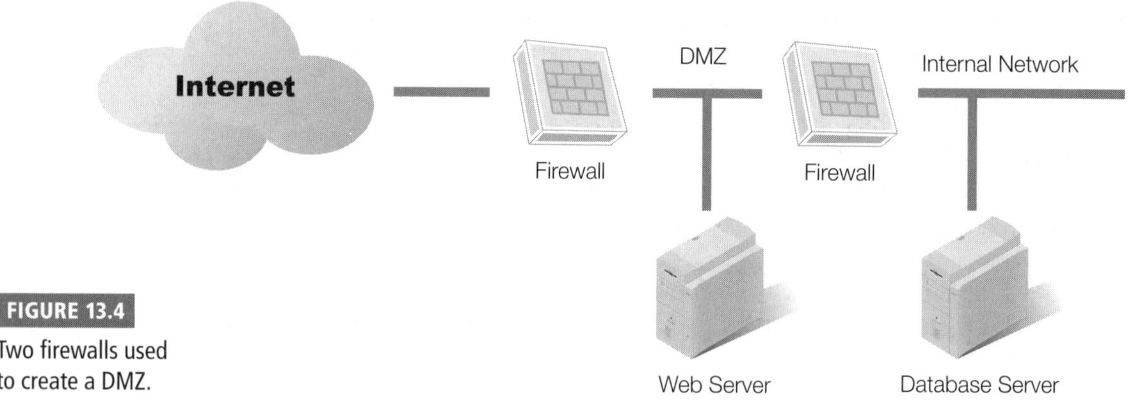

FIGURE 13.4

Two firewalls used to create a DMZ.

Selecting a Firewall

Before you select a firewall, you should make sure that your organization has created a written security policy. You would then select the firewall that can fulfill and comply with the policy. When evaluating firewalls, take the time to evaluate the levels of security they provide. Quite simply, some are better than others, and a high cost doesn't necessarily mean high quality.

The basic concept of any firewall is the same, so you should evaluate a firewall based on the level of security and features it offers. First and foremost, the firewall should be able to fulfill and comply with your security policy. Some other characteristics to consider are:

- **Security Assurance**—Independent assurance that the relevant firewall technology meets its specifications.
- **Privilege Control**—The degree to which the product can impose user access restrictions.
- **Authentication**—The ability to authenticate clients and allow different types of access control for different users.
- **Audit Capabilities**—The ability to monitor network traffic, generate logs, and provide statistical reports. Logs may include both authorized traffic and unauthorized attempts and may be able to trigger alarms in response to certain events.

When considering the features, consider the product's ability to meet the needs of the organization. A good firewall product should provide:

- **Flexibility**—The firewall should be open enough to accommodate the security policy of your organization, as well as allow for changes. Security policies can change, and security procedures should also be able to change and adapt to different needs.
- **Performance**—A firewall should be fast enough that users don't notice the screening of packets. The volume of data throughput and transmission speed associated with the product should be reasonable and consistent with the organization's network bandwidth to the Internet.
- **Scalability**—Firewalls should be able to handle additional workload. The additional workload can be due to growth within the organization or due to increased use of the Internet connection.

When considering integrated features, consider the ability of the firewall to meet your network and users' needs. This includes:

- **Ease of use**—The firewall product should ideally have a Graphical User Interface (GUI), which simplifies the job of installing, configuring, and managing it.
- **Customer support**—Vendors that sell firewalls provide support for them. This includes providing prompt access to technical expertise for installation, use, and maintenance. It also includes training.

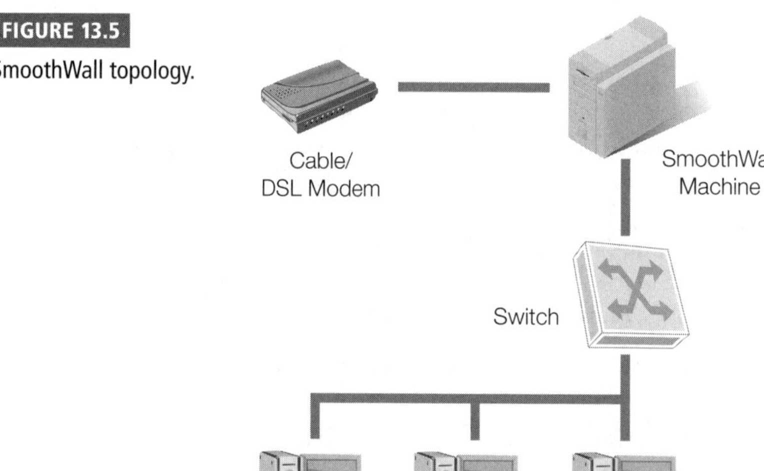

FIGURE 13.5
SmoothWall topology.

Hardware Requirements for SmoothWall

As mentioned previously, one of the main advantages of SmoothWall is that it will run on a variety of hardware. It's recommended you use a machine that is 166 MHz or faster. In any case, you will need at least two network cards (NICs) in your SmoothWall machine, as firewalls traverse two or more network connections. You may or may not need a crossover cable as well. The Dell Powerconnect 2650 switch performs auto-sensing, so there is no need to use a crossover cable. This is common with many switches today. Figure 13.5 depicts the topology of SmoothWall.

The minimum requirements for a computer running SmoothWall are:

- Processor running 166 MHZ or greater
- 512 MB PC133 **synchronous dynamic random access memory (SDRAM)**
- 20 GB Hard Drive
- Two NICs

Planning a Firewall Implementation with SmoothWall

As a software appliance, SmoothWall will convert a computer server or PC into a dedicated hardware security appliance, running the security-hardened Linux operating system and all other necessary software. When planning a firewall, you should use standard hardware, typically from major manufacturers such Dell, HP, or IBM, which will provide you with considerable benefits including:

- **Flexibility**—You can easily add RAID, redundant power supplies, additional RAM, and a range of network interface cards.
- **Performance and value for the money**—The average desktop PC will have many times the processing power and memory complement of most mid-range hardware firewall appliances. Office PCs have become a commodity, offering exceptional value for the money.
- **Support**—The major PC manufacturers can support their products virtually anywhere in the world, including rapid, on-site repair or replacement if the customer requires. Alternatively, in most major cities, several computer support companies also support such hardware. In contrast, the support available for smaller manufacturers' equipment is often limited to repairs done after you've had to ship the machine back to the factory.

What kind of firewall is right for an organization? Truthfully, no single correct and definite answer exists. A security policy developed by a Fortune 500 company certainly will not be suitable for a small business owner.

The following are brief fictitious scenarios, to illustrate different firewall designs to meet different needs.

Firewalling a Big Organization: Application-Level Firewall and Package Filtering, a Hybrid System

Employees at Other People's Money, Inc. (OPM) access the Internet on a daily basis for a wide variety of different business purposes. Additionally, they host a Web server that has a high volume of access from OPM customers. Finally, mobile workers use a VPN server to access internal resources.

OPM might decide a DMZ with two application-level firewalls (see Chapter 14, Fundamentals of Network Security, Firewalls, and VPNs) and packet filtering adequate for its needs. The Web server and VPN server would go in the DMZ so that they are accessible from the Internet, but the internal network has additional layers of protection.

Firewalling a Small Organization: Packet Filtering or Application-Level Firewall, a Proxy Implementation

Imagine a smaller organization that requires Internet access by employees, but doesn't host a Web server or a VPN server. All users in the organization require access to the Internet, and they need a layer of protection against Internet-based attacks.

A proxy server or a firewall such as SmoothWall would be enough. All users could access the Internet through the SmoothWall firewall, and it would provide protection against external attacks. While SmoothWall was the example examined in depth in this chapter, many other products can provide the same level of service for a small organization.

Firewalling in a Subnet Architecture

Imagine a larger organization with multiple subnets. They may want to limit specific types of traffic within subnets. For example, they may want to ensure that traffic within a specific subnet is encrypted with IPSec. Additionally, they may want to allow NNTP traffic on one subnet, but not on others.

You can configure routers to provide basic packet filtering. In other words, they can block or allow traffic based on IP addresses, ports such as port 119 for NNTP, and some protocols such as ICMP or IPSec.

If the organization wants to protect subnets within the network, basic packet filtering provided by routers might be the most appropriate choice. This model supports each type of client and service within the internal network. No hardware or software modifications or special client software would be necessary. The access through the routers used as packet-filtering firewalls is transparent for both the user and the applications. The existing routers can handle the packet filtering. This solution doesn't require the purchase of a host or firewall product. Buying an expensive UNIX host or firewall product would be unnecessary.

Installing a Firewall with SmoothWall

The installation of SmoothWall is easy. As long as you ensure you have the computer BIOS set to boot from a CD, the installation process will begin automatically.

SmoothWall Express runs on a workstation with a bootable CD-ROM drive. After booting, it will automatically check the workstation and hardware components.

 **WARNING**

During the installation process SmoothWall will delete all data you may have on your hard disk. So, before you start the installation, ensure that all valuable data is safely backed up.

The common interfaces on the installation screen of SmoothWall are listed below:

- **Red**—Internet. This interface is protected by the `iptables` firewall rules.
- **Orange**—Filtered/Special Purpose. This is commonly used for a DMZ or other special section you want to allocate.
- **Green**—Trusted network. All traffic is permitted to and from this interface.

Note the green + red configuration. The green interface card connects to the internal network and the red interface to the external network. If you have a different setup or hardware, please use the appropriate configuration.

At this point, you should read the information that appears on the following screen and hit the enter key on your keyboard.

At this point you should see the screen alerting you that your hard drive will be prepared for installing the firewall.

If you have two of the same NICs, you may want to pay attention to the Media Access Control (MAC) addresses so you know which cable to connect to the modem and which one goes to your switch. If your red interface connects to an ISP, ensure you configure it based on the requirements of the ISP. For example, some ISPs will assign manual IP addresses, while others use DHCP. When DHCP is used, all the Transmission Control Protocol/Internet Protocol (TCP/IP) configuration information such as DNS, gateway, and IP address happens automatically.

The green interface should have a static IP (such as 192.168.0.1) to connect to the internal network. Once you have the interfaces setup correctly, it's time to reboot the computer. Also, it's very important that you power-cycle the modem. Often ISPs will assign a different IP when the MAC address of the device attached to the modem changes.

> **TIP**
> An excellent Web site is available that will walk you step by step through SmoothWall installation. Just check *http://www.linux-tip.net/cms/content/view/316/26/*

When configuring the NICs for the green and red interfaces, you can use static IP addresses for both interfaces.

Now you will need to set up the DNS and Default Gateway accordingly.

Now enter the SmoothWall admin password. You will need it for logging into the Web interface later. Then, setup the root password.

At this point the setup of SmoothWall is now complete and your network should be protected. You should see a screen showing that the installation is complete. Now, remove the CD and restart SmoothWall.

Configuring a Firewall with SmoothWall

Once you have finished installing SmoothWall, you will have to configure the firewall via a Web browser. The interface is clean and well laid out, and works well with Mozilla Firefox, Google Chrome, and Microsoft Internet Explorer. Once you reboot the computer, you can access it via a browser from a Web interface (usually *https://192.168.0.1:441*) to start configuring the firewall. SmoothWall Express version 2.0 added the ability to use HTTPS. You can also access it using port 81. Without logging in, you should be able to see part of the management menu, the version, and load averages.

Since the install connected the red interface to the Internet, your first access of the home page should lead you to the following message: "There are updates available for your system. Please go to the 'Updates' section for more information." You will find the Updates menu item under Maintenance.

At this point, if you want to verify or change anything, you must log in. During the configuration process you were asked to specify some passwords. To log in to the Web interface, you must use "admin" as the user name and the password you specified. Logging in as "root" will work only over Secure Shell (SSH) or from the console. You cannot log in as "root" using the Web interface.

For most scenarios, the out-of-the-box SmoothWall installation should work without any additional configuration. But additional customization can bring out the real power of SmoothWall features. The Services tab allows you to monitor each advanced feature, including time, remote access, intrusion detection, dynamic DNS updates, and proxy services. Some services such as SSH access services are not started by default. Interestingly, ICMP is configured to reply to both external and internal `ping` requests, making the firewall susceptible to DoS attacks.

The Networking tab exposes the interface settings, IP address blocking, timed access, and traffic rules. Incoming and outgoing rules are easy to create and maintain. You can view the status of the system at all times with various options. Configuration and resources appear in text form. You can also view a summary screen of all the services running on the SmoothWall system (computer).

In the quality of service (QoS) configuration section, you can use drop-down boxes to select upload and download connection speeds and enable the service. The QoS engine prioritizes different types of traffic to make the connection speed seem faster. The settings are combo boxes, which makes them understandable even to non-technical users. By default, instant messaging traffic is set to low priority, VPN traffic to normal, and gaming traffic to high.

Elements of Firewall Deployment

At this point, you should start thinking about deploying the firewall and think about the services you want it to run. You should pay special attention to the services tab. You have the ability to run:

- Web Cache/Proxy (SQUID)
- DHCP Server
- DDNS (for dynamic IPs)
- Intrusion Detection System (Snort)
- Secure Shell (Open SSH)

To enable the Web proxy, you must select it by checking the box. The Web proxy information needs to be changed.

The "Transparent" option simply means that every client on the network will be forced to connect through the proxy server. Browser settings will not need to be changed, and the clients will not even know they are using the proxy. You should change the cache size from 50 to 5000 MB. You shouldn't change the other options, as caching objects too large or too small can create problems.

One of the great features of SmoothWall is the ability to view network usage. You can view graphs of network traffic generated by **Round-Robin Database Tool (RRDtool)** every five minutes.

You can also view the logs of Web usage through the proxy. You can even dig further by filtering the log by IP. This way, you can see all the Web sites visited by a certain IP (or user).

Performing Testing with SmoothWall

To test SmoothWall's ability to mitigate attacks, you can enable Snort intrusion detection software and run a few attacks against the firewall over the red interface. For example, you can use NMap, the Metasploit framework, and some other port scanning and attacking tools. In all cases, the firewall should be able to deal with them. The Snort and firewall logs should identify most types of attacks, the IP address of the attacker, and the time and date of the attack. SmoothWall's IP lookup feature can determine and report the origin of an attacker.

Once SmoothWall is up and running, the next step is to test its ability to access Internet resources. You should first ensure you can access the Internet from the SmoothWall box. To do this, run the following command: `ping www.google.com`

> **TIP**
> ICMP may be blocked by the host you ping. If the ping fails, consider pinging another host that you know will respond.

If you get a successful reply, it means your host can access the Internet.

Now, if you have an internal client configured, try to ping one by running the command, substituting the actual IP address of an internal client. An example would be `Ping 172.16.0.1`.

You can also test a client's ability to traverse the firewall. Start a Web browser on a client system and enter the IP address of the SmoothWall router. For example, if the IP address for the green NIC on the SmoothWall machine is 172.16.1.95, then you would enter *http://172.16.1.95* in the location bar of the browser. You should be able to see the SmoothWall startup screen. If you see the screen, then the firewall is up and running. Next, try to access any Web site to confirm that you can surf the Internet. If you encounter problems accessing the Internet, try checking the following:

- Check the TCP/IP settings on the SmoothWall host. Make sure all of the addresses and subnet masks are correct.
- Make sure the NIC accessing your ISP (red) is the correct card. Some ISPs will provide access only when the MAC address on the NIC is correct.
- Check the TCP/IP settings on the client computer.

Firewall Troubleshooting

Sometimes, right after installing SmoothWall, you may have problems being able to SSH into the system. This is typically because port 22 is not open. In this case, you should make sure that SSH is enabled and that port 22 or 222 is open. This enables you to tunnel different SSH connections at the same time.

One small disadvantage with using SmoothWall from the console is that some traditional Linux tools are modified. For example, some shell commands such as `whereis` and `locate` are not included, which can make it a little hard to find items. Also, `config` files are stored in non-traditional Linux locations, and partitions are not named according to standards. For instance, the `snort.conf` file is stored in `/etc` and the `squid.conf` file is stored in `/var/SmoothWall/proxy`.

If you are still having trouble with the networking aspect of the firewall during the configuration process, you still have access to traditional tools such as `ping`, **`traceroute`**, and **`tcpdump`**. They are all useful in determining what your network problem may be. Another factor to watch for is the crossover cable. Some networking devices require a crossover cable when they are connected together, while others have auto-sensing capabilities and will automatically switch to crossover mode even when you're using a regular cable. The cable from your green interface may or may not need to be a crossover cable.

While SmoothWall does not natively contain an FTP server, you can still transfer files to and from the system via SCP/SFTP. To do so, you simply need to connect to port 22 or 222 with a client such as WinSCP3, which is nearly the same as using another FTP client.

Additional SmoothWall Features

SmoothWall is a versatile product that gives power to network security administrators, allowing them to decide how to control their networks by making it easy to do so. The Web-based GUI is clean, easy to read, and provides a wealth of information about the status of a network's traffic and security.

The Web-based interface is organized into broad areas with tabs that allow navigation for specific features. You can run SmoothWall as a proxy server, or a DHCP server, or forward ports to machines in the green zone, and more. You can even set up advanced proxy server features such as per-user authentication or delay pools. Larger organizations may want to use a dedicated proxy server to get these functions, however.

You can configure the address range, WINS server, and static hosts for the DHCP server. You can specify dynamic DNS, offer remote access for SHH, and synchronize with a Network Time Protocol server. SmoothWall also lets you enable Snort, a popular open-source intrusion detection system.

Some of the network settings you can control include:

- **Port forwarding**—This allows you to forward a port from the firewall to a machine inside the green or orange zones. You can use this feature to hide your Web servers behind a single IP address.
- **External service access**—You can access any services running on the SmoothWall machine by opening the ports you need.
- **DMZ pinholes**—As the name implies, this allows you to open a pinhole from the DMZ to the green zone. This is useful if your external servers need to communicate with servers inside the green zone. For example, your Web server may need to communicate with a database server inside the green zone.
- **PPP settings**—You can set up various profiles, configure up to four modems, and use dial on demand.
- **IP block**—You can ban specific IP addresses or ranges here.

Firewall Implementation Best Practices

You must keep the firewall and your protected network logically secure. Sound security logic should be the starting point in putting together a security policy that will use secure systems such as **Kerberos**, IPSec, and many others. The requirements to run a secure firewall, such as SmoothWall, also include a series of "good habits" that administrators should cultivate. It's a good policy to try to keep the strategies simple, so that the system is easier to maintain.

Most bastion hosts and firewall applications, have the capability to generate traffic logs. You can record user-browsing patterns on these servers, this may include information about the users, their connections, their address, or even specifications about their organization. These logs usually include:

- The IP address
- The server/host name
- The time of the access
- The user's name (if known by user authentication or, with UNIX, obtained by the `identd` protocol)
- The URL requested
- The data variables submitted through forms users usually fill out during their session
- The status of the request
- The size of the data transmitted

CHAPTER SUMMARY

Firewalls provide protection to servers and workstations from Internet threats. They can be configured to allow only specific traffic based on what an organization wants to allow. Organizations typically define what traffic is acceptable in a comprehensive, written security policy. IT professionals then identify a firewall solution that can fulfill and comply with the policy within the established budget.

SmoothWall Express is an Internet firewall that can protect an organization's network. This chapter demonstrated how to configure and use a firewall such as SmoothWall using a Web-based GUI. SmoothWall is an open-source firewall, requiring no knowledge of Linux to install or use. SmoothWall purposely to turns any typical PC into a network appliance whose sole function is to route network traffic to and from the Internet, assign IP addresses, and protect the private side of the network from intrusion.

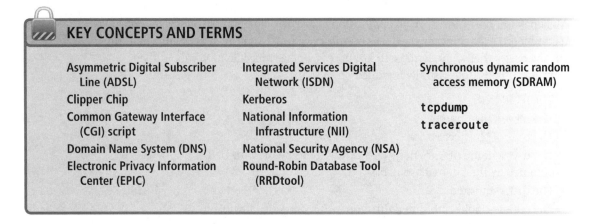

KEY CONCEPTS AND TERMS

Asymmetric Digital Subscriber Line (ADSL)
Clipper Chip
Common Gateway Interface (CGI) script
Domain Name System (DNS)
Electronic Privacy Information Center (EPIC)
Integrated Services Digital Network (ISDN)
Kerberos
National Information Infrastructure (NII)
National Security Agency (NSA)
Round-Robin Database Tool (RRDtool)
Synchronous dynamic random access memory (SDRAM)
`tcpdump`
`traceroute`

CHAPTER 13 ASSESSMENT

1. The following are all key features of SmoothWall, *except*:

A. POP3
B. Static and dynamic DNS support
C. Cybercash support
D. Snort IDS support
E. DHCP and Network time server support

2. According to the ________ ________ ________, attacks to systems connected to the Internet are becoming more and more complex.

A. National Systems Agency
B. National Security Agency
C. Central Intelligence Agency
D. Navy Security Agency
E. Federal Bureau of Investigation

3. Firewalling involves two distinct areas that must be protected:

A. Network and transaction security
B. Access and controls
C. File sharing and printing capabilities
D. Access to the Internet and from the Internet
E. None of the above

4. The ________ was created to alert the public on the emerging privacy issues relating to the National Information Infrastructure.

A. EDIP
B. EPIC
C. NII
D. CERN
E. W3C

5. The following are characteristics we should be looking for in a firewall, *except*:

A. Security Assurance
B. Privilege Control
C. Digital Switches
D. Authentication
E. Audit Capabilities

6. A good firewall product should provide:

A. Flexibility
B. Performance
C. Scalability
D. All the above
E. A and C

7. The following are all characteristics of SmoothWall firewall, *except*:

A. It is a simple Linux kernel
B. It cannot use iptables to control and route traffic
C. It is built to run as a dedicated firewall/router
D. It provides a way to gain extra capability with NAT
E. It runs on a variety of hardware

8. The following are all common interfaces used by SmoothWall, *except*:

A. green: Trusted network
B. blue: DMZ connection
C. red: Internet
D. orange: Filtered/Special Purpose

9. The following are attributes of a minimum hardware specification to run SmoothWall, *except*:

A. 512 MB PC133 SDRAM
B. 20 GB hard drive
C. 10/100 on-board NIC
D. AMD Duron 1100
E. Flat LCD screen

10. To install SmoothWall, you need to make sure the computer BIOS is set to boot from a CD. True or False? ________

11. In a typical SmoothWall firewall installation the green interface should have:

A. A static IP
B. Software bugs but not flaws
C. Dynamic addressing
D. Proxy servers connected to it
E. Internal code connecting to an external service

12. When configuring the NICs for the green interface, it is advisable to use ________.

A. capacity planning
B. maximum utilization
C. a static IP address
D. wirespeed settings
E. factory defaults

13. Which of the following is not related to SmoothWall offered services?

A. Web Cache/Proxy
B. Fingerprint authentication
C. DHCP Server
D. DDNS
E. Intrusion Detection System

14. What does the "Transparent" option means when configuring Web proxying in SmoothWall?

A. It allows you to create a tunnel mode
B. Every client on the network will be forced to connect through the proxy server
C. Every client on the network will be waived access to the network
D. The proxy server is on stealth mode
E. Collisions on the network are not seen

15. SmoothWall does not work well with Mozilla Firefox and Google Chrome. True or False?

16. The following are services found in the service tab of SmoothWall, *except*:

A. SQUID
B. Web Cache/Proxy
C. DDNS
D. Diskcopy
E. SSH

17. The following are tools we can use when troubleshooting a firewall installation, *except*:

A. `ping`
B. `traceroute`
C. `robocopy`
D. `ipconfig`
E. `tcpdump`

CHAPTER

14 Real-World VPNs

VIRTUAL PRIVATE NETWORKS (VPN) are a key technology and component in today's computer security environment. Recall that the Internet is open to virtually any user, while an intranet is open only to individuals within your organization. A third kind of network is the extranet. Extranets lie somewhere between the Internet and an intranet.

Companies use extranets to connect with suppliers and customers, two constituencies that are essential to business processes. Extranets usually use VPN technology to ensure confidentiality and integrity of information. VPNs are becoming an increasingly important component of any successful business's information technology plan. VPNs can substantially enhance the technological architecture of any organization's network through the use of efficient collaborative and flexible technology.

In this chapter, you'll learn how to do a complete VPN installation at your organization, from operating systems and VPN appliances to remote desktops.

Chapter 14 Topics

This chapter will cover the following topics and concepts:

- What operating system-based VPNs are
- What VPN appliances are
- What a remote desktop protocol is
- How to use remote control tools
- How to perform remote access
- What terminal services are
- What Microsoft DirectAccess is

- What DMZ, extranet, and intranet VPN solutions are
- What Internet café VPNs are
- What the online remote VPN options are
- What the Tor application is
- How to plan a VPN implementation
- What VPN implementation best practices are

Chapter 14 Goals

Upon completion of this chapter, you will be able to:

- Create a remote control VPN using Remote Desktop
- Evaluate hardware VPN devices
- Experiment with TOR
- Set up an Internet café VPN client
- Assess online remote control products, such as GoToMyPC and LogMeIn
- Configure an IPSec VPN

Operating System-Based VPNs

An operating system-based VPN is very convenient because you can refer to remote servers by their assigned Internet Protocol (IP) addresses, not by network-address-translated ("NATted") IP addresses. This avoids problems inherent in connecting to servers behind a many-to-one NAT configuration. You can choose from several ways to install a VPN using computers running commercial operating systems. You can configure a VPN connection from a client computer using a variety of operating systems, including Windows XP, Vista®, Windows 7, Linux, and Unix.

A VPN, as discussed earlier in this book, is a hardware and software solution for remote workers, providing users with a data-encrypted gateway through a firewall and into a corporate network. VPNs were once practical only for large businesses, but today, most businesses—large and small—can afford the technology, and VPNs are becoming increasingly popular in the small- to midsized business market. VPNs are ideal for companies with telecommuters, satellite offices, or employees who travel and need to connect to the corporate network via the Internet. If used properly, VPNs block hackers attempting to access your network to steal sensitive data. They can also save your organization a lot of money on long-distance phone calls.

As a data-encrypted tunnel over the Internet, a VPN can offer a robust and secure Internet connection for your organization. It can also be a cheap alternative to a dedicated phone line. Some solutions for small companies start as low as $200. How can you know if your organization needs a VPN? That depends on some key factors you should consider before deciding to use a VPN:

- Does your organization traffic in sensitive data? For most businesses, the answer is probably "yes." Most companies have customer information and records, financial records, and proprietary information in their internal networks that merit protection. On the other hand, if your organization stores its sensitive data offline or you don't have anything online of interest to hackers, perhaps your organization doesn't need to invest in a VPN.
- Does your organization employ telecommuters, traveling employees, or other remote workers? If so, a VPN can provide two main advantages: It can offer secure network access to employees away from the office, traveling or working off-site, and it can extend the corporate network to them, enabling them to remain productive outside your office.
- Does your company already use Secure Sockets Layer (SSL)—encrypted Internet pages? Some companies using Microsoft Exchange servers for e-mail, for example, may already have the encryption protection necessary for remote workers—at least for accessing their e-mail (via Outlook Web Access). In this case, the VPN is a built-in feature of the operating system. Businesses without sensitive information can use operating system-based VPNs and Web-based alternatives to a VPN for authentication and encryption, though these may be less secure.
- Does your organization have more than a few employees? A VPN may be an expensive solution for a company with fewer than five employees, so some alternatives might work better for such an environment.

Suppose you've considered these issues and concluded that your organization does need a VPN. In this case, here are six further important factors to consider:

- Consider the difference between a VPN based on **Customer Premise Equipment (CPE)** and one based on an operating system. A CPE solution represents the majority of VPNs on the market and is commonly referred to as a VPN appliance. This solution is easy to set up, manage, and maintain. Windows Server 2008 Network Access is an example of an operating system-based VPN. If you have a server running Windows Server 2008, you can install the Network Policy and Access Services role and configure the server as a VPN server. This requires some expertise with Windows Server 2008 and can be a little more challenging than a CPE solution. However, the operating system–based VPN can be cheaper and easier to manage than a CPE.

- Should you install the VPN yourself or use a managed service? Any competent IT staff can probably install leading commercial products from vendors such as Cisco or SonicWall. While the DIY approach provides more control over setup and usage, installing a VPN incorrectly can inadvertently open a security hole in your organization's network. In addition, the administration and management of a VPN in-house can sometimes be complicated. Telecommunications companies such as Qwest, Verizon, and BellSouth, as well as several Internet service providers, offer managed security solutions that can save you time and money.
- Do you have a firewall? As you learned in Chapter 13, a VPN cannot replace a firewall. Some administrators tend to use a VPN instead of a firewall, which is not a smart choice. The purposes of a VPN are to create an encrypted tunnel or gateway through your network's firewall and to keep out hackers. The VPN encrypts the pieces of data, but the firewall still protects the internal network from outside threats. A VPN without a firewall doesn't make good security sense.
- Do you have an operating system-based VPN? Regardless of the strategy you end up using, make sure you have an IPSec (Internet Protocol Security)–compliant operating system. IPSec is a VPN-supporting technology included in Windows XP, Vista®, Windows 7, Windows Server 2008, and Windows Server 2008 R2. Used with compatible VPNs, IPSec guarantees the authenticity, integrity, and confidentiality of network traffic. Interoperability with a VPN may be an issue with Macintosh systems or some variants of UNIX or Linux. If you decided to buy a VPN, make sure it is compatible with your operating system.
- Does you have a wireless local area network (LAN)? The VPN should operate securely with it. A VPN can enhance the capabilities of a wireless LAN, but improperly "layering" a VPN on a wireless network can result in security holes. One method places the wireless LAN outside the firewall, hosting the VPN behind the firewall to ensure security. Otherwise, wireless network traffic can access systems behind the firewall, canceling the benefits of the VPN. Many organizations use layered firewalls so that the wireless network is protected from the outside while restricting access to the inside. In essence, the LAN operates in what is called a demilitarized zone (DMZ).
- Can your organization tolerate a potential decrease in network performance? A VPN may cause a performance lag for internal users accessing the Internet. This happens when 10 to 15 percent of the Internet bandwidth serves as security overhead. While VPNs are great for setting up a secure connection, they can take a measurable toll on connection speed. The tradeoff is that VPNs are worthwhile investments for providing a secure connection for remote and traveling workers.

VPN Usage in Organizations

VPNs serve an organizations computer network in two primary ways. They give remote users access to internal networks or they connect two separate offices. These are the host-to-gateway model and the gateway-to-gateway model:

- **Host-to-gateway VPN**—The mobile user takes specific actions to connect to the VPN. For example, the mobile user would first connect to the Internet from a remote location outside the organization. Once connected to the Internet, the user could then initiate the VPN to tunnel through the Internet. The VPN appliance or server then acts as a gateway for the user to access resources on the internal network.
- **Gateway-to-gateway VPN**—This is used to connect two offices in different locations. For example, an organization could have a main office in Virginia Beach and a remote office in Miami. VPN appliances or servers can operate in both locations with an always-on VPN connection between them. Now users in Miami can connect to resources in Virginia Beach using this gateway-to-gateway model. In this model, users in the remote office don't need to take any additional steps to connect. The gateway-to-gateway model is also called a site-to-site model.

VPN Appliances

One of the easiest and most cost-effective ways to provide secure access to a network is to purchase an inexpensive VPN appliance and set it up, which will take about an hour of your time. VPN appliances can make secure remote access easy.

When considering the purchase of a VPN appliance, ensure that you have the required complementary hardware in place. First, the VPN appliance must have access to the Internet. Remote users will use the public IP address assigned to the appliance to connect to it. Second, the VPN server must have access to the internal network. It will use internal routing to connect remote users from the Internet to the internal network. Of course, resources in the internal network must be on and available for the VPN users to access them.

Not long ago, VPN appliances were expensive and required client licenses for each computer in addition to the appliance itself. VPN technology was too expensive for all but the largest companies. But new products made it possible to install a VPN appliance on virtually any size network for budget-minded organizations SMBs and small offices/home offices (SOHOs). For example, Buffalo Technology's 125 High-Speed Mode Wireless Secure Remote Gateway is a VPN Gateway/Firewall router and a wireless access point rolled into one neat package. Another great product is the Linksys WRV54 Wireless-G VPN Broadband Router, a similar product that provides robust protection for your network.

You should know that some VPN appliance products on the market are designed for home installations. While these products are very easy to install, they allow only a very limited number of accounts and some of them provide relatively slow access.

Configuring a Typical VPN Appliance

Most VPN appliances are designed for simple and quick installations, with plenty of wizards and automated setup that makes it easy even for non-computer-savvy people. All you typically need to do is to plug the appliance into your network between your ISP provider's connection and your internal network. If your network does not have a router or hub, this device can serve that purpose as well. Once you turn on the VPN appliance, you can use any computer on the network to login to a Web page, complete your configuration, and add user access accounts.

While VPN appliances are a secure technology, you need to take basic security measures to preserve the security of your network and remote connections. When you are configuring user account access on the VPN gateway system, for instance, always change the default settings and never use the default passwords. Also, you should give each VPN user an individual access account. In practice, that means if an employee leaves the company, you don't have to change the access passwords for everyone—you just turn off the associated account.

Client-Side Configuration

Once you have configured your appliance, you will need to configure the software on the computers (clients) connected to the network. The systems designed for small installations assume that you will use Microsoft or Macintosh VPN client software. Some variants of Linux and UNIX may have built-in client VPN software.

Adding a VPN appliance to your office network gives you a remote access solution that lets you and your staff be more productive from anywhere in the world—not a bad return on a few hundred dollars and an hour of your time.

Remote Desktop Protocol

Remote Desktop Protocol (RDP) is a proprietary protocol developed by Microsoft, which provides a user with a graphical interface to another computer. The protocol is an extension of the ITU-T T.128 application sharing protocol. Clients exist for most versions of Microsoft Windows, Windows Mobile, Linux, UNIX, Mac OS X and other modern operating systems. By default RDP uses TCP port 3389.

Remote Desktop Connection (RDC) is a built-in application that uses RDP. When RDC is enabled, you can connect to another computer, log on, and perform almost any action as if you are sitting in front of the remote computer. You can do this from a desktop PC to another desktop PC, using the same operating system. In large organizations, administrators commonly use this to remotely manage servers from their desktop PCs.

> **NOTE**
> Microsoft changed the name of Terminal Services to Remote Desktop Services in Windows Server 2008 R2. However, the MSTSC command still works. It's also worth noting that Terminal Services and Remote Desktop Services have much broader usage than just connecting to remote desktops. For example, you can use these services when a Microsoft server is configured as VPN server.

RDC must be enabled on the remote computer. In most Windows operating systems, you do this by right-clicking over Computer in Windows Explorer or from the Start menu, and selecting Properties. You'll then change the Remote settings to allow Remote Desktop connections. This also opens port 3389 on the remote computer. If the connection goes through a firewall, port 3389 must also be open on the firewall. You can launch RDC differently in different Windows operating systems. However, one method that works in all current Windows versions is to enter `MSTSC` from the command line. The initials represent MicroSoft Terminal Services Connection.

The client can run other operating systems, such as Mac OS, Linux, or UNIX, as long as the terminal services protocol is supported. When connecting to Windows Server 2008, Windows Vista, or newer systems, you'll need to weaken security to support the non-Microsoft clients.

GoToMyPC is another remote desktop technology that allows you to remotely access your computer from any other Internet-connected computer in the world with almost any operating system through a secure, private connection. The application is ideal for organizations that need remote desktop access for up to 20 computers. It's an easy and secure remote-access solution that enables you to conveniently access e-mail, files, programs, and network resources from home or the road.

Using Remote Control Tools

As companies continue to expand their networks and increasingly use remote offices and telecommuting, they need the ability to manage devices from virtually any location.

Microsoft has offered a built-in Remote Control solution called Remote Assistance for modern operating systems since Windows XP. It allows help desk professionals or other IT administrators to remotely control a user's system, while the user is watching.

For example, a user may not know how to configure an application. The user calls the help desk for assistance. Instead of trying to talk the user through the steps, the help desk pro can show the user how to do it. The help desk pro can use remote assistance to take control of the user's desktop. While connected, the helper will have control of the user's desktop as long as the user allows it. The user is able to disconnect the helper at any time.

While the built-in Remote Assistance is great as a free tool, it doesn't meet the needs of every organization. Several third-party tools are available that can provide additional features. For example, Symantec offers pcAnywhere as a solution for organizations to access and securely manage remote computers.

pcAnywhere supports multiple platforms for both host and remote systems, including Windows (including Vista® and Windows Server 2008), Linux, and Mac. Systems can also be securely accessed from Windows Mobile/Pocket PC devices and Web browsers. The application allows organizations to easily connect to servers and endpoint devices.

Some of the main features of pcAnywhere include:

- Feature-rich, secure, reliable remote control solution
- Compatibility with heterogeneous host and remote platform support across Windows, Linux, and Mac OS X. All hosts can also be accessed from Microsoft Pocket PC devices or Web browsers
- Supports 64-bit environments
- Gateway option enables real-time discovery of and connection to multiple devices behind firewalls and NAT devices, which mitigates private and dynamic IP

Performing Remote Access

VPNs allow remote users to connect to a private network over a public network. The private network is the organization's internal network. The public network is often the Internet, but it's also possible for an organization to use leased lines from a telecommunications company to create the VPN connection.

Remote users can be:

- Salespeople on the road
- Field technicians
- Consultants working in customer work sites
- Anyone that needs to have access to internal company resources while away

Since data transmits over a public network, you need to protect it. VPNs use tunneling protocols to establish secure connections. These tunneling protocols include different types of encryption to protect the data.

The Technology for Remote Use

Several protocols support VPNs. These include:

- **Point-to-point (PPTP) tunneling protocol**—This protocol supports Microsoft's remote access servers and has known issues. It uses Microsoft Point-to-Point Encryption (MPPE). While PPTP is still used for some remote access solutions, IPSec and SSL-based solutions are replacing it.
- **Layer 2 Tunneling Protocol (L2TP)**—Cisco and Microsoft collaborated to create this by combining strengths from Cisco's Layer 2 Forwarding (L2F) protocol and Microsoft's PPTP. It uses IPSec for encryption. A significant weakness is that IPSec can't go through a Network Address Translation (NAT) server, since NAT breaks IPSec. For a period of time, you had to either bypass NAT or use older PPTP or L2F protocols.
- **Secure Sockets Layer (SSL)–based tunneling protocols**—Due to the limitations of IPSec with NAT, newer tunneling protocols use SSL for encryption. For example, Microsoft can use Secure Socket Tunneling Protocol (SSTP). Cisco and other vendor VPN appliances can also has SSL-based tunneling protocols. SSL requires Public Key Infrastructure (PKI) support to obtain and use a certificate.

- **Internet Key Exchange v2 (IKEv2)**—IKEv2 is an IPSec based VPN protocol that uses NAT-Traversal (NAT-T). NAT-T allows IPSec traffic to pass through a NAT server. IKEv2 provides significant improvements over IKE and has been adopted by several companies such as Microsoft, in Windows Server 2008 R2; Cisco; and OpenSwan. OpenSwan is a Linux-based solution presented later in this chapter. IKEv2 requires Public Key Infrastructure (PKI) support to obtain and use a certificate.

Each method has its advantages based on the access requirements of your users and your organization's IT processes. While many solutions only offer either IPSec or SSL, some vendors, such as Microsoft and Cisco, offer multiple technologies integrated on a single platform with unified management. Offering both IPSec and SSL technologies can enable organizations to customize their remote-access VPN without any additional hardware or management complexity.

SSL-based VPNs also enable remote-access connectivity from almost any Internet-enabled location using a Web browser and its native SSL encryption. It does not require any special-purpose client software to be pre-installed on the system. This makes remote access SSL VPNs capable of "anywhere" connectivity from company-managed desktops and non-company-managed desktops, such as employees' PCs, contractor or business partner desktops, and Internet kiosks. Any software required for application access across the SSL VPN connection is dynamically downloaded on an as-needed basis, thereby minimizing desktop software maintenance.

IPSec-based VPNs are the deployment-proven remote-access technology used by most organizations today. IPSec VPN connections use pre-installed VPN client software on the user desktop, thus focusing it primarily on company-managed desktops. IPSec-based remote access also offers versatility and customizability through modification of the VPN client software. Using APIs in IPSec client software, organizations can control the appearance and function of the VPN client for use in applications such as unattended kiosks, integration with other desktop applications, and other special use cases.

Both IPSec and SSL VPN technologies offer access to virtually any network application or resource. SSL VPNs offer additional features such as easy connectivity from non-company-managed desktops, little or no desktop software maintenance, and user-customized Web portals upon login.

Choosing Between IPSec and SSL Remote Access VPNs

Both IPSec and SSL can provide the level of security needed for a VPN. The primary drawback with IPSec is that it can't traverse a NAT server. If you are deploying a VPN server and want the connection to go through a NAT server, SSL is sound solution.

While it is possible to use NAT-Traversal (NAT-T) to allow IPSec traffic to pass through a NAT server, be aware of some issues with it. For example, Microsoft has specifically recommended that NAT-T not be used, though IT professionals still recommend NAT-T with non-Microsoft hosts.

Terminal Services

Terminal Services is a built-in Microsoft Server product with multiple uses. It works in two modes—Terminal Services for Administration and Terminal Services for Applications. Other vendors also use terminal services for remote applications.

Terminal Services for Administration allows administrators to remote into servers from their desktop computers. It allows them to remotely administer the server as described in the Remote Desktop section earlier in this chapter.

Terminal Services for Applications is the focus of this section. It allows a single server to host one or more applications for remote users. For example, a legacy application may not run on Windows 7. A Terminal Services server could be configured to host the application and multiple Windows 7 clients could then connect to the server to run the application. Each client would run a separate instance of the application in a separate memory space.

It's also possible for a Terminal Services server to host entire desktops. For example, older computers may be running Windows 2000 and they don't have the hardware to support Windows 7. An organization can configure a Terminal Services server to host Windows 7 desktops for these clients. The users would start the Windows 2000 computer, connect to the Terminal Services server, and then run a Windows 7 desktop.

As mentioned earlier, Microsoft renamed Terminal Services to Remote Desktop Services when it released Windows Server 2008 R2. Windows Server 2008 R2 increased the capabilities and features, but supports the older capabilities and features.

Over the past few years, many software publishers have experimented with offering hosted services. The basic idea behind hosted services architecture is that an organization does not have to purchase licenses for software applications or have the hassles of installing or maintaining those applications. Instead, an ISP or a software vendor leases the applications to the organization. The application actually runs on the service provider's servers, and users interact with the application over the Internet.

Nonetheless, this arrangement has some other drawbacks as well. For instance, terminal services take an application's configuration out of an organization's direct control. It's not uncommon to hear about network administrators who were put out of a job because the companies that they work for decided to outsource all of their applications to a hosting provider. Another compelling argument against the use of hosted services has to do with service availability. If your Internet connection goes down, then nobody can access the hosted applications. Of course Internet service is more reliable in some areas than others.

Terminal services for hosted applications has many benefits. The primary one is that the service provider takes care of all of the application maintenance for you. Many of these benefits are things that you just don't get if you install the applications locally on each individual workstation or if you outsource your applications to a hosting provider. Microsoft products can provide hosted applications using TS RemoteApp and TS Web Access.

TS RemoteApp

One of the challenges with running applications on remote servers is that it looks odd to users and they have trouble adapting. TS RemoteApp is a Microsoft solution that runs on a Microsoft Terminal Services server but appears, to end users, as if it were actually running on their systems.

They don't need to open a Terminal Services session, but instead launch the application from their Start menu or a shortcut on their computer. The application appears in a window on the users' computers just as if it's running on the local computer.

TS Web Access

An extension of TS RemoteApp is TS Web Access. This allows TS RemoteApp applications to launch from a Web browser. This provides many possible benefits.

The TS RemoteApp applications can intertwine into Web pages and appear to launch from a Web server. In other words, the clients use a Web browser to access a Web site. From within this Web site, they can then click on a link for the TS RemoteApp application. TS WebAccess can be configured in an internal intranet or accessible to users from the Internet.

Notice that TS Web Access allows remote clients to connect to internal resources without the need for a VPN. Depending on what your remote clients need, this is a suitable substitute.

Microsoft DirectAccess

DirectAccess is a newer Microsoft solution that can be used as an alternative to a traditional Internet Engineering Task Force (IETF) VPN. It allows remote clients to connect to internal servers without initiating a VPN connection. As long as a client has Internet connectivity, they will be able to access internal resources using DirectAccess.

Microsoft introduced DirectAccess in Windows 7 and Server 2008 R2 products. Once it's configured on the clients and servers, it is relatively invisible to the clients. Client computers connect to the DirectAccess computer, which acts as a gateway to internal resources. Only resources configured to be accessible with DirectAccess can be accessed from clients. In other words, you could have 10 servers in the internal network, but choose to make only a few of them accessible.

For example, you could configure a Microsoft Exchange server (used for e-mail) with DirectAccess. When a DirectAccess enabled Windows 7 client connects to the Internet, it would automatically connect with a DirectAccess server. When the user starts Microsoft Outlook, DirectAccess automatically makes the connection to the internal Microsoft Exchange server. In other words, users can be on the road and still use their e-mail client just as if they are in the office. The same process works for any servers that an administrator wants to make accessible on the Internet. DirectAccess can be enhanced by combining it with Forefront Unified Access Gateway (UAG). UAG gives administrators more control over the connections and enhances security. When UAG is run, a UAG server acts as the gateway between the client and the internal network. This is similar to how DirectAccess works by itself in that clients don't need to establish a separate VPN connection.

A significant added benefit of DirectAccess is that administrators can execute control over the remote clients. For example, in a Microsoft environment, Group Policy can ensure that a system has minimum-security settings. While this is normally not possible for systems that are disconnected from the internal network, DirectAccess with UAG allows an administrator to apply Group Policy to these remote computers.

It's also possible to use Network Access Protocol with DirectAccess. You can create policies to ensure that the remote system has other security measures in place. For example, you can ensure that the system is up-to-date with current security updates and that it has up-to-date antivirus software installed and enabled.

DMZ, Extranet, and Intranet VPN Solutions

A demilitarized zone (DMZ) is a physical or logical sub-network that contains and exposes an organization's external services to a larger untrusted network, usually the Internet. The purpose of a DMZ is to add an additional layer of security to an organization's LAN. An external attacker can gain access to equipment in the DMZ, but not parts of the network behind the firewall.

For example, public-facing servers that need to be accessible from the Internet are placed in the DMZ. This could include Web servers, e-mail servers, FTP servers, and more. Organizations that employ VPN servers for remote users often place them in the DMZ.

In a network, the hosts most vulnerable to attack are those that provide services such as e-mail, Web, and FTP servers to users outside of the local area network. Because of the increased potential of these hosts being compromised, they are placed into their own subnetwork to protect the rest of the network if an intruder were to succeed.

Hosts in the DMZ have limited connectivity to specific hosts in the internal network, though communication with other hosts in the DMZ and to the external network is allowed. For example, a Web server in the DMZ may be able to connect to a database server in the internal network, but not to any other hosts in the internal network. This allows hosts in the DMZ to provide services to both the internal and external network, while an intervening firewall controls the traffic between the DMZ servers and the internal network clients.

Intranet VPNs

An intranet is an internal network. While users within the intranet can access the Internet using different resources such as a proxy server, access to the internal network is severely restricted. Since traffic in the intranet is primarily from internal clients, the intranet is a trusted zone and needs fewer security measures.

An intranet VPN is a VPN that connects two or more internal networks. Earlier in this chapter, you learned about the concept of gateway-to-gateway VPNs. A gateway-to-gateway VPN provides connectivity between two locations such as a main office and a branch office. This is also known as an intranet VPN.

It's important to realize that even though the VPN may be called an intranet VPN, it will still have to traverse a wide area network (WAN) link. Most organizations will rent access to this WAN link and it's very rare that a company has exclusive access to it. In other words, the WAN link will be accessible to users outside the organization. The same level of security measures used in a DMZ VPN should also secure an intranet VPN.

Extranet VPNs

Extranet VPNs link customers, suppliers, partners, or communities of interest to a corporate intranet over a shared infrastructure. For example, an organization may hire a consulting company to look at different processes within the organization and provide recommendations to improve them. The organization could create an extranet VPN to allow the consultants access to some internal resources.

Extranets are commonly configured to connect via the Internet, but can use leased lines or even dedicated connections. Extranets differ from intranets in that they allow access to remote users outside of the enterprise.

Figure 14.1 illustrates an extranet VPN topology. Using digital certificates, clients establish a secure tunnel over the Internet to the enterprise. A certification authority (CA)

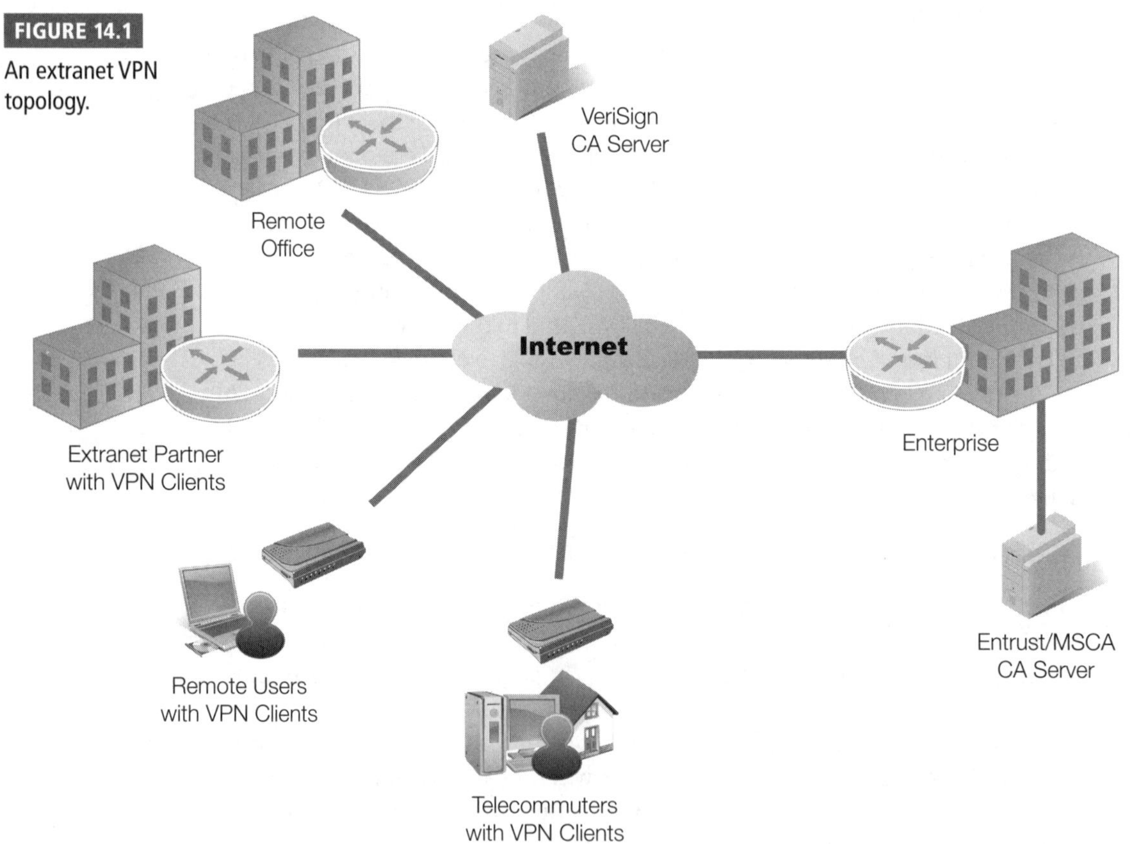

FIGURE 14.1
An extranet VPN topology.

issues a digital certificate to each client for device authentication. The CA server checks the identity of remote users and then authorizes remote users to access information relevant to their functions.

Internet Café VPNs

An Internet café is a public location that sells Internet access, often by the minute. The café will often sell typical café items such as coffee and sandwiches. However, with the explosion of wireless in recent years, many eateries provide free wireless Internet access to bring in customers. For example, many Starbucks and McDonald's locations provide free WiFi.

The challenge when using an Internet café or even an open wireless connection at an eatery is security. Others in the local area may be able to view data in the connection unless it's encrypted. Since the majority of Internet traffic is not encrypted, attackers may be able to gain valuable information by capturing another user's Internet use.

The owner of the Internet café can capture any data that passes through with a free packet sniffer such as Wireshark. Additionally, many free wireless sniffers are available that an attacker can use over a shared wireless connection to capture all of the traffic.

An alternative is to use an Internet café VPN connection. As soon as you connect with the Internet café or the wireless connection, you would connect to the Internet café VPN. This would be hosted at your organization. It will encrypt all the traffic and prevent any sniffing attacks.

For example, HotSpotVPN is a product your organization can purchase to and use as an Internet café VPN connection. Once you set it up, you can direct your users to connect to it for all Internet access.

> **NOTE**
> You can get more details about HotSpotVPN at *http://www.hotspotvpn.com/overview/*.

Online Remote VPN Options

GoToMyPC, LogMeIn and NTRconnect are remote access and control solutions, which all perform extremely well. Each product is easy to set up, easy to use, and all offer a similar set of features. While each product is similar, you should know about a few noteworthy differences.

Security

While each technology handles security slightly differently, all are extremely secure and can be safely used in any environment. LogMeIn and NTRconnect do offer a few more features than GoToMyPC. Both LogMeIn and NTRconnect provide 256-bit end-to-end encryption—GoToMyPC, on the other hand, provides only 128-bit. For example, LogMeIn and NTRconnect allow you to restrict the times that your computer can be remotely accessed and specify the IP addresses from which it can be remotely accessed—functionality which is not offered by GoToMyPC. Also, NTRconnect is the only product to provide keycard security. If you feel that you need to limit remote access times and/or restrict access to only certain IPs, then you will want to consider either LogMeIn or NTRconnect.

Wake-on-LAN Support

Wake-on-LAN is an extremely valuable feature. Most computers include power management capabilities allowing them to turn off, or go to a low power state when they aren't being used for a time. These computers can then be awakened up when they are sent a specific string of bits in a "magic packet." When the computer receives the magic packet, it wakes up. If it was off, it will turn on. If it was in a lower power state, it will go to a full-power state.

Of the products mentioned, only NTRconnect enables you to remotely start your computer. To use GoToMyPC or LogMeIn, the remote computer must be switched on. If you work away from your home or office computer for extended periods and switch off your computer while away, you'll probably find NTRconnect's wake-on-LAN support to be a real benefit.

File Sharing

LogMeIn provides file-sharing functionality that enables you to e-mail a link to a file on your computer that the recipient can use to download the file (directly from your computer) at any time. To share files in this manner, you do not need to invite the person to share your desktop and you do not need to be at your computer at the time he or she downloads the file. This feature is especially useful if you frequently need to share files that are too big to e-mail.

This feature is not available with GoToMyPC or NTRconnect.

Remote Printing

GoToMyPC and LogMeIn enable you to easily print a document on the host using the printer attached to the client. However, NTRconnect does not support this feature. NTRconnect's lack of support for remote printing is not too much of a problem as you can easily copy a document from the host to the client (and then print it). That said, if remote printing is something that you need to do on a regular basis, you'll probably prefer the convenience of GoToMyPC or LogMeIn.

Mac Support

With all three products, you can use a Mac as the client, but only NTRconnect enables you to use a Mac as the host. So, if you need to be able to remotely access a Mac, NTRconnect is your only choice.

The Tor Application

Tor is an application that uses onion routing. Generically, onion routing was designed as an architecture to limit a network's vulnerability to eavesdropping and traffic analysis. It uses multiple proxy servers or relays to provide anonymous connections. Each proxy server knows only the details from the previous proxy server or the next proxy server.

The proxy servers provide anonymity for users by requesting access to resources and making it appear as if the proxy server is requesting the access, not the original user.

FYI

Data leakage is also a common problem with peer-to-peer (P2P) networks such as BitTorrent. Users share data they didn't intend to. As an example, the Top Secret plans for the U.S. president's helicopter were leaked through a P2P network and found on servers in Iran. Some people think that organizations forbid these types of application to prevent piracy of copyrighted material. However, the primary reason is due to the inherent security risks that most people simply don't understand. Of course, there's nothing wrong with helping prevent the theft of copyrighted material in the process.

Tor was derived from the Onion Routing Project managed by the U.S. Naval Research Lab. However, Tor is not an acronym for The Onion Routing project. Instead, it is simply a brand name—similar to Kleenex for facial tissues. The *torproject.org* Web site still uses an onion as a logo; however, Tor is not all upper case.

The goal of Tor is to allow users to browse the Internet anonymously. Instead of going directly to an Internet site, Tor uses the computers of other Tor users as relays or proxies. Any single Tor connection will go through multiple other computers.

Interestingly, even though the U.S. Naval Research Lab originally designed Tor, it's forbidden on most government systems. The primary reason is related to data leakage. While the Tor network does provide a level of anonymity, the user never knows what other computers the request will go through. Data sent and received can be captured by any of these computers.

For example, in 2007 Dan Egerstad, a security professional in Sweden, collected usernames and passwords for 100 e-mail accounts of users at different embassies. He simply installed Tor on his system and then captured all the data that went through it. His computer was used as a proxy in the Tor network for thousands of users and a simple protocol analyzer captured the data. More than the credentials, he also captured a significant number of sensitive e-mail messages from embassies and Fortune 500 companies.

Planning a VPN Implementation

VPNs create a secure data link with a branch office, remote employee, business partner, or customer that will enable or require server access behind a firewall. VPNs can provide a secure and encrypted data stream between a firewall and a remote client or server.

This section provides you with the configuration of a permanent site-to-site VPN tunnel using Openswan, one of the most popular VPN packages for Linux.

NOTE

You can download the Openswan RPM package at *www.openswan.org*. The RPM package has an extension of `.rpm` (from the original Red-hat Package Manager) standard used by many Linux distributions today. Be aware that to download the RPM version of Openswan you must have the IPSec-tools RPM package installed on your system.

> **NOTE**
> In this implementation, the external IP of the machine is listed as 12.34.56.78. The gateway IP is listed as 12.34.56.1. The internal IP of the VPN server (since it has a NIC on both the inside and the outside) is 192.168.1.1 in this example. You can change it to fit your needs.

Requirements

For this implementation you will need:

- Linux Kernel 2.0, 2.2, 2.4 or 2.6 based
    - For Linux 2.0 or 2.2, use Openswan 1.0.10
    - For Linux Kernels 2.4 and 2.6, use Openswan 2.4.x
    - For FreeBSD, OpenBSD, NetBSD, and OSX, use Openswan 2.5.x

Before you attempt this simple SOHO Linux VPN, keep the following in mind:

- The IPSec protocol on which VPNs are based will not tolerate its data packets being network address translated. If your firewall does NAT, then you'll have to disable it specifically for the packets that will traverse the VPN.
- You should set up your Linux VPN box also as a firewall. Configure and test the firewall first, as you did in Chapter 13, then configure the VPN.
- The networks at both ends of the VPN tunnel must use different IP address ranges. For example, the organization's internal network may be using an IP address range of 192.168.0.1 to 192.168.0.254. The other network must use a different address range such as 192.168.1.1 through 192.168.1.254. To avoid confusion, you may want to use completely different private address ranges for each network such as 172.16.y.z. or 10.x.y.z.
- Permanent site-to-site VPNs require firewalls at both ends that use staticIP addresses.

Figure 14-2 depicts an Openswan sample topology diagram of a VPN between two environments.

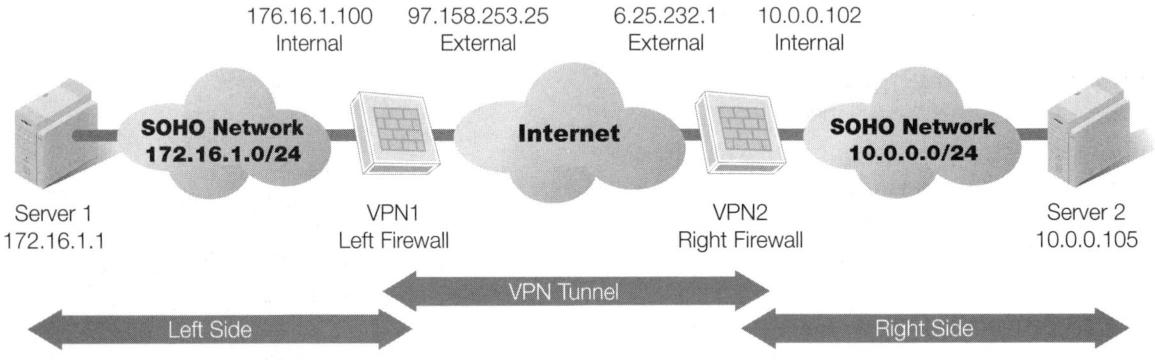

FIGURE 14.2

Openswan sample topology diagram.

```
su
mv openswan-2.#.#.tar.gz /usr/src
cd /usr/src
tar -xzf openswan-2.#.#.tar.gz
```

FIGURE 14.3
Installing Openswan from the source.

```
cd /usr/src/openswan-2.#.#
make programs
make install
```

FIGURE 14.4
Using Openswan's userland-only install.

Installation

You can install Openswan in two different ways: by performing a RPM install or by installing it from source libgmp development libraries.

Performing a RPM Install

You'll find different instructions for installing Openswan depending on what version of Unix/Linux you're using. Openswan hosts a Wiki site that includes instructions for many different types of RPM installations at *http://wiki.openswan.org/*. This site also includes a lot of other details on installing, configuring, and troubleshooting Openswan.

Install from the Source

As root, unpack your Openswan source somewhere in your drive, such as /usr/src. Figure 14.3 provides an example.

You now need to choose your install method. You can choose a userland-only, for 2.6 kernels, or a KLIPS install for kernels 2.6 or earlier (2.0, 2.2, and 2.4). If you decide to use the userland-only install, change your new Openswan directory, and then make and install Openswan's userland tools, as depicted in Figure 14.4.

NOTE
Kernel IP Security (KLIPS) modifies the Linux kernel to support IPSec protocols.

Once you finish entering these commands you should be done with the install. Now, all you need to do is to start Openswan and test your new install. If you decide to use KLIPS, you will have to make a modular of it, along with other Openswan programs you'll need for the VPN. To do so, enter the command sequence shown in Figure 14.5, which will change to your new Openswan directory, make the Openswan module, and install it all.

```
cd /usr/src/openswan-2.#.#
export KERNELSRC=/usr/src/kernels/linux-2.6.18/
make module
make module_install
```

FIGURE 14.5
Performing an Openswan's KLIPS install.

FIGURE 14.6

Link KLIPS statically into your kernel.

```
cd /usr/src/openswan-2.#.#
patch -p1 -s < openswan-2.4.7-klips.patch
patch -p1 -s < openswan-2.4.7-natt.patch
make oldconfig [answer Y to klips and nat-t options]
make dep [linux < 2.6 only]
make bzImage
```

FIGURE 14.7

Starting Openswan.

```
service ipsec start
```

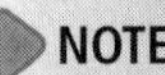

NOTE

For more information on installing NAT-T, check the Openswan Web site at *http://wiki.openswan.org/index.php/Openswan/NATTraversal*.

At this point, you can actually enhance the security of the VPN by using NAT Traversal (NAT-T) support. NAT-T is a method for encapsulating IPSec ESP packets into UDP packets for passing through routers or firewalls employing Network Address Translation (NAT). To deploy NAT-T you need to patch and rebuild your kernel. However, rebuilding the kernel is a risky operation so should be approached cautiously.

To link KLIPS statically into your kernel (using your old kernel settings), and install other Openswan components, just follow the commands listed on Figure 14.6, then reboot your system and test your install.

Start Openswan

To start Openswan enter the command as shown in Figure 14.7.

This step is not necessary if you have rebooted your system, as Openswan will launch automatically after it's been successfully installed.

You can take additional steps to secure the VPN connection. For example, you can use certificate-based keys to secure the connection. You can follow the steps in an excellent walk-through here: *http://www.linuxhomenetworking.com/wiki/index.php/Quick_HOWTO_:_Ch35_:_Configuring_Linux_VPNs.*

Deployment

Before you deploy your VPN, you need to start Openswan on both VPN devices, for the new /etc/ipsec.conf settings to take effect. You can do that by issuing the following commands:

```
[root@vpn2 tmp]# service ipsec restart
ipsec_setup: Stopping Openswan IPSec...
ipsec_setup: Starting Openswan IPSec U2.2.0/K2.6.8-1.521...
[root@vpn2 tmp]#
```

Once that's done, it's time now for you to initialize the tunnel. To initialize it you can use the `ipsec` command to start the tunnel net-to-net. Be sure to issue the command simultaneously on the VPN boxes at both ends of the tunnel. The "IPSec SA established" message highlighted in Figure 14.8 signifies a successful deployment.

```
[root@vpn2 tmp]# ipsec auto --up net-to-net
104 "net-to-net" #1: STATE_MAIN_I1: initiate
106 "net-to-net" #1: STATE_MAIN_I2: sent MI2, expecting MR2
108 "net-to-net" #1: STATE_MAIN_I3: sent MI3, expecting MR3
004 "net-to-net" #1: STATE_MAIN_I4: ISAKMP SA established
112 "net-to-net" #2: STATE_QUICK_I1: initiate
004 "net-to-net" #2: STATE_QUICK_I2: sent QI2, IPsec SA established
{ESP=>0xe0bdd0e9 <0x13ac7645}
[root@vpn2 tmp]#
```

FIGURE 14.8

Successfully deploying the Openswan VPN.

Testing and Troubleshooting

To check that you have a successfully installed VPN you should run the command `ipsec verify`. If your installation was successful you should see at least a screen display similar to the one depicted in Figure 14.9.

If any of these first four checks fails, check the section below titled "Troubleshooting."

At least a couple of things on your system can interfere with Openswan, so you should verify them:

- **Firewalls**—Make sure you allow UDP 500 and ESP (protocol 50) through the firewall. This is necessary because for IPSec traffic to traverse through a firewall you need the following ports/protocols open in both directions:
  - Protocol 50 ESP
  - Protocol 51 AH (Optional)
  - UDP port 500 IKE
  - UDP port 4500 (If you are using NAT-Traversal to tunnel through NAT/other Firewalls)

The Smoothwall firewall presented in Chapter 13 works well with OpenSwan. You will need:

- To create some name for the remote VPNs in the zones file
- To describe which IPSec interface to use based on the names in the zone file
- To describe how the networks named in the zones file interact in the policy file
- To define the public IP address of the remote sites in the tunnels file

Smoothwall automatically makes the rules necessary to allow IPSec for the networks named in the tunnels file.

NOTE

Another alternative for a firewall to work with Openswan is Shorewall. This firewall also works well with IPSec and Openswan. Best of all, you will find comprehensive documentation at their Web site at *http://www.shorewall.net.*


```
   Checking your system to see if IPsec got installed and started
correctly
   Version check and ipsec on-path                          [OK]
   Checking for KLIPS support in kernel                     [OK]
   Checking for RSA private key (/etc/ipsec.secrets)        [OK]
   Checking that ninigapa is running                        [OK]
```

FIGURE 14.9

Testing Openswan's install.

TABLE 14-1 VPN Implementation best practices.

	DO	DON'T
Passwords	• Do change the original password to something you will remember.	• Don't write down your password unless it will be stored in a safe.
Software	• Buy or upgrade antivirus detection software. • Update your virus definitions daily. • Check frequently for updated OS (operating system) patches and application patches	• Don't go without antivirus software • Don't ignore OS and application updates/patches • Don't use unsafe applications, such as peer-to-peer file sharing tools or applications of unknown origin.
Firewalls	• Enable built-in firewalls • Use external standalone firewalls whenever possible	• Don't go without either a built-in or standalone firewall
Hardware	• If connecting via a wireless interface disconnect or disable the wired network interface. • If connecting via wired interface disconnect the wireless. • Use the VPN for work purposes only.	• Don't enable or connect more than one network interface while using a VPN connected computer. • Don't allow people to use the computer who might do so unsafely.
Services and protocols	• Disable any unneeded services or protocols.	• Don't run default services and protocols if they aren't needed.

VPN Implementation Best Practices

The VPN is only as safe as the machine it is used on. Before deploying a VPN, review the implementation best practices, listed as dos and don'ts, in Table 14.1.

Additional steps you can use for the VPN server include:

- **Use strong authentication**—Ensure that only authorized clients can connect. Since the VPN server will have a public IP address, it's accessible from an Internet user anywhere in the world. If they can easily log on to the VPN server, they can easily access your Internet network.

- **Use strong encryption**—The two primary encryption protocols used in VPNs today are IPSec and SSL. Either of these is strong enough to protect a VPN but other protocols should be closely evaluated before using them.
- **Protect the VPN server behind a firewall**—Whether you're using a host-to-gateway or gateway-to-gateway configuration, you should not put the VPN server directly on the Internet. Instead, place it behind a firewall such as in a DMZ configuration. This will provide a layer of protection from Internet attacks.

CHAPTER SUMMARY

This chapter has discussed the different types, design, configuration, implementation, and testing of VPNs. It has also discussed the main VPN technologies available on the market and best practices implementations. VPNs can provide remote clients access to your internal network in a host-to-gateway configuration. They can also provide access between two offices in the same organization using a gateway-to-gateway model.

Many different VPN applications are available. Microsoft provides VPN solutions built into the server operating system. Cisco and other vendors sell VPN appliances you can install and configure easily. You can also use UNIX or Linux systems and install free VPN solutions such as Openswan.

VPNs are increasingly becoming a part of everyday life on the Internet. Many people use them to gain access to resources in their offices, such as e-mail servers and other intranet resources. This trend is certain to become more popular as many companies are finding it cheaper for their employees to work from home, relieving them of the need to lease additional office space.

Site-to-site VPNs will also continue to be deployed as companies; both small and large find it increasingly necessary to share access to their main networks with remote offices. One notable area is in the realm of IP telephony, where VPNs enable all remote offices to use a single IP switchboard at the center of a VPN hub and spoke network. Intra-office communication is encrypted and the use of a single switchboard saves money.

KEY CONCEPTS AND TERMS

Customer Premise Equipment (CPE)
Gateway-to-gateway VPN
Host-to-gateway VPN
Internet Key Exchange v2 (IKEv2)

CHAPTER 14 ASSESSMENT

1. ________ provide(s) secure communications between external users and internal servers located behind a firewall. (Multiple answers may be correct.)

A. VPNs
B. IPSec
C. Intranets
D. Extranets
E. SSL

2. A desirable feature of an operating system-based VPN is the ability to refer to remote servers by their network address translated IP addresses. True or False?

A. True
B. False

3. A VPN is also known as:

A. A Neural Network
B. A data-encrypted tunnel over the Internet
C. A file sharing and printing server
D. A bastion host
E. None of the above

4. Encrypted communications using Web browsers usually use the ________ protocol.

5. An easy and cost-effective way to secure access to a network is by purchasing (an) inexpensive ________.

A. Switch
B. Router
C. Antivirus software
D. Remote terminal
E. VPN appliance

6. Most VPN appliances are designed for complex installations. True or False?

A. True
B. False

7. VPN appliances are ________.

A. Not readily available
B. OS specific
C. Very expensive
D. Secure technologies
E. A and B

8. What does RDP stands for?

A. Remote Desktop Processing
B. Remote Desktop Protocol
C. Radio Demilitarized Processing
D. Recovery Dispatching Process
E. Remote Dial-up Process

9. Another name for Terminal Services is:

A. Remote Dial-up System
B. Remote Desktop Services
C. Remote Desktop System
D. Radius Dial-up Services

10. GoToMyPC is a remote desktop technology that allows you to remotely access your computer from any other Internet-connected computer in the world with almost any operating system through a secure, private connection.

A. True
B. False

11. What are two primary methods for deploying remote-access VPNs?

A. SSL and SSH
B. SSL and API
C. IPSec and SSL
D. IPSec and SSH
E. None of the above

12. Terminal Services provides the ability to:

A. Host multiple, simultaneous client sessions
B. Implement software bugs
C. Implement dynamic addressing
D. Sync proxy servers
E. All of the above

13. Terminal Services RemoteApp applications appear to users as if the applications are installed locally when they are actually running a remote server.

A. True
B. False

14. Microsoft's DirectAccess:

A. Is an alternative to a traditional VPN
B. Is not a VPN
C. Is a mix of Microsoft Access database served through a VPN
D. Is a DDNS
E. Intrusion Detection System

15. Users must have physical connectivity with the internal network for the DirectAccess connection to be established.

A. True
B. False

16. When performing a download and install of the RPM version of Openswan, you do not need to have the IPSec-tools RPM package installed on your machine.

A. True
B. False

17. What are the two methods of installing Openswan?

A. KLIPS and IPSec
B. RPM and source libgmp development libraries
C. By hand or automatically
D. Remotely and through a diskette
E. None of the above

18. To check that you have a successfully installed Openswan VPN you should run the command `ipsec verify`.

A. True
B. False

CHAPTER 15

Perspectives, Resources, and the Future

THE FOCUS OF THIS BOOK thus far has been to look at the tools, technologies, processes, and procedures you can use as a security professional to secure your organization's IT assets, networks, and systems. You've learned about using firewalls to secure the perimeter of the network and VPNs for securing data in transit. You've learned how malicious people might try to attack your network. An understanding of these topics and the others discussed here is critically important for success in the information security field. In this chapter you'll learn about what's next.

Today's information security professionals face a daunting task. Not only do you need to understand how to secure a complex, diverse, and rapidly changing IT environment, but you also need to be aware of the challenges and threats to come. An in-depth understanding of security technologies such as VPNs and firewalls and of threats like malware or social engineering provides the foundation of your arsenal. To be truly successful, however, you also need the ability to identify and respond to trends in both the technologies and the threats under development. To keep up with attackers, you need to know what's coming and where to get reliable, current information.

Throughout your career as an information security professional, you will encounter situations in which you will need to apply security best practices to new technologies or new architectures. You may find that you are conducting investigations, trying to determine how your infrastructure was compromised. You may be monitoring new attacks and trying to develop new defenses. Whatever challenges you face in the future will require that you leverage the experience, understanding, and best practices you've learned to ensure you are effective against new risks and threats.

Chapter 15 Topics

This chapter will cover the following topics:

- What the future holds for network security, firewalls, and VPNs
- What some resources sites for network security technologies, techniques and threats are
- What some useful network security tools are
- What the impact of ubiquitous wireless connectivity is
- What potential uses of security technologies are
- What specialized firewalls are available
- What the impact of anti-hacker technologies like honeypots, honeynets, and padded cells is
- What emerging network security technologies are

Chapter 15 Goals

Upon completion of this chapter, you will be able to:

- Discuss the different types of integrated and specialized firewalls, as well as the advantages and disadvantages of each.
- List additional sources of information related to network security.
- Describe emerging IT and security trends and their impact on network security.
- Identify challenges and advantages presented by the new technologies and emerging threats to network security.
- Understand the difference between an IDS and an IPS.
- Discuss the future of network security, firewalls and VPNs.

What the Future Holds for Network Security, Firewalls, and VPNs

Throughout this book you have learned about the present state of network security, firewalls, and VPNs. In this chapter you will be looking to the future.

How does a security expert discern what the future holds? A number of factors should influence your planning as you try to draw a road map for your information security strategy:

- **Historical progression of threats**—If you are familiar with how threats have progressed over time, you have a better understanding of where those threats may be headed in the future. For example, 10 years ago virtually all malware attacks were focused on operating systems. Today malware attacks go after applications far more than operating systems. Browsers are a particularly popular target for attacks today.
- **Your industry**—Each industry has different focuses when looking to the future. A bank will have very different requirements from a shoe store, for example. Understand your industry, network with your peers, and make sure you are looking at the proper framework for your planning.
- **Experts**—It's always a good idea to see what the people who predict the future of the industry think before doing your planning. While experts can disagree over certain specific predictions, if you keep an eye on the major information sources (some of which are provided later in this chapter) you will find you can develop a pretty good idea of where information security is headed.
- **Vendors**—Since they are frequently trying to sell you their next-generation solution, vendors usually have a biased view of the future; they can also provide valuable information for your planning, however. If the vendors you work with or follow are all targeting a particular threat or technology, they view it as an area to generate revenue. If an industry targets a specific area as a source of revenue, it's a good bet that a threat lurks there somewhere.

Here are some of the areas you should pay attention to as you plan your information security strategy.

Threats

One area evolving almost faster than you can imagine is the variety of threats to your infrastructure. Several years ago the threats most prevalent were from unsophisticated attackers whose main goal was to accomplish something they could brag about in chat rooms with their buddies. Today, organized crime has zeroed in on the huge amounts of money to be made in computer hacking. We now see targeted attacks against specific industries and companies, viruses that target credit card numbers, bank account information and Social Security numbers, and rootkits that, once installed on a computer, turn it into a host the attacker can control remotely to attack other systems and networks. Some attackers will threaten to crash networks with denial of service attacks, unless the system owner pays extortion money—the high-tech equivalent of a protection racket.

In the future, you will see more resilient networks that will mitigate the risk of traffic-based attacks, more secure operating systems and applications to resist malware, and intrusion prevention systems that will respond instantly to attacks, choking them off before they can damage your infrastructure.

Firewall Capabilities

Firewalls have been adding capabilities since they were first introduced. Early firewalls contained some limited filtering and NAT capabilities and not much else. You will learn about the wide range of today's firewall capabilities and specialties later in this chapter.

Encryption

Encryption is a constantly evolving standard. In 1977, the Data Encryption Standard (DES) was specified in the Federal Information Processing Standards (FIPS) Publications. It became a national standard. We have gone from DES, a 56-bit algorithm, to 3DES, an effective 168-bit algorithm, to the algorithm encryption standard (AES), which supports a 256-bit algorithm. The problem with encryption is the constantly improving processing power of computers. As computers get faster and more capable, with bigger and bigger memory space, encryption algorithms become easier and easier to break, through brute force and other techniques.

Encryption's popularity has grown as concerns about protecting data at rest, in transit, and while archived have come to the forefront of many industries. How many stories have you seen about the stolen laptop with 100,000 Social Security numbers on it or an application compromised by an attacker able to read data directly from a hard drive because it was stored in clear text? Today, some government agencies (the Department of Defense, for example) require full-drive encryption for all laptops.

Recognizing the growing need for encryption, the industry is responding quickly. The AES standard was designated as the replacement for DES. It is designed to scale upward with longer keys. Keep in mind as you look into encryption solutions whether they support AES or an equivalent algorithm and be sure that you encrypt your data everywhere it's vulnerable. The days of relying on your VPN as the only data protection are gone. You need to secure data with encryption everywhere it can be accessed.

Authentication

Another area where you can expect to see dramatic changes in future capabilities is in authentication, especially with respect to identity and access management. In the past, much of user security was based on a user ID and password. Years were spent trying to teach users what a strong password is, why they need a strong password, and why they need to change their passwords every 90 days. The effort has been largely ineffective. Users still choose poor passwords, and even when they select strong passwords, the passwords can still be cracked with sufficient computer power.

The other challenge associated with authentication is actually a user-management issue. All too often in a complex environment, the creation, permissioning, management, and eventual retiring of user accounts doesn't work. Accounts retain permissions long after users move on to other roles, accounts remain on systems long after employees have left the organization, and, in many cases, no auditing of actions using privileged accounts takes place. Collectively, these critical tasks are known as identity and access management.

How will these challenges evolve in the future? One trend is moving away from passwords to tokens, smart cards, and biometric authentication as a replacement to user ID and password solutions.

On the identity and account management front, a number of solutions automate these activities, providing full account life-cycle management and the associated auditing capabilities many companies look for. The one challenge with these solutions is that, due to the sophistication of most corporate computing environments, they are very complex to install and maintain. It's not just a matter of automating the creation of Active Directory accounts in most cases. Companies have multiple application systems and authentication requirements. Making all of these components work together is not easy. Once you get them working together, however, you've removed a significant threat to your security landscape.

Metrics

One of the biggest complaints from CIOs about information security is the lack of measures for the success of a program. Information security has moved from being an esoteric discipline practiced by a few misunderstood experts to a core business function vital to support the bottom line. While this evolution has been long overdue, today management expects you to quantify your contribution to the company and justify the expenditures they make to support security.

The good news is that the industry has been moving this direction for some time and has developed a number of performance metrics. The most popular is the **Information Technology Infrastructure Library (ITIL)**, which is a set of concepts you can use to formalize your security management practice and the associated reporting. In addition, a number of solutions allow you to automate not only these processes, but also the associated measurements.

Focus

Another area of significant evolution in information security is in the nature of what you are trying to protect. Initially, information security was all about keeping the bad guys out of your network. As a result, companies invested significant amounts of money in firewalls and other network security technologies.

Then focus shifted from the network to the host, however, and organizations focused more on managing patches, hardening operating systems, and installing host-based firewalls.

Once the industry secured the host, attackers shifted to threatening the applications running on those hosts. IT then started focusing on integrating security into the software development lifecycle, testing and evaluating code, hiring penetration testers to try to break our code deliberately, and deploying firewalls and proxy servers specifically to secure applications.

The next shift in focus for information security is a growing focus on what is truly valuable—the data itself. Ultimately, all the measures developed to date, from the network firewalls, to the host hardening, to the penetration testing, have all been about securing the data. The industry is now moving toward a data-centric security model, which is a significant paradigm shift from previous models. A data-centric model will force companies to focus on classifying and applying values to their data. While this will undoubtedly be a painful process for many companies, this approach will ultimately yield a much more secure environment.

Securing the Cloud

Cloud computing is a relatively new phenomenon in computing infrastructure that involves moving computing resources out to the Internet. Resources are then shared by multiple applications and, in many cases, shared by multiple corporations. Think of how the phone networks or the electrical grid operates. These clouds are typically built using virtualization that allows for exceptional efficiencies, but also opens up a number of new security challenges.

First, to leverage the true benefits of cloud computing, you have to trust the vendor providing your cloud. This requires a shift in focus from deploying security technologies to ensuring that your vendors are contractually obligated and physically able to keep your data secure. You also need to be able to evaluate vendors to determine how trustworthy they are. If you have the available resources, you should be auditing the vendor(s) to ensure they consistently keep your data secure.

You'll learn about the security challenges specific to virtualization later in the chapter.

Securing Mobile Devices

A rapidly growing sector of the end user computing space is the use of mobile devices like smart phones, netbooks, or tablet computers. These devices present some unique challenges. Think about how many people today receive e-mail on their smart phone. Or ran out to get a new iPad and are now reviewing confidential documents while riding the train to work. How do you secure these devices?

The good news is that once the industry identifies issues like these, it concentrates resources to work and ultimately solve the problem. The computer security industry has very few "unsolvable" issues. Already virus protection, mobile device management, and encryption applications are available for mobile devices. The challenge you'll typically see in both current and future technology is that these types of devices are frequently overlooked or discounted when documenting security risks. Be sure to keep these devices on your list of risks. They possess an alarming amount of storage and processing capacity, which makes it easy for an employee to inadvertently place confidential information on them.

Resources Sites for Network Security, Firewalls, and VPNs

A variety of resource sites are available to you for more information on network security, firewalls, and VPNs. While this list of online and offline resources provides a good start to for finding additional information, it's impossible to cover every source. Here are some sites and books covering the critical topics just to get you started. If you need additional information, you are only a search engine click or a bookstore trip away from the answer.

At press time, all Web sites listed here were valid; however, with the mergers, acquisitions, and other changes in the industry, some of these links may change over time.

Many of the vendors listed here have products in multiple areas—so they are listed once to avoid confusion.

Firewall Vendors

- Check Point Software —*www.checkpoint.com*
- Cisco—*www.cisco.com*
- Juniper Networks—*www.juniper.net*
- Fortinet—*www.fortinet.com*
- McAfee—*www.mcafee.com*
- Palo Alto Networks—*www.paloaltonetworks.com*
- Astaro—*www.astaro.com*
- SonicWall—*www.sonicwall.com*
- Watchguard—*www.watchguard.com*

Virtual Private Network Vendors

- Microsoft—*www.microsoft.com*
- Citrix—*www.citrix.com*
- F5 Networks—*www.f5.com*
- Nortel—*www.nortel.com*
- OpenVPN—*www.openvpn.net*
- Openswan—*www.openswan.org*

Network Security Web Sites

- National Institute of Standards and Technology/Computer Security Research Center—*csrc.nist.gov*
- HackerWhacker (Firewall Testing Website)—*www.hackerwhacker.com*
- Gibson Research Corporation (Security testing and tools)—*www.grc.com*
- Hack Yourself (Security Testing and Tools)—*www.hackyourself.org*
- CERT (Security Research)—*www.cert.org*
- SANS (Security Research and Training)—*www.sans.org*
- ISACA (Standards/Certifications)—*www.isaca.org*
- $(ISC)^2$ (Standards/Certifications)—*www.isc2.org*
- Symantec (Security Vendor)—*www.symantec.com*

Network Security Magazine Web Sites

- SC Magazine—*www.scmagazineus.com*
- Information Security Magazine—*searchsecurity.techtarget.com*
- CSO Magazine—*www.csoonline.com*

Tools for Network Security, Firewalls, and VPNs

As you review the information security technologies that you may encounter as your information security career progresses, one of the questions you'll probably have is, where will you find these tools?

In the previous chapters you've learned about a number of commercial and open-source solutions for network security. A wealth of both commercial and open-source solutions for network security tools, firewalls and VPNs are available. Where will you find the tools of the future?

Commercial Off-the-Shelf (COTS) Software

Commercial software remains the choice of corporations everywhere, and this won't be changing any time in the future. A number of reasons account for the dominance of commercial solutions in the information security industry. They include:

- The popularity of combining hardware and software into an appliance. Many of the most popular firewall, VPN, vulnerability management, intrusion detection and other security applications will be developed and distributed in an appliance format. While some open-source solutions will allow you to use standard server hardware to create an appliance-like solution, a truly open-source appliance will probably be distributed as a commercial solution.
- Companies rely on solutions they can support. One of the ongoing challenges with open-source software is the lack of commercial support for the solutions. Highly technical people can work well within the open-source support community. Support from an open-source community is typically better than what comes from a commercial help desk, but corporations are generally reluctant to trust security-related solutions to that model.
- Many of the most popular open-source solutions are being commercialized, as their developers look to generate revenue off the products. Two examples would be the Snort intrusion detection solution as well as the Nessus vulnerability scanner. Both tools were widely used and extremely popular open-source security solutions, and both are now available commercially.

Open-Source Applications and Tools

While it is pretty common to see companies embrace commercial tools in their production environments, you can't discount the sheer innovation available in the open-source community. Most of the tools referenced in this book are open-source, and you can expect to see continued development on most of them.

Keep in mind a couple of other advantages to open-source tools as you build your security tool kit. First, working with open-source tools is a great way to build your information security skill set. Most security professionals cannot afford to purchase multiple commercial security applications to learn with, so leveraging open-source is a cost-effective career builder.

The other value that open-source security tools bring to a security professional is that these are the same tools many of the people attacking your network will use. One of the most important skills you can develop is the ability to understand the people trying to get into your systems. Learning the tools and techniques they may use by developing parallel expertise will take you far in your career. Commercial applications seldom offer the same learning opportunities. Attackers generally are not using commercial applications in their attacks, and they typically don't draw from the same community available with open-source solutions as you will to help your learning.

The Impact of Ubiquitous Wireless Connectivity

No chapter on the future of information security would be complete without a discussion of the influence of wireless connectivity on security technologies. The first thing to realize as you think about wireless is that you need to consider a variety of wireless technologies. Be sure not to focus too narrowly and miss something critical.

Consider the types of wireless technologies that impact your environment:

- **Wireless deployed as a LAN technology**—The original wireless nightmare for information security professionals, deploying of wireless as part of the office LAN caused constant sleepless nights for security departments. Security departments used to invest countless hours test-driving their locations, searching for unsecured wireless access points on their networks. The real challenge with this technology, other than the fact that it permitted the bypassing of your perimeter security controls, was that it was so convenient. Setup was so easy for an employee— at least to set up in the default configuration, with all the attendant security issues.

  The good news is that the industry has made great strides in wireless security. Stronger authentication technologies like 802.1x, which requires connecting systems to be authenticated using PKI machine certificates, stronger encryption technologies, and significant improvements in user awareness have made wireless LAN in the office a viable replacement for the wired LAN, while still affording the security you need to keep your data secure.

- **Public and Home Office Wireless**—Public/Home Office wireless is a great thing for your employees. Take out your laptop, connect to the wireless, and you're on the Internet ready to surf. You can connect to the corporate network, do your banking, shop online, or just catch up on the news. What could be more convenient? As is often the case, convenience is the enemy of security. A number of security challenges present themselves with public/home office wireless. First, any unencrypted traffic sent over these wireless networks can be intercepted. Counting on Starbucks (or an employee's cable company) to configure their wireless with the most advanced security capabilities enabled is not reasonable. Work with your users to make sure they understand the risks associated with these types of wireless.

  The good news from a corporate network perspective is that you are probably running a VPN for business connections, so that data should be secure.

- **Mobile Wireless**—The ubiquity of smart phones and other devices that can connect to the cellular networks presents the third challenge when discussing the impact of wireless connectivity on information security. Now employees don't need to search for a wireless hot spot before connecting to the network—they can access their mail from just about anywhere. The best defense against these risks is a combination of policy and technology. First, your policy should restrict access to company systems and e-mail to company-owned devices. That allows you some level of control over the types and configurations of devices with access to your data. Next, make sure the devices you're using leverage the appropriate security technologies like encryption and antivirus scanning. While it's virtually impossible to physically secure something as portable as a smart phone, you can ensure that the data on the device can't be recovered if it is stolen or lost.

Potential Uses of Security Technologies

One ever-expanding area of discussion when looking at security technologies like firewalls, VPNs, intrusion detection, honeypots, vulnerability management, and others is the many uses for this technology. Obviously you use security technologies to secure your data, networks, and systems. And that is certainly the primary use for security technologies. But you should be aware of some additional uses for this technology.

The core security concepts can be summed up with the acronym "CIA." This stands for confidentiality, integrity, and availability.

- **Confidentiality**—Confidentiality deals with keeping information, networks, and systems secure from unauthorized access. This issue is particularly critical in today's environment in light of the high-profile leaking of people's personal information by several large companies. These breaches in confidentiality made the headlines largely because the thefts exposed people to the potential of identity theft.

  Several technologies support confidentiality in an enterprise security environment. These include:

  - Strong encryption
  - Strong authentication
  - Stringent access controls

- **Integrity**—Integrity is the consistency, accuracy, and validity of data or information. One of the goals of successful information security is to ensure that the information is protected against any unauthorized or accidental changes. The architecture should include processes and procedures to manage intentional changes, as well as the ability to detect changes.

- **Availability**—Availability is the third core security principle, defined as a characteristic of a resource being accessible to a user, application, or computer system when required. In other words, when users need information, it's available to them. Typically, threats to availability come in two types: accidental and deliberate. Accidental threats include natural disasters such as storms, floods, fire, power outages, earthquakes, and so forth. This category also includes outages due to equipment failure, software issues, and other unplanned system, network, or user issues. The second category is related to outages that result from the exploitation of a system vulnerability. Some examples of this threat include a denial of service attack, or a network worm that impacts vulnerable systems and their availability. In some cases, one of the first actions you need to take following an outage is determining which category an outage fits into. Companies handle accidental outages very differently from deliberate ones.

As you continue to work in the information security field, another acronym you will encounter is "GRC." This stands for governance, risk, and compliance. This is the best way to look at your security technologies from a business perspective. Look at how the security technologies you're deploying provide much more than just securing data:

- **Governance**—Governance is the processes and procedures that ensure employees are following your organization's security policy. For example, you have a policy that says that data in transit across a public network must be secured with at least 56-bit encryption. You would ensure that the only way to connect to the network is through a VPN that uses at least 56-bit encryption. This mechanism would be part of your governance efforts.

  Governance is generally used to demonstrate to management, customers, and auditors that your information security program is operating as outlined in your policies, procedures, and practices. If you are a service provider, you can leverage your governance capabilities to show that you can be trusted to keep clients' information secure.

- **Risk**—One of the foundations of any information security program is a robust risk management practice. If you don't identify your risks, how do you know which security technologies to deploy and where? A risk is the likelihood or potential for a threat to take advantage of a vulnerability and cause harm or loss. Risk is a combination of an asset's value, exposure level, and rate of occurrence. A goal of security is to recognize, understand, and eliminate risk.

  A risk management process starts with a risk assessment of your environment. Start with your critical data, applications, systems, and networks. Document the risks associated with them in a risk matrix. A typical risk matrix will contain the following:

  - A description of the risk
  - The likelihood that the risk will actually occur
  - The impact of the risk

- A total risk score
- The relevant business owner for the risk
- Which of the core security principles the risk impacts: confidentiality, integrity, and/or availability.
- The appropriate strategy or strategies to deal with the risk

The last bullet is the one that's critical with respect to security technologies—you leverage security technologies as part of the strategy to deal with the risks. One of the fastest-growing sectors in the information security career field is compliance. Compliance means ensuring your company obeys internal policies, as well as any applicable laws or other regulatory requirements. A good example of this is the Sarbanes-Oxley act, which requires publicly traded companies to validate the controls securing all financial data. You will find that your security program, in conjunction with the security technologies supporting it, are critical to ensuring compliance with a growing number of regulations.

What Happens When There Is No Perimeter?

If you look back to the first uses of network security, security professionals essentially put a firewall between the corporate network and the Internet. That firewall marked the perimeter of the network. As networks have become more complex, companies started finding they were connecting to the Internet in more locations, so more firewalls were installed. The perimeter remained the demarcation between the Internet and the corporate network. Today, the vanishing perimeter has been the subject of many presentations, white papers, and sales pitches, as vendors try to convince organizations to invest to protect their perimeter-less environments.

VPNs extended the internal network outside the nice, neat network perimeter defined by the firewall/Internet interface. Suddenly your network could be in any hotel or coffee shop in the country, as your employees discovered the benefits of mobile computing. To make matters worse, high capacity drives and portable storage meant that not only was your network being extended into places that you had never imagined, but you data storage was no longer contained within your office space. Critical information could be stored easily anywhere your employees wanted.

Unfortunately, that wasn't the end of the challenges you face as an information security professional. In addition to your employees taking your network and data anywhere they wanted, your business discovered the benefits of interconnecting with customers, vendors, suppliers, and partners. Each of these groups needed varying levels of access to your systems, networks, and data.

In addition to all the challenges with connections and data beyond your network, businesses also discovered the benefits of online commerce over the Internet. That seems harmless enough, until you realize that to do business on the Internet, you need to punch holes in the network perimeter to provide access from the Internet to your systems, networks, and data. It's a little like installing skylights in your roof: you want the benefit of the sunlight in the house, but you don't want leaks when it rains.

In a perfect world, your upper-level management would have consulted with you before they embarked on these projects. They would have given you an unlimited budget to deploy network zones separating each of the different types of data, with firewalls and intrusion detection deployed at each level, and enough staff to monitor all the infrastructure to ensure nothing is getting past your security measures.

In reality, the first few connections were most likely put in without input from security, and these might not even be firewalled. It's so much easier than having to justify purchasing firewalls, setup firewall rules, monitor logs, and all the other things an organization needs to do as it opens holes in its protective perimeter.

What's needed in this case is a clear, well-established policy with strong senior management support. The appropriate controls should be put in place to re-establish your perimeter. If you treat the risk of all these new technologies connecting to your network the same way you treat the risks posed by the Internet, you'll mitigate the risks associated the increasingly fluid perimeter you will be dealing with.

Specialized Firewalls Available

In this chapter you'll learn about some of the specialized firewalls that are available—or are coming soon, such as:

- **Hybrid**—A hybrid firewall combines a number of different functions in a single appliance. You learned about firewalls with integrated VPN capabilities, but you can also expect to see firewalls combined with vulnerability management, intrusion detection and prevention, antivirus/anti-spyware, content filtering, or a variety of other network and security-related technologies. The key when looking into hybrid firewalls is ensuring that they will meet your specific security needs while not creating a performance bottleneck. The more functions you put on a single system, the more chances you'll run into a performance bottleneck.
- **Data Protection**—A data protection firewall is a hybrid firewall, but deserves some additional explanation. The focus of a mature security program is to ensure that data is secure. An emerging technology is **data leakage prevention (DLP)**, which is a technology specifically designed to ensure that your data stays within your network. When combined with firewall technologies at the perimeter of the network, a data protection firewall becomes an invaluable tool in keeping your data out of Gmail and Facebook accounts and within the internal network where it belongs.
- **Application**—An application firewall is specifically designed to control input, output, and/or access to an application. This type of firewall became very popular when the focus of attacks shifted from operating systems to applications. An application firewall operates by monitoring the input, output, and system calls made in an application, and blocking any that do not conform to the firewall rules. An application firewall can block buffer overflow attacks, SQL injection attacks, and the majority of other application-focused attacks.

Application firewalls are either network-based or host-based applications. One drawback of application firewalls is they are typically designed for specific types of applications (i.e., Web applications or databases), whereas a standard firewall can secure many different types of applications, though not to the level an application firewall provides.

- **Database**—A database firewall is an application designed to control the input, output, and system calls made to a database. While limited to database security, this firewall offers very granular security for databases.
- **Ubiquitous**—This is ultimately the direction that firewalls will likely take in the future. The industry current supports a variety of firewalls integrated into the network and the host, that run on the perimeter and the core to protect demarcation between network zones. Now firewalls are moving into the virtualization area. Eventually this intelligence and control will be pushed directly into the infrastructure and managed from a single console. Instead of controlling isolated ports on a firewall-by-firewall basis, you'll be able to manage secure data as it flows into, out of, and through your environment from the originating host to the perimeter of your network and at all connections in between. This will allow you to re-establish the perimeter that disappeared with all the external connections to your network.

Intrusion Detection Systems (IDS) and Intrusion Prevention Systems (IPS)

Two other security technologies available to secure networks are intrusion detection systems (IDS) and intrusion prevention systems (IPS). An IDS detects unauthorized user activities, attacks, and network compromises. IDSs come in two types, host-based and network-based.

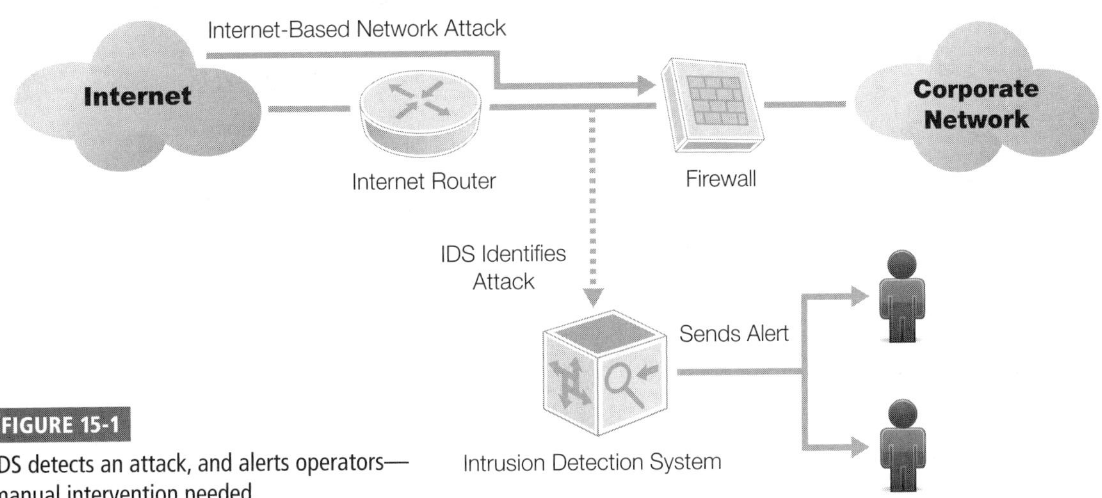

FIGURE 15-1

IDS detects an attack, and alerts operators—manual intervention needed.

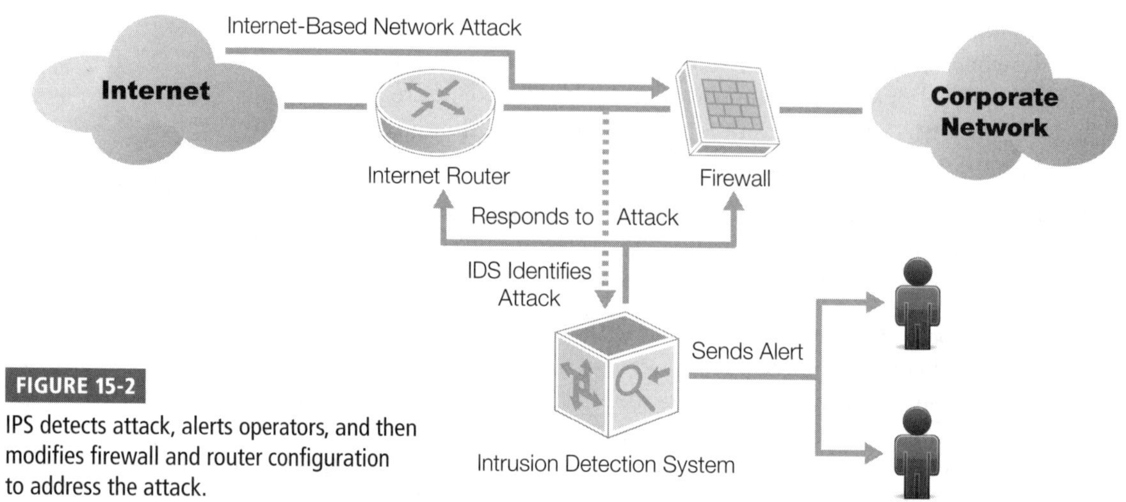

FIGURE 15-2

IPS detects attack, alerts operators, and then modifies firewall and router configuration to address the attack.

> **NOTE**
>
> IDS/IPS is used largely on Internet connections, since those connections typically present the largest threat to the network. You can also deploy IDS/IPS in strategic locations on the internal network. This is an excellent idea if your internal network has connections to third-party networks such as customers, vendors, or business partners.

An intrusion prevention system (IPS) is very similar to an IDS, except that in addition to detecting and alerting, an IPS can also take action to prevent a breach from occurring.

Two common deployment methods are used when placing an IDS/IPS for protecting a network from the Internet. Each has its own advantages and disadvantages.

An unfiltered IDS/IPS installation examines the raw Internet data stream before it crosses the firewall. This provides the highest amount of visibility to attacks, but also means that a significantly higher volume of data will be monitored, with a higher possibility of false positives. During periods of high traffic, the IDS/IPS might not be able to process all the packets, and attacks can be missed.

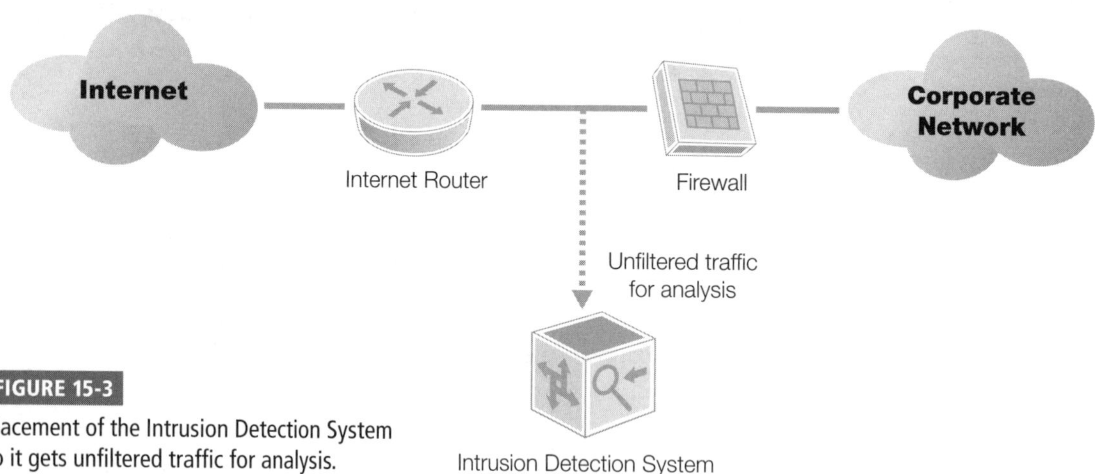

FIGURE 15-3

Placement of the Intrusion Detection System so it gets unfiltered traffic for analysis.

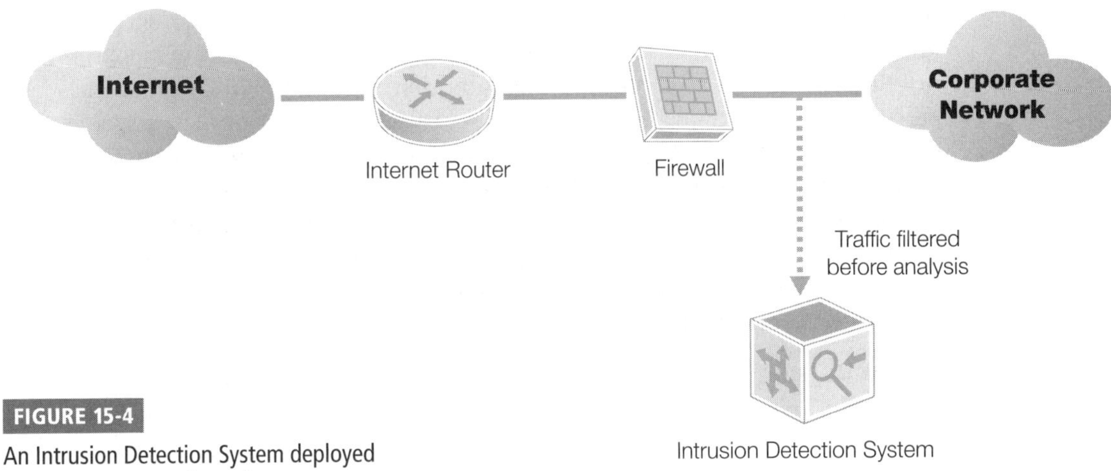

FIGURE 15-4
An Intrusion Detection System deployed behind a screening firewall.

A screened IDS/IPS solution monitors traffic that gets through the screening firewall. The advantage to this model is it dramatically reduces the amount of traffic to be monitored, reducing the chances of false positives and lost packets during high traffic volumes. A loss of visibility accompanies this model, as you cannot see attacks blocked by the screening firewall.

Effect of Honeypots, Honeynets, and Padded Cells

Honeypots, honeynets, and padded cells are complementary technologies to IDS/IPS deployments. A honeypot is a trap for hackers. A honeypot is designed to distract hackers from real targets, detect new exploitations, and learn about the identity of hackers. A honeynet is just a collection of honeypots used to present an attacker an even more realistic attack environment. A **padded cell** is a system that waits for an IDS to detect attackers and then transfers the attackers to a special host where they cannot do any damage to the production environment.

While these are all extremely useful technologies, not many corporate environments deploy them. You generally see these deployed by educational institutions and security research firms. Generally corporate information security professionals are so busy securing their environment from attacks that they don't spend time researching attack patterns. As long as the attack doesn't succeed, they are satisfied.

Emerging Network Security Technologies

In addition to these future enhancements to security technologies, you should also be aware of three more areas of emerging security technology:

- **Data Leakage Prevention (DLP)**—DLP technologies are systems that identify, monitor, and protect data in use, data in motion, and data at rest from inappropriate use, distribution, transmission, or other unauthorized actions. DLP technologies perform deep-content inspection within a scope defined by a central management console and are usually deployed at multiple locations within the environment to ensure full coverage. As the value of data continues to climb, this technology should see wider implementation. The technology is already used heavily in the financial industry. New government regulations will help drive the implementation in other sectors, most likely healthcare. HIPAA, HITECH, and PCI have specific data protection requirements.
- **Biometrics**—Identifies a user based on anatomical characteristics such as fingerprint, voice print, or iris patterns. These methods of identification have a number of advantages over passwords, tokens, or ID cards.

  First, biometric authentication requires the person being authenticated be physically present. Second, biometric security removes the need to remember complicated passwords. No more passwords taped under keyboards—you carry your password with you wherever you go. Finally, biometrics remove the need to carry a token or ID card with you—you don't have to worry about not being able to work when you leave your token on the kitchen table at home.

  The areas where biometrics are currently being investigated include ATMs, laptops, and computer networks.
- **Virtualization Security**—As virtualization and cloud computing continue to gain ground, a new generation of virtualization-aware security tools are under development. Antivirus, vulnerability management, data leakage prevention, and IDS/IPS technologies are all being developed to run against the underlying hypervisor layer. This gives the security applications direct access to the underlying data transport layer of the virtual environment rather than forcing them to run against each virtual server, dramatically improving performance, visibility to security issues, and ease of use.

  In multi-tenant environments (multiple companies sharing the same virtual environment) additional security tools are being developed to ensure that no access occurs between the virtual environments.

IP Version 6

You learned about IPv6 in some detail in Chapter 12, VPN Technologies, so you should be aware that IPv6 is the next-generation IP version and the successor to IPv4. While the main driving force for the redesign of Internet Protocol was the rapidly approaching exhaustion of IPv4 addresses, IPv6 has significant implications to future information security professionals.

IPv6 includes a native information security framework (IPsec) that provides for both data and control packets. This means that what you currently do with a traditional VPN you will be able to do natively with any IPv6 device. At a high level, that means you can run your IPsec VPN without requiring a client, but the implications are significantly more profound than just that.

In a fully IPv6 environment, any connection can use an IPsec connection. This means that any connection from a user to an application, host-to-host, or even peer-to-peer connection authenticate and encrypt as it passes across the network.

While the thought of a network featuring nothing but secure connections seems like a security professional's dream configuration, you should also consider some drawbacks before kicking off your IPv6 migration project. One of the challenges with encryption is that it not only secures data from the bad guys, but it also secures the data from the good guys. A number of security technologies like IDS/IPS, content filtering, network-based antivirus, data leakage prevention, and even firewall technologies rely on being able to look at packets as they cross the network to determine how to handle them. Once those packets are encapsulated in a secure IPsec connection, all the security tools you have relied on stop working.

With the limited deployment of IPv6, significant development on solutions to overcome these challenges hasn't occurred yet, but it will be a subject of great interest as the use of IPv6 expands.

VPNs, Firewalls, and Virtualization

Chapter 12, VPN Technologies, looked at some of the types of virtualization and how they impact the current use of VPNs. You should think about some additional areas that look to the future of virtualization.

Virtualization and VPN deployment are examples—some SSL VPNs have the ability to provide a unique virtual VPN configuration for each individual user group. Much like other types of virtualization, a virtualized SSL VPN allows you to separate the physical and logical use of the VPN. In the future, this capability could extend to IPsec VPNs, as well. While this technology offers some unique abilities when configuring secure VPN contexts for different user groups, the additional complexity is something you need to know. A misconfigured virtual VPN context could expose parts of your network to groups that should not have access to them. For example, if you are using a virtualized VPN to provide customers access to a help desk ticketing system, and you inadvertently grant that context access to your intranet where all your pricing information resides, you expose the organization's proprietary data to unnecessary risk.

Firewalls are another technology that is starting to permit virtualization. Currently some firewalls on the market can partition into multiple virtual firewalls. Each virtual firewall appears to be a separate firewall with its own security policy, interfaces, and configuration. This allows you to use your firewall hardware more efficiently than you might otherwise, but once again additional risks occur with the deployment of virtual firewalls.

First, while firewalls exist that support this technology, not all of them support all their features in the virtualized environment. Before you deploy a virtualized firewall, be sure it supports all the features you need to meet your business and security requirements. While this is a very promising technology, it's also very new, and sometimes early adopters can find themselves encountering issues the vendor didn't discover during their quality assurance processes.

Next, you are relying on logical segregation of firewalls rather than the physical separation offered by multiple physical firewalls. While this technology remains new, do some testing before deploying virtual firewalls into a critical environment. Finding that there's a way to bypass the virtual security and move from one virtual environment to another would not be good if you are using the firewall to separate two customers connected to your network.

Finally, this model suffers from the same complexity challenges with respect to the virtual VPNs. Any time you have a solution that offers greater flexibility, you also open the possibility for greater complexity. Complex environments are almost always more difficult to secure, monitor, and manage than simple environments.

However, assuming all the challenges associated with virtualizing security technologies like VPN and firewalls, a compelling business case exists for leveraging hardware more effectively in a virtualized environment. Be sure you understand the technology thoroughly before deploying it. Information security is seldom a forgiving field for learning as you go.

Steganography

Steganography is the art and science of writing hidden messages so that only the sender and intended recipient know a message exists. Steganography is the ultimate security through obscurity technology.

Probably the most well known technique for steganography in the modern era is the embedding of additional information in a digital image. An image before and after a message has been embedded in it appears unchanged to the naked eye. In reality, run the image through the proper program and the secret message appears. However, steganography has been around a lot longer than digital images, and it can take many forms. Simply writing a message in invisible ink on the page of a book is a form of steganography.

The main advantage of steganography is that messages do not arouse suspicion. If you encrypt an e-mail message and send it, and the message is intercepted, then whoever intercepted the message assumes there's something sensitive in the message. If however, you send a copy of a picture of your kids at the amusement park with a message embedded in the photo, unless the intercepting party knows the coded message is coming, they will not give it any special attention. Encrypted messages protect the message. Steganographic messages protect the data as well as the intentions of the sender and the receiver.

Anti-Forensics

The final topic for discussion in this chapter is the use of **anti-forensics**. Anti-forensics are a series of techniques designed to try to frustrate forensic investigators and their **digital forensic techniques**.

Forensic techniques are well known to the information security community, and by extension, to the hacker community, as well. As a result, hackers have developed an arsenal of counter-techniques they use to foil investigations. If they can prevent the investigator from recovering usable evidence, they stand a better chance of avoiding discovery or prosecution. Some of these techniques are also used to hide rootkits and other malware.

Some examples of anti-forensic tools and techniques include:

- Securely overwriting data
- Overwriting metadata
- Designing code that won't run when the system is in debugging mode
- Designing code that won't run in a virtual machine
- Preventing a system from entering safe mode or debugging mode
- Running all code from an external device like a USB drive
- Tampering with file system date and time stamps
- Running in read-only mode to prevent the system from updating file information.

You should be familiar with the concepts associated with anti-forensics, but unless you are planning on becoming a forensic investigator you probably won't encounter any of these except possibly securely overwriting data.

CHAPTER SUMMARY

In this chapter you learned about a number of topics dealing with the future of security technologies and some of the significant emerging security threats. Future information security tools may come from the commercial or the open-source communities, and you learned about the pros and cons of both of those areas of development.

Governance, Risk, and Compliance are the pillars of good policy for guiding your use of security technologies. While the obvious use for security technologies is to provide security, when all is said and done, information security needs to be a business enabler, created with an understanding of the business requirements and the bottom line. The days of deploying information security technologies based solely on management's fear of security incidents are long gone.

Changes in networking technologies on the security perimeter can affect how network security operates. Firewall specialization includes hybrid, data protection, application, database, and ubiquitous firewalls. IDS, IPS and other complementary technologies, such as honeypots, honeynets, and padded cells, steganography, and anti-forensics are essential elements in modern secure networks.

KEY CONCEPTS AND TERMS

Anti-forensics
Data leakage prevention (DLP)
Digital forensic techniques
Information Technology Infrastructure Library (ITIL)
Padded Cell

CHAPTER 15 ASSESSMENT

1. Pick the two most common IDS/IPS deployment models:
   A. Bypass
   B. Unfiltered
   C. Tunneled
   D. Intranet
   E. Screened
2. Which of the following are types of specialized firewalls?
   A. Data protection
   B. Host
   C. Application
   D. Hybrid
   E. Network
3. Two technologies used to identify attack techniques and patterns include ________ and ________.
4. Techniques used to counter digital investigations are known as: ________.
5. Pick the two changing areas to watch when developing your information security road map.
   A. Security industry focus
   B. Vendors
   C. Computer processing power
   D. Cloud computing
   E. Network design
6. The technique of hiding a secret message in plain sight is known as ________.
7. Which of the following is a potential disadvantage of IPv6 from a security perspective?
   A. Additional address space
   B. Less flexible than IPv4
   C. Industry support
   D. Maturity of the standard
   E. Ubiquitous encryption
8. Identifying a user based on anatomical characteristics is known as ________.
9. Which of the following are biometric characteristics?
   A. Default password
   B. Fingerprint
   C. Iris pattern
   D. Voice print
   E. Token
10. Which of the following are considered complementary technologies to an IDS/IPS implementation?
    A. Honeypot
    B. Encryption
    C. VPN
    D. Padded cell
    E. Virtual firewall
11. A device that monitors network traffic and alerts during an attack is an ________.
12. A device that monitors network traffic and alerts and takes action without manual intervention during an attack is an ________.

13. Which of the following contribute to the erosion of the network perimeter?

A. Specialized firewalls
B. VPN
C. IPS/IDS
D. Cloud computing
E. Business partner connections

14. The act of ensuring your company obeys internal policies and any applicable laws is known as ________.

15. The processes and procedures used to ensure employees are following corporate security policies are known collectively as ________.

16. Identify one risk associated with the use of a public wireless connection.

A. Encryption
B. Virus
C. Data interception
D. Data corruption
E. Social engineering

17. What is one advantage to commercial security solutions that might make a company select them over open-source equivalents?

A. Flexibility
B. Support
C. Cost
D. Availability
E. Value

18. Which of the following might be included in a risk register?

A. Risk description
B. Impact
C. Cost
D. Business owner
E. Continuity planning

19. Which of the following are considered core security principles when discussing the uses of security technologies?

A. Confidentiality
B. Governance
C. Integrity
D. Risk
E. Compliance

20. When an IDS detects an attack it can direct the attacker to a host where the attacker cannot do any damage. This host is known as a ________.

APPENDIX

A

Answer Key

CHAPTER 1 Fundamentals of Network Security

1. C 2. E 3. A 4. B 5. C 6. E 7. D 8. B 9. B 10. A 11. A 12. E 13. B and C 14. D 15. E 16. B 17. D 18. C 19. E 20. E

CHAPTER 2 Firewall Fundamentals

1. B 2. C 3. A 4. E 5. D 6. B 7. C 8. B 9. A 10. E 11. E 12. E 13. D 14. A 15. D 16. D 17. B 18. C 19. D 20. B 21. C 22. A 23. E

CHAPTER 3 VPN Fundamentals

1. D 2. B 3. E 4. A 5. B 6. C 7. A 8. E 9. A 10. C 11. D 12. D 13. D 14. D 15. A 16. B 17. A 18. B 19. A 20. D 21. C 22. C 23. B 24. A 25. D

CHAPTER 4 Network Security Threats and Issues

1. C 2. A 3. D 4. E 5. C 6. D 7. E 8. C 9. B 10. E 11. A 12. A 13. C 14. B 15. D 16. D 17. C 18. E 19. A 20. C

CHAPTER 5 Network Security Implementation

1. C 2. E 3. C 4. A 5. A 6. D 7. D 8. C 9. B 10. A 11. E 12. B 13. D 14. A 15. D 16. C 17. B 18. D 19. C 20. A

CHAPTER 6 Network Security Management

1. D 2. B 3. E 4. C 5. D 6. A 7. E 8. E 9. A 10. E 11. D 12. B 13. C 14. C 15. E 16. E 17. B 18. E 19. A 20. D

CHAPTER 7 Exploring the Depths of Firewalls

1. B 2. A 3. D 4. C 5. E 6. D 7. E 8. D 9. B 10. C 11. C 12. wirespeed 13. A 14. C 15. E 16. E 17. C 18. C 19. C 20. E

CHAPTER 8 Firewall Deployment Considerations

1. B 2. E 3. D 4. B 5. A 6. D 7. B 8. C 9. D 10. B 11. E 12. D 13. C 14. A 15. D 16. D 17. B 18. D 19. A 20. B

CHAPTER 9 Firewall Management and Security Concerns

1. B 2. E 3. D 4. B 5. B 6. A 7. C 8. B 9. D 10. E 11. A
12. C 13. C 14. C 15. B 16. A 17. B 18. D 19. B 20. D

CHAPTER 10 Using Common Firewalls

1. A, C, and E 2. D 3. B and D 4. B 5. A 6. inbound, outbound
7. B 8. A, C, and E 9. C 10. B 11. A 12. B 13. A, C, D, and E
14. D 15. A, B, C, D, and E (all) 16. outside 17. post forwarding
18. A 19. B 20. throughput

CHAPTER 11 VPN Management

1. E 2. C 3. Three of the following: Denial of service attack, missing patches, backdoor attack, unpublished vulnerability in the code, weak client security, weak authentication, weak encryption key selection, social engineering
4. SSL, IPSec 5. A and D 6. anonymity 7. C and E 8. VPN policy
9. B, C, and D 10. A, B, and D 11. privacy 12. patch/update 13. B
14. two-factor or token/biometric 15. redundant 16. C and D 17. B
18. A, B, and D 19. A and C 20. circuits

CHAPTER 12 VPN Technologies

1. B and D 2. C and E 3. 3DES 4. SSL and IPSec 5. A and B 6. network address translation (NAT) 7. C and D 8. platform independent 9. B, C, and D
10. B and D 11. request for comments (RFC) 12. virtualization 13. A, B, and E
14. L2F and PPTP 15. SSH 16. A, C, and E 17. B, C, and F 18. A, B, D, and E
19. A and D 20. Secure Socket Layer

CHAPTER 13 Firewall Implementation

1. C 2. B 3. A 4. B 5. C 6. D 7. B 8. B 9. E 10. True 11. A
12. C 13. B 14. B 15. False 16. D 17. C

CHAPTER 14 Real-World VPNs

1. A and D 2. B 3. B 4. Secure Socket Layer (SSL) 5. E 6. B 7. D 8. B
9. B 10. A 11. C 12. A 13. A 14. A 15. B 16. B 17. B 18. B

CHAPTER 15 Perspectives, Resources, and the Future

1. B and E 2. A, C, and D 3. honeypots and honeynets 4. anti-forensics
5. A and D 6. steganogrophy 7. E 8. biometrics 9. B, C, and D
10. A and D 11. IDS or IPS 12. IPS 13. B, D, and E 14. compliance
15. governance 16. C 17. B 18. A, B, and D 19. A and C 20. padded cell

APPENDIX B

Standard Acronyms

3DES	triple data encryption standard
ACD	automatic call distributor
AES	Advanced Encryption Standard
ANSI	American National Standards Institute
AP	access point
API	application programming interface
B2B	business to business
B2C	business to consumer
BBB	Better Business Bureau
BCP	business continuity planning
C2C	consumer to consumer
CA	certificate authority
CAP	Certification and Accreditation Professional
CAUCE	Coalition Against Unsolicited Commercial Email
CCC	CERT Coordination Center
CCNA	Cisco Certified Network Associate
CERT	Computer Emergency Response Team
CFE	Certified Fraud Examiner
CISA	Certified Information Systems Auditor
CISM	Certified Information Security Manager
CISSP	Certified Information System Security Professional
CMIP	common management information protocol
COPPA	Children's Online Privacy Protection
CRC	cyclic redundancy check
CSI	Computer Security Institute
CTI	Computer Telephony Integration
DBMS	database management system
DDoS	distributed denial of service
DES	Data Encryption Standard
DMZ	demilitarized zone
DoS	denial of service
DPI	deep packet inspection
DRP	disaster recovery plan
DSL	digital subscriber line
DSS	Digital Signature Standard
DSU	data service unit
EDI	Electronic Data Interchange
EIDE	Enhanced IDE
FACTA	Fair and Accurate Credit Transactions Act
FAR	false acceptance rate
FBI	Federal Bureau of Investigation
FDIC	Federal Deposit Insurance Corporation
FEP	front-end processor
FRCP	Federal Rules of Civil Procedure
FRR	false rejection rate
FTC	Federal Trade Commission
FTP	file transfer protocol
GIAC	Global Information Assurance Certification
GLBA	Gramm-Leach-Bliley Act
HIDS	host-based intrusion detection system
HIPAA	Health Insurance Portability and Accountability Act
HIPS	host-based intrusion prevention system
HTTP	hypertext transfer protocol
HTTPS	HTTP over Secure Socket Layer
HTML	hypertext markup language
IAB	Internet Activities Board
IDEA	International Data Encryption Algorithm
IDPS	intrusion detection and prevention
IDS	intrusion detection system

IEEE Institute of Electrical and Electronics Engineers
IETF Internet Engineering Task Force
InfoSec information security
IPS intrusion prevention system
IPSec IP Security
IPv4 Internet protocol version 4
IPv6 Internet protocol version 6
IRS Internal Revenue Service
(ISC)^2 International Information System Security Certification Consortium
ISO International Organization for Standardization
ISP Internet service provider
ISS Internet security systems
ITRC Identity Theft Resource Center
IVR interactive voice response
LAN local area network
MAN metropolitan area network
MD5 Message Digest 5
modem modulator demodulator
NFIC National Fraud Information Center
NIDS network intrusion detection system
NIPS network intrusion prevention system
NIST National Institute of Standards and Technology
NMS network management system
OS operating system
OSI open system interconnection
PBX private branch exchange
PCI Payment Card Industry
PGP Pretty Good Privacy
PKI public-key infrastructure
RAID redundant array of independent disks
RFC Request for Comments
RSA Rivest, Shamir, and Adleman (algorithm)
SAN storage area network
SANCP Security Analyst Network Connection Profiler
SANS SysAdmin, Audit, Network, Security
SAP service access point
SCSI small computer system interface
SET Secure electronic transaction
SGC server-gated cryptography
SHA Secure Hash Algorithm
S-HTTP secure HTTP
SLA service level agreement
SMFA specific management functional area
SNMP simple network management protocol
SOX Sarbanes-Oxley Act of 2002 (also Sarbox)
SSA Social Security Administration
SSCP Systems Security Certified Practitioner
SSL Secure Socket Layer
SSO single system sign-on
STP shielded twisted cable
TCP/IP Transmission Control Protocol/Internet Protocol
TCSEC Trusted Computer System Evaluation Criteria
TFTP Trivial File Transfer Protocol
TNI Trusted Network Interpretation
UDP User Datagram Protocol
UPS uninterruptible power supply
UTP unshielded twisted cable
VLAN virtual local area network
VOIP Voice over Internet Protocol
VPN virtual private network
WAN wide area network
WLAN wireless local area network
WNIC wireless network interface card
W3C World Wide Web Consortium
WWW World Wide Web

Glossary of Key Terms

802.1x | Port or portal authentication. A mechanism commonly used by network devices, such as firewalls, routers, switches, and wireless access points, to perform authentication of users before allowing communication to continue across or through the device. The authentication can take place locally on the device or go to an authentications service, such as a credit card payment system, PKI, or directory service.

A

AAA services | Combination of authentication, authorization, and accounting on a dedicated system. Examples include RADIUS, TACACS, and directory services such as LDAP and Active Directory.

Access control | The process or mechanism of granting or denying use of a resource; typically applied to users or generic network traffic.

Access control list (ACL) | Mechanism defining traffic or an event to apply an authorization control of allow or deny against. Often used interchangeably with the terms *rule* and *filter* in relation to firewalls. An ACL focuses on controlling a specific user or client's access to a protocol or port.

Active threats | A form of threat that takes some type of initiative to seek out a target to compromise. These can be hackers, intruders, or automated worms. In any case, an active threat seeks out vulnerable targets. If you don't have reasonable security measures and the active threat discovers your system, you might be at risk for a compromise.

ADSL | Asymmetric Digital Subscriber Line (ADSL); one form of the Digital Subscriber Line technology, a data communications technology that enables faster data transmission over copper telephone lines than a conventional voice band modem can provide.

Adware | Unwanted software that displays advertisements. Often linked with spyware.

Agents | Malicious software programs distributed by hackers to take over control of victims' computers. Also known as bots or zombies. Agents are commonly used to construct botnets.

Alert | A notification from a firewall that a specific event or packet was detected. Alerts notify administrators of events that may need real-time human response or attention.

Algorithm | A set of rules and procedures, usually mathematical in nature. Algorithms can define how the encryption and decryption processes operate. Often very complex, many algorithms are publicly known; anyone can investigate and analyze the strengths and weaknesses of an algorithm.

Allow by default | A security stance that allows all communications except those prohibited by specific deny exceptions. Also known as default allow.

Alternate data stream (ADS) | A feature added to the NTFS file system to support files from POSIX, OS/2, and Macintosh. ADS supports multiple resource forks for file objects. Hackers use ADS to hide files.

Annualized loss expectancy (ALE) | The calculation of the total loss potential across a year for a given asset and a specific threat. ALE calculations are part of risk assessment. ALE = SLE × ARO.

Annualized rate of occurrence (ARO) | A probability prediction based on statistics and historical occurrences on the likelihood of how many times in the next year is a threat going to cause harm. ARO is used in the ALE calculation.

Anomaly-based detection | A form of Intrusion Detection System/Intrusion Prevention System (IDS/IPS) detection based on a defined normal, often defined using rules similar to firewall rules. All traffic or events that fail to match defined normal are considered anomalies and potentially malicious.

Anonymity | The ability for a network or system user to remain unknown. A number of tools and techniques provide anonymity when connected to a network, although the underlying network protocols make true anonymity very difficult.

Anti-forensics | Refers to a series of tools and techniques used to prevent forensic examination from identifying an attack or attacker.

AppleTalk | A legacy protocol developed by Apple Inc. for use in networks hosting mainly Macintosh computers. Mostly replaced by TCP/IP.

Appliance | A hardware product that is dedicated to a single primary function. The operating system or firmware of the hardware device is hardened and its use is limited to directly and only supporting the intended function. Firewalls, routers, and switches are typical appliances.

Appliance firewall | A hardened hardware firewall.

Application layer (Layer 7) | The top or seventh layer of the OSI model. This layer is responsible for enabling communications with host software, including the operating system. The application layer is the interface between host software and the network protocol stack. The sub-protocols of this layer support specific applications or types of data.

Application proxy/firewall/gateway | A type of firewall that filters on a specific application's content and session information.

Arbitrary code execution | An exploit that allows a hacker to run any command line function on a compromised system. Buffer overflow attacks and SQL injection attacks can often allow arbitrary code execution.

ARP spoofing | The falsification of ARP replies to trick the requestor into sending frames to a system other than its intended destination.

Asset | Anything you use in a business process to accomplish a business task is considered an asset.

Asset value (AV) | The cumulative value of an asset based on both tangible and intangible values. AV supports the SLE calculation.

Asymmetric cryptography | A means of encoding and decoding information using related but different keys for each process. A key used to encode cannot decode, and vice versa. Cryptography based on algorithms that use either key pairs or some other special mathematical mechanism. Asymmetric cryptography that uses key pairs is commonly known as public-key cryptography. Different keys serve different purposes. Different keys are used by different members of the communication session. Some systems use something different from keys altogether.

Attack surface | Portions of a software system that unauthenticated users can run.

Auditing | Act of conducting an audit. Auditing can be the action of a system that is recording user activity and system events into an audit log. Auditing can also be the action of an auditor who checks for compliance with security policies and other regulations.

Auditor | Either an outside consultant or an internal member of the Information Technology staff. The auditor performs security audits, confirms that auditing is sufficient, and investigates audit trails produced by system auditing. In the case of regulatory compliance, auditors should be external and independent of the organization under audit.

Authentication | The process of confirming the identity of a user. Also known as logon.

Authenticity | The security service of the combination of authentication and access control (authorization) that provides either the identity of the sender of a message or controls who is the receiver of a message.

Authorization | Defining what users are allowed and not allowed to do. Also known as access control.

Availability | When a system is usable for its intended purpose. The security service that supports access to resources in a timely manner. If availability becomes compromised, a denial of service is taking place.

Avalanche effect | A common feature of hash algorithms. This effect ensures that small changes in the input data produce large changes in the outputted hash value. A single binary digit change in a file should produce a clearly recognizable difference in the resultant hash value.

Awareness | Basic security training that focuses on common or basic security elements that all employees must know and abide by. Less rigorous than training or education.

B

Backdoor | Unauthorized access to a system. A backdoor is any access method or pathway that circumvents access or authentication mechanisms.

Backup | The process of making copies of data onto other storage media. The purpose of a backup is to protect against data loss by having additional onsite or offsite copies of data that can be restored when necessary.

Banner | A message sent by a service in response to a valid or invalid query. A banner can confirm communication is functioning properly or announce an error. Some banners disclose the product name and version number of the service.

Banner grabbing | The act of capturing or extracting banners from services. Hackers often perform banner grabbing after port scanning to learn what service is active on a port.

Bastion host | A firewall positioned at the initial entry point where a network interfaces with the Internet. It serves as the first line of defense for the network. Also known as a sacrificial host.

Behavioral-based detection | A form of IDS/IPS detection based on a recording of real-world traffic as a baseline for normal. All traffic or events that fail to match the normal baselines are considered abnormal and potentially malicious.

Black list | A type of filtering in which all activities or entities are permitted except for those on the black list. Also known as a block list.

Blog | A contraction of the words "web" and "log," it is a form of Web site where the site owner posts messages, images, and videos for the public to view and potentially comment on. Blogs are commonly a platform for discussing issues, causes, or interests.

Border sentry | A description often applied to firewalls positioned on network zone transitions or gateway locations.

Botnet army | A network of zombie/bot/agent–compromised systems controlled by a hacker. The network consists of the bots, agents, or zombies that intercommunicate over the Internet. Another term for zombie.

Botnets | A network of zombie/bot/agent–compromised systems controlled by a hacker. The network consists of the bots, agents, or zombies that intercommunicate over the Internet.

Bots | Malicious software programs distributed by hackers to take over control of victims' computers. Also known as agents or zombies. Bots are commonly used to construct botnets.

Bottleneck | Any restriction on the performance of a system. Can be caused by a slower component or a pathway with insufficient throughput. A bottleneck causes other components of system to work slower than their optimum rate.

Breach | Any compromise of security. Any violation of a restriction or rule whether caused by an authorized user or an unauthorized outsider.

Bridge | A network device that forwards traffic between networks based on the MAC address of the Ethernet frame. A bridge forwards only packets whose destination address is on the opposing network.

Brute force attack | A form of password or encryption key cracking attack that tries all possible valid combinations from a defined set of possibilities (e.g., a set of characters or hex values). Brute force attacks will eventually generate a valid solution given enough time, assuming the hacker uses the correct set of possibilities.

Buffer overflow | A condition in which a memory buffer exceeds its capacity and extends its contents into adjacent memory. Often used as an attack against poor programming techniques or poor software quality control. Hackers can inject more data into a memory buffer than it can hold, which may result in the additional data overflowing into the next area of memory. If the overflow extends to the next memory segment designated for code execution, a skilled attacker can insert arbitrary code that will execute with the same privileges as the current program. Improperly formatted overflow data may also result in a system crash.

Business continuity plan | A plan to maintain the mission-critical functions of the organization in the event of a problem that threatens to take business processes offline. The goal of business continuity planning is to prevent the interruption of business tasks, even with a damaged environment and reduced resources.

Business task | Any activity necessary to meet an organization's long-term goals. Business tasks are assigned to employees and other authorized personnel via their job descriptions.

Bus topology | A network design based on a single backbone cable to which all host segments connect. Ethernet is logically a bus topology-based technology, although it can operate in numerous other physical topologies.

C

Caching | Specifically, caching by a proxy server is the retention of Internet content. Various internal clients may access this content and provide it to subsequent requesters without the need to retrieve the same content from the Internet repeatedly.

Centralized logging system | A technique of storing or copying log events to a centralized logging server. This mechanism is used to create a redundant copy of all log files in a single warehousing location. A common example of this is syslog.

Certificate Authority (CA) | A trusted third-party entity that issues digital certificates to verify and validate identities of people, organizations, systems, and networks digitally.

Channel | A communication pathway, circuit, or frequency dedicated or reserved for a specific transmission.

Chip creep | The slow movement of a chip out of its socket or solder points because of expansion and contraction caused by extreme temperature fluctuations.

Choke point | Similar to a bottleneck, but deliberately created within a network infrastructure. A choke point is a controlled pathway through which all traffic must cross. At this point, filtering to block unwanted communication or monitoring can occur.

Ciphertext | The seemingly random and unusable output from a cryptographic function applied to original data. Ciphertext is the result of encryption. Decryption converts ciphertext back into plain text.

Circuit | A logical connection between a client and a resource server. May exist at Layer 3, 4, or 5 of the OSI model. Also known as a session or a state.

Circuit proxy/firewall | A filtering device that allows or denies the initial creation of a circuit, session, or state, but performs no subsequent filtering on the circuit once established.

Client | A host on a network. A client is the computer system, which supports user interaction with the network. Users employ a client to access resources from the network. Users can also employ a client generically as any hardware or software product to access a resource. For example, standard e-mail software is a client.

Client/server network | A form of network where certain computers are designated as "servers" to host resources shared with the network. The remaining computers are designated as "clients" to enable users to access shared resources. Most client/server networks employ directory services and single sign-on. Also known as a domain.

Client-to-server VPN | A VPN created between a client and a server either within the same local network or across a WAN link or intermediary network to support secure client interaction with the services of a resource host. Also known as a host-to-host VPN.

Clipper Chip | A chipset developed and promoted by the U.S. Government as an encryption device to be adopted by telecommunications companies for voice transmission. It was announced in 1993 and was discontinued in 1996.

Closed source | A type of software product that is pre-compiled and whose source code is undisclosed.

Cluster | A logical division of data composed of one or more sectors on a hard drive. A cluster is the smallest addressable unit of drive storage, usually 512, 1,024, 2,048, or 4,096 bytes, depending on the logical volume size.

Cold calling | A tactic of pursuing and extracting information for the purpose of making a sale or performing a social engineering attack. A cold call presupposes little or no knowledge of the person answering the phone. It requires the caller to be able to pick up on vocal and word clues, be knowledgeable about human nature, and adapt quickly to changes in conversation.

Command shell | A software interface with a system that allows code execution. A command shell is often the focus of an attack. If a hacker gains access to a command shell, he or she can perform arbitrary code execution. Also known as a terminal window or a command prompt. For example, in Windows, the command shell prompt is usually "C:\>".

Commercial firewall | A firewall product designed for larger networks. Usually a commercial firewall is a hardware device.

Common Gateway Interface (CGI) script | The Common Gateway Interface (CGI) is a standard that defines how Web server software can delegate the generation of Web pages to a console application. Such applications are known as CGI scripts. They can be written in many programming languages, although scripting languages are often used.

Compliance audit | A detailed and thorough review of the deployed security infrastructure compared with the organization's security policy and any applicable laws and regulations.

Compression | Removal of redundant or superfluous data or space to reduce the size of a data set. Compression consumes less storage space and increases the speed of data transmission.

Confidentiality | The security service of preventing access to resources by unauthorized users, while supporting access to authorized users.

Content filtering | A form of filtering that focuses on traffic content. Application proxies perform most content filtering.

Contract workers | Outsiders brought into an organization to work on a temporary basis. Contracted workers can be consultants, temporary workers, seasonal workers, contractors, or even day-laborers. Contracted workers potentially represent a greater risk than regular, full-time regular employees because they might lack loyalty, not see the company as worthy of protection, might not be accountable after a project ends, and so on.

Cookie filter | A cookie is a small text file used by Web browsers and servers to track Web sessions. A cookie filter blocks the sending and receiving of cookies. Blocking cookies can reduce some threats of session tracking and identify theft, but can also disable many Web-based services such as online purchasing.

Corporate firewall | An appliance firewall placed on the border or edge of an organization's network.

Cost/benefit | The final equation of risk analysis to assess the relative benefit of a countermeasure against the potential annual loss of a given asset exposed to a specific threat.

Covert channel | An unknown, secret pathway of communication. Covert channels can be timing or storage-based.

Cross-site scripting (XSS) | The malicious insertion of scripting code onto a vulnerable Web site. The results of an XSS attack can include the corruption of the data on the Web site or identity theft of the site's visitors.

Cryptography | The art and science of hiding information from unauthorized third parties. Cryptography is divided into two main categories: encryption and decryption.

Customer Premise Equipment (CPE) | A customer premise equipment-based VPN. This VPN is also known as a VPN appliance.

D

Data Leakage Prevention (DLP) | A distributed data protection technology that leverages deep analysis, context evaluation, and rules configured from a central console to ensure confidential information remains secure while in use, in transit, and at rest

Data link layer (Layer 2) | The second layer of the OSI model responsible for physical addressing (MAC addresses) and supporting the network topology, such as Ethernet.

Database-based detection | A form of IDS/IPS detection based on a collection of samples, patterns, signatures, and so on stored in a database of known malicious traffic and events. All traffic or events that match an item in the database is considered abnormal and potentially malicious. Also known as signature, knowledge, and pattern-matching based detection.

Dead-man switch | A form of auto-initiation switch that triggers when the ongoing prevention mechanism fails. Common dead-man switches include firewalls and hand grenades. If the firewall stops functioning, the connection is severed. If a person dies while holding a live grenade, the safety latch opens and the grenade explodes.

Decryption | The process of converting cipher text back into plain text.

Dedicated connection | A network connection that is always on and available for immediate transmission of data. Most leased lines are dedicated connections.

Dedicated leased lines | See dedicated connection and leased line.

De-encapsulation | The action of processing the contents of a header, removing that header, and sending the remaining payload up to the appropriate protocol in the next higher layer in the OSI model.

Default allow | A security stance that allows all communications except those prohibited by specific deny exceptions. Also known as allow by default.

Default deny | A security stance that blocks all access to all resources until a valid authorized explicit exception is defined.

Default permit | A security stance that allows all access to all resources until an explicit exception is defined.

Defense in depth | A tactic of protection involving multiple layers or levels of security components. Based on the idea that multiple protections create a cumulative effect that will require an attacker to breach all layers, not just one.

Demilitarized zone (DMZ) | A type of perimeter network used to host resources designated as accessible by the public from the Internet.

Denial of service (DoS) | A form of attack that attempts to compromise availability. DoS attacks are usually of two types: flaw exploitation and flooding. DDoS (Distributed Denial of Service) often involves the distribution of robots, zombies, or agents to thousands or millions of systems that are then used to launch a DoS attack against a primary target.

Deny by default | A security stance that prevents all communications except those enabled by specific allow exceptions. Also known as default deny.

Deterrent | A form of security defense that focuses on discouraging a perpetrator with disincentives such as physical harm, social disgrace, or legal consequences. A deterrent can also be a defense that is complex or difficult to overcome, such as strong encryption, multifactor authentication, or stateful inspection filtering.

Dialer | A rogue program that automatically dials a modem to a pre-defined number. Sometimes this is to auto-download additional malware to the victim or to upload stolen data from the victim. In other cases, the dialer calls premium rate telephone numbers to rack up massive long distance charges.

Dictionary attack | A form of password or encryption key-cracking attack that uses a pre-constructed list of potential passwords or encryption keys.

Digital certificate | An electronic proof of identity issued by a certificate authority (CA). A digital certificate is an entity's public key encoded by the CA's private key.

Digital envelope | A secure communication based on public-key cryptography that encodes a message or data with the public key of the intended recipient.

Digital forensic techniques | Identifying, extracting, and evaluating evidence obtained from digital media such as computer hard drives, CDs, DVDs and other digital storage device

Digital signature | A public-key cryptography–based mechanism for proving the source (and possibly integrity) of a signed dataset or message. A digital signature uses the private key of a sender. Not the same as a "digitized signature," which is a digital image of handwriting.

Directory service | A network service that maintains a searchable index or database of network hosts and shared resources. Often based on a domain name system (DNS). An essential service of large networks.

Disaster recovery plan | A plan to restore the mission-critical functions of the organization once they have been interrupted by an adverse event. The goal of disaster recovery planning is to return the business to functional operation within a limited time to prevent the failure of the organization due to the incident

Disgruntled employees | Workers who feel wronged by their employer and who may take malicious, unethical, potentially illegal actions to exact revenge on the organization.

Distributed denial of service (DDoS) | An attack that uses multiple remotely controlled software agents disseminated across the Internet. Because the denial of service attack comes from multiple machines simultaneously, it is "distributed." DDoS attacks can include flooding, spam, eavesdropping, interception, MitM, session hijacking, spoofing, packet manipulation, distribution of malware, hosting phishing sites, stealing passwords, cracking encryption, and more.

Distributed LAN | A LAN whose components are in multiple places that are interconnected by WAN VPN links.

DNS poisoning | A form of exploitation in which the data on a DNS server are falsified so subsequent responses to DNS resolution queries are incorrect. DNS poisoning can wage man-in-the-middle attacks.

DNS spoofing | A form of exploitation in which unauthorized or rogue DNS server responds to DNS queries with false, spoofed resolutions. DNS poisoning can wage man-in-the-middle attacks.

Domain | A client/server network managed by a directory service.

Domain name system (DNS) | A network service that resolves fully qualified domain names (FQDNs) into their corresponding IP address. DNS is an essential service of most networks and their directory services.

Domain registration | The information related to the owners and managers of a domain name accessed through domain registrar's Web sites and whois lookups. A domain registration might include a physical address, people's names, e-mail addresses, and phone numbers. This information is useful in waging social engineering attacks.

Downtime | Any planned or unplanned period when a network service or resource is not available. Downtime can be caused by attack, hardware failure, or scheduled maintenance. Most organizations strive to minimize downtime through security and system management.

Dual-homed firewall | A firewall that has two network interfaces. Each network interface is located in a unique network segment. This allows for true isolation of the segments and forces the firewall to filter all traffic moving from one segment to another.

Dumpster diving | A type of reconnaissance in which an attacker examines an organization's trash or other discarded items to learn internal or private information. The results of dumpster diving are often used to wage social engineering attacks.

Dynamic packet filtering | The process of automatically created temporary filters. In most cases, the filters allow inbound responses to previous outbound requests. Also called stateful inspection.

E

Eavesdropping | The act of listening in on digital or audio conversations. Network eavesdropping usually requires a sniffer, protocol analyzer, or packet capturing utility. Eavesdropping may be able to access unencrypted communication, depending on where it occurs.

Edge router | A router positioned on the edge of a private network. Usually an edge router is the last device owned and controlled by an organization before an ISP or telco connection.

Education | The third and highest level of obtaining security knowledge that leads to career advancement. Security education is broad and not necessarily focused on specific job tasks or assignments. More rigorous than awareness or training.

Egress filtering | Filtering traffic as it attempts to leave a network, which can include monitoring for spoofed addresses, malformed packets, unauthorized ports and protocols, and blocked destinations.

Electronic Privacy Information Center (EPIC) | A public interest research group in Washington, D.C., established in 1994 to focus public attention on emerging civil liberties issues and to protect privacy, the First Amendment, and Constitutional values in the information age. It pursues a wide range of activities, including privacy research, public education, conferences, litigation, publications, and advocacy. It maintains two of the world's most popular privacy sites—epic.org and privacy.org—and publishes the online EPIC Alert every two weeks with information about emerging privacy and civil liberties issues.

Encapsulation | The process of enclosing or encasing one protocol or packet inside another protocol or packet. Also known as "tunneling." Encapsulation allows for communications to cross intermediary networks that might be incompatible with the original protocol. Encapsulation is distinct from encryption, but many encapsulation protocols include encryption.

Encryption | The process of converting original data into a chaotic and unusable form to protect it from unauthorized third parties. Decryption returns the data back to its original, usable form.

Enumeration | The process of discovering sufficient details about a potential target to learn about network or system vulnerabilities. Enumeration often starts with operating system identification, followed by application identification, then extraction of information from discovered services.

Exploit | An attack tool, method, or technique a hacker uses to take advantage of a known vulnerability or flaw in a target system.

Exposure factor (EF) | The potential amount of harm from a specific threat stated as a percentage. Used in the calculation of SLE.

Extranet | A type of perimeter network used to host resources designated as accessible to a limited group of external entities, such as business partners or suppliers, but not by the public. Often, access to an extranet requires the use of a virtual private network or VPN, especially when access originates from the Internet.

Extranet VPN | A VPN used to grant outside entities access into a perimeter network; used to host resources designated as accessible to a limited group of external entities, such as business partners or suppliers, but not the general public.

F

Fail-open | A failure response resulting in open and unrestricted access or communication.

Fail-safe | A failure response resulting in a secured or safe level of access or communication.

Fail-secure | A failure response resulting in a secured or safe level of access or communication.

Fair queuing | A technique of load balancing that operates by sending the next transaction to the firewall with the least current workload.

False negative | An event that does not trigger an alarm but should have, due to the traffic or event actually being abnormal and/or malicious. This is the unwanted non-detection of a malicious event.

False positive | An event that triggers an alarm but should not have, due to the traffic or event actually being benign. This is the unwanted false alarm that wastes time and resources pursuing a non-malicious event.

File encryption | A form of security protection that protects individual files by scrambling the contents in such a way as to render them unusable by unauthorized third parties.

File Transfer Protocol (FTP) | A protocol and a data exchange system commonly used over TCP/IP networks, including the Internet, but which is unencrypted and performs authentication and data transfer in plaintext.

Filter | A written expression of an item of concern (protocol, port, service, application, user, IP address) and one or more actions to take when the item of concern appears in traffic. A filter expresses the intention to block or deny unwanted items of concern. Also known as a rule or ACL.

Filtering | The process of inspecting content against a set of rules or restrictions to enforce allow-and-deny operations on that content. Firewalls and other security components use filtering.

Firewalking | A hacking technique used against static packet filtering firewalls to discover the rules or filters controlling inbound traffic.

Firewall | A network security device or host software that filters communications, usually network traffic, based on a set of predefined rules. Unwanted content is denied and authorized content is allowed. Also known as a sentry device.

Flaw exploitation | A form of DoS that uses a software specific exploit to cause the interruption of availability. Once you apply the appropriate patch, the system is no longer vulnerable to this particular exploit.

Flooding | An attack, usually resulting in a DoS, in which hackers direct massive amounts of traffic toward a target to fully consume available bandwidth or processing capabilities.

Footprinting | The act of researching and uncovering information about a potential attack target. Also known as reconnaissance.

Fragmentation | This occurs when a dataset is too large for maximum supported size of a communication container, such as a segment, packet, or frame. The original dataset divides into multiple sections or fragments for transmission across the size-limited medium, then reassembles on the receiving end. Fragmentation can sometimes corrupt or damage data or allow outsiders to smuggle malicious content past network filters.

Frame | The collection of data at the Data Link layer (Layer 2) of the OSI model, defined by the Ethernet IEEE 802.3 standard, that consists of a payload from the Network layer (Layer 3) to which an Ethernet header and footer have been attached.

Full mesh topology | A network design that establishes all possible connections between hosts. A full mesh topology is the most fault-tolerant topology possible, but is also the least resistant to propagation of malware.

Fully qualified domain name (FQDN) | A complete Internet host name including a top-level domain name, a registered domain name, possibly one or more sub-domain names, and a host name. Examples include: *www.itttech.edu* and *maps.google.com*. A DNS is used to resolve FQDNs into IP addresses.

Fuzzing tools | Hacking and testing utilities that use a brute force technique to craft packets and other forms of input directed toward the target. Fuzzing tools stress a system to push it to react improperly, to fail, or to reveal unknown vulnerabilities.

G

Gateway | An entrance or exit point to a controlled space. A firewall is often positioned at a gateway of a network to block unwanted traffic.

Gateway-to-gateway VPN | A VPN model used to connect to offices together such as a main office and a remote office. It is also referred to as a site-to-site VPN.

H

Hacker | A person who performs hacking. Modern use of this term now implies malicious or criminal intent by the hacker, although criminals are more correctly known as "crackers." An "ethical hacker" obtains the permission of the owner of a system before hacking.

Hacking | The act of producing a result not intended by the designer of a system. Hackers may perform such acts out of curiosity or malice. Malicious hacking is known as "cracking," but many people typically call all these actions "hacking," regardless of intent.

Hardening | The process of securing or locking down a host against threats and attacks. This can include removing unnecessary software, installing updates, and imposing secure configuration settings.

Hardware address | The physical address assigned to a network interface by the manufacturer. Also known as the MAC address.

Hardware firewall | An appliance firewall. A hardened computer product that hosts firewall software exclusively.

Hardware VPN | A dedicated device hosting VPN software. Also known as an appliance VPN. Hardware VPNs can connect hosts and/or networks.

Hash algorithm | A set of mathematical rules and procedures that produces a unique number from a dataset. See hash and hashing.

Hash or hash value | The unique number produced by a hash algorithm when applied to a dataset. A hash value verifies the integrity of data.

Hashing | The process of verifying data integrity. Hashing uses hash algorithms to produce unique numbers from datasets, known as hash values. If before and after hash values are the same, the data retain integrity.

Header | The additional data added to the front of a payload at each layer of the OSI model that includes layer-specific information.

Hierarchical File System (HFS) | A storage device file system developed by Apple Inc. for use on Macintosh computers. HFS supports multiple resource forks for file objects.

Hijacking | This attack occurs when a hacker uses a network sniffer to watch a communications session to learn its parameters. The hacker then disconnects one of the session's hosts, impersonates the offline system, and then begins injecting crafted packets into the communication stream. If successful, the hacker takes over the session of the offline host, while the other host is unaware of the switch.

Honeynet | A collection of multiple honeypots in a network for the purposes of luring and trapping hackers.

Honeypot | A closely monitored system that usually contains a large number of files that appears to be valuable or sensitive, and serves as a trap for hackers. A honeypot distracts hackers from real targets, detects new exploitations, and learns the identities of hackers.

Host | A node that has a logical address assigned to it, usually an IP address. This typically implies that the node operates at and/or above the network layer. This would include clients, servers, firewalls, proxies, and even routers. The term excludes switches, bridges, and other physical devices such as repeaters and hubs. In most cases, a host either shares or accesses resources and services from other hosts.

Host firewall | A software firewall installed on a client or server.

Host VPN | A VPN endpoint located on a host client or server. A host VPN relies on either a native feature of the operating system or a third-party application.

Host-to-gateway VPN | A VPN model where the remote client connects to the VPN server to gain access to the internal network.

Host-to-host VPN | A VPN created between two individual hosts across a local or intermediary network. Host-to-host VPNs is also known as client-to-server or remote-to-office or remote-to-home VPNs.

Host-to-site VPN | A VPN created between a host and a network across a local or intermediary network. Also known as a remote access VPN.

HOSTS file | A static file on every IP enabled host where FQDN to IP address resolutions can be hard coded.

Hybrid attack | A form of password or encryption key-cracking attack that combines dictionary attacks with brute force attacks. A dictionary list provides seed values to a brute force attack tool that makes modifications to the seed value. A very effective attack against users who mistakenly believe that changing a few characters or adding a few characters to a base password is actually improving the password's strength. For example, hybrid attacks may combine dictionary words with a digit or two to increase the likelihood of obtaining a successful result.

Hybrid VPN | A form of VPN establishing a secure VPN over trusted VPN connections.

I

IEEE 802.1x | A networking mechanism to hand off or pass off the task of authentication to a third-party dedicated authentication system. Also known as port authentication, portal authentication, or port-based network access (admission) control (PNAC).

ICMP redirect | An announcement message sent to hosts to adjust the routing table. ICMP type 5 messages are known as redirects. Hackers can use ICMP redirects to perform man-in-the-middle or session hijacking attacks.

Identity proofing | The act of authentication. Confirming the identity of a user or host.

IDS insertion | An attack that exploits the nature of a network focused IDS to collect and analyze every packet to trick the IDS into thinking an attack took place when it actually hasn't. The common purpose of IDS injection attacks is to trick signature or pattern matching detection of malicious network events.

Incident response plan | A predefined procedure to react to security breaches to limit damage, contain the spread of malicious content, stop compromise of information, and promptly restore the environment to a normal state.

Information Technology Infrastructure Library (ITIL) | A set of concepts and practices that provide detailed descriptions and comprehensive checklists, tasks and procedures for common IT practices. The Security Management section is based on the ISO 27002 standard.

Ingress filtering | Filtering traffic as it attempts to enter a network. This can include monitoring for spoofed addresses, malformed packets, unauthorized ports and protocols, and blocked destinations.

Insertion attack | An exploit-based on the introduction of unauthorized content or devices to an otherwise secured infrastructure. Three common insertion-based attacks include SQL injection, IDS insertion, and rogue devices.

Instant message (IM) | A form of near real-time text communication. Also known as chat, IRC, and SMS messaging.

Intangible cost/value | Costs or values not directly related to budgetary funds. They can include, but are not limited to: research and development, marketing edge, competition value, first to market, intellectual property, public opinion, quality of service, name recognition, repeat customers, loyalty, honesty, dependability, assurance, reliability, trademarks, patents, privacy, and so on.

Integrated Services Digital Network (ISDN) | A set of communications standards for simultaneous digital transmission of voice, video, data, and other network services over the traditional circuits of the public switched telephone network.

Integrity | The security service of preventing unauthorized changes to data.

Interception attack | Any attack that positions the attacker inline with a session between a client and server. Such attacks typically allow the hacker to eavesdrop and manipulate the contents of the session. Also known as a man-in-the-middle attack.

Intermediary network | Any network, network link, or channel located between the endpoints of a VPN. Often the Internet.

Internal personnel | Any worker or person who is physically present within the building or who has authorization to remotely connect into the network. Internal personnel are the most common cause of security violations.

International Assigned Numbers Authority (IANA) | The entity responsible for global coordination of IP addressing, DNS root, and other Internet protocol resources.

Internet Control Message Protocol (ICMP) | A commonly used protocol found in the Network layer (Layer 3). ICMP rides as the payload of an IP packet. ICMP supports network health and testing. Commonly abused by hackers for flooding and probing attacks.

Internet Key Exchange (IKE) | The protocol used to set up a security association (SA) in the IPSec protocol suite.

Internet Relay Chat (IRC) | A real-time text communication system. Hackers commonly use IRC as a way to communicate anonymously and control botnets.

Internetwork Packet Exchange/Sequenced Packet Exchange (IPX/SPX) | A legacy protocol developed by Novell for their NetWare networking product. Mostly replaced by TCP/IP.

Intrusion detection system (IDS) | A security mechanism to detect unauthorized user activities, attacks, and network compromise. An IDS can respond in a passive manner through alerts and logging or in an active manner by disconnecting an offending session.

Intrusion prevention system (IPS) | A security mechanism to detect and prevent attempts to breach security.

IP address | The temporary logical address assigned to hosts on a network. An IP address is managed and controlled at the Network layer (Layer 3) of the OSI model by IP (Internet Protocol). IPv4 addresses are 32-bit addresses presented in human-friendly dotted-decimal notation. IPv6 addresses are 128-bit address presented in a special hexadecimal grouping format.

IPSec | IP protocol encryption services extracted from IPv6 to be used as an add-on component for IPv4. IPSec provides tunnel mode and transport mode encrypted network layer connections between hosts and/or networks.

Job description | An essential part of security and an extension of the written security policy. The job description defines the business tasks for each person within the organization. This in turn prescribes the authorization personnel need to accomplish these assigned tasks.

K

Kerberos | A computer network authentication protocol that allows nodes communicating over a non-secure network to prove their identity to one another in a secure manner. It is also a suite of free software published by Massachusetts Institute of Technology (MIT) that implements this protocol. It was designed as a client-server model, and it provides mutual authentication—both the user and the server verify each other's identity. Kerberos protocol messages are protected against eavesdropping and replay attacks.

Key or **encryption key** | The unique number used to guide an algorithm in the encryption and decryption process. A valid key must be within the key space of an algorithm.

Key exchange | The cryptographic function ensuring that both endpoints of a commutation have the same symmetric key. Key exchange occurs by simultaneous key generation or with a digital envelope.

Key pair | The set of associated keys including a public key and a private key used by public key cryptography. Only the public key can decrypt data encrypted by the private key, and vice versa.

Key space | The range of valid keys used by an algorithm. Key space is the bit length of the keys supported by the algorithm.

Keystroke logger | Malware that records all keyboard input and transmits the keystroke log to a hacker.

Knowledge-based detection | A form of IDS/IPS detection based on a collection of samples, patterns, signatures, and so on stored in a database of known malicious traffic and events. All traffic or events that match an item in the database is considered abnormal and potentially malicious. Also known as signature, database, and pattern-matching–based detection.

L

LAN-to-LAN VPN | A VPN between two networks over an intermediary network. Also known as WAN VPN and site-to-site VPN.

Latency | The accumulation of delay each time a communication signal crosses a node or host. Some amount of delay occurs between reception on one interface and transmission out another interface. Too much latency causes communication timeouts.

Leased line | A network communications line leased from an ISP or telco service. A leased line is usually a dedicated line between network locations or to the Internet.

Leetspeak | A somewhat secret form of communication or language hackers use based on replacing letters with numbers, symbols, or other letters that somewhat resemble the original characters. For example, "elite" becomes "eleet," and then becomes "31337."

Line topology | A network design in which hosts are connected end-to-end, each system being connected to no more than two others.

Load balancing | A network traffic management technique to spread the workload or traffic levels across multiple devices to maintain availability, uptime, and high-performance at wirespeed.

Local area network (LAN) | A network confined to a limited geographic distance. Generally, a LAN is comprised of segments that are fully owned and controlled by the host organization as opposed to using lines leased from telcos.

Log | A log is a recording or notation of activities. Many security services, applications, and network resources automatically create a log of all events. Also known as an event log or a log file.

Logging | The act of creating or recording events into a log. Similar to auditing and monitoring.

Logic bomb | Malware that acts like an electronic land mine. Once a hacker places a logic bomb in a system, it remains dormant until a triggering event takes place. The trigger can be a specific time and date, the launching of a program, the typing of a specific keyword, or accessing a specific URL. Once the trigger occurs, the logic bomb springs its malicious event on the unsuspecting use.

Logical address | A temporarily assigned address given to a host. IP address is a common example of a logical address. Most logical addresses exist at the Network layer (Layer 3) of the OSI model.

Logical topology | A description of the arrangement of network devices and how they communicate with each other. Logical topology is a function of network protocols and may not reflect the actual physical topology of the network.

M

MAC (Media Access Control) address | The physical address assigned to a network interface by the manufacturer. The MAC address is a 48-bit binary address presented in as hexadecimal pairs separated by colons. The first half of a MAC address is known as the Organizationally Unique Identifier (OUI) or vender ID, the last half is the unique serial number of the NIC.

MAC spoofing | The act of a hacker changing the MAC address of their network interface. Commonly used to bypass MAC filtering on a wireless access point by impersonating a valid client.

Malicious code (or malware) | Any software that was written with malicious intent. Administrators use antivirus and anti-malware scanners to detect and prevent malicious code (also known as malware) from causing harm within a private network or computer.

Management interface | The command line or graphical interface used to control and configure a device. Often accessible through a console (CON) port on the device or through a logical interface across the network.

Man-in-the-middle (MinM) | This attack occurs when a hacker is positioned between a client and a server and the client is fooled into connecting with the hacker computer instead of the real server. The attack performs a spoofing attack to trick the client. As a result, the connection between the client and server is proxied by the hacker. This allows the hacker to eavesdrop and manipulate the communications.

Maximum Transmission Unit (MTU) | The largest amount of data that a datagram can hold based on the limitations of the networking devices managing a given segment. As an MTU changes across a communication path, a datagram may be fragmented to comply with the MTU restriction.

Mean Time Between Failures (MTBF) | A rating on some hardware devices expressing the average length of time between significant failures.

Mean Time To Failure (MTTF) | A rating on some hardware devices expressing the average length of time until the first significant failure is likely to happen.

Metacharacter | A character that has a special meaning assigned to it and recognized as part of a scripting or programming language. Metacharacters should be filtered, escaped, or blocked to prevent script injection attacks. Escaping metacharacters is a programmatic tactic to treat all characters as basic ASCII rather than as something with special meaning or purpose.

Mission-critical | The state or condition of an asset or process vitally important to the long-term existence and stability of an organization. If a mission-critical element is interrupted or removed, it often results in the failure of the organization.

MITRE | The MITRE Corporation is a not-for-profit organization chartered to work in the public interest. It sponsors a vulnerability research, cataloging, and information organization: *http://cve.mitre.org/*.

Mobile code | A form of software transmitted to and executed on a client. Hackers can use mobile code for malicious purposes.

Modeling | The process of simulating and testing a new concept, design, programming, technique, and so forth before deployment into a production environment. Modeling often occurs before piloting.

Modem | An acronym for MOdulator-DEModulator. A device that communicates computer data across a telephone connection.

Monitor or monitoring | The act of watching for abnormal or unwanted circumstances. Commonly used interchangeably with logging and auditing.

Monkey-in-the-middle | Another term for man-in-the-middle.

Multi-factor authentication | Authentication that requires multiple valid proofs of identity used in simultaneous combination.

N

National Information Infrastructure (NII) | The product of the High Performance Computing and Communication Act of 1991. It was a telecommunications policy buzzword, which was popularized during the Clinton administration under the leadership of Vice President Al Gore. It was a proposed advanced, seamless web of public and private communications networks, interactive services, interoperable hardware and software, computers, databases, and consumer electronics to put vast amounts of information at users' fingertips.

National Institute of Standards and Technology (NIST) | NIST is a non-regulatory federal agency within the U.S. Department of Commerce whose mission is to promote U.S. innovation and industrial competitiveness by advancing measurement science, standards, and technology. As part of its mission, the NIST performs vulnerability research, cataloging, and information distribution: *http://nvd.nist.gov/*.

National Security Agency (NSA) | The National Security Agency/Central Security Service (NSA/CSS) is a cryptologic intelligence agency of the United States government, administered as part of the United States Department of Defense. It is responsible for the collection and analysis of foreign communications and foreign signals intelligence, which involves cryptanalysis. It is also responsible for protecting U.S. government communications and information systems from similar agencies elsewhere, which involves cryptography.

Native firewall | A firewall within an operating system or hardware device placed there by the vendor or manufacturer. Can also include firewalls not necessarily installed by default, but which you can add to a system through an update or patch installation.

NetBIOS | A transport layer protocol used for file and printer sharing over TCP/IP. Originally developed in 1983 as an application-programming interface (API) for software communications, the protocol was extended to encapsulate NetBIOS information in TCP and UDP packets, also known as NetBIOS over TCP/IP (NBT).

NetBIOS Extended User Interface (NetBEUI) | An application-programming interface (API) developed by IBM in 1985 to emulate NetBIOS on a token ring network. Still used by Microsoft to describe a transport layer protocol for file and print sharing over Ethernet, which technically is better termed NetBIOS Frames (NBF). NBF makes extensive use of broadcast messages and thus introduces additional traffic to a network.

Network access control (NAC) | A mechanism that limits access or admission to a network based on the security compliance of a host.

Network address translation (NAT) | A service that converts between internal addresses and external public addresses. This conversion is performed on packets as they enter or leave the network to mask and modify the internal client's configuration. The primary purpose of NAT is to prevent internal IP and network configuration details from being discovered by external entities, such as hackers.

Network layer (Layer 3) | The third layer of the OSI model. This layer is responsible for logical addressing (IP addresses) and routing traffic.

Network News Transfer Protocol (NNTP) | The protocol used by the USENET message service. USENET is a persistent message service that allows anyone to post and read messages from over 100,000 named, categorized, topical newsgroups.

Network security | The collection of security components assembled in a network to support secure internal and external communications. Network security depends on upon host security. Network security operates to protect the network as a whole, rather than as individual systems.

New Technology File System (NTFS) | A file format developed by Microsoft commonly used on Windows systems. NTFS offers file security, large volume size, large file size, and alternate data streams (ADS).

Nmap | A network mapping tool that performs network scanning, port scanning, OS identification, and other types of network probing. Nmap is available at *http://www.insecure.org/*.

Node | Any device on the network that can act as the endpoint of a communication. This includes clients, servers, switches, routers, firewalls, and anything with a network interface that has a MAC address. A node is a component that can receive communication with, rather than one that communication only through or across. For example, network cables and patch panels are not nodes.

Non-authenticating query service | Any communication exchange that does not verify the identity of the endpoints of a communication and accepts any properly formed response as valid. DNS and ARP are common examples. Hackers can easily spoof such a service.

Non-dedicated connection | A network connection not always on and available for immediate transmission of data. A connection must be established through a negation process before the channel is open and ready for data transmission. Dial-up, ISDN, and DSL lines are non-dedicated connections.

Non-repudiation | A security service that ensures that a sender cannot deny sending a message. This service can be provided by public key cryptography, typically through a digital signature.

O

One-time pad | A form of cryptography in which each encryption key is used once before being discarded. Keys are pseudorandom and never repeat. Key length must match message length, so that each character is encrypted with a unique key character.

One-way function | A mathematical operation performed in one direction relatively easily; reversing the operation is impossible—or nearly so.

Open source | A type of software product that may or may not be pre-compiled and whose source code is freely disclosed and available for review and modification.

Opportunistic hackers | A person who takes advantages of unique or abnormal situations to perform malicious actions, but who would not initiate such actions otherwise.

Optical carrier (OC) | A form of network carrier line, often leased or dedicated, which uses fiber optic cables for very high-speed connections. An OC-1 connection supports a throughput of 51.84 Mbps.

OS/2 | A multi-tasking operating system developed jointly by Microsoft and IBM. First released in 1987, it lost nearly its entire market share to Windows after the two companies ceased collaboration in 1990. IBM discontinued support in 2006.

OSI model | Open systems interconnect (OSI) is a standard conceptual tool used to discuss protocols and their functions. The OSI model has seven layers. Each layer can communicate with its peer layer on the other end of a communication session. While the OSI model helps to discuss protocols, most protocols are not in full compliance with it.

Out of band | A method of communication through an alternative route, mechanism, or pathway than the current one employed (the current communication is known as "in band"). Commonly used as a technique for secured data exchange or verification of an identity.

P

Packet | The collection of data at the Network layer (Layer 3) of the OSI model. It consists of the payload from the Transport layer (Layer 4) above and the Network layer header. IP packets are a common example.

Packet manipulation | Any modification of network communications performed mid-session by a hacker. Commonly used in session hijacking, man-in-the-middle, and spoofing attacks.

Padded cell | Specialized host used to place an attacker into a system where the intruder cannot do any harm.

Partial mesh topology | A mesh network design that establishes many but not all possible host-to-host links. Not as fault tolerant as a full-mesh topology.

Partition | A logical division of a hard drive that can be formatted with a file system.

Passive threats | Any harmful code or site that depends upon the user's actions to be accessed or activated. If users never visit an infected site or do not perform the risky activity, the threat never reaches them. A passive threat is similar to a virus in that it depends upon the activity of the user to activate, infect, and spread.

Patch management | The procedure of watching for the release of new updates from vendors, testing the patches, obtaining approval, then overseeing the deployment and implementation of updates across the production environment.

Payload | The non-header component of a PDU/segment/packet/frame. The payload is the data received from the layer above that includes the above layer's header and its payload.

Permission | An ability to interact with a resource that is granted or denied to a user through some method of authorization or access control, such as access control lists (ACLs)

Personal firewall | Typically a software host firewall installed on a home computer or network client. Can also refer to SOHO hardware firewalls such as those found on DSL and cable modems and wireless access points.

Phishing | An attack that seeks to obtain information from a victim by presenting false credentials or luring victims to an attack site. Phishing can occur face to face, over the phone, via e-mail, on a Web site, or through IM.

Physical address | The hardware address assigned to a network interface by the manufacturer. Also known as the MAC address.

Physical layer (Layer 1) | The bottom or first layer of the OSI model. This layer converts data into transmitted bits over the physical network medium.

Physical topology | The actual cable structure connecting hosts and nodes together. Physical topology may be independent of logical topology.

Piloting | Using a new service, device, configuration, software, and so on to a limited number of testing hosts before rolling out the new component to the entire production environment. Piloting often occurs after modeling. Also called beta testing.

Ping sweep | A network scan that sends ICMP type 8 echo requests to a range of IP addresses to obtain ICMP type 0 echo responses. A ping sweep can discover active systems and identify the IP addresses in use.

Playback attack | See replay attack.

Pop-up blocker | A software tool that prevents or restricts Web sites from automatically opening additional tabs or windows without the user's consent. These additional windows are known as pop-ups or pop-unders. Pop-ups are commonly used as methods of advertising, as well as elements in social engineering and distribution of malicious code.

Port-based network access (admission) control (PNAC) | A form of network access control or admission control (NAC) used on individual network access devices, such as firewalls, VPN gateways, and wireless routers, to offload authentication to a dedicated authentication server/service. Only after valid authentication are communications with or across the network device allowed.

Port forwarding | The function of routing traffic from an external source received on a specific pre-defined IP address and port combination (also known as a socket) to an internal resource server. Also known as reverse proxy and static NAT.

Port number | The addressing scheme used at the Transport layer (Layer 4) of the OSI model. There are 65,535 ports, each of which can in theory support a single simultaneous communication.

Port scanning | A network scan that sends various constructions of TCP or UDP packets to determine the open or closed state of a port. Tools such as nmap are used to perform port scanning.

POSIX | A variant of the UNIX operating system. Supported by Windows NT 4.0, but not in any subsequent version of Windows. POSIX used the ADS feature of NTFS.

Post Office Protocol (POP) | An application layer protocol used by e-mail clients to receive messages from an e-mail server. The default TCP/IP port is 110, and it does not encrypt communications. The companion SMTP protocol sends messages to an e-mail server.

Presentation layer (Layer 6) | The sixth layer of the OSI model translates the data received from host software into a format acceptable to the network. This layer also performs this task in reverse for data coming from the network to host software.

Principle of least privilege | The guideline that all users should be granted only the minimum level of access and permission required to perform their assigned job tasks and responsibilities.

Privacy | Keeping information about a network or system user from being disclosed to unauthorized entities. While typically focused on private information like a Social Security number, medical records, credit card number, cellular phone number, etc., privacy concerns extend to any data that represents personally identifiable information (also known as PII).

Private branch exchange (PBX) | A type of business telephone network. PBX systems allow for multiple phone extensions, voice mailboxes, and conference calling. PBX systems require specialized equipment. PBX systems are largely being replaced by VOIP (Voice over IP) solutions.

Private IP address | The ranges of IP addresses defined in RFC 1918 for use in private networks that are not usable on the Internet.

Private key | The key of the public key cryptography key pair kept secret and used only by the intended entity. The private key decodes information encoded with its associated public key, encrypting information that can be decrypted only by its associated public key. This process validates the identity of the originator and creates a digital signature.

Privilege | An increased ability to interact with and modify the operating system and desktop environment granted or denied to a user through some method of authorization or access control, such as user rights on a Windows system.

Privilege escalation | The act of obtaining a higher level of privilege or access for a user account or a session. A tactic employed by hackers once they intrude into a network through the compromise of a normal user account.

Professional hackers | Criminals whose objective is to compromise IT infrastructures. Whether operating as individuals, offering mercenary hacking services, or functioning as members of a criminal ring, professional hackers focus time and energy on becoming effective cyber attackers. A professional hacker is someone who contracts out his or her hacking skills to others.

Protocol Data Unit (PDU) | The collection of data at the Session, Presentation, and Application layers (Layers 5–7) of the OSI model.

Proxy | A network service that acts as a "middle man" between a client and server. A proxy can hide the identity of the client, filter content, perform NAT services, and cache content.

Proxy attack | See man-in-the-middle.

Proxy manipulation | An attack in which a hacker modifies the proxy settings on a client to redirect traffic to another system, such as the hacker's own machine. The hacker may host a proxy server in addition to eavesdropping and manipulating the redirected traffic.

Pseudo random number generator (PRNG) | The mechanism of computer systems that produces partially random numbers using a complex algorithm and a seed value that is usually time based. Computers are currently unable to produce true random numbers and a PRNG approximates randomness.

Public IP address | Any address that is valid for use on the Internet. This excludes specially reserved addresses such as loopback (127.0.0.1–127.255.255.255), RFC 1918 addresses, and the Windows APIPA addresses (169.254.0.0–169.254.255.255). Organizations lease public addresses from an Internet Service Provider (ISP).

Public key | The key of the public key cryptography key pair shared with other entities with whom the holder of the private key wishes to correspond. The public key decodes messages encoded with its associated private key, originates messages that only the holder of the associate private key can decrypt, and creates digital envelopes.

Public key cryptography | A subset of asymmetric cryptography based on the use of key pair sets. Public key cryptography uses public and private keys to create digital envelopes and digital signatures.

Public Key Infrastructure (PKI) | A combination of several cryptographic components to create a real-world solution that provides secure communications, storage, and identification services. Commonly uses symmetric encryption, asymmetric/public key encryption, hashing, and digital certificates. In most cases, when PKI refers to authentication, digital certificates are used as credentials.

Public network | Any network that accessible by entities from outside an organization. Most often, use of this term implies the Internet, but many other public networks exist.

Pwned | A leetspeak word derived from a common IRC typo of "owned." Used to mean hacking and taking over control of a computer or network.

R

Reconnaissance | The act of learning as much as possible about a target before attempting attacks. Reconnaissance consists of collecting data about the target from multiple sources online and offline. Effective reconnaissance is done covertly, without tipping off the target about the research. Reconnaissance can also be called footprinting, discovery, research, and information gathering.

Recreational hackers | People those who enjoy learning and exploring, especially with computing technology. However, they might make poor choices as to when to use their newfound skills. Bringing in unapproved software from home, experimenting on the company network, or just trying out an exploit to "see if it works" are all potential problems caused by recreational hackers.

Redundancy or **redundant** | The feature of network design that ensures the existence of multiple pathways of communication. The purpose is to prevent or avoid single points of failure.

Redundant Array of Independent Disks (RAID) | A disk set management technology that gains speed and fault tolerance. RAID can provide some protection against hard drive failure, but does not protect against software or data compromises, such as virus infection.

Regional Internet Registry (RIR) | The five regional organizations that oversee and monitor the allocation and registration of IP addresses (both IPv4 and IPv6). RIR consists of American Registry for Internet Numbers (ARIN), RIPE Network Coordination Center (RIPE NCC), Asia-Pacific Network Information Centre (APNIC), Latin American and Caribbean Internet Address Registry (LACNIC) and African Network Information Centre (AfriNIC).

Rekeying | The process of triggering the generation of a new symmetric encryption key and secure exchange of that key. Rekeying can take place based on time, idleness, volume, randomness, or election.

Remote access | A communications link that enables access to network resources using a wide area network (WAN) link to connect to a geographically distant network. In effect, remote access creates a local network link for a system not physically local to the network. Over a remote access connection, a client system can technically perform all the same tasks as a locally connected client, with the only difference being the speed or the bandwidth of the connection.

Remote access server (RAS) or network access server (NAS) | A network server that accepts inbound connections from remote clients. Also known as a network access server (NAS).

Remote-to-home VPN | A VPN used to connect a remote or mobile host into a home computer or network. Also known as a host-to-host VPN.

Remote-to-office VPN | A VPN used to connect a remote or mobile host into office network workstation. Also known as a host-to-host VPN.

Remote control | The ability to use a local computer system to remotely take control of another computer over a network connection. Often used for remote technical assistance.

Replay attack | This attack occurs when a hacker uses a network sniffer to capture network traffic and then retransmits that traffic back on to the network at a later time. Replay attacks often focus on authentication traffic in the hope that retransmitting the same packets that allowed the real user to log into a system will grant the hacker the same access.

Request for comment (RFC) | A document that defines or describes computer and networking technologies. RFCs exist for hardware, operating systems, protocols, security services, and much more.

Resources | Any data item or service available on a computer or network accessible by a user to perform a task.

Return on Investment (ROI) | A business evaluation technique to determine whether an investment will earn back equivalent or greater benefit within a specific time.

Reverse proxy | The function of routing traffic from an external source received on a specific pre-defined IP address and port combination (also known as a socket) to an internal resource server. Also known as port forwarding and static network address translation (NAT).

RFC 1918 addresses | IP addresses that, by convention, are not routed outside a private or closed network. Class A: 10.0.0.0–10.255.255.255; Class B: 172.16.0.0–172.31.255.255; Class C: 192.168.0.0–192.168.255.255

Ring topology | A network design where host segments are attached to a central cable ring.

Risk | The likelihood or potential for a threat to take advantage of a vulnerability and cause harm or loss. Risk is a combination of an asset's value, exposure level, and rate of occurrence of the threat. A goal of security is to recognize, understand, and eliminate risk.

Risk assessment | Risk assessment is the process of examining values, threat levels, likelihoods, and total cost of compromise versus the value of the resource and the cost of the protection. This involves the use of values and calculations, such as AV, EF, SLE, ARO, ALE, and the cost/benefit equation.

Risk management | Performing risk assessment, and then acting on the results to reduce or mitigate risk. Often risk assessment establishes a new security policy and then aids in revising it over time.

Roles or **job roles** | A collection of tasks and responsibilities defined by a security policy or job description for an individual essential productivity, or security position.

Rootkit | A form of malware that hackers can upload and deploy on a target system. It often replaces multiple components of the host operating system with altered code. A rootkit may have stealth capability, which means that when activated, it can camouflage itself, logs, other files, or resources by intercepting calls to the operating system and generating its own reply. For example, the directory command "DIR" can be reprogrammed to suppress the display of the rootkit files A rootkit acts a somewhat like a device driver and positions itself between the kernel (the core program of an operating system) and the hardware. From there, the rootkit can selectively hide files on storage devices and active process in memory from being viewable, accessible, or detectible by the OS. Rootkits often hide other forms of malware or hacker tools. Rootkits can include other malware functions in addition to their stealth abilities.

Round-robin | A form of load balancing which hands out tasks in a repeating non-priority sequence.

Round-robin database Tool (RRDtool) | Round-Robin Database Tool, aimed to handle time-series data like network bandwidth, temperatures, CPU load, and so on. The data are stored in a round-robin database (circular buffer), thus the system storage footprint remains constant over time.

Router | A network device responsible for directing traffic towards its stated destination along the best-known current available path.

Rule | A written expression of an item of concern (protocol, port, service, application, user, IP address) and one or more actions to take when the item of concern appears in traffic. Also known as a filter or ACL.

Rule set | The list of rules on a firewall (or router or switch) that determine what traffic is and is not allowed to cross the filtering device. Most rule sets employ a first-match-apply-action process.

S

Sacrificial host | A firewall positioned at the initial entry point where a network interfaces with the Internet serving as the first line of defense for the network. Also known as a bastion host.

Scalability | The ability of a product or service to provide adequate performance across changes in size, load, scope, or volume.

Scanning | The act of probing a network using custom crafted packets. Scanning can determine the IP addresses in use and whether ports are open or closed. The tool nmap can be used to perform scanning.

Screening router | A router that can perform basic static packet filtering services in addition to routing functions. A screening router is the predecessor of modern firewalls.

Script kiddie | A new, inexperienced, or ignorant hacker who uses pre-built attack tools and scripts instead of writing his or her own or customizing existing ones. Even though a derogatory term in the hacker community, "script kiddie" still describes a serious threat to network security.

Sector | A subdivision of computer storage medium that represents a fixed size of user-accessible data. Magnetic disks typically have 512-byte sectors; optical disks have 2,048-byte sectors. When a device is formatted, sectors are grouped into clusters.

Secure Shell (SSH) | A network protocol that allows data exchange using a secure channel between two networked devices. It is used primarily on GNU/Linux and UNIX based systems to access shell accounts. SSH was a replacement for Telnet and other insecure remote shells, which send information, notably passwords, in plaintext, rendering them susceptible to packet analysis. The encryption used by SSH provides confidentiality and integrity of data over an insecure network, such as the Internet.

Secure Sockets Layer (SSL) | A security protocol that operates at the top of the Transport layer (Layer 4) and resides as the payload of a TCP session. Netscape designed SSL in 1997 for secure Web e-commerce, but it can encrypt any traffic above the Transport layer. It uses public key certificates to identify the endpoints of session and uses symmetric encryption to protect transferred data. SSL v3.0 is the last version of SSL; TLS is replacing SSL.

Secured VPN | A VPN that uses encryption to protect the confidentiality of its transmissions.

Security goals and security objectives | Sets of stated purposes or targets for network security activity. Standard goals include confidentiality, integrity, and availability. Objectives are generally more oriented towards achieving or maintaining the goals, such as ensuring the confidentiality of resources.

Security policy | A written document prescribing security goals, missions, objectives, standards, procedures, and implementations for a given organization. Also identifies what assets need protection based on their value.

Security Technical Implementation Guides (STIGS) | A security guideline, procedure, or recommendation manual.

Security through obscurity | A form of security based on hiding details of a system, or creating convolutions that are difficult to understand. Such strategies do not usually resist a persistent attack, and are used when true security is poorly understood or the perceived threat is insufficient to overcome the obscure methodology. For example, proprietary source encryption algorithms can be labeled security through obscurity, as no forum for peer review or for formal testing exists to examine whether the methodology is cryptographically sound.

Segment | The collection of data at the Transport layer (Layer 4) of the OSI model. It consists of the payload from the Session layer (Layer 5) above and the Transport layer header. TCP segments are a common example. (Note: UDP segments are called datagrams as they are connectionless, rather than connection-oriented).

Senior management | The individual or group of highest controlling and responsible authority within an organization. Ultimately the success or failure of network security rests with senior management.

Separation of duties | An administrative rule whereby no single individual possesses sufficient rights to perform certain actions. Achieved by dividing administrative level tasks and powers among compartmentalized administrators.

Server | A host on a network. A server is the computer system that hosts resources accessed by users from clients.

Session | A logical connection between a client and a resource server. May exist at Layer 3, 4, or 5 of the OSI model. Also known as a circuit or a state.

Session hijacking | When a hacker is able to take over a connection after a client has authenticated with a server. To perform this attack, a hacker must eavesdrop on the session to learn details, such as the addresses of the session endpoints and the sequencing numbers. With this information, the hacker can desynchronize the client, take on the client's addresses, and then inject crafted packets into the data stream. If the server accepts the initial false packets as valid, then the session has been hijacked.

Session layer (Layer 5) | The fifth layer of the OSI model. This layer manages the communication channel, known as a session, between the endpoints of the network communication. A single transport layer connection between two systems can support multiple simultaneous sessions.

Shell code | The content of an exploit to be executed on or against a target system.

Signature-based detection | A form of IDS/IPS detection based on a collection of samples, patterns, signatures, and so on stored in a database of known malicious traffic and events. All traffic or events that match an item in the database is considered abnormal and potentially malicious. Also known as database, knowledge, and pattern-matching–based detection.

Simple Mail Transfer Protocol (SMTP) | An application-layer protocol used by e-mail clients to send messages to an e-mail server and is also used to relay messages between e-mail servers. The default TCP/IP port is 25, and it does not encrypt communications. The companion POP protocol receives messages from an e-mail server.

Single-factor authentication | The use of only a single element of validation or verification to prove the identity of a subject. Considered much weaker than multi-factor authentication.

Single loss expectancy (SLE) | The calculation of the loss potential across of a single incident for a given asset and a specific threat. SLE calculations are part of risk assessment. SLE = AV × EF.

Single point of failure | Any element of a system or network infrastructure, which is the primary or only pathway through which a process occurs. The compromise of such an element could result in system failure. Network design should avoid single points of failure by including redundancy and defense in depth.

Single sign-on (SSO) | A network security service that allows a user to authenticate to an entire domain through a single client log on process. All domain members will accept this single authentication. Local authorization is used to control access to individual resources. Such a single authentication can be more complex, since multiple logons for each individual server are not required.

Site-to-site VPN | A VPN used to connect networks. Also known as a LAN-to-LAN VPN and WAN VPN.

Slack space | The unused portion of the last cluster allocated to a stored file. It may contain remnants of prior files stored in that location. Hackers can hijack slack space to create hidden storage compartments.

Slideware | An industry term referring to any product that appears in a vendor's PowerPoint slide deck, but is not yet available in one of its products. Also sometimes known as "vaporware."

Sniffer | A software utility or hardware device that captures network communications for investigation and analysis. Also known as packet analyzer, network analyzer, and protocol analyzer.

Social engineering | The craft of manipulating people into performing tasks or releasing information that violates security. Social engineering relies on telling convincing lies to manipulate people or take advantage of the victim's desire to be helpful.

Socket | The combination of an IP address and a port number as a complete address.

Software firewall | A host firewall installed on a client or server.

Software VPN | A VPN crafted by software rather than hardware. Software VPN may be a feature of the operating system or a third-party application.

SOHO (small office, home office) network | Any small network, workgroup, or client/server, deployed by a small business, a home-based business, or just a family network in a home.

Spam | Unwanted and often unsolicited messages. Spam is not technically malicious software, but spam can have a serious negative effect on IT infrastructures through sheer volume. Estimates vary, but spam may represents up to 95 percent of all e-mail (which implies for every legitimate e-mail there are up to 19 unrelated spam e-mails.)

Split tunnel | A VPN connection that allows simultaneous access to the secured VPN link and unsecured access to the Internet across the same connection.

Spoofing | The falsification of information. Often spoofing is the attempt to hide the true identity of a user or the true origin of a communication.

Spyware | An advancement of keystroke logging to monitor and record many other user activities. Spyware varies greatly, but it can collect a list of applications launched, URLs visited, e-mail sent and received, chats sent and received, and names of all files opened. It can also record network activity, gather periodic screen captures, and even recording from a microphone or Web cam. Can be linked with adware.

SQL injection | A form of Web site/application attack in which a hacker submits SQL expressions to cause authentication bypass, extraction of data, planting of information, or access to a command shell.

Star topology | A network design in which host segments radiate from a central node.

State | A logical connection between a client and a resource server. May exist at Layer 3, 4, or 5 of the OSI model. Also known as a session or a circuit.

Stateful inspection | The process of automatically tracking sessions or states to allow inbound responses to previous outbound requests. Also called dynamic packet filtering.

Static electricity discharge (SED) or Electrostatic discharge (ESD) | A sudden and momentary electric current, usually of high voltage and low amperage, that flows between two objects. Commonly caused by low humidity environments. Humans, polyester, and plastics are prone to static build-up. SED can damage most computer components.

Static NAT | The static coding of a translation pathway across a NAT service. Also known as port forwarding and reverse proxy.

Static packet filtering | A method of filtering using a static or fixed set of rules to filter network traffic. The rules can focus on source or destination IP address, source or destination port number, IP header protocol field value, ICMP types, fragmentation flags, and IP options. Static packet filtering is therefore mainly focused on the Network layer (Layer 3), but can also include Transport layer (Layer 4) elements. Static packet filtering focuses on header contents and does not examine the payload of packets or segments.

Subnetting | The process of dividing a block of computer network addresses into smaller blocks that contain a common set of high-order address bits, called a routing prefix. A subnet is typically served by a single router.

Sunk cost | Time, money, and effort already spent on a project, event, or device. In economics, sunk costs are irrelevant to future decisions. Emotionally, however, people often use sunk costs as a rationalization to continue failing processes or procedures.

Switch | A device, which provides network segmentation through hardware. Across a switch, temporary dedicated electronic communication pathways are created between the endpoints of a session (such as a client and server). This switched pathway prevents collisions. Additionally, switches allow the communication to use the full potential throughput capacity of the network connection, instead of 40 percent or more being wasted by collisions (as occurs with hubs).

Symmetric cryptography | Cryptography based on algorithms that use a single shared secret key. The same key encrypts and decrypts data and the same key must be shared with all communication partners of the same session.

Synchronous dynamic random access memory (SDRAM) | Dynamic random access memory (DRAM) that has a synchronous interface. Traditionally, dynamic random access memory (DRAM) has an asynchronous interface, which means that it responds as quickly as possible to changes in control inputs. SDRAM has a synchronous interface, meaning that it waits for a clock signal before responding to control inputs and is therefore synchronized with the computer's system bus.

Systems Network Architecture (SNA) | A legacy networking protocol developed by IBM commonly used to support communications between mainframes. Mostly replaced by TCP/IP.

T

Tangible cost/value | Costs or values directly related to budgetary funds. They can include, but are not limited to: purchase, license, maintenance, management, administration, support, utilities, training, troubleshooting, hardware, software, updates/upgrades, and so forth.

Tcpdump | A common packet analyzer that runs at the command line. It allows the user to intercept and display TCP/IP and other packets being transmitted or received over a network to which the computer is attached.

Telco | Short for telecommunications company or corporation. Used to refer to any company that sells or leases WAN connection services whether wired or wireless.

Telecommuting | The act of working from a home, remote, or mobile location while connecting into "the employer's private network, often using a VPN.

Telnet | A protocol and a service used to remotely control or administer a host through a plaintext command line interface.

Terminal server/services/session | A modern form of legacy thin client operation. A thin client software utility connects to a central terminal server, which simulates remote control. A terminal service system can support multiple simultaneous terminal client connections. When terminal services are in use, the client workstation coverts to thin client status. All operations of storage and processing then take place on the terminal server.

Thin client | A legacy terminal concept used to control mainframes. Thin clients had no local processing or storage capability. Modern thin clients simulate these limitations and perform all operations on the terminal server, remote control server, or thin client server.

Threat | Any potential harm to a resource or node on the network. Threats can be natural or artificial, caused by mother nature or man, or by the result of ignorance or malicious intent. Threats originate internally and externally.

Topology | An arrangement of networking segments, hosts, and nodes. Common examples include bus, star, ring, full mesh, partial mesh, tree, and line.

Traceroute | A computer network tool used to show the route taken by packets across an IP network. An IPv6 variant, traceroute6, is also widely available.

Traffic congestion | The problem when too much data crosses a network segment. This results in reduced throughput, increased latency, and lost data.

Training | The second level of knowledge distribution offered by an organization to educate users about job task focused security concerns. More rigorous than awareness; less rigorous than education.

Transmission Control Protocol (TCP) | The connection-oriented protocol operating at the Transport layer (Layer 4) of the OSI model.

Transport layer (Layer 4) | The fourth layer of the OSI model. This layer formats and handles data transportation. This transportation is independent of and transparent to the application.

Transport Layer Security (TLS) | A security protocol that operates at the top of the Transport layer (Layer 4) and resides as the payload of a TCP session. It uses public key certificates to identify the endpoints of session and uses symmetric encryption to protect transferred data. TLS 1.0 is the replacement for SSL 3.0.

Transport mode encryption | A form of encryption also known as point-to-point or host-to-host encryption. Transport mode encryption protects only the payload of traffic and leaves the header in plain-text original form.

Trapdoor | A form of unauthorized access to a system. A trapdoor is any access method or pathway that circumvents access or authentication mechanisms. Also known as a backdoor.

Tree topology | A network design that organizes hosts into a hierarchy. Each host is connected upstream to a single parent, but can be connected downstream to none, one, or many hosts.

Triple-homed firewall | A firewall that has three network interfaces. Each network interface is located in a unique network segment. This allows for true isolation of the segments and forces the firewall to filter all traffic traversing from one segment to another.

Trojan horse | A mechanism of distribution or delivery more than a specific type of malware. The Trojan horse embeds a malicious payload within a seemingly benign carrier or host program. When the host program is executed or otherwise accessed, the malware is delivered. The gimmick of a Trojan horse is the act of fooling someone (a type of social engineering attack) into accepting the Trojan program as safe.

Trust | Confidence in the expectation that others will act in your best interest, or that a resource is authentic. On computer networks, trust is the confidence that other users will act in accordance with the organization's security rules and not attempt to violate stability, privacy, or integrity of the network and its resources.

Trusted Platform Module (TPM) | A dedicated microchip found on some motherboards that host and protect the encryption key for whole hard drive encryption.

Trusted third party | A mechanism of authentication using a third entity known and trusted by two parties. The trusted third party allows the two communicating parties, who were originally strangers to each other, to establish an initial level of inferred trust.

Trusted VPN | A VPN that uses dedicated channels, rather than VPNs, to provide privacy to its transmissions.

Tunnel mode encryption | A form of encryption also known as site-to-site, LAN-to-LAN, gateway-to-gateway, host-to-LAN, and remote access encryption. Tunnel mode encryption performs a complete encapsulation of the original traffic into a new tunneling protocol. The entire original header and payload are encrypted and a temporary link or tunnel header guides the data across the intermediary network.

Tunneling | The act of transmitting a protocol across an intermediary network by encapsulating it in another protocol. See encapsulation.

Two-factor authentication | A method of proving identity using two different authentication factors. Authentication factors are something you know, something you have, or something you are. Examples include a smart card (something you have) with a PIN (something you know), a biometric device (something you are) coupled with a password (something you know), or a proximity card (something you have) that activates a fingerprint reader (something you are).

U

Unified threat management (UTM) | The deployment of a firewall as an all-encompassing primary gateway security solution. The idea behind UTM is a single device can be designed to perform firewall filtering, IPS, antivirus scanning, anti-spam filtering, VPN end-point hosting, content filtering, load-balancing, detailed logging, and potentially other security services, performance enhancements, or extended capabilities.

Unpartitioned space | The area on a storage device not contained within a partition. Unpartitioned space is not directly accessible by the OS.

Upstream filtering | The management of traffic by a firewall or other filtering device located one or more hops away (upstream) from a private network.

URL injector | Malware that replaces URLs in HTTP GET requests for alternative addresses. These injected URLs cause a different Web page to appear in the browser than the one requested by the user's request. These replaced Web pages could be advertisement sites, generate traffic to falsify search engine optimization (SEO), or lead to fake or spoofed sites.

USENET newsgroups | Persistent public messaging forums accessed over the NNTP (Network News Transfer Protocol). USENET has existed since 1980. Although the Web, e-mail, and BitTorrent are more widely known, USENET is still in use today.

User Datagram Protocol (UDP) | The connectionless protocol operating at the Transport layer (Layer 4) of the OSI model.

V

Virtual private network (VPN) | A mechanism to establish a secure remote access connection across an intermediary network, often the Internet. This allows inexpensive insecure links to replace expensive security links. VPNs allow for cheap long-distance connections established over the Internet. Both endpoints need only a local Internet link.

The Internet itself serves as a "free" long-distance carrier. VPNs employ encapsulation and tunneling protocols, such as IPSec.

Virus | Malware that needs a host object to infect. Most viruses infect files, such as executables, device drivers, DDLs, system files, and sometimes even document, audio, video, and image files. Some viruses infect the boot sector of a storage device, including hard drives, floppies, optical discs, and USB drives. Viruses are spread through the actions of users, and spread file-to-file (compare to worms).

VPN appliance | A hardware VPN device.

VPN Fingerprinting | A technique used by an attacker to identify the vendor, and in some cases, the software version, of a VPN server.

Vulnerability | A weakness or flaw in a host, node, or any other infrastructure component that a hacker can discover and exploit. Security management aims to discover and eliminate such vulnerabilities.

Vulnerability management | The technology and business processes used to identify, track, and mitigate known weaknesses on hosts within a computing environment.

Vulnerability scanning | A form of investigation that aims at checking whether or not a target system is subject to attack based on a database of tests, scripts, and simulated exploits.

W

WAN VPN | A VPN between two networks over an intermediary network. Also known as LAN-to-LAN VPN and site-to-site VPN.

War dialing | A method of discovering active modems by dialing a range of phone numbers.

War driving | A method of discovering wireless networks by moving around a geographic area with a detection device.

White list | A type of filtering concept where the network denies all activities except for those on the white list. Also known as an "allow" or "permissions list."

Whois | A tool used to view domain registration information. Whois is a command line function of Linux and Unix, but is also a tool on most domain registrar Web sites.

Whole hard drive encryption | The process of encrypting an entire hard drive rather than just individual files. In most cases, whole hard drive encryption provides better security against unauthorized access than file encryption, because it encrypts temporary directories and slack space.

Wide area network (WAN) | A network not limited by any geographic boundaries. A WAN network can span a few city blocks, reach across the globe, and even extend into outer space. A distinguishing characteristic of a WAN is its use of leased or external connections and links. Often, telcos own these external connections.

Wirespeed | The maximum communication or transmission capability of a network segment. Often used to describe a network device's ability to perform tasks on traffic, while being able to maintain overall network transmission speeds without introducing delay, lag, or latency.

Workgroup | A form of networking where each computer is a peer. Peers are equal to each other in terms of how much power or controlling authority any one system has over the other members of the same workgroup. All workgroup members are on equal footing because they can manage their own local resources and users, but not those of any other workgroup member.

Worm | Malware that does not need a host object; instead, a worm is a self-sustaining program in its own right. Worms are designed around specific system flaws. The worm scans other systems for this flaw and exploits the flaw to gain access to another victim. Once hosted on another system, the worm seeks to spread itself by repeating the process. Worms can act as carriers to deposit other forms of malicious code as they multiply and spread across networked hosts.

Wrapper | A tool used to create Trojan horses by embedding malware inside of a host file or program.

Write-once read-many (WORM) | A form of storage device that can be written to once, but once written cannot be electronically altered. Examples include DVD-R, WORM tapes, and WORM hard drives.

Z

Zero-day exploits | New and previous unknown attacks for which are there no current specific defenses. "Zero day" refers to the newness of an exploit, which may be known in the hacker community for days or weeks. When such an attack occurs for the first time, defenders are given zero days of notice (hence the name.) Such attacks usually exploit previously unidentified system flaws.

Zeroization | The process of purging a storage device by writing zeros to all addressable locations on the device. A zeroized device contains no data remnants that other users could potentially recover.

Zombie army | A network of zombie/bot/agent-compromised systems controlled by a hacker. The network consists of the bots, agents, or zombies that intercommunicate over the Internet. Another term for botnet.

Zombies | Malicious software programs distributed by hackers to take over control of victims' computers. Also known as bots or agents. Zombies are commonly used to construct botnets (or zombie armies).

Zone of risk | Any segment, subnet, network, or collection of networks that represent a certain level of risk. The higher the risk, the higher the security need to protect against that risk. The less the risk of a zone, the lower security need because fewer threats exist or existing threats are less harmful. The flip side of risk zones is zones of trust.

Zone of trust | Any segment, subnet, network, or collection of networks that represent a certain level of trust. Highly trusted zones require less security, while low trusted zones require more security. The flip side of trust zones is zones of risk.

References

Beaver, Kevin. *Hacking For Dummies*. 3rd ed. Indianapolis: Wiley Publishing, Inc., 2010.

Bhaiji, Yusuf. *Network Security Technologies and Solutions*. Indianapolis: Cisco Press, 2008.

Cheswick, William R., Steven M. Bellovin, and Aviel D. Rubin. *Firewalls and Internet Security: Repelling the Wily Hacker*. 2nd ed. Boston: Addison-Wesley Professional, 2003.

Cisco Systems. *Internetworking Technologies Handbook, Virtual Private Networks*. http://www.cisco.com/en/US/docs/internetworking/technology/handbook/VPN.html (accessed July 15, 2010).

CNN. "How the President's secret helicopter plans wound up in Iran." March 2009. http://ac360.blogs.cnn.com/2009/03/10/how-the-presidents-secret-helicopter-plans-wound-up-iran/ (accessed July 15, 2010).

Cole, Eric. *Hiding in Plain Sight: Steganography and the Art of Covert Communication*. Indianapolis: Wiley Publishing, Inc., 2003.

———. *Network Security Bible*. Indianapolis: Wiley Publishing, Inc., 2009.

Comer, Douglas E. *Internetworking with TCP/IP, Vol 1*. 5th ed. Upper Saddle River, NJ: Prentice Hall, 2005.

Davies, Joseph, and Elliot Lewis. *Deploying Virtual Private Networks with Microsoft Windows Server 2003 (Technical Reference)*. Redmond, WA: Microsoft Press, 2003.

Davis, Michael, Sean Bodmer, and Aaron LeMasters. *Hacking Exposed Malware and Rootkits*. New York: McGraw-Hill Osborne Media, 2009.

Defense Information Systems Agency (DISA). "Information Assurance Support Environment (IASE), Security Checklists." http://iase.disa.mil/stigs/checklist/index.html (accessed July 15, 2010).

Defense Information Systems Agency (DISA). "Information Assurance Support Environment (IASE), Security Technical Implementation Guides (STIGS)." http://iase.disa.mil/stigs/stig/index.html (accessed July 15, 2010).

DeLaet, Gert, and Gert Schauwers. *Network Security Fundamentals*. Indianapolis: Cisco Press, 2004

Douligeris, Christos, and Dimitrios N. Serpanos. *Network Security: Current Status and Future Directions*. Hoboken, NJ: Wiley-IEEE Press, 2007.

Dr. K. *Hackers' Handbook 3.0 (Expanded, Revised and Updated): Includes WiFi, Identity Theft, Information Warfare and Web 2.0*. New York: Carlton Books, 2009.

Erickson, Jon. *Hacking: The Art of Exploitation*. 2nd ed. San Francisco: No Starch Press, 2008.

Feilner, Markus. *OpenVPN: Building and Integrating Virtual Private Networks*. Packt Publishing, 2006.

Ford, Jerry Lee Jr. *Absolute Beginner's Guide to Personal Firewalls*. Indianapolis: Que, 2007.

Frenkel, Sheila, et al. "Guide to Ipsec VPNs: Recommendations of the National Institute of Standards and Technology." Special publication 800-77. Computer Security Division, Information Technology Laboratory, National Institute of Standards and Technology, 2005.

Gibson, Darril. *MCITP Windows Server 2008 Server Administrator Study Guide*. Indianapolis: Sybex, 2008.

Graves, Kimberly. *CEH Certified Ethical Hacker Study Guide.* Indianapolis: Sybex, 2010.

Gregg, Michael. *Certified Ethical Hacker Exam Prep.* Indianapolis: Que, 2006.

Harris, Shon. *CISSP All-in-One Exam Guide.* 5th ed. New York: McGraw-Hill Osborne Media, 2010.

———, Allen Harper, Chris Eagle, and Jonathan Ness. *Gray Hat Hacking, Second Edition: The Ethical Hacker's Handbook*. New York: McGraw-Hill Osborne Media, 2007.

Huang, Qiang, and Jazib Frahim. *SSL Remote Access VPNs.* Indianapolis: Cisco Press, 2008.

IETF RFC Repository. http://www.ietf.org/rfc.html (accessed July 15, 2010).

Internet Engineering Task Force (IETF). "Internet Key Exchange (IKEv2) Protocol." December 2005. http://tools.ietf.org/html/rfc4306 (accessed July 15, 2010).

Irwin, Mike, Charlie Scott, and Paul Wolfe. *Virtual Private Networks.* 2nd ed. Sebastopol, CA: O'Reilly Media, 1998.

ISA Server.org. "Setting Up the Windows XP PPTP and L2TP/IPSec client." http://www.isaserver.org/img/upl/vpnkitbeta2/xpvpnclient.htm (accessed July 15, 2010).

Katz, Jonathan, and Yehuda Lindell. *Introduction to Modern Cryptography: Principles and Protocols.* Chapman & Hall/CRC, 2007.

Komar, Brian, Ronald Beekelaar, and Joern Wettern. *Firewalls for Dummies.* 2nd ed. Indianapolis: Wiley Publishing, Inc., 2003.

Kozierok, Charles. *The TCP/IP Guide: A Comprehensive, Illustrated Internet Protocols Reference.* San Francisco: No Starch Press, 2005.

Krawetz, Neal. *Introduction to Network Security*. Charles River Media, 2006.

Lewis, Mark. *Comparing, Designing, and Deploying VPNs.* Indianapolis: Cisco Press, 2006.

Linux Home Networking. "Configuring Linux VPNs." http://www.linuxhomenetworking.com/wiki/index.php/Quick_HOWTO_:_Ch35_:_Configuring_Linux_VPNs (accessed July 15, 2010).

Liu, Dale, and Stephanie Miller, Mark Lucas, Abhishek Singh, and Jennifer Davis. *Firewall Policies and VPN Configurations.* Rockland, MA: Syngress, 2006.

Long, Johnny, Jack Wiles, Scott Pinzon, and Kevin D. Mitnick. *No Tech Hacking: A Guide to Social Engineering, Dumpster Diving, and Shoulder Surfing*. Rockland, MA: Syngress, 2008.

Lyon, Gordon Fyodor. *Nmap Network Scanning: The Official Nmap Project Guide to Network Discovery and Security Scanning*. City: Nmap Project, 2009.

Mairs, John. *VPNs: A Beginner's Guide*. New York: McGraw-Hill Osborne Media, 2001.

Maiwald, Eric. *Network Security: A Beginner's Guide.* 2nd ed. New York: McGraw-Hill Osborne Media, 2003.

McClure, Stuart, Joel Scambray, and George Kurtz. *Hacking Exposed: Network Security Secrets and Solutions.* 6th ed. New York: McGraw-Hill Osborne Media, 2009.

Merkow, Mark S. *Virtual Private Networks for Dummies*. Indianapolis: Wiley Publishing, Inc., 1999.

Metheringham, Nigel. "IPSec/Netkey interaction with IPTables/Netfilter." Openswan open forum entry. http://lists.openswan.org/pipermail/users/2005-August/006101.html (accessed July 15, 2010).

Microsoft Technet. "DirectAccess Technical Overview." http://technet.microsoft.com/library/dd637827.aspx (accessed July 15, 2010).

Mitnick, Kevin D., William L. Simon, and Steve Wozniak. *The Art of Deception: Controlling the Human Element of Security*. Indianapolis: Wiley Publishing, Inc., 2003.

———, and William L. Simon. *The Art of Intrusion: The Real Stories Behind the Exploits of Hackers, Intruders and Deceivers*. Indianapolis: Wiley Publishing, Inc., 2005.

MITRE Corporation. "MITRE's Common Vulnerability Database (CVE)." http://cve.mitre.org/ (accessed July 15, 2010).

National Institute of Standards and Technology (NIST), National Vulnerability Database. http://nvd.nist.gov/ (accessed July 15, 2010).

Nichols, Randall K., and Panos C. Lekkas. *Wireless Security: Models, Threats, and Solutions*. New York: McGraw-Hill Osborne Media, 2001.

Noonan, Wes, and Ido Dubrawsky. *Firewall Fundamentals*. Indianapolis: Cisco Press, 2006.

Off-line certificate enrolment on Windows 2000/XP. http://www.jacco2.dds.nl/networking/certutil.html (accessed June 21, 2010).

Peltier, Thomas R. *Information Security Risk Analysis*. 3rd ed. Auerbach Publications, 2010.

Philipp, Aaron, David Cowen, and Chris Davis. *Hacking Exposed Computer Forensics*. 2nd ed. New York: McGraw-Hill Osborne Media, 2009.

PopTop + MSCHAPv2 + Samba + Radius + Microsoft Active Directory + Fedora Howto. http://www.members.optushome.com.au/~wskwok/poptop_ads_howto_1.htm (accessed July 15, 2010).

Real Time Enterprises, Incorporated. "Create a IPSEC + Certificates MMC." http://support.real-time.com/open-source/ipsec/index.html (accessed July 15, 2010).

Rhodes-Ousley, Mark, Roberta Bragg, and Keith Strassberg. *Network Security: The Complete Reference*. New York: McGraw-Hill Osborne Media, 2003.

Ruston, Chris, and Chris Peiris. *How to Cheat at Designing Security for a Windows Server 2003 Network*. Rockland, MA: Syngress, 2006.

SANS. "The Top Cyber Security Risks." http://www.sans.org/top-cyber-security-risks/?ref=top20 (accessed July 15, 2010).

Scarfone, Karn, and Paul Hoffman. *Guidelines on Firewalls and Firewall Policy: Special Publication 800-41, Revision 1*. Washington: National Institute of Standards and Technology (NIST), 2009.

Schneier, Bruce. *Schneier's Cryptography Classics Library: Applied Cryptography, Secrets and Lies, and Practical Cryptography*. Indianapolis: Wiley Publishing, Inc., 2007.

———. *Secrets and Lies: Digital Security in a Networked World*. Indianapolis: Wiley Publishing, Inc., 2004.

Schudel, Gregg, and David J. Smith. *Router Security Strategies: Securing IP Network Traffic Planes*. Indianapolis: Cisco Press, 2008.

Security Focus. "Embassy leaks highlight pitfalls of Tor. September, 2007." http://www.securityfocus.com/news/11486 (accessed July 15, 2010).

Shinder, Thomas W. *The Best Damn Firewall Book Period.* 2nd ed. Rockland, MA: Syngress, 2008.

SmoothWall Community Forums. http://community.smoothwall.org/forum/ (accessed July 15, 2010).

SmoothWall Limited. http://www.smoothwall.net/ (accessed July 15, 2010).

SmoothWall Open Source Project. http://www.smoothwall.org/ (accessed July 15, 2010).

Snader, Jon C. *VPNs Illustrated: Tunnels, VPNs, and IPsec.* Boston: Addison-Wesley Professional, 2005.

Stevens, W. Richard, and Gary R. Wright. *TCP/IP Illustrated, Volumes 1–3.* Boston: Addison-Wesley Professional, 1994.

Stewart, James Michael. *CompTIA Security+ Review Guide: SY0-201.* Indianapolis: Sybex, 2008.

———, Ed Tittel, and Mike Chapple. *CISSP: Certified Information Systems Security Professional Study Guide.* 4th ed. Indianapolis: Sybex, 2008.

Strassberg, Keith, Gary Rollie, and Richard Gondek. *Firewalls: The Complete Reference.* New York: McGraw-Hill Osborne Media, 2002.

Sweeney, T., (2000, April 3). Businesses Lock In On VPN Outsourcing Options Providers of virtual private network services put a new spin on the outsourcing spiel. InformationWeek. http://www.informationweek.com/780/vpn.htm (accessed July 15, 2010).

"Using a Linux L2TP/IPsec VPN server." May 2010. http://www.jacco2.dds.nl/networking/openswan-l2tp.html (accessed July 15, 2010).

Virtual Private Network Consortium. http://www.vpnc.org/ (accessed July 15, 2010).

Volonino, Linda, and Ian Redpath. *e-Discovery for Dummies.* Indianapolis: Wiley Publishing, Inc, 2009.

Vyncke, Eric, and Christopher Paggen. *LAN Switch Security: What Hackers Know About Your Switches.* Indianapolis: Cisco Press, 2007.

Whitman, Michael E., Herbert J. Mattord, Richard Austin, and Greg Holden. *Guide to Firewalls and Network Security.* Florence, KY: Course Technology/Cengage Learning Inc., 2008.

Yuan, Ruixi, and W. Timothy Strayer. *Virtual Private Networks: Technologies and Solutions.* Boston: Addison-Wesley Professional, 2001.

Zwicky, Elizabeth D., Simon Cooper, and D. Brent Chapman. *Building Internet Firewalls.* 2nd ed. Sebastopol, CA: O'Reilly Media, 2000.

Index

E

N

O